Oxford *Smart*

KEY STAGE 3 MATHEMATICS
MOSAIC

Craig Barton

Jemma Sherwood • Dan Draper
Charlotte Hawthorne • Helen Konstantine
Katie Wood • Ian Bettison

1

OXFORD
UNIVERSITY PRESS

Great Clarendon Street, Oxford, OX2 6DP, United Kingdom

Oxford University Press is a department of the University of Oxford. It furthers the University's objective of excellence in research, scholarship, and education by publishing worldwide. Oxford is a registered trade mark of Oxford University Press in the UK and in certain other countries.

British Library Cataloguing in Publication Data
Data available

978-138-203492-0

978-138-203493-7 (ebook)

10 9 8 7 6 5 4 3 2

The manufacturing process conforms to the environmental regulations of the country of origin.

Printed in the UK by Bell and Bain Ltd, Glasgow.

Acknowledgements
The authors would like to thank the following:

Dan Draper:
I would like to thank every mentor, mentee, pupil and colleague that has shared in the delight and wonder of mathematics.

Charlotte Hawthorne:
A huge thank you to my wonderful boys, Oliver and Henry, for being patient while mummy worked and making me smile every day.

Helen Konstantine:
A thank you to my daughter, Alexis and my parents for all of their support and to all the students I've taught, past and present, who gave me the ideas and inspiration.

Thank you to Julia Smith for her authoring of the chapter hooks and to Rose Parkin and Catherine Baker for their expert reviews.

Thank you to our partners at Eedi for their support in developing *Oxford Smart* Mosaic and for the use of their data taxonomy.

Cover and character illustrations: Michal Bednarski

The publisher and authors would like to thank the following for permission to use photographs and other copyright material:

Photos: Throughout: OoddySmile Studio/Shutterstock; Seth Gallmeyer/ Shutterstock; **pIV:** © Simon Vine Photography; **pXIII:** Rattanapon Ninlapoom/Shutterstock; **p2:** Christian Bertrand / Shutterstock; **p46:** Halfpoint/Shutterstock; **p46(inset):** Kutlayev Dmitry/Shutterstock; **p47:** BSVIT/Shutterstock; **p90:** Triff/Shutterstock; **p91:** Hyejin Kang/ Shutterstock; **p158:** Lukasz Kochanek/Shutterstock; **p216:** chuckchee / Shutterstock; **p217:** Jut / Shutterstock; **p246:** Teenasparkler/Shutterstock; **p290(t):** Pablo Wilson/Shutterstock; **p290(b):** Sony Herdiana/ Shutterstock; p291L zhenya/123RF; **p348:** AlenKadr/Shutterstock; **p384:** Sachinda Perera/Shutterstock; **p402(l):** RVV-DESIGN / Shutterstock; **p402(r):** ANNA ZASIMOVA / Shutterstock; **p403:** Denys Po / Shutterstock.

Artwork by PDQ Media, Q2A Media, Mark Daisy, Lorna Kent, Judy Musette, Dave Russell, Graham Smith, John Wood, Jan McCafferty and Oxford University Press.

Every effort has been made to contact copyright holders of material reproduced in this book. Any omissions will be rectified in subsequent printings if notice is given to the publisher.

Links to third party websites are provided by Oxford in good faith and for information only. Oxford disclaims any responsibility for the materials contained in any third party website referenced in this work.

The manufacturer's authorised representative in the EU for product safety is Oxford University Press España S.A. of el Parque Empresarial San Fernando de Henares, Avenida de Castilla, 2 – 28830 Madrid (www.oup.es/en).

Contents

Welcome to Mosaic

My name is Craig. I have been lucky enough to teach maths for 15 years.

Now, Maths often gets a bad name. Maybe you have heard maths described as boring, hard, painful, and even pointless - heck, maybe you have used these words yourself. And at times maths certainly can be all of those things.

But it doesn't have to be.

I have worked closely with our expert authors to design *Oxford Smart* Mosaic - a maths course that is challenging and fun, and one that will help all the tricky ideas maths can throw at you make a lot more sense.

For each topic there are lots of worked examples that you can follow, together with a similar example for you to try. This means you will always have something you can use to support you any time you need it.

Then there are loads of practice questions to help build up your confidence. But you won't be asked to just do hundreds of the same type of question until you are bored out of your mind. Oh no, instead you will be asked to make predictions about the answer to a question based on what you noticed about the last question, or to think creatively about how you might tackle a problem that looks a bit weird. There are multiple choice questions to vote on, quizzes to answer, and mistakes to explain. In fact, anything anyone could ever wish to do with maths is in this course.

Now, the work you will be asked to do will not always be easy. At times the answer to a question will not be obvious, and you may struggle, feel frustrated and want to give up. But keep thinking, keep asking questions, keep trying, and you will get there. And soon (I hope!) you will start to see maths as the beautiful, fun subject that geeks like me love.

If you are ready, let's do some maths.

About this book

This book is the first of three in the *Oxford Smart* Mosaic series. These books will help you learn all the maths you need for Key Stage 3, and to become confident (or even more confident!) in your skills as a mathematician.

This book contains nine chapters. Each chapter is about a different topic. Most of the topics only appear once during Key Stage 3, and you will study each topic for a few weeks to make sure you have time to learn it properly. Each chapter is split into sections so you can focus on one part of the topic at a time.

There are some important principles for learning maths well, and over the next few pages we'll show you how we've included them in this book, and in the digital resources that go with it.

Build on what you already know

Learning maths is a bit like building a house. You don't add a new layer of bricks if some of the bricks below are missing. To be successful with a new topic in maths, you need to build on things you learnt in previous years.

So, it's important to check what you've remembered before starting a new topic, and to fill any gaps before you move on. **Reactivate your knowledge** exercises at the start of each chapter help you to do this.

For example, when you start learning about properties of numbers in Year 7, you'll need to remember these areas that you covered in Primary school.

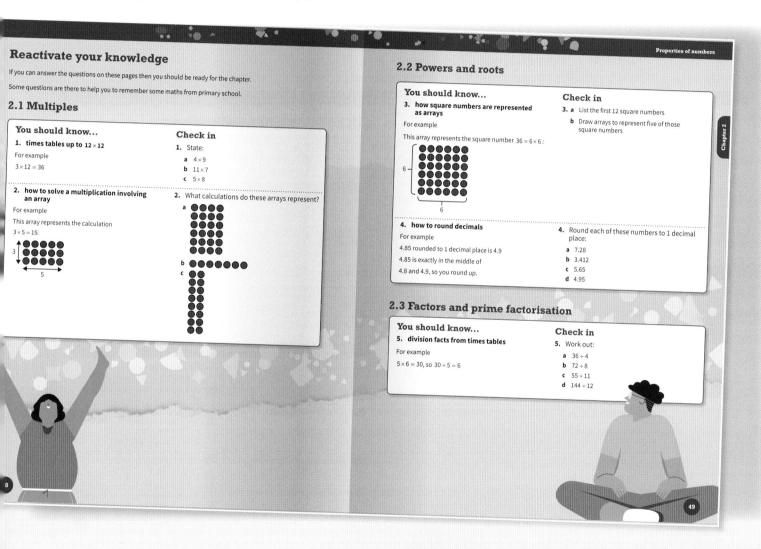

Your teacher might also ask you some multiple-choice questions in class before you start the new work. These help your teacher to see if you've misunderstood anything, or whether you have any gaps they need to help you with.

Learn new topics in small steps

It's easier to learn maths if you don't have to think about too many new things at once. So, we've broken each topic down into small steps. The **Objective** shows you what you will be learning about on each page.

Your teacher will usually go through the new work with you, but we've included exposition and examples in case you missed something in class or want to look back over anything.

The worked examples are called **Example-problem pairs** because each example is paired with a similar question for you to try on your own. The worked examples mean you always have something to look back on if you get stuck. And the **Your turn!** questions let you check your understanding with a bit of support before you move on. There's more information on how to get the most out of the **Example-problem pairs** on page **xi**.

Objective   Exposition

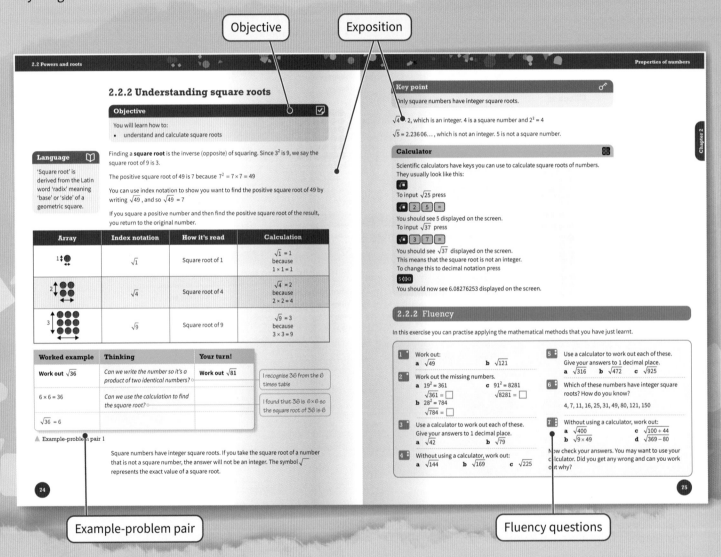

Example-problem pair   Fluency questions

The **Fluency questions** at the end of the page are for you to practise what you've just learned. This helps you and your teacher check that you're confident with the basics before you move on.

There may be lots of small steps in a section! Don't worry, we'll go through each of them in turn to make sure you're confident with everything before we move on to anything more complex.

Master each topic in depth

Once you've learnt all the separate steps, it's time to put them together. We help you do this with lots of different opportunities to practise and apply what you have learned. This is an important stage in your learning because it helps your brain to make connections, which helps you to remember the topic and recognise when to use it. The aim is to learn the topic once, and learn it really well, so you don't have to relearn it in the future!

To help you master each topic, there are three different ways to practise maths that we've included at the end of every section. They may look a little bit different to what you've seen in maths before, because each exercise works in a particular way to help you become a better mathematician. Let's look at each of them now.

Intelligent practice

Intelligent practice may look like another fluency exercise, but it's much more than that. There are hidden connections between the different questions which we want you to find. Use your best detective skills to spot how each question is related to the one before, then try to predict the answer based on your previous answer.

This type of thinking helps you develop good reasoning skills, which are an important part of being a mathematician.

You can use the **Reflect**, **Expect**, **Check**, **Explain** framework to help you with this exercise. This is explained in more detail on page **xii**.

2.1 Intelligent practice

"Why is it intelligent?" You might notice a connection when you move on from one question to the next. You can use the Reflect, Expect, Check, Explain process to:

- *reflect* on what's different between each question and the one that came before
- decide how you *expect* this answer to be different
- complete the question and *check* your answer
- *explain* to yourself why your expectation was correct or incorrect

> **EXAMPLE**
>
> **Question 2a**
> Is 72 a multiple of 9? How do you know?
> *I recognise 72 from times tables $72 = 9 \times 8$. So, yes, 72 is a multiple of 9.*
> *Or, I could use the divisibility rule for 9.*
> *The digit sum is $7 + 2 = 9$ and 9 is a multiple of 9 so 72 must be a multiple of 9*
>
> **Question 2b**
> Is 720 a multiple of 9? How do you know?
> **Reflect:** This question is like Q2a because it deals with multiples of 9. The number is just larger.
> **Expect:** $720 = 10 \times 72$. So, 720 must be a multiple of 9 too.
> **Check:** Using the divisibility rule for 9: the digit sum $7 + 2 + 0$ is 9 and 9 is a multiple of 9.
> **Explain:** I was right!
> *720 is a multiple of 9 because the digit sum is a multiple of 9 and $72 = 9 \times 8$ so $720 = 9 \times 80$*

1 Write down the:
  a 8th multiple of 9
  b 9th multiple of 8
  c 8th multiple of 6
  d 6th multiple of 8
  e 12th multiple of 4
  f 4th multiple of 12
  g 3rd multiple of 16
  h 16th multiple of 3

2 Are these statements true or false? How do you know?
  a 72 is a multiple of 9
  b 720 is a multiple of 9
  c 721 is a multiple of 9
  d 144 is a multiple of 9
  e 144 is a multiple of 3
  f 144 is a multiple of 6
  g 153 is a multiple of 6

Method selection

The **Method selection** exercises give you regular practice in choosing what methods to pick. You may need to use methods from earlier in the topic, or even from previous topics. This helps things stick in your long-term memory and gives you confidence that you can work out what to do.

2.1 Method selection

In these questions you'll need to think carefully about which methods to apply. For some questions you might need to use skills from earlier chapters.

1 28, 42, and 70 are multiples of which of these numbers?
Copy the table and tick the numbers that 28, 42 and 70 are multiples of.

	2	3	4	5	6
28					
42					
70					

2 Tables have 4 legs. If there are 48 legs in total, how many tables are there?

3 The timetable at a bus stop says a bus arrives at 8 a.m., and every 25 minutes after that time. Will there be a bus at 9:50 a.m.?

4 Each egg box holds 6 eggs. How many eggs do you need to fill 15 boxes?

Purposeful practice

Purposeful practice questions give you an opportunity to be creative. There might be more than one way to tackle the question, or you might be able to spot patterns and make generalisations about your answers.

> These exercises help to develop your problem-solving skills, which are another important part of being a mathematician.

2.2 Purposeful practice

There may be more than one way to approach these questions.
Once you have answered a question one way, can you think of another way?

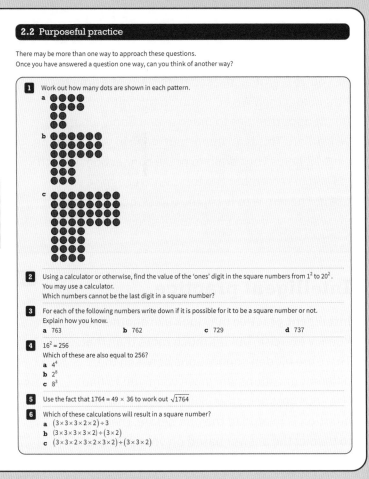

1 Work out how many dots are shown in each pattern.

  a

  b

  c

2 Using a calculator or otherwise, find the value of the 'ones' digit in the square numbers from 1^2 to 20^2.
You may use a calculator.
Which numbers cannot be the last digit in a square number?

3 For each of the following numbers write down if it is possible for it to be a square number or not.
Explain how you know.
  a 763   b 762   c 729   d 737

4 $16^2 = 256$
Which of these are also equal to 256?
  a 4^4
  b 2^8
  c 8^3

5 Use the fact that $1764 = 49 \times 36$ to work out $\sqrt{1764}$

6 Which of these calculations will result in a square number?
  a $(3 \times 3 \times 3 \times 2 \times 2) \div 3$
  b $(3 \times 3 \times 3 \times 3 \times 2) \div (3 \times 2)$
  c $(3 \times 3 \times 2 \times 3 \times 2 \times 3 \times 2) \div (3 \times 3 \times 2)$

Watch out!

At the end of each chapter, there's also an exercise called **Watch out!** This is all about explaining mistakes, so it's another exercise that needs a bit of detective work.

To work out what someone has done wrong you need to use good reasoning skills. Then try to explain the mistake convincingly enough that they believe you!

> Spotting mistakes will also help you get better at checking your own work.

Watch out! exercise

Some students have tried to answer the questions below but have unfortunately made some mistakes.
For each question do the following:
  a answer the question correctly
  b write down the mistake that each student has made
  c comment on why they might have made that mistake
  d write an explanation for each student to convince them (nicely!) that their answer cannot be correct.

1 Aisha and Cameron have each tried to answer the question "Write $9 \times 9 \times 9 \times 9 \times 9$ in index notation."
  Aisha wrote
  $9 \times 9 \times 9 \times 9 \times 9 = 5 \times 9$
  Cameron wrote
  $9 \times 9 \times 9 \times 9 \times 9 = 5^9$

2 Yousef and Oona have each tried to answer the question "Evaluate 6^3"
  Yousef wrote
  $6 \times 3 = 18$
  Oona wrote
  $3 \times 3 \times 3 \times 3 \times 3 \times 3 = 729$

3 Adisa, Paige and Evan have each tried to answer the question "Express 180 as a product of its prime factors."
  Adisa wrote
  $1 \times 2 \times 2 \times 3 \times 3 \times 5$
  Paige wrote
  $2^2 + 3^2 + 5$
  Evan wrote
  $2 \times 2 \times 5 \times 9$

4 Nia, Jacob and Mustafa have each tried to answer the question "Find the HCF of 12 and 30"
  Nia wrote
  60
  Mustafa wrote
  3
  Jacob wrote
  12

5 Ralph, Mollie and Suchin have each tried to answer the question "Find the LCM of 12 and 15"
  Ralph wrote
  24
  Mollie wrote
  3
  Suchin wrote
  $12 \times 15 = 180$

6 Luka and Zainab have each tried to answer the question "Evaluate $\sqrt{64}$"
  Luka wrote
  32
  Zainab wrote
  4

7 Clare and Pete have each tried to answer the question "Write down all the factors of 28"
  Clare wrote
  1, 2, 4, 14, 28
  Pete wrote
  1×28
  2×14
  4×9

Make sure it sticks

After you've mastered a topic, you still need to make sure it stays in your memory. The key to this is revisiting the topic every so often. The Review exercise at the end of each chapter helps you to revisit each part of the topic a few days or weeks after you last practised the material.

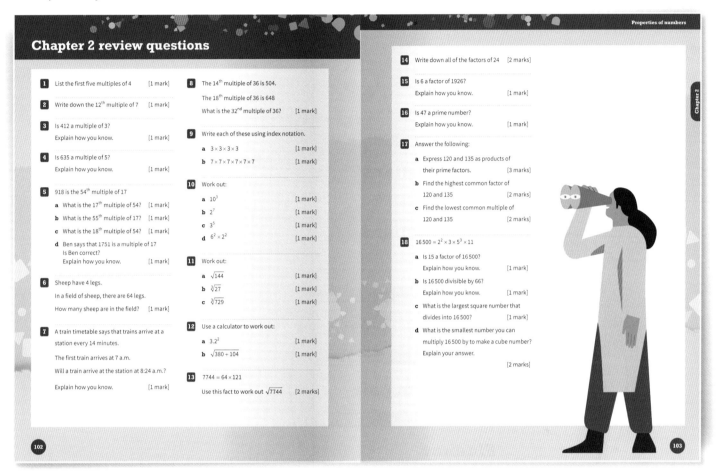

Chapter 2 review questions

1. List the first five multiples of 4 [1 mark]

2. Write down the 12th multiple of 7 [1 mark]

3. Is 412 a multiple of 3?
   Explain how you know. [1 mark]

4. Is 635 a multiple of 5?
   Explain how you know. [1 mark]

5. 918 is the 54th multiple of 17?
   a What is the 17th multiple of 54? [1 mark]
   b What is the 55th multiple of 17? [1 mark]
   c What is the 18th multiple of 54? [1 mark]
   d Ben says that 1751 is a multiple of 17
      Is Ben correct?
      Explain how you know. [1 mark]

6. Sheep have 4 legs.
   In a field of sheep, there are 64 legs.
   How many sheep are in the field? [1 mark]

7. A train timetable says that trains arrive at a station every 14 minutes.
   The first train arrives at 7 a.m.
   Will a train arrive at the station at 8:24 a.m.?
   Explain how you know. [1 mark]

8. The 14th multiple of 36 is 504.
   The 18th multiple of 36 is 648
   What is the 32nd multiple of 36? [1 mark]

9. Write each of these using index notation.
   a $3 \times 3 \times 3 \times 3$ [1 mark]
   b $7 \times 7 \times 7 \times 7 \times 7 \times 7$ [1 mark]

10. Work out:
    a 10^3 [1 mark]
    b 2^7 [1 mark]
    c 3^5 [1 mark]
    d $6^2 \times 2^2$ [1 mark]

11. Work out:
    a $\sqrt{144}$ [1 mark]
    b $\sqrt[3]{27}$ [1 mark]
    c $\sqrt[3]{729}$ [1 mark]

12. Use a calculator to work out:
    a 3.2^2 [1 mark]
    b $\sqrt{380 + 104}$ [1 mark]

13. $7744 = 64 \times 121$
    Use this fact to work out $\sqrt{7744}$ [2 marks]

Properties of numbers

14. Write down all of the factors of 24 [2 marks]

15. Is 6 a factor of 1926?
    Explain how you know. [1 mark]

16. Is 47 a prime number?
    Explain how you know. [1 mark]

17. Answer the following:
    a Express 120 and 135 as products of their prime factors. [3 marks]
    b Find the highest common factor of 120 and 135 [2 marks]
    c Find the lowest common multiple of 120 and 135 [2 marks]

18. $16\,500 = 2^2 \times 3 \times 5^3 \times 11$
    a Is 15 a factor of 16 500?
       Explain how you know. [1 mark]
    b Is 16 500 divisible by 66?
       Explain how you know. [1 mark]
    c What is the largest square number that divides into 16 500? [1 mark]
    d What is the smallest number you can multiply 16 500 by to make a cube number?
       Explain your answer. [2 marks]

Chapter 2

102   103

Assess what you know

Assessing what you know on a regular basis means you and your teacher can take action quickly to fill any gaps or correct misunderstandings. Then you can continue to learn new topics secure in the knowledge that you have the necessary building blocks in place.

Assessment takes many different forms. Often it's as simple as the teacher checking everybody has understood something using mini whiteboards or voting, or a few questions in your book. This sort of assessment helps the teacher know whether they should explain something again, or give you more practice, or whether in fact you're all ready to move on to the next thing.

If your school has a Kerboodle subscription, your teacher may also set online quizzes at the end of each section and chapter. These quizzes check whether you are secure with each of the objectives, then offer you extra help if you need it, or extra challenge if you're ready for it.

At a glance…
The Learning Episode Model

The last few pages have shown you many of the different features of this book, and how they help you to be a confident, capable mathematician.

All of these features fit together to create what we call the Learning Episode Model. This diagram shows you everything at a glance:

Introduction

1

Reactivate questions

Diagnostic questions

Build on what you already know

Exposition

2

Example-problem pair

Fluency

Learn new topics in small steps

Intelligent practice

3

Method selection

Purposeful practice

Master each topic in depth

4

Review questions and quizzes

Make sure it sticks

How to use...
Example-problem pairs

One of the things you'll see a lot of in this book is **Example-problem pairs**. These are a special type of worked example that really help you understand what you are doing at each step and why.

There are lots of different ways you can use the **Example-problem pairs**. Here's one possible approach.

1 Start with the Worked example on the left

2 Think about each line of working using the questions in the Thinking column. You might be able to talk through your thinking with a partner, or as a class.

4 One you've thought about the example on the left, move to the Your turn! question on the right. This question will be very similar to the example you've just been through.

You can use the same Thinking questions to answer this equation one step at a time.

Worked example	Thinking	Your turn!
Write $8 \times 8 \times 8 \times 8 \times 8$ **in index notation**	*Are we repeatedly multiplying the same number?*	**Write** $9 \times 9 \times 9 \times 9 \times 9 \times 9$ **in index notation**
There are 5 copies of the number 8 being multiplied	*How many times are we multiplying that number?*	
8 is the base number and 5 is the exponent	*Which value is the exponent and which is the base number?*	
So $8 \times 8 \times 8 \times 8 \times 8 = 8^5$		

Yes, so I need to count how many times 8 has been multiplied

I counted the number of 8s that were written

The number being multiplied is the base number and the number of copies is the exponent

3 Try to predict what the next line of working will be before you look at it.

The questions in the Thinking column help you to think more generally about the example, so that you understand how to approach a different question.

The **Your turn!** question lets you apply the new concept with some support, so that you can be confident in what you need to do before you move on to the Fluency questions.

How to use...
Reflect, Expect, Check, Explain

In the **Intelligent practice** exercise, we ask you to use the Reflect, Expect, Check, Explain framework. This means you think about the question you're about to do, compare it to the one you've just done, and predict how the answer will be different. This is a great technique for developing your reasoning skills – plus it gives you an opportunity to discuss things with your partner, or as a class, which helps you to become more confident talking about maths.

When completing the **Intelligent practice** questions, follow the steps of the framework by asking yourself these questions.

1 **Reflect**: Read the question. What has changed in this question compared to the previous one? What has stayed the same?

2 **Expect**: Using your reflection from Step 1 and the answer to the previous question, what do you think the answer will be? Can you explain why you think that?

3 **Check** your expectation by carrying out the usual method to answer the question.

4 **Explain**: Was your expectation in Step 2 correct? If the answer surprises you, can you explain why? If the answer is what you expected, how could you explain your reasoning to someone else? If you weren't able to make a prediction in Step 2, can you explain the relationship now?

Here's an example of this in action.

EXAMPLE

Question 2a
Is 72 a multiple of 9? How do you know?

I recognise 72 from times tables $72 = 9 \times 8$. So, yes, 72 is a multiple of 9.

Or, I could use the divisibility rule for 9.

The digit sum is $7 + 2 = 9$ and 9 is a multiple of 9 so 72 must be a multiple of 9

Question 2b
Is 720 a multiple of 9? How do you know?

Reflect: This question is like Q2a because it deals with multiples of 9. The number is just larger.

Expect: 720 is 10×72. So, 720 must be a multiple of 9 too.

Check: Using the divisibility rule for 9: the digit sum $7 + 2 + 0$ is 9 and 9 is a multiple of 9.

Explain: I was right!

720 is a multiple of 9 because the digit sum is a multiple of 9 and $72 = 9 \times 8$ so $720 = 9 \times 80$

You may also want to use this framework when you are working through the Your turn! question in an Example-problem pair.

How to use...
your calculator

Learning how to use your calculator well is an important skill at Key Stage 3. This may feel like quite a change from Primary school.

Some of the topics in this book, like square roots, would be almost impossible without a calculator. In other topics your calculator will be useful for doing a lot of calculations quickly, or for checking answers. It's still really important that you can carry out calculations confidently, both mentally and using written methods, so you shouldn't rely on your calculator for all your calculations. Your teacher may let you know when they expect you to use a calculator and when they expect you to work things out for yourself. We've indicated topics where we think a calculator is important with this symbol: ▣.

A calculator makes calculations easy and can save you a lot of time. However, unless you are careful, it is also easy to make mistakes. To reduce the possibility of making mistakes make sure you get to know the keys on your calculator and what they mean.

Calculator

This box shows you how to use your calculator. This is an important skill as you will need to use your calculator throughout Key Stage 3 and beyond.

Another way of reducing mistakes when using your calculator is to estimate the answer first and then compare this to the answer your calculator gives you. They should be similar.

How to use...
the other features of this book

Investigate Further

This box provides you with ideas for how to take your learning further and discover something outside of the curriculum.

Language

Key words are in bold when they are first introduced. Sometimes there is a language box to tell you more about the history and usage of these words. Definitions of the key words can also be found in the Glossary.

Key point

Key points of the learning that you will need to remember are highlighted in this box.

1 Place value

How many people do you think are in this crowd? Hundreds? Thousands? Millions?

What comes before?

Primary school

- Tenths, hundredths, and thousandths
- Reading, writing, ordering, and comparing numbers up to 10 000 000
- Multiplication and division by multiples of 10
- Measurement

This chapter

- 1.1 Place value in integers
- 1.2 Place value in decimals
- 1.3 Ordering and comparing numbers
- 1.4 Measures

What comes after?

Book 1

- Ordering positive and negative numbers
- Comparing and ordering fractions
- Scale diagrams

Book 2

- Estimation and rounding

Book 3

- Standard form

Introduction

You can write any number using just the digits 0 to 9. Two things tell us what the number is: the digits used and where they appear in the number.

The way you write numbers has developed over the last two thousand years from Roman numerals into the base-10 system you use today. The base-10 system uses the position of digits to tell you how much each digit is worth. You can use this system because of the invention of 0, the number that distinguishes 102 from 12 and 120.

In this chapter you'll learn about the place value of digits in numbers and look at comparing and ordering numbers.

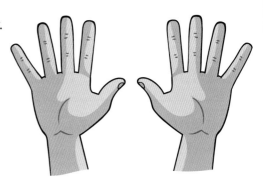

In this chapter you will learn how to...

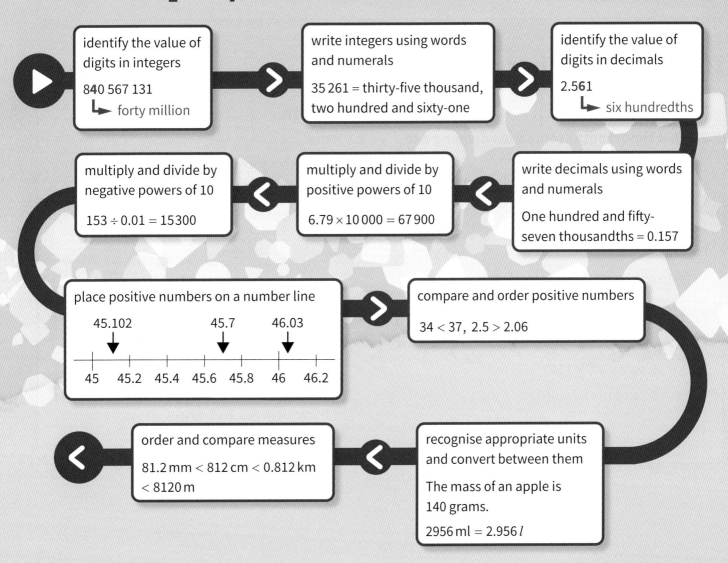

identify the value of digits in integers

84**0** 567 131
↳ forty million

write integers using words and numerals

35 261 = thirty-five thousand, two hundred and sixty-one

identify the value of digits in decimals

2.5**6**1
↳ six hundredths

multiply and divide by negative powers of 10

$153 \div 0.01 = 15300$

multiply and divide by positive powers of 10

$6.79 \times 10\,000 = 67\,900$

write decimals using words and numerals

One hundred and fifty-seven thousandths = 0.157

place positive numbers on a number line

45.102   45.7   46.03

45   45.2   45.4   45.6   45.8   46   46.2

compare and order positive numbers

$34 < 37$, $2.5 > 2.06$

order and compare measures

81.2 mm < 812 cm < 0.812 km < 8120 m

recognise appropriate units and convert between them

The mass of an apple is 140 grams.

2956 ml = 2.956 l

Reactivate your knowledge

If you can answer the questions on these pages then you are ready for this chapter.

Some questions are there to help you to remember some maths from primary school.

1.1 Place value in integers

You should know...

1. how to round whole numbers

For example

236 to the nearest 10 is 240 because 236 is closer to 240 than 230

345 to the nearest 10 is 350

23 456 to the nearest 1000 is 23 000

Check in

1. Round:

    a 4365 to the nearest 10

    b 56 345 to the nearest 100

    c 2457 to the nearest 1000

1.2 Place value in decimals

You should know...

2. that thousandths come from dividing one into a thousand equal parts

Hundredths come from dividing into one hundred equal parts.

Tenths come from dividing into ten equal parts.

For example

15 thousandths, written as a fraction, is $\dfrac{15}{1000}$

Check in

2. Write:

    a three thousandths as a fraction

    b fourteen hundredths as a fraction

    c $\dfrac{7}{10}$ in words

---

3. how to use place value to help you multiply

For example

$3 \times 5 = 15$, so $3 \times 500 = 1500$

$11 \times 6 = 66$, so $110 \times 60 = 6600$

3. Work out:

    a 12×40
       (Hint: work out 12×4 first)

    b 800×9

    c 700×50
       (Hint: work out 7×5 first)

    d 300×120

4. how to divide numbers by 10 or 100

For example

$790 \div 10 = 79$

$400 \div 100 = 4$

$38 \div 10 = 3.8$

$2 \div 100 = 0.02$

4. Work out:

   a $140 \div 10$

   b $600 \div 100$

   c $9 \div 100$

   d $51 \div 100$

1.3 Ordering and comparing numbers

You should know...

5. how to estimate the position of a whole number on a number line

For example

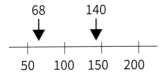

Check in

5. Estimate the positions of these numbers on a copy of the number line shown:

   a 650

   b 724

   c 591

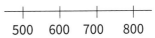

1.4 Measures

You should know...

6. the common units of length, mass, and volume

For example

l is litres and measures volume

mm is millimetres and measures length

kg is kilograms and measures mass

Check in

6. For each of these units, state whether they measure length, mass, or volume:

   a g

   b ml

   c km

Place value in integers

1.1.1 Understanding place value in integers

Language

The word digit comes from the Latin word *digitus*, meaning a finger or a toe. It came to refer to numbers because people counted on their fingers.

Objectives

You will learn how to:

- understand the place value of digits in integers
- write integers as words and numerals and use positive powers of 10 in place-value tables

The position of a **digit** in an **integer** (whole number) tells you its value. From the right, the digits tell you how many ones, tens, hundreds, thousands (and so on) the integer is made up of.

The integer 21 395 is made up of 5 ones, 9 tens, 3 hundreds, 1 thousand, and 2 ten thousands. You can show this in a place-value table. It can be easier to write the column headings using digits.

Ten thousands	Thousands	Hundreds	Tens	Ones
10 000	1000	100	10	1
2	1	3	9	5

The place-value table helps you to see how to write a number in words. 21 395 is written twenty-one thousand three hundred and ninety-five. The column headings carry on to the left. You will see a pattern in each group of three headings.

Millions			Thousands			Ones		
Hundred millions	Ten millions	Millions	Hundred thousands	Ten thousands	Thousands	Hundreds	Tens	Ones
100 000 000	10 000 000	1 000 000	100 000	10 000	1000	100	10	1

Worked example	Thinking	Your turn!
What is the value of the digit 5 in the integer 510 762?	*Which column in the place-value table is the digit in?*	What is the value of the digit 8 in the integer 789 053?
$5 \times 100\,000 = 500\,000$		

The 5 is in the 6th column going from right to left, the hundred thousands column.

▲ Example-problem pair 1

You know the integer 21 395 starts in the ten thousands column. If you write zeros before the first digit, they will belong to columns to the left of the ten thousands.

00 021 395 = 21 395

These extra zeros before the first digit are called **leading zeros**. If you removed these leading zeros the size of the number would not change, so you know they are not needed.

Often zeros cannot be ignored. In the integer 203 you have 2 hundreds, 0 tens, and 3 ones. You cannot ignore the zero because if you did, the number would read 23 and you would have 2 tens and 3 ones. This is a different number from 203

203 is not equal to 23. You write this as $203 \neq 23$

Here the zero is not needed: 0516

Here the zeros are needed: 40 950

Here the first zero is not needed but the second is needed: 07 203

1.1.1 Fluency

In this exercise you can practise applying the mathematical methods that you have just learnt.

1 8 940 372 is an integer.
What is the value of the digit
  a 7?   **b** 4?   **c** 8?

2 Write each of these numbers in words.
  a 23 076   **b** 1 432 607

3 Write each of these numbers using numerals.
  a seventeen thousand, eight hundred and twenty
  b four million, eight hundred and sixteen thousand, six hundred and one

4 120 743 905 is an integer.
What is the value of the digit
  a 4?   **b** 1?

5 12 057 346 009 is an integer.
What is the value of the digit
  a 5?   **b** 1?

6 Write each of these numbers in words.
  a 720 041   **c** 3 000 060
  b 9 042 007

7 Write each of these numbers using numerals.
  a eighty-five thousand and seven
  b nine hundred and seven thousand and sixty-three
  c eight million, sixty-four thousand, three hundred and four

8 Which zeros are not needed in each of these numbers? Copy each number and underline the zeros that are not needed. Write 'none' if they are all needed.
  a 0134   **c** 230 000 000 681
  b 000 040 056   **d** 008 901 320

9 **a** Write 123 706 041 in words.
  b Write the number four hundred and seventy million, six hundred and fifty-four thousand, three hundred and one using numerals.

Now check your answers. Did you get any wrong and can you work out why?

1.1.2 Representing place value in integers using powers of 10

Objective

You will learn how to:

- write integers as words and numerals and use positive powers of 10 in place-value tables

You can also write the column headings of a place-value table as **powers of 10** in index form.

Millions			Thousands			Ones		
Hundred millions	Ten millions	Millions	Hundred thousands	Ten thousands	Thousands	Hundreds	Tens	Ones
100 000 000	10 000 000	1 000 000	100 000	10 000	1000	100	10	1
10^8	10^7	10^6	10^5	10^4	10^3	10^2	10^1	10^0

Investigate Further

The column headings carry on to the left, using higher powers of 10. Research what the next few columns are.

Notice the pattern in the powers of 10:

$10^0 = 1$

$10^1 = 10$

$10^2 = 10 \times 10 = 100$

$10^3 = 10 \times 10 \times 10 = 1000$

$10^4 = 10 \times 10 \times 10 \times 10 = 10\,000$

$10^5 = 10 \times 10 \times 10 \times 10 \times 10 = 100\,000$

You can see that a digit becomes 10 times greater in value each time it moves one place to the left.

Worked example	Thinking	Your turn!
In 264 368 how many times greater is the first 6 than the second 6?	*What do we multiply by to move from one column to the next?* *How many columns do we move from one digit to the other?*	In 5 164 172 how many times greater is the first 1 than the second 1?
$10 \times 10 \times 10 = 1000$ times greater.		

To move left I multiply by 10

There are three places to move between the sixes.

▲ Example-problem pair 1

You can write a number in expanded form using powers of 10 to show the place value of each digit:

$21\,395 = 2 \times 10\,000 + 1 \times 1000 + 3 \times 100 + 9 \times 10 + 5 \times 1$

You can also write this using powers of 10 in **index form** as:

$21\,395 = 2 \times 10^4 + 1 \times 10^3 + 3 \times 10^2 + 9 \times 10^1 + 5 \times 10^0$

Worked example	Thinking	Your turn!	Calculator
Write the integer 510 762 in expanded form using powers of 10 in a) numerals and b) index form.	What is each digit multiplied by in the number?	Write the integer 789 053 in expanded form using powers of 10 in a) numerals and b) index form.	To enter a power of 10 in index form, such as 10^5, on a calculator, press

a $510\,762 =$
$5 \times 100\,000 + 1 \times 10\,000 +$
$0 \times 1000 + 7 \times 100 +$
$6 \times 10 + 2 \times 1$

What powers of 10 in index form represent each of the columns?

b $510\,762 =$
$5 \times 10^5 + 1 \times 10^4 +$
$0 \times 10^3 + 7 \times 10^2 +$
$6 \times 10^1 + 2 \times 10^0$

Calculator:
To enter a power of 10 in index form, such as 10^5, on a calculator, press

[1][0][$x^\square$][5]

The exponent key may look like ◉

The digits are multiplied by 100 000, 10 000, 1000, 100, 10, and 1 in that order.

100 000 is 10^5, 10 000 is 10^4, and so on.

▲ Example-problem pair 2

1.1.2 Fluency

In this exercise you can practise applying the mathematical methods that you have just learnt.

1 Here is a number written in a place-value table.

Thousands	Hundreds	Tens	Ones
7	4	2	1

Fill in the numbers in these sentences.

a The value of the digit 4 in the hundreds column is $4 \times 10^\square$

b The value of the digit 7 in the thousands column is $7 \times 10^\square$

c The value of the digit 2 in the tens column is $2 \times 10^\square$

2 Here is a number: 12 057 346 009
Which digit is in the place that has a value 10 times more than the place of the digit 3?

3 Here is a number written in a place-value table.

Ten millions	Millions	Hundred thousands	Ten thousands	Thousands	Hundreds	Tens	Ones
6	2	1	7	3	0	8	9

Fill in the numbers in these sentences.

a The value of the digit 1 in the hundred thousands column is $1 \times 10^\square$

b The value of the digit 6 in the ten millions column is $6 \times 10 \times 10^\square$

4 Write each of these numbers in expanded form using powers of 10 in numerals and index form. The first one has been done for you.
$6700 = 6 \times 1000 + 7 \times 100 = 6 \times 10^3 + 7 \times 10^2$

a 5200

b 78 200

c 91 030

d 145 607

5 Write the number shown in the place-value table in words.

10^8	10^7	10^6	10^5	10^4	10^3	10^2	10^1	10^0
6	0	2	2	1	4	0	7	6

1.1 Exercises

1.1 Intelligent practice

"Why is it intelligent?" You might notice a connection when you move on from one question to the next. You can use the Reflect, Expect, Check, Explain process to:

- *reflect* on what's different between each question and the one that came before
- decide how you *expect* this answer to be different
- complete the question and *check* your answer
- *explain* to yourself why your expectation was correct or incorrect.

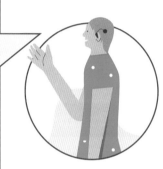

EXAMPLE

Question 1a

What is the value of the digit 3 in each integer?

315

The digit is in the hundreds column so its value is 300

Question 1b

What is the value of the digit 3 in each integer?

0315

Reflect: *This is like question 1a but there is one extra digit in this number.*

Expect: *The extra digit is a leading zero, so I don't think the number has changed.*

Check: *Looking from the right, the 3 is still in the hundreds column, so its value is 300*

Explain: *I was right! The leading zero did not change the value of the digits.*

---

1 What is the value of the digit 3 in each integer?

   a 315   **d** 3150

   b 0315   **e** 31 500

   c 00315   **f** 301 050

2 What is the ten millions digit in each integer?

   a 52 342 456   **c** 678 523 424 567

   b 523 424 567   **d** 6 783 523 424 567

3 What is the ten millions digit in each integer?

   a 456 000 000   **c** 00 456 000 000

   b 056 000 000   **d** 45 600 000 000

4 Here are some integers written in expanded form. Write them in ordinary form.

   a $7 \times 100 + 3 \times 10 + 5 \times 1$

   b $7 \times 1000 + 0 \times 100 + 3 \times 10 + 5 \times 1$

   c $7 \times 1000 + 3 \times 10 + 5 \times 1$

   d $7 \times 10000 + 3 \times 100 + 5 \times 10$

5 Here are some integers written in expanded form. Write them in ordinary form.

   a $9 \times 10^4 + 3 \times 10^3 + 8 \times 10^2 + 5 \times 10^1 + 1 \times 10^0$

   b $9 \times 10^4 + 8 \times 10^3 + 3 \times 10^2 + 1 \times 10^1 + 5 \times 10^0$

   c $9 \times 10^4 + 0 \times 10^3 + 0 \times 10^2 + 5 \times 10^1 + 1 \times 10^0$

   d $9 \times 10^4 + 5 \times 10^1 + 1 \times 10^0$

   e $9 \times 10^4 + 1 \times 10^1 + 5 \times 10^0$

6 Explain which zeros in these numbers are needed and which are not, and why.

   a 00 567

   b 56 700

1.1 Method selection

In these questions you'll need to think carefully about which methods to apply.

1 This table shows the names of the place-value columns in words, numerals, and powers of 10
Copy the table and fill in the gaps.

				Hundreds	Tens	Ones
		10 000		100	10	1
10^6				10^2	10^1	

2 Copy these and fill in the boxes to make each of the calculations correct.
  a $36 \times \square = 360$
  b $36 \times \square = 3600$
  c $36 \times \square = 36\,000$
  d $\square \times 100\,000 = 360\,000\,000$
  e $\square \times 10 = 360\,000\,000$

3 Write the correct symbol, $=$ or $\neq$, for each box.
  a $5068 \,\square\, 5 \times 1000 + 0 \times 100 + 6 \times 10 + 8 \times 1$
  b $5068 \,\square\, 5 + 1000 \times 0 + 100 \times 6 + 10 \times 8 + 1$
  c $5068 \,\square\, 5 \times 10^3 + 6 \times 10^1 + 8 \times 10^0$
  d $5 \times 1000 + 6 \times 10 + 8 \times 1 \,\square\, 5068$

4 Write the number 2304 in expanded form with powers of 10 in three different ways
(using numerals or index form).

5 Write down five numbers, each greater than the one before, which contain 7 hundreds.

6 In the place-value table, the column headings can be grouped in threes:

	Millions			Thousands			Ones		
...	Hundred millions	Ten millions	One millions	Hundred thousands	Ten thousands	One thousands	Hundreds	Tens	Ones

Describe the pattern you see in the column headings.

7 Write these numbers in ascending order.
0450, 4500, 4050, 4005, 0405, 0045

8 Paul says, "The number 80 000 is greater than the number 7000 just because 8 is greater than 7."
Is Paul correct? Explain your reasoning.

9 Explain how you know that the number 3×10^4 is greater than the number 4×10^3

1.1 Purposeful practice

There may be more than one way to approach these questions.
Once you have answered a question one way, can you think of another way?

1 Here are two integers with some of their digits hidden.
Which number is greater? How do you know?

4▓▓19   **9▓▓1**

2 Complete the questions.

a Copy and complete the Venn diagram by filling each section with an integer.
If a section cannot be filled, explain why.

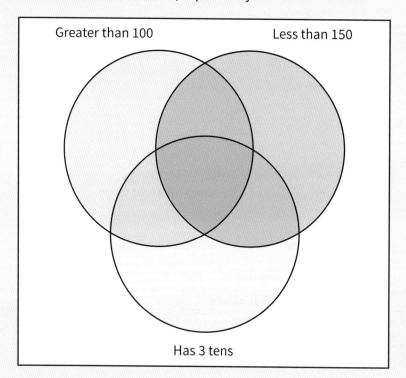

Greater than 100

Less than 150

Has 3 tens

b Is there more than one number that can go in the centre section?
Explain how you know.

3 Here are five digits.

5   1   0   4   6

Use all these digits to make

a the greatest possible integer

b the least possible integer

c the greatest possible odd integer

d the least possible five-digit, even integer

e the integer closest to 60 000

4 Answer the questions.
  a By putting the digits 1, 2, 3, and 4 into the boxes once only, make
    i the greatest possible sum
      □□ + □□
    ii the least possible sum
      □□ + □□
    iii the greatest possible difference
      □□ − □□
    iv the least possible positive difference.
      □□ − □□
  b How do your answers to part **a** change if you can move the + or − symbol anywhere between the four digits?

5 Using all the digits 1 to 9 once only, make
  a the integer closest to 100 000 000
  b the integer closest to 1 000 000 000
  c the integer closest to five hundred million
  d the least integer greater than $4 \times 100\,000\,000$
  e the greatest integer less than 7×10^8

6 Using any of the digits from 1 to 9 no more than once, make
  a the integer closest to 3000
  b the greatest integer less than $2 \times 100\,000$
  c the least integer greater than 10^4

Place value in decimals

1.2.1 Understanding place value in decimals

Objectives

You will learn how to:

- understand the place value of digits in decimals
- write decimals as words and numerals and use negative powers of 10 in place-value tables

If you split the number 1 into 10 equal-sized parts, each part is one tenth of the whole. You write this as $\frac{1}{10}$ in fraction notation or 0.1 in decimal notation. In a decimal, the whole numbers go to the left of the decimal point, and the parts of a whole number go to the right of the decimal point. The parts of a whole are shown to the right of the ones in a place-value table.

Ones	Tenths	Hundredths	Thousandths	Ten-thousandths	Hundred-thousandths	Millionths
1	$\frac{1}{10}$	$\frac{1}{100}$	$\frac{1}{1000}$	$\frac{1}{10\,000}$	$\frac{1}{100\,000}$	$\frac{1}{1\,000\,000}$
1	0.1	0.01	0.001	0.000 1	0.000 01	0.000 001
0	2	1	7	4	8	3

Language

When reading numbers, many people say 'nought' instead of 'zero', so you will often hear "nought point …".

The column names for parts of a whole have the same patterns as for integers. You can write the column headings as fractions or decimals.

The place-value table shows the number 0.217 483. The number 0.217 483 is read "zero point two one seven four eight three" and is made up of 2 tenths, 1 hundredth, 7 thousandths, 4 ten-thousandths, 8 hundred-thousandths, and 3 millionths.

$0.217\,483 = 0 \times 1 + 2 \times 0.1 + 1 \times 0.01 + 7 \times 0.001 + 4 \times 0.0001 + 8 \times 0.000\,01 + 3 \times 0.000\,001$

Worked example	Thinking	Your turn!
What is the value of the digit 6 in the number 5.107 62?	*Which column in the place-value table is the digit in?*	What is the value of the digit 3 in the number 7.890 53?
$6 \times 0.000\,1 = 0.000\,6$, or 6 ten-thousandths		

The 6 is in the 4th column to the right of the decimal point, the ten-thousandths column.

▲ Example-problem pair 1

The number 0.213 95 ends in the hundred-thousandths column. If you write zeros after the last digit, they will belong to columns to the right of the hundred-thousandths.

0.213 950 00 = 0.213 95

These extra zeros are called **trailing zeros**. If you removed these trailing zeros the size of the number would not change, so you know they are not needed.

Often zeros cannot be ignored. In the number 1.203 you have 1 one, 2 tenths, 0 hundredths, and 3 thousandths. You cannot ignore the zero because if you did, the number would read 1.23 and would have 1 one, 2 tenths, and 3 hundredths. This is an entirely different number from 1.203

1.203 is not equal to 1.23. You write this as $1.203 \neq 1.23$

Here the zeros are needed: 4.0905

Here the zeros are not needed: 495.00

Here the first zero is needed but the second is not needed: 0.7230

1.2.1 Fluency

In this exercise you can practise applying the mathematical methods that you have just learnt.

1 Here is a number: 0.5423
What is the value of the digit
a 5? **b** 2?

2 Write each of these numbers in words.
a 0.12 **b** 0.045

3 Write each of these numbers using numerals.
a seven tenths
b seventeen hundredths

4 Here is a number: 0.123 984
What is the value of the digit
a 9? **b** 8?

5 Here is a number: 15.942 307 006
What is the value of the digit
a 7? **b** 6?

6 Write each of these numbers in words.
a 0.2456 **c** 0.941 245
b 0.0364 **d** 0.875 016

7 Write each of these numbers using numerals.
a five hundred and seven thousandths
b eighty-five ten-thousandths
c one thousand, four hundred and seventeen ten-thousandths
d eight hundred and seventy-one thousand, six hundred and fifty-seven millionths

8 Which zeros are not needed in each of these numbers? Copy each number and underline the zeros that are not needed. Write 'none' if they are all needed.
a 0.40 **d** 0.005 000 000 100
b 0.024 500 **e** 0.000 000 123 547
c 0.145 000 030

9 Write the number nineteen and sixty-five millionths using numerals.

Now check your answers. Did you get any wrong and can you work out why?

1.2.2 Representing place value in decimals using powers of 10

> **Objective** ☑️
>
> You will learn how to:
> - write decimals as words and numerals and use negative powers of 10 in place-value tables

You can also write the column headings of a place-value table as powers of 10 in index form.

Ones		Tenths	Hundredths	Thousandths	Ten-thousandths	Hundred-thousandths	Millionths
1	•	$\frac{1}{10}$	$\frac{1}{100}$	$\frac{1}{1000}$	$\frac{1}{10\,000}$	$\frac{1}{100\,000}$	$\frac{1}{1\,000\,000}$
1	•	0.1	0.01	0.001	0.0001	0.000 01	0.000 001
10^0	•	10^{-1}	10^{-2}	10^{-3}	10^{-4}	10^{-5}	10^{-6}
0	•	2	1	7	4	8	3

Notice the pattern in the powers of 10:

$$10^3 = 10 \times 10 \times 10 = 1000$$

$$10^2 = 10 \times 10 = 100$$

$$10^1 = 10$$

$$10^0 = 1$$

$$10^{-1} = \frac{1}{10} = 0.1$$

$$10^{-2} = \frac{1}{10 \times 10} = 0.01$$

$$10^{-3} = \frac{1}{10 \times 10 \times 10} = 0.001$$

As you move from each column to the one on its right, the value of the column is divided by 10. The negative powers of 10 show that you are looking at parts of a whole.

Worked example	Thinking	Your turn!
In 0.056 2306 how many times greater is the first 6 than the second 6?	*What do we multiply by to move from one column to the next?* *How many columns do we move from one digit to the other?*	In 1.000 01 how many times bigger is the first 1 than the second 1?
$10 \times 10 \times 10 \times 10 = 10\,000$ times greater.		

To move left, I multiply by 10

There are four places to move between the sixes.

▲ Example-problem pair 1

The place-value table helps you to see how to write a number in expanded form.

$$0.217\,483 = 0 \times 1 + 2 \times 0.1 + 1 \times 0.01 + 7 \times 0.001 + 4 \times 0.0001 + 8 \times 0.000\,01 + 3 \times 0.000\,001$$

You can use powers of 10 in index form to write a decimal in expanded form.

$$0.217\,483 = 0 \times 10^0 + 2 \times 10^{-1} + 1 \times 10^{-2} + 7 \times 10^{-3} + 4 \times 10^{-4} + 8 \times 10^{-5} + 3 \times 10^{-6}$$

Calculator

To enter a power of 10 in index form, such as 10^{-5}, on a calculator, press

The Exponent key may look like 🔲

Worked example	Thinking	Your turn!
Write the number 5.107 62 in expanded form using a) numerals and b) powers of 10	*What is each digit multiplied by in the number?*	Write the number 7.890 53 in expanded form using a) numerals and b) powers of 10
a $5.107\,62 = 5 \times 1 + 1 \times 0.1 + 0 \times 0.01 + 7 \times 0.001 + 6 \times 0.0001 + 2 \times 0.000\,01$	*What powers of 10 represent each of the columns?*	
b $5.107\,62 = 5 \times 10^0 + 1 \times 10^{-1} + 0 \times 10^{-2} + 7 \times 10^{-3} + 6 \times 10^{-4} + 2 \times 10^{-5}$		

The digits are multiplied by 1, 0.1, 0.01, 0.001, 0.0001, and 0.000 01, in that order.

1 is 10^0, 0.1 is 10^{-1}, 0.01 is 10^{-2}, and so on.

▲ Example-problem pair 2

1.2.2 Fluency

In this exercise you can practise applying the mathematical methods that you have just learnt.

1 Here is a number written in a place-value table.

Ones	Tenths	Hundredths	Thousandths
0	6	7	3

Fill in the numbers in these sentences.

a The value of the digit 7 in the hundredths column is $7 \times 10^{\square}$

b The value of the digit 6 in the tenths column is $6 \times 10^{\square}$

c The value of the digit 3 in the thousandths column is $3 \times 10^{\square}$

2 Here is a number: 15.942 307 006
Which digit is in the place that has a value 10 times less than the place of the digit 4?

3 Here is a number written in a place-value table.

Ones	Tenths	Hundredths	Thousandths	Ten-thousandths	Hundred-thousandths	Millionths
0	4	5	8	1	0	6

Fill in the numbers in these sentences.

a The value of the digit 8 in the thousandths column is $8 \times 10^{\square}$

b The value of the digit 6 in the millionths column is $6 \times 10 \times 10^{\square}$

4 Write each of these numbers in expanded form using powers of 10 in numerals and index form. The first one has been done for you.

$$0.67 = 6 \times 0.1 + 7 \times 0.01 = 6 \times 10^{-1} + 7 \times 10^{-2}$$

a 0.56   **b** 0.871   **c** 0.7021   **d** 0.0306

5 Write the number shown in the place-value table in words.

10^0	10^{-1}	10^{-2}	10^{-3}	10^{-4}	10^{-5}	10^{-6}	10^{-7}
3	0	7	5	2	1	0	3

1.2.3 Multiplying and dividing by positive powers of 10

You know that the value of each column in a number is ten times greater than the column to the right. This means that when you multiply a number by 10, all the digits get ten times greater and move one column to the left.

$45 \times 10 = 450$

Since 100 is 10×10 multiplying by 100 moves the digits two places to the left. In a similar way, multiplying by 1000 moves them three places, multiplying by 10 000 moves them four places, and so on.

Worked example	Thinking	Your turn!	
Work out $6.7 \times 10\,000$	*Which way do the digits move when we multiply by 10, 100, 1000, …?* ○— *How many places do the digits need to move?* ○—	Work out 0.23×1000	They move to the left. $10\,000 = 10^4$, so the digits move four places
$6.7 \times 10\,000 = 67\,000$			

▲ Example-problem pair 1

You know that dividing by 10 makes the digits in a number move one place to the right.

$4.5 \div 10 = 0.45$

In the same way, dividing by 100 moves the digits two places to the right, dividing by 1000 moves three places, and so on.

Worked example	Thinking	Your turn!	
Work out $4300 \div 100\,000$	*Which way do the digits move when we divide by 10, 100, 1000, …?* ○— *How many places do the digits need to move?* ○—	Work out $45.8 \div 10\,000$	They move to the right. $100\,000 = 10^5$, so the digits move five places
$4300 \div 100\,000 = 0.043$			

▲ Example-problem pair 2

1.2.3 Fluency

In this exercise you can practise applying the mathematical methods that you have just learnt.

1 Work out each of these.

  a 34×10

  b 57×100

  c $91 \div 10$

  d $69\,751 \div 1000$

2 Work out each of these.

  a $2.3 \times 10\,000$

  b $36 \times 100\,000$

  c $6.31 \times 1\,000\,000\,000$

  d $452 \div 10\,000$

  e $694\,125 \div 1\,000\,000$

  f $947\,254.63 \div 1\,000\,000$

3 Work out each of these.

  a 6.12×10^3

  b 3.41×10^5

  c 0.82×10^6

  d 12.73×10^7

  e $6790 \div 10^3$

  f $123\,540 \div 10^5$

4 Work out each of these.

  a $6.1 \times 10 \times 1000 \times 100$

  b $45.102 \times 10 \times 100 \times 1000 \times 100$

  c $675\,124 \div 100 \div 1000 \div 100$

  d $641\,312 \div 1\,000\,000 \times 1000 \times 10\,000\,000 \div 10\,000$

5 Work out each of these.

  a $5.4 \times 10^2 \times 10^3$

  b $16.2 \times 10^4 \times 10^5$

  c $8.7 \times 10^6 \div 10^4$

  d $91.5 \times 10^8 \div 10^7 \times 10^2$

Now check your answers. You may want to use your calculator.

Did you get any wrong and can you work out why?

1.2.4 Multiplying and dividing by negative powers of 10

Objective

You will learn how to:

- multiply and divide by negative powers of 10

You can also multiply and divide by numbers such as 0.1, 0.01, 0.001, …

Since 0.1 is $\frac{1}{10}$, multiplying by 0.1 is the same as dividing by 10

$45 \times 0.1 = 45 \div 10 = 4.5$

This means multiplying by 0.01 is the same as dividing by 100, multiplying by 0.001 is the same as dividing by 1000, and so on. Notice the pattern in these calculations.

$6 \times 1000 = 6000$

$6 \times 100 = 600$

$6 \times 10 = 60$

$6 \times 1 = 6$

$6 \times 0.1 = 0.6$

$6 \times 0.01 = 0.06$

$6 \times 0.001 = 0.006$

Worked example	Thinking	Your turn!	
Work out 905×0.1	*Which way do the digits move when we multiply by 0.1, 0.01, 0.001, …?* *How many places do the digits need to move?*	Work out 1.05×0.01	Multiplying by 0.1 is the same as dividing by 10, so they move to the right of the decimal point. $10 = 10^1$, so the digits move one place
$905 \times 0.1 = 90.5$			

▲ Example-problem pair 1

You have seen that multiplying by 0.1 is the same as dividing by 10. In a similar way, you can show that dividing by 0.1 is the same as multiplying by 10

$6 \div 1000 = 0.006$

$6 \div 100 = 0.06$

$6 \div 10 = 0.6$

$6 \div 1 = 6$

$6 \div 0.1 = 60$

$6 \div 0.01 = 600$

$6 \div 0.001 = 6000$

Worked example	Thinking	Your turn!
Work out $0.012 \div 0.001$	*Which way do the digits move when we divide by 0.1, 0.01, 0.001, …?* *How many places do the digits need to move?*	Work out $0.0054 \div 0.00001$
12		

Dividing by 0.001 is the same as multiplying by 1000, so they move to the left of the decimal point.

$1000 = 10^3$, so the digits move three places

▲ Example–problem pair 2

1.2.4 Fluency

In this exercise you can practise applying the mathematical methods that you have just learnt.

1 Work out each of these.
  a 52×0.1 **c** $85 \div 0.1$
  b 7.3×0.1 **d** $6.1 \div 0.1$

2 Work out each of these.
  a 46×0.001 **d** $645 \div 0.01$
  b 590×0.0001 **e** $8430 \div 0.001$
  c $92\,700 \times 0.000\,001$ **f** $0.6987 \div 0.000\,01$

3 Work out each of these.
  a 81×10^{-3} **c** $45 \div 10^{-2}$
  b 761×10^{-5} **d** $34.79 \div 10^{-4}$

4 Work out each of these.
  a $5.31 \times 1000 \div 0.1 \times 0.001 \div 10$
  b $732 \div 0.000\,001 \times 1\,000\,000 \div 0.1 \div 100\,000$
  c $8.2146 \times 0.000\,001 \times 1000 \div 0.01 \div 0.001$

5 Work out each of these.
  a $67.2 \times 10^2 \div 10^{-3} \times 10^{-4}$
  b $19.2 \div 10^{-5} \times 10^{-4} \div 10^{-2}$
  c $0.754 \times 10^{-6} \div 10^{-5} \div 10^{-4} \times 10^{-7}$

Now check your answers. You may want to use your calculator.
Did you get any wrong and can you work out why?

1.2 Exercises

1.2 Intelligent practice

"Why is it intelligent?" You might notice a connection when you move on from one question to the next. You can use the Reflect, Expect, Check, Explain process to:

- *reflect* on what's different between each question and the one that came before
- decide how you *expect* this answer to be different
- complete the question and *check* your answer
- *explain* to yourself why your expectation was correct or incorrect.

EXAMPLE

Question 1a

What is the value of the digit 3 in this number?

3.15

The digit is in the ones column so its value is 3

Question 1b

What is the value of the digit 3 in this number?

0.315

Reflect: *This is like question 1a but there is one extra digit in this number.*

Expect: *The extra digit is in the ones column, so I think the value of the 3 has changed.*

Check: *The 3 is immediately after the decimal point, putting it in the tenths column.*

Its value is $\dfrac{3}{10}$

Explain: *I was right! The 3 has a different value because it is in a different column, this time after the decimal place.*

---

1 What is the value of the digit 3 in each number?

a 3.15
b 0.315
c 0.0315
d 0.3150
e 31.500
f 0.003 010 50

2 What is the ten millionths digit in each number?

a 0.523 424 56
b 0.523 424 567
c 0.678 523 424 567
d 0.678 520 024 567

3 What is the ten millionths digit in each number?

a 0.000 004 56
b 0.456 000 00
c 0.004 560 000 00
d 0.000 000 456 00

4 Here are some numbers written in expanded form. Write them in ordinary form.

a $7 \times 0.1 + 3 \times 0.01 + 5 \times 0.001$
b $7 \times 0.1 + 0 \times 0.01 + 3 \times 0.001 + 5 \times 0.0001$
c $7 \times 0.1 + 3 \times 0.001 + 5 \times 0.0001$
d $7 \times 1 + 3 \times 0.01 + 5 \times 0.0001$

5 Here are some numbers written in expanded form. Write them in ordinary form.

a $9 \times 10^{-1} + 3 \times 10^{-2} + 8 \times 10^{-3} + 5 \times 10^{-4} + 1 \times 10^{-5}$
b $9 \times 10^{-1} + 8 \times 10^{-2} + 3 \times 10^{-3} + 1 \times 10^{-4} + 5 \times 10^{-5}$
c $9 \times 10^{-1} + 0 \times 10^{-2} + 0 \times 10^{-3} + 5 \times 10^{-4} + 1 \times 10^{-5}$
d $9 \times 10^{-1} + 5 \times 10^{-4} + 1 \times 10^{-5}$
e $9 \times 10^{-1} + 1 \times 10^{-4} + 5 \times 10^{-5}$

6 Explain which zeros in these numbers are needed and which are not, and why.

a 5.6700
b 0.0567

1.2 Method selection

In these questions you'll need to think carefully about which methods to apply.

1 This table shows the names of the place-value columns in words, numerals, fractions, and powers of 10. Copy the table and fill in all the gaps.

Ones	Tenths	Hundredths				
1	0.1	0.01			0.000 01	
	$\dfrac{1}{10}$		$\dfrac{1}{1000}$			
	10^{-1}			10^{-4}		

2 Copy these and fill in the boxes to make the calculations correct.

a $36 \times \square = 360$

b $36 \div \square = 360$

c $360 \times \square = 36$

d $3600 \times \square = 36$

e $36\,000 \div \square = 36$

f $36\,000 \times \square = 36$

g $\square \times 0.000\,01 = 3.6$

h $\square \div 0.000\,01 = 3.6$

Now check each answer using your calculator.

3 Copy these and put the correct symbol, $=$ or $\neq$, into each box.

a $5.068 \,\square\, 5 \times 1 + 0 \times 0.1 + 6 \times 0.01 + 8 \times 0.001$

b $5.068 \,\square\, 5 + 1 \times 0 + 0.1 \times 6 + 0.01 \times 8 + 0.001$

c $5.068 \,\square\, 5 \times 10^0 + 6 \times 10^{-2} + 8 \times 10^{-3}$

d $5 \times 1 + 6\dfrac{1}{100} + 8 \times \dfrac{1}{1000} \,\square\, 5.068$

4 Write the number 23.045 in expanded form with powers of 10 in three different ways (using numerals or index form).

5 Write down five numbers, each less than the one before, which contain 7 hundredths.

6 If I multiply by 10, then again by 10, then again by 10, it is the same as multiplying by 1000, because $10 \times 10 \times 10 = 1000$

Write down a single multiplication that is the same as each of these.

a $\times 100 \times 10$

b $\times 10 \times 10 \times 1000$

c $\times 100 \times 100 \times 100$

d $\times 0.1 \times 0.1$

e $\times 0.01 \times 0.01$

f $\times 0.001 \times 0.1 \times 0.1$

g $\times 10 \times 0.01 \times 100$

h $\times 1000 \times 0.001$

7 If I divide by 10, then again by 10, then again by 10, it is the same as dividing by 1000, so $\div 10 \div 10 \div 10$ is equivalent to $\div 1000$ because $10 \times 10 \times 10 = 1000$

Write down a single division that is the same as each of these.

a $\div 100 \div 10$

b $\div 10 \div 10 \div 10\,000$

c $\div 100 \div 100 \div 100$

d $\div 0.1 \div 0.1$

e $\div 0.01 \div 0.01$

f $\div 0.1 \div 0.01 \div 0.001$

g $\div 1000 \div 0.001$

h $\div 100 \div 0.1 \div 1000$

8 Jayla says, "The number 0.000 07 is less than the number 0.0008 because 7 is less than 8." Is Jayla correct? Explain your reasoning.

9 Explain how you know that the number 4×10^{-3} is greater than the number 3×10^{-4}

1.2 Purposeful practice

There may be more than one way to approach these questions.

Once you have answered a question one way, can you think of another way?

1 Copy the Venn diagram.

a Complete the Venn diagram with a number that fits each section. If a section cannot be filled, explain why.

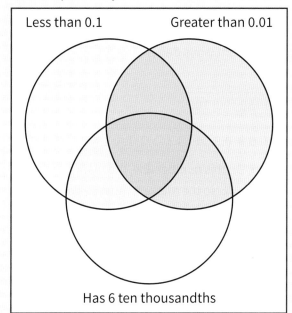

Less than 0.1   Greater than 0.01

Has 6 ten thousandths

b Is there more than one number that can go in the centre section? Explain how you know.

2 Here are five digits.

7 9 0 1 8

Use all of these digits, and a decimal point if necessary, to make

a the least possible number

b the number closest to 1

c the number closest to 80

d the greatest number less than 10

e the least number greater than 7

3 Here are two numbers with some of their digits hidden. Which number is the greatest? How do you know?

0.62⬛⬛8   0.7⬛⬛1

4 By putting the digits 5, 6, 7 and 8 into the boxes once only, make

a the greatest possible sum
☐.☐ + ☐.☐

b the least possible sum
☐.☐ + ☐.☐

c the greatest possible difference
☐.☐ − ☐.☐

d the least possible positive difference
☐.☐ − ☐.☐

5 Using any of the digits from 1 to 9 no more than once, along with two zeros, make

a the number closest to 0.5

b the greatest number less than 2×0.01

c the least number greater than 10^{-1}

6 Write four decimal numbers, each closer to zero than the one before, in expanded form with powers of 10. Each number should contain a maximum of four digits when written as a numeral.

7 Here is a number written in expanded form using powers of 10.

$5 \times 10^0 + 9 \times 10^{-1} + 2 \times 10^{-3}$

a Multiply the number by

i 10   **iv** 0.1

ii 100   **v** 0.01

iii 10 000

Write each answer in expanded form using powers of 10. What do you notice about the original number and your answer?

b Divide the number by

i 10   **iv** 0.01

ii 100   **v** 0.0001

iii 0.1

Write each answer in expanded form using powers of 10. What do you notice about the original number and your answer?

Ordering and comparing numbers

1.3.1 Placing integers and decimals on number lines

> ### Objective
>
> You will learn how to:
> - place positive numbers on a number line

Number lines can be split up in different ways depending on the size of the numbers you are working with.

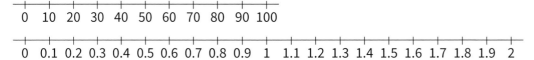

You don't always label every marker. On this number line, the markers split the gap between 0 and 10 into 5 parts. $10 \div 5 = 2$, so the markers must be going up by 2 each time.

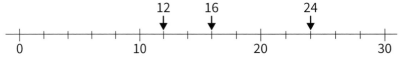

On the line below the markers split the gap between 14 and 15 into 20 parts.
$15 - 14 = 1$, and $1 \div 20 = 0.05$, so the markers must be going up by 0.05 each time.

Worked example	Thinking	Your turn!	
Copy this number line and write the numbers 0.35, 0.38, and 0.31 in the correct places on the number line.	*How many parts is this number line being split into?*	Copy this number line and write the numbers 5.7, 6.1 and 6 in the correct places on the number line.	The difference between 0.3 and 0.4 is 0.1 and this is split into 10 parts.
0.3 ————— 0.4	*What value does each marking on the number line have?*	5.5 ————— 6.5	The line is split into 10 parts, so each mark adds $0.1 \div 10 = 0.01$
	How far along the line is the number we want to place?		0.31 comes first. It is 0.01 greater than 0.3
0.31 0.35 0.38			0.35 is halfway between 0.3 and 0.4
0.3 ————— 0.4			0.38 is 0.02 less than 0.4

▲ Example-problem pair 1

1.3.1 Fluency

In this exercise you can practise applying the mathematical methods that you have just learnt.

1 Copy this number line and draw arrows to show the correct place for each of these numbers.

a 2   **c** 8
b 5   **d** 6.5

2 Copy this number line and draw arrows to show the correct place for each of these numbers.

a 0.1   **c** 0.7
b 0.5   **d** 0.85

3 Write the value of the numbers indicated by each letter.

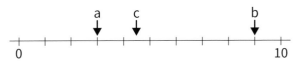

4 Write the value of the numbers indicated by each letter.

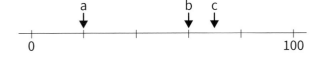

5 Write the value of the numbers indicated by each letter.

6 Copy this number line and draw arrows to show the approximate place for each of these numbers.

a 0.5   **c** 0.75
b 0.2   **d** 0.9

7 Copy this number line and draw arrows to show the approximate place for each of these numbers.

a 30   **c** 23
b 15   **d** 41

Now check your answers. Did you get any wrong and can you work out why?

1.3.2 Comparing the size of integers and decimals

Objective

You will learn how to:

- compare positive numbers using <, >, and =

When you compare the size of numbers, you think about their positions on the number line. If you look at two numbers, you say the one on the right is 'greater than' the one on the left, or the one on the left is 'less than' the one on the right.

Here are the numbers 0.4 and 0.7 on a number line.

0				0.4		0.7			1

You say that 0.4 is less than 0.7 and write $0.4 < 0.7$. You also say that 0.7 is greater than 0.4 and write $0.7 > 0.4$

When comparing two numbers, it can help to look at the value of their digits. Compare the integers 32 174 201 and 32 125 309. Here they are in the place-value table.

Ten millions	Millions	Hundred thousands	Ten thousands	Thousands	Hundreds	Tens	Ones
3	2	1	7	4	2	0	1
3	2	1	2	5	3	0	9
They both have 3 ten millions	They both have 2 millions	They both have 1 hundred thousand	32 174 201 has 7 ten thousands and 32 125 309 has 2 ten thousands. This means 32 174 201 is greater.				

You can see that $32\,174\,201 > 32\,125\,309$

Worked example	Thinking	Your turn!
Write these two numbers with the correct symbol, < or >, between them. 4320 4230	*What is the first digit that is different in each number?* *Which number has the greater or lesser digit?*	Write these two numbers with the correct symbol, < or >, between them. 23 502 23 052
4320 > 4230		

The numbers both have 4 thousands, but their hundreds digits are different.

4320 has 3 hundreds but 4230 only has 2 hundreds.

▲ Example-problem pair 1

This works with decimal numbers too. You still compare the value of the digits, starting with the first column. Compare the numbers 0.314 and 0.34

Ones	Tenths	Hundredths	Thousandths
0	3	1	4
0	3	4	
They both have 0 ones	They both have 3 tenths	0.314 has 1 hundredth and 0.34 has 4 hundredths. This means 0.314 is less.	

You can see that $0.314 < 0.34$

Worked example	Thinking	Your turn!
Write these two numbers with the correct symbol, < or >, between them. 3.567 3.57	*What is the first digit that is different in each number?* *Which number has the greater or lesser digit?*	Write these two numbers with the correct symbol, < or >, between them. 15.045 15.45
$3.567 < 3.57$		

Both numbers have 3 ones and 5 tenths, but their hundredths digits are different.

3.57 has 7 hundredths but 3.567 only has 6 hundredths.

▲ Example-problem pair 2

1.3.2 Fluency

In this exercise you can practise applying the mathematical methods that you have just learnt.

1 Write <, >, or = in the box to make each of these statements correct.
  a 650 ☐ 605
  b 875 ☐ 857
  c 906 ☐ 960
  e 5120 ☐ 5.12 × 100
  f 6282 ☐ 628.2 × 10

2 Write <, >, or = in the box to make each of these statements correct.
  a 512 000 ☐ 521 000
  b 604 000 ☐ 600 400
  c 1 540 000 ☐ 1 054 000
  d 60 120 458 ☐ sixty million, one hundred and twenty thousand, four hundred and fifty-eight

3 Write <, >, or = in the box to make each of these statements correct.
  a 9.01 ☐ 9.1
  b 12.054 ☐ 12.504
  c 0.0674 ☐ 0.0647
  d 0.0102 ☐ one hundredth and two thousandths

Now check your answers. Did you get any wrong and can you work out why?

1.3.3 Ordering integers and decimals

Objective

You will learn how to:
- order positive numbers

When you order numbers, you need to use the values of their digits to find out which are greater and which are lesser.

Here is a list of numbers:

3.907, 3.097, 3.97, 3.79

They all have 3 ones, which means you must now compare the next column, tenths.

The numbers with 9 tenths are greater than those with 7 or 0 tenths, so you know that 3.97 and 3.907 are greater than 3.79, which is greater than 3.097

To compare 3.97 and 3.907, you then look at the hundredths. The number with fewer hundredths is the lesser number. 3.97 has 7 hundredths and 3.907 has 0 hundredths so 3.907 is lesser.

The numbers, in order from least to greatest, are:

3.097, 3.79, 3.907, 3.97

When you are ordering a list of numbers you can use the same strategies that you used to compare two numbers, either using a number line or place-value tables.

When you are asked to put numbers in order of size from least to greatest? (increasing size), this is called **ascending** order.

When you are asked to put numbers in order of size from greatest to least (decreasing size), this is called **descending** order.

Language

'Ascending' means going up. It comes from the Latin word *ascendere*, meaning 'to climb up'. 'Descending' means going down. It comes from the Latin word *descendere*, meaning 'to climb down'.

Worked example	Thinking	Your turn!
Write the numbers in order, least first. 907, 790, 970, 709	*What do we need to look at when ordering integers?*	Write the numbers in order, least first. 8020, 8200, 2800, 2008
709, 790, 907, 970		

▲ Example-problem pair 1

Which numbers have the fewest hundreds, then tens, then ones. The numbers with 7 hundreds are less than those with 9 hundreds.

709 has 0 tens, 790 has 9 tens.

907 has 0 tens, 970 has 7 tens.

You may need to order a list of integers, decimals, or both, in either ascending or descending order.

Worked example	Thinking	Your turn!
Write the numbers in ascending order. 0.54, 0.504, 0.405, 0.054	*What do we have to look at when ordering decimals?*	Write the numbers in ascending order. 1.46, 1.064, 1.604, 1.406
0.054, 0.405, 0.504, 0.54		

Which numbers have the fewest ones, tenths, hundreths and so on. They all have 0 ones.

The number with 0 tenths is less than that with 4 tenths, which is less than those with 5 tenths.

0.54 has 4 hundredths but 0.504 has 0 hundredths.

🔺 Example-problem pair 2

When numbers are given in different formats, the first step will be to put them all into the same format to make them easier to compare.

For example, you can rewrite the list: ten million, 909 188, 6×10^6
as 10 000 000, 909 188, 6 000 000

You can then apply the same strategies as before to put these in the correct order.

1.3.3 Fluency

In this exercise you can practise applying the mathematical methods that you have just learnt.

1 Place each group of numbers in ascending order.
  a 420, 402, 1402, 42, 4002
  b 610, 601, 61, 106, 1600, 1060

2 Place each group of numbers in ascending order.
  a 0.506, 0.56, 0.056, 5.6, 0.0506
  b 1.302, 1.32, 1.032, 0.1032, 1.0302
  c 7301.24, 7031.42, 70 314.2, 730 142, 703.142, 37 012.4
  d 642 027.3, 64 202.73, 624 072.3, 46 202.73, 6420.273, 6 420 273

3 Place each group of numbers in ascending order.
  a two million, 19 541 321, 2×10^5, 1.9×10^{-6}
  b eighteen million, 181 364 510, 18×10^8, 1.82×10^7
  c ninety-two million, 9 200 000, 92.1×10^6, $9 210 000 \times 10^{-9}$

Now check your answers. Did you get any wrong and can you work out why?

1.3 Exercises

1.3 Intelligent practice

"Why is it intelligent?" You might notice a connection when you move on from one question to the next. You can use the Reflect, Expect, Check, Explain process to:

- *reflect* on what's different between each question and the one that came before
- decide how you *expect* this answer to be different
- complete the question and *check* your answer
- *explain* to yourself why your expectation was correct or incorrect.

Question 1a   **EXAMPLE**

Copy the number line and draw arrows to place the numbers on the number line.

3200

The number line is divided into 10 parts, so each part is worth 100. This means 3200 must be on the second marker.

3000   4000

Question 1b

Copy the number line and draw arrows to place the numbers on the number line.

3600

Reflect: The first number was less than 3500, this number is greater than 3500, so it will be past halfway.

Expect: Since 3600 is 400 more than 3200, it will be four markers on from the last answer.

Check:

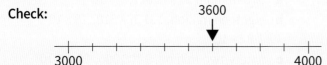

3600

3000   4000

Explain: I was right! 3600 is one marker past halfway and four markers on from 3200

---

1   Copy each number line and draw arrows to place the numbers on the number lines.

a   3200   3600   3700   3850

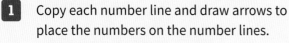

3000   4000

b   320   360   370   385

300   400

c   32   36   37   38.5

30   40

d   3.2   3.6   3.7   3.85

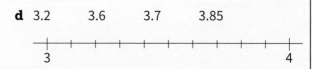

3   4

Look back at each part and compare them. What do you notice? Explain why this is happening.

2 Write the value of each of the numbers shown with an arrow on the number lines.

a

10   30

b

100   300

c

130   330

d

180   320

e

1   6

f

2   4

g

1.5   1.6

3 Copy the number line and draw arrows to show the approximate place of each number on the number line.

a 20   55   75   89

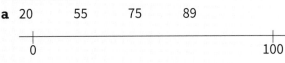
0   100

b 20   55   75   89

0   200

c 0.2   0.55   0.75   0.89

0   1

4 Write these numbers in ascending order.
a 312, 213, 321, 231, 132, 123
b 3.12, 2.13, 3.21, 2.31, 1.32, 1.23
c 0.312, 0.213, 0.0321, 0.0231, 1.32, 0.001 23

5 Write the correct symbol, >, <, or = in the box to make each statement correct.
a 248 000 ☐ 240 800
b 248 000 ☐ 24 800
c 24.08 ☐ 24.8
d 0.248 ☐ 0.2048
e 00.248 ☐ 0.248 00

1.3 Method selection

In these questions you'll need to think carefully about which methods to apply.

1 Write >, <, or = in the box to make these statements correct.
a 3040 ☐ three thousand four hundred
b 0.45 ☐ four tenths
c 3.6 million ☐ $4 \times 1\,000\,000$
d Five hundredths and three thousandths ☐ 0.0053

2 Write >, <, or = in the box to make these statements correct.
a Two point three million ☐ $2 \times 10^4 + 3 \times 10^3$
b $0 \times 10^0 + 1 \times 10^{-1} + 7 \times 10^{-2}$ ☐ 0.17
c 5×10^{-6} ☐ 5×10^6

3 Write these numbers in ascending order.

$3 \times 10^2 + 1 \times 10^1 + 2 \times 10^{-2}$

two point one three

0.321

twenty-three and one tenth

$1 \times 1 + 3 \times 0.1 + 2 \times 0.01$

12.3

4 Write these numbers in descending order.

twelve million

1 200 000

1.2×10^9

one hundred and twenty thousand

12×10^{10}

5 Draw a copy of this number line and use arrows to show the approximate place for each of these numbers.

1.2×10 0.14×100 1100×0.01 $0.19 \div 0.01$

```
  ┼─────────────────────────────┼
  10                            20
```

6 Draw a copy of this number line and use arrows to show the approximate place for each of these numbers.

9600×0.001 $0.93 \div 0.01$ 150×0.1 $0.07 \div 0.001$

```
  ┼────────┼────────┼────────┼────────┼
  0                                  100
```

1.3 Purposeful practice

There may be more than one way to approach these questions.
Once you have answered a question one way, can you think of another way?

1 Find the missing endpoints of each number line.

a
```
┼──┼──┼──┼──┼──┼──┼──┼──┼──┼──┼
10         25                  ?
```

b
```
┼──┼──┼──┼──┼──┼──┼──┼──┼──┼──┼
176                    194  ?
```

c
```
┼──┼──┼──┼──┼──┼──┼──┼──┼──┼──┼
?            11            13
```

d
```
┼──────┼──────┼──────┼──────┼
3.1         3.18              ?
```

e
```
┼──┼──┼──┼──┼──┼──┼──┼──┼──┼──┼
7    8.5                      ?
```

2 Here is a number line. The number 10 is exactly halfway between the two ends.

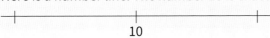

10

   a If the left end of the line is the number 5, what number is at the right end?

   b If the right end of the line is the number 13, what number is at the left end?

   c If the left end of the line is the number 1, what number is at the right end?

   d If the right end of the line is the number 15.5, what number is at the left end?

   e If the left end of the line is the number 8.8, what number is at the right end?

   f If the right end of the line is the number 17.65, what number is at the left end?

   g If you know one of the endpoints and the middle, explain how you work out the other endpoint.

3 The maximum temperature in five towns is recorded on the same day in July.

Barnet	24.54 °C
Barking	24.35 °C
Barnsley	24.7 °C
Barry	24.5 °C
Bath	24.95 °C

Write the towns in order of temperature, warmest first.

4 Using the fact that $34 \times 7 = 238$, write down the answer to

   a 3.4×7

   b 0.34×7

   c 34×0.7

   d 340×7

   e 340×70

   f 0.034×7000

Now check each answer using your calculator.

5 Here are some numbers in ascending order, with one missing.

23.24, ☐, 23.81, 24.25

Using each of the digits 5, 2, 6, 9, 3 exactly once, write down all the numbers that could go in the box.

Measures

1.4.1 The metric system

Objectives

You will learn how to:
- recognise and convert between units of measure
- compare measurements using <, >, and =

When measuring quantities, you use units in the **metric system**. The main units are:

Quantity	Unit	Abbreviation
mass	gram	g
length	metre	m
capacity	litre	l

There are **prefixes** that you put in front of these units to help you talk about large or small quantities. The most common of these prefixes are:

Prefix	Symbol	Meaning (multiplier)	Meaning in words	Meaning in index form
giga	G	1 000 000 000	1 billion	10^9
mega	M	1 000 000	1 million	10^6
kilo	k	1000	1 thousand	10^3
deci	d	0.1	1 tenth	10^{-1}
centi	c	0.01	1 hundredth	10^{-2}
milli	m	0.001	1 thousandth	10^{-3}
micro	μ	0.000 001	1 millionth	10^{-6}
nano	n	0.000 000 001	1 billionth	10^{-9}

This table shows you how to understand units with prefixes. Here are some examples:

one kilogram = 1 kg = 1000 g   one millilitre = 1 ml = 0.001 l

one nanometre = 1 nm = 0.000 000 001 m

For example, the diameter of a gold particle is about 0.000 000 000 14 m, but it is much easier to write this as 0.14 nm.

Another unit that is commonly used is the tonne, which is a unit of mass equal to 1000 kg or 1 000 000 g. This means 1 tonne = 1 Mg

Worked example	Thinking	Your turn!
Write these measurements in descending order. 25 cm, 0.2 m, 230 mm, 0.23 km, 270 µm	What is the best unit to convert all these into so that we can compare the size of the numbers?	Write these measurements in ascending order. 40 m, 450 cm, 0.45 km, 4000 mm, 45 000 nm
25 cm = 0.25 m 0.2 m = 0.2 m (no need to convert) 230 mm = 0.23 m 0.23 km = 230 m 270 µm = 0.000 27 m	What is the multiplier associated with each prefix?	
In descending order, you have 0.23 km, 25 cm, 230 mm, 0.2 m, 270 µm		

If I convert to metres, I remove all the prefixes.

centi: 0.01

milli: 0.001

kilo: 1000

micro: 0.000 001

▲ Example-problem pair 1

1.4.1 Fluency

In this exercise you can practise applying the mathematical methods that you have just learnt.

1 Copy and complete each sentence with a unit of measure.
   a The mass of an egg is 70 ☐.
   b The length of a football pitch is 120 ☐.
   c The capacity of a jug is 6 ☐.

2 Write these measurements in ascending order.
   a 30 cm, 350 cm, 35 cm, 0.35 cm
   b 85 g, 8.5 g, 80 g, 850 g

3 Write <, >, or = in the box to make each statement correct.
   a 18 km ☐ 2.1 km   **b** 95 l ☐ 96 l

4 Copy and complete these conversions.
   a 45 mm = ☐ cm
   b 6.7 cm = ☐ m
   c 0.000 000 86 m = ☐ nm

5 Copy and complete these conversions.
   a 71 g = ☐ mg   **c** 52 Mg = ☐ g
   b 3700 g = ☐ kg

6 Write these measurements in ascending order.
   a 720 mm, 7.2 cm, 7 m, 0.72 km
   b 85 g, 8.5 g, 0.85 kg, 0.08 kg
   c 12 l, 1.2 l, 120 ml, 1020 ml

7 Copy and complete these conversions.
   a 31 l = ☐ cl
   b 85 ml = ☐ l
   c 12 cl = ☐ ml
   d 0.095 l = ☐ nl

8 Write the calculation you would do to work out each of these conversions.
   a a measurement with centi- into one with milli-
   b a measurement with kilo- into one with centi-
   c a measurement with milli- into one with kilo-

Now check your answers. You may want to use your calculator. Did you get any wrong and can you work out why?

1.4.2 Money and time

Objectives ☑

You will learn how to:

- recognise and convert between units of measure
- compare measurements using <, >, and =

There are two more sets of units you should be familiar with.

The first is for money. In the UK you use pounds (£) and pence (p). There are 100 pence in 1 pound, so you write £1 = 100 p

One UK pound is divided into 100 pence, but a dollar or a euro is divided into 100 'cents'. You already know that 'centi-' is a prefix that means 'one hundredth', and one cent is one hundredth of a dollar or a euro.

Worked example	Thinking	Your turn!
How many pence are there in £146?	*How many pence are in 1 pound?*	**How many pence are there in £153?**
$146 \times 100 = 14\,600$ p		

£1 = 100 p

▲ Example-problem pair 1

We also need to know the common units for time. We measure time in hours (h), minutes (min), and seconds (s). This set of units is different from all the others because they don't use multipliers that are powers of 10 to convert between the units. Instead, they are powers of 60. There are 60 seconds in a minute and 60 minutes in an hour.

$1 \, \text{min} = 60 \, \text{s}$

$1 \, \text{h} = 60 \, \text{min}$

$1 \, \text{h} = 60 \times 60 = 3600 \, \text{s}$

Worked example	Thinking	Your turn!
How many minutes are there in 300 seconds?	*How many seconds are there in a minute?*	**How many minutes are there in 480 seconds?**
	Do we need to multiply or divide?	
$300 \div 60 = 5 \, \text{minutes}$		

1 minute = 60 seconds

Minutes are greater, so there will be fewer minutes than seconds and I need to divide.

▲ Example-problem pair 2

Remember that there are 24 hours in one day and 365 days in one year (366 days in a leap year). There are 7 days in one week and 52 weeks in one year.

Worked example	Thinking	Your turn!
How many minutes are there in 10 days?	*How many hours are there in a day?*	How many minutes are there in 6 days?
$10 \text{ days} = 10 \times 24 = 240 \text{ h}$	*How many minutes in an hour?*	
$240 \text{ h} = 240 \times 60 = 14\,400 \text{ min}$		

1 day = 24 hours

1 hour = 60 minutes

▲ Example-problem pair 3

1.4.2 Fluency

In this exercise you can practise applying the mathematical methods that you have just learnt.

1 Copy and complete each sentence with a sensible unit of measure.
   a The cost of a book is ☐ 4.99
   b The length of time it took an athlete to run a marathon is 2 ☐ 43 ☐ and 17 ☐

2 Copy and complete these conversions.
   a 370 pence = £ ☐
   b £9.10 = ☐ pence
   c 1471 pence = £ ☐
   d £17.93 = ☐ pence

3 Copy and complete these conversions.
   a 4 hours = ☐ minutes
   b 360 minutes = ☐ hours
   c 8 minutes = ☐ seconds
   d 720 seconds = ☐ minutes
   e 6.5 hours = ☐ seconds

4 Write these amounts of money in ascending order.
   a 2530 pence, £2.53, £253, 253 000 pence
   b £83.72, 83 720 pence, £837, 837 pence

5 Write these times in ascending order.
   a two hours and seventeen minutes, 135 minutes, 2.4 hours, 8280 seconds
   b eight hours and nine minutes, 8.1 hours, 490 minutes, 29 124 seconds

Now check your answers. You may want to use your calculator. Did you get any wrong and can you work out why?

1.4 Exercises

1.4 Intelligent practice

"Why is it intelligent?" You might notice a connection when you move on from one question to the next. You can use the Reflect, Expect, Check, Explain process to:

- *reflect* on what's different between each question and the one that came before
- decide how you *expect* this answer to be different
- complete the question and *check* your answer
- *explain* to yourself why your expectation was correct or incorrect.

> **EXAMPLE**
>
> **Question 1a**
> Write <, >, or = in the box to make each of these statements correct. 20 cm ☐ 25 cm
>
> *20 cm < 25 cm because 20 < 25*
>
> **Question 1b**
> Write <, >, or = in the box to make each of these statements correct. 0.2 cm ☐ 0.25 cm
>
> **Reflect:** *The numbers look similar, but there are decimal points here.*
>
> **Expect:** *The digit 2 is in the tenths column for both numbers. The first number has nothing in the hundredths column, but the second number has 5 in the hundredths column, so I think the first number is less than the second number.*
>
> **Check:** *0.2 cm < 0.25 cm*
>
> **Explain:** *I was right! 0.2 is 5 hundredths less than 0.25*

1 Write <, >, or = in the box to make each of these statements correct.
- **a** 20 cm ☐ 25 cm
- **b** 0.2 cm ☐ 0.25 cm
- **c** 0.2 cm ☐ 25 cm
- **d** 20 cm ☐ 0.25 cm

2 Convert
- **a** 500 g to kg
- **b** 5 g to kg
- **c** 5 km to m
- **d** 50 km to m
- **e** 50 km to mm
- **f** 5000 ml to *l*
- **g** 500 ml to *l*

3 Convert
- **a** 25 cm to mm
- **b** 25 cm to μm
- **c** 25 kg to mg
- **d** 25 kg to μg
- **e** 25 Mg to Gg
- **f** 25 kg to tonnes

4 Convert
- **a** 15 600 p to £
- **b** £15.60 to p
- **c** £1.56 to p

5 Convert
- **a** 4 minutes to seconds
- **b** 4 hours to seconds
- **c** 4 days to hours
- **d** 4 hours to days

1.4 Method selection

In these questions you'll need to think carefully about which methods to apply.

1 Put these measures in descending order from greatest to least.
  a 62 *l*, 62 cl, 62 ml, 62 dl
  b 70 000 mg, 7 kg, 700 g, 700 000 µg
  c 250 m, 2.5 km, 2 500 000 cm, 2500 mm
  d 214.5 p, £2.41, 2145 p, £24.10

2 Put these measures in ascending order
  a 75 dl, 0.75 *l*, 7500 cl, 0.75 kl
  b 15 tonnes, 150 000 kg, 1.5 Gg, 1.5 Mg

3 Write <, >, or = in the box to make each of these statements correct.
  a 72 cm ☐ 720 mm   **c** 840 ml ☐ 0.84 *l*
  b 920 g ☐ 9.2 kg   **d** 95 km ☐ 9500 cm

4 Write <, >, or = in the box to make each of these statements correct.
  a 38 cl ☐ 380 ml   **c** 8 *l* ☐ 8100 cl
  b 27 cl ☐ 2.7 *l*   **d** 931 ml ☐ 93.1 cl

5 Here are some weighing scales showing the mass of a parcel in grams. A parcel which weighs more than 1.2 kg costs more to send. Does this parcel weigh more than 1.2 kg?

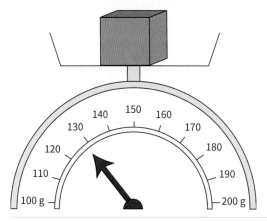

6 Here are the lengths of some films. Write them in order from shortest to longest.

1 h 45 min, 85 min, 1½ h, 125 min, 2.2 h

1.4 Purposeful practice

There may be more than one way to approach these questions.
Once you have answered a question one way, can you think of another way?

1 Sally is 1.83 m tall. Suzie is 5 cm taller than Sally. How tall is Suzie?

2 A vet weighs a kitten at 106 g. Two weeks later the kitten weighs 0.12 kg. How much heavier is the kitten?

3 A runner is training for a race. She runs 1500 m every day. How far will she run in one week? Give your answer in kilometres.

4 A bottle contains 2 *l* of sparkling water. A glass can be filled with 150 ml of liquid. Daoud wants to fill 20 glasses. How many bottles will he need?

5 Write down five measures that are equivalent to
  a 1800 g
  b 20 km
  c 250 cl

6 One portion of spaghetti weighs 75 g. What mass of spaghetti is needed for 25 people? Give your answer in kg.

7 One lap of a running track is 400 m long. Eryn wants to run 10 km on the track. How many laps must Eryn run?

Watch out! exercise

Some students have tried to answer the questions below but have unfortunately made some mistakes.
For each question do the following:

a answer the question correctly

b write down the mistake that each student has made

c comment on why they might have made that mistake

d write an explanation for each student to convince them (nicely!) that their answer cannot be correct.

1 Jacqueline has tried to answer the question, "Is the number 0407 the same as the number 407?"

Jacqueline wrote: *The number 0407 is different to the number 407*

2 Arjun tried to answer the question, "Remove any unnecessary zeros from the number 0.6010"

Arjun wrote: $0.6010 = 0.61$

3 Karl tried to answer the question, "Insert >, <, or = in the box to make this statement correct:

$0.304 \square 0.34$"

Karl wrote: $0.304 > 0.34$

4 Zara and Matt have answered this question, "What number is the arrow pointing to?"

A. Zara wrote: 1.2

B. Matt wrote: 0.7

5 Akin and Isabella have answered this question, "What number is the arrow pointing to?"

A. Akin wrote: 4.535

B. Isabella wrote: 4.58

6 Tom knows that there are 1000 m in 1 km. He tried to answer the question, "Convert 45 m to kilometres."

Tom wrote: $45\text{ m} = 45\,000\text{ km}$

7 Lisa answered this question, "Write down the value of 10^{-2}"

Lisa wrote: $10^{-2} = -100$

8 Peter knows that 0.1 is the same as one tenth. He used this to answer this question, "Work out $480 \div 0.1$"

Peter wrote: $480 \div 0.1 = 480 \div \dfrac{1}{10} = 48$

9 Taio had a question that uses a time of 0.5 h. He decided to convert this to minutes.

Taio wrote: $0.5\text{ h} = 50\text{ minutes}$

10 Carla answered this question, "Convert 9 hours to minutes."

Carla wrote: $9\text{ hours} \div 60 = 0.15\text{ minutes}$

Check your understanding

Turn over to find the review questions

1.1 Place value in integers

You should now be able to...	Questions
understand the place value of digits in integers	1
write integers as words and numerals and use positive powers of 10 in place-value tables	2, 3, 4, 5

1.2 Place value in decimals

You should now be able to...	Questions
understand the place value of digits in decimals	7
write decimals as words and numerals and use negative powers of 10 in place-value tables	8, 9
multiply and divide by positive powers of 10	10a, 10b, 10c
multiply and divide by negative powers of 10	10d, 10e, 10f, 10g

1.3 Ordering and comparing numbers

You should now be able to...	Questions
place positive numbers on a number line	12, 13
compare positive numbers using <, >, and =	18a, 18b
order positive numbers	6, 11, 14

1.4 Measures

You should now be able to...	Questions
know and convert between units of measure	15, 16, 17, 20
compare measurements using <, >, and =	18c–f, 19

Chapter 1 review questions

1 Here is a number:

45 031

  a What is the value of the digit 3? [1]

  b What is the value of the digit 4? [1]

  c Which digit has a value 100 times greater than the digit 3? [1]

2 Copy and complete:

$6230 = 6 \times 1000 + 2 \times 100 + 3 \times 10$

$ = 6 \times 10^{\square} + 2 \times 10^{\square} + 3 \times 10^{\square}$ [3]

3 Write the number 540 073 in words. [1]

4 Write $8 \times 10^5 + 3 \times 10^3 + 2 \times 10^2$ in ordinary form. [1]

5 Write eighty-five thousand, seven hundred fourteen using numerals. [1]

6 Write these numbers in ascending order:

0320   3200   0032   0302   3020   3002 [2]

7 Here is a number:

5.137 062

  a What is the value of the digit 1? [1]

  b What is the value of the digit 2? [1]

  c Which digit has a value 100 times less than the digit 7? [1]

8 Copy and complete:

$0.432 = 4 \times \dfrac{1}{10} + 3 \times \dfrac{1}{100} + 2 \times \dfrac{1}{\square}$

$ = 4 \times 10^{\square} + 3 \times 10^{\square} + 2 \times 10^{-3}$ [3]

9 Write $6 \times 10^0 + 5 \times 10^{-2} + 2 \times 10^{-3} + 1 \times 10^{-5}$ in ordinary form. [1]

10 Work out

  a 34×100 [1]

  b $7.31 \times 10\,000$ [1]

  c $854 \div 1000$ [1]

  d 63×0.1 [1]

  e $8.9 \div 0.1$ [1]

  f 936×0.0001 [1]

  g $61.5 \div 0.001$ [1]

11 Write these numbers in ascending order.

0.603 0.63 0.063 0.0063 0.0603 0.6003 [2]

12 Copy this number line and draw arrows to place the numbers on it. [3]

220   260   285

200   300

13 Write down the value of each letter on this number line. [3]

a b c

2 7

14 Write these numbers in ascending order.
a 423 234 243 342 324 432 [2]
b 0.457 0.475 0.754 0.745 0.574 0.0547 [2]

15 Convert 0.74 kg into grams. [1]

16 Convert 5400 ml into litres. [1]

17 Convert £82.71 into pence. [1]

18 Write <, >, or = in the box to make each statement true.
a 540 □ 504 [1]
b 0.041 □ 0.401 [1]
c 2.4 litres □ 2400 ml [1]
d 850 g □ 8.5 kg [1]
e 3 hours □ 160 minutes [1]
f 452 pence □ £45.20 [1]

19 Write these units of length in ascending order.
3 cm 3000 mm 0.3 m 0.03 km [2]

20 Convert 2.4 hours into minutes. [1]

Key words

Make sure you can write a definition for these key terms.

digit • integer • power • leading zero • power of 10
index form • trailing zero • ascending • descending • metric system • prefix

What do you notice about the arrangement of these boxes? How many boxes are there?

What comes before?

Primary school
- Times tables
- Multiplication and division facts
- Square numbers
- Factors, multiples, and primes

This chapter

- 2.1 Multiples
- 2.2 Powers and roots
- 2.3 Factors and prime factorisation

What comes after?

Book 1
- Arithmetic
- Factorising algebraic expressions

Book 2
- Sequences

Introduction

In this chapter you will develop your understanding of numbers, including multiples and factors. For example, because $3 \times 4 = 12$, 12 is a multiple of 3 and 4, and 3 and 4 are factors of 12.

You will learn that some numbers have special properties, such as primes, squares, and cubes. Prime numbers only have two factors: themselves and 1. For example, 3 is prime because there are no other positive whole numbers that multiply together to give 3, except for 1 and 3.

These special properties have lots of uses. For example, prime numbers are used in encryptions to keep data safe online.

In this chapter you will learn how to...

understand and use multiples

Multiples of 7 are 7, 14, 21, 28, 35, 42, ...

understand and calculate powers of numbers

$5^2 = 25$, $5^3 = 125$, 12×12

identify a prime number

3, 17 and 59 are prime, while 6, 42 and 105 are not prime

understand and calculate square and cube roots

$\sqrt{64} = 8$, $\sqrt[3]{64} = 4$

understand and use factors, including prime factors

$24 = 2^3 \times 3$, $77 = 7 \times 11$

find the lowest common multiple of two numbers

Lowest common multiple of 18 and 30 is $6 \times 3 \times 5 = 90$

find the highest common factor of two numbers

$18 = 2 \times 3 \times 3$, $30 = 2 \times 3 \times 5$

Highest common factor of 18 and 30 is $2 \times 3 = 6$

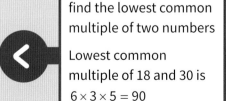

Reactivate your knowledge

If you can answer the questions on these pages then you should be ready for the chapter.

Some questions are there to help you to remember some maths from primary school.

2.1 Multiples

You should know...

1. times tables up to 12×12

For example

$3 \times 12 = 36$

2. how to solve a multiplication involving an array

For example

This array represents the calculation

$3 \times 5 = 15$:

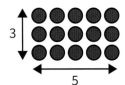

Check in

1. State:

    a 4×9

    b 11×7

    c 5×8

2. What calculations do these arrays represent?

    a 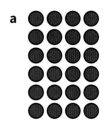

    b ⬤⬤⬤⬤⬤⬤⬤⬤

    c 

2.2 Powers and roots

You should know...

3. how square numbers are represented as arrays

For example

This array represents the square number $36 = 6 \times 6$:

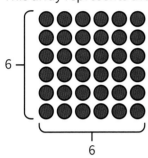

4. how to round decimals

For example

4.85 rounded to 1 decimal place is 4.9

4.85 is exactly in the middle of

4.8 and 4.9, so you round up.

Check in

3. a List the first 12 square numbers

b Draw arrays to represent five of those square numbers

4. Round each of these numbers to 1 decimal place:

a 7.28

b 3.412

c 5.65

d 4.95

2.3 Factors and prime factorisation

You should know...

5. division facts from times tables

For example

$5 \times 6 = 30$, so $30 \div 5 = 6$

Check in

5. Work out:

a $36 \div 4$

b $72 \div 8$

c $55 \div 11$

d $144 \div 12$

Multiples

2.1.1 Understanding multiples

Language

'Multiple' and 'multiply' come from the Latin *multi* meaning many or much. Use of the term 'multiple' as a noun first occurred in the 1680s.

Objectives

You will learn how to:

- understand and list multiples of a number
- identify whether a number is a multiple of another number

If you list some of the numbers in a particular times table, it means you have listed some of the **multiples** of that number. For example: 3, 6, 9, 12, 15… are the first five numbers in the 3 times table and so they are the first five multiples of 3.

Key point

A multiple of a given number is the product of that number and an integer.

Worked example	Thinking	Your turn!
Write down the first five multiples of 7	*Which number do we start with?*	Write down the first five multiples of 8
7,	*How do we find the next multiple?*	
7, 14	*What do the numbers increase by?*	
7, 14, 21, 28, 35		

I start with $7 \times 1 = 7$

The next multiple would be 7×2

The numbers go up by 7 each time

▲ Example-problem pair 1

If a smaller number divides a larger number exactly (with no remainder), the larger number is a multiple of the smaller number.

33 is a multiple of 3 because $33 \div 3 = 11$ exactly or $3 \times 11 = 33$

You can represent this in an array as 3 rows of 11

33 is also a multiple of 11 because $11 \times 3 = 33$. This can be represented by the same array shown.

41 is not a multiple of 11 because $41 \div 11 = 3$ remainder 8

41 is not in the 11 times table. When you try to represent this as an array you can clearly see the remainder as an incomplete row.

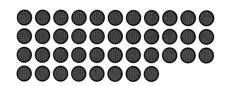

44 is another multiple of 11 because $11 \times 4 = 44$

11 is not a multiple of 44 because $11 = 44 \times \dfrac{1}{4}$ and $\dfrac{1}{4}$ is not an integer.

When you add two multiples of a number, the result is also a multiple of that number, e.g. 33 and 44 are both multiples of 11, so $33 + 44 = 77$ is also a multiple of 11.

Worked example	Thinking	Your turn!
Is 87 a multiple of 7?	*Can we do this without listing all the multiples in order?*	Is 92 a multiple of 8?
$7 \times 12 = 84$ $87 \div 7 = 12$ remainder 3	*Do we know any nearby times table results?*	
No, 87 isn't a multiple of 7 because 7 doesn't divide 87 exactly		

I need to check if 87 is in the 7 times table

I remember from the 7 times table $7 \times 12 = 84$

▲ Example-problem pair 2

2.1.1 Fluency

In this exercise you can practise applying mathematical methods that you have just learnt.

1 List the first five multiples of 3

2 List the first 10 multiples of 11

3 Decide if each statement is true or false.
  a 7 is a multiple of 14
  b 25 is a multiple of 5
  c 42 is a multiple of 7
  d 12 is a multiple of 36

4 List the first four multiples of 14

5 List the first six multiples of 23

6 List the first five multiples of 34

7 List the first four multiples of 85

8 $210 = 7 \times 30$

Use this fact to explain why each of these numbers is, or is not, a multiple of 7
  a 230   **b** 280

9 42 is a multiple of 6 since $6 \times 7 = 42$
54 is a multiple of 6 since $6 \times 9 = 54$

Use this information to explain how you know each of these numbers is a multiple of 6
  a 96   **b** 138

Now check your answers. You may want to use your calculator. Did you get any wrong and can you work out why?

2.1.2 Divisibility rules

Objective

You will learn how to:

- identify whether a number is a multiple of another number

You can use division to check if a number is a multiple of another number.

You can refer to divisibility rules to help you determine whether a number is a multiple or not. Saying a number is divisible by 3, for instance, means the number is a multiple of 3. The table shows some of the main divisibility rules.

Divisible by	Rule	Divisible	Not divisible
2	If it's even (last digit is 0, 2, 4, 6 or 8)	432**0**	382**7**
3	If the digit sum is divisible by 3	741 $7 + 4 + 1 = 12$	913 $9 + 1 + 3 = 13$
4	If the last two digits form a number divisible by 4 Or, halve the number and check if the result is even	25**32** 32 is divisible by 4	35**22** 22 is not divisible by 4
5	If the last digit is 0 or 5	71 53**0**	35 05**1**
6	If the number is even and divisible by 3	67**2** $6 + 7 + 2 = 15$	46**6** $4 + 6 + 6 = 16$
8	Halve the number and check if the last two digits are divisible by 4 Or, halve the number, halve the number again and check if the result is even	4544 Half of 4544 is 22**72** 72 is divisible by 4	2532 Half of 2532 is 12**66** 66 is not divisible by 4
9	If the digit sum is divisible by 9	567 $5 + 6 + 7 = 18$	813 $8 + 1 + 3 = 12$
10	If the last digit is 0	57**0**	30**8**

Calculator

A calculator can help you check if a number is divisible by a particular number. To check if 2534 divides by 7 you press these keys

[2][5][3][4][÷][7][=]

You will see 362 on the screen. This is an integer so 2534 divides by 7
To check if 2354 divides by 6 you press these keys

[2][3][5][4][÷][6][=]

You will see $\dfrac{1177}{3}$ or 392.333333 on the screen. This is not an integer so 2354 is not divisible by 6.

Worked example	Thinking	Your turn!
Is 1544 divisible by 8?	*What is the divisibility rule we could use to check if this number is a multiple?*	**Is 2756 divisible by 8?**
Half of 1544 is 772 72 = 4 × 18, so it's divisible by 4	*What do we need to do to apply the rule?* *Is this number divisible using this rule?*	
1544 is divisible by 8		

A divisibility rule for 8 is to halve the number and check if the last 2 digits are divisible by 4

I have halved 1544 and it's 772, now I can check the last two digits

Yes, 72 divides by 4 with no remainder

▲ Example-problem pair 1

2.1.2 Fluency

In this exercise you can practise applying mathematical methods that you have just learnt.

1 Decide if each statement is true or false.
 a 21 is a multiple of 3
 b 32 is a multiple of 5
 c 56 is a multiple of 7
 d 48 is a multiple of 12
 e 121 is a multiple of 11
 f 71 is a multiple of 9

2 Which of these numbers are a multiple of 2? Explain how you know.
 a 18   c 106
 b 85   d 193

3 Which of these numbers are a multiple of 3? Show your working.
 a 54   c 145
 b 102   d 345

4 Which of these numbers are a multiple of 9? Explain how you know.
 a 45   c 153
 b 72   d 819

5 Is 4203 a multiple of 3? Explain how you know.

6 Is 7623 a multiple of 9? Explain how you know.

7 Is 91 302 a multiple of 6? Explain how you know.

8 Is 85 926 a multiple of 4? Explain how you know.

Now check your answers. You may want to use your calculator. Did you get any wrong and can you work out why?

2.1 Exercises

2.1 Intelligent practice

"Why is it intelligent?" You might notice a connection when you move on from one question to the next. You can use the Reflect, Expect, Check, Explain process to:

- *reflect* on what's different between each question and the one that came before
- decide how you *expect* this answer to be different
- complete the question and *check* your answer
- *explain* to yourself why your expectation was correct or incorrect.

> **EXAMPLE**
>
> **Question 2a**
> Is 72 a multiple of 9? How do you know?
> I recognise 72 from times tables $72 = 9 \times 8$. So, yes, 72 is a multiple of 9.
> Or, I could use the divisibility rule for 9.
> The digit sum is $7 + 2 = 9$ and 9 is a multiple of 9 so 72 must be a multiple of 9
>
> **Question 2b**
> Is 720 a multiple of 9? How do you know?
> **Reflect:** This question is like Q2a because it deals with multiples of 9. The number is just larger.
> **Expect:** 720 is 10×72. So, 720 must be a multiple of 9 too.
> **Check:** Using the divisibility rule for 9: the digit sum $7 + 2 + 0$ is 9 and 9 is a multiple of 9.
> **Explain:** I was right!
> 720 is a multiple of 9 because the digit sum is a multiple of 9 and $72 = 9 \times 8$
> so $720 = 9 \times 80$

1 Write down the:
   a 8th multiple of 9
   b 9th multiple of 8
   c 8th multiple of 6
   d 6th multiple of 8
   e 12th multiple of 4
   f 4th multiple of 12
   g 3rd multiple of 16
   h 16th multiple of 3

2 Are these statements true or false?
   How do you know?
   a 72 is a multiple of 9
   b 720 is a multiple of 9
   c 721 is a multiple of 9
   d 144 is a multiple of 9
   e 144 is a multiple of 3
   f 144 is a multiple of 6
   g 153 is a multiple of 6

3 Copy and complete the Venn diagram shown using these numbers.

751, 754, 755, 756, 758, 759, 760

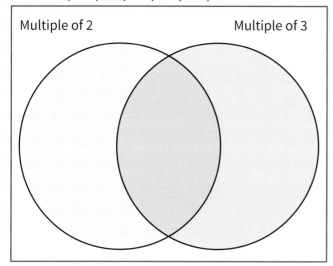

Multiple of 2   Multiple of 3

4 The 56th multiple of 13 is 728
  a What Is the 13th multiple of 56?
  b What is the 57th multiple of 13?
  c How many multiples of 13 are there between 720 and 750?

2.1 Method selection

In these questions you'll need to think carefully about which methods to apply.

For some questions you might need to use skills from earlier chapters.

1 28, 42, and 70 are multiples of which of these numbers?
Copy the table and tick the numbers that 28, 42 and 70 are multiples of.

	2	3	4	5	6
28					
42					
70					

2 Tables have 4 legs. If there are 48 legs in total, how many tables are there?

3 The timetable at a bus stop says a bus arrives at 8 a.m., and every 25 minutes after that time. Will there be a bus at 9:50 a.m.?

4 Each egg box holds 6 eggs. How many eggs do you need to fill 15 boxes?

5 A school buys 240 cakes and 240 cookies to sell at break.
If cakes come in boxes of 8 and cookies come in packs of 5,
how many boxes and how many packs should the school buy?

6 Rearrange these digits to make 3-digit numbers.

| 5 | 4 | 1 |

Is it possible to make a 3-digit number that is a multiple of:

a 2

b 3

c 4

d 5?

7 Here is a number with a missing digit: 561□
The number is a multiple of 6. What could the missing digit be?

8 $130 + 65 = 195$

Use the calculation to complete the sentence.

195 is the □th multiple of 13

9 $170 + 170 + 67 = 407$

Use the calculation to determine if 407 is a multiple of 17

10 In the school hall, the chairs are in rows of 18. How many chairs are there in 13 rows?

11 If today is Wednesday, what day will it be in 91 days' time?

12 Which is bigger: the 23rd multiple of 20 or the 21st multiple of 22?

13 If a number is a multiple of 24, what other numbers is it a multiple of?

2.1 Purposeful practice

There may be more than one way to approach these questions.
Once you have answered a question one way, can you think of another way?

1 42 and 98 are both multiples of several numbers.
Which numbers are both 42 and 98 multiples of?
What is the largest number that both 42 and 98 are multiples of?

2 A padlock has a 3-digit number code.
The first digit is 4 and the 3-digit number is a multiple of both 3 and 7
How many possible number codes could there be?

3 Calculate the following and in each case work out if the result is a multiple of 5:
a $(37 \times 5) + (63 \times 5)$
b $(55 \times 2) + (63 \times 3)$
c $(55 \times 2) + (45 \times 7)$

4 The digits in the number 123 are consecutive.
Find five other 3-digit numbers like this and work out how many of them are multiples of 3

5 A 5-digit number has these digits:

1☐234

Find three different digits that could fill the box to make a number that is a multiple of 3.

6 The 17th multiple of 34 is 578 and the 9th multiple of 34 is 306
What is the 26th multiple of 34?

7 By partitioning 398 into smaller numbers that total 398,
work out whether 398 is a multiple of 19

8 A teacher puts her students into pairs, but there is 1 student left over.
Then she puts them in groups of 3, but there are 2 students left over.
Finally, she puts them in groups of 4 and there are 3 students left over.
How many students could there be in the class, if there are fewer than 40 students?

9 Arrange the digits 2, 3, and 5 to make a 3-digit number that is a multiple of 11 and 2

Powers and roots

2.2.1 Square and cube numbers

Objectives ☑

You will learn how to:
- understand and calculate square numbers
- understand and calculate cube numbers

Calculator

Scientific calculators have a key you can use to calculate squares.

It is usually labelled x^2

To input 15^2 press

The squared key may look like (■²)

You will see 225 displayed on the screen.

A **square number** is the result of multiplying a number by itself.

You can use **index notation** (^{2}) to show that you want to square a number.

$$3^2$$

— **exponent** (or index)

— **base** number

You read this as "three **squared**" or "three to the **power** of two".

3^2 is the same as 3×3. So $3^2 = 9$

9 is a square number. You know the first 12 square numbers from times tables. The first three are shown in the table below represented by a square array.

Array	Index notation	How it's read	Calculation
●	1^2	one squared	$1 \times 1 = 1$
●● ●●	2^2	two squared	$2 \times 2 = 4$
●●● ●●● ●●●	3^2	three squared	$3 \times 3 = 9$

Worked example	Thinking	Your turn!	
Work out 7^2	*What does the exponent 2 mean?*	**Work out 9^2**	Squaring a number means multiplying it by itself
$7^2 = 7 \times 7$	*Can we calculate the result?*		I know 7×7 from my times table facts
$= 49$			

▲ Example-problem pair 1

A **cube number** is the result of multiplying three copies of a number (a number multiplied by itself and then by itself again).

2^3 is read as "two **cubed**" or "two to the power of three". 2^3 is the same as $2 \times 2 \times 2$. So $2^3 = 8$.

8 is a cube number because it's the result of 2^3. The first five cube numbers are found by working out 1^3, 2^3, 3^3, 4^3, 5^3

Calculator

Scientific calculators also have a key you can use to calculate cubes.
It is usually labelled x^3. On some calculators it is found above another key like x^2. In that case you will need to press the shift key first to access it.
To input 7^3 press

You will see 343 displayed on the screen.
Scientific calculators also have a key you can use to enter any exponent at all. See 2.2.4 for more details.

Worked example	Thinking	Your turn!
Work out 2^3	*What does the exponent 3 mean?*	**Work out 3^3**
$2^3 = 2 \times 2 \times 2$	*Can we calculate the result?*	
$= 8$		

Cubing a number means multiplying three copies of the number

First, I do $2 \times 2 = 4$ then $4 \times 2 = 8$

▲ Example-problem pair 2

2.2.1 Fluency

In this exercise you can practise applying the mathematical methods that you have just learnt.

1 Which of these is the correct calculation for 5^3?

5×3 $3 \times 3 \times 3 \times 3 \times 3$ $5 \times 5 \times 5$ 3×5

2 Write the correct exponent to complete each of these statements.

a $2 \times 2 = 2^{\square}$ **c** $2 \times 2 \times 2 = 2^{\square}$

b $3 \times 3 = 3^{\square}$ **d** $7 \times 7 \times 7 = 7^{\square}$

3 Work out:

a 1^3 **b** 4^3 **c** 5^3

4 Work out:

a $2^2 \times 3^2$ **d** $5^2 \times 2^3$

b $3^3 \times 5^2$ **e** $2^2 \times 6^2$

c $2^3 \times 4^2$ **f** $2^2 \times 3^2 \times 4^2$

5 Work out:

a $2^2 + 3^3$ **d** $6^3 + 2^3$

b $4^3 - 5^2$ **e** $7^2 + 3^2 - 2^3$

c $5^3 - 3^3$ **f** $9^2 - 4^3 + 5^2$

Now check your answers. You may want to use your calculator. Did you get any wrong and can you work out why?

2.2.2 Understanding square roots

Objective

You will learn how to:

- understand and calculate square roots

Language

'Square root' is derived from the Latin word *radix* meaning 'base' or 'side' of a geometric square.

Finding a **square root** is the inverse (opposite) of squaring. Since 3^2 is 9, we say the square root of 9 is 3.

The positive square root of 49 is 7 because $7^2 = 7 \times 7 = 49$

You can use index notation to show you want to find the positive square root of 49 by writing $\sqrt{49}$, and so $\sqrt{49} = 7$

If you square a positive number and then find the positive square root of the result, you return to the original number.

Array	Index notation	How it's read	Calculation
1 ↕ ● ↔	$\sqrt{1}$	Square root of 1	$\sqrt{1} = 1$ because $1 \times 1 = 1$
2 ↕ ●● ●● ↔	$\sqrt{4}$	Square root of 4	$\sqrt{4} = 2$ because $2 \times 2 = 4$
3 ↕ ●●● ●●● ●●● ↔	$\sqrt{9}$	Square root of 9	$\sqrt{9} = 3$ because $3 \times 3 = 9$

Worked example	Thinking	Your turn!	
Work out $\sqrt{36}$	*Can we write the number so it's a product of two identical numbers?* ○	Work out $\sqrt{81}$	I recognise 36 from the 6 times table
$5 \times 6 = 36$	*Can we use the calculation to find the square root?* ○		I found that 36 is 6×6 so the square root of 36 is 6
$\sqrt{36} = 6$			

▲ Example-problem pair 1

Square numbers have integer square roots. If you take the square root of a number that is not a square number, the answer will not be an integer. The symbol $\sqrt{}$ represents the exact value of a square root.

Chapter 2

Key point

Only square numbers have integer square roots.

$\sqrt{4} = 2$, which is an integer. 4 is a square number and $2^2 = 4$

$\sqrt{5} = 2.236\,06\ldots$, which is not an integer. 5 is not a square number.

Calculator

Scientific calculators have a key you can use to calculate square roots of numbers.
It usually looks like this:

To input $\sqrt{25}$ press

You should see 5 displayed on the screen.
To input $\sqrt{37}$ press

You should see $\sqrt{37}$ displayed on the screen.
This means that the square root is not an integer.
To change this to decimal notation press the conversion key. It may look like

 or FORMAT

You should now see 6.08276253 displayed on the screen.

2.2.2 Fluency

In this exercise you can practise applying the mathematical methods that you have just learnt.

1 Work out:
  a $\sqrt{49}$ **b** $\sqrt{121}$

2 Work out the missing numbers.
  a $19^2 = 361$
  $\sqrt{361} = \square$
  b $28^2 = 784$
  $\sqrt{784} = \square$
  c $91^2 = 8281$
  $\sqrt{8281} = \square$

3 Use a calculator to work out each of these.
  Give your answers to 1 decimal place.
  a $\sqrt{42}$ **b** $\sqrt{79}$

4 Without using a calculator, work out:
  a $\sqrt{144}$ **b** $\sqrt{169}$ **c** $\sqrt{225}$

5 Use a calculator to work out each of these.
  Give your answers to 1 decimal place.
  a $\sqrt{316}$ **b** $\sqrt{472}$ **c** $\sqrt{925}$

6 Which of these numbers have integer square roots? How do you know?

  4, 7, 11, 16, 25, 31, 49, 80, 121, 150

7 Without using a calculator, work out:
  a $\sqrt{400}$ **c** $\sqrt{100 + 44}$
  b $\sqrt{9 \times 49}$ **d** $\sqrt{369 - 80}$

Now check your answers. You may want to use your calculator. Did you get any wrong and can you work out why?

2.2.3 Understanding cube roots

Objective

You will learn how to:

- understand and calculate cube roots

Finding a **cube root** is the inverse of cubing. Since $4^3 \times 4 \times 4 \times 4 = 64$, we say the cube root of 64 is 4.

You can use index notation to show you want to find the cube root of 64 by writing $\sqrt[3]{64}$, and so $\sqrt[3]{64} = 4$

Worked example	Thinking	Your turn!
Work out $\sqrt[3]{125}$	*What are the first few cube numbers?*	Work out $\sqrt[3]{27}$
$5^3 = 5 \times 5 \times 5 = 125$	*How can we use our knowledge of cube numbers to find a cube root?*	
So $\sqrt[3]{125} = 5$		

I know that the first 5 cube numbers are 1, 8, 27, 64, 125

I remember that 125 is 5^3

▲ Example-problem pair 1

Cube numbers have integer cube roots. If you work out the cube root of a number that is not a cube number, the answer is not an integer. The symbol $\sqrt[3]{}$ represents the exact value of a cube root.

Worked example	Thinking	Your turn!
Which of these numbers have an integer cube root? 1, 2, 3	*What are the first few cube numbers?* *How do the cube numbers tell me which numbers have integer cube roots?*	Which of these numbers have an integer cube root? 6, 7, 8
1 is a cube number as $1 \times 1 \times 1 = 1$, so 1 has an integer cube root 2 and 3 are not cube numbers, so don't have integer cube roots		

The first few cube numbers are
$1 \times 1 \times 1 = 1$
$2 \times 2 \times 2 = 8$
$3 \times 3 \times 3 = 27$

A number will only have an integer cube root if it is a cube number

▲ Example-problem pair 2

Calculator

Scientific calculators have a key that allow you to calculate cube roots or other roots.
They usually look like this:

To input $\sqrt[3]{216}$ press

You should see 6 displayed on the screen.
To input $\sqrt[3]{30}$ press

You should see 3.107232506 displayed on the screen.

2.2.3 Fluency

In this exercise you can practise applying the mathematical methods that you have just learnt.

1 Work out the missing numbers.
a $9^3 = 729$
$\sqrt[3]{729} = \square$
b $8^3 = 512$
$\sqrt[3]{512} = \square$
c $12^3 = 1728$
$\sqrt[3]{1728} = \square$

2 Use a calculator to work out each of these. Give your answers to 1 decimal place.
a $\sqrt[3]{40}$
b $\sqrt[3]{261}$

3 Work out:
a $\sqrt[3]{64}$
b $\sqrt[3]{1000}$
c $\sqrt[3]{343}$
d $\sqrt[3]{1331}$

4 Use a calculator to work out each of these. Give your answers to 1 decimal place.
a $\sqrt[3]{150}$
b $\sqrt[3]{420}$
c $\sqrt[3]{776}$
d $\sqrt[3]{900}$

5 Which of these numbers have integer cube roots?

8, 27, 65, 120, 216, 1000

6 Use a calculator to work out $\sqrt[3]{27 \times 216}$

What do you notice about your result?

7 Work out:
a $\sqrt[3]{27 + 64 + 125}$
b $\sqrt[3]{1000 \div 8}$

Now check your answers. You may want to use your calculator. Did you get any wrong and can you work out why?

2.2.4 Higher powers of numbers

Calculator

Scientific calculators have a key that allows you to calculate higher powers of numbers. They usually look like:

 or

To input 3^7 press

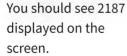

You should see 2187 displayed on the screen.

You can calculate powers with exponents higher than 2 or 3. Using index notation:

$$10^4 = 10 \times 10 \times 10 \times 10 = 10\,000$$

You saw higher powers of ten in Chapter 1. 10^4 can be read as "ten to the power of four" and means that four copies of the same number are multiplied together. $10\,000$ is the fourth power of 10

In the same way, 10^5 can be read as "ten to the power of five" and means that five copies of the same number are multiplied together so

$$10^5 = 10 \times 10 \times 10 \times 10 \times 10 = 100\,000.\ 100\,000 \text{ is the fifth power of 10.}$$

Worked example	Thinking	Your turn!	
Write $8 \times 8 \times 8 \times 8 \times 8$ in index notation	*Are we repeatedly multiplying the same number? If so, how many times are we multiplying that number?*	**Write $9 \times 9 \times 9 \times 9 \times 9 \times 9$ in index notation**	*Yes, so I need to count how many times 8 has been multiplied. There are 5 copies of the number 8 being multiplied.*
8 is the base number and 5 is the exponent	*Which value is the exponent and which is the base number?*		*The number being multiplied is the base number and the number of copies is the exponent*
So $8 \times 8 \times 8 \times 8 \times 8 = 8^5$			

▲ Example-problem pair 1

Products of numbers with different exponents and bases can be simplified.

For example, $4 \times 4 \times 4 \times 6 \times 6$ can be written as $(4 \times 4 \times 4) \times (6 \times 6) = 4^3 \times 6^2$

Calculator

You can use your calculator to solve questions involving numbers with a mix of exponents and bases.

To calculate $5^3 \times 2^4$ you would press

You should see 2000 displayed on the screen.

You should be able to recognise the first 12 square numbers: 1, 4, 9, 16, 25, 36, 49, 64, 81, 100, 121, 144

And the first five cubes numbers: 1, 8, 27, 64, 125

You can use these to help you solve problems with higher exponents.

For example, you know $2^3 = 8$ so you can use this to work out higher powers of 2.

$$2^4 = 2^3 \times 2 = 8 \times 2 = 16 \qquad 2^5 = 2^4 \times 2 = 16 \times 2 = 32$$

2.2.4 Fluency

In this exercise you can practise applying the mathematical methods that you have just learnt

1 Work out the first four powers of 2

2 Which of these is the correct calculation for 6^4?

$6 \times 4 \qquad 4 \times 4 \times 4 \times 4 \times 4 \times 4 \qquad 6 \times 6 \times 6 \times 6 \qquad 4 \times 6$

3 Write the correct exponent to complete each of these statements.

a $5 \times 5 \times 5 \times 5 = 5^{\square}$

b $7 \times 7 \times 7 \times 7 \times 7 = 7^{\square}$

c $2 \times 2 \times 2 \times 2 \times 2 \times 2 \times 2 = 2^{\square}$

4 Work out the first four powers of:

a 3   **b** 4   **c** 5

5 Write each of these numbers as a power of 2, 3, 4, or 5

a 25   **c** 256

b 8   **d** 625

6 Work out:

a $2^3 \times 5^2$ **b** $3^2 \times 2^4$ **c** $5^3 \times 6^2$

7 Work out

a $2^3 \times 2^2 \times 2^4$

b $3^2 \times 2^3 \times 5^2$

c $3^3 \times 5^2 \times 10^3$

8 **a** Which of these numbers are powers of 2?

4, 12, 60, 128, 256

b Which of these numbers are powers of 3?

9, 18, 30, 81, 243

c Which of these numbers are powers of 5?

25, 125, 500, 625, 3125

Now check your answers. You may want to use your calculator. Did you get any wrong and can you work out why?

2.2 Exercises

2.2 Intelligent practice

"Why is it intelligent?" You might notice a connection when you move on from one question to the next. You can use the Reflect, Expect, Check, Explain process to:

- *reflect* on what's different between each question and the one that came before
- decide how you *expect* this answer to be different
- complete the question and *check* your answer
- *explain* to yourself why your expectation was correct or incorrect.

EXAMPLE

Question 3a

Work out 10^4

$10^4 = 10 \times 10 \times 10 \times 10 = 10\,000$

Question 3b

Work out 5^4

Reflect: This question is like 3a but this time it's 5 to the power of 4, not 10 to the power of 4.

Expect: 5 is 10 divided by 2 so the answer will be half.

Check: $5^4 = 5 \times 5 \times 5 \times 5 = 625$

Explain: I was wrong! I need to divide the answer for 10 by 2 not just once but 4 times, once for each time 5 is multiplied in 5^4.

---

1 Write out the calculation for each of the following. For example $4^2 = 2 \times 2$

  a 5^3

  b 3^5

  c Which do you think is larger, **a** or **b**?

  d 7^2

  e 2^7

  f Which do you think is larger, **d** or **e**?

2 Write each of these in index notation.

  a $3 \times 3 \times 3 \times 3 \times 3 \times 3$

  b $9 \times 9 \times 9 \times 9$

  c $6 \times 6 \times 6$

  d $4 \times 4 \times 4 \times 4 \times 4 \times 4 \times 4 \times 4 \times 4$

  e Order the calculations in **a** to **d** from smallest to biggest

3 Work out:

  a 10^4 **c** 2^6 **e** 3^4

  b 5^4 **d** 4^3

4 Use the fact that:

  a $11^2 = 121$ to find $\sqrt{121}$

  b $11^3 = 1331$ to find $\sqrt[3]{1331}$

  c $11^4 = 14\,641$ to find $\sqrt{14\,641}$

5 Use a calculator to work out:

  a 6^2

  b 6.5^2

  c 7^2

  d Jaylah says that 6.5 is the midpoint of 6 and 7 so 6.5^2 is the midpoint of 6^2 and 7^2 Work out if she is correct or not.

6 Estimate which integer these calculations are closest to, then use a calculator to evaluate them.

a $\sqrt{101}$

b $\sqrt{123}$

c $\sqrt{145}$

7 Write these calculations using a single index number.

a $2^2 \times 2$

b $2^2 \times 2^5$

c $9^2 \times 9^5$

d $9^4 \times 9^3$

e $9^4 \times 9^3 \times 9^2$

2.2 Method selection

In these questions you'll need to think carefully about which methods to apply.

For some questions you might need to use skills from earlier chapters.

1 **a** How many dots are there in the image?

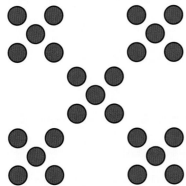

b A triangle has 3 vertices. How many vertices are there in total in the image shown?

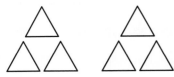

c A square has 4 vertices. How many vertices are there in total in the image shown?

2 Which is bigger:
a 5^2 or the 6th multiple of 4
b 15^2 or the 16th multiple of 14?

3 Copy and complete these statements. (The first has been done for you.)
$2^2 \times 7^2 = 196 = 14^2$
a $2^2 \times 5^2 = \square = \square^2$
b $3^2 \times 11^2 = \square = \square^2$
c $2^3 \times 7^3 = \square = \square^3$
d $2^4 \times 3^4 = \square = \square^4$

4 Copy and complete these statements. (The first has been done for you.)
$\sqrt{4} \times \sqrt{25} = 10 = \sqrt{100}$
a $\sqrt{25} \times \sqrt{16} = \square = \sqrt{\square}$

b $\sqrt{100} \times \sqrt{9} = \square = \sqrt{\square}$

c $\sqrt{1600} \times \sqrt{2500} = \square = \sqrt{\square}$

5 Find:
a two square numbers that sum to 85
b two cube numbers that have a difference of 61
c two square numbers that have a product of 225

6 Which two consecutive integers does each of these square roots lie between?
a $\sqrt{18}$
b $\sqrt{72}$
c $\sqrt{162}$

7 Use a calculator to evaluate each of these calculations.
a 7^3 c 1.1^3 e 2.1^5
b $\sqrt{225}$ d $\sqrt[3]{4.096}$ f $\sqrt{25 \times 36}$

8 Use squares and cubes that you recognise to help you to write down the missing number that goes in each box.
a $10^{\square} = 100\,000$
b $3^{\square} = 243$
c $2^{\square} = 64$
d $\square^4 = 256$

2.2 Purposeful practice

There may be more than one way to approach these questions.
Once you have answered a question one way, can you think of another way?

1 Work out how many dots are shown in each pattern.

a

b

c

2 Using a calculator or otherwise, find the value of the 'ones' digit in the square numbers from 1^2 to 20^2.
You may use a calculator.
Which numbers cannot be the last digit in a square number?

3 For each of the following numbers write down if it is possible for it to be a square number or not.
Explain how you know.

a 763   b 762   c 729   d 737

4 $16^2 = 256$
Which of these are also equal to 256?

a 4^4

b 2^8

c 8^3

5 Use the fact that $1764 = 49 \times 36$ to work out $\sqrt{1764}$

6 Which of these calculations will result in a square number?

a $(3 \times 3 \times 3 \times 2 \times 2) \div 3$

b $(3 \times 3 \times 3 \times 3 \times 2) \div (3 \times 2)$

c $(3 \times 3 \times 2 \times 3 \times 2 \times 3 \times 2) \div (3 \times 3 \times 2)$

Factors and prime factorisation

2.3.1 Understanding factors of numbers

Language

The word 'factor' originally comes from Latin and meant 'a maker'. You multiply two factors together to 'make' a number. The word was first used in a mathematical sense in the 1670s.

Objective

You will learn how to:

- understand and identify factors of a number

Two integers that you multiply together to give a product are **factors** of that product.

e.g. $8 \times 3 = 24$, so 8 and 3 are both factors of 24. They make a **factor pair.**

Look for factors in pairs to make sure you don't miss any. Start with 1 and the number. To find the factors of 24, start with 1 and 24 because $1 \times 24 = 24$

Trying 2 gives us 2 and 12 because $2 \times 12 = 24$

Trying 3 gives us 3 and 8 because $3 \times 8 = 24$

Trying 4 gives us 4 and 6 because $4 \times 6 = 24$

24 isn't in the 5 times table so 5 is not a factor.

We already have 6 as a factor so we know we have all the factors of 24: 1, 2, 3, 4, 6, 8, 12 and 24

Worked example	Thinking	Your turn!
Write down all the factors of 18	*Which factor pair can we always include?*	**Write down all the factors of 20**
1, 18	*What other times tables is the number in?*	
1, 18 2, 9 3, 6	*How can we check we have found all the pairs?*	

I can always include 1 and the number itself, $1 \times 18 = 18$ so 1 and 18 are factors

I will check each times table starting with 2 and then 3…

4 and 5 are not factors. I've already got 6 since 3 and 6 make a factor pair so I've got them all

▲ Example-problem pair 1

Key point

A factor of a number divides that number exactly (without a remainder).

$24 \div 7 = 3$ remainder 3, so 7 is not a factor of 24

$24 \div 6 = 4$ with no remainder, so 6 is a factor of 24

Worked example	Thinking	Your turn!
Is 6 a factor of 716?	*What divisibility rules can we use here?*	**Is 4 a factor of 614?**
716 is divisible by 2 because its last digit is 2		
It has a digit sum of 14 $(= 7 + 1 + 6)$ which isn't divisible by 3		
So 6 isn't a factor of 716		

I can use the divisibility rule for 6 – check if a number is even and divisible by 3

If it is divisible by 2 it is even. If the digit sum is divisible by 3, the number is also divisible by 3.

716 is even but it isn't divisible by 3 so it can't be divisible by 6

🔺 Example-problem pair 2

Since factors come in pairs, all integers have an even number of factors, apart from square numbers.

24 is not a square number, and has eight factors: 1, 2, 3, 4, 6, 8, 12, and 24

25 is a square number, and has three factors: 1, 5, and 25

You can also say that 25 is a multiple of each of the numbers: 1, 5, and 25

2.3.1 Fluency

In this exercise you can practise applying the mathematical methods that you have just learnt.

1 Write the factors of each number.
  a 5 **b** 12 **c** 120

2 Are these statements true or false?
  a 4 is a factor of 20
  b 3 is a factor of 82
  c 5 is a factor of 70
  d 6 is a factor of 74

3 Write the factors of each number.
  a 200 **c** 340
  b 225 **d** 1000

4 Which of these numbers are *not* factors of 256?
  2, 3, 4, 5, 16, 32, 36, 40, 128

5 Which of these numbers are *not* factors of 700?
  4, 7, 8, 15, 25, 35, 70, 140, 175, 350

6 State whether each of these integers has an odd or even number of factors.
  a 60 **c** 121 **e** 400
  b 81 **d** 200 **f** 625

Now check your answers. You may want to use your calculator. Did you get any wrong and can you work out why?

2.3.2 Prime numbers

Language 📖

'Prime' used to describe numbers originates from the Latin word *primus*, meaning first in importance.

Objective ☑️

You will learn how to:

- identify whether a number is prime

A **prime number** is an integer greater than 1 that has just two factors. The factors are 1 and the number itself.

To work out if a number is prime, try dividing it by smaller prime numbers to see if it has any factors other than itself and 1. You only need to check the primes up to the square root of the number. If no prime number divides the larger number exactly, then the larger number is prime.

Worked example	Thinking	Your turn!	
Is 91 a prime number?	*What does prime mean?* ○	**Is 87 a prime number?**	A prime number is only divisible by 1 and itself
91 is odd so 2 is not a factor The digit sum is $9 + 1 = 10$ which isn't divisible by 3 so 3 is not a factor The last digit isn't a 0 or a 5 so 5 is not a factor	*Is the number divisible by 2, 3, 5, 7, or any larger prime numbers?* ○		I can use the divisibility rules to work through each number
91 divides by 7 with no remainder $7 \times 13 = 91$	*How does this tell us if the number is prime or not?* ○		91 is divisible by something other than 1 and itself so it isn't prime
So 91 isn't prime			

▲ Example-problem pair 1

An integer greater than 1 that is not prime is called a **composite number.** Composite numbers have more than two factors

14 is a composite number. Its factors are 1, 2, 7, and 14

11 is not a composite number. It is a prime number. Its factors are 1 and 11

You can write a composite number as a product of two other numbers. For example, $14 = 2 \times 7$

Worked example	Thinking	Your turn!
Sort these numbers into composite numbers and prime numbers: 28, 100, 19, 74	*How do we know if a number is composite?*	Sort these numbers into composite numbers and prime numbers: 10, 144, 11, 12
$28 = 2 \times 14$ $100 = 2 \times 50$ $74 = 2 \times 37$	*Is the number divisible by 2, 3, 5, 7 or any larger prime numbers?*	
28, 100, 74 are all composite numbers 19 is prime. Its only factors are 1 and 19		

▲ Example-problem pair 2

> I know a number is composite if it has factors other than 1 and itself

> 28, 100, and 74 are all even so must be divisible by 2 and can't be prime. 19 is not divisible by 2, 3, 5 or 7 or any larger prime numbers.

Investigate Further 🔍

Research how prime numbers are used in encryption to keep information safe online.

2.3.2 Fluency

In this exercise you can practise applying the mathematical methods that you have just learnt.

1 Fill in the gaps in this definition.
A **prime number** is a number that has _____ factors, _____ and _____.

2 Write the first six prime numbers.

3 Which of these numbers are prime?
9, 13, 15, 17, 19, 20

4 Which of these numbers are prime?
21, 29, 65, 67, 81, 89

5 Show that 93 is *not* a prime number.

6 Show that 73 is a prime number.

7 Write the smallest prime number that has three digits.

8 Patrick says that 1041 is prime. Show that Patrick is incorrect.

9 Show that 887 is a prime number.

Now check your answers. You may want to use your calculator. Did you get any wrong and can you work out why?

2.3.3 Prime factorisation

Objective

You will learn how to:
- write a number as a product of its prime factors

The number 24 is a composite number. The factors of 24 that are also prime numbers are 2 and 3. These are called **prime factors.**

5 is a prime factor of 30 because it's a factor of 30 and it's a prime number.

6 is not a prime factor of 30 because even though it's a factor of 30, it's not prime.

7 is not a prime factor of 30 because even though it's prime, it's not a factor of 30

Key point

All positive integers greater than 1 are either prime or can be written as a product of prime factors.

You can use a factor tree to help you write a number as a product of its prime factors.

Start by finding two numbers whose product equals your starting number. Keep breaking each factor down in this way until you are left with only prime numbers.

Here are three different ways to find the prime factors of 24. Notice that each way results in the same prime factors.

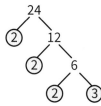 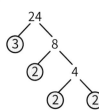 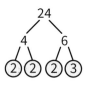

We now use the factor tree to help us write the **prime factorisation** (or prime factor decomposition) of 24:

$24 = 2 \times 2 \times 2 \times 3$

This prime factorisation is unique. This means it is the only possible answer.

If any factors are repeated, write them using index notation:

$24 = 2^3 \times 3$

Worked example	Thinking	Your turn!
Express 72 as a product of its prime factors.	*Can we find a factor pair that has a product equal to the number given?*	**Express 60 as a product of its prime factors.**
72 2 36	*Can we identify any prime factors and circle them?*	
72 ② 36 6 6 ③②③②	*Can we find further factors pairs for the composite numbers?*	
$72 = 2 \times 2 \times 2 \times 3 \times 3$	*How do we write this in index notation?*	
$= 2^3 \times 3^2$		

I can see that 72 is even so it must divide by 2

2 is a prime factor so I'll circle it

36 is composite and I know it is 6 × 6 so I can decompose it and keep going because 6 is also a composite number

Once I'm down to 2 and 3, those are both prime so I can circle them. There are no more composite numbers after that

There are three copies of the 2 so 2 is cubed

There are two copies of 3 so 3 is squared

▲ Example-problem pair 1

Calculator

Scientific calculators often have a key that allows you to express a number as a product of prime factors. Look for the key with the word FACT written above it in yellow. You will need to press shift before using the key.

To express 72 as a product of prime factors press

You should see $2^3 \times 3^2$ displayed on the screen.

2.3.3 Fluency

In this exercise you can practise applying the mathematical methods that you have just learnt.

1 Express each of these numbers as a product of prime factors.
- **a** 12
- **b** 90
- **c** 100
- **d** 144

2 Express each of these numbers as a product of prime factors.
- **a** 120
- **b** 200
- **c** 320
- **d** 475
- **e** 650
- **f** 1000

3 Express each of these numbers as a product of prime factors.
- **a** 539
- **b** 1001
- **c** 833
- **d** 49 049

Now check your answers. You may want to use your calculator. Did you get any wrong and can you work out why?

2.3.4 Using prime factorisation to identify properties of numbers

> ## Objective ☑
>
> You will learn how to:
> - use prime factorisation to identify features of a number

Once you have written a number as a product of prime factors, you can use it to find out things about the number, such as whether it's a square number or if a particular number is a factor.

For example, by writing 168 as a product of prime factors, you can determine whether 168 is divisible by 24

$168 = 2 \times 2 \times 2 \times 3 \times 7$

$24 = 2 \times 2 \times 2 \times 3$

All the factors of 24 are factors of 168:

$168 = \boxed{2 \times 2 \times 2 \times 3} \times 7$

You can see that $168 = 24 \times 7$, and so 24 is a factor of 168

Worked example	Thinking	Your turn!
By writing 405 as a product of prime factors, show that 45 is a factor of 405	*Can we express both numbers as products of their prime factors?*	**By writing 392 as a product of prime factors, show that 49 is a factor of 392**
$405 = 3 \times 3 \times 3 \times 3 \times 5$ $45 = 3 \times 3 \times 5$	*Are the factors of the smaller number also all factors of the larger number?*	
$405 = ③ \times ③ \times 3 \times 3 \times ⑤$ $45 = ③ \times ③ \times ⑤$	*How does this show us if it is a factor?*	
Yes 45 is a factor of 405 $405 = 3 \times 3 \times \boxed{3 \times 3 \times 5} = 3 \times 3 \times 45$		

I can draw factor trees for 405 and 45

I can circle the common factors to check

405 contains all the prime factors of 45, so I can write it as $405 = 45 \times ?$ showing that 45 is a factor of 405

▲ Example-problem pair 1

In the previous section, you looked at square numbers.

A square number is the result of multiplying a number by itself.

Look at some square numbers:

$196 = 14^2 = 14 \times 14$ which is $(2 \times 7) \times (2 \times 7) = (2 \times 2) \times (7 \times 7) = 2^2 \times 7^2$

$2025 = 45^2 = 45 \times 45$ which is $(3 \times 3 \times 5) \times (3 \times 3 \times 5) = (3 \times 3 \times 3 \times 3) \times (5 \times 5) = 3^4 \times 5^2$

Notice how, in these square numbers, all the exponents of the prime factors are *even* numbers. This is true for all square numbers.

Worked example	Thinking	Your turn!
By expressing 432 as a product of prime factors, show that 432 isn't a square number	*Can we express the given number as a product of prime factors?*	By expressing 675 as a product of prime factors, show that 675 isn't a square number
$432 = 2 \times 2 \times 2 \times 2 \times 3 \times 3 \times 3$ $= 2^4 \times 3^3$	*Are all the exponents even?*	
No, 432 isn't a square number, $432 = 2^4 \times 3^{\textcircled{3}}$ The prime factor 3 has an odd exponent.		

I can draw a factor tree for 432

No, 3 has an odd exponent

▲ Example-problem pair 2

Similarly, for cube numbers, all of the exponents of the prime factors are divisible by 3

For example, $216 = 6^3 = 6 \times 6 \times 6$, which is $(2 \times 3) \times (2 \times 3) \times (2 \times 3) = 2^3 \times 3^3$

2.3.4 Fluency

In this exercise you can practise applying the mathematical methods that you have just learnt.

 1 $56 = 2^3 \times 7$
Use this fact to determine if each of these numbers is a factor of 56

   a 9   **c** 21

   b 14   **d** 28

 2 $820 = 2^2 \times 5 \times 41$
Use this fact to determine if each of these numbers is a factor of 820

   a 4   **c** 10   **e** 60

   b 6   **d** 82   **f** 205

3 Here are some numbers written as the product of prime factors. Work out whether each number is a square, a cube, both or neither.

   a $64 = 2^6$ **b** $500 = 2^2 \times 5^3$

   c $9261 = 3^3 \times 7^3$ **d** $2704 = 2^4 \times 13^2$

   e $2\,775\,556 = 2^2 \times 7^4 \times 17^2$

Now check your answers. You may want to use your calculator. Did you get any wrong and can you work out why?

2.3.5 Highest common factor using prime factorisation

Objective ☑️

You will learn how to:
- find the highest common factor of two or more numbers

The **highest common factor (HCF)** of two or more integers is the largest integer that is a factor of all of them.

One way to find the HCF of two numbers is to list all the factors of the two numbers and select the largest that appears in both lists.

To find the HCF of 24 and 36, you could list the factors of both numbers.

24: **1, 2, 3, 4, 6,** 8, ⑫ 24

36: **1, 2, 3, 4, 6,** 9, ⑫ 18, 36

1, 2, 3, 4, 6, and 12 are common factors of 24 and 36. The HCF of 24 and 36 is 12 because it is the largest factor in both lists.

Another way to find the HCF of two numbers is to use their prime factorisation.

For example, to find the HCF of 24 and 36, you first write both numbers as products of their prime factors. Here are their prime factor trees:

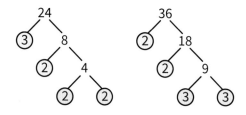

$24 = ② \times ② \times 2 \times ③$

$36 = ② \times ② \times ③ \times 3$

The HCF is the product of all the prime factors common to both numbers. In this case there are two lots of 2 and one 3 common to both numbers, so the HCF is $2 \times 2 \times 3 = 12$

Worked example	Thinking	Your turn!	
Find the highest common factor of 72 and 126	*How do we express the numbers as products of their prime factors?*	**Find the highest common factor of 42 and 105**	I'll draw factor trees for both 72 and 126 then I can write them as a product of their prime factors

$72 = 2 \times 2 \times 2 \times 3 \times 3$ $126 = 2 \times 3 \times 3 \times 7$

How do we use the prime factorisation for each number to find the HCF?

I need to check which prime factors are found in both

$72 = 2 \times 2 \times ⨀2 \times ⨀3 \times ⨀3$

$126 = ⨀2 \times ⨀3 \times ⨀3 \times 7$

How can we use the common factors to find the HCF?

I have circled the factors that appear in both lists. Multiplying these will give me the HCF

HCF is $2 \times 3 \times 3 = 18$

▲ Example-problem pair 1

2.3.5 Fluency

In this exercise you can practise applying the mathematical methods that you have just learnt.

1 Find the highest common factor of each pair of numbers.
  a 24 and 46   **b** 60 and 80

2 The factors of four numbers are shown.

16: 1, 2, 4, 8, 16	**24**: 1, 2, 3, 4, 6, 8, 12, 24	**60**: 1, 2, 3, 4, 5, 6, 10, 12, 15, 20, 30, 60	**72**: 1, 2, 3, 4, 6, 8, 9, 12, 18, 24, 36, 72

Find the highest common factor of each of these pairs of numbers.
  a 16 and 24   **c** 24 and 60
  b 16 and 60   **d** 24 and 72

3 $45 = 3^2 \times 5$ $85 = 5 \times 17$
     $75 = 3 \times 5^2$ $90 = 2 \times 3^2 \times 5$
Use these prime factorisations to find the highest common factor of each pair of numbers.
  a 45 and 85   **c** 45 and 75
  b 75 and 90   **d** 85 and 90

4 Write each pair of numbers as the product of prime factors and use this to find the highest common factor.
  a 62 and 70   **c** 120 and 156
  b 90 and 108   **d** 240 and 324

5 Find the highest common factor of each set of numbers.
  a 12, 40, and 60   **c** 121, 363, and 385
  b 100, 140, and 180   **d** 145, 725, and 870

Now check your answers. You may want to use your calculator. Did you get any wrong and can you work out why?

2.3.6 Lowest common multiple using prime factorisation

The **lowest common multiple (LCM)** of two or more integers is the smallest integer that is a multiple of all of them.

To find the LCM of two numbers, you could list multiples of the two numbers and select the smallest that appears in both lists.

For example, to find the LCM of 24 and 36 you could list the multiples of both numbers.

24: 24, 48, **72**, 96, …

36: 36, **72**, 108, …

72 is the LCM of 24 and 36 because it is the smallest multiple that appears in both lists.

For larger numbers especially, it is quicker and easier to use the prime factorisations of both numbers. To find the lowest common multiple, you need to multiply together all of the factors of both numbers, without repeating the factors they have in common.

To do this, first write out the prime factors of each number and use this to find the HCF. This tells you which factors are included in both the numbers, because all factors of the HCF must be all the factors that the two numbers have in common.

$24 = ② × ② × 2 × ③$

$36 = ② × ② × ③ × 3$

HCF $= 2 × 2 × 3 = 12$

To work out what other factors to include in the calculation for the LCM, cross out the factors from the HCF as they have already been included.

$24 = \cancel{②} × \cancel{②} × 2 × \cancel{③}$

$36 = \cancel{②} × \cancel{②} × \cancel{③} × 3$

To find the LCM, multiply the HCF by any remaining factors from both lists.

LCM $= 12 × 2 × 3 = 72$

When finding the LCM of three numbers, you must be careful to only use the remaining factors once, even if they appear in more than one number.

Worked example	Thinking	Your turn!	
Find the lowest common multiple of 18 and 60	*How can we find the LCM?*	**Find the lowest common multiple of 42 and 105**	I need to list their multiples or use prime factorisation.
$18 = 2 \times 3 \times 3$ $60 = 2 \times 2 \times 3 \times 5$	*How do we use our answer to find the HCF?*		I need to circle the common factors and multiply them together.
$18 = 2 \times 3 \times 3$ $60 = 2 \times 2 \times 3 \times 5$ $HCF = 2 \times 3 = 6$	*How can we use the HCF to find the LCM?*		I need to cross out the factors I used to find the HCF and then multiply the HCF by the remaining factors.
$18 = 2 \times 3 \times 3$ $60 = 2 \times 2 \times 3 \times 5$			
So the LCM is $6 \times 2 \times 3 \times 5 = 180$			

▲ Example-problem pair 1

2.3.6 Fluency

In this exercise you can practise applying the mathematical methods that you have just learnt.

1 Find the lowest common multiple of each pair of numbers.

   a 5 and 7   **c** 9 and 15

   b 8 and 12   **d** 18 and 27

2 $45 = 5 \times 3^2$

   $75 = 3 \times 5^2$

   $85 = 5 \times 17$

   $90 = 2 \times 3^2 \times 5$

   Use these prime factorisations to find the lowest common multiple of each pair of numbers.

   a 45 and 85   **c** 45 and 75

   b 75 and 90   **d** 85 and 90

3 Find the lowest common multiple of each pair of numbers.

   a 62 and 70   **c** 120 and 156

   b 90 and 108   **d** 240 and 324

4 Find the lowest common multiple of each set of numbers.

   a 145, 725 and 870   **c** 121, 363 and 385

   b 100, 140 and 180   **d** 12, 40 and 60

Now check your answers. You may want to use your calculator. Did you get any wrong and can you work out why?

2.3 Exercises

2.3 Intelligent practice

"Why is it intelligent?" You might notice a connection when you move on from one question to the next. You can use the Reflect, Expect, Check, Explain process to:

- *reflect* on what's different between each question and the one that came before
- decide how you *expect* this answer to be different
- complete the question and *check* your answer
- *explain* to yourself why your expectation was correct or incorrect.

EXAMPLE

Question 4b

Express 28 as a product of prime factors.

$28 = 2 \times 2 \times 7$

Question 4c

Express 280 as a product of prime factors.

Reflect: The number in this question is 10 times bigger than in Q4b

Expect: If I take my answer from Q4b and multiply it by another 2 and a 5, I will have the prime factorisation for 280. So $280 = (2 \times 2 \times 7) \times 2 \times 5$

Check:

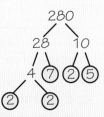

$280 = 2 \times 2 \times 2 \times 5 \times 7$

Explain: I was correct! Because $2 \times 2 \times 7 \times 2 \times 5 = 2 \times 2 \times 2 \times 5 \times 7$

---

1 Write the factors of each of these numbers.
   a 28   **b** 42   **c** 77
   d Which factors are common to 28, 42 and 77?

2 How many factors does each of these numbers have?
   a 13   **b** 61   **c** 89   **d** 113
   e What do you notice about your answers to parts **a** to **d**?

3 How many factors does each of these numbers have?
   a 49   **b** 64   **c** 81
   d What do you notice about your answers to parts **a** to **c**?

4 Express each of these numbers as a product of prime factors.

a	14	**d**	70	**g**	500
b	28	**e**	35	**h**	50
c	280	**f**	3500	**i**	2500

5 189, 198 and 918 have been written as a product of their prime factors.

$189 = 3^3 \times 7$

$198 = 2 \times 3^2 \times 11$

$918 = 2 \times 3^3 \times 17$

Write which of them have a factor of:

a 3

b 6

c 18

d 27

6 10, 12, 20 and 30 have been written as a product of their prime factors.

$10 = 2 \times 5$ $20 = 2 \times 2 \times 5$

$12 = 2 \times 2 \times 3$ $30 = 2 \times 3 \times 5$

Find the HCF of:

a	5 and 10	**e**	20 and 30
b	5 and 20	**f**	12 and 30
c	10 and 20	**g**	7 and 30
d	10 and 30		

7 6, 10, 15, 30, 45 and 60 have been written as a product of their prime factors.

$6 = 2 \times 3$ $30 = 2 \times 3 \times 5$

$10 = 2 \times 5$ $45 = 3 \times 3 \times 5$

$15 = 3 \times 5$ $60 = 2 \times 2 \times 3 \times 5$

Find the LCM of:

a	6 and 7	**d**	6 and 30
b	6 and 10	**e**	6 and 45
c	6 and 15	**f**	60 and 45

2.3 Method selection

In these questions you'll need to think carefully about which methods to apply.

For some questions you might need to use skills from earlier chapters.

1 **a** Express 42 as a product of prime factors

b Use your answer to part a to decide which of these numbers are factors of 42:

2   3   5   7   11   13   17   19

c What other factors does 42 have?

2 List the prime numbers between 80 and 90

3 Two friends are building towers with identical building bricks. Ali has 48 bricks and Bella has 32 bricks.

a Ali uses all 48 of his bricks to make towers that are all the same height. How many bricks tall could his towers be?

b Bella uses all 32 of her bricks to make towers that are all the same height. How many bricks tall could her towers be?

c After they have built their towers, Bella notices that Ali's towers are the same height as hers. What heights could their towers be? What are the tallest possible towers they could have built?

4 A red light flashes every 8 seconds, and a blue light flashes every 20 seconds. If they both flash together, after how many seconds will they flash together again?

5 Are these statements true or false?
  a 7 is a factor of 7^3
  b 7 is a factor of 3^7
  c 7 is a factor of $3^2 \times 7$
  d 7 is a factor of $2^7 \times 17$

6 Express 455 and 585 as a product of prime factors. Copy and complete the Venn diagram.

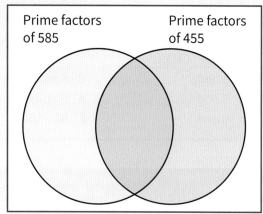

7 Express 187 and 935 as a product of prime factors and use your answers to help you find the LCM of 187 and 935. What do you notice about your answer?

8 **a** By expressing 450 as a product of its prime factors, show that it isn't a square number.
  b What is the smallest number you can multiply 450 by to make a square number?
  c What is the square root of the square number made?

9 $588 = 2^2 \times 3 \times 7^2$
Use the prime factorisation of 588 to find the missing numbers in these calculations.
  a $588 = \square \times 6$
  b $588 = \square \times 21$
  c $588 = 14 \times \square$

10 90, 135, and 315 have been written as a product of their prime factors.
$90 = 2 \times 3^2 \times 5$
$135 = 3^3 \times 5$
$315 = 3^2 \times 5 \times 7$
Use these products to find the LCM of 90, 135 and 315.

11 Use your calculator to express 1728 as a product of prime factors and determine whether 1728 is a square number, cube number or both.

2.3 Purposeful practice

There may be more than one way to approach these questions.
Once you have answered a question one way, can you think of another way?

1 What is the smallest sum of two positive integers whose product is 196?

2 Write down the smallest integer that has:
  a 1 factor   **d** 4 factors
  b 2 factors   **e** 5 factors
  c 3 factors

3 85 800 has been written as a product of its prime factors. Use this to determine which of these numbers are factors of 85 800
$85\,800 =$
$2^3 \times 3 \times 5^2 \times 11 \times 13$

2	3	4	5	6	7	8	9	10	11	12	13

4 Use your calculator to help you express each of these numbers as a product of its prime factors. Then identify the square number, the cube number, the multiple of 11 and the prime number.

   a 1764   **c** 2310

   b 2221   **d** 2744

5 $15\,750 = 2 \times 3^2 \times 5^3 \times 7$

Which of these statements are true?

   a 90 is a factor of 15 750

   b 25 is the largest square factor of 15 750

   c 15 750 has 24 factors

   d $15\,750 \div \left(3^2 \times 5^2\right) = 70$

6 A semi-prime is a number that is the product of exactly two prime numbers.

25 is a semi-prime because it can be written as

$25 = 5 \times 5$

26 is a semi-prime because it can be written as

$26 = 2 \times 13$

How many semi-primes are there between 30 and 40?

7 Find two numbers that have four factors and two of the factors total 20.

8 The Manchester bus leaves the bus station at 8 a.m. and every 15 minutes after that until the last bus at 5 p.m.

The Newcastle bus leaves the bus station at 8 a.m. and every 25 minutes after that until the last bus at 4:45 p.m.

   a After 8 a.m., what is the next time the two buses leave the bus station at the same time?

   b How many times between 8 a.m. and 5 p.m. do the two buses leave the bus station together?

9 How many unique arrays can be made with 315 dots?

10 The highest common factor of 31 and 29 is 1. Find the lowest common multiple of the two numbers.

If the highest common factor of two numbers is 1, how would you find their lowest common multiple?

11 The highest common factor of two numbers is 2 and the product of the two numbers is 1276. What is the lowest common multiple of the two numbers?

12 Explain what the lowest common factor of two or more numbers would be.

13 Explain why you can't find the highest common multiple of two or more numbers.

14 'The product of two square numbers is always a square number.'

Thinking about prime factorisation, explain why this statement is true.

Watch out! exercise

Some students have tried to answer the questions below but have unfortunately made some mistakes.

For each question do the following:

a answer the question correctly

b write down the mistake that each student has made

c comment on why they might have made that mistake

d write an explanation for each student to convince them (nicely!) that their answer cannot be correct.

1 Aisha and Cameron have each tried to answer the question "Write $9 \times 9 \times 9 \times 9 \times 9$ in index notation."

Aisha wrote
$9 \times 9 \times 9 \times 9 \times 9 = 5 \times 9$

Cameron wrote
$9 \times 9 \times 9 \times 9 \times 9 = 5^9$

2 Yousef and Oona have each tried to answer the question "Evaluate 6^3"

Yousef wrote
$6 \times 3 = 18$

Oona wrote
$3 \times 3 \times 3 \times 3 \times 3 \times 3 = 729$

3 Adisa, Paige and Evan have each tried to answer the question "Express 180 as a product of its prime factors."

Adisa wrote
$1 \times 2 \times 2 \times 3 \times 3 \times 5$

Evan wrote
$2 \times 2 \times 5 \times 9$

Paige wrote
$2^2 + 3^2 + 5$

4 Nia, Jacob and Mustafa have each tried to answer the question "Find the HCF of 12 and 30"

Nia wrote
60

Mustafa wrote
3

Jacob wrote
12

5 Ralph, Mollie and Suchin have each tried to answer the question "Find the LCM of 12 and 15"

Ralph wrote
24

Mollie wrote
3

Suchin wrote
$12 \times 15 = 180$

6 Luka and Zainab have each tried to answer the question "Evaluate $\sqrt{64}$"

Luka wrote
32

Zainab wrote
4

7 Clare and Pete have each tried to answer the question "Write down all the factors of 28"

Clare wrote
1, 2, 4, 14, 28

Pete wrote
1×28

2×14

4×9

Check your understanding

Turn over to find the review questions

2.1 Multiples

You should now be able to...	Questions
understand and list multiples of a number	1, 2, 5a–c, 8
identify whether a number is a multiple of another number	3, 4, 5d, 6, 7

2.2 Powers and roots

You should now be able to...	Questions
understand and calculate square numbers	10d, 12a
understand and calculate cube numbers	10a
understand and calculate square roots	11a, 12b, 13
understand and calculate cube roots	11b, 11c
understand and calculate powers of numbers	9, 10b, 10c
recognise powers of 2, 3, 4, and 5	13

2.3 Factors and prime factorisation

You should now be able to...	Questions
understand and identify factors of a number	14, 15
identify whether a number is prime	16
write a number as a product of its prime factors	17a
use prime factorisation to identify features of a number	18
find the highest common factor of two or more numbers	17b
find the lowest common multiple of two or more numbers	17c

Chapter 2 review questions

1 List the first five multiples of 4 [1]

2 Write down the 12th multiple of 7 [1]

3 Is 412 a multiple of 3?

Explain how you know. [1]

4 Is 635 a multiple of 5?

Explain how you know. [1]

5 918 is the 54th multiple of 17

    a What is the 17th multiple of 54? [1]

    b What is the 55th multiple of 17? [1]

    c What is the 18th multiple of 54? [1]

    d Ben says that 1751 is a multiple of 17
       Is Ben correct?
       Explain how you know. [1]

6 Sheep have 4 legs.

In a field of sheep, there are 64 legs.

How many sheep are in the field? [1]

7 A train timetable says that trains arrive at a station every 14 minutes.

The first train arrives at 7 a.m.

Will a train arrive at the station at 8:24 a.m.?

Explain how you know. [1]

8 The 14th multiple of 36 is 504.

The 18th multiple of 36 is 648

What is the 32nd multiple of 36? [1]

9 Write each of these using index notation.

    a $3 \times 3 \times 3 \times 3$ [1]

    b $7 \times 7 \times 7 \times 7 \times 7 \times 7$ [1]

10 Work out:

    a 10^3 [1]

    b 2^7 [1]

    c 3^5 [1]

    d $6^2 \times 2^2$ [1]

11 Work out:

    a $\sqrt{144}$ [1]

    b $\sqrt[3]{27}$ [1]

    c $\sqrt[3]{729}$ [1]

12 Use a calculator to work out:

    a 3.2^2 [1]

    b $\sqrt{380 + 104}$ [1]

13 $7744 = 64 \times 121$

Use this fact to work out $\sqrt{7744}$ [2]

14 Write down all of the factors of 24 [2]

15 Is 6 a factor of 1926?

Explain how you know. [1]

16 Is 47 a prime number?

Explain how you know. [1]

17 Answer the following:

a Express 120 and 135 as products of

their prime factors. [3]

b Find the highest common factor of

120 and 135 [2]

c Find the lowest common multiple of

120 and 135 [2]

18 $16\,500 = 2^2 \times 3 \times 5^3 \times 11$

a Is 15 a factor of 16 500?

Explain how you know. [1]

b Is 16 500 divisible by 66?

Explain how you know. [1]

c What is the largest square number that

divides into 16 500? [1]

d What is the smallest number you can

multiply 16 500 by to make a cube number?

Explain your answer.

[2]

Key words

Make sure you can write a definition for these key terms.

*multiple • square number • index notation • exponent • base • squared • power • cube number
cubed • square root • cube root • factor • factor pair • prime number • composite number
prime factor • prime factorisation • highest common factor (HCF) • lowest common multiple (LCM)*

3

Arithmetic

NASA's rover, Curiosity, gathers information about the weather on Mars, including high and low temperatures. How do temperatures on Mars compare with temperatures on Earth? How does the temperature change throughout a single day on Mars?

Date	21 July	22 July	23 July	24 July	25 July	26 July	27 July
High temperature	−1°C	−2°C	−2°C	1°C	0°C	−4°C	−1°C
Low temperature	−68°C	−69°C	−69°C	−68°C	−69°C	−69°C	−69°C

What comes before?

Primary school
- Column addition and subtraction
- Written methods of multiplication and division
- Priority of operations

Book 1
- Comparing and ordering numbers
- Multiplying and dividing numbers by powers of 10

This chapter

- 3.1 Addition and subtraction with negative integers
- 3.2 Multiplication and division with negative integers
- 3.3 Addition and subtraction with decimals
- 3.4 Multiplication and division with decimals
- 3.5 Efficient calculations

What comes after?

Book 1
- Expressions and equations
- Arithmetic procedures with fractions
- Multiplicative relationships and ratio

Book 2
- Estimation

Introduction

You need to add, subtract, multiply, and divide numbers all the time; when you go to the shop, when you convert from kilometres to miles, or when you share pizza between friends.

In this chapter, you will also learn how to carry out all four operations on negative numbers, just as you can for positive numbers. Negative numbers are used in lots of situations, such as for temperature or to describe a downhill slope. For example, ice cream tubs are normally stored in freezers under $-18°C$ to make sure they stay frozen.

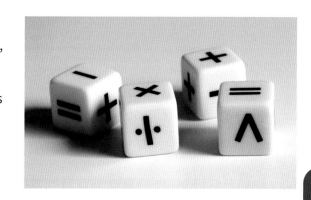

In this chapter you will learn how to...

order and compare positive and negative numbers

$-2 < -1.7 < 1.7 < 2$

add and subtract positive and negative numbers

$-0.65 + 0.03 = -0.62$

$11 + (-20) = -9$

multiply positive and negative numbers

$32 \times (-6) = -192$

$-5 \times (-1.6) = 8$

use the commutative law

$14 + 17$ is equal to $17 + 14$

$56 \div 8.3$ is not equal to $8.3 \div 56$

divide positive and negative numbers

$-1.44 \div 12 = -0.12$

$-72 \div (-8) = 9$

use the associative law

$(11 \times 6) \times 0.5$ is equal to $11 \times (6 \times 0.5)$

$(22 - 4.6) - 0.9$ is not equal to $22 - (4.6 - 0.9)$

use the distributive law

$6 \times (104 - 70)$ is equal to $(6 \times 104) - (6 \times 70)$

$(24 + 3.6) \div 1.2$ is equal to $(24 \div 1.2) + (3.6 \div 1.2)$

calculate using priority of operations

1. Brackets
2. Powers and roots

$3 \times (5.9 - 0.9)^2 + 51 \div 4.5$

3. Multiplication and division
4. Addition and subtraction

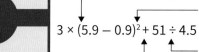

Reactivate your knowledge

If you can answer the questions on these pages then you should be ready for the chapter.

Some questions are there to help you to remember some maths from primary school and some are to help you remember maths from earlier in the book.

If you see this symbol  it tells you where that information was introduced in an earlier chapter. If you are struggling with those questions you could go back and read through it again.

3.1 Addition and subtraction with negative integers

You should know...

1. how to place positive numbers on a number line

For example

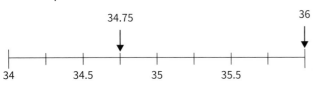

Look back to Subsection 1.1.3

2. how to compare and order positive numbers

For example

Is 47 greater or less than 49?

The tens digits are the same, so look at the units digits.

4⑦ < 4⑨

7 < 9, so 47 < 49

2.5⑨4 > 2.5①6

Is 2.594 greater or less than 2.516?

The units and tenths are the same, so look at the hundredths digits.

9 > 1, so 2.594 > 2.516

Look back to Subsection 1.1.3

Check in

1. Place each of these numbers on a copy of this number line:

   a 13

   b 14.5

   c 12.5

2. Insert < or > to make each of these statements correct.

   a 114 ☐ 113

   b 71.5 ☐ 71.9

   c 92.2 ☐ 86.7

3.2 Multiplication and division with negative integers,
3.3 Addition and subtraction with decimals, and
3.4 Multiplication and division with decimals

You should know...

3. how to solve a multiplication or division involving an array

For example

This array represents the multiplication $3 \times 5 = 15$:

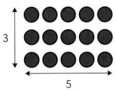

It also represents the division $15 \div 5 = 3$

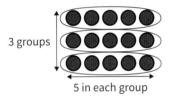

3 groups

5 in each group

Check in

3. What multiplications and divisions do these arrays represent?

a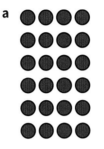

b ●●●●●●●●

c ●●
  ●●
  ●●
  ●●
  ●●
  ●●
  ●●
  ●●

---

4. what the multiples of a number are

For example

The first ten multiples of 6 are:

6, 12, 18, 24, 30, 36, 42, 48, 54, 60

4. Write the first ten multiples of:

a 3

b 7

c 12

---

5. how to partition numbers in different ways

For example

12 341 can be partitioned into ten thousands, thousands, hundreds, tens, and units as

$10\,000 + 2000 + 300 + 40 + 1$

5. Partition these numbers in different ways:

a 563

b 6293

c 20 937

---

6. how to divide positive numbers using short division

For example

```
    5 9.2
8 | 4 7⁷3 ¹6
```

6. Using short division, work out:

a $1458 \div 6$

b $923 \div 4$

c $436.1 \div 7$

You should know...

7. how to use place value to help you multiply and divide

For example

$3 \times 5 = 15$, so $3 \times 500 = 1500$

$11 \times 6 = 66$, so $110 \times 60 = 6600$

$36 \div 4 = 9$, so $360 \div 9 = 40$

$18 \div 3 = 6$, so $180\,000 \div 300 = 600$

8. how to multiply and divide numbers by positive powers of 10

For example

$79.1 \times 10\,000 = 791\,000$

$1476 \div 100 = 14.76$

 Look back to Subsection 2.1.2

9. how to multiply and divide numbers by negative powers of 10

For example

$435 \times 0.1 = 43.5$

$16 \div 0.001 = 16\,000$

 Look back to Subsection 1.1.2

Check in

7. Work out:

a 12×40
(Hint: work out 12×4 first)

b 700×50
(Hint: work out 7×5 first)

c $240 \div 8$
(Hint: work out $24 \div 8$ first)

d $48\,000 \div 600$
(Hint: work out $48 \div 6$ first)

8. Work out:

a 16.4×100

b 873×1000

c $24.05 \div 10$

d $63\,822 \div 10\,000$

9. Work out:

a 4850.3×0.001

b 820×0.1

c $193 \div 0.01$

d $65.8 \div 0.0001$

3.5 Efficient calculations

You should know...

10. how to calculate powers of numbers on a calculator

For example

$2.5^2 = 2.5 \times 2.5 = 6.25$

$7^3 = 7 \times 7 \times 7 = 343$

$6^4 = 6 \times 6 \times 6 \times 6 = 1296$

 Look back to Subsection 2.2.2

11. how to work out square roots and cube roots on a calculator

For example

Square root is the inverse of square.

$6.2^2 = 38.44$, so $\sqrt{38.44} = 6.2$

Cube root is the inverse of cube.

$4^3 = 64$, so $\sqrt[3]{64} = 4$

 Look back to Subsection 2.2.2

Check in

10. Using a calculator, work out:

   a 17^2

   b 4.5^3

   c 1.8^4

   d 9^5

11. Using a calculator, work out:

   a $\sqrt{324}$

   b $\sqrt{19.4}$

   c $\sqrt[3]{512}$

   d $\sqrt[3]{43.6}$

Chapter 3

3.1.1 Negative integers

Objectives

You will learn:
- how to order and compare positive and negative integers
- that there are infinitely many integers

Floors in tall buildings are often numbered with the ground floor as 0 and upper floors as 1, 2, 3, and so on. Underground floors are given **negative numbers**. If you went down one level below the ground floor you would be at level −1. If you went down two levels below the ground floor you would be at level −2.

Count backwards using whole numbers; keep going past zero and you are using negative numbers!

Investigate Further

Brahmagupta, a Hindu mathematician who lived about 1400 years ago, wrote a set of rules for dealing with fortunes (positive numbers) and debts (negative numbers). Mathematicians argued for centuries about negative numbers and whether they were useful or could be calculated with. They only began to be used more widely about 300 years ago. Research the history of negative numbers and how they have been used.

Language

'Ascending' means going up. With numbers, this means going from left to right on the number line. 'Descending' is the opposite of ascending and means going down. With numbers, this means going from right to left on the number line.

Up to now, you may have only met number lines that start at 0 and extend to the right. However, if you continue the number line to the left of 0, you will show negative numbers. For every **positive number** there is a corresponding negative number, e.g. 4 and −4

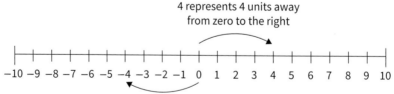

4 represents 4 units away from zero to the right

−4 represents the same distance from zero but in opposite direction, to the left

The whole numbers shown above are examples of integers. An integer is a whole number and can be positive, negative, or zero. Zero is neither positive nor negative. You don't need to show a positive sign in front of a positive number, but you must always include the negative sign for negative numbers.

You can order integers by thinking about their position on a number line.

This number line shows the integers from negative 10 to positive 10 in ascending order. You use the phrases 'less than' ($<$) or 'greater than' ($>$) when you are talking about ordering numbers (see Section 1.3).

-9 is to the left of -7, so -9 is less than -7
We write this as: $-9 < -7$

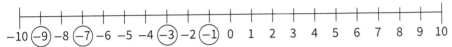

-1 is to the right of -3, so -1 is greater than -3
We write this as: $-1 > -3$

Key point

Greater than means that a number's position on the number line is further right than the number you are comparing it with.
Less than means that a number's position is further to the left than the number you are comparing it with.

Worked example	Thinking	Your turn!
Write these two numbers with the correct symbol $<$ or $>$ between them.	*Which number is further right on the number line?*	Write these two numbers with the correct symbol $<$ or $>$ between them. $-4 \square -2$
$-5 \square -9$ $\begin{array}{ccccccc} \mid & \mid & \mid & \mid & \mid & \mid & \mid \\ -10 & -9 & -8 & -7 & -6 & -5 & -4 \end{array}$ $-5 > -9$		

-5 is to the right of -9 on a number line, so it is greater than -9

▲ Example-problem pair 1

When you need to order a list of numbers where some are positive and some are negative, you can use a number line. Another method would be to deal with the positive and negative numbers separately.

Worked example	Thinking	Your turn!
Write these numbers in ascending order: 23, −22, 0, 21, 25, −26, −29	*What is the first step we can take?*	Write these numbers in ascending order: 57, −52, 53, −55, −58, 0, −50
Ordering the positive numbers: 21, 23, 25	*How do we know what the least positive number is?*	
Ordering the negative numbers: −29, −26, −22	*How do we know what the least negative number is?* *Where do we put the zero?*	
So the correct order is: −29, −26, −22, 0, 21, 23, 25		

 Example-problem pair 2

I can start by pulling out the positive numbers and ordering them. Ascending means I need to order them from least to greatest.

They all have the same value in the tens column, so I need to compare the ones.

I can think about the negative part of a number line.

The zero goes between the negative and the positive numbers.

Language 📖

The word 'infinite' comes from the Latin word *in*, meaning not or opposite, and *finis* meaning end (also seen in the word finish), together meaning endless. This is the symbol for 'infinite': ∞

When you count using positive integers, you can always keep going. If you get to 100, you can count on to 101, 102, 103, and so on. If you get to a million, you can still count on. For any positive number there will always be a greater number. This is because there are infinitely many positive integers. This means they continue forever!

For every positive number you write, there is a negative number that represents the same distance from zero but in the opposite direction. So the number line continues infinitely in the negative direction too. For any negative number there will always be another lesser number that is further from zero.

3.1.1 Fluency

In this exercise you can practise applying mathematical methods that you have just learnt.

1 Draw a number line that goes from -5 to 5

2 Write the numbers that are represented by each letter on this number line.

$-8 \quad a \quad -6 \quad -5 \quad -4 \quad -3 \quad -2 \quad b \quad 0 \quad 1 \quad 2 \quad 3 \quad 4 \quad c \quad 6 \quad 7 \quad 8$

3 Write the numbers that are represented by each letter on this number line.

$-6 \qquad a \qquad b \quad 6$

4 Use the number line to write these numbers in ascending order.

$6, -4, 1, -3, 0$

$-10 \quad -9 \quad -8 \quad -7 \quad -6 \quad -5 \quad -4 \quad -3 \quad -2 \quad -1 \quad 0 \quad 1 \quad 2 \quad 3 \quad 4 \quad 5 \quad 6 \quad 7 \quad 8 \quad 9 \quad 10$

5 Copy and complete each of these using $<$, $>$, or $=$.

a $4 \,\square\, -3$

b $-7 \,\square\, 5$

c $-11 \,\square\, -13$

d $-10 \,\square\, -10$

e $0 \,\square\, -8$

6 Draw arrows on a copy of this number line to show the position of each number.

$-7, 4, -9, 8, 2$

$-10 \qquad\qquad\qquad\qquad\qquad\qquad\qquad 10$

7 Write these numbers in descending order.

$2, 15, -6, 11, -12, 6$

8 There is an integer missing in this inequality.

$-4 < \square < 2$

Write all the possible values for the missing integer.

9 There is an integer missing in this inequality.

$-6 < \square < 1$

Write all the possible values for the missing integer.

Now check your answers. Did you get any wrong and can you work out why?

3.1.2 Addition with negative integers

You will learn how to:
- add positive and negative integers

As well as using a number line, you can represent integers using counters. Because integers can be positive or negative, you use two-colour counters to represent them.

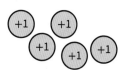

This is the number 5

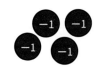

This is the number −4

You can use these two-colour counters to model the **sum** of positive and negative numbers. For example,

$1 + 2$ (+1) + (+1)(+1)   = 3

$1 + 1$ (+1) + (+1)   = 2

$1 + 0$ (+1) +   = 1

$1 + (−1)$ (+1) + (−1)   = 0

In the last row something is *added* to 1 to make 0! You say that −1 is the **additive inverse** of 1, because together they add up to 0. You can also say that positive 1 and negative 1 make a **zero pair**.

Key point

The additive inverse of a number is what you need to add to it to make zero. For example, the additive inverse of 1 is −1 since when you add them, they make zero. The additive inverse of 3 is −3, as $3 + −3 = 0$. The additive inverse of −2 is 2. You call a number and its additive inverse a zero pair.

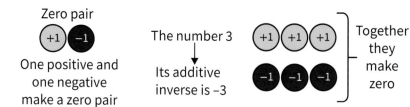

Sometimes, to make calculations clearer, you use brackets to separate the operation in front (e.g. + or −) from the negative sign. For example, $3 + (−4)$ or $−4 − (−5)$

Notice that you don't need brackets around the negative 4 in the last calculation as there is no operation in front.

Worked example	Thinking	Your turn!
Evaluate this calculation: $7 + -5$	*What model can we use to help us?*	Evaluate this calculation: $8 + -3$

Positive 7 add negative 5 can be modelled like this:

How should we arrange the counters?

(+1) (+1) (+1) (+1) (+1) (+1) (+1)   +   (−1) (−1) (−1) (−1) (−1)

> I can use two-colour counters to model positive 7 and negative 5.

> I will line up the positives and negatives to make zero pairs. There are two yellow (positive) counters left.

(+1) (+1) (+1) (+1) (+1) (+1) (+1)
(−1) (−1) (−1) (−1) (−1)

After making the zero pairs there are two yellow counters left.

This means the answer to the calculation:

$7 + -5$ is positive 2

You can write

$7 + -5 = 2$

▲ Example-problem pair 1

When adding positive and negative numbers, sometimes the answer is positive and sometimes it is negative. Sometimes the answer is less than the first number. If the positive number is further from zero than the negative number, the answer will be positive. If the negative number is further from zero than the positive number, the answer will be negative. Check that your answer has the sign (positive or negative) that you expect.

3.1.2 Fluency

In this exercise you can practise applying mathematical methods that you have just learnt.

1 Work out:

a $7 + 11$	**f** $-12 + 15$
b $3 + (-4)$	**g** $-7 + 19$
c $6 + (-2)$	**h** $-7 + (-2)$
d $8 + (-11)$	**i** $-6 + (-4)$
e $-8 + 5$	**j** $-12 + (-5)$

c $-2 + (-13) + 6$ **e** $17 + 11 + (-10)$
d $-8 + (-9) + (-2)$ **f** $-14 + 5 + 6$

3 Copy and complete each of these using $<$ or $>$.
   a $18 + -7 \square 18$ **b** $-7 + -6 \square -7$

Now check your answers. You may want to use your calculator. Did you get any wrong and can you work out why?

2 Work out:
   a $8 + (-12) + (-5)$ **b** $-7 + 9 + (-15)$

Chapter 3

3.1.3 Introduction to subtraction with negative integers

> ### Objective
>
> You will learn how to:
> - subtract positive and negative integers

You sometimes use the words '**minuend**' and '**subtrahend**' as a sort of short-cut to describe the different parts of a subtraction. The number you are subtracting from is the minuend, and the number you are subtracting is the subtrahend.

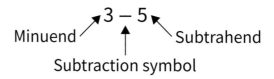

Minuend $3 - 5$ Subtrahend

Subtraction symbol

> ### Language
>
> 'Plus' and 'minus' are everyday words people use when talking about numbers. Sometimes they mean add and subtract, and sometimes they mean positive and negative.

Look at this pattern of subtractions.

Subtractions		Equivalent additions

Change the — to a +   Flip the subtrahend

$$(+1) - (+1) = \quad (+1) + (-1)$$
$$1 - 1 \quad = \quad 1 + (-1) \quad = 0$$

$$(+1) - \quad = \quad (+1) +$$
$$1 - 0 \quad = \quad 1 + 0 \quad = 1$$

$$(+1) - (-1) = \quad (+1) + (+1)$$
$$1 - (-1) \quad = \quad 1 + 1 \quad = 2$$

You can see that any subtraction can be rewritten as an addition of the additive inverse. You swap the sign of the second number (the subtrahend) and add the numbers instead.

> ### Key point
>
> The subtraction symbol means the same thing as addition of the additive inverse.

Worked example	Thinking	Your turn!
Calculate: $-4 - -7$	How do we subtract using the model?	Calculate: $-3 - -8$

> Subtraction is addition of the additive inverse, so I need to add the additive inverse of negative 7.

| | How can we tell if there will be zero pairs before we build the model? | |

> I flip my counters for negative 7, then I can add.

$-4 - (-7) = 3$

▲ Example-problem pair 1

3.1.3 Fluency

In this exercise you can practise applying mathematical methods that you have just learnt.

1 Use counters to work out:
   a $7 - 2$
   b $3 - 5$
   c $-2 - (-6)$
   d $-7 - (-2)$
   e $-5 - (-4)$
   f $-3 - (-5)$

2 Use counters to work out:
   a $-2 - 10$
   b $6 - (-2)$
   c $-5 - 4$
   d $8 - (-3)$

3 Copy and complete each of these using < or >.
   a $4 - 2 \square 4$
   b $-3 - (-4) \square -3$
   c $6 - (-5) \square 6$
   d $-4 - 7 \square -4$

Now check your answers. You may want to use your calculator. Did you get any wrong and can you work out why?

3.1.4 More addition and subtraction with negative integers

Once you understand the principles of adding and subtracting with negative numbers, you can work with number lines, additive inverses (zero pairs), and part-part-whole models to help you think about larger numbers.

To work out $12 - 26$ you can partition 26 into 12 and 14 so $12 - 26 = 12 - 12 - 14 = -14$.

Partitioning a number means writing it as an equivalent calculation involving addition (or subtraction).

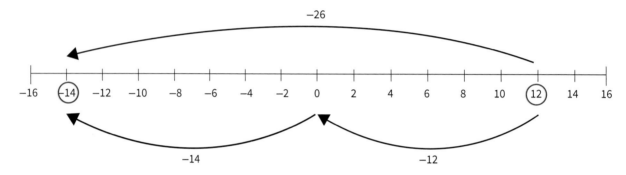

In another example, 27 could also be partitioned as $(25 + 2)$ or $(20 + 5 + 2)$ or $(30 - 3)$.

A number's **absolute value** is its distance from zero. For example, negative 3 and positive 3 are both a distance of 3 from zero, so both have an absolute value of 3.

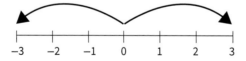

When you have a mix of positive and negative numbers in an addition, check the absolute value of the positives and the absolute value of the negatives. If you have a greater value of positives, the answer will be positive. If you have a greater value of negatives, the answer will be negative.

In $-3 + 4$ the absolute value of the positive (4) is greater than the absolute value of the negative (3), so the answer will be positive: $-3 + 4 = 1$

In $3 + -4$ the absolute value of the positive (3) is less than the absolute value of the negative (4), so the answer will be negative: $3 + -4 = -1$

Worked example	Thinking	Your turn!
Work out the value of: $-38 + 15 - 27 + 19 - (-24)$	*How can we rewrite subtractions?*	Work out the value of: $-26 + 19 - 37 + 24 - (-29)$
$-38 + 15 + (-27) + 19 + 24$	*Which numbers are positive and which are negative?*	
$15 + 19 + 24 + (-38) + (-27)$ $\begin{array}{r} 1\ 5 \\ 1\ 9 \\ +\ 2\ 4 \\ \hline 5\ 8 \\ \scriptstyle 1 \end{array}$ $\begin{array}{r} 3\ 8 \\ +\ 2\ 7 \\ \hline 6\ 5 \\ \scriptstyle 1 \end{array}$	*What do we do with the positive and negative numbers?* *What do we need to do with the signs?*	
$58 + -65$ $58 + -58 + -7 = -7$	*How can we partition one of the numbers to make this easier to calculate?*	

I rewrite them as additions of the additive inverse.

The positive numbers are $+15, +19$, and $+24$
The negative numbers are -38 and -27

I find the sum of the positives and the sum of the negatives (using absolute values).

65 is the sum of the negatives, so I need to add 58 and -65

I can partition -65 into -58 and -7

▲ Example-problem pair 1

3.1.4 Fluency

In this exercise you can practise applying mathematical methods that you have just learnt.

1 Work out:
a $15 - 7$
b $6 - 11$
c $-12 - (-16)$
d $-7 - (-3)$
e $-5 - 18$
f $9 - (-7)$
g $85 + (-19)$
h $-134 - (-61)$

2 Copy and complete each of these by putting the correct mathematical symbol in place of the □
a $10 - -3 = 10\ \square\ 3 = 13$
b $17 - \square\ 12 = 17 + 12 = 29$
c $21\ \square - 5 = 21 + 5 = 26$

3 Work out:
a $12 - (-15) + (-7)$
b $18 + (-9) - (-16)$
c $-71 + 18 - (-22)$
d $123 + (-16) + (-22)$
e $-48 + 23 - (-7) + (-19)$
f $18 + (-29) - (-91) + 16 - (-33)$

4 Copy and complete each of these using < or >.
a $14 - 12\ \square\ 14$
b $-5 - -4\ \square - 5$
c $8 - -5\ \square\ 8$
d $-9 - 12\ \square - 9$

Now check your answers. You may want to use your calculator. Did you get any wrong and can you work out why?

Chapter 3

3.1 Exercises

3.1 Intelligent practice

"Why is it intelligent?" You might notice a connection when you move on from one question to the next. You can use the Reflect, Expect, Check, Explain process to:

- *reflect* on what's different between each question and the one that came before
- decide how you *expect* this answer to be different
- complete the question and *check* your answer
- *explain* to yourself why your expectation was correct or incorrect.

EXAMPLE

Question 1a
Work out $-7 + 9$

$-7 + 9 = 2$

Question 1b
Work out $7 + -9$

Reflect: This is like question 1a, but the numbers have the opposite signs.

Expect: Since the numbers are the same but the signs are opposite, I expect the answer will be the same value but negative.

Check: $7 + -9 = -2$

Explain: I was right! It's still 2 but negative this time because the larger number in the calculation is negative.

1 Work out:

   a $-7 + 9$

   b $7 + -9$

   c $-7 + -9$

   d $-70 + -90$

   e $70 + -90$

   f $80 + -100$

   g $-80 + 100$

   h $-8 + 10$

   i $-8 + 10 + -7 + 9$

   j $-8 + 10 + -9 + 9$

   k $-9 + 27 + 10 + -8 + 9 + -27$

2 Decide if each statement is true or false.

   a $-3 < 0$

   b $-3 > 0$

   c $3 > 0$

   d $3 > 4$

   e $-3 > 4$

   f $-3 > -4$

   g $3 > -4$

   h $3 > -3$

3 Copy and complete these questions by:
  i rewriting any subtractions as additions of the additive inverse,
  ii drawing positive and negative counters to model the addition,
  iii writing the answer.

The first one has been done for you.

Question	Rewritten	Model	Answer
$-3-5$	$-3+(-5)$		-8

a $-3--5$ $-3+(+5)$

b $-5+-3$

c $-3+5$

d $6+-5+3$

e $6-5-3$

f $5-6-3$

3.1 Method selection

In these questions you'll need to think carefully about which methods to apply.
For some questions you might need to use skills from earlier chapters.

1 The temperature in Bratislava was $7\,°C$ at 1 pm. By 11 pm the temperature had gone down by 9 degrees. What was the temperature at 11 pm?

2 Below is part of a bank statement. Credits are money going into the account. Debits are money going out of the account. The balance is the current amount in the account, which could be positive or negative.

Complete the missing amounts in the statement.

An amount goes in either the credit or debit column in each row, not both.

Date	Credit	Debit	Balance
29th March	348		870
30th March		50	
1st April			523
7th April		85	
9th April			480
14th April		124	

3 Each brick in the number pyramids is the sum of the two bricks below it. Copy and complete these number pyramids:

a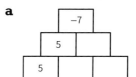

c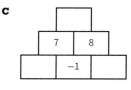

b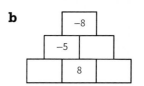

d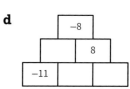

4 Find the missing number in each calculation:

a $-4+\square=-7$

b $\square+6=-11$

c $-5+\square=0$

d $5-\square=12$

e $7+-5=6+\square$

f $8--3=\square-9$

g $3-\square+-5+4=8$

5 Find the values which replace each shape in the calculations. A shape is worth the same value in both calculations.

△ + ☆ = 2

△ − ☆ = −8

◇ + ☁ = −13

◇ − ☁ = 5

6 This is a variation on the column subtraction method. Instead of exchanging when you are subtracting a digit which is greater than the one above, you use negative numbers.

$$
\begin{array}{r}
6 \ \ 2 \ \ 1 \\
- \ 3 \ \ 4 \ \ 5 \\
\hline
3 \ {-2} \ {-4}
\end{array}
$$

= 300 − 20 − 4

= 280 − 4

= 276

Try out this method for these calculations:

a 523 − 165

b 2304 − 1089

c 105 − 57

What do you think about this method compared with the usual column subtraction method?

3.1 Purposeful practice

There may be more than one way to approach these questions.

Once you have answered a question one way, can you think of another way?

1 Using −2, 2, 5, −5 and the operations + and − only, how many different calculations can you write that use all four numbers? What do you notice about the results?

2 This sequence of patterns is made from two–colour counters.

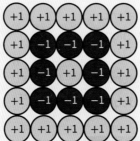

Pattern 1   Pattern 2   Pattern 3

a Find the value of each pattern.

b Build the next two patterns and find their values. What do you notice?

3 Answer questions a and b.

a Using the digits −2, −1, 0, 1, 2, 3, 4, 5, 6, 7, or 8 in the square boxes, and either the + or − operation in the circle, write as many statements as you can where the answer is −3

☐ ○ ☐

b Using the digits and operations as in part a, but this time you can have more than one operation, e.g. $-2+5-8$, write as many statements as you can where the answer is -3

4 Use the numbers -3, 5, -8, 11 once each in the calculation:

$$(\square - \square) + (\square - \square)$$

a Can you make the calculation equal 21?

b How many different answers can you make?

5 Below is an addition pyramid, where each brick is the sum of the two directly below it. Make a copy of the pyramid.

a Using the numbers 3, 2, and -7 in the base of this addition pyramid:

   i how can you make the top brick equal zero?

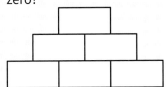

   ii how many different totals can the top brick have?

b Choose three different starting numbers for the base. How can you make the top brick equal zero?

c Add another level at the bottom of your pyramid.

   i Choose four different numbers from -5, -4, -3, -2, -1, 1, 2, 3, 4, and 5 for the bottom level. What different totals can you make at the top of the pyramid now?

   ii Describe your strategy for finding the digits that give you the largest top number.

d Investigate different sizes of addition pyramids. Explore what types of total you can make when your starting numbers are all positive, all negative, one negative, and so on.

6 Calculate the following and reflect on your answers to each set.

a Calculate i to v.

   i $3 - 4 + 5 - 6$

   ii $10 - 11 + 12 - 13$

   iii $11 - 10 + 9 - 8$

   iv $2 - 1 + 0 - -1$

   v What do you notice?

b Calculate i to v.

   i $3 - 4 - 5 + 6$

   ii $12 - 13 - 14 + 15$

   iii $8 - 7 - 6 + 5$

   iv $-1 - -2 - -3 + -4$

   v What do you notice?

c Calculate i to v.

   i $3 + 4 - 5 - 6$

   ii $10 + 11 - 12 - 13$

   iii $9 + 8 - 7 - 6$

   iv $-5 + -6 - -7 - -8$

   v What do you notice?

d What happens if you change the order of additions and subtractions, or use five or more integers?

7 In this question, bigger circles have a bigger absolute value. Copy and complete the calculations by thinking about whether the sum will be positive or negative and the size of the result. The first one is done for you as an example.

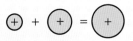

Multiplication and division with negative integers

3.2.1 Multiplying integers

In primary school you learnt to multiply larger numbers using the column method of multiplication shown, but you can model multiplication in different ways.

For example, to calculate 14×27:

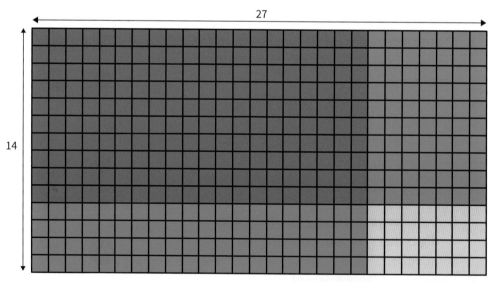

×	20	7
10	200	70
4	80	28

Each number inside the grid shows the answer to one of the multiplications used in the column method (from left to right): 4×7, 10×7, 4×20, 10×20. You could also build an array with 14 rows of 27 counters, or use base-ten blocks to show this calculation.

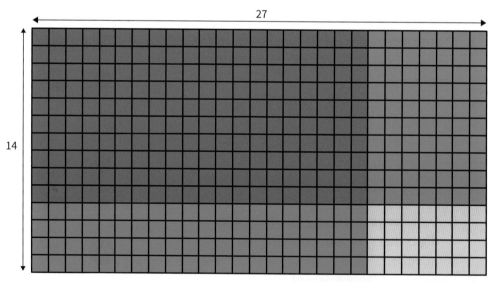

So far, all the multiplications you have done have been with positive numbers, and the result has always been positive. If you use two-colour counters to make arrays, 3×4 can be seen as 4 copies of 3, or 3 copies of 4, but that both show a result of positive 12.

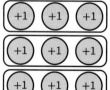

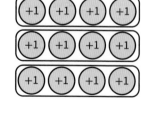

4×3
4 copies of 3

3×4
3 copies of 4

You can also use two-colour counters to make arrays when you multiply a negative number by a positive number. For $4 \times (-3)$ you can see this as 4 copies of negative 3. Similarly, the calculation $3 \times (-4)$ can be seen as 3 copies of negative 4. Both show a result of negative 12.

$4 \times (-3)$
4 copies of negative 3

$3 \times (-4)$
3 copies of negative 4

Key point

The product of a positive number and a negative number is always negative.

You can use this to work out multiples of negative numbers, e.g. multiples of -5

Worked example	Thinking	Your turn!	
Write down the first four multiples of -5	*Which number do we start with?* *How do we find the next multiple?*	Write down the first four multiples of -6	I start with $-5 \times 1 = -5$ The next multiple is -5×2 The numbers will decrease by 5 each time.
-5 $-5, -10$ $-5, -10, -15, -20$	*Will the numbers decrease or increase?* *How are these multiples different or the same as the multiples of a positive number?*		The first four multiples of 5 are 5, 10, 15, 20 so I need the same absolute values but negative rather than positive.

▲ Example-problem pair 1

3.2.1 Fluency

In this exercise you can practise applying the mathematical methods that you have just learnt.

1 Work out:

a 4×5 **c** 6×-5 **e** -9×3

b 3×-7 **d** -8×4

2 Work out:

a 4×60 **c** 7×-50 **e** -9×300

b 20×-6 **d** -400×8

3 List the first five multiples of -7

4 List the first six multiples of -12

5 Work out each of these calculations.

a 13×12 **b** 8×-15 **c** -7×20

d Explain why each of your answers is positive or negative.

6 Copy each statement and insert either $<$ or $>$ to make the statement true.

a 5×-7 _____ 6×-7

b -3×8 _____ -4×8

c 6×-8 _____ -5×8

d -3×12 _____ 2×-12

Now check your answers. You may want to use your calculator. Did you get any wrong and can you work out why?

3.2.2 Multiplying two or more negative numbers

You will now look at how to multiply two numbers that are both negative.

In Subsection 3.2.1, you saw that $3 \times (-4)$ can be shown as making 3 copies of negative 4

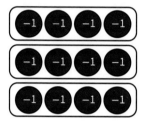

You know that $3 \times 4 = 12$, but when one of those numbers was negative, all the counters were flipped over, showing that -3×4 and 3×-4 both equal -12

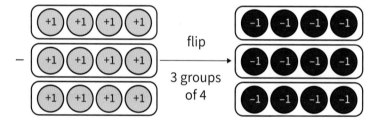

If you make both numbers negative, that means the counters would be flipped twice, giving a positive answer, so $-3 \times -4 = 12$

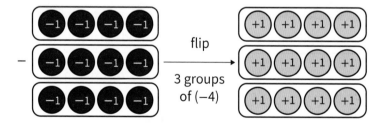

When multiplying, find the absolute value of the answer by ignoring any negative signs. Then, every time you see a negative number, change the sign of the answer.

Key point

$(\text{positive}) \times (\text{positive}) = \text{positive}$

$(\text{positive}) \times (\text{negative}) = \text{negative}$

$(\text{negative}) \times (\text{positive}) = \text{negative}$

$(\text{negative}) \times (\text{negative}) = \text{positive}$

Worked example	Thinking	Your turn!
Work out: -35×-19	What calculation is this the same as?	Work out: -3×-19

×	30	5
10	300	50
9	270	45

```
    3 0 0
      5 0
    2 7 0
 +    4 5
  ───────
    6 6 5
      1
```

What method can we use to calculate this?

$-35 \times -19 = 665$

-35×-19 is the same as 35×19

I can use a grid or a column method.

▲ Example-problem pair 1

When multiplying more than two numbers, you can use the same idea.

For example,
$1 \times -2 \times 3 \times -4$
First work out:
$1 \times 2 \times 3 \times 4 = 24$
There are two negatives in the question, meaning two flips. The answer is 24

You can see that **even** powers of negative numbers give a positive answer, but **odd** powers of negative numbers give negative answers.

Looking at powers of -1:
$(-1)^2 = -1 \times -1 = 1$
$(-1)^3 = -1 \times -1 \times -1 = -1$
$(-1)^4 = -1 \times -1 \times -1 \times -1 = 1$
$(-1)^5 = -1 \times -1 \times -1 \times -1 \times -1 = -1$

Calculator

You can use your calculator to work out powers of negative numbers. For example, try $(-2)^2, (-2)^3, (-2)^4$ and so on. You need to include brackets when calculating powers of negative numbers. For example, to work out $(-5)^4$, enter:

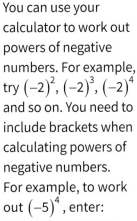

The power key may instead look like

You should see 625 displayed on the screen.

3.2.2 Fluency

In this exercise you can practise applying the mathematical methods that you have just learnt.

1 Work out:

  a -3×-7 **c** -8×-9

  b -4×-6 **d** -11×-8

2 Work out:

  a -15×-4 **d** -21×-5 **g** -31×-6

  b -6×-20 **e** -25×-7 **h** -7×-41

  c -4×-18 **f** -19×-8

Explain the sign of your answer.

3 Work out each of these calculations. Explain the sign of your answer for each calculation.

  a $(-6)^2$ **c** $(-3)^3$ **e** 5^4

  b 4^3 **d** $(-10)^4$ **f** $(-2)^5$

Now check your answers. You may want to use your calculator. Did you get any wrong and can you work out why?

3.2.3 Dividing integers

Objective

You will learn how to:

- divide positive and negative integers

Division is the inverse of multiplication. You can use the array model and what you've learnt about multiplication to make sense of division of positive and negative numbers.

The array 4×3 shows that $4 \times 3 = 12$ and that $3 \times 4 = 12$. It can also show $-4 \times -3 = 12$ and $-3 \times -4 = 12$. The array also shows the related division facts.

$4 \times 3 = -12$

$3 \times 4 = 12$

$12 \div 4 = 3$

$12 \div 3 = 4$

$-4 \times -3 = 12$

$-3 \times -4 = 12$

$12 \div -4 = -3$

$12 \div -3 = -4$

If you look at the array for -12 for the related division facts, you get these eight facts.

$3 \times -4 = -12$

$-4 \times 3 = -12$

$-12 \div -4 = 3$

$-12 \div 3 = -4$

$4 \times -3 = 12$

$-3 \times 4 = 12$

$-12 \div -3 = 4$

$-12 \div 4 = -3$

Investigate Further

If you arranged these 12 negative counters in a different array, what other facts could you write?

Worked example	Thinking	Your turn!
Work out: $-24 \div 4$  $-24 \div 4 = -6$	*How can we show this using counters?* *How can we use this to work out the answer?*	Work out: $-32 \div 8$

I need 24 counters, red side up in rows or columns of 4 (or I could group in 4s).

I have divided -24 into four rows. Each row is made of six -1 counters $= -6$

▲ Example-problem pair 1

You can work out division answers using the same ideas that worked for multiplication. First find the absolute value of the calculation, then use the negative signs to decide how many flips you have made and what the sign of the answer is.

Key point

(positive) × (positive) = positive
(positive) × (negative) = negative
(negative) × (positive) = negative
(negative) × (negative) = positive

(positive) ÷ (positive) = positive
(positive) ÷ (negative) = negative
(negative) ÷ (positive) = negative
(negative) ÷ (negative) = positive

Worked example	Thinking	Your turn!
Work out: $-132 \div -3$	*How do we determine the sign of the result before calculating?*	Work out: $204 \div -6$
The result will be positive. Using short division: $\begin{array}{r} 4\ \ 4 \\ 3\overline{\smash{)}1\ \ 3\ ^1 2} \end{array}$	*What different methods could we use to find the answer?*	
$-132 \div -3 = 44$		

A negative divided by a negative gives a positive, so I can work out $132 \div 3$ instead.

I could use a mental or written strategy.

▲ Example-problem pair 2

3.2.3 Fluency

In this exercise you can practise applying the mathematical methods that you have just learnt.

1 Work out:
   a $35 \div 7$
   b $48 \div -6$
   c $-15 \div 3$
   d $-90 \div -10$

2 Work out each of these calculations. Explain the sign of your answer for each calculation.
   a $200 \div 25$
   b $125 \div -5$
   c $-320 \div 16$
   d $-147 \div -7$

3 Work out:
   a $90 \div -18$
   b $-240 \div 12$
   c $102 \div -6$
   d $-126 \div 9$
   e $-208 \div -16$
   f $-288 \div -24$

Now check your answers. You may want to use your calculator. Did you get any wrong and can you work out why?

3.2 Exercises

3.2 Intelligent practice

"Why is it intelligent?" You might notice a connection when you move on from one question to the next. You can use the Reflect, Expect, Check, Explain process to:

- *reflect* on what's different between each question and the one that came before
- decide how you *expect* this answer to be different
- complete the question and *check* your answer
- *explain* to yourself why your expectation was correct or incorrect.

EXAMPLE

Question 1b

Work out -9×8

$-(9 \times 8) = -72$

Question 1c

Work out 9×-8

Reflect: This question looks like 1b, but the 8 is negative instead of the 9

Expect: I expect that my answer will be the same as I can multiply numbers in any order, and a negative number multiplied by a positive number is a negative number.

Check: $9 \times -8 = -(9 \times 8) = -72$

Explain: I was right! Both calculations have the same absolute value, and they are both a positive and a negative multiplied together, so they both have negative answers.

1 Work out:

  a 9×8

  b -9×8

  c -8×9

  d $-9 \times (-8)$

  e -90×8

  f -9×80

  g -90×80

  h $30 \times (-3) \times (-80)$

  i $9 \times (-10) \times (-4) \times (-20)$

  j $3 \times (-10) \times (-5) \times 2 \times 4 \times 3 \times 2$

2 Work out:

  a $27 \div 3$

  b $(-27) \div 3$

  c $27 \div (-3)$

  d $(-27) \div (-3)$

  e $270 \div (-3)$

  f $(-270) \div (-30)$

  g $540 \div (-3)$

  h $(-540) \div (-30)$

  i $540 \div (-9)$

  j $(540 \div 3) \div (-3)$

  k $(-540) \div (-6)$

  l $270 \div (-9)$

3 Copy and complete these questions using the grid method of multiplication.

a

×	10	−5
10		
−8		

b

×	12	−7
−10		
12		

c

×	22	−17
−5		
7		

4 Work out:

a 3^2 **b** $(-3)^2$ **c** $(-3)^3$ **d** $(-3)^4$ **e** $(-30)^4$ **f** $(-30)^5$

3.2 Method selection

In these questions you'll need to think carefully about which methods to apply.

For some questions you might need to use skills from earlier chapters.

1 Calculate each of these, giving your answers in numerals and words.
  a thirty thousand × nine thousand
  b twenty-three thousand × one thousand four hundred
  c twelve × three hundred and two thousand
  d eleven thousand ÷ eighty-eight
  e ninety-six thousand ÷ sixty four
  f one hundred and twenty-three thousand four hundred fifty-six ÷ twelve

2 List the first five multiples of:
  a −3
  b −9
  c −12
  d −4
  e −40
  f −80

3 A diver enters the sea and descends 30 feet per minute.
How far below sea level will she be after 7.5 minutes?

4 Copy and complete these sum-product puzzles. The first one has been completed as an example.

In each puzzle there are two numbers in the middle row. The brick above is the sum of the numbers in the middle row. The brick below is the product of the numbers in the middle row.

E.g. Sum 10 | middle 3, 7 | Product 21

d Sum [ ] | middle 4, 6 | Product [ ]

h Sum 12 | middle 4, [ ] | Product [ ]

l Sum [ ] | middle 4, [ ] | Product 12

a Sum [ ] | middle 8, 2 | Product [ ]

e Sum [ ] | middle 4, 4 | Product [ ]

i Sum 8 | middle [ ], [ ] | Product 12

m Sum 13 | middle [ ], [ ] | Product 12

b Sum [ ] | middle [ ], −2 | Product −18

f Sum −7 | middle [ ], [ ] | Product −18

j Sum [ ] | middle [ ], 6 | Product −24

n Sum [ ] | middle 5, −6 | Product [ ]

c Sum 9 | middle [ ], [ ] | Product 18

g Sum −9 | middle [ ], [ ] | Product 18

k Sum [ ] | middle −5, −6 | Product [ ]

o Sum [ ] | middle −10, 3 | Product [ ]

5 Copy and complete the missing parts of these tables using the grid method of multiplication.

a

×	−7	−3
	49	
		9

c

×	5	
	25	
4		−16

e

×		
−6	36	
8		−64

b

×	−7	−3
	49	
		−9

d

×	9	
4		−28
		35

f

×	−9	
−4		−28
		−35

3.2 Purposeful practice

There may be more than one way to approach these questions.

Once you have answered a question one way, can you think of another way?

1 Copy and complete each of these calculations by using three different numbers from:

$-5, 6, -7, 8$ and -9

a $\square \times \square + \square = -49$

b $\square \times \square + \square = 38$

c $\square \times \square + \square = -46$

d $\square \times \square - \square = 37$

e $\square \times \square - \square = -49$

f $\square \times \square - \square = -51$

2 For each region of this Venn diagram, write a calculation. If there is a region where it is impossible to write a calculation, you must be able to explain why.

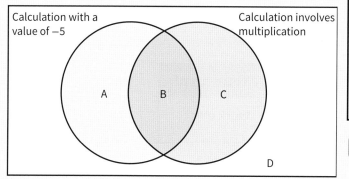

3 Answer questions a and b.

a For each region of this Venn diagram, write a calculation. If there is a region where it is impossible to write a calculation, you must be able to explain why.

b Write a calculation with a result of -2 that could belong in each region.

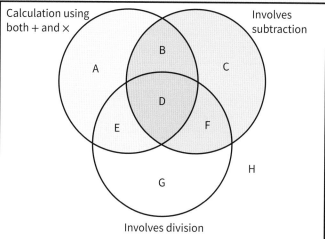

4 Use the numbers $-3, 4, -7,$ and 8, and the operations $+, -,$ and $\times$ to make each of these target results.

You can use one or more of the operations and you can use operations more than once, but use each number at most once for each target result.

a -17 **b** -57 **c** 25

3.3 Addition and subtraction with decimals

3.3.1 Adding and subtracting positive decimals

Objective

You will learn how to:

- add and subtract positive decimals

You can add and subtract decimals in the same way as integers, using the column method.

Remember to line up all the numbers correctly according to place value when you use the column method for addition or subtraction.

align units

$$
\begin{array}{r}
3\ 0\ 4\ .\ 0 \\
+\quad 1\ 0\ .\ 2 \\
\hline
3\ 1\ 4\ .\ 2
\end{array}
$$

align decimal points

$$
\begin{array}{r}
6\ .\ 2\ 4 \\
+\ 1\ 0\ 4\ .\ 1\ 0 \\
\hline
1\ 1\ 0\ .\ 3\ 4
\end{array}
$$

You will sometimes need to include trailing zeros in numbers to help you carry out the calculation.

Worked example	Thinking	Your turn!
Work out: $32.7 - 8.56$	*How do we line up the calculation?*	**Work out:** $43.8 - 9.57$
$\begin{array}{r} 3\ 2\ .\ 7 \\ -\quad 8\ .\ 5\ 6 \\ \hline \end{array}$	*Do we need to add trailing zeros?* *Do I need to make any exchanges?*	
$\begin{array}{r} 3\ 2\ .^6\not{7}\ ^1 0 \\ -\quad 8\ .\ 5\ 6 \\ \hline .\ 1\ 4 \end{array}$	*Do I need to make another exchange?*	
$\begin{array}{r} ^2\not{3}\ ^1 2\ .^6\not{7}\ ^1 0 \\ -\quad 8\ .\ 5\ 6 \\ \hline 2\ 4\ .\ 1\ 4 \end{array}$ So, $32.7 - 8.56 = 24.14$	*How can we check our answer?*	

I line up the units digit in 32.7 (2) with the units digit of 8.56 (8) The decimal points should also line up.

I need to add a trailing zero to 32.7

I need to subtract 6 hundredths from 0 hundredths, so I need to exchange a tenth.

I need to subtract 8 units from 2 units, so I need to exchange a ten.

I can check that this is correct by adding 24.14 to 8.56 to check that this makes 32.7

▲ Example-problem pair 1

3.3.1 Fluency

In this exercise you can practise applying the mathematical methods that you have just learnt.

1 Copy and complete each of these calculations.

a
```
  4 5 . 6
+   3 . 2
_____
```

b
```
  1 3 6 . 7
+   4 5 . 9
_____
```

c
```
  9 4 . 6
-   2 . 3
_____
```

d
```
  2 1 4 . 5
-   3 2 . 7
_____
```

2 Use the column method to calculate each of these.

a $154.4 + 23.7$

b $364.15 + 9.324$

c $89.7 - 65.3$

d $105.34 - 19.6$

e $3.7894 + 16.352$

f $18.247 - 6.3781$

3 Without doing the calculation, work out which of these numbers the answer to the calculation $1398.74 - 421.93$ is closest to: 10, 100, 1000

4 Without doing the calculation, work out which of these numbers the answer to the calculation $239.5 + 114.36$ is closest to: 250, 350, 420, 450

Now check your answers. You may want to use your calculator. Did you get any wrong and can you work out why?

3.3.2 Negative decimals

Objectives

You will:
- learn how to order and compare positive and negative decimals
- know that given two numbers, you can always find another number between them

In Chapter 1, you learnt how to order positive decimals. You can order negative decimals using the same principle. Remember, negative numbers further from zero are less than negative numbers closer to zero.

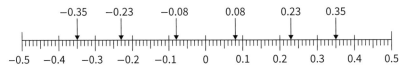

Worked example	Thinking	Your turn!	
Write these two numbers with the correct symbol, < or >, between them: $-1.305 \,\square\, -1.55$	*Are the signs the same?*	Write these two numbers with the correct symbol, < or >, between them: $-4.817 \,\square\, -4.801$	Yes. Both these numbers are negative.
  −1.55 −1.305 number line $-1.305 > -1.55$	*Which number is closer to zero on the number line?*		−1.305 is closer to zero than −1.55, so −1.305 is greater.

▲ Example-problem pair 1

Remember that when ordering lists of positive and negative numbers, you can order the positive and negative numbers separately, as the positive numbers will all be bigger than all of the negative numbers.

Between any two integers you can divide the number line up as much as you want. When looking at decimals you can first consider tenths, where you split the space between two integers into ten equal sections. For example, between 3 and 4 you can find 3.1, 3.2, and so on.

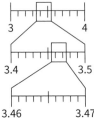

To find hundreths, you take the section between any two tenths and 'zoom in' some more and split that space up into ten equal sections.

You can keep going to find thousandths.

Between any two decimals, you can continue to split the space up as much as you like.

This means that between any two decimals, there are infinitely many decimals.

3.3.2 Fluency

In this exercise you can practise applying the mathematical methods that you have just learnt.

1 Write five decimals that are greater than 43.1

2 Write the numbers that are represented by each letter on the number line.

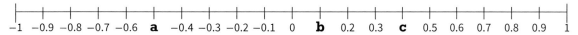

3 Write the numbers that are represented by each letter on the number line.

4 Use this number line to write these numbers in ascending order: $4, -2.8, 3, 3.6, -4.8, 2, -2.2$

5 Copy and complete each of these using $<$, $>$, or $=$.

a $-4.7 \square -4.9$ b $-8.6 \square 7.1$ c $-8.3 \square -8.3$ d $-15.9 \square -16.1$

6 Draw arrows on a copy of this number line to show the position of each number.

$1, -3, 3.4, -1.8, -4.8$

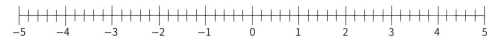

7 Answer questions a and b.

a Write five integers that are greater than -7 b Write five decimals that are less than -3.5

8 Write three possible decimal numbers that could complete this inequality.

$-5 < \square < -3$

9 Copy and complete each of these sentences.

a There are _____ many positive numbers.

b There are _____ many negative numbers.

c For every positive number, there is a _____ negative number.

d There are _____ many decimals.

Now check your answers. You may want to use your calculator. Did you get any wrong and can you work out why?

3.3.3 Adding and subtracting positive and negative decimals

> **Objective**
>
> You will learn how to:
> - add and subtract positive and negative decimals

To calculate with negative decimals, you need to understand absolute value (see Subsection 3.1.4) and compare decimal numbers accurately.

Remember that any subtraction can be written as an addition of the additive inverse.

When you add two negative integers, the result will be the negative sum of the absolute values of the two numbers. This is the same with decimals. For example, knowing that $3.45 + 7.8 = 11.25$ means that you know $(-3.45) + (-7.8) = -11.25$

To work out the sum of a mixture of positive and negative numbers you can add the positive numbers and the negative numbers separately. You can use the column method for the separate parts, being careful to align the numbers using place value. Then you need to work out whether the overall sum will be positive or negative using the absolute values of the sum of the positives and the sum of the negatives.

Worked example	Thinking	Your turn!
Work out: $-7.8 + 3.02 - 5.8 + 16 - (-8.5)$	*How can we rewrite the subtractions?*	Work out: $4.9 + (-13) - 21.08 + 24 - (-32.5)$
$-7.8 + 3.02 + (-5.8) + 16 + 8.5$ $\begin{array}{r} 0\,3\,.\,0\,2 \\ 1\,6\,.\,0\,0 \\ +\,0\,8\,.\,5\,0 \\ \hline 2\,7\,.\,5\,2 \\ {\scriptstyle 1} \end{array}$ $\qquad \begin{array}{r} 7\,.\,8 \\ +\quad 5\,.\,8 \\ \hline 1\,3\,.\,6 \end{array}$	*What do we do with the positive and negative numbers?* *Why do we add in extra zeros here?*	
$27.52 + (-13.6)$ $\begin{array}{r} 2\,{}^{6}\!7\,.\,{}^{1}5\,2 \\ -\,1\,3\,.\,6\,0 \\ \hline 1\,3\,.\,9\,2 \end{array}$	*How can we do this calculation?*	

> I rewrite them as additions.

> I use the absolute values and find the sum of the positives and the sum of the negatives separately.

> I add in extra zeros to keep the place value columns clearly aligned.

> The negative amount is less than the positive, so I can set this up as a column subtraction.

▲ Example-problem pair 1

Just like with negative integers, you cannot always easily use the column method for adding and subtracting negative decimals. You may need to use additive inverses (zero pairs) to partition numbers, as the following example shows.

Worked example	Thinking	Your turn!
Work out: $17.2 - 28.83$	*Why can't we just use a column subtraction?*	Work out: $18 - 62.78$
 	−28.83	
−17.2	−11.63 | $17.2 + (-28.83)$ $= 17.2 + (-17.2) + (-11.63)$ So the answer is -11.63	*How do we partition the number?*	
Alternatively, $17.2 - 28.83$ $= -(28.83 - 17.2)$ $= -(11.63)$ $= -11.63$	*Can we do this another way?*	

Notes boxes:
- The number being subtracted has a larger absolute value, so column subtraction would give me an incorrect answer.
- I partition it so that -17.2 can form a zero pair with 17.2
- I can use column subtraction to work out $28.83 - 17.2$, as this is the negative of $17.2 - 28.83$

▲ Example-problem pair 2

3.3.3 Fluency

In this exercise you can practise applying the mathematical methods that you have just learnt.

1 Work out:
a $-7.2 + 3.8$
b $-24.81 + 32.7$
c $8.93 + (-11.6)$
d $-9.12 - (-8.73)$

2 Work out:
a $-5.4 + 8.1 - (-9.25) + (-18.32)$
b $-18.71 + (-13.65) + 5.18$
c $-8.9 + 13.71 - (-4.53) + (-15.2)$
d $51.7 - 23.91 - (-4.83) + (-16.9) - 13.78$

3 Without doing the calculations, complete each of these using $<$ or $>$.
a $1.8 + -2.1 \square 1.8$
b $14.35 - 10.47 \square 14.35$
c $-15.67 - -3.81 \square -15.67$
d $-7.043 + -18.91 \square -7.043$
e $48.54 - -32.98 \square 48.54$
f $-103.7 - 92.3781 \square -103.7$

Now check your answers. You may want to use your calculator. Did you get any wrong and can you work out why?

3.3 Exercises

3.3 Intelligent practice

"Why is it intelligent?" You might notice a connection when you move on from one question to the next. You can use the Reflect, Expect, Check, Explain process to:

- *reflect* on what's different between each question and the one that came before
- decide how you *expect* this answer to be different
- complete the question and *check* your answer
- *explain* to yourself why your expectation was correct or incorrect.

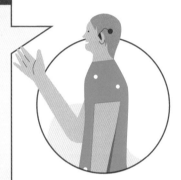

Question 2a   **EXAMPLE**

Copy and complete using the correct symbol, > or <.

4 ☐ 4.5

4 < 4.5

Question 2b

Copy and complete using the correct symbol, > or <.

−4 ☐ − 4.5

Reflect: The numbers are the same as in part a but the signs have changed.

Expect: I think the correct symbol is the same as for part a, <, since 4 is smaller than 4.5

Check: −4 is greater than −4.5 as it is closer to zero and they are both negative, so you write −4 > −4.5. I got this one wrong.

Explain: On a number line −4 is on the right of −4.5 so −4 is the greater number. −4 is closer to zero than −4.5

---

1   Write the numbers indicated by the arrows on these number lines:

a

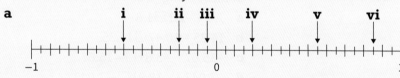

b

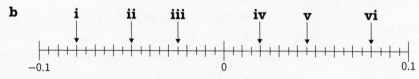

c

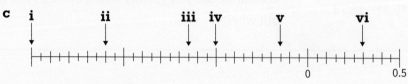

2 Copy and complete each of these using the correct symbol, $>$ or $<$.

a $4 \square 4.5$

b $-4 \square -4.5$

c $-4 \square 4.5$

d $4 \square -4.5$

e $4.04 \square 4.5$

f $-4.04 \square -4.5$

g $-4.94 \square -4.5$

h $-4.94 \square 4.95$

i $4.94 \square -4.95$

3 Calculate:

a
```
    3 . 5
 +  4 . 2
_____
```

b
```
    3 . 5
 +  4 . 6
_____
```

c
```
   1 3 . 5
 +    4 . 6
_____
```

d
```
   1 3 . 5 2
 +    4 . 6 2
_____
```

e
```
   1 3 . 5 2
 -    4 . 6 2
_____
```

f
```
   1 . 3 5 2
 - 0 . 4 6 2
_____
```

g
```
   1 . 3 5
 - 0 . 4 6
_____
```

4 Work out:

a $4.7 + 2.8$

b $4.8 + 2.7$

c $4.8 - 2.7$

d $4.7 - 2.8$

e $47 - 2.8$

f $4.7 - 0.28$

g $4.71 - 0.29$

h $4.69 - 0.27$

5 Calculate:

a $4.5 + 3.2 - 7.7$

b $4.5 + 3.2 - 8$

c $-4.5 + (-3.2) + 8$

d $4.5 + (-3.2) - 8$

e $4.5 - 3.2 - 8$

f $0.45 - 0.32 - 0.8$

g $0.32 - 0.45 - 0.8$

h $0.32 - 0.45 + 0.8$

i $0.8 - 0.32 + 0.45$

j $0.8 + (-0.32) + 0.45$

k $8 + (-3.2) + 4.5$

l $7.9 + (-3.1) + 4.5$

m $7.9 + (-3.1) + 4.5 - 79.31$

n $10.9 + (-3.1) + 4.5 - 82.31$

3.3 Method selection

In these questions you'll need to think carefully about which methods to apply.

For some questions you might need to use skills from earlier chapters.

1 Each brick in the number pyramids is the sum of the two bricks below it. Copy and complete these number pyramids.

a
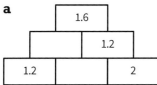

b
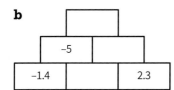

c

d
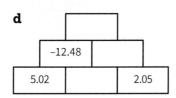

2 Find the missing number in each calculation:

a $-5 + \square = -7.8$

b $2.8 - \square = 9.8$

c $10 + \square = 7.3$

d $\square + 1.2 = 0.5$

e $3.4 - \square = 7$

f $8.5 + 10.6 = -5.2 + \square$

g $4.3 - \square + -6.03 + 7.2 = -5.5$

3 Work out:

a $5 - 7.5$

b $25 - 7.5$

c $-5 + 7.5$

d $247 - 302$

e $10.8 - 8.53$

f $12 + 5.8 + (-9)$

g $1.5 + 0.63 - 10 + 3.37$

h $14.8 - 21.7$

i $32.06 - 1.74 - 0.26$

j $72 - 135.8$

4 Here is a variation on the column subtraction method. Instead of exchanging when you are subtracting a digit which is greater than the one above, you simply use negative numbers, then use place value to calculate the correct answer.

Look at how $5.2 - 3.47$ has been worked out using this method:

$$
\begin{array}{r}
5\,.\;2\;\;0 \\
-\;3\,.\;4\;\;7 \\
\hline
2\,.{-}2\,{-}7
\end{array}
$$

$$= 2 - 0.2 - 0.07$$
$$= \quad 1.8 - 0.07$$
$$= \quad 1.73$$

Try out this method for these calculations:

a $12.8 - 7.5$

b $23.7 - 8.52$

c $60 - 42.87$

What do you think about this method compared with the usual column subtraction method?

3.3 Purposeful practice

There may be more than one way to approach these questions.
Once you have answered a question one way, can you think of another way?

1 Use the digits 1 to 6 exactly once each in the calculation:

□.□+□+□.□□

a Find the greatest possible result and the least possible result of the calculation.
b Find the calculation with the result closest to 3.5

2 Use the digits 1 to 6 only once each in the calculation:

□.□−□−□.□□

a Find the greatest possible result and the least possible result of the calculation.
b Find the calculation with the result closest to 0

3 Copy and complete this Venn diagram. For each region,
a write an addition problem
b write a subtraction problem.

If there is a region where it is impossible to write a calculation, explain why.

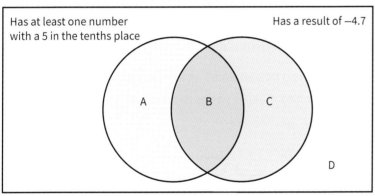

Multiplication and division with decimals

3.4.1 Multiplying positive decimals

Objectives

You will learn how to:
- multiply positive and negative decimals
- multiply and divide efficiently using powers of 10

You have learnt to multiply large numbers such as 3000×700. You can write 3000 and 700 in expanded form and then reorder the multiplication to make it easier to work out mentally. Look back at Subsection 1.2.3 to remind yourself how to do this.

$$3000 \times 700 = 3 \times 1000 \times 7 \times 100 = 3 \times 7 \times 1000 \times 100$$

Write in expanded form

Calculate the products separately

You can use this same approach to multiply decimals such as 0.003×0.07

You can rewrite the numbers 0.003 and 0.07 as integers divided by a power of 10 and then reorder the calculation to make it easier to work out mentally.

$$0.003 \times 0.07 = 3 \div 1000 \times 7 \div 100 = 3 \times 7 \div 1000 \div 100 = 21 \div 100\,000 = 0.00\,021$$

Calculate separately

Worked example	Thinking	Your turn!
Calculate: 0.4×0.009	*What is the first step?*	Calculate: 0.04×0.0002
$0.4 = 4 \div 10$ $0.009 = 9 \div 1000$		
$\begin{aligned} 0.4 \times 0.009 &= 4 \div 10 \times 9 \div 1000 \\ &= 4 \times 9 \div 10 \div 1000 \\ &= 36 \div 10000 \\ &= 0.0036 \end{aligned}$	*Why do we reorder the calculation and how do we know it's equivalent?*	

> I write the numbers as integers multiplied or divided by a power of 10

> I reorder the calculation with the powers of 10 at the end to help work out the answer mentally. Dividing by 10 then dividing by 1000 is the same as dividing by 10 000. I could have worked it out in two steps: $36 \div 10 = 3.6$ and then $3.6 \div 1000 = 0.0036$

▲ Example-problem pair 1

Once you have rewritten the multiplication, you can use your normal methods.

Worked example	Thinking	Your turn!
Calculate: 2.8×4.35	*How can we rewrite this without using decimals?*	Calculate: 3.42×5.8

> I can write the decimals using expanded form.

$2.8 = 28 \div 10$ $4.35 = 435 \div 100$ $2.8 \times 4.35 = 28 \div 10 \times 435 \div 100$ $\qquad = 28 \times 435 \div 10 \div 100$	*How do we decide whether to use a mental or written strategy?*	

> I will use a written strategy here as the numbers are quite large and I can't see an obvious way to simplify the calculation.

Work out 28×435 using a written method:

×	400	30	5
20	8000	600	100
8	3200	240	40

$$
\begin{array}{r}
8\ 0\ 0\ 0 \\
6\ 0\ 0 \\
1\ 0\ 0 \\
3\ 2\ 0\ 0 \\
2\ 4\ 0 \\
+ \qquad 4\ 0 \\
\hline
1\ 2\ 1\ 8\ 0 \\
\end{array}
$$

$2.8 \times 4.35 = 28 \times 435 \div 10 \div 100$

$= 12\,180 \div 10 \div 100$

$= 1218 \div 100$

$= 12.18$

▲ Example-problem pair 2

3.4.1 Fluency

In this exercise you can practise applying mathematical methods that you have just learnt.

1 Work out:

   a 20×600 **b** 40×8000 **c** 900×3000

2 Work out:

   a 4.1×2.3 **b** 5.2×6.4 **c** 15.9×3.1

3 Calculate:

   a 0.3×0.07

   b 0.05×0.06

   c 0.08×0.002

   d 0.004×0.006

   e 0.0007×0.005

4 Work out:

   a 3.12×1.5 **c** 5.48×7.1 **e** 6.37×2.86

   b 4.26×3.4 **d** 4.6×9.15

5 Without doing the calculations, decide which two calculations have a different answer from the others.

   a 2.4×18 **c** 1.8×24 **e** 2400×0.018

   b 24×0.18 **d** 240×0.18 **f** $18 \times 24\,000$

Now check your answers. You may want to use your calculator. Did you get any wrong and can you work out why?

3.4.2 Dividing positive decimals

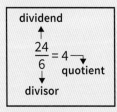
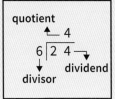
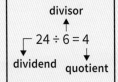
Objective

You will learn how to:

- divide positive and negative decimals

Bar models can be useful to show divisions and multiplications.

Look at the two divisions shown.

$1.2 \div 4$ is difficult to calculate mentally but it is similar to the calculation $12 \div 4$

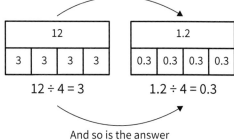

The number being divided is 10 times smaller

$12 \div 4 = 3$

$1.2 \div 4 = 0.3$

And so is the answer

If both the numbers in a division are multiplied or divided by the same amount, then the answer stays the same.

$$12 \div 4 = 3$$
$$\div 10 \downarrow \quad \downarrow \div 10$$
$$1.2 \div 0.4 = 3$$

You can use this property to divide decimals. If you want to calculate $6 \div 0.3$, you could add 0.3 repeatedly until you make 6, counting how many lots of 0.3 you need. But a more efficient way would be to make 0.3 into an integer by multiplying it by 10.

To make sure the answer stays the same, you have to also multiply 6 by 10:

$$6 \div 0.3 = ?$$
$$\times 10 \downarrow \quad \downarrow \times 10$$
$$60 \div 3 = 20$$

$60 \div 3 = 20$, so $6 \div 0.3$ must also be 20

Worked example	Thinking	Your turn!
Work out: $1.08 \div 0.4$	*How can we rewrite this to make it easier to work out?*	Work out: $2.94 \div 0.3$
$1.08 \div 0.4$ $\times 10 \downarrow \quad \downarrow \times 10$ $10.8 \div 4$	*Why do we need to adjust both numbers?*	
So the calculation becomes: $10.8 \div 4$ Using short division: $\begin{array}{r} 2\,.\,7 \\ 4\,\overline{)1\,0\,.^2 8} \end{array}$ So $1.08 \div 0.4 = 2.7$		

I want to divide by an integer not a decimal, so I'll multiply by 10

If I do the same to both numbers in the division the answer will be the same as the original question.

▲ Example-problem pair 1

Simplify divisions as much as you can to make them easier to do. You have seen how you can multiply both numbers in a division by powers of 10, but you can also multiply or divide both numbers by any amount to simplify the calculation.

For example, to calculate $78 \div 1.5$, you could multiply both numbers by ten so that the divisor is an integer. Then you can work out $780 \div 15$. But dividing by 15 is not as simple as it could be, so you could divide both numbers by 5 as they are both multiples of 5

$$780 \div 15$$
$$\div 5 \downarrow \quad \downarrow \div 5$$
$$156 \div 3$$

This is now much easier to calculate as the 3 times table is easier to recall.

Investigate Further 🔍

Sometimes, no matter how many trailing zeros you add, you still have remainders.

$$1.7571428 57\ldots$$
$$7\overline{)12.5^340^50^10^30^20^60^40^50\ldots}$$

Try calculating $12.3 \div 7$ and see if you can spot any patterns after the decimal point.

Worked example	Thinking	Your turn!
Work out: $15 \div 2.4$	How can we rewrite this to make it easier?	Work out: $30 \div 1.6$
$15 \div 2.4$ $\times 10 \downarrow \quad \downarrow \times 10$ $150 \div 24$	What could we do to simplify this division further?	
$150 \div 24 = 75 \div 12$ Set up as a short division: $$\begin{array}{r} 6.2\,5 \\ 12\overline{)7\,5.^30\,^60} \end{array}$$ So, $15 \div 2.4 = 6.25$	What other equivalent calculations could work here?	

I want to divide by an integer not a decimal, so I'll multiply by 10

I can divide both the dividend and divisor by 2 to make them smaller.

75 and 12 both have a common factor of 3 I could instead have calculated $25 \div 4$

▲ Example-problem pair 2

3.4.2 Fluency

In this exercise you can practise applying mathematical methods that you have just learnt.

1 Work out:
  a $120 \div 30$ b $2400 \div 60$ c $540 \div 9000$

2 Work out:
  a $23.4 \div 3$ b $4.64 \div 4$ c $111.24 \div 9$

3 Work out:
  a $0.24 \div 0.006$ c $0.064 \div 0.0008$
  b $0.35 \div 0.0007$ d $12 \div 0.0004$

4 Work out:
  a $711 \div 0.3$ c $464 \div 0.04$
  b $825 \div 0.5$ d $2940 \div 0.06$

5 Work out:
  a $0.8 \times 400 \div 0.02$
  b $600 \times 0.05 \times 3000 \div 0.09$
  c $0.04 \times 70 \div 0.002 \times 200$

6 Without doing the calculations, work out which two calculations have different answers from the others.
  a $25 \div 0.8$ c $250 \div 8$ e $2500 \div 80$
  b $250 \div 0.08$ d $2.5 \div 0.08$ f $2500 \div 0.008$

Now check your answers. You may want to use your calculator. Did you get any wrong and can you work out why?

3.4.3 Multiplying and dividing negative decimals

Objectives

You will learn how to:

- multiply positive and negative decimals
- divide positive and negative decimals

Remember the rules that you met in Subsection 3.2.3:

$(\text{positive}) \times (\text{positive}) = \text{positive}$ $(\text{positive}) \div (\text{positive}) = \text{positive}$
$(\text{positive}) \times (\text{negative}) = \text{negative}$ $(\text{positive}) \div (\text{negative}) = \text{negative}$
$(\text{negative}) \times (\text{positive}) = \text{negative}$ $(\text{negative}) \div (\text{positve}) = \text{negative}$
$(\text{negative}) \times (\text{negative}) = \text{positive}$ $(\text{negative}) \div (\text{negative}) = \text{positive}$

Worked example	Thinking	Your turn!
Work out: -3.2×-1.94	*What calculation is this the same as?*	**Work out:** -2.39×-1.3
$-3.2 \times -1.94 = 3.2 \times 1.94$ $3.2 = 32 \div 10$ $1.94 = 194 \div 100$ 3.2×1.94 $= 3.2 \div 10 \times 194 \div 100$ $= 32 \times 194 \div 10 \div 100$	*How can we rewrite this without using decimals?*	
Work out 32×194 using a written method: $\begin{array}{r} 3\ 0\ 0\ 0 \\ 2\ 7\ 0\ 0 \\ 1\ 2\ 0 \\ 2\ 0\ 0 \\ 1\ 8\ 0 \\ +\qquad 8 \\ \hline 6\ 2\ 0\ 8 \\ {\scriptstyle 1}\ {\scriptstyle 1} \end{array}$ $32 \times 194 \div 10 \div 100$ $= 6208 \div 10 \div 100$ $= 6.208$ So $-3.2 \times -1.94 = 6.208$	*How do we decide whether to use a mental or written strategy when solving these types of problems?*	

Speech bubbles (Your turn! column):

-3.2×-1.94 is the same as $-(3.2 \times -1.94) = 3.2 \times 1.94$

I can write the decimals using expanded form.

I will use a written strategy here as the numbers are quite large and I can't see an obvious way to simplify the calculation.

×	100	90	4
30	3000	2700	120
2	200	180	8

▲ Example-problem pair 1

When calculating with a mixture of positive and negative numbers, always check the sign of your final answer.

Worked example	Thinking	Your turn!
Work out: $-3.54 \div 0.06$	How do we work out the sign of the result before calculating?	Work out: $-2.72 \div 0.04$
$-3.54 \div 0.06 = -\square$ $0.06 \times 100 = 6$ $3.54 \times 100 = 354$ So the calculation becomes: $-354 \div 6$	How can we rewrite this to make it easier to work out? Why do we need to adjust both numbers?	
Using short division: $\begin{array}{r} 5\ 9 \\ 6\overline{\smash{)}3\,^35\,^54} \end{array}$ So $-3.54 \div 0.06 = -59$		

A negative divided by a positive gives a negative.

I want to divide by an integer not a decimal, so I'll multiply 0.06 by 100

If I do the same to both numbers in the division, the answer will be the same as the original question.

▲ Example-problem pair 2

3.4.3 Fluency

In this exercise you can practise applying mathematical methods that you have just learnt.

1 Work out:
a -3.2×-1.4 **b** -8.3×2.6 **c** 12.6×-4.5

2 Work out:
a $-8.5 \div 5$ **b** $3.72 \div -3$ **c** $-116.24 \div -8$

3 Calculate:
a -0.4×0.05 **c** 0.007×-0.006
b -0.08×-0.03 **d** -0.0009×0.004

4 Work out:
a $0.18 \div -0.003$ **c** $-0.032 \div 0.0004$
b $-0.27 \div -0.0009$ **d** $-0.00042 \div -0.0007$

5 Work out:
a 4.55×-1.2 **c** -6.4×8.95
b -2.37×-3.6 **d** -3.62×-4.73

6 Work out:
a $-684 \div -0.6$ **c** $-768 \div 0.08$
b $-660 \div 0.5$ **d** $1650 \div -0.03$

7 Without doing the actual calculations, work out which two of these calculations have a different answer from the other four.
a -3.8×14 **d** -38×0.14
b -3800×0.014 **e** 1.4×-38
c 380×-0.14 **f** $-0.0014 \times -38\,000$

8 Without doing the actual calculations, work out which two of these calculations have a different answer from the other four.
a $-49 \div 0.6$ **d** $4.9 \div -0.06$
b $-4900 \div 60$ **e** $490 \div -0.06$
c $-49\,000 \div -600$ **f** $490 \div -6$

Now check your answers. You may want to use your calculator. Did you get any wrong and can you work out why?

3.4 Exercises

3.4 Intelligent practice

"Why is it intelligent?" You might notice a connection when you move on from one question to the next. You can use the Reflect, Expect, Check, Explain process to:

- *reflect* on what's different between each question and the one that came before
- decide how you *expect* this answer to be different
- complete the question and *check* your answer
- *explain* to yourself why your expectation was correct or incorrect.

Question 2a   EXAMPLE

Calculate 0.9×0.8

$0.9 \times 0.8 = 9 \times 8 \div 10 \div 10 = 72 \div 100 = 0.72$

Question 2b

Calculate 0.9×0.16

Reflect: This is 0.9 multiplied by a number as in part a and 16 is twice 8

Expect: I think the answer will be the answer from part a multiplied by 2, so 1.44

Check: $0.9 \times 0.16 = 0.144$

Explain: I forgot to divide by 10! The answer should be smaller than part a since I'm multiplying by a smaller positive number $(0.16 < 0.8)$

---

1   Calculate:

   a 1.2×4.3 **d** 4.2×0.68

   b 2.1×3.4 **e** $4.2 \times 0.68 \times 0.1$

   c 4.2×3.4 **f** 0.42×0.68

2   Calculate:

   a 0.9×0.8 **e** 0.09×2.7

   b 0.9×0.16 **f** 0.009×2.7

   c 0.9×0.26 **g** 0.9009×2.7

   d 0.09×2.6 **h** 0.3003×0.81

3   Work out:

   a 1.44×1.5

   b 0.144×0.015

   c 14.4×0.15

   d $2.88 \times 7.5 \times 0.001$

   e $0.02 \times 1.44 \times 0.75 \times 10$

   f $1.2^2 \times 0.075 \times 0.04$

   g $2.4^2 \times 0.075 \times 0.04$

4   Work out:

   a $1.5 \times (-1.6)$

   b $(-1.5) \times (-1.6)$

   c $1.5 \times (-3.2)$

   d $(-4.5) \times (-3.2)$

   e $(-4.5) \times 0.8$

   f $(-0.8) \times (-4.5) \times (-0.02)$

   g $0.3 \times (-5) \times 8 \times 30 \times (-2)$

   h $0.09 \times 0.5 \times 800 \times (-20)$

   i $15 \times 16 \times (-10) \times (-0.03) \times (-2)$

5   Work out:

   a $12.6 \div 5$ **h** $1.26 \div 0.7$

   b $12.6 \div 9$ **i** $1.26 \div 1.4$

   c $0.126 \div 9$ **j** $1.26 \div 0.06$

   d $0.126 \div 3$ **k** $(-1.26) \div 0.06$

   e $1260 \div 0.3$ **l** $1.26 \div (-0.06)$

   f $126 \div 0.9$ **m** $(-12.6) \div (-0.21)$

   g $126 \div 0.7$

6 Work out:

a $4.05 \div 9$

b $(1.35 \div 9) \div 0.5$

c $(1.35 \div 0.5) \div 9$

d $(0.27 \div 9) \times (-100)$

e $\left[(6 \times 0.9) \div (-3)\right] \times 0.5$

3.4 Method selection

In these questions you'll need to think carefully about which methods to apply.

For some questions you might need to use skills from earlier chapters.

1 Calculate each of these, giving your answers in numerals and words.

a three tenths × five hundredths

b sixteen tenths × twenty-three hundredths

c thirteen thousandths × twenty-four tenths

d one thousand one hundred ÷ eight tenths

e nine hundred and sixty ÷ four hundredths

2 Copy and complete these sum-product puzzles. In each puzzle there are two numbers in the middle row. The brick above is the sum of the numbers in the middle row. The brick below is the product of the numbers in the middle row.

a
Sum [ ]
1.4 | 6
Product [ ]

b
Sum [ ]
0.7 | 6
Product [ ]

c
Sum [ ]
0.4 | [ ]
Product 2.4

d
Sum 2.4
0.4 | [ ]
Product [ ]

e
Sum [ ]
3 | 2.8
Product [ ]

f
Sum [ ]
1.5 | 5.6
Product [ ]

g
Sum [ ]
−5 | [ ]
Product −20

h
Sum [ ]
−15 | [ ]
Product 60

3 Copy and complete these tables using the grid method of multiplication.

a

×	0.3	0.7
0.78		
		2.73

b

×	0.08	0.12
5.73		
	0.144	

c

×		
−0.2	0.654	−0.111
−3.8		

4 An adult rabbit is 2.4 kg. A young rabbit weighs 80 g.

How many times heavier is the adult than the young rabbit?

5 A partially filled van has room for an extra of 70 kg of parcels.
The driver has 300 parcels, each weighing 240 g, that need to be loaded.
Can all of these parcels safely be loaded onto the van?

6 A 5 m length of ribbon is to be cut into 85 mm pieces.
How many pieces can be cut? What length of ribbon will be left over?

7 Answer questions a to h.
  a Pencils can be bought in boxes of 500. How many pencils are there in 60 boxes?
  b Find the cost of 30 chairs at £49 each.
  c The cost of six coffees is £14.70. What does one coffee cost?
  d Tickets to an event cost £24.50 each. Cara bought tickets for her and her friends
    and she spent £147 in total. How many tickets did she buy?
  e A school council has raised £150 to purchase new books for the library.
    The books cost £4.90 each. How many new books can they buy?
  f Find the cost of six chairs at a cost of £14.70 each.
  g Karim bought some boxes of tiles and the total came to £176.40.
    If each box costs £14.70, how many boxes did he buy?
  h A length of wood which is 176.4 cm long is cut into 24 equal pieces.
    How long is each piece?

3.4 Purposeful practice

There may be more than one way to approach these questions.

Once you have answered a question one way, can you think of another way?

1 Complete parts a and b.

  a Calculate:

    i 3×4

    ii 3.5^2

    iii 5×6

    iv 5.5^2

    v 6.5^2

    vi 10.5^2

  b Looking at the answers in part a, describe a quick way to square numbers that end in 5 tenths. Can you explain why it works?

2 Write a calculation for each section of the Venn diagram.

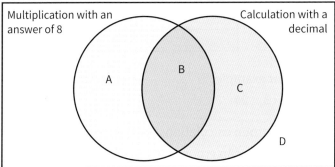

3 Write a calculation for each section of the Venn diagram.

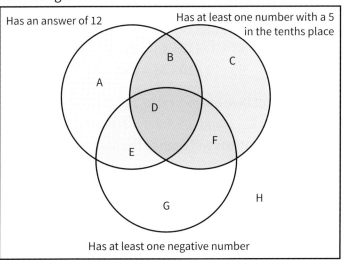

4 Use the digits 2, 3, 4, 5 exactly once each in the calculation:

$$\square.\square \times \square.\square$$

  a Try to get a result close or equal to:

    i 8.5

    ii 14.5

    iii 15

  b Change the operation to division. Try to get a result close to:

    i 1.5

    ii 0.5

    iii 1

5 Here is a price list for different colours of ribbon. The prices are per metre and you can only purchase ribbon in whole metre lengths.

Colour	Price per metre
Gold	63p
Red	27p
Blue	32p
Silver	45p
Green	20p

  a Can you work out a way to spend exactly £35? Is there more than one way?

  b If you are allowed to buy the ribbon in multiples of 0.5 m instead, what is the least number of different colours you can buy while still spending exactly £35?

Efficient calculations

3.5.1 The commutative and associative laws

Objectives

You will:
- know and use the commutative law
- know and use the associative law

The **commutative law** means that if you have a string of additions, you can do them in any order and the result will always be the same.

For example, the bar model shows that
$3 + 4 + 5 = 12$ no matter in which order 3, 4, and 5 are added.

12		
3	4	5
3	5	4
4	3	5
4	5	3
5	3	4
5	4	3

Multiplication is also commutative. For example,
$$2 \times 3 \times 4 = 3 \times 4 \times 2 = 3 \times 2 \times 4 = 4 \times 2 \times 3 = 24$$

The **associative law** says that you can group calculations involving only addition or only multiplication in any way you like. You can group calculations using brackets and do the calculation in the brackets before the others. You will still get the same final result, whichever way you group the calculations.

$60 + 3 + 10 + 5 = 78$ $60 \times 3 \times 10 \times 5 = 9000$

$60 + (3 + 10) + 5 = 78$ $60 \times (3 \times 10) \times 5 = 9000$

$60 + 3 + (10 + 5) = 78$ $60 \times 3 \times (10 \times 5) = 9000$

$60 + (3 + 10 + 5) = 78$ $60 \times (3 \times 10 \times 5) = 9000$

Subtraction and division are *not* commutative operations or associative operations. The order matters. For example, $3 - 4 \neq 4 - 3$ and $3 \div 4 \neq 4 \div 3$. Adding brackets and changing the order that you do the calculations will change the final result.

$60 - 3 - 10 - 5 = 42$ $60 \div 3 \div 10 \div 5 = 0.4$

$60 - (3 - 10) - 5 = 62$ $60 \div (3 \div 10) \div 5 = 40$

$60 - 3 - (10 - 5) = 52$ $60 \div 3 \div (10 \div 5) = 10$

$60 - (3 - 10 - 5) = 72$ $60 \div (3 \div 10 \div 5) = 1000$

You can use these laws to make mental or written calculations more efficient.

Worked example	Thinking	Your turn!
Use the commutative and associative laws to calculate this efficiently: $4 \times 2 \times 15 \times 5$	*Can we change the order of calculation to make this easier?*	Use the commutative and associative laws to calculate this efficiently: $5 \times 8 \times 4 \times 7$
$4 \times 2 \times 15 \times 5$ $= 2 \times 5 \times 4 \times 15$ $= (2 \times 5) \times (4 \times 15)$ $= 10 \times 60$ $= 600$	*Which laws can be used to make the calculation more efficient?* *What other order could we have done this in?*	

I can rearrange the numbers because multiplication is commutative and group the multiplications because multiplication is associative.

I can look for pairs of numbers that multiply to give 10 or a multiple of 10

I could have done $(4 \times 5) \times 15 = 20 \times 15 = 300$ then $\times 2$ to get 600, since multiplying by 20 can be done mentally by doubling and multiplying by ten.

▲ Example-problem pair 1

3.5.1 Fluency

In this exercise you can practise applying mathematical methods that you have just learnt.

1 Here are two calculations:

$3 + 13 + 7 = 3 + 7 + 13 = 10 + 13 = 23$

$5 \times 7 \times 4 = 5 \times 4 \times 7 = 20 \times 7 = 140$

  a Using these calculations, explain what is meant by the commutative law.

  b Use the commutative law to work out:

    i $8 + 17 + 2$ **iii** $5 \times 18 \times 2$

    ii $12 + 37 + 8$ **iv** $4 \times 29 \times 25$

2 Here are two calculations:

$4 \times 5 \times 3 = 20 \times 3 = 4 \times 15$

$8 + 3 + 4 = 11 + 4 = 8 + 7$

  a Using these calculations, explain what is meant by the associative law.

  b Use the associative law to work out:

    i $19 \times 5 \times 2$ **iii** $18 + 7 + 3$

    ii $13 \times 25 \times 4$ **iv** $31 + 47 + 53$

3 Which of these statements are true, and which are false? Explain your answers.

  a $7 + 3 - 5 = 7 - 5 + 3$

  b $9 + 12 - 8 = 12 - 8 + 9$

  c $11 - 6 + 3 = 11 - 3 + 6$

  d $16 - 9 = 9 - 16$

  e $5 \times 6 \div 2 = 6 \div 2 \times 5$

  f $8 \div 2 \times 7 = 2 \times 7 \div 8$

  g $20 \div 5 \times 4 = 20 \times 4 \div 5$

  h $32 \div 8 = 8 \div 32$

4 Here is a calculation:

  a Explain each step in the working.

$1.08 - 0.2 - (-0.12) = 1.08 - 0.2 + 0.12$
$= 1.08 + 0.12 - 0.2$
$= 1.2 - 0.2$
$= 1$

  b Use the same method to calculate:

    i $2.51 - 0.8 - (-0.29)$

    ii $3.64 + 0.49 - (-0.36)$

    iii $9.53 + 1.78 - 0.53$

    iv $3.84 - (-0.77) - (-0.16)$

5 Here is a calculation:

$2.1 \times -2 \times -5 = 2.1 \times 10 = 21$

  a Explain each step of the working.

  b Use the same method to calculate:

    i $-3.6 \times 2 \times (-5)$ **iii** $8.32 \times (-4) \times (-25)$

    ii $8.1 \times (-5) \times (-2)$ **iv** $9.23 \times 2 \times (-50)$

Now check your answers. You may want to use your calculator. Did you get any wrong and can you work out why?

3.5.2 Factorising numbers to multiply and divide

You learnt about factors and prime factorisation in Chapter 2. You can use the **factorisation** of numbers to make some calculations more efficient. Being able to quickly write numbers as a product of prime factors, or even do this mentally, will give you an advantage for calculations like this. Look back at Chapter 2 for a reminder of how to do this and for definitions of prime and composite numbers.

Worked example	Thinking	Your turn!	
Work out, by factorising, 35×14	*What factors would be good to use?*	Work out, by factorising, 55×12	Factors of 2 and 5 make 10, so these factors are good to find.
$35 = 5 \times 7$ $14 = 2 \times 7$	*How can we use these factors to calculate efficiently?*		
35×14 $= 5 \times 7 \times 2 \times 7$ $= 7 \times 7 \times 2 \times 5$ $= 49 \times 10$ $= 490$			I'll leave $\times 2 \times 5$ until the end as that's just $\times 10$ and I can do that mentally.

▲ Example-problem pair 1

Other examples of using factorisation to calculate efficiently that you may have used:

- doubling and doubling again to multiply by 4
- multiplying by 3 and then doubling to multiply by 6

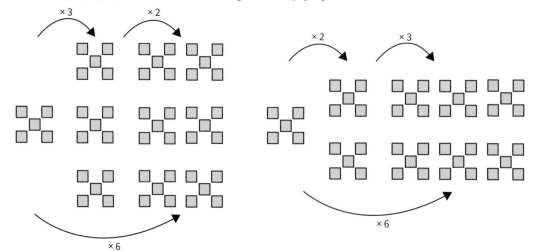

Since division is the inverse of multiplication you can reverse this process to divide by composite numbers. If something is multiplied by 6 this is the same as multiplying by 2 and then 3 (or 3 and then 2), so to divide by 6 you can divide by 2 and then 3 (or 3 and then 2). You can divide by larger numbers more efficiently by using factors of the divisor.

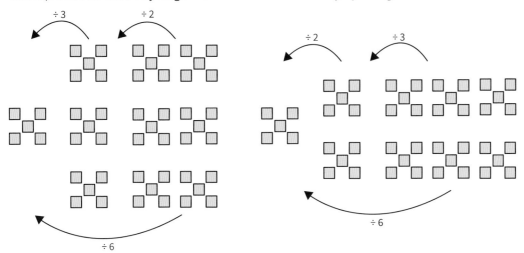

Worked example	Thinking	Your turn!
Work out, by factorising, $306 \div 6$	*Which number should we look to factorise?*	Work out, by factorising, $258 \div 6$
$6 = 2 \times 3$ $306 \div 6 = 306 \div 2 \div 3$ $\quad 1\ 5\ 3 \qquad\qquad 5\ 1$ $2\,\overline{)3^{1}0\ 6} \quad\ \ 3\,\overline{)1\ 5\ 3}$ $306 \div 6 = 51$	*Does it matter which order we divide by each factor?*	

I can factorise either number, but I chose 9 as I can do the prime factorisation quicker than 306

I could divide by 2 and then 3, or divide by 3 and then 2. I'd still be dividing by 6 overall.

▲ Example-problem pair 2

3.5.2 Fluency

In this exercise you can practise applying mathematical methods that you have just learnt.

 1 Here is a calculation:

$45 \times 12 = 9 \times 5 \times 2 \times 6 = 9 \times 10 \times 6 = 540$

a Explain each step of the working.
b Use the same method to calculate:

   i 65×14 **iv** 45×80
   ii 55×18 **v** 122×250
   iii 24×35 **vi** 144×450

 2 Here is a calculation:

$210 \div 6 = 210 \div 3 \div 2 = 70 \div 2 = 35$

a Explain each step of the working.

b Use the same method to calculate:

   i $440 \div 8$ **iv** $1500 \div 6$
   ii $783 \div 9$ **v** $3360 \div 14$
   iii $420 \div 12$ **vi** $8640 \div 16$

3 Use factorisation to work out:

   a $-840 \div 12$ **d** 3.5×-1.8
   b $-960 \div -24$ **e** -7.2×-7.5
   c 5.5×1.4 **f** $-134.4 \div 16$

Now check your answers. You may want to use your calculator. Did you get any wrong and can you work out why?

3.5.3 The distributive law

> **Objective** ☑
>
> You will:
> - know and use the distributive law

To multiply 26 by 5 you can partition 26 into $20 + 6$, multiply 20 by 5, multiply 6 by 5, and add these together. You write this as:

$$5 \times 26 = 5 \times (20 + 6)$$
$$= 5 \times 20 + 5 \times 6$$
$$= 100 + 30$$
$$= 130$$

You call this the **distributive law** of multiplication over addition. You can use any numbers in the calculation.

Multiplication is also distributive over subtraction, and division is distributive over addition and subtraction. For division, the distributive law applies only if the addition or subtraction is the dividend and not the divisor.

For example, $4 \times (5 - 3) = (4 \times 5) - (4 \times 3)$

$$(5 + 3) \div 4 = (5 \div 4) + (3 \div 4)$$

$$(5 - 3) \div 4 = (5 \times 4) - (3 \div 4)$$

You can partition a number any way you like.

The distributive law for division only works if the addition or subtraction is the dividend.

> **Investigate Further** 🔍
>
> Try calculations by partitioning the numbers in multiple ways. Are some partitions easier than others? Try calculating 17×28 by working out $(15 + 2) \times (20 + 8)$ or $(20 - 3) \times (30 - 2)$.

Worked example	Thinking	Your turn!
Work out: 8×29	*What number could we partition and how?*	Work out: 7×19
Using the distributive law: $8 \times (30 - 1)$ $= 8 \times 30 - 8 \times 1$ $= 240 - 8$ $= 232$		

I partitioned 29 into 30 and -1 as I think this is easier than multiplying by 20 and 9

▲ Example-problem pair 1

When you use the grid method, you normally partition by place value (e.g. $27 = 20 + 7$ and $14 = 10 + 4$), but you can partition the numbers you are multiplying however you like and the total will always be the same. Remember, partitioning a number means writing it as an equivalent calculation involving addition (or subtraction).

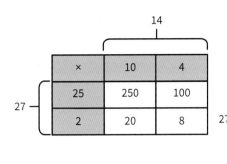

×	10	4
25	250	100
2	20	8

(14 above, 27 at left)

```
  2 5 0
  1 0 0
    2 0
+     8
  3 7 8
```

×	7	7
20	140	140
5	35	35
2	14	14

(14 above, 27 at left)

```
  2 8 0
    7 0
+   2 8
  3 7 8
```

×	10	4
30	300	120
−3	−30	−12

(14 above, 27 at left)

$$300 - 30 = 250$$
$$120 - 12 = 108 \; +$$
$$\underline{378}$$

Using the partitioning method, you can calculate $27 \times 14 = 378$

3.5.3 Fluency

In this exercise you can practise applying mathematical methods that you have just learnt.

1 Here is a calculation:

$$15 \times 6 = (10 + 5) \times 6 = 10 \times 6 + 5 \times 6 = 60 + 30 = 90$$

a Using this calculation, explain what is meant by the distributive law.

b Use the distributive law to work out:

   i 18×3 **iii** 22×5

   ii 24×6 **iv** 28×9

2 Here is a calculation:

$$18 \times 13 = 10 \times 13 + 8 \times 13 = 130 + 8 \times 10 + 8 \times 3$$
$$= 130 + 80 + 24 = 234$$

a Explain each step of the working.

b Use the same method to calculate:

   i 16×14 **iv** 24×23

   ii 23×12 **v** 34×42

   iii 19×21

3 Here is a calculation:

$$153 \div 9 = (90 + 63) \div 9 = 90 \div 9 + 63 \div 9$$
$$= 10 + 7 = 17$$

a Explain each step of the working.

b Use the same method to calculate:

   i $136 \div 8$ **iv** $374 \div 11$

   ii $138 \div 6$ **v** $312 \div 8$

   iii $168 \div 7$

4 Here is a calculation:

$$99 \times 3.2 = 100 \times 3.2 - 1 \times 3.2 = 320 - 3.2 = 316.8$$

a Explain each step of the working.

b Use the same method to calculate:

   i 99×1.8 **iii** 999×1.25

   ii 98×4.5 **iv** 998×2.5

Now check your answers. You may want to use your calculator. Did you get any wrong and can you work out why?

3.5.4 Priority of operations

You will learn how to:
- calculate using the priority of operations
- use a calculator fluently

Any mathematical calculation involving more than one operation obeys the following order of calculation.

Priority 1. Brackets or groups

Calculations which are grouped by brackets should be carried out before any others.

Sometimes, a symbol includes a 'hidden' pair of brackets. Treat root symbols and fractions as if they are contained in brackets. For example:

$\sqrt{9+16}$ with the square root symbol extending over the sum means the same as $\sqrt{(9+16)}$, and $\dfrac{1}{9+16}$ with the dividing line extending over the sum means the same as $\dfrac{1}{(9+16)}$

Priority 2. Powers and roots

Once all the brackets have been calculated, calculations involving powers (indices/exponents) and roots have the next highest priority.

For example, $(7-2)+3^2 = 5+3^2 = 5+9 = 14$

You calculate the brackets first and then you calculate the power before you do the addition.

Priority 3. Multiplication and division

Once any brackets or groups and powers or roots have been calculated, the next priority is multiplication and division.

For example, $1+2^2 \times 3 = 1+4 \times 3 = 1+12 = 13$

First you calculate the power and then you multiply before you add.

Priority 4. Addition and subtraction

Finally, any additions and subtractions can be calculated.

Brackets or groups

Powers and roots

Multiplication and division

Addition and subtraction

Order of operation

Worked example	Thinking	Your turn!
Work out: $\dfrac{20 - \sqrt{3 + 22}}{9 - 2 \times 3}$	*Are there any bracketed or grouped calculations?*	Work out: $\dfrac{5 + 5 \times 3}{10 - \sqrt{29 + 7}}$
$= \dfrac{20 - \sqrt{25}}{9 - 2 \times 3}$ $= \dfrac{20 - 5}{9 - 6}$ $= \dfrac{15}{3}$ $= 15 \div 3$ $= 5$	*What other groups are there?* *What do we work out next?*	

The root symbol is grouping the calculation $3 + 22$, so I calculate this first.

There are two groups, one in the numerator of the fraction and one in the denominator. I can work out either one first.

I finish calculating the groups in the numerator and in the denominator, before I work out the fraction as a division.

▲ Example-problem pair 1

Scientific calculators use priority of operations. Some basic calculators do not, and simply work out each operation one at a time as you enter them. Sometimes you will need to use brackets on your calculator to make sure operations are done in the correct order.

Calculator

To work out $\dfrac{2 + 6 \times 5}{8 + 2}$ using a calculator press these keys:

Or press:

You should see 3.2 displayed on the screen.

Worked example	Thinking	Your turn!
Work out: $$\dfrac{\sqrt{12+17}-8.5}{3.2^2-2.7}$$ Give your answer to 2 decimal places.	Can we work this out mentally or any parts of it?	Work out: $$\dfrac{-100+8.8^2}{\sqrt{2\times 8.1}-9}$$ Give your answer to 2 decimal places.
$$=\dfrac{\sqrt{29}-8.5}{3.2^2-7}$$	On the calculator, how do we make sure the square root is the correct length and the division is correct?	
$\boxed{\tfrac{\square}{\square}}\ \boxed{\sqrt{\square}}\ \boxed{2}\ \boxed{9}\ \boxed{\rightarrow}\ \boxed{-}$ $\boxed{8}\ \boxed{.}\ \boxed{5}\ \boxed{\downarrow}\ \boxed{3}\ \boxed{.}$ $\boxed{2}\ \boxed{x^2}\ \boxed{-}\ \boxed{7}\ \boxed{=}$ $= -0.9613688867$		
$= -0.96$ (to 2 d.p.)	How many decimal places should we give in our answer?	
(Check: $\sqrt{29}-8.5 \approx 5.5-8.5=-3$ $3.2^2-7 \approx 10-7=3$ Estimate: $-3 \div 3 = -1$)	Does our result look about right?	

I know $12+17=29$, but I'll use a calculator for the rest.

After I have typed everything in the square root, I need to press the right arrow to type -8.5

The question says to use 2 decimal places.

I've got nearly -1

▲ Example-problem pair 2

3.5.4 Fluency

In this exercise you can practise applying mathematical methods that you have just learnt.

1 Work out:
   a $(3+4) \times 5$

   b $8 \times (15-9)$

   c $24 \div (3+5)$

2 Use a calculator to work out:
   a $(3.7+4.5) \times 1.2$

   b $8.3 \times (6.7-5.5)$

   c $(8.1+3.9) \div 0.12$

3 Work out:
   a $(16-12)^2 \times 3 - 18 \div 3$

   b $(4+3) \times 2^2 + 12 \div 4$

   c $8 \times (7-4)^2 \div (12-9)$

   d $50 \div (12-7)^2 \times (18-5)$

   e $(19+4) - 6^2 + 15 \div 3$

4 Use a calculator to work out:
   a $(1.3+4.1)^2 - (3.7+1.8) \div 1.1$

   b $-(1.2+5.6)^2 - \sqrt{4.41}$

   c $15.6 \div 0.3 + \sqrt{1.54 + 2.07}$

   d $(8.5+1.7)^3 - 13.2 \div 0.3 - (6.4-3.25)$

   e $16.2 \div 0.03 + (8.4-7.2)^2 - \sqrt{9.81 - 8.37}$

5 Work out:
   a $(8-11)^2 + 28 \div 7 - (3+1)$

   b $(7-9)^3 \div 4 + 8 \times 6 - 9$

   c $54 \div (12-9)^3 + (25-27)^2 \div (15-13)$

   d $(25-16)^2 \div (12-9) + (18-23)^2 + 24 \div 6$

6 Here is a calculation:
   $3.9 \times (1.9 + 3.01) \div (10.1 - 6.2)$

   Amit works out the answer on his calculator and gets 49.1

   Without working out the actual answer, explain why Amit must be wrong.

7 Here is a calculation:
   $(4.2+1.9)^2 - (7.9+2.03) \div (12.1 - 5 \times 2.1)$

   Jenna works out the answer on her calculator and gets 31.003 75

   Without working out the actual answer, work out whether Jenna's answer is likely to be correct.

Now check your answers. You may want to use your calculator. Did you get any wrong and can you work out why?

3.5 Exercises

3.5 Intelligent practice

"Why is it intelligent?" You might notice a connection when you move on from one question to the next. You can use the Reflect, Expect, Check, Explain process to:

- *reflect* on what's different between each question and the one that came before
- decide how you *expect* this answer to be different
- complete the question and *check* your answer
- *explain* to yourself why your expectation was correct or incorrect.

EXAMPLE

Question 3a

Work out $1 + 2 - 3$

$1 + 2 - 3 = 1 + 2 + (-3) = 3 + (-3) = 0$

Question 3b

Work out $1 - 2 + 3$

Reflect: This question has the same numbers as 3a, but the add and subtract symbols have been swapped.

Expect: I expect that my answer will be the same as addition and subtraction have the same priority so they can be done in any order.

Check: $1 - 2 + 3 = 1 + (-2) + 3 = (-1) + 3 = 2$

Explain: Oh, that's different to the last answer! But that makes sense because although addition and subtraction have the same priority, subtraction is not commutative like addition so you can't just add and subtract the numbers in any order.

Do not use your calculator in this exercise.

1 Using commutative, associative and distributive laws, work out:

- **a** $8 + 7 + 2 + 4 + 3$
- **b** $80 + 70 + 20 + 40 + 30$
- **c** $-8 + 7 + (-2) + 4 + 3$
- **d** $3 + 4 + 2 + 7 + 8$
- **e** $0.7 + 0.2 + 0.8 + 0.4 + 0.3$
- **f** $3.7 + 8.2 + 1.8 + 1.4 + 3.3$
- **g** $37 + 82 + 18 + 14 + 33$

2 Work out:

- **a** $3 \times 2 \times 2 \times 2 \times 5$
- **b** $3 \times 2 \times 4 \times 5$
- **c** $2 \times 3 \times 5 \times 4$
- **d** $2 \times 3 + 5 \times 4$
- **e** $2 \times 3 + 8 + 5 \times 4$
- **f** $2 \times 3 + 8 + 8 \times 4$
- **g** $12 \times 3 + 8 + 8 \times 4$
- **h** $12 \times 3 + 8 \times 4$
- **i** $12 \times 4 + 8 \times 4$
- **j** $12 \times 6 + 8 \times 6$
- **k** $12 \times 13 + 8 \times 13$
- **l** $1.2 \times 1.3 + 0.8 \times 1.3$

3 Work out:

- **a** $17 + 28 - 36$
- **b** $17 - 28 + 36$
- **c** $12 + 39 - 20$
- **d** $39 - 20 + 12$
- **e** $25 - 31 + 42$
- **f** $25 + 31 - 42$
- **g** $20 + 30 - 40$
- **h** $20 - 40 + 30$
- **i** $(-40) + 20 + 30$

4 Calculate:

- **a** $1.2 - 3.4 + 5.6$
- **b** $1.2 + 5.6 - 3.4$
- **c** $2.3 - 4.56 + 7.7$
- **d** $3.4 - 5.76 + 6.6$
- **e** $3.05 - 5.67 + 6.94$
- **f** $3.14 - 5.68 + 6.8$

5 Work out:

- **a** $3 + 4 \times 8 + 24 \div 6$
- **b** $(3 + 4) \times 8 + 24 \div 6$
- **c** $3 + 4 \times (8 + 24 \div 6)$
- **d** $(3 + 4) \times (8 + 24 \div 6)$

6 Work out:
- **a** $420 \div 14 \div 10$
- **b** $420 \div (14 \div 10)$
- **c** $420 \div 7 \div 2 \div 10$
- **d** $420 \div 14 \div 5 \times 2$

7 Work out:
- **a** $10 + 4 \times 6 + 24$
- **b** $4 + 10 \times 6 + 24$
- **c** $(4 + 10) \times 6 + 24$
- **d** $4 + 10 \times (6 + 24)$
- **e** $10 + 4 \times (6 + 24)$
- **f** $(10 + 4) \times (6 + 24)$

8 Work out:
- **a** $24 + 52 + 32 \div 4$
- **b** $24 + (52 + 32) \div 4$
- **c** $(24 + 52 + 32) \div 4$
- **d** $2.4 + 5.2 + 3.2 \div 4 + 8 \times 0.2$
- **e** $2.4 + (5.2 + 3.2) \div 4 + 8 \times 0.2$
- **f** $(2.4 + 5.2 + 3.2) \div 4 - 8 \times 0.2$
- **g** $(2.4 + 5.2 + 3.2) \div 4 - 2 \times 0.3$
- **h** $(5.2 + 3.2) \div 4$
- **i** $(2.4 + 5.2 + 3.2) \div 4 - 2 \times 0.3 - 2 \times 0.6$

9 Work out:
- **a** $6 \div (12 \div 2) + 3$
- **b** $6 \div 12 \div 2 + 3$
- **c** $6 \times (12 \div 2) + 3$
- **d** $6 \times 12 \div (2 + 3)$
- **e** $6 - 12 \div 2 + 3$
- **f** $6 - (12 \div 2) + 3$
- **g** $6 - (12 \div 2 + 3)$
- **h** $6 - (12 - 2) \times 3$
- **i** $6 - 12 \div (2 \times 3)$
- **j** $6 - (12 \div 2 \times 3)$
- **k** $(6 - 12) \div (2 \times 3)$
- **l** $6^2 - 12 \div 2 \times 3$
- **m** $6^2 - 12 \times 2 \div 3$
- **n** $(6^2 - 12) \times 2 \div 32 \times 3 - 6^2 \div 12$
- **o** $2 \times (3 - 6^2 \div 12)$
- **p** $(2 \times 3)^2 - 2 \times 3^2$
- **q** $(2 \times 3 - 6^2) \times (6 - 8 + 4)$
- **r** $(2 \times 3 - 6^2) \times (6 - (8 + 4))$
- **s** $(2 \times 3 - 6^2) \times (6 - (8 + 4))^2$

3.5 Method selection

In these questions you'll need to think carefully about which methods to apply.

For some questions you might need to use skills from earlier chapters.

1 What is the units digit in the answers to these calculations?
- **a** 125×7787
- **b** 678×3456
- **c** 899×788
- **d** $10\,244 \times 1667$

2 Copy and complete the calculations, replacing the □ with the correct operation(s) from $+$, $-$, $\times$, or $\div$.
- **a** $5 \square - 2 = -10$
- **b** $8 \square - 4 = -2$
- **c** $-8 \square - 2 = -10$
- **d** $7 \square - 4 = 11$
- **e** $18 \square - 6 = -3$
- **f** $-8 \square (-5 \square 2) = 56$
- **g** $5 \square - 2 \square 8 = -11$

3 Copy the calculations and insert brackets so they are correct.
- **a** $3 \times 2 + 7 - 1 = 26$
- **b** $6 \times 2 + 3 \times 5 = 150$
- **c** $7 + 5 \times 2 - 3 = 2$
- **d** $2 + 3 \times 4 + 7 = 55$
- **e** $2 + 3 \times 5 - 7 \times 4 = 34$

4 Copy each array and match it to the calculation it represents using the priority of operations.

a $3 \times 2 + 4$ **d** $5 \times (-2) + 4$ **g** $5 + (-2) \times 4$

b $5 + 6 \times 2$ **e** $2 + 3 \times 5$ **h** $4 + 4 \times 4$

c $3 + 2 \times 4$ **f** $2 \times 2 + 2 \times 3$

A (+1)(+1)(+1)(+1)(+1) (+1)(+1)(+1)(+1)(+1)(+1)
(+1)(+1)(+1)(+1)(+1)(+1)

B (+1)(+1)(+1) (+1)(+1)(+1)(+1)
(+1)(+1)(+1)

C (−1)(−1) (+1)
(−1)(−1) (+1)
(−1)(−1) (+1)
(−1)(−1) (+1)
(+1)

D (+1)(+1) (+1)(+1)(+1)(+1)(+1)
(+1)(+1)(+1)(+1)(+1)
(+1)(+1)(+1)(+1)(+1)

E (+1)(+1) (+1)(+1)(+1)
(+1)(+1) (+1)(+1)(+1)

F (+1)(+1)(+1)(+1) (+1)(+1)(+1)(+1)
(+1)(+1)(+1)(+1)
(+1)(+1)(+1)(+1)
(+1)(+1)(+1)(+1)

G (+1)(+1)(+1) (+1)(+1)
(+1)(+1)
(+1)(+1)
(+1)(+1)

H (−1)(−1) (+1)
(−1)(−1) (+1)
(−1)(−1) (+1)
(−1)(−1) (+1)
(−1)(−1)

5 Charlie buys four yoghurts at 89 p each, two packets of biscuits at £1.20 each, and some bottles of water which cost 85 p each. Charlie pays with a £10 note and gets £1.49 change. How many bottles of water did he buy?

6 Paper is often sold in packs called reams. A ream contains 500 sheets of paper.

a How many sheets of paper are there in:

   i 20 reams,

   ii 200 reams,

   iii 600 reams?

b A quire is the name for 25 sheets of paper. How many quires are there in a ream?

c A bundle of paper contains 40 quires.

   i How many sheets of paper are there in a bundle?

   ii How many reams are there in a bundle?

d A pallet of paper contains 200 000 sheets of paper.

   i How many bundles are there in a pallet?

   ii How many quires are in a pallet?

   iii How many reams are in a pallet?

   iv How many pallets would you need if you wanted 72 000 000 sheets of paper?

   v Ten sheets of paper together are 1 mm thick. If you stacked all the paper in a pallet in a single tower, how tall would the tower be? Give your answer in metres.

7 A car can travel 43.5 miles for each gallon of fuel. Fuel costs £6.25 per gallon. To travel 300 miles, how much will the fuel cost? (You may use a calculator.)

8 The lift in a building has a weight limit of 1300 kg. Mario plans to send 120 boxes of electrical equipment up to the top floor using the lift. He plans to send them up using a remote control device instead of getting into the lift himself. 50 boxes have a mass of 9.2 kg each; 25 boxes have a mass of 15.4 kg each; and the rest have a mass of 10.5 kg each. Will Mario be able to send all these supplies up in the lift in just one trip?

3.5 Purposeful practice

There may be more than one way to approach these questions.
Once you have answered a question one way, can you think of another way?

1 Copy and complete the calculations, using the numbers given, so they are correct.

a $\square \times \square + \square = -19$ Use $-4, 5, 6$ **f** $\square \times \square - \square = 34$ Use $-4, 5, 6$

b $\square \times \square + \square = 34$ Use $4, -5, -6$ **g** $\square \times \square - \square = -26$ Use $4, -5, 6$

c $\square \times \square + \square = -39$ Use $3, -6, 7$ **h** $\square \times \square - \square = 27$ Use $3, -6, 7$

d $\square \times \square + \square = 27$ Use $-3, 6, -7$ **i** $\square \times \square - \square = -11$ Use $-3, 6, -7$

e $\square \times \square + \square = -18$ Use $2, -8, -5$ **j** $\square \times \square - \square = -2$ Use $2, -8, -5$

2 For each region of this Venn diagram, write a calculation which contains at least three operations and has a result of 15

If there is a region where it is impossible to write a calculation you must be able to explain why.

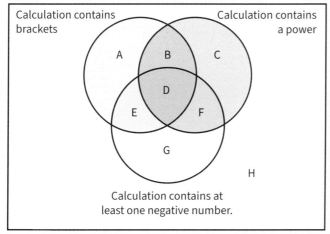

3 Using the numbers 3, 4, and 5, and any of the operations $+$, $-$, and $\times$, but no brackets, write as many different calculations and their answers as you can. Find some calculations that look different but have the same answer.

4 State which of the commutative, associative, and distributive laws are being used for each statement.

a $4.3 \times 25 \times 4 = 4.3 \times 100$

b $25 \times 4.3 \times 4 = 4.3 \times 25 \times 4$

c $-218 + 40 + 118 = -218 + 118 + 40$

d $2023 \times 98 = 2023 \times 100 - 2023 \times 2$

e $642 \div 6 = (600 + 42) \div 6 = 600 \div 6 + 42 \div 6 = 100 + 7 = 107$

f $15 \times 72 - 64 \times 15 + 15 \times (-8) = 15 \times (72 - 64 - 8)$

5 Using four 4s and the operations $+$, $-$, $\times$, $\div$, squaring, and square rooting, which of the integers from 1 to 20 can you make?

Watch out! exercise

Some students have tried to answer the questions below but have unfortunately made some mistakes.

For each question do the following:

- **a** answer the question correctly
- **b** write down the mistake that each student has made
- **c** comment on why they might have made that mistake
- **d** write an explanation for each student to convince them (nicely!) that their answer cannot be correct.

1 Anna and Bastian have tried to answer the question, "Calculate $(-10)+(-8)$"

Anna wrote 18

Bastian wrote -2

2 Cameron answered the question, "Calculate $8-(-2)$"

Cameron wrote 6

3 Zuri and Melanie answered the question, "Calculate $(-5)\times(-6)$"

Zuri wrote -11

Melanie wrote -30

4 Jake tried to answer the question, "Calculate $(-7)\times 0$"

Jake wrote -7

5 Sam, Elena, and Rhys tried to answer the question, "Calculate $5\div 0.5$"

Sam wrote 1

Elena wrote 2.5

Rhys wrote 0.1

6 Maryam and Isla tried to answer the question, "Calculate $(-1)^2$"

Maryam wrote -1

Isla wrote -2

7 Oscar tried to answer the question, "Calculate $2+5\times 3$"

Oscar wrote $2+5\times 3=21$

8 Max and Shaun answered the question, "Calculate $\dfrac{2+6\times 5}{8+2}$"

Max wrote 6

Shaun wrote 7

Check your understanding

Turn over to find the review questions

3.1 Addition and subtraction with negative integers

You should now be able to...	Questions
order and compare positive and negative integers	1a–b
know that there are infinitely many integers	1c–d
add and subtract positive and negative integers	2, 9

3.2 Multiplication and division with negative integers

You should now be able to...	Questions
multiply positive and negative integers	10a – c, 11, 14
divide positive and negative integers	10d, 10e

3.3 Addition and subtraction with decimals

You should now be able to...	Questions
add and subtract positive and negative decimals	4, 5, 6, 7, 8
order and compare positive and negative decimals	3
know that given two numbers, you can always find another number between them	1c

3.4 Multiplication and division with decimals

You should now be able to...	Questions
multiply and divide efficiently using powers of 10	11
multiply and divide positive and negative decimals	10f–h, 12, 13

3.5 Efficient calculations

You should now be able to...	Questions
know and use the commutative, associative, and distributive laws	15, 16, 17
calculate using the priority of operations	17
use a calculator fluently	18

Chapter 3 review questions

1 Complete questions a to d.

   a Write these numbers in order, smallest first. [1]

      5, −6, 2, −2, 0

   b Draw arrows on a copy of this number line to show the position of each number. [1]

   c Jamal says, "There are 19 numbers between −10 and 10 since there are 19 marks on the number line."

      Is Jamal correct? Explain your answer. [1]

   d Ellie says, "The largest number is 10 since that is where the number line stops."

      Is Ellie correct? Explain your answer. [1]

2 Work out:

   a $5 + -7$ [1]

   b $-8 + 3$ [1]

   c $-9 + -12$ [1]

   d $-3 + 5 + (-2)$ [1]

   e $6 - (-5)$ [1]

   f $-8 - (-12)$ [1]

3 Write these numbers in order, smallest first. [1]

   2.3, −2.2, −1.6, 0.8, −0.5

4 Work out $4.51 + 7.32$ [2]

5 Work out $6.87 - 3.54$ [2]

6 Barry buys a magazine costing £3.25 and a bag of snacks costing £8.79

   How much does Barry spend in total? [2]

7 Zaina has £11.34 in her wallet. She buys a book costing £8.85

   How much money does Zaina have left after buying the book? [2]

8 Josef's bank balance was −£63.28. He pays in £54.31

   What is Josef's bank balance now? [2]

9 The temperature in Birmingham was 12 °C at 8 am. By 11 pm, the temperature had gone down by 17 °C.

   What was the temperature at 11 pm? [1]

10 Work out:

   a -7×5 [1]

   b $4 \times (-6)$ [1]

   c $-12 \times (-7)$ [1]

   d $18 \div (-3)$ [1]

   e $-200 \div (-25)$ [1]

   f $7.2 \times (-2.5)$ [1]

   g -3.6×4.5 [1]

   h $-11.05 \div (-8.5)$ [1]

11 Tiles come in boxes of 24

   Mia buys 60 boxes. How many tiles does Mia buy? [2]

12 The cost of 8 cakes is £6.08

   How much does each cake cost? [2]

13 A piece of string of length 4.56 metres is cut into 19 equal pieces.

   How long is each piece? [2]

14 Work out:

   a $(-3)^2$ [1]

   b $(-2)^3$ [1]

15 Arthur says, "$7 + 3 = 3 + 7$ is an example of the commutative law."

   a Is Arthur correct? [1]

   b Write your own example of the commutative law. [1]

16 Brianna says, " $2 \times 4 \times 7 = 8 \times 7 = 2 \times 28$ is an example of the distributive law."

a Is Brianna correct? [1]

b Write your own example of the distributive law. [1]

17 Work out:

a $4 \times (6 - 3)$ [1]

b $8^2 + 3 \times 2$ [1]

c $(7 + 9) \div (-5 + 3)$ [1]

d $18 \times 3 \div (11 - 2)$ [1]

e $(2 - 5)^2 + 7 \times 2^3$ [1]

f $\dfrac{2^2 - 18}{3 - -4}$ [1]

18 Use a calculator to work out:

a $3.6 \times (4.1 - 2.7)^2$ [1]

b $-5.6 + 3.2 \times (-4.8)^2 - (12 + 4.7)$ [1]

Key words

Make sure you can write a definition for these key terms.

negative number • *positive number* • *sum* • *additive inverse* • *zero pair* • *minuend* • *subtrahend*
partitioning • *absolute value* • *even* • *odd* • *dividend* • *divisor* • *quotient*
commutative law • *associative law* • *factorise* • *distributive law*

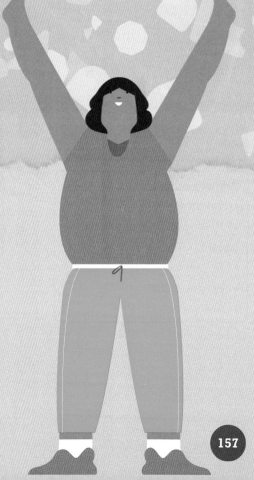

4 Expressions and equations

Speed can be measured in miles per hour (mph) or kilometres per hour (km/h).

The photo shows that 100 mph is about the same as 160 km/h. What other facts about speed can you work out from the photo?

What comes before?	This chapter	What comes after?
Primary school • Simple formulae • Missing number problems **Book 1** • Square numbers • Finding factors • Arithmetic	• 4.1 Introduction to algebra • 4.2 Formulae and equations • 4.3 Simplifying expressions • 4.4 Using the distributive law	**Book 2** • Linear equations • Sequences **Book 3** • Expressions and formulae **GCSE** • Quadratic equations • Functions

Introduction

Sometimes it's helpful to have a shorthand way to refer to an unknown number or to represent a quantity that varies. You can use algebra to do this, by using a letter to represent the unknown number. You might use algebra to give a formula for the area of a shape or the volume of a solid. You can also use algebra to describe graphs and sequences, which is something you'll cover later in your studies.

In this chapter you will learn how to...

 use a letter to represent a number

The number of faces in a set of regular dice is $6n$, where n represents the number of dice in the set

 identify terms, coefficients, constants, expressions, formulae, and equations

$2x$ is a term and 2 is the coefficient of x in this term

$3x - 9$ is an expression

$2x + 3 = 7$ is an equation

use an algebraic expression or formula to represent a relationship

'The area of a triangle is half the base (b) times the height (h)' can be written as $A = \dfrac{bh}{2}$

 read and use algebraic notation

$4 \times a$ is written as $4a$

$b \div 3$ is written as $\dfrac{b}{3}$

$y \times y$ is written as y^2

substitute numbers into an algebraic expression, function machine, or formula

If $y = 2x + 5$, when $x = 3$,

$y = 2(3) + 5 = 6 + 5 = 11$

 identify and simplify like terms in an algebraic expression

$2a + 8b - 3 - 2b$ can be simplified to

$2a + 6b - 3$

 factorise expressions

$5x + 10 = 5(x + 2)$

 expand and simplify brackets

$4(a - b) = 4a - 4b$

Reactivate your knowledge

If you can answer the questions on these pages then you should be ready for the chapter.

Some questions are there to help you to remember some maths from primary school and some are to help you remember maths from earlier in the book.

If you see this symbol it tells you where that information was introduced in an earlier chapter. If you are struggling with those questions you could go back and read through it again.

4.1 Introduction to algebra

You should know...

1. how to multiply numbers using commutativity and associativity

For example

The commutative law means that if you have a string of additions or multiplication you can do them in any order.

$3 \times 8 = 8 \times 3$

The associative law means that you can group calculations involving only addition or only multiplication in any way you like.

$(4 + 7) + 3 = 4 + (7 + 3)$

You can use both to calculate more efficiently.

$5 \times 7 \times 2 = (5 \times 2) \times 7 = 10 \times 7 = 70$

🔗 Look back to Book 1 Section 3.5

2. a fraction represents a division

For example

$\dfrac{3}{5}$ represents $3 \div 5$

3. square numbers come from squaring an integer

For example

$3^2 = 3 \times 3 = 9$

9 is a square number, it is the square of 3

🔗 Look back to Book 1 Section 2.2.1

Check in

1. Work out:

  a $4 \times 9 \times 3$

  b $2 \times 7 \times 4$

  c $0.5 \times 11 \times 6$

2. Write a fraction that represents these divisions:

  a $5 \div 11$ **b** $30 \div 13$

  Write a division that is represented by these fractions:

  c $\dfrac{4}{25}$ **d** $\dfrac{19}{6}$

3. Work out:

  a 4^2

  b 1^2

  c 12^2

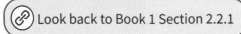

4. how to add and subtract with negative numbers

For example

$-2 + 5 = 3$

$4 + -7 = 4 - 7 = -3$

$-6 - -1 = -6 + 1 = -5$

 Look back to Book 1 Section 3.1

4. Work out:

a $-8 + 10$

b $4.25 - 12.3$

c $3 + -9$

d $-3.9 - 4.2$

e $-7 - -5$

f $-1.56 + -8.3$

5. how to multiply and divide negative numbers

For example

$6 \times -3 = -18$

$-6 \times -3 = 18$

$6 \div -3 = -2$

$-6 \div -3 = 2$

 Look back to Book 1 Section 3.2

5. Calculate:

a -3×5

b -2×-6

c $-8 \div 4$

d $-15 \div -3$

6. the order of operations

For example

$(2 \times 5) - 3 \times 2^2$ Brackets first

$= 10 - 3 \times 2^2$ then Indices or roots

$= 10 - 3 \times 4$ then Multiplication and Division

$= 10 - 12$ then Addition and Subtraction

$= -2$

 Look back to Book 1 Section 3.5.4

6. Work out:

a $15 - 3 \times 4$

b $1 + 20 \div 5$

c $4 \times 5^2 - (6 \times 7)$

d $19 + (5 - 2)^2$

Chapter 4

4.2 Formulae and equations and
4.3 Simplifying expressions

You should know...

7. how to solve missing number problems

For example

$3 \times \square = 18$

$3 \times 6 = 18$, so the number that goes in the box to make this statement correct is 6

Check in

7. Find the missing number that makes each calculation correct:

a $\square + 19 = 27$

b $50 \div \square = 12.5$

c $\square - 13 = -6$

d $0.9 \times \square = 4.5$

4.4 Using the distributive law

You should know...

8. how to find highest common factors (HCF) of numbers

For example

Find the HCF of 60 and 10

First write them as a product of their prime factors:

$60 = ② \times 2 \times 3 \times ⑤$

$10 = ② \times ⑤$

Multiply common prime factors:

The HCF of 60 and 10 is $2 \times 5 = 10$

 Look back to Book 1 Section 2.3.5

9. how to use the distributive law

For example

$2 \times (1 + 0.3) = 2 \times 1 + 2 \times 0.3$

$= 2 + 0.6$

$= 2.6$

 Look back to Book 1 Section 3.5.3

Check in

8. Find the HCF of:

  a 4 and 10

  b 60 and 15

  c 24 and 36

9. Using the distributive law, work out:

  a $5 \times (10 + 7)$

  b $3 \times (120 - 6)$

  c $8 \times (4 + 0.5)$

Chapter 4

4.1 Introduction to algebra

4.1.1 Algebraic thinking

Language

The word 'algebra' comes from the Arabic word الجبر *al-jabr*. It was first used by the mathematician al-Khwarizmi around 1200 years ago. The word meant 'the reunion of broken parts'. It was also used to describe mending a broken bone.

Language

'Variable' comes from the Latin word *variabilis* meaning 'changeable' and was used to describe the weather.

Objective

You will:

- understand how to use a letter to represent a number

You can use algebraic thinking to solve problems where the quantities may change.

One car has:	Two cars will have:	Three cars will have:
4 wheels	$4 \times 2 = 8$ wheels	$4 \times 3 = 12$ wheels

In each case you need to multiply 4 by the number of cars to find the total number of wheels. You can use a letter in place of a number to represent the number of cars.

n cars will have $4 \times n$ wheels.

The letter n is a **variable**; here it represents the number of cars.

The number 4 is not a variable because its value does not vary.

Key point

A **variable** is a letter that can represent different numbers.

Here the variable n is used to write a rule to find the total number of wheels on *any* number of cars.

Worked example	Thinking	Your turn!
Simon is three years older than Natasha. Find Simon's age when Natasha is		Mia is 8 years older than James. Find Mia's age when James is
a 5 years old	*What information do we have and what are we trying to find?*	**a** 4 years old
Simon's age $= 5 + 3$ $= 8$ years old	*How could we represent the situation?*	

I know Natasha's age, and the difference between Natasha's and Simon's ages. I am trying to find out Simon's age.

I can draw a bar model to compare Natasha's and Simon's ages.

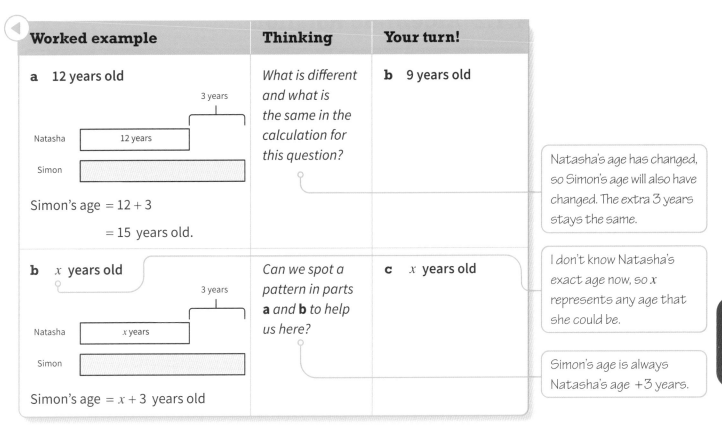

Worked example	Thinking	Your turn!
a 12 years old	*What is different and what is the same in the calculation for this question?*	**b** 9 years old

Natasha's age has changed, so Simon's age will also have changed. The extra 3 years stays the same.

Simon's age $= 12 + 3$

$= 15$ years old.

b x years old	*Can we spot a pattern in parts* **a** *and* **b** *to help us here?*	**c** x years old

I don't know Natasha's exact age now, so x represents any age that she could be.

Simon's age $= x + 3$ years old

Simon's age is always Natasha's age $+3$ years.

▲ Example-problem pair 1

4.1.1 Fluency

In this exercise you can practise applying mathematical methods that you have just learnt.

1 Joe has three more pens than Naomi. Find the number of pens Joe has when Naomi has
   a 3 pens   **c** 10 pens
   b 4 pens   **d** n pens

2 There are three fewer apples than bananas. Find the number of apples when there are
   a 9 bananas   **c** 20 bananas
   b 10 bananas   **d** n bananas

3 When Sara packs for a camping trip, she packs two snack bars for every day she is away plus one spare bar. Find the number of bars that she should pack when she goes away for
   a 2 days   **c** 10 days
   b 7 days   **d** n days

4 Luke completes a race in half the time taken by Kenji. Find the time taken by Luke to complete the race if Kenji takes
   a 6 minutes   **c** 25 minutes
   b 12 minutes   **d** n minutes

5 The monthly cost of a mobile phone contract is given by
- the price of the phone divided by 20
- plus the network access charge of £5

Find the monthly cost of the mobile phone contract when the price of the phone is
   a £200   **c** $£(x - 1)$
   b £x **d** $£(3 \times x)$

Now check your answers. You may want to use your calculator. Did you get any wrong and can you work out why?

4.1.2 Algebraic notation

Objectives

You will learn how to:

- understand and use algebraic notation
- identify terms, products, and expressions

In the example from the previous page, the answer $x + 3$ is called an **algebraic expression**. It has two **terms**: x and 3.

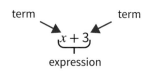

Key point

An **algebraic expression** (often just called an **expression**) is a combination of symbols that can include numbers, variables, and mathematical operations (such as +, −, × or ÷). It does not include an equals sign.
A **term** is a number, a variable, or two or more numbers or variables multiplied together.

When you work with algebraic terms, you write them without multiplication or division signs. This is to make them quicker to write and easier to work with. The multiplication sign × looks similar to the variable x, so using them together could make expressions very difficult to read.

Here are some rules on the correct way to write algebraic terms.

Key point

Write $3 \times a$ or $a \times 3$ as $3a$: the number always goes in front of the letter
Write $a \div 2$ as $\dfrac{a}{2}$
Write $1a$ as just a
Write $-1a$ as just $-a$
Write $a \times a$ as a^2
Write $a \times a \times a$ as a^3

A term can have two or more different variables multiplied together.

Key point

Write the **product** $a \times b$ or $b \times a$ as ab: when letters are multiplied together, write them in alphabetical order.
Write $a \div b$ as $\dfrac{a}{b}$

The 3 in $x + 3$ is a term. The 3 in $3x + 1$ is not a term by itself, it's part of the $3x$ term. $3x$ means $3 \times x$ and is a product of 3 and x.

$4y^2 - 2$ is an expression. $4y^2 - 2 = 6$ is not an expression, because it includes an equals sign. The term $4y^2$ in $4y^2 - 2$ means $4 \times y \times y$ and is also a product.

Worked example	Thinking	Your turn!
There are k doughnuts in a box. Work out the total number of doughnuts in:	What is the variable and how can we represent it?	There are q pens in a pack. Work out the total number of pens in:
a 3 boxes Total number of doughnuts $= k \times 3 = 3k$	How do we write this in the correct way?	**a** 3 packs
b n boxes Total number of doughnuts $= k \times n = kn$	What is different between this question and the previous one? How do we write this in the correct way?	**b** n packs

I don't know exactly how many doughnuts there are in a box, so k represents any number that there could be.

I write the number before the letter in a product.

The number of boxes has changed from a known number, 3, to an unknown number, n

I don't need to write the multiplication sign between variables and k comes first alphabetically so goes first in the term.

▲ Example-problem pair 1

4.1.2 Fluency

In this exercise you can practise applying mathematical methods that you have just learnt.

1 Which of the following are expressions?
- **a** $2a$
- **b** $x + 1 = 7$
- **c** $\dfrac{n}{3} - 2$
- **d** $ab - 2 = 5$
- **e** $7 = a - b$
- **f** $2x^2 + 9$

2 How many terms are there in each expression?
- **a** $a + 4$
- **b** $p + 20 - 5$
- **c** x^2
- **d** $2n - 5$

3 Simplify these algebraic expressions.
- **a** $5 \times x$ **b** $y \times 7$ **c** $a \times -4$ **d** $b \div 3$

4 A bookshop stores x books on a shelf.

Work out the total number of books on
- **a** 5 shelves
- **b** n shelves
- **c** $2n$ shelves

5 How many terms are there in each expression?
- **a** $y^3 + 4$
- **b** $p + q - 5$
- **c** $a^2 - b$
- **d** $5n^2 + \dfrac{n}{2} - 1$

6 Simplify these algebraic expressions.
- **a** $6 \div w$ **c** $y \times y$ **e** $z \times y \times 2$
- **b** 6×6 **d** $x \times x \times x$

7 Simplify these algebraic expressions.
- **a** $x \times 3 \times x \times x$ **c** $y \times 2 \times m$
- **b** $2 \times x \times 4 \times x$ **d** $2 \times x \times 6 \times y \times x \div c$

Now check your answers. Did you get any wrong and can you work out why?

4.1.3 Generalising relationships

> **Objective** ☑️
>
> You will:
> - understand how to use an algebraic statement or formula to represent a relationship

Look at these calculations: $\quad 4 \times 5 + 8 \qquad 4 \times 6 + 8 \qquad 4 \times 7 + 8$

Notice which parts of the calculations are different and which parts are the same. You can **generalise** the calculation as $4 \times n + 8$, which you write as $4n + 8$

Worked example	Thinking	Your turn!	
A journey by train takes half the time it takes by bus, plus an extra 5 minutes. Find the time of the journey by train if the bus journey takes:		A journey by train takes a third of the time it takes by bus, plus an extra 10 minutes. Find the time of the journey by train if the bus journey takes:	
a 60 minutes 60 minutes Bus Train [5] Journey time $= 60 \div 2 + 5$ $= 30 + 5$ $= 35$ minutes	*What information do we have and what are we trying to find?* *How can we represent the situation?*	**a** 30 minutes	I know how long the bus takes, and the difference in time between the bus and the train. I am trying to find out how long the train takes. I can draw a bar model to compare the bus and train times.
b 30 minutes 30 minutes Bus Train [5] Journey time $= 30 \div 2 + 5$ $= 15 + 5$ $= 20$ minutes	*What is different and what is the same in the calculation for this question?*	**b** 60 minutes	The time for the bus has changed so the time for the train will have changed. The extra 5 stays the same.
c x minutes x minutes Bus Train [5] Journey time $= x \div 2 + 5$ $= \dfrac{x}{2} + 5$ minutes	*Is there a pattern in parts **a** and **b** that will help us?* *Can we write this in a simpler way?*	**c** x minutes	I don't know the exact time for the bus now, so x represents this time. The train time is always half of this plus 5 minutes. I write the division using a fraction.

▲ Example-problem pair 1

Algebra is useful for solving problems because it is often easier to use an algebraic expression than to explain using words. Look at the table to see this.

Words	Algebra
10 more than a number	$x + 10$
10 less than a number	$x - 10$
A number subtracted from 10	$10 - x$
Double a number	$2x$
Half a number	$\dfrac{x}{2}$

Words	Algebra
A number divided by 10	$\dfrac{x}{10}$
10 divided by a number	$\dfrac{10}{x}$
The product of two different numbers	xy
The sum of two different numbers	$x + y$

4.1.3 Fluency

In this exercise you can practise applying mathematical methods that you have just learnt.

1 Write algebraic expressions to show each of these relationships.
  a 5 more than x **c** 8 lots of x
  b 7 less than y **d** z divided into 3 parts

2 There are 5 times more red counters than blue counters. Write an expression for the number of red counters when there are n blue counters.

3 Write algebraic expressions to show each of these relationships.
  a Two of the same number, x, are added together.
  b Two of the same number, x, are multiplied together.
  c One number, x, is divided by another number, y
  d Three times one number, x, is added to two times another number, y
  e Two times one number, x, is divided by another number, y
  f A number, x, is multiplied by itself.

4 Write down an expression for
  a the sum of a and b
  b the difference between a and b
  c the product of a and b
  d double the number a

5 Tristan has a £10 voucher he wants to use towards buying some sweets. Each pack of sweets costs £3
Work out how much Tristan will still need to pay if he buys
  a 4 packs of sweets   **b** y packs of sweets

6 Cinema tickets cost £4 for a child and £6 for an adult. Write an expression for the total cost for
  a x children and 2 adults
  b x children and y adults

7 Three consecutive numbers are added together. Write an expression for this sum.

8 Write an expression that can represent any multiple of 3

Now check your answers. You may want to use your calculator. Did you get any wrong and can you work out why?

4.1.4 Substitution

Objective

You will learn how to:

- substitute numbers into an algebraic expression

The value of an expression changes when the variable has different values.

Key point

Substitution is where a variable is replaced by a numerical value.

For example, the cost per person of hiring a minibus is £$\left(\dfrac{120}{n}\right)$ where n is the number of people.

You can substitute different values for n and the cost per person will change.

When $n = 12$

$$\frac{120}{n} = \frac{120}{12}$$
$$= 120 \div 12$$
$$= 10$$

So the cost per person is £10

When $n = 20$

$$\frac{120}{n} = \frac{120}{20}$$
$$= 120 \div 20$$
$$= 6$$

So the cost per person is £6

Worked example	Thinking	Your turn!
Find the value of the expression $8x - 3$ when $x = 5$ When $x = 5$, $8x - 3 = 8 \times 5 - 3$ $\quad = 40 - 3$ $\quad = 37$	*What do we do with the information about the value of the variable?*	Find the value of the expression $4x + 1$ when $x = 9$

I know that the value of x is 5, so I replace every instance of x in this expression with 5

I need to remember that $8x$ means $8 \times x$

▲ Example-problem pair 1

You can substitute more than one variable into the same expression if it has more than one unknown. Be careful to substitute each variable in the right place; if you are given a value for y you cannot substitute it for x.

Worked example	Thinking	Your turn!
Find the value of the expression $5x^2 - 2y$ when $x = 3$ and $y = -4$	What is the correct order of operations?	Find the value of the expression $3 + 7xy$ when $x = -5$ and $y = 2$
When $x = 3$ and $y = -4$, $5x^2 - 2y = 5 \times 3^2 - 2 \times (-4)$ $\qquad = 5 \times 9 + 8$ $\qquad = 45 + 8$ $\qquad = 53$	What do we do with the information about the value of the variable?	

> I need to remember to use the correct order of operations, so to work out 5×3^2, I first work out 3^2 then multiply by 5

> I know that the value of x is 3 and the value of y is -4, so I replace every instance of x with 3 and every instance of y with -4

▲ Example-problem pair 2

4.1.4 Fluency

In this exercise you can practise applying mathematical methods that you have just learnt.

1 Here is an expression:

$x + 6$

Find the value of the expression when

a $x = 1$
b $x = 7$
c $x = 31$
d $x = -11$

2 Here is an expression:

$5x + 2$

Find the value of the expression when

a $x = 1$
b $x = 4$
c $x = 31$
d $x = -7$

3 Here is an expression

$\dfrac{x}{3} + 5$

Find the value of the expression when

a $x = 3$ **c** $x = 36$
b $x = 12$ **d** $x = -18$

4 Here is an expression:

$x^2 - 1$

Find the value of the expression when

a $x = 2$ **c** $x = 9$
b $x = 4$ **d** $x = -3$

5 Here is an expression:

$3a - 6b$

Find the value of the expression when

a $a = 7$, $b = 1$
b $a = 3$, $b = 8$
c $a = 6$, $b = -2$
d $a = -1$, $b = -3$

6 Find the value of each expression when $x = 5$ and $y = -2$

a $2x^2$ **c** $6xy$
b $x^2 + y^2$ **d** $x^2 - y^3$

Now check your answers. You may want to use your calculator. Did you get any wrong and can you work out why?

4.1 Exercises

4.1 Intelligent practice

"Why is it intelligent?" You might notice a connection when you move on from one question to the next. You can use the Reflect, Expect, Check, Explain process to:

- *reflect* on what's different between each question and the one that came before
- decide how you *expect* this answer to be different
- complete the question and *check* your answer
- *explain* to yourself why your expectation was correct or incorrect.

> **Question 1a**   **EXAMPLE**
>
> Write the term $3 \times a$ in the correct way.
>
> In algebra we don't need to include the multiplication sign so $3 \times a$ is written as $3a$
>
> **Question 1b**
>
> Write the term $a \times 3$ in the correct way.
>
> **Reflect:** This is similar to question **1a**, except the product is written the other way around.
>
> **Expect:** I think that the answer will be the same as question **1a** since the order does not matter with multiplication.
>
> **Check:** $a \times 3$ is written $3a$ since we always write the number in front of the letter.
>
> **Explain:** I was right! $3 \times a$ and $a \times 3$ are the same.

1   Write each term in the correct way.

   a $3 \times a$ **c** $a \div 3$

   b $a \times 3$ **d** $3 \div a$

2   Write each term in the simplest way.

   a $1 \times a$ **c** $a \div 1$

   b $a \times 1$ **d** $1 \div a$

3   Write each term in the correct way.

   a $2 \times a$ **f** $a \times a \times 2 \times 3$

   b $a \times 2$ **g** $a \times a \div 6$

   c $a \times a$ **h** $6 \div (a \times a)$

   d $6 \times a \times a$ **i** $a \times 2 \times a \times 3 \times a$

   e $a \times a \times 6$

4   Write each term in the correct way.

   a $c \times 8$ **d** $d \times c$

   b $c \times 1$ **e** $c \times d \times 8$

   c $c \times d$ **f** $2 \times d \times c \times 4$

   g $d \times c \div 8$ **i** $8 \times d \times d \times c$

   h $8 \times d \times c \times c$

5   Work out the value of each expression when $x = 6$

   a $x - 2$ **f** $\dfrac{x}{2} - 3$

   b $x + 2$

   c $2x$ **g** $3 - \dfrac{x}{2}$

   d $2x + 3$ **h** $\dfrac{3 - x}{2}$

   e $2x - 3$

6   Work out the value of each expression when $x = 4$

   a $8 - x$ **f** $2x^2 - 8x$

   b $x - 8$ **g** $\dfrac{x^2}{2} - 8x$

   c $2x - 8$

   d $x^2 - 8$ **h** $\dfrac{x^2 - 8x}{2}$

   e $2x^2 - 8$

4.1 Method selection

In these questions you'll need to think carefully about which methods to apply.
For some questions you might need to use skills from earlier chapters.

1 Match up the statements on the left with a algebraic expression on the right.

Statement	Algebraic expression
9 less than a number	$\dfrac{9}{x}$
9 more than a number	x^2
a number subtracted from 9	$x - 9$
9 lots of a number	xy
a number divided by 9	$x - y$
9 divided by a number	$x + 9$
a number added to itself	$2x$
a number multiplied by itself	$9 - x$
the sum of two different numbers	$9x$
the product of two different numbers	$\dfrac{x}{9}$
the difference between two different numbers	$x + y$

2 Copy and complete the table to work out the value of each algebraic expression when $x = 3$ and $y = 12$

Algebraic expression	Value when $x = 3$ and $y = 12$
$x + 9$	
$9 - x$	
$\dfrac{9}{x}$	
x^2	
$x - 9$	
$2x$	
$9x$	
$\dfrac{x}{9}$	
xy	
$x - y$	
$x + y$	

3 Copy and complete the table.

Expression written out in full	Expression written in the simplest way	Value of the expression when $a = 10$	Value of the expression when $a = -3$
$a \times 6$			
	$2a$		
$a + 6$			
$6 - a$			
$6 \div a$			
	$\dfrac{a}{2}$		
$6 \times a + 2$			
	$6 - 2a$		
$a \times a$			
$a \times 6 \times a$			
	$\dfrac{3a^2}{2}$		

4 Use written methods to find the value of the expression $12x - 38$ when

a $x = 9$ **c** $x = -7$ **e** $x = 24.8$

b $x = 23$ **d** $x = 3.5$ Now check your answers using a calculator.

5 Use written methods to find the value of the expression $xy - 27$ when

a $x = 5$ and $y = 13$ **c** $x = -24$ and $y = 15$ **e** $x = 6.3$ and $y = 12.9$

b $x = 41$ and $y = 62$ **d** $x = -24$ and $y = -15$ Now check your answers using a calculator.

6 Simplify the expressions by writing each term in the correct way.

a $a \times a \div b + a \times b \times 3$

b $3 \times a \times b + a \times a \times a - b \times 2 \times 3$

c $a \times b^2 \div 3 - b \times 3 \times a^2 + b \div (a \times 3)$

d $2 \times a \div (b \times b) + b \times 5 \times 3 \times a \times b \times b$

4.1 Purposeful practice

There may be more than one way to approach these questions.

Once you have answered a question one way, can you think of another way?

1 Use the letters x and y and the number 8 to create some different expressions.
Can you find some pairs of expressions that look different but have the same meaning?

2 Create some expressions that have value 50 when
a $x = 5$ **b** $x = -5$
c Is it possible to have the same expression for part **a** and part **b**? Explain your answer.

3 Look at the expressions shown.

$3x$ $\qquad$ $x + 3$ $\qquad$ $\dfrac{x}{3}$ $\qquad$ $x - 3$ $\qquad$ $3 + x$ $\qquad$ $3 - x$ $\qquad$ $\dfrac{3}{x}$ $\qquad$ $(3x)^2$ $\qquad$ $x + x + x$ $\qquad$ $3x^2$

a Work out the value of each expression when $x = 3$. Do any of the expressions have the same value?

b Choose a different value of x and work out the value of each expression in this case.
Do any of the expressions have the same value?

c Investigate with different values of x. Can you find pairs of expressions that
 i always have the same value $\qquad$ **iii** never have the same value?
 ii sometimes have the same value

4 Using $a = 3$ and $b = 5$, think of expressions using a and b that could belong in each of the regions. If you think a region is impossible to fill, explain why.

a

| value of expression is a multiple of 4 | value of expression is a factor of 12 |

A $\quad$ B $\quad$ C

D

b

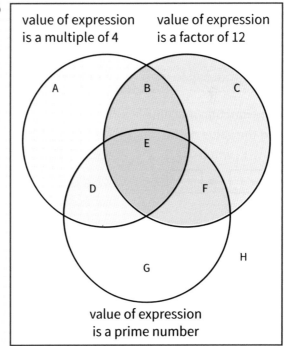

| value of expression is a multiple of 4 | value of expression is a factor of 12 |

A $\quad$ B $\quad$ C

E

D $\quad$ F

G $\quad$ H

value of expression is a prime number

Formulae and equations

4.2.1 Function machines

> ### Objective
>
> You will learn how to:
> * substitute numbers into function machines

A function machine tells you how to use an input number to calculate an output number. You need to apply the operations in the order they appear in the function machine.

Here is a function machine:

$$\text{input} \longrightarrow \boxed{\times 3} \longrightarrow \boxed{-1} \longrightarrow \text{output}$$

This machine tells you that to find the output you must:
* multiply the input by 3
* then subtract 1

So, if the input is 7 then

$$\begin{aligned}\text{output} &= 7 \times 3 - 1 \\ &= 21 - 1 \\ &= 20\end{aligned}$$

Worked example	Thinking	Your turn!
Use the function machine to find the value of the output, y, when $x = 3$ $x \longrightarrow \boxed{\times 4} \longrightarrow \boxed{+6} \longrightarrow y$ When $x = 3$, $\quad y = 3 \times 4 + 6$ $\quad\quad = 12 + 6$ $\quad\quad = 18$	*What is the first calculation we do?* *What is the correct order of operations here?*	Use the function machine to find the value of the output, y, when $x = 5$ $x \longrightarrow \boxed{\times 8} \longrightarrow \boxed{-2} \longrightarrow y$

> The first box tells me what to do first to the value of x

> I need to multiply first and then add.

▲ Example-problem pair 1

When you write down the instructions from the function machine you may need to use brackets.

Worked example	Thinking	Your turn!
Use the function machine to find the value of the output, y, when $x = 3$ $$x \rightarrow \boxed{+6} \rightarrow \boxed{\times 4} \rightarrow y$$ When $x = 3$, $$y = (3+6) \times 4$$ $$= 9 \times 4$$ $$= 36$$	*How do we show which operation should be done first?*	Use the function machine to find the value of the output, y, when $x = 5$ $$x \rightarrow \boxed{-2} \rightarrow \boxed{\times 8} \rightarrow y$$

> I need to add first, so I can put that in brackets to make sure I add before multiplying.

▲ Example-problem pair 2

4.2.1 Fluency

In this exercise you can practise applying the mathematical methods that you have just learnt.

1 Here is a function machine.

$$x \longrightarrow \boxed{+7} \longrightarrow y$$

Find the value of y when

a $x = 2$ **b** $x = 19$ **c** $x = -4$ **d** $x = -15$

2 Here is a function machine.

$$x \longrightarrow \boxed{\times 2} \longrightarrow \boxed{+5} \longrightarrow y$$

Find the value of y when

a $x = 3$ **b** $x = 17$ **c** $x = -1$ **d** $x = -8$

3 Here is a function machine.

$$x \longrightarrow \boxed{+2} \longrightarrow \boxed{\times 5} \longrightarrow y$$

Find the value of y when

a $x = 3$ **b** $x = 17$ **c** $x = -1$ **d** $x = -8$

4 Here is a function machine.

$$x \longrightarrow \boxed{\div 3} \longrightarrow \boxed{+5} \longrightarrow \boxed{\times 2} \longrightarrow y$$

Find the value of y when

a $x = 9$ **b** $x = 15$ **c** $x = -3$ **d** $x = -30$

Now check your answers. You may want to use your calculator.

Did you get any wrong and can you work out why?

4.2.2 Formulae and substitution

Objective ☑

You will learn how to:

- identify and substitute numbers into an algebraic formula

A **formula** shows how one variable relates to another variable (or variables).

There are lots of occasions when it is helpful to use a formula. For example, you have probably used a formula to find the area of a triangle or the perimeter of a rectangle. Can you remember a formula for either of these?

$y = 2x$ is a formula for y

$2x = y$ is a formula for y

$v = u + at$ is a formula for v

$A = x^2$ is a formula for A

$x = 2x - 1$ is not a formula as there is only one variable.

You can substitute into a formula to see how the value of one variable changes in response to another variable.

Investigate Further 🔍

In your future studies, you will learn about and use lots of other formulae that are used in maths, science, engineering, and many other subjects. One very famous formula is $E = mc^2$. Can you find out who discovered this formula and what it is about? What do the letters E, m and c represent?

Worked example	Thinking	Your turn!
$y = 7(x + 5)$ Use the formula to find the value of y when $x = 4$ When $x = 4$, $\quad y = 7(4 + 5)$ $\qquad = 7 \times 9$ $\qquad = 63$	*What do we need to do with the information about the value of x?*	$y = 8(x - 9)$ Use the formula to find the value of y when $x = 10$

I know that the value of x is 4, so I replace every instance of x in this formula with 4

▲ Example-problem pair 1

The value that you substitute into a formula can be negative.

Worked example	Thinking	Your turn!
$y = 7(x + 5)$ **Use the formula to find the value of y when $x = -6$** When $x = -6$, $$y = 7((-6) + 5)$$ $$= 7 \times (-1)$$ $$= -7$$	*What mistake might somebody make here?*	$y = 8(x - 9)$ **Use the formula to find the value of y when $x = -3$**

I must be careful not to forget the negative sign when substituting $x = -6$ into this formula.

▲ Example-problem pair 2

4.2.2 Fluency

In this exercise you can practise applying the mathematical methods that you have just learnt.

1 Which of these could be formulae?

  a $6x - 1 = 10$

  b $7x - 3$

  c $y = 2x + 1$

  d $3x + y$

  e $A = 5xy$

2 Use the formulae below to find the value of y when $x = 6$

  a $y = x + 3$

  b $y = 4x$

  c $y = \dfrac{x}{2}$

3 $y = 10x + 9$

Use the formula to find the value of y when

  a $x = 1$

  b $x = 3$

  c $x = 5$

  d $x = -5$

  e $x = -0.5$

4 $y = 20 - \dfrac{x}{2}$

Use the formula to find the value of y when

  a $x = 14$

  b $x = 21$

  c $x = -12$

  d $x = 8.5$

5 $p = \dfrac{q^2}{2} + 1$

Use the formula to find the value of p when

  a $q = 4$

  b $q = 10$

  c $q = -8$

  d $q = 5$

6 Here is a formula:

$F = ma$

Find the value of F when

  a $m = 7, a = 3$

  b $m = 5, a = -4$

  c $m = 3.2, a = -3$

  d $m = 1.7, a = 4.5$

Now check your answers. You may want to use your calculator. Did you get any wrong and can you work out why?

4.2.3 Creating formulae using function machines

You can use a function machine to write a formula that links the input to the output. The formula is the rule that shows the relationship between the input and the output.

For example, look at this function machine.

$$x \longrightarrow \boxed{+1} \longrightarrow y$$

To find the output, y, you add 1 to the input, x. So the value of y will always be one more than the value of x. Therefore, the formula that shows that the relationship between x and y is: $y = x + 1$

When there is more than one step to the function machine, you must be careful to follow the steps in the order they appear.

Worked example	Thinking	Your turn!
Write a formula that shows the relationship between x and y for the function machine. $x \longrightarrow \boxed{\times 3} \longrightarrow \boxed{-7} \longrightarrow y$ $y = 3 \times x - 7$ $y = 3x - 7$	*What is the order of the steps for the input x?*	Write a formula that shows the relationship between x and y for the function machine. $x \longrightarrow \boxed{\times 6} \longrightarrow \boxed{+5} \longrightarrow y$

This function machine shows that I have to first multiply the input x by 3, and then subtract 7

▲ Example-problem pair 1

The order of the steps in a function machine is important. Sometimes you will need to use brackets in the formula to ensure that it represents the steps in the correct order.

Worked example	Thinking	Your turn!	
Write a formula that shows the relationship between x and y for the function machine. $x \rightarrow \boxed{-7} \rightarrow \boxed{\times 3} \rightarrow y$ $y = (x - 7) \times 3$ You normally write this as $y = 3(x - 7)$	What is the order of the steps for the input x?	Write a formula that shows the relationship between x and y for the function machine. $x \rightarrow \boxed{+5} \rightarrow \boxed{\times 6} \rightarrow y$	The order of operations would normally mean I multiply first, but in this case I need to subtract first. I can use brackets to show that I first have to subtract 7 from the input x, and then multiply the result by 3

▲ Example-problem pair 2

4.2.3 Fluency

In this exercise you can practise applying the mathematical methods that you have just learnt.

1 The area of a rectangle is length multiplied by width. Find the area of a rectangle with
   a length 4 cm and width 7 cm
   b length 8 cm and width 12 cm

2 The perimeter of a rectangle is twice the sum of the length and the width.
   Find the perimeter of a rectangle with
   a length 5 cm and width 8 cm
   b length 10 cm and width 15 cm

3 Write a formula that shows the relationship between x and y for each function machine.
   a $x \rightarrow \boxed{-8} \rightarrow y$
   b $x \rightarrow \boxed{\times 8} \rightarrow y$
   c $x \rightarrow \boxed{+8} \rightarrow y$

4 For each part of the question
   i   Draw a function machine to show the information.
   ii Write a formula to show the relationship between x and y
   a I start with a number, x, I add 8 to give the value of y
   b I start with a number, x, I multiply by 4 to give the value of y

   c I start with a number, x, I subtract 2 to give the value of y
   d I start with a number, x, I divide by 3 to give the value of y

5 Write a formula that shows the relationship between x and y for each function machine.
   a $x \rightarrow \boxed{+8} \rightarrow \boxed{\times 3} \rightarrow y$
   b $x \rightarrow \boxed{\times 3} \rightarrow \boxed{+8} \rightarrow y$
   c $x \rightarrow \boxed{\times 3} \rightarrow \boxed{+8} \rightarrow \boxed{\div 2} \rightarrow y$
   d $x \rightarrow \boxed{\times 3} \rightarrow \boxed{-8} \rightarrow \boxed{\times 2} \rightarrow y$

6 For each part of the question
   i   Draw a function machine to show the information
   ii Write a formula to show the relationship between x and y
   a I start with a number, x, and I subtract 4 and then multiply by 7 to give the value of y
   b I start with a number, x, and I add 6 and then divide by 2 to give the value of y

Now check your answers. You may want to use your calculator. Did you get any wrong and can you work out why?

4.2.4 Equations and inequalities

Objectives

You will learn how to:

- identify equations and inequalities
- write linear equations and determine whether a value satisfies an equation

You have seen how letters can be used as *variables* where their value can *vary*. Sometimes a letter can only take particular values.

Key point

An **equation** is a statement which shows two algebraic expressions that are *equal*.

For example, $2x + 8 = 7$ or $3x + 7 = x - 9$

Worked example	Thinking	Your turn!
Write an equation for the number Nathan is thinking of. "I am thinking of a number; I multiply by 2 then add 5, and the answer is 7."	*How could we represent this?*	Write an equation for the number Maryam is thinking of. "I am thinking of a number; I multiply by 4 and subtract 3, and the answer is 9."
$x \rightarrow \boxed{\times 2} \rightarrow \boxed{+5} \rightarrow y$ $x \times 2 + 5 = 7$	*What do equations look like?*	
$2x + 5 = 7$	*How can we write in the correct way?*	

I can represent this as a function machine or an equation.

The number is first multiplied by 2 and then 5 is added, so the steps must be this way round.

I need to use an equals sign.

I don't write the multiplication sign between 2 and x

▲ Example-problem pair 1

When an equation is true for a certain unknown value (or values), this value is called the **solution** of the equation.

For example, $x = 4$ satisfies the equation $5x = 20$ (since $5 \times 4 = 20$), so you say that 4 is a solution to the equation $5x = 20$. 3 would not be a solution to the equation $5x = 20$ because 5×3 does not equal 20

Key point

A **solution** to an equation is a value for a variable that satisfies the equation (makes it true).

You can check if a value is a solution to an equation by substituting it for a variable in the equation, and checking if both sides of the equation have the same value.

Worked example	Thinking	Your turn!
Decide if $x = 5$ **is a solution to the equation** $3(x+1) = 16$	*How can we decide if it is a solution to the equation?*	**Decide if** $x = 4$ **is a solution to the equation** $2(x-9) = -1$
When $x = 5$, $3(x+1) = 3(5+1) = 3 \times 6 = 18$	*Does this satisfy the equation?*	
So $x = 5$ is not a solution to the equation $3(x+1) = 16$		

If both sides of the equation have the same value when I substitute $x = 5$ in, then $x = 5$ is a solution.

The left-hand side of the equation has a value of 18 when $x = 5$, this is not the same as 16

▲ Example-problem pair 2

Another type of mathematical statement is an **inequality**. An inequality compares two expressions or values. The symbols $< \neq >$, $<$ or $>$ may be used. $a < \neq > b$ means a is not equal to b, $a < b$ means a is less than b, $a > b$ means a is greater than b. You can check if a value satisfies an inequality using substitution in a similar way to how you check with an equation.

4.2.4 Fluency

In this exercise you can practise applying the mathematical methods that you have just learnt.

1 Which of these are equations?
a $3x + 2 = 5$ **d** $7 = 2 - x$
b $6x + 2y$ **e** $2x + 3 \neq 5$
c $14x^2$ **f** $y + 3 = 7 - 2y$

2 Decide if the value of x given is a solution to the equation in each part.
a $3x = 21; x = 7$ **b** $x - 12 = 20; x = 8$

3 Write an equation for the number Emir is thinking of in each case.
a "I am thinking of a number; I add 3 and the answer is 10"
b "I am thinking of a number; I multiply by 6 and the answer is 10"

4 Write an equation for the number that Mira is thinking of in each case.
a "I am thinking of a number; I subtract 2 then multiply by 3 and the answer is 10"
b "I am thinking of a number; I subtract 2, multiply by 3, then divide by 5 and the answer is 10"

c "I am thinking of a number; I square it, then subtract 2 and the answer is 10"

5 Decide if each of these is an equation or an expression.
a $4x - 1 = 7$ **c** $\frac{1}{2}x - 3 = 6$
b $2x + 2y$ **d** $7 = 18x - 5$

6 Decide if the value of x given is a solution to the equation in each part.
a $2(x + 8) = 30; x = 11$
b $4(x - 3) = 16; x = 7$
c $\frac{x + 37}{-2} = -16; x = 7$
d $\frac{13 - x}{6} = 2; x = -1$
e $x - 6 = 24 - 3x; x = 7.5$
f $2x + 5 = 18 - 7x; x = 1.4$

7 Decide if the value of x given is a solution to the inequality in each part.
a $5x - 9 < 4; x = 3$ **b** $24 - 3x \neq 9; x = 5$

Now check your answers. Did you get any wrong and can you work out why?

4.2 Exercises

4.2 Intelligent practice

"Why is it intelligent?" You might notice a connection when you move on from one question to the next. You can use the Reflect, Expect, Check, Explain process to:

- *reflect* on what's different between each question and the one that came before
- decide how you *expect* this answer to be different
- complete the question and *check* your answer
- *explain* to yourself why your expectation was correct or incorrect.

EXAMPLE

Question 1a

Find the value of y when $x = 7$ for the function machine.

$$x \longrightarrow \boxed{\times 5} \longrightarrow y$$

When $x = 7$, $y = 7 \times 5 = 35$

Question 1b

Find the value of y when $x = 7$ for the function machine.

$$x \longrightarrow \boxed{\times 10} \longrightarrow y$$

Reflect: This is similar to question **1a**, except the function machine multiplies the value of x by 10 instead of multiplying it by 5

Expect: I think that the answer will be double the answer from **1a**

Check: When $x = 7$, $y = 7 \times 10 = 70$

Explain: I was right, 70 is double 35

---

1 Find the value of y when $x = 7$ for each function machine.

a $x \longrightarrow \boxed{\times 5} \longrightarrow y$

b $x \longrightarrow \boxed{\times 10} \longrightarrow y$

c $x \longrightarrow \boxed{\times 10} \longrightarrow \boxed{+3} \longrightarrow y$

d $x \longrightarrow \boxed{+3} \longrightarrow \boxed{\times 10} \longrightarrow y$

e $x \longrightarrow \boxed{+3} \longrightarrow \boxed{\times 10} \longrightarrow \boxed{-4} \longrightarrow y$

f $x \longrightarrow \boxed{-4} \longrightarrow \boxed{\times 10} \longrightarrow \boxed{+3} \longrightarrow y$

g $x \longrightarrow \boxed{-4} \longrightarrow \boxed{\times 10} \longrightarrow \boxed{+3} \longrightarrow \boxed{\div 2} \longrightarrow y$

h $x \longrightarrow \boxed{-4} \longrightarrow \boxed{\times 10} \longrightarrow \boxed{\div 2} \longrightarrow \boxed{+3} \longrightarrow y$

i $x \longrightarrow \boxed{-4} \longrightarrow \boxed{\div 2} \longrightarrow \boxed{\times 10} \longrightarrow \boxed{+3} \longrightarrow y$

2 $y = \dfrac{x}{3}$

Use the formula to find the value of y when

$x = 36$

$x = 72$

$x = 75$

$x = -75$

3 A formula for the speed of a car is given by $v = u + 3t$

Find the speed of the car when

a $u = 0$ and $t = 5$

b $u = 20$ and $t = 5$

c $u = 20$ and $t = 6$

d $u = 20$ and $t = 12$

4 Use the formulae as instructed below.

a $y = 4x^2 - 7$

Use the formula to find the value of y when

i $x = 3$

ii $x = -3$

b $y = (4x)^2 - 7$

Use the formula to find the value of y when

i $x = 3$

ii $x = -3$

c $y = (4x - 7)^2$

Use the formula to find the value of y when

i $x = 3$

ii $x = -3$

5 Decide whether $x = 8$ satisfies each equation or inequality.

a $x + 3 = 11$ **d** $2x + 4 < 24$

b $x + 4 = 12$ **e** $2x + 6 < 24$

c $2x + 4 = 24$ **f** $2x + 6 > 24$

4.2 Method selection

In these questions you'll need to think carefully about which methods to apply.

For some questions you might need to use skills from earlier chapters.

1 Look at the examples in the box.

$3x + 5$ $7x - 14 = 2$ $x^2 + 3x$

$3x > 18$ $9 - x$

$A = \dfrac{1}{2}bh$ $xy + y^2$ $x + 5 = 2x$

$x \neq 6$ $y = 2x$

Write examples of each of these from the box.

a an expression

b an equation

c a formula

d an inequality

2 Work out the perimeter of each rectangle when $x = 20$ and $y = 6$

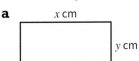

a x cm, y cm

b $(x - 5)$ cm, y cm

3 The perimeter of each rectangle is $20\,\text{cm}$

Write an equation involving x

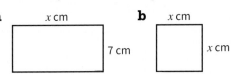

a x cm, 7 cm

b x cm, x cm

4 Write an expression for the perimeter of each rectangle.

a x cm, y cm

b $2x$ cm, y cm

5 Write a formula for the area, $A\,\text{cm}^2$, of each rectangle.

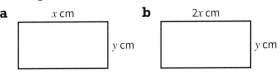

a x cm, y cm

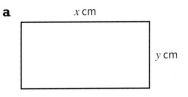

b $2x$ cm, y cm

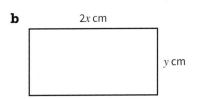

c $2x$ cm, x cm

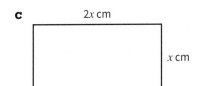

6 $P = 6n + 1$

Copy and complete the table to show the value of P for different values of n and state whether P is a prime number.

n	P	Is P a prime number?
1		
2		
3		
4		
5		
6		
7		
8		
9		
10		

7 A formula for the number of tables, T, needed for an event is $T = \dfrac{p}{6}$

where p is the total number of people.

A formula for the number of vases, v, needed is $v = T + 2$

a Work out the number of tables needed when $p = 54$

b Work out the number of vases needed when

    i $T = 12$

    ii $p = 30$

8 Answer the problems below.

a A plumber charges £50 per hour plus a £90 callout charge.

    i Write a formula for the amount the plumber will charge, £c, for a job that takes t hours.

    ii Use your formula to find the amount the plumber will charge for a job that takes 3 hours.

b A plumber charges £50 per hour plus a callout charge of £P.

    i Write a formula for the amount the plumber will charge, £c, for a job that takes t hours.

    ii Use your formula to find an expression for the amount the plumber will charge for a job that takes 3 hours.

c A plumber charges £H per hour plus a callout charge of £P.

    i Write a formula for the amount the plumber will charge, £c, for a job that takes t hours.

    ii Use your formula to find an expression for the amount the plumber will charge for a job that takes 3 hours.

9 $y = 2x^2, z = (2x)^2$

Use the formulae to find the values of y and z when

a $x = 3$ **c** $x = 6$ **e** $x = 65$

b $x = 0$ **d** $x = -6$ **f** $x = 1.6$

Show all your working.

10 $y = \sqrt{2x - 5}$

a Use the formula to find the possible values of y when

    i $x = 7$ **ii** $x = 27$

b Explain why you cannot find the value of y when $x = 2$

11 Decide whether $x = 17$ is a solution to each equation or inequality.

Show all your working clearly and then use a calculator to check your answer.

a $12x - 70 = 134$ **f** $3x^2 = 2601$

b $63 - 18x = 243$ **g** $987 - 3x^2 = 120$

c $3(9 - x) = 78$ **h** $\dfrac{24}{x - 41} = 1$

d $\dfrac{x}{4} + 12.75 = 17$ **i** $2x - 12 < 25$

e $5.8x - 32.9 = 65.7$

4.2 Purposeful practice

There may be more than one way to approach these questions.
Once you have answered a question one way, can you think of another way?

1

| $+4$ | -4 | $\times 6$ | $\div 3$ | $\times -1$ | $\div 2$ |

a Use any of the functions above to make some different function machines.

b Write a formula from each of your function machines to link the input, x, with the output, y

c Investigate if the order in which the boxes are drawn makes a difference to the formula.

2 Answer the following:

a Write some equations or inequalities that have $x = 8$ or $x < 8$ as a solution. Try to use different mathematical operations and think of ways to make your equations or inequalities interesting and different from each other.

b Change each of your equations or inequalities in part **a** as little as possible to have $x = 5$ as a solution.

3 This shape is a rectangle. Use the diagram to write some formulae.

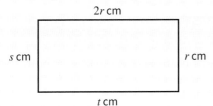

$2r$ cm

s cm r cm

t cm

4 Think of values of a and b that could belong in each of the regions.
If you think a region is impossible to fill, explain why.

a

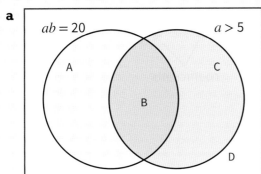

$ab = 20$ $a > 5$

A

B

C

D

b

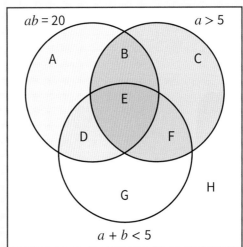

$ab = 20$ $a > 5$

A   B   C

E

D   F

G   H

$a + b < 5$

Simplifying expressions

4.3.1 Identifying like terms

Objectives

You will learn how to:
- identify constants and coefficients
- identify like terms

Expressions and equations can involve many terms, for example the expression $3 + 2x - 7y$ has three terms: 3, $2x$, and $-7y$. The term without any letters, 3, is called a **constant** (it does not vary).

Key point

A constant is a term that does not involve a variable.

The other two terms in this expression involve variables: x and y. Each of them is multiplied by a number, called the **coefficient**. The coefficient of x is 2 and the coefficient of y is -7

Key point

The coefficient in a term is the number the variable or variables are multiplied by, for example in the term $5z$ the coefficient of z is 5

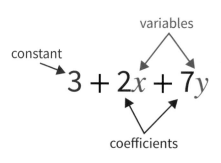

Worked example	Thinking	Your turn!
$4a + b - 3b^2 + 6$ **a** What is the coefficient of b in the expression? b is the same as $1b$, so the coefficient of b is 1	*What number is the variable multiplied by?*	$x - 3y - 8 + 5yz + 7y^2$ **a** What is the coefficient of y in the expression?
b What is the coefficient of b^2 in the expression? The coefficient of b^2 is –3 Remember to include the negative sign.	*What number is the variable multiplied by?*	**b** What is the coefficient of yz in the expression?
c What is the constant in the expression? The constant is 6 since this is a term that involves only a number and no variable.	*What is the definition of a constant?*	**c** What is the constant in the expression?

I am looking for a term with only b and no other variables.

I am looking for a term with only b^2 and no other variables.

I am looking for a term that does not involve a variable and only involves a number.

▲ Example-problem pair 1

You can **simplify** some expressions by adding up terms involving the same variables. These are called **like terms** since they are 'alike'. For example, $7x$ and $4x$ are like terms so you can simplify $7x + 4x$ to $11x$

Key point ⚿

Like terms involve exactly the same variable, or variables, so they can be simplified by adding them together.

3a and 6a are 'like terms' (they are both a number multiplied by a)

$3y$ and $\dfrac{y}{2}$ are 'like terms' (they are both a number multiplied by y). $\dfrac{y}{2}$ is y multiplied by $\dfrac{1}{2}$

$3y$ and $3x$ are 'unlike terms' (the letters are different)

$3xy$ and $4yx$ are 'like terms' (the order of the variables does not matter when you multiply)

$3xy$ and $4x$ are 'unlike terms' (y is in one term but not the other)

$3y^2$ and $y \times 5y$ are 'like terms' (y is in both terms twice since $y^2 = y \times y$)

$3x$ and $3x^2$ are 'unlike terms' (x is in the first term once but the second term twice)

4.3.1 Fluency

In this exercise you can practise applying mathematical methods that you have just learnt.

1 Here is an expression:
$6x + y + 4 - 8xy$
  a How many terms are there in the expression?
  b Which term in the expression is a constant?

2 Answer these problems.
  a Arjan has 8 bags each containing 10 sweets. Angelica has 6 bags each containing 10 sweets. How many sweets do Arjan and Angelica have in total?
  b Brittany has 8 bags each containing x sweets. Amrita has 6 bags each containing x sweets. Write an expression for the number of sweets Brittany and Amrita have in total.

3 Here is an expression:
$-2x^2 + 6xy - 9 + 10y^2$
  a What is the coefficient of y^2?
  b What is the coefficient of x^2?

4 Here are some cards.

| $4a$ | a^2 | 6 | $3a$ | $-5a$ |

| 10 | $-3a^2$ | $4a$ | $4a^2$ | -7 |

| $2a$ | $5b$ | $-b^2$ | $-4a$ | $12a$ |

Group the cards so that they are in sets containing like terms.

5 Here is an expression:
$6x + x^2 - 7x + 3 + 8x - 3x^2 - 5 + 4x$
Write down all the terms that are
  a like $6x$
  b like x^2
  c like 3

6 Here is an expression:
$8p + 7q - 3p^2 - 9 + p^2 + 8 - 3q + 4q^2$
Write down all the terms that are
  a like $7q$
  b like p^2
  c like $8p$

7 In the expression $y - y^2 + \dfrac{x^2}{4}$, what is the coefficient of x^2?

8 Here are some cards.

| $4ab$ | a^2b | $3ab$ | $-2ab$ |

| $6ab$ | $-ab$ | $7b^2a$ | $-3a^2b$ |

| $-2ab$ | $12a^2b^2$ | $4ab^2$ | $2ab^2$ |

Group the cards so that they are in sets containing like terms.

9 Here is an expression:
$8xy + 3x^2y - 4xy + 2xy^2 - 7xy + 2x^2y + 5x^3y - 6xy^3$
a Write down all the terms that are
  i   like $8xy$ ii   like $3x^2y$
b Johan says that $2xy^2$ and $-6xy^3$ are like terms since both are multiples of x times a power of y.
Explain why Johan is incorrect.

Now check your answers. You may want to use your calculator.
Did you get any wrong and can you work out why?

Chapter 4

4.3.2 Simplifying expressions

Objective

You will learn how to:

- simplify expressions by collecting like terms

Why do you think you might want to simplify expressions? Have a look at this example.

Nabila is selling badges for charity. At breaktime she sells $2n$ badges, at lunchtime she sells $4n$ badges and after school she sells $3n$ badges.

You can write an expression for the total number of badges Nabila has sold.

$2n + 4n + 3n$

$2 + 4 + 3 = 9$ so $2n + 4n + 3n = 9n$

So you can simplify the expression to $9n$

Simplifying expressions makes them quicker to write and easier to work with.

Key point

Simplifying an expression by adding the like terms is called **collecting like terms.**

For example, the terms x and $3x$ can be collected together to give $4x$, but the terms x and y or x and x^2 cannot be collected together since they are not like terms.

Terms involving different variables cannot be simplified when added together, for example $2x + 3y$ cannot be simplified since $2x$ and $3y$ are not like terms.

You can use algebra discs to represent expressions and help you to simplify. You lay out discs to represent each term in the expression and then group together terms that add up to zero (remember from Chapter 3, these are called zero pairs). Then you can see what is left.

For example, look at this expression:

$6x - 5 + x$

All the terms are like terms since they are all terms in the variable x

You know that subtracting 5 is the same as adding -5. In the same way, subtracting $5x$ is the same as adding $-5x$

You can then rearrange the algebra discs to see the pairs that add up to zero (remember from chapter 3 that these are called zero pairs).

In this case you have $5x + (-5x) = 0$ leaving $2x$ remaining.

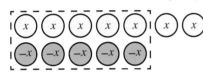

You can see that:

$6x - 5x + x = 2x$

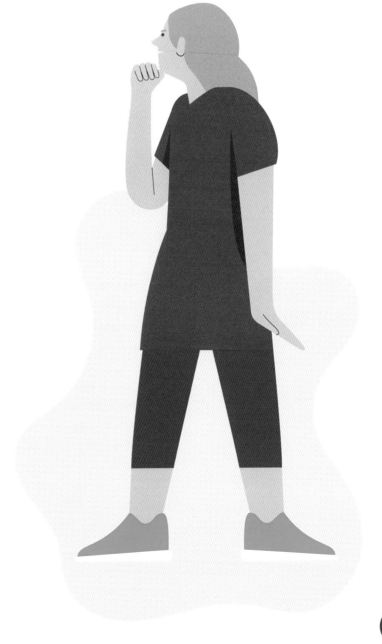

Worked example	Thinking	Your turn!
Simplify the expression $3x + 8y - 4x - 5y$	How can we represent this expression?	Simplify the expression $2x - 3y - 5x + y$

I can represent this expression using algebra discs.

x x $+$ y y y y $+$ $-x$ $-x$ $+$ $-y$ $-y$ $-y$ x — y y y y — $-x$ $-x$ — $-y$ $-y$	How can we represent terms with negative coefficients?	

Subtracting $4x$ is the same as adding $-4x$ and subtracting $5y$ is the same as adding $-5y$

x x x y y y y y y y y $-x$ $-x$ $-x$ $-x$ $-y$ $-y$ $-y$ $-y$ $-y$	How can we work out which terms we will be left with?	

I can group together terms that add up to zero to cancel them out (zero pairs).

$3x + 8y - 4x - 5y = (3x - 4x) + (8y - 5y)$ $\qquad\qquad\qquad\quad = -x + 3y$		

▲ Example-problem pair 1

Terms involving different powers of the same variable cannot be simplified when added together. For example, $x^2 - 5x$ cannot be simplified since x^2 and $5x$ do not involve the same power of x, so are not like terms.

Worked example	Thinking	Your turn!
Simplify the expression $2x + 4x^2 - 3x^2 + x - 2$		Simplify the expression $3x^2 + 2x - 5 - x^2 + 4$

x $+$ x^2 x^2 $+$ $-x^2$ $-x^2$ $+$ x $+$ -1 x — x^2 x^2 — $-x^2$ — — -1	How do we represent different terms?	

x^2 and x terms don't have the same power of x, so they are not like terms and so I represent them as discs with different colours.

x^2 x^2 x^2 x^2 x x x -1 -1 $-x^2$ $-x^2$ $-x^2$	How can we work out which terms we will be left with?	

I can group together terms that add up to zero to cancel them out.

$2x + 4x^2 - 3x^2 + x - 2$ $= (4x^2 - 3x^2) + (2x + x) - 2$ $= x^2 + 3x - 2$		

▲ Example-problem pair 2

In the previous examples, there were some equations:

$3x + 8y - 4x - 5y = -x + 3y$

$2x + 4x^2 - 3x^2 + x - 2 = x^2 + 3x - 2$

They look like ordinary equations; however, these are special because they are true for *all* values of the variables. Equations like these that are true for all values of the variable are called **identities**. For example, $x + 2x = 3x$ and $x + y = y + x$ are identities, but $2x - 3 = x$ is not an identity. This is an equation which is only true when $x = 3$

Key point 🔑

An **identity** is an equation that is true for all values of the variable or variables.

4.3.2 Fluency

In this exercise you can practise applying mathematical methods that you have just learnt.

1 Simplify by collecting like terms.

   a $x + 2x + 4x + 6x$

   b $a + a + b + a + b + a + b$

   c $6p + 5q + 2p - 7q$

   d $-5a - 8b + 3a + 5b - 12a + 7b$

   e $8x - 7y + 3z - 6y - 5x + 10y - z + 4z$

2 Simplify by collecting like terms.

   a $3x^2 + 2x^2 + 7x^2$

   b $9x^2 - 5x^2 + 3x^2 - x^2$

   c $8x + 4x^2 + 7x + 3x^2 + x^2$

   d $5a + 3a^2 - 2a - 2a^2 + 8a - 4a^2$

   e $p^2 + 3p + 5p^2 - 6p - 2p^2 + 8p - 7p^2$

   f $4x + 6y + 2x^2 + 3x - x^2 + 7y^2 - 3y - x - 4y^2$

   g $c^2 - 7c + 8d - 5c^2 - 3d^2 + 3c^2 - 5d - 8d^2 + e$

   h $-4x^2 - 12 + 3y^2 - 7y^2 + 9 + 9x^2 - 3x + 5y - 2y + 10x + 7$

3 Simplify by collecting like terms.

   a $3ab + 5ab + 3ab^2 + 7ab^2$

   b $9x + 10xy + 3x + 12xy + 2x - 8xy$

   c $7p^2q + 8pq^2 - 3p^2q + 5pq^2 - 6p^2 + 2p^2q - 5p^2$

   d $12xy + 6x^2y + 4x^3y - 3xy - 2x^3y - 4x^2y + 3x^2y$

   e $5xy + 7yx - 3x^2y + 4xz - 2yx^2 - 2xy^2 - 3yz$

Now check your answers. Did you get any wrong and can you work out why?

4.3 Exercises

4.3 Intelligent practice

"Why is it intelligent?" You might notice a connection when you move on from one question to the next. You can use the Reflect, Expect, Check, Explain process to:

- *reflect* on what's different between each question and the one that came before
- decide how you *expect* this answer to be different
- complete the question and *check* your answer
- *explain* to yourself why your expectation was correct or incorrect.

EXAMPLE

Question 1a

Suri has 5 pens in her pencil case and 8 pens on her desk.

How many pens does she have in total?

The number of pens is $5 + 8 = 13$ *pens*

Question 1b

Suri has x pens in her pencil case and 8 pens on her desk.

How many pens does she have in total?

Reflect: *This is similar to question* **1a**, *except instead of 5 pens in her pencil case she has* x *pens.*

Expect: *I think that instead of 13 pens she will have* $13x$ *pens.*

Check: *The number of pens is given by* $x + 8$

Explain: *I was wrong, the number of pens is* $x + 8$ *and this cannot be simplified because* x *and 8 are not like terms.*

---

1 Answer the problems below.

a Suri has 5 pens in her pencil case and 8 pens on her desk.
How many pens does she have in total?

b Suri has x pens in her pencil case and 8 pens on her desk.
How many pens does she have in total?

c Suri has x pens in her pencil case and x pens on her desk.
How many pens does she have in total?

d Suri has x pens in her pencil case and $4x$ pens on her desk.
How many pens does she have in total?

e Suri has $3x$ pens in her pencil case and $4x$ pens on her desk.
How many pens does she have in total?

2 Anton has 3 boxes of eggs in the fridge and 2 boxes of eggs in the cupboard.
Work out the total number of eggs if

a each box contains 6 eggs

b each box contains 12 eggs

c each box contains x eggs

d each box contains $2x$ eggs

---

3 Simplify these expressions as much as possible.

a $d + d + d + d$

b $d + d + e + d$

c $d + d + e + e$

d $d + e + d + e$

e $d + e + d - e$

f $d + e - d - e$

g $d - e - d - e$

h $d - e + d + e$

i $2d - e + d + e$

j $2d + e + d + e$

k $2d + 7e + d + e$

l $2d + 7e + d - e$

m $2d + 7e + d - 2e$

n $2d + 7e + 3d - 2e$

o $2d + 7e - 3d - 2e$
p $-2d + 7e - 3d - 2e$
q $-2d + 7e + 3d - 2e$

r $-2d - 7e + 3d - 2e$
s $-2 - 7e + 3 - 2e$
t $-7e - 2 - 2e + 3$

e $3x + y^2 + 5xy + 3x$
f $3xy + y^2 + 5xy + 3x$
g $3xy + y^2 - 5xy + 3x$
h $3xy + 2y^2 - 5xy + 3x$
i $3xy + 2y^2 - 5y^2 + 3x$
j $3xy - 2y^2 - 5y^2 + 3x$
k $3xy - 2y^2 - 5y^2 + 3xy$
l $-3xy - 2y^2 - 5y^2 + 3xy$
m $-3xy - 2y^2 - 5y^2 + 3xy^2$
n $-3xy - 2y^2 - 5x^2 + 3xy^2$
o $-3xy - 2y^2 - 5x^2 + 3x^2y$
p $-3x^2y - 2y^2 - 5x^2 + 3x^2y$
q $-3x^2y - 2xy^2 - 5x^2 + 3x^2y$
r $3x^2y - 2xy^2 - 5x^2 + 3x^2y$
s $3x^2y - 2xy^2 - 5xy^2 + 3x^2y$

4 Simplify these expressions as much as possible.

a $x^2 + x^2$
b $x^2 + 5x^2$
c $x + 5x^2$
d $x + 5x^2 + 2x$
e $3x + 5x^2 + 2x$
f $3x - 5x^2 + 2x$
g $3x - 5x^2 - 2x$

h $3x - 5x^2 - 2x + 5x^2$
i $3x - 5x^2 - 2x + 8x^2$
j $-3x - 5x^2 - 2x + 8x^2$
k $-3x - 5 - 2x + 8x^2$
l $-3x - 5 - 2 + 8x^2$
m $-5 + 8x^2 - 2 - 3x$

5 Simplify these expressions as much as possible.

a $3x + y + 5x$
b $3x + y^2 + 5x$

c $3x + y^2 + 5xy$
d $3x + y^2 + 5xy + 2x^2$

4.3 Method selection

In these questions you'll need to think carefully about which methods to apply.

For some questions you might need to use skills from earlier chapters.

1 Here is an expression: $3x + y - 5$
   a Write down
     i the number of terms
     ii the variables
     iii the coefficient of x
     iv the coefficient of y
   b Work out the value of the expression when
     $x = 6$ and $y = 4$

2 Here is an expression: $3x^2 - 5x + 4y$
   a Write down:
     i the number of terms
     ii the variables
     iii the coefficient of x
     iv the coefficient of x^2
     v the coefficient of y
   b Work out the value of the expression when
     $x = -2$ and $y = 1.5$

3 Here is an expression:
   $8x + 3x - x + 7x + 4x - 9x$
   a Without simplifying first, find the value of
     the expression when $x = 2$
   b Simplify the expression.
   c Work out the value of your simplified
     expression when $x = 2$

4 Here is an expression: $3x + 4x^2 - 8x + x^2 + 6x$
   a Without simplifying first, find the value of
     the expression when $x = 7$
   b Simplify the expression.
   c Work out the value of your simplified
     expression when $x = 7$

5 Write an expression for the perimeter, P cm,
   of each triangle. Simplify your expression as
   much as possible.
   a 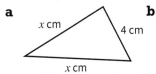   **b**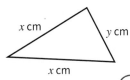

c
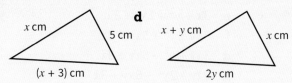
x cm · 5 cm · $(x + 3)$ cm

d
$x + y$ cm · x cm · $2y$ cm

e
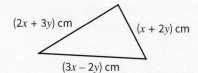
$(2x + 3y)$ cm · $(x + 2y)$ cm · $(3x - 2y)$ cm

6 The perimeter of each triangle is $6x + 8y$. Work out an expression for the missing side length.

a
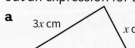
$3x$ cm · x cm

b $(x + 3y)$ cm · $2x$ cm

c
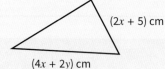
$(2x + 5)$ cm · $(4x + 2y)$ cm

7 In the number pyramids, the expression in each 'brick' is found by adding the expressions in the two bricks below it. Copy and complete the number pyramids.

a

| x | $x + y$ | y |

b
| $3x$ | $2x - y$ | $x + 2y$ |

c
| | $7x - y$ | |
| $4x - y$ | $6x + 5y$ | |

d
	$4y + 5$	
	$-2x + 7$	
$x + y - 2$		

e
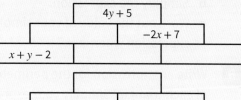
| $6x + x^2$ | $x^2 - x$ | $4x$ |

f
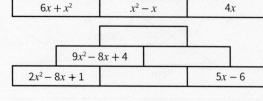
| | $9x^2 - 8x + 4$ | |
| $2x^2 - 8x + 1$ | | $5x - 6$ |

g
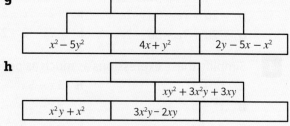
| $x^2 - 5y^2$ | $4x + y^2$ | $2y - 5x - x^2$ |

h
| | $xy^2 + 3x^2y + 3xy$ | |
| $x^2y + x^2$ | $3x^2y - 2xy$ | |

8 Write these algebraic expressions in the simplest way.

a $x + x$
b $x \times 2$
c $x \times x$
d $x \times y$
e $y \times x$
f $x + y$
g $y - x$
h $y \times x \times 6$
i $y \times x \times x$
j $y \times x \times y$

9 Simplify these algebraic expressions.

a $a + a + a$
b $a + 3a + b$
c $a - 3a + b$
d $a \times 3a + b$
e $a + 3a \times b$
f $a + 3a \times a$
g $a + 3a \times a - a^2$
h $b \times a + 3a \times a - a^2$
i $b \times a + 3a \times a - a^2b$
j $b \times a^2 + 3a \times a - a^2b$
k $b^2 \times a + 3a \times a - a^2b$
l $b^2 \times a + 3a \times b - a^2b$
m $b^2 \times a + 3a^2 \times b - a^2b$

10 Find the value of these expressions when $x = 6$ and $y = -3$

a $x + 2x + 7x$
b $x + 8x - 4x + 2x$
c $8y + 7 - 4y + 8 - 3y + 1$
d $3x - x^2 + x + x^2 - 1$
e $8x - 1 + 3y - 7x - 4y + 7$
f $8x - xy + 5x - 3xy + x$
g $-3x^2 + 2x - y^2 + 3x + 6x^2$
h $5xy^2 + 3xy - 7x^2y - 6xy^2 - 9xy + 10x^2y$

11 Fill in the boxes to make these mathematical statements true for all values of x.

a $x \, \square \, 3x = 4x$
b $2x \, \square \, x + 3y = x + 3y$
c $5x \, \square \, 6x \, \square \, y \, \square \, 3y = 11x - 2y$
d $\square \, 7x \, \square \, 6y \, \square \, 5y \, \square \, 4x = -11x - y$
e $x \, \square \, x = x^2$
f $x \, \square \, y \, \square \, 3 = 3xy$
g $5x^2y \, \square \, 3yx \, \square \, 8x^2y = 3xy - 3x^2y$
h $5xy^2 \, \square \, 8yx \, \square \, 4x^2y \, \square \, 9xy - yx^2$
$ = -xy \, \square \, 5x^2y + 5xy^2$

4.3 Purposeful practice

There may be more than one way to approach these questions.
Once you have answered a question one way, can you think of another way?

1 Some thin strips of length x cm and y cm are used to form rectangles.
  a The length of the rectangle below is $(x + y)$ cm and its width is $2y$ cm

  x cm y cm

  y cm

  y cm

  Write down a formula for the perimeter of the rectangle. Simplify the formula as much as possible.

  b The formula for the perimeter of a different rectangle is $P = 8x + 10y$
  See how many possible expressions for the length and width of the rectangle you can find.

2 Write some expressions that simplify to
  a x **b** $x + 1$ **c** $x^2 - x + 1$

3 In these number pyramids, the expression in each "brick" is found by adding the expressions in the two bricks below it. Make copies of each number pyramid and find different ways to complete them.

  a

  | | $8x$ | |

  b

  | | $9x^2 + 4x$ | |

4 Look at the table below.

  a Copy and complete the table. Decide whether the mathematical statements in the table are always true, sometimes true or never true.

  Make sure you can explain your answers.

  Make up your own equations that can fit in the final three rows of the table. If you have time you can think of more than one for each row.

Mathematical statements	Always true	Sometimes true	Never true
$x + 3x = 5x - x$	✓		
$3x + 5x + 3 - 8x = 4$			
$2x + 7 - 8x + 7x = 3x + 2x - 1$			
$6x - 9 - 4x + 13 = 2x + 5$			
$x^2 + 7x - 5x + 3x^2 - 2x = 36$			
$-xy + 3x - 2y + 7xy - 3x = 6xy - 2y$			
	✓		
		✓	
			✓

  b Which of the mathematical statements in the table are identities?

Using the distributive law

4.4.1 Expanding brackets

Objective

You will learn how to:

- expand brackets by multiplying an expression by a term

In algebra, you will sometimes need to multiply a number or a term by an expression in brackets. For example: $9(x+3)$ or $a(b-2)$

Key point

If there is no operator (e.g. +, -, ÷) between a number or letter and a bracket then the number or letter is multiplied by the expression inside the brackets.

$$3(x+2) = 3 \times (x+2) \qquad y(x+2) = y \times (x+2)$$

You can treat the brackets in the same way as you did with numbers in Chapter 3 using the distributive law.

Key point

Expanding the brackets means writing an expression such as $3(x+2)$ or $y(x+2)$ so that it does not have any brackets. You do this by multiplying the term next to the brackets by each of the terms inside the brackets.

You can use a grid to help you to expand the brackets.

Worked example	Thinking	Your turn!	
Expand the brackets $b(3a-4)$	*What do we need to multiply each term in the brackets by?*	**Expand the brackets** $d(4c-3)$	I need to multiply each term in the brackets by b
$b(3a-4) = b \times 3a + b \times (-4)$	*How can we make sure that we don't get confused with the minus sign?*		Putting the −4 in brackets means I won't forget the sign!
$= 3ab - 4b$	*How can we simplify this?*		
Using a grid: 	×	3a	−4
---	---	---
b	3ab	−4b		*How can we represent this problem?*		I can use a grid to help me work this out.

▲ Example-problem pair 1

You may need to use powers in your simplified expression after you have expanded brackets.

Worked example	Thinking	Your turn!
Expand the brackets $a(4a-5)$ <table><tr><td>×</td><td>$4a$</td><td>-5</td></tr><tr><td>a</td><td>$4a^2$</td><td>$-5a$</td></tr></table> $a(4a-5)=4a^2-5a$	*How can we represent this problem in a grid?* *How do we write out our answer from the grid?*	Expand the brackets: $c(4c-3)$

Each term in the brackets goes at the top of a column and the term outside the brackets goes at the start of the row.

▲ Example-problem pair 2

4.4.1 Fluency

In this exercise you can practise applying the mathematical methods that you have just learnt.

1 Here is an example of the distributive law used to expand brackets:
$2(5+7)=2\times5+2\times7=10+14$
Use this example to help you write expansions for each of these:
  a $2(x+7)$
  b $2(5+y)$
  c $2(x+y)$

2 Expand
  a $3(x+2)$
  b $4(y+7)$
  c $9(x-2)$
  d $7(a-4)$
  e $6(p-8)$
  f $5(3-x)$

3 Expand
  a $x(x+4)$
  b $x(2x+5)$
  c $2x(x-4)$
  d $3x(x+8)$
  e $2a(3a+4)$
  f $3a(4a-3)$
  g $6p(5-p)$
  h $7q(6-5q)$

4 Expand
  a $8(x+y)$
  b $2x(3x-2y+4)$
  c $2x^2(3x-5y)$
  d $-4x^2(2x-y-3)$
  e $1.5a(5a-6b)$
  f $0.2xy(3x-4y+2)$

Now check your answers. Did you get any wrong and can you work out why?

4.4.2 Expanding and simplifying

Objective

You will learn how to:

- expand and simplify brackets

Look at this expression: $3(x+1)+2(6-x)-(x+10)$

You can use what you have learnt about expanding the brackets and collecting like terms to simplify the expression.

Start by expanding the brackets:

$$3(x+1)=3\times x+3\times 1 \qquad 2(6-x)=2\times 6+2\times(-x) \qquad -1(x+10)=(-1)\times x+(-1)\times 10$$
$$=3x+3 \qquad\qquad\qquad =12-2x \qquad\qquad\qquad =-x-10$$

Remember, with algebraic terms you do not write the coefficient if it is a 1
For example, $1a$ is written as just a and $-1a$ is written as $-a$. The same thing applies to brackets. $-1(x+10)$ is just written $-(x+10)$

Key point

If there is no number in front of a bracket then this means $1\times$ the expression in the bracket. For example, $(a+b)$ means $1\times(a+b)$ and $-(a+b)$ means $-1\times(a+b)$

Now you have expanded all the brackets you can simplify by collecting like terms:

$$3(x+1)+2(6-x)-(x+10)=3x+3+12-2x-x-10$$
$$=(3x-2x-x)+(3+12-10)$$
$$=5$$

Can you see what has happened to the x terms in this case?

Worked example	Thinking	Your turn!
Expand and simplify $5(t+9)-2t(t-6)$	*What do we do first?*	Expand and simplify $2x(x+5)-3(x-1)$
$5(t+9)=5\times t+5\times 9=5t+45$ Using a grid:		

×	t	9
5	$5t$	45

I can deal with each set of brackets separately.

Worked example	Thinking	Your turn!

$-2t(t-6) = (-2t) \times t + (-2t) \times (-6)$
$= -2t^2 + 12t$

How can we make sure that we don't get confused with the minus signs?

> I will put the terms with negative coefficients in brackets to help me remember the minus signs.

Using a grid:

×	t	-6
$-2t$	$-2t^2$	$12t$

$5(t+9) - 2t(t-6) = 5t + 45 - 2t^2 + 12t$

How do we find the final answer?

> Now I can gather the results from expanding both brackets and add them together.

$5(t+9) - 2t(t-6) = 5t + 45 - 2t^2 + 12t$
$= -2t^2 + (5t + 12t) + 45$
$= -2t^2 + 17t + 45$

How many different kinds of terms are there in this expression?

> The terms involving t and t^2 are not like terms so I can't group them together. I will finish with three terms.

▲ Example-problem pair 1

4.4.2 Fluency

In this exercise you can practise applying the mathematical methods that you have just learnt.

1 Expand and simplify.
 a $2 + 3(x+1)$
 b $7(x-2) - 5$

2 Expand and simplify.
 a $3(x+2) + 2(x-1)$
 b $2(3x-1) + 4(x+3)$
 c $3(x+4) - 2(x-2)$
 d $6(4x-3) - 3(2x-7)$

3 Expand and simplify.
 a $8 + 3(x+6)$
 b $15 - 5(x-8)$
 c $4(a+2b) + 6(ab+3b)$
 d $9(ab-3b) - 2(a-2ab)$
 e $4(a+b) + 3(2a+3ab) - 2(6b-ab)$
 f $a(2a-3b) + b(3a+4b) + 6(ab-b^2)$

4 A rectangle has sides $3x - y$ cm and $4x + 3y$ cm. Brice writes an expression for the perimeter of the rectangle:
$2(3x-y) + 3(4x+3y)$
 a Explain the mistake the Brice has made and write a correct, unsimplified expression for the perimeter of the rectangle.
 b Expand and simplify your answer to part a.

5 Expand and simplify.
 a $p(p^2q - 3p^2) + q(p^3 - 4p^2)$
 b $x^2(4xy^2 + 3xy) - y(2x^3y + 8x^3)$
 c $4x(y^2 - 3xy) + 2y(3xy + 7x^2) - 3xy(6y - 5x)$
 d $8x(4x^3y^2 - 3xy^3) - 2xy(xy^2 - 3x^3y) + 4x^2y^2(3y - 2x^2)$

Now check your answers. You may want to use your calculator. Did you get any wrong and can you work out why?

4.4.3 Identifying algebraic factors

Objective ☑

You will learn how to:

- identify algebraic factors and find the highest common factor of algebraic terms

In Chapter 2 you learnt that any number can be written as a product of its prime factors. For example, $30 = 2 \times 3 \times 5$

You can also write algebraic terms as a product of their factors. For example, $xy = x \times y$ or $x^2 = x \times x$

Some terms consist of variables and numbers multiplied together, such as $3x$, $6x^2$ or $-15xy$. For these, recall that the number part of the term is called the coefficient.

You can write a term as a product of its factors by considering any coefficient and algebraic parts separately, for example:

$$3x = 3 \times x \qquad\qquad 6x^2 = 2 \times 3 \times x \times x$$

If a term has a negative coefficient, then you can write it with –1 as a factor, for example

$$-15xy = (-1) \times 3 \times 5 \times x \times y$$

Worked example	Thinking	Your turn!
Write each term as a product of its prime and algebraic factors.		Write each term as a product of its prime and algebraic factors.
a $18ab$ $18ab = 2 \times 3 \times 3 \times a \times b$	How do we write the number as a product of primes?	**a** $22xy$
b $-26a^2$ $-26a^2 = (-1) \times 2 \times 13 \times a \times a$	What can we do with a negative coefficient?	**b** $-24x^2$

> I know two numbers that multiply to give 18 from times tables and I write those using primes.

> A negative coefficient means I will have a factor of negative one.

▲ Example-problem pair 1

To find the **highest common factor (HCF)** of two terms you multiply together the prime and algebraic factors that are the same in both terms.

For example, to find the highest common factor of $16xy$ and $12y$, first write them both as products of their prime and algebraic factors:

$$16xy = ②\times②\times 2 \times 2 \times x \times ⓨ \qquad\qquad 12y = ②\times②\times 3 \times ⓨ$$

The prime factor of 2 appears twice in each term and y appears once in both, so the highest common factor is $2 \times 2 \times y = 4y$

The highest common factor (HCF) can be numerical or algebraic, e.g. the highest common factor of $12x$ and $18y$ is 6 and the highest common factor of $6ab$ and $4a$ is $2a$

Worked example	Thinking	Your turn!
Find the HCF of the pairs of terms.		Find the HCF of the pairs of terms.
a $42a$ and $14b$ $42a = ②× 3 ×⑦× a$ $14b = ②×⑦× b$ $2 × 7 = 14$ HCF is 14	*What do we do if more than one number or letter is circled?*	**a** $16x$ and $12y$
b $50a^2$ and $10ab$ $50a^2 = ②×⑤× 5 ×ⓐ× a$ $10ab = ②×⑤×ⓐ× b$ $2 × 5 × a = 10a$ HCF is $10a$		**b** $22xy$ and $33x^2$

I multiply the circled numbers or letters together to find the highest common factor.

I can't include a^2 as a common algebraic factor because the $10a$ only has a as a factor, not a^2

🔺 Example-problem pair 2

4.4.3 Fluency

In this exercise you can practise applying the mathematical methods that you have just learnt.

1 Write each number as a product of prime factors.
   a 6   **b** 10   **c** 35   **d** 42

2 Write each of these terms as a product of prime and algebraic factors.
   a xy **c** $18x$ **e** $21x^2$ **g** $24x^2$
   b x^2 **d** $21x$ **f** $30x^2$

3 Write each of these terms as a product of prime and algebraic factors.
   a $24x^2y$ **c** $24xy^2$ **e** $24x^2y^2z$
   b $24xy$ **d** $24x^2y^2$

4 Work out the highest common factor of each of these pairs of terms.
   a 3 and $3x$ **c** $5y$ and $15x$
   b $4y$ and $7y$

5 Work out the highest common factor of each of these pairs of terms.
   a $49x$ and $7x$ **e** $25b$ and $10b^2$
   b $18y^2$ and $9y$ **f** $20p^2$ and $25p$
   c $9x$ and $12x^2$ **g** $16z$ and $24z^3$
   d $18a^2$ and $12a$

6 Work out the highest common factor of each of these pairs of terms.
   a $12az^2$ and $39bz$ **c** $25x^2y$ and $30xy^2$
   b $32ab^2$ and $24ac$

Now check your answers. You may want to use your calculator. Did you get any wrong and can you work out why?

4.4.4 Factorising expressions

Objective

You will learn how to:

*   factorise expressions

The reverse of expanding brackets is called **factorising**.

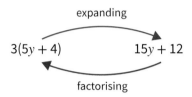

expanding

$3(5y + 4)$ $15y + 12$

factorising

Factorising an expression is when you write it using brackets. Expressions can sometimes be factorised by putting common factors in front of the brackets. For example, the expression $2a + 6$ can be factorised as $2(a + 3)$ since 2 is a common factor of both terms in the expression.

To factorise an expression fully you must find the highest common factor of the terms and place this in front of the brackets. Then you put the remaining factors for each term inside the bracket.

For example, $3(x + 5)$ is **fully factorised** since the highest common factor of x and 5 is 1. However, $3(10x + 5)$ is not fully factorised since the highest common factor of $10x$ and 5 is 5. The fully factorised expression is $15(2x + 1)$.

Key point

An expression is fully factorised into a single set of brackets if the highest common factor of the terms inside the bracket is 1.

You can use grids to represent factorising. For example, if you want to factorise the expression $6x + 9$ then the terms $6x$ and 9 must go on the bottom of the grid, and you need to work out what to put at the top and side of the grid.

×	?	?
?	$6x$	9

→

×	?	?
3	$6x$	9

→

×	$2x$	3
3	$6x$	9

The highest common factor of $6x$ and 9 goes here.

$6x = 2 \times 3 \times x$

$9 = 3 \times 3$

So HCF = 3

To work out the numbers at the top of the grid you can see what factors remain for each of the terms.

So $6x + 9 = 3(2x + 3)$

You can see that the expression is fully factorised since the HCF of $2x$ and 3 is 1

You can check the answer by expanding the brackets:
$3(2x + 3) = 3 \times 2x + 3 \times 3 = 6x + 9$

The highest common factor may not be a constant (number without a variable).
You can also factorise expressions so that the term outside the bracket contains one or more variables.

Worked example	Thinking	Your turn!	
Fully factorise $15p - 5p^2$		Fully factorise $15a^2 - 18a$	I have listed the factors of each term and circled the common factors . To find the HCF I will multiply the common factors.
$15p = 3 \times 5 \times p$ $-5p^2 = (-1) \times 5 \times p \times p$	How can we find the highest common factor?		
So HCF $= 5 \times p = 5p$	What is the highest common factor?		The HCF is what goes outside the brackets then I can use a grid to work out what goes inside.
Using a grid: 	×	3	$-p$	 	$5p$	$15p$	$-5p^2$	 HCF Terms from the question	How can we use a grid to help us to work out what would go in the brackets?		I can find what goes in the top of each column by looking at the remaining factors of each term, those are what will go in the brackets.
$15p - 5p^2 = 5p(3 - p)$	How do we know that our answer is fully factorised?		The terms inside the bracket have no common factors other than 1, so my answer is fully factorised.

▲ Example-problem pair 1

4.4.4 Fluency

In this exercise you can practise applying the mathematical methods that you have just learnt.

1 Factorise fully

  a $4a + 16$ **d** $8a - 12$

  b $6x + 18$ **e** $9x - 33$

  c $3y - 6$ **f** $18p + 60$

2 Factorise fully

  a $x^2 + 2x$ **e** $16p^2 + 20$

  b $3a^2 + 9a$ **f** $18x^2 + 14x$

  c $2a^2 - 6a$ **g** $12b^2 - 16b$

  d $9x^2 + 12x$ **h** $9y^2 - 21y$

3 Factorise fully

  a $3ab + 6a$

  b $5pq - 5p$

  c $6x^2y + 3xy$

  d $8xy^2 + 12x^2y$

  e $6xy + 3x^2y - 9xy^2$

Now check your answers. Did you get any wrong and can you work out why?

4.4 Exercises

4.4 Intelligent practice

"Why is it intelligent?" You might notice a connection when you move on from one question to the next. You can use the Reflect, Expect, Check, Explain process to:

- *reflect* on what's different between each question and the one that came before
- decide how you *expect* this answer to be different
- complete the question and *check* your answer
- *explain* to yourself why your expectation was correct or incorrect.

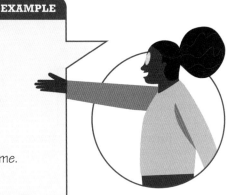

Question 2a   **EXAMPLE**

Expand the brackets $3(8 + x)$

$3(8 + x) = 3 \times 8 + 3 \times x = 24 + 3x$

Question 2b

Expand the brackets $3(7 + x)$

Reflect: This is similar to question **2a**, except inside the brackets we have $7 + x$ instead of $8 + x$

Expect: I think that the constant term will change but the x term will stay the same.

Check: $3(7 + x) = 3 \times 7 + 3 \times x = 21 + 3x$

Explain: I was right! The constant term is 21 so that has changed, but the x term is $3x$ so that has stayed the same.

---

1 Expand the brackets.

a $2(3 + 7)$		**g** $5(x - 1)$	
b $2(5 + 7)$		**h** $5(2x - 1)$	
c $3(5 + 7)$		**i** $5(2x - 9)$	
d $3(x + 7)$		**j** $5x(2x - 9)$	
e $3(x - 7)$		**k** $5x(2x - 9y)$	
f $5(x - 7)$		**l** $-5x(2x - 9y)$	

2 Expand the brackets.

a $3(8 + x)$		**g** $4(7 + 5y)$	
b $3(7 + x)$		**h** $4y(7 + 5y)$	
c $3(7 + y)$		**i** $4y(8 + 5y)$	
d $4(7 + y)$		**j** $4y(8 - 5y)$	
e $4(7 - y)$		**k** $4x(8 - 5y)$	
f $4(7 - 5y)$		**l** $4x(8x - 5y)$	

3 Expand the brackets.

a $2(10 + 3)$		**d** $10(a - 3)$	
b $10(2 + 3)$		**e** $10a(a - 3)$	
c $10(a + 3)$		**f** $-10a(a - 3)$	

g $-10a(2a - 3)$	**j** $-10a(2a - 3b + ac)$
h $-10a(2a - 3b)$	**k** $10a(2a - 3b + ac)$
i $-10a(2a - 3b + c)$	**l** $10a(2a - 3bc + ac)$

4 Expand the brackets and simplify.

a $2 + 5(x + 4)$	**g** $3 - 5(3x + 4)$
b $3 + 5(x + 4)$	**h** $3 - 5x(3x + 4)$
c $3 + 5(x - 4)$	**i** $3 - 5x(3x - 4)$
d $3 + 5(2x - 4)$	**j** $3 - 5x(3x - 4y)$
e $3 - 5(2x - 4)$	**k** $-3 - 5x(3x - 4y)$
f $3 - 5(2x + 4)$	**l** $-3 - 5xy(3x - 4y)$

5 Expand the brackets and simplify.

a $2(x + 3) + 3(x + 5)$
b $2(x + 3) + 3(x - 5)$
c $2(x - 3) + 3(x - 5)$
d $2(x - 3) - 3(x - 5)$
e $2(5x - 3) - 3(x - 5)$
f $2(5x - 3) - 3(7x - 5)$
g $2(5x - 3) - 3x(7x - 5)$

h $2x(5x-3)-3x(7x-5)$
i $2x(5x-3y)-3x(7x-5)$
j $2x(5x-3y)-3x(7x-5y)$
k $2xy(5x-3y)-3x(7x-5y)$
l $2xy(5x-3y)-(7x-5y)$

e $3a+12$
f $3a-12$
g $3a-4$
h $3a^2-4$
i $3a^2-4a$

j $3a^2-24a$
k $9a^2-24a$
l $-9a^2-24a$
m $-9a^2b-24a$
n $-9a^2b-24ab$

6 Work out the highest common factor of each pair of terms.
a 12 and 18
b $12x$ and 18
c $12x$ and 30
d $12x^2$ and 30
e $12x^2$ and $30x$
f $12x^2$ and $30y$
g $12x^2$ and $30xy$
h $12x^2y$ and $30xy$
i $12x^2y$, $30xy$ and $3y$

8 Factorise each of these expressions fully.
a $10x+5$
b $5+10x$
c $5-10x$
d $15-10x$
e $15-10x^2$
f $15x-10x^2$
g $10x^2-15x$
h $10x^2-15y$
i $10x^2-15y^2$
j $10x^2-15xy^2$
k $10x^2y-15xy^2$
l $10x^2y-15xy^2+x$
m $10x^2y-15xy^2+xy$
n $10x^2y-15xy^2+x^2y^2$

7 Factorise each of these expressions fully, if possible.
a $3\times5+3\times2$
b $3\times a+3\times2$
c $3a+3\times2$
d $3a+6$

Chapter 4

4.4 Method selection

In these questions you'll need to think carefully about which methods to apply.

For some questions you might need to use skills from earlier chapters.

1 Complete the problems.
a Write all the factors of 36
b Write 36 as a product of its prime factors.
c Work out the highest common factor of 36 and 45
d Factorise $36x+45$

2 Complete the problems.
a Factorise $4x+14$
b Work out the value of $4x+14$ when $x=2$
c Expand $2(4x+14)$

3 Complete the problems.
a Factorise $3x^2-5x$
b Work out the value of $3x^2-5x$ when $x=4$
c Expand $4(3x^2-5x)$

4 Fill in the boxes to make the statements always true.
a $3(x+5)=\square\,x+\square$
b $9(x+\square)=\square\,x+36$
c $7(\square-4)=7x\,\square\,28$
d $2(3x-4)=\square\,x-\square$
e $8(\square\,x+7)=24x+\square$
f $\square\,(x-5)=4x\,\square\,\square$
g $\square(\square\,x+5)=18x+15$
h $\square(5x-\square)=45x-9$
i $x(3x+\square)=\square+7x$
j $\square(5x+\square)=25x^2+30x$
k $\square(\square\,x+\square)=39x^2+13x$
l $3y(3x+\square)=\square+33y$
m $3xy(2x+5y)=6\,\square+15\,\square$
n $\square(2y-4)=8xy^2-\square$

5 In this question, write all your expressions without brackets and fully simplified.

a Work out an expression for the area of this rectangle.

2 cm

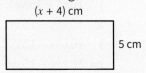

$(x + 3)$ cm

b Work out an expression for the perimeter of this rectangle.

$(x + 4)$ cm

5 cm

c Work out an expression for the length of this rectangle.

Area = $(3x + 12)$ cm²

3 cm

d Work out an expression for the area of this rectangle.

$(2x + 5)$ cm

7 cm

e Work out an expression for the perimeter of this rectangle.

$(8 - 3x)$ cm

5 cm

f Work out an expression for the width of this rectangle.

$(3x - 8)$ cm

Area = $(21x - 56)$ cm²

g Work out an expression for the length of this rectangle.

Area = $(14x - 8x^2)$ cm²

$2x$ cm

h Work out an expression for the area of this rectangle.

$(3x + 2)$ cm

x cm

i Work out an expression for the length of this rectangle.

Area = $(8x + 24xy)$ cm²

$8x$ cm

j Work out an expression for the width of this rectangle.

$(x + 2y)$ cm

Area = $(15x^2 + 30xy)$ cm²

6 Decide whether each expression is fully factorised.

a $5(x + 7)$ **e** $8x(3x + 4)$

b $2(4x + 8)$ **f** $9y(7x + 3y)$

c $3(x^2 + x)$ **g** $7xy(15xy - 18y)$

d $2(6x - 9)$

7 Find the odd one out in each part.

a $4(x + 6)$ $4(6 + x)$ $6(x + 4)$

b $3(2x + 4)$ $6(x + 3)$ $2(3x + 6)$

c $5(8 - 2x)$ $10(4 - x)$ $8(5 - x)$

d $3(x^2 - 1)$ $3x(x - 1)$ $-3x(1 - x)$

e $x(12 - 4x)$ $-4x(x - 3)$ $2(6x - 2)$

f $3xy(2 + x)$ $3y(2x + x^2)$ $x(6y + 3x)$

g $12xy(2x - y)$ $6x(4xy - 6y^2)$ $4y(6x^2 - 9xy)$

8 Work out if each statement is true for all values of x

a $3(x + 2) + 5(x - 4) = 2(4x - 7)$

b $5(2x + 1) + 3(x - 8) = 7(x - 3)$

c $6(5x + 2) - 2(3x - 14) = 8(3x + 5)$

d $8x(x + 3) - x(3 - x) = 3x(x - 7)$

9 Expand the brackets and simplify.

a $0.3(x + 7)$ **c** $24(0.6 - 3x)$

b $1.5(2x - 5)$ **d** $1.6(0.2x + 1.5)$

e $7(0.3x - 2) - 3(0.8x - 1.5)$

f $2.5(3.1x + 2.4y) - 0.1(0.3y + 7x)$

10 A square has side length $(2x + 5)$ cm
Write down an expression for the perimeter of the square that does not use brackets.

11 A rectangle has side lengths $(3x + 2)$ cm and $(4x - 1)$ cm. Write down a simplified expression for the perimeter of the rectangle.

12 A rectangle has side lengths 6 cm and $(8x - 5)$ cm
    a Write down an expression for the area of the rectangle that does not use brackets.
A smaller rectangle is cut from the one above.
The smaller rectangle has side lengths 2 cm and $(2x + 1)$ cm
    b Write down a simplified expression for the area that is left.

13 A standard box of chocolates contains x truffles and $2y$ plain chocolates.
A deluxe box of chocolates contains $2x$ truffles and $3y$ plain chocolates.
Barney buys 8 standard boxes and 5 deluxe boxes.
Write down an expression for the total number of truffles and plain chocolates that Barney buys.

14 A rectangle has side lengths $(2x + 3)$ cm and $(4x - 1)$ cm
Show that the perimeter of the rectangle can be written as $4(3x + 1)$

15 Ben has $3x + 7$ counters and Danni has twice as many counters as Ben.
Fenella has $8x - 1$ counters and Gerald has 9 fewer counters than Fenella.
Show that they have $5(5x + 2)$ counters between all four people.

4.4 Purposeful practice

There may be more than one way to approach these questions.
Once you have answered a question one way, can you think of another way?

1 Combine these expressions in different ways and simplify the result.
How many different results can you find?

$4x$	$x + 7$	$y - 3$
	2	$6y$

2 The area of a rectangle is $(24x + 36)$ cm^2
Find possible pairs of expressions for the length and width of the rectangle.

3 The area of a rectangle is $(63x^2 - 42x)$ cm^2
Find possible pairs of expressions for the length and width of the rectangle.

4 Think of expressions that could belong in each of the regions of each Venn diagram.
If you think a region is impossible to fill, explain why.

a

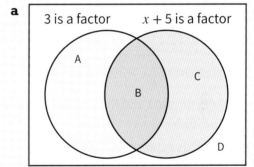

3 is a factor $x + 5$ is a factor

b

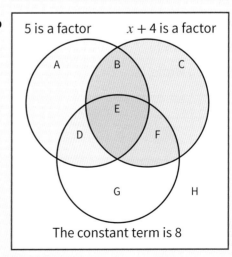

5 is a factor $x + 4$ is a factor

The constant term is 8

Chapter 4 summary

Watch out! exercise

Some students have tried to answer the questions below but have unfortunately made some mistakes.

For each question do the following:

a answer the question correctly

b write down the mistake that each student has made

c comment on why they might have made that mistake

d write an explanation for each student to convince them (nicely!) that their answer cannot be correct.

1 Anna and Cameron tried to answer the question:

Write the expression $3 \times a \times a$ in a simpler way.

Anna wrote $6a$ Cameron wrote $9a^2$

2 Bronwen and Alex tried to answer this question:

Write a formula for the function machine.

$$x \longrightarrow \boxed{+4} \longrightarrow \boxed{\times 7} \longrightarrow y$$

Bronwen wrote $7x + 28$ Alex wrote $y = 7x + 4$

3 Amanda, Rowena and Ricardo tried to answer this question:

Simplify this expression if possible:
$7x - 3y - x + 8y$

Amanda wrote $6x + 11y$

Rowena wrote $7x + 5y$

Ricardo wrote $8x + 5y$

4 James and Ashley tried to answer this question:

Simplify this expression if possible: $x^2 + x$

James wrote x^3

Ashley wrote $2x^2$

5 Nazreen and Maeve answered this question:

Expand the brackets $m(m - 1)$

Nazreen wrote $2m - m$

Maeve wrote $m^2 - 1$

6 Lena and Noah tried to answer this question:

Factorise fully $18x^2 - 12x$

Lena wrote $6(3x^2 - 2x)$

Noah wrote $2x(9x^2 - 6)$

Check your understanding

Turn over to find the review questions

4.1 Introduction to algebra

You should now be able to...	Questions
understand how to use a letter to represent a number	1, 2, 3, 4, 5
identify terms, products, and expressions	
understand how to use an algebraic statement or formula to represent a relationship	
understand and use algebraic notation	All questions
substitute numbers into an algebraic expression	6, 8, 10, 11

4.2 Formulae and equations

You should now be able to...	Questions
substitute numbers into function machines	7
identify and substitute numbers into an algebraic formula	8
use a simple formula written in words and write a formula from given information	9, 12
identify equations and inequalities	10, 11
write linear equations and determine whether a value satisfies an equation	

4.3 Simplifying expressions

You should now be able to...	Questions
identify constants and coefficients	14
identify like terms	13
simplify expressions by collecting like terms	

4.4 Using the distributive law

You should now be able to...	Questions
expand brackets by multiplying an expression by a term	15
expand and simplify brackets	16
identify algebraic factors and find the highest common factor of algebraic terms	17
factorise expressions	18

Chapter 4 review questions

1 Meena has 7 more counters than Josh.

Find the number of counters Meena has if Josh has

a 11 counters [1 mark]

b n counters. [1 mark]

2 Finn has four times as many pencils as Hana.

Find the number of pencils Finn has if Hana has

a 8 pencils [1 mark]

b x pencils. [1 mark]

3 Malak has a third of the number of carrots that Dean has.

Find the number of carrots Malak has if Dean has

a 36 carrots [1 mark]

b y carrots. [1 mark]

4 Boxes of chocolates contain x chocolates.

Work out the total number of chocolates in

a 7 boxes [1 mark]

b p boxes. [1 mark]

5 Tickets to a theme park are £9 for children and £12 for adults.

Find the total cost for

a 3 children and 2 adults [1 mark]

b a children and b adults. [1 mark]

6 Work out the value of each expression when $t = 3$

a $7 - t$ [1 mark]

b $8t$ [1 mark]

c $t^2 + 7$ [1 mark]

d $4t^2 - 9$ [1 mark]

7 Find the value of y when $x = 3$

$x \longrightarrow \boxed{+3} \longrightarrow \boxed{\times 5} \longrightarrow y$ [1 mark]

8 $y = 3(x + 7)$

Find the value of y when

a $x = 6$ [1 mark]

b $x = -12$ [1 mark]

c $x = 3.2$ [1 mark]

9 Write a formula that shows the relationship between x and y for each function machine.

a $x \longrightarrow \boxed{\times 2} \longrightarrow \boxed{+5} \longrightarrow y$ [1 mark]

b $x \longrightarrow \boxed{-7} \longrightarrow \boxed{\times 4} \longrightarrow y$ [1 mark]

10 Maddy says that $x = 7$ is a solution to the equation $3x - 5 = 16$

Show that Maddy is correct. [1 mark]

11 Zara says that $x = 3.2$ is a solution to the inequality $6x - 1 < 20$

Is Zara correct? Explain your answer. [1 mark]

12 A taxi company charges £2 per mile plus £1.50

Write a formula for £C, the total cost of a journey of m miles. [1 mark]

13 Simplify

a $2x + 6 + 5x - 2$ [1 mark]

b $4x + 8y - 3x - 5y$ [1 mark]

c $7x^2 + 3x - 2x^2 - 8x$ [1 mark]

d $8xy + 7y - 3xy - 6x$ [1 mark]

14 Here is an expression: $7x - 3y^2 + 5$

Write down

a the number of terms [1 mark]

b the value of the constant [1 mark]

c the coefficient of x [1 mark]

d Dina says that the coefficient of y^2 is 3
Is Dina correct? Explain your answer.
[1 mark]

15 Expand

a $2(x - 5)$ [1 mark]

b $p(2q + 7)$ [1 mark]

c $x(3x - 4)$ [1 mark]

d $y(2x - 4y + 1)$ [1 mark]

16 Expand and simplify

a $4 + 3(x + 2)$ [1 mark]

b $3t - 2(t + 6)$ [1 mark]

c $4(x + 3) + 2(3x - 1)$ [2 marks]

d $7(2x - 1) - 4(x - 5)$ [2 marks]

17 Work out the highest common factor of each of these pairs of terms:

a $63x$ and $12x$ [1 mark]

b $60x$ and $25x^2$ [1 mark]

c $14x^3y$ and $49x^2y^2$ [2 marks]

18 Factorise fully

a $6x - 12$ [1 mark]

b $5x - 5y$ [1 mark]

c $y + y^2$ [2 marks]

d $18x^2 + 6x$ [2 marks]

e $xy^2 - 2xy$ [2 marks]

f $5x^2 - 10xy + 15x$ [2 marks]

Chapter 4

Key words

Make sure you can write a definition for these key terms.

variable • expression • term • product • generalise • substitute • function machine • formula
equation • solution • inequality • constant • coefficient • simplify • like terms • collect like terms
identity • expand brackets • highest common factor (HCF) • factorise • fully factorise

Greg is a character in a video game. How could you describe Greg's position on the grid? How could you describe a route for the monster to catch Greg?

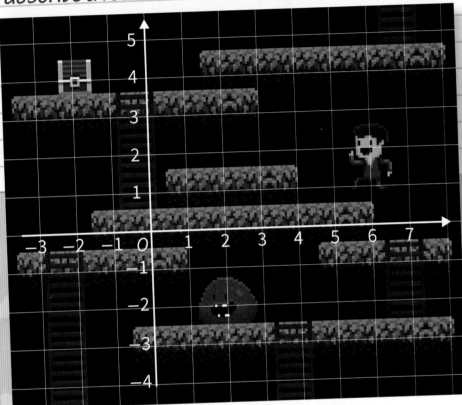

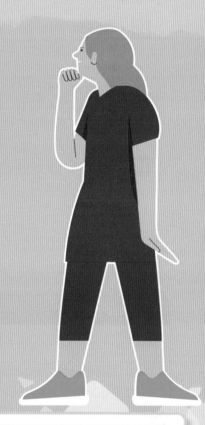

What comes before?	This chapter	What comes after?
Primary school • Quadrilaterals • Coordinate grids • Axes **Book 1** • Coordinates • Arithmetic	• 5.1 Plotting coordinates • 5.2 Coordinates, formulae, and graphs	**Book 1** • Transformations **Book 2** • Linear graphs **Book 3** • Linear and non-linear graphs **Key stage 4** • Graphs • Functions

Introduction

In this chapter you will learn how to describe and plot points and shapes using coordinate pairs. You will then solve problems involving coordinates, for example, finding the midpoint of two points. You will also use your knowledge of the properties of shapes in other coordinate problems, such as suggesting the coordinates of points to complete a shape on a grid.

You will also discover how coordinates can be used to describe a straight line on a coordinate grid. These straight line graphs show the relationship between two variables. A straight line graph can also be described with an equation, which you will learn to plot points from and draw.

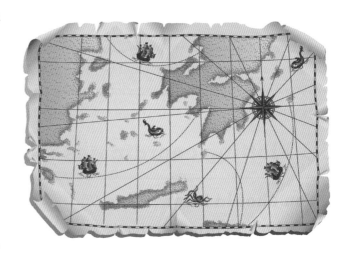

In this chapter you will learn how to...

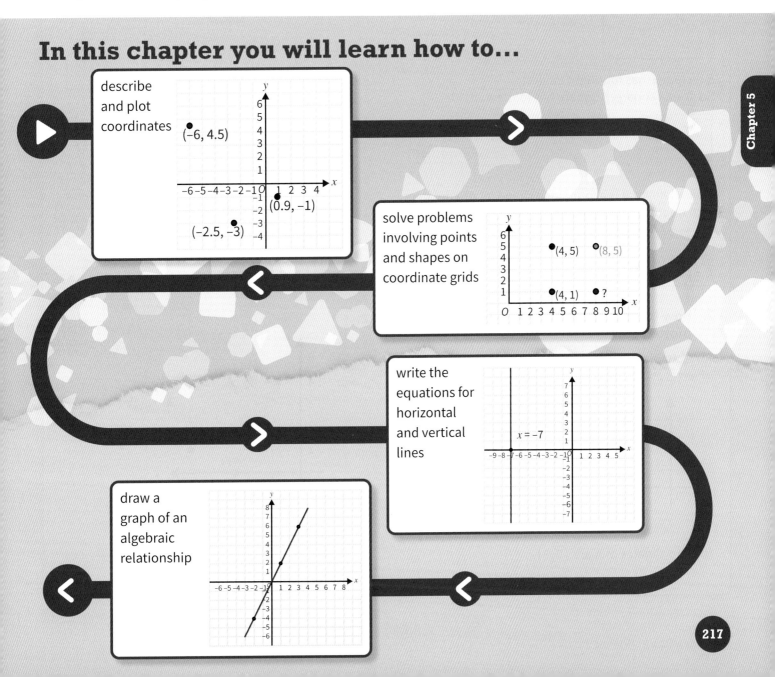

describe and plot coordinates

solve problems involving points and shapes on coordinate grids

write the equations for horizontal and vertical lines

draw a graph of an algebraic relationship

Reactivate your knowledge

If you can answer the questions on these pages then you should be ready for the chapter.

Some questions are there to help you to remember some maths from primary school and some are to help you remember maths from earlier in the book. If you see this symbol 🔗 it tells you where that information was introduced in an earlier chapter. If you are struggling with those questions you could go back and read through it again.

5.1 Plotting coordinates

You should know...

1. properties of quadrilaterals

For example

A rectangle has four right angles.
So does a square. A square has four equal sides.

A parallelogram is a four-sided shape, or quadrilateral, with opposite sides parallel.

2. how to write the coordinates of plotted points

For example

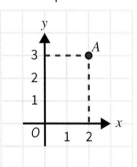

The coordinates of A are $(2,3)$.

Check in

1.

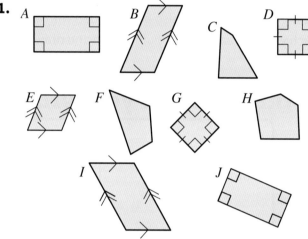

Write the letters of:

a the squares,

b the rectangles,

c the parallelograms.

2.

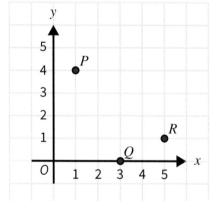

Write the coordinates of:

a P b Q c R

5.2 Coordinates, formulae, and graphs

You should know...

3. how to work out pairs of values which satisfy an equation with two variables

For example

$x = 5$, $y = 7$ and $x = 8$, $y = 4$ satisfy the equation $x + y = 12$

 Look back to Section 4.2

Check in

3. Find three pairs of values that satisfy each of these equations:

a $2 \times \boxed{} = 4 \times \boxed{}$

b $x + y = 18$

c $y = 5x$

5.1.1 Coordinates in all four quadrants

> ### Objective
>
> You will learn how to:
> * describe and plot coordinates

A coordinate grid can be used to describe the positions of points and to solve geometric and algebraic problems. You use a grid with two perpendicular number lines called axes to describe the position of a point.

The horizontal number line on a coordinate grid is called the **x-axis** and the vertical number line is called the **y-axis**.

> ### Key point
>
> The axes split the grid into four sections, called **quadrants**. The quadrants are labelled anticlockwise starting from the top right.

You use a **coordinate pair** to describe a position on the coordinate grid. The first number is the horizontal position of the point, and the second number is the vertical position. For example, in the diagram shown:

* the point A is in the first quadrant and has coordinates $(4, 2)$,
* the point B is on the x-axis and has coordinates $(-4, 0)$,
* the point C is in the fourth quadrant and has coordinates $(2, -5)$.

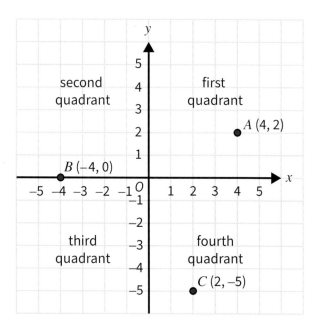

The point with coordinates $(0, 0)$ is called the **origin**.

> ### Key point
>
> A coordinate pair is written (x, y) where x is the position from the origin in the x-direction and y is the position from the origin in the y-direction.

Worked example	Thinking	Your turn!
Plot these points on a coordinate grid: $A\ (4,3)$ $B\ (-2,4)$ $C\ (0,-2)$ $D\ (3,-2.5)$	Which number tells us the horizontal position and which number tells us the vertical position? Where do we put a point with a zero coordinate?	Plot these points on a copy of the coordinate grid: $A\ (-1,2)$ $B\ (2,0)$ $C\ (-3,-4)$ $D\ (3.5,2.5)$

I need to remember that the first number is the horizontal position, and the second number is the vertical position.

A zero x-value means the point is on the vertical y-axis.

▲ Example-problem pair 1

You can draw your own axes. When you draw coordinate axes, you should use a ruler, label the axes, and number the axes with equally spaced intervals.

5.1.1 Fluency

In this exercise you can practise applying the mathematical methods that you have just learnt.

1 Write the coordinates of each point A to E.

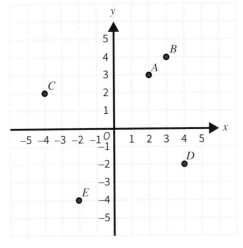

2 Plot each of these points on a coordinate grid. Use a copy of the axes from question **1**.

a $A\ (2.5,3)$ d $D\ (2.5,-5.5)$
b $B\ (-3.5,4)$ e $E\ (-3,-4.5)$
c $C\ (-2.5,3.5)$ f $F\ (-2.5,-3.5)$

3 Draw a suitable coordinate grid and plot each of these points on the grid.

a $A\ (1.2,5.6)$ d $D\ (-2.8,5.2)$
b $B\ (3.5,2.4)$ e $E\ (4.5,-3.4)$
c $C\ (-3.6,2.2)$ f $F\ (-4.4,-5.8)$

Now check your answers. Did you get any wrong and can you work out why?

Chapter 5

5.1.2 Points and midpoints on coordinate grids

You can find the **midpoint** of two points using their coordinates. The midpoint of two points is the point halfway between the two. You can work it out by finding the value halfway between the x-coordinates of the two points and the value halfway between the y-coordinates.

You find the value halfway between two numbers by adding them up then dividing by two.

For example, the midpoint of $A(3,1)$ and $B(5,9)$ is $(4,5)$ since:

- the midpoint of the x-coordinates is $(3+5)\div 2 = 4$
- the midpoint of the y-coordinates is $(1+9)\div 2 = 5$

You can use capital letters to label a line segment. For example, AB is the straight line connecting points A and B.

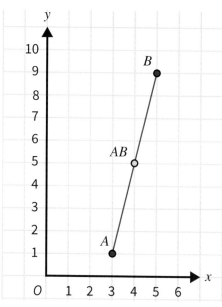

Investigate Further 🔍

Sita and Jen want to meet somewhere that is the same distance from both of their homes. On a map, Sita's home has coordinates $(9,2)$ and Jen's has coordinates $(1,10)$. How many points are the same distance from their homes? Where might be the most sensible place to meet?

Worked example	Thinking	Your turn!
The points A and B have these coordinates: $A(7,2)$, $B(9,-8)$. Find the midpoint of A and B.		The points A and B have these coordinates: $A(3,-7)$, $B(-3,-1)$. Find the midpoint of A and B.
Midpoint of x-coordinates $= (7+9)\div 2$ $= 16\div 2$ $= 8$ Midpoint of y-coordinates $= (2+-8)\div 2$ $= -6\div 2$ $= -3$ So the midpoint of A and B is $(8,-3)$.	*What rule can we use to find the midpoint?*	

I need to add up the x-coordinates of both points and divide by two, and then repeat for the y-coordinates.

▲ Example-problem pair 1

Investigate Further 🔍

Algebraic points can also be reflected, can you work out the coordinates of the point (a, b) after it has been reflected in the x-axis or the y-axis?

If you know the coordinates of a midpoint and one of the points, you can use a diagram to find the coordinates of the other point.

You can **reflect** a point in the x-axis or the y-axis.

For example, the point $(6, 2)$ when reflected in the x-axis is $(6, -2)$ and the point $(8, 4)$ when reflected in the y-axis is $(-8, 4)$.

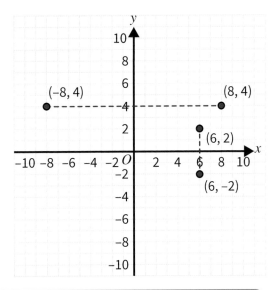

5.1.2 Fluency

In this exercise you can practise applying the mathematical methods that you have just learnt.

1 Look at this graph.

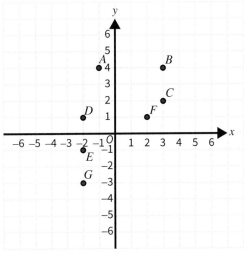

a Write the coordinates of the midpoint of:
   i AB,   ii BC.

b Which of points E, F, and G is a reflection of point D in the x-axis?

2 Point A has coordinates $(-2, 3)$.

a Write the coordinates of point A when it is reflected in:
   i the x-axis,   ii the y-axis.

Point B has coordinates $(5, 3)$ and point C has coordinates $(4, -3)$.

b Write the coordinates of the midpoint of:
   i AB,   ii AC,   iii BC.

3 Point C has coordinates $(5, -3)$.

a Write the coordinates of point C when it is reflected in:
   i the x-axis,   ii the y-axis.

Point A has coordinates $(-3, 0)$ and point B has coordinates $(2, 2)$.

b Write the coordinates of the midpoint of:
   i AB,   ii AC,   iii BC.

4 Point P has coordinates $(4, 6)$.

a K is the midpoint of the line segment PQ and has coordinates $(3, 8)$.
Find the coordinates of Q.

b L is the midpoint of the line segment PR and has coordinates $(7, -2)$.
Find the coordinates of R.

c M is the midpoint of the line segment PS and has coordinates $(-1, 11)$.
Find the coordinates of S.

d N is the midpoint of the line segment PT and has coordinates $(-5, -6)$.
Find the coordinates of T.

Now check your answers. Did you get any wrong and can you work out why?

5.1.3 Shapes on coordinate grids

Objective

You will learn how to:

- solve problems involving shapes on coordinate grids

Language

The word 'vertex' for a corner of a shape comes from the Latin word *vertere* which means 'to turn'.

You can solve problems with shapes by drawing them on a coordinate grid and using your knowledge of their properties.

Squares, rectangles, and parallelograms all have two pairs of parallel sides. You can use this fact to find the coordinates of a corner, which is also called a **vertex**.

Worked example	Thinking	Your turn!
A square $PQRS$ has vertices at $P\,(3,4)$, $Q\,(0,6)$, and $R\,(-2,3)$. Plot these points on a coordinate grid with axes that go from -6 to 6. Work out the coordinates of S.	*What properties of a square help us to do this?*	A rectangle $PQRS$ has vertices at $P\,(-1,5)$, $Q\,(-4,6)$, and $R\,(-6,0)$. Plot these points on a coordinate grid with axes that go from -7 to 7. Work out the coordinates of S.

I know that a square has two pairs of parallel sides.

Looking at side QR, you can see that point R is 2 units to the left and 3 units down from point Q.

So, since side PS is parallel and the same length as QR, the point S must be 2 units to the left and 3 units down from point P.

So the coordinates of S must be at $(1, 1)$

▲ Example-problem pair 1

5.1.3 Fluency

In this exercise you can practise applying the mathematical methods that you have just learnt.

1 Points A, B, C, and D have coordinates $(-2, 4)$, $(4, 4)$, $(4, 2)$, and $(-2, 2)$ respectively.
a Plot the points on a suitable set of axes.
The points are joined to make a shape $ABCD$.
b What is the name of the shape?

2 $A(-4, 3)$, $B(2, 3)$, and $C(2, -3)$ are three vertices of a square.
a Plot the given points on a suitable set of axes.
b Write the coordinates of the fourth vertex, D.

3 Points A, B, C, and D have coordinates $(-2, 4)$, $(2, 2)$, $(2, -4)$, and $(-2, -2)$ respectively.
a Plot the points on a suitable set of axes.
The coordinates are joined to make a shape $ABCD$.
b What is the name of the shape?

4 The points A, B, and C are vertices of a rectangle.

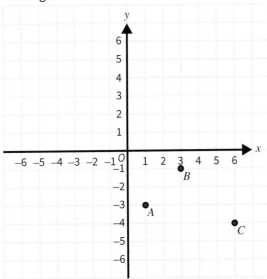

Write the coordinates of the fourth vertex, D.

5 Look at this graph.

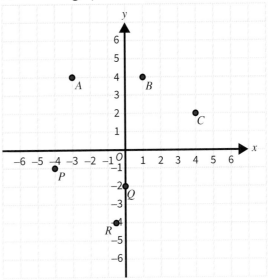

a P, Q, and R are three vertices of a rectangle. Write the coordinates of the fourth vertex, S.
b A, B, and C are three vertices of a parallelogram $ABCD$. Write the coordinates of the fourth vertex, D.

6 $ABCD$ is a parallelogram.

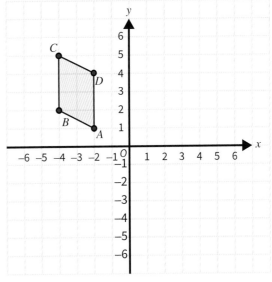

Write the coordinates of the vertices of parallelogram $A'B'C'D'$ when $ABCD$ is reflected in the y-axis.

Now check your answers. Did you get any wrong and can you work out why?

5.1 Exercises

5.1 Intelligent practice

"Why is it intelligent?" You might notice a connection when you move on from one question to the next. You can use the Reflect, Expect, Check, Explain process to:

- *reflect* on what's different between each question and the one that came before
- decide how you *expect* this answer to be different
- complete the question and *check* your answer
- *explain* to yourself why your expectation was correct or incorrect.

Question 1a   **EXAMPLE**

Write the coordinates of point A.

A has coordinates $(2, 1)$.

Question 1b

Write the coordinates of point B.

Reflect: Point B is directly above point A.

Expect: I think that the x-coordinate of B will be the same but the y-coordinate will be bigger.

Check: The coordinates of B are $(2, 2)$.

Explain: I was right! Points A and B have the same x-coordinate but the y-coordinate of B is bigger since it is above A.

---

1   Use the diagram to write the coordinates of points A, B, C, D, E, and F.

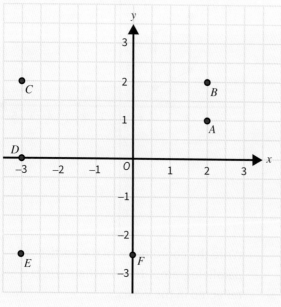

2   **a**   Copy the axes shown.

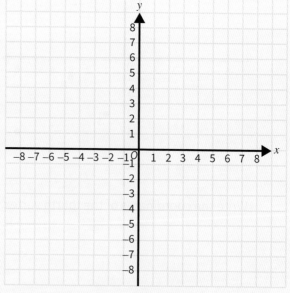

    b   Plot these points on the axes:

       $A\,(3, 8)$, $B\,(3, 2)$, $C\,(3, -2)$, $D\,(0, -2)$,
       $E\,(0, 5)$, $F\,(-4, 5)$, and $G\,(-2, 5)$.

3 Find the midpoint of each pair of coordinates.
a $(0,0)$ and $(8,6)$
b $(0,0)$ and $(6,8)$
c $(0,0)$ and $(12,16)$
d $(12,16)$ and $(0,0)$
e $(12,16)$ and $(2,2)$
f $(12,16)$ and $(4,4)$
g $(-12,16)$ and $(-4,4)$
h $(-12,-16)$ and $(-4,-4)$
i $(-120,-160)$ and $(-40,-40)$
j $(-120,-160)$ and $(40,40)$
k $(-30,-40)$ and $(10,10)$
l $(-0.3,-0.4)$ and $(0.1,0.1)$
m $(0.7,-0.4)$ and $(1.1,0.1)$

4 Draw a suitable coordinate grid and use the points to plot the quadrilateral $ABCD$. Write its name in each case.
a $A\,(2,3),\ B\,(4,3),\ C\,(4,5),\ D\,(2,5)$
b $A\,(3,3),\ B\,(5,3),\ C\,(5,5),\ D\,(3,5)$
c $A\,(3,3),\ B\,(5,3),\ C\,(5,6),\ D\,(3,6)$
d $A\,(2,3),\ B\,(5,3),\ C\,(5,6),\ D\,(2,6)$
e $A\,(2,-2),\ B\,(5,-2),\ C\,(5,6),\ D\,(2,6)$
f $A\,(4,-4),\ B\,(10,-4),\ C\,(10,12),\ D\,(4,12)$
g $A\,(4,-4),\ B\,(10,-4),\ C\,(6,12),\ D\,(0,12)$
h $A\,(4,4),\ B\,(10,4),\ C\,(6,-12),\ D\,(0,-12)$

5 Use copies of the axes from question 2. Use the points to plot a square and write the coordinates of the fourth vertex.
a $(2,1),\ (6,1),\ (6,5)$
b $(3,1),\ (7,1),\ (7,5)$
c $(3,-4),\ (7,-4),\ (7,0)$
d $(-3,-4),\ (-7,-4),\ (-7,0)$
e $(-3,4),\ (-7,4),\ (-7,0)$
f $(-1.5,2),\ (-3.5,2),\ (-3.5,0)$

6 You have the coordinates of three vertices of a square. Plot the square on a coordinate grid using axes from -12 to 12 for x and y. Write the coordinates of the fourth vertex.
a $(0,4),\ (-4,0),\ (0,-4)$
b $(0,2),\ (-4,-2),\ (0,-6)$
c $(2,2),\ (-2,-2),\ (2,-6)$
d $(2,4),\ (-2,0),\ (2,-4)$
e $(4,8),\ (-4,0),\ (4,-8)$
f $(-4,8),\ (4,0),\ (-4,-8)$
g $(-1,2),\ (1,0),\ (-1,-2)$

7 You have the coordinates of three vertices of a parallelogram $ABCD$. Plot the parallelogram on a coordinate grid and write the coordinates of the fourth vertex, D.
a $A\,(0,0),\ B\,(8,0),\ C\,(10,4)$
b $A\,(2,0),\ B\,(8,0),\ C\,(10,4)$
c $A\,(2,0),\ B\,(8,2),\ C\,(10,6)$
d $A\,(2,0),\ B\,(8,-2),\ C\,(10,-6)$
e $A\,(0.5,0),\ B\,(2,-2),\ C\,(2.5,-6)$

5.1 Method selection

In these questions you'll need to think carefully about which methods to apply.
For some questions you might need to use skills from earlier chapters.

1 Use the diagram to answer the questions.

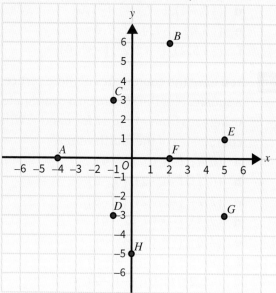

a Write the name and coordinates of a point on the x-axis.

b Write the name and coordinates of a point on the y-axis.

c Write the name and coordinates of a point in the first quadrant.

d Write the name and coordinates of a point in the third quadrant.

e Work out the midpoint of the points B and F.

f Work out the midpoint of the points C and E.

g Work out the midpoint of the points G and H.

h What type of quadrilateral is $ADFC$?

i What type of triangle is CFB?

j What type of triangle is DGE?

k Write the name of a point that won't change if it is reflected in the x-axis.

l Write the coordinates of C following reflection in the y-axis.

m The points $D, A,$ and B are three vertices of a rectangle. Work out the coordinates of the fourth vertex.

2 A quadrilateral $PQRS$ has vertices at $P\,(2,-4)$, $Q\,(2,6)$, $R\,(-3,6)$ and $S\,(-3,-4)$. The quadrilateral is drawn on a grid where one unit $= 1\,\text{cm}$.

a Write the name of the quadrilateral.

b Work out the perimeter of the quadrilateral.

c Work out the area of the quadrilateral.

3 Two villages are shown on a map at the points $(2,27)$ and $(12,14)$.
A mobile phone mast needs to be placed as close as possible to each village and the same distance from both villages. Work out the point where the mast should be placed.

4 Copy and complete the table.

Point A	Point B	Midpoint
$(3,9)$	$(7,1)$	$(\ldots,\ldots)$
$(-2,8)$	$(-8,-6)$	$(\ldots,\ldots)$
$(5,-4)$	$(2,\ldots)$	$(\ldots,4)$
$(13,\ldots)$	$(\ldots,15)$	$(12,7)$
$(\ldots,-11)$	$(19,24)$	$(0,\ldots)$
$(-13,21)$	$(\ldots,\ldots)$	$(-4,-3)$

5 A rectangle $PQRS$ has vertices at $P\,(6,-1)$, $Q\,(6,-5)$ and $R\,(-8,-5)$.

a Find the coordinates of the point S.

The rectangle $P'Q'R'S'$ is the reflection of $PQRS$ in the x-axis.

b Find the coordinates of P', Q', R' and S'.

6 A quadrilateral $ABCD$ has vertices at $A\,(-0.8,-0.2)$, $B\,(-0.8,-1.4)$, $C\,(0.4,-1.4)$ and $D\,(0.4,-0.2)$.

a Plot the points and draw the quadrilateral on a coordinate grid.

b Write the name of the quadrilateral.

The quadrilateral is now drawn on a grid where one unit = 1 cm.

c Work out the perimeter of the quadrilateral.

d Work out the area of the quadrilateral.

7 A square $ABCD$ has vertices at $A\,(2,6)$, $B\,(-6,8)$ and $C\,(-8,0)$.

a Find the coordinates of the point D.

The points E, F, G, and H are the midpoints of AB, BC, CD, and DA respectively.

b Find the coordinates of E, F, G, and H.

c Write the name of the quadrilateral $EFGH$.

8 The diagonals of a parallelogram cross each other at their midpoints.

P has coordinates $(4,9)$, Q has coordinates $(-1,2)$, and the midpoint of the diagonals, M, has coordinates $(11,7)$.

Work out the coordinates of R and S.

5.1 Purposeful practice

There may be more than one way to approach these questions. Once you have answered a question one way, can you think of another way?

1 Write the coordinates of:
a a point in the first quadrant,
b a point in the second quadrant,
c a point in the third quadrant,
d a point in the fourth quadrant,
e a point on the x-axis,
f a point on the y-axis,
g the origin.

Find possible positions for the other two vertices of the square.

b One vertex of a square is at the origin. Find possible positions for the other three vertices of the square.

c One vertex of a square is at the point $(2,1)$. Find possible positions for the other three vertices of the square.

2 Look at this graph.
a Two vertices of a square are at the points shown.

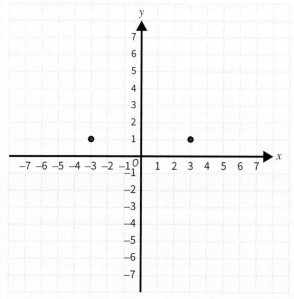

3 A rectangle is drawn on a grid where one unit = 1 cm.
The area of the rectangle is $30\,\text{cm}^2$.
Write possible coordinates of the vertices of the rectangle.

4 A rectangle is drawn on a grid where one unit = 1 cm.
The perimeter of the rectangle is $20\,\text{cm}$.
Write possible coordinates of the vertices of the rectangle.

5 The midpoint of the points A and B is $(3,5)$. Write possible coordinates for A and B.

Chapter 5

Coordinates, formulae, and graphs

5.2.1 Horizontal and vertical lines

Objective

You will:

- understand that on a horizontal or vertical line either x or y is constant

Look at the points on the coordinate grid shown.

Their coordinates are: $A\,(2,-1)$, $B\,(2,-2)$, $C\,(2,3)$, $D\,(2,0)$ and $E\,(2,1.5)$.

The x-coordinate of each of the points is 2, but the y-coordinates are all different.

You can draw a line that goes through these points, as shown in the diagram. This line could continue forever in both directions.

All the points on this line have x-coordinate 2. Using algebra, this rule is written as $x = 2$

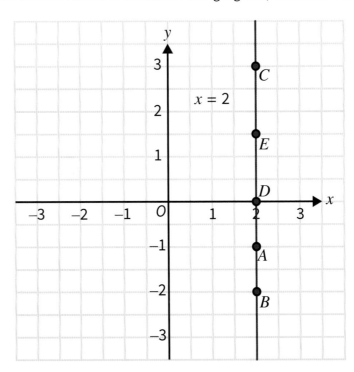

Key point

- An algebraic rule that describes all the points on a line is called the equation of that line.
- The equation of a horizontal line is $y = a$ where a is a constant.
- The equation of a vertical line is $x = b$ where b is a constant.

Worked example	Thinking	Your turn!
These points are plotted on a coordinate grid and a line is drawn through them: $(-1,-2),(2,-2),(4.2,-2)$. Write a rule to describe the points on the line. 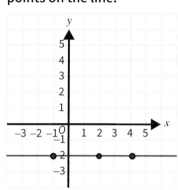	*What do all the points have in common?*	These points are plotted on a coordinate grid and a line is drawn through them: $(-3,3),(-3,-2),(-3,1.8)$. Write a rule to describe the points on the line. 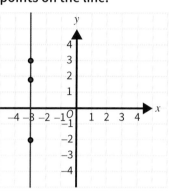
The y-coordinate of every point is -2	*Can we use algebra to write this?*	
Using algebra this is written $y=-2$		

I look at the three points and see that the y-coordinate is the same in all of them but the x-coordinate changes.

I know that horizontal lines always have equation $y=a$ for some constant a

Chapter 5

▲ Example-problem pair 1

5.2.1 Fluency

In this exercise you can practise applying the mathematical methods that you have just learnt.

1 On a single coordinate grid:
 a plot these points $(1,3),(-4,3),(2,3)$
 b draw a line through the points,
 c write a rule to describe the points on the line.

2 On a single coordinate grid:
 a plot these points $(2,5),(2,-3),(2,0)$
 b draw a line through the points,
 c write a rule to describe the points on the line.

3 On a single coordinate grid, draw the line with equation:
 a $x=5$ **b** $x=-2$ **c** $y=4$ **d** $y=-6$

4 Write the equation of lines A to D

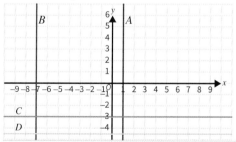

5 Draw each of these lines on a coordinate grid. Label each line with its equation
 a $y=2.5$ **b** $x=-3.2$ **c** $x=5.8$ **d** $y=-1.3$

Now check your answers. Did you get any wrong and can you work out why?

5.2.2 Graphs of relationships

Objective

You will:
- understand that a graph shows all the points (within a range) that satisfy a relationship

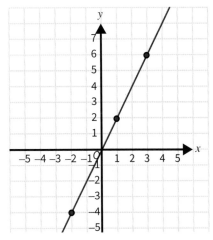

You can represent the relationship between two variables **graphically**.

For example, a rule could be that the y-coordinate is double the x-coordinate. Some examples of points that satisfy this rule are $(1, 2)$, $(3, 6)$ and $(-2, -4)$. You can represent this relationship graphically by plotting and joining up the points that satisfy it, as shown.

This line could continue forever in both directions. Every point on the line satisfies the rule that the y-coordinate is double the x-coordinate. Between any two points on the line there are an infinite number of points that satisfy the relationship. Any point not on the line will not satisfy the rule.

Worked example	Thinking	Your turn!
Plot these points on a coordinate grid and draw a line that passes through them all: $(0, 1)$, $(3, 4)$, $(-4, -3)$. Explain whether the point $(-2.3, -1.3)$ lies on the line.	*Can we describe the relationship between the x-coordinates and the y-coordinates?*	Plot these points on a coordinate grid and draw a line that passes through them all: $(0, 0)$, $(2, 8)$, $(-1, -4)$. Explain whether the point $(-2, -0.5)$ lies on the line.

> The y-coordinate is always one more than the x-coordinate.

> If I have plotted the points correctly then I should be able to use a ruler to draw a straight line through them all.

> I need to check whether this point satisfies the rule that the y-coordinate is one more than the x-coordinate.

What would the relationship between the x- and y-coordinates be if the given point lies on the line?

Worked example	Thinking	Your turn!
The x-coordinate is -2.3 and the y-coordinate is -1.3 $-2.3 + 1 = -1.3$ So the y-coordinate is one more than the x-coordinate. Therefore, the point $(-2.3, -1.3)$ does lie on the line.		

Investigate Further 🔍

Plot each set of points and decide whether the relationship can be represented graphically by a straight line or a curve.

a $(-2, -2), (1, 3), (3, 8)$
b $(-2, 5), (1, 3), (5, -2)$
c $(-2, 4), (0, 0), (2, 4)$

▲ Example-problem pair 1

All the graphs you have seen in this section have been straight lines. But not all relationships are represented graphically by a straight line. You will learn more about graphs that are curves in Book 3.

5.2.2 Fluency

In this exercise you can practise applying the mathematical methods that you have just learnt.

1 Here are some points: $(2, 10), (3, 15), (-1, -5)$.
  a Describe the relationship between the x-coordinate and the y-coordinate for each of these points.
  b Plot the points on a coordinate grid and draw a line that passes through them all.
  c Does $(1.5, 7.5)$ lie on the line you have drawn?

2 A line is drawn.

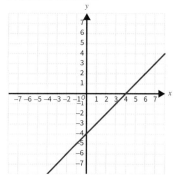

  a Which of these coordinates lie on the line?
    i $(4, 0)$ iii $(0, 0)$ v $(-1, -5)$
    ii $(3, -1)$ iv $(2, 2)$ vi $(-2, 2)$

b Describe what all of the points you have chosen in part **a** have in common.
c Does $(0.5, -3.5)$ lie on the line?

3 Here are some points:
$(-5, 5), (-2, 2), (1, -1), (3, -3)$.
  a Describe the relationship between the x-coordinates and the y-coordinates.
  b Plot the points on a coordinate grid and draw a line that passes through them all.
  c If the line was extended, explain whether the point $(2178, -2178)$ would lie on it.

4 Here are some points:
$(0, 0), (1, 1), (2, 4), (3, 9), (4, 16)$.
  a Describe the relationship between the x-coordinates and the y-coordinates.
  b Plot the points. Is it possible to draw a straight line through them?

Now check your answers. Did you get any wrong and can you work out why?

Chapter 5

5.2.3 Representing relationships algebraically and graphically

Objective

You will learn how to:
- plot points and draw a graph of an algebraic relationship

Remember from Chapter 4 that a formula is a rule that shows the relationship between two or more variables. For example, $y = x + 3$ is a formula.

When you have a relationship that is represented graphically, you can write a formula to describe it **algebraically**.

Key point

Representing a relationship algebraically means using a formula to describe the relationship.

You can use a table of values to help you work out the relationship. The x-coordinates go along the top row and the corresponding y-coordinates go below them in the bottom row.

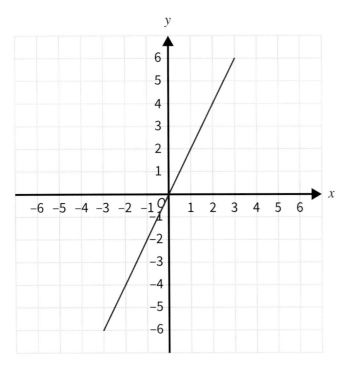

For example, for the graph shown, you could draw a table of values like this:

x	−3	−2	−1	0	1	2	3
y	−6	−4	−2	0	2	4	6

For all of these points, you can see that the y-coordinate is double the x-coordinate.

You could write a formula to show this relationship: $y = 2x$

When you have a relationship expressed algebraically you can use substitution to find some points that satisfy the relationship. Then you can use these points to represent the relationship graphically. A table of values is also useful for this.

Worked example	Thinking	Your turn!
Copy and complete the table of values for the relationship $y = 6x$, and then draw a graph to represent the relationship. What shape is the graph?	How can we use a formula to find the value of a variable?	Copy and complete the table of values for the relationship $y = x + 6$, and then draw a graph to represent the relationship. What shape is the graph?

x	-2	-1	0	1	2
y					

x	-2	-1	0	1	2
y					

> I need to substitute each of the x-values into the formula to find the corresponding y-value to fill in the table.

Substitute into the formula.

When $x = -2$, $y = 6 \times (-2) = -12$

When $x = -1$, $y = 6 \times (-1) = -6$

When $x = 0$, $y = 6 \times 0 = 0$

When $x = 1$, $y = 6 \times 1 = 6$

When $x = 2$, $y = 6 \times 2 = 12$

The completed table is

x	-2	-1	0	1	2
y	-12	-6	0	6	12

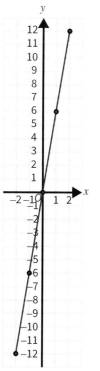

What do we need to remember when we draw coordinate axes?

> I need to remember to use a ruler, label the axes, and number the axes with equally spaced intervals.

The graph is a straight line.

▲ Example-problem pair 1

Chapter 5

5.2.3 Fluency

In this exercise you can practise applying the mathematical methods that you have just learnt.

1 Use a coordinate grid for this question.
a Copy and complete the coordinates so that the y-coordinate is two more than the x-coordinate.
   i $(1,...)$
   ii $(2,...)$
   iii $(3,...)$
   iv $(0,...)$
   v $(-1,...)$
   vi $(-2,...)$
   vii $(-3,...)$
b Plot the points from part **a** on a coordinate grid.
c Draw a line that passes through the points.

2 Here are some incomplete coordinates.
a Copy and complete the coordinates so that the y-coordinate is three times the x-coordinate.
   i $(1,...)$
   ii $(2,...)$
   iii $(0,...)$
   iv $(-1,...)$
   v $(-2,...)$
b Plot the points from part **a** on a coordinate grid.
c Draw a line that passes through the points.

3 Look at this table.

x	-3	-2	-1	0	1	2	3
y							

a Copy and complete the table of values for the relationship $y = x - 3$
b Represent the relationship graphically.

4 Look at this table.

x	-3	-2	-1	0	1	2	3
y							

a Copy and complete the table of values for the relationship $y = 2x$
b Represent the relationship graphically.

5 Represent these relationships graphically on separate coordinate grids.
a $y = x$ **b** $y = \dfrac{x}{2}$

6 Here is a set of coordinates:

$(-3, -12)$

$(-2, -8)$

$(-1, -4)$

$(0, 0)$

$(1, 4)$

$(2, 8)$

$(3, 12)$

a Represent the relationship between the x and y coordinates graphically.
b Express algebraically the mathematical relationship that connects the x and y coordinates.

7 The graph shows the relationship between two variables. Express this relationship algebraically.

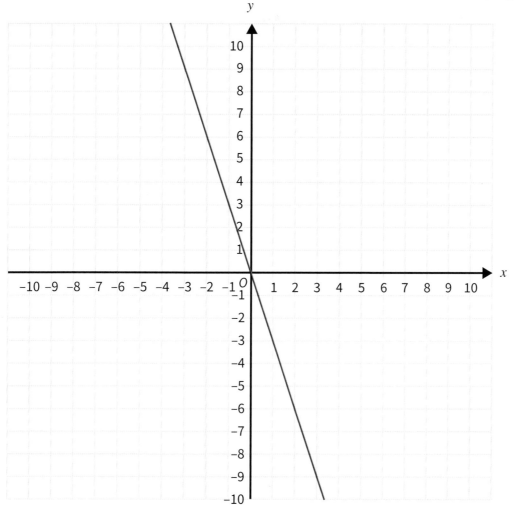

8 Look at this table.

x	−3	−2	−1	0	1	2	3
y							

a Copy and complete the table of values for the relationship $y = 2 - x^2$

b Represent the relationship graphically.

c Describe the shape of the graph you have drawn.

Now check your answers. Did you get any wrong and can you work out why?

5.2 Exercises

5.2 Intelligent practice

"Why is it intelligent?" You might notice a connection when you move on from one question to the next. You can use the Reflect, Expect, Check, Explain process to:

- *reflect* on what's different between each question and the one that came before
- decide how you *expect* this answer to be different
- complete the question and *check* your answer
- *explain* to yourself why your expectation was correct or incorrect.

> **EXAMPLE**
>
> **Question 1a**
>
> A graph is drawn to represent the relationship 'y is 8 times x'.
>
> Decide whether the point $(2, 16)$ lies on the line.
>
> Yes since $16 = 8 \times 2$
>
> **Question 1b**
>
> Decide whether the point $(16, 2)$ lies on the line.
>
> **Reflect:** This is similar to question **1a**, except the x and y coordinates have been swapped.
>
> **Expect:** I think this will mean that the point is no longer on the line since the relationship between x and y will be the other way around.
>
> **Check:** $8 \times 16 = 128$ and not 2
>
> **Explain:** I was right! The point $(16, 2)$ is not on the line since the y-coordinate is not 8 times the x-coordinate.

---

1 A graph is drawn to represent the relationship 'y is 8 times x'.

Decide whether each of these points lies on the line.

- **a** $(2, 16)$
- **b** $(16, 2)$
- **c** $(16, 128)$
- **d** $(-16, -128)$
- **e** $(-1.6, -12.8)$

2 A graph is drawn to represent the relationship 'y is 5 more than x'.

Decide whether each of these points lies on the line.

- **a** $(0, 5)$
- **b** $(1, 6)$
- **c** $(-1, -6)$
- **d** $(-6, -1)$
- **e** $(-60, -10)$

3 A line is drawn on a graph to represent the relationship 'y is half of x'.

Copy and complete the coordinate pairs so that each point lies on the line.

- **a** $(20, \ldots)$
- **b** $(10, \ldots)$
- **c** $(-10, \ldots)$
- **d** $(-1, \ldots)$
- **e** $(0, \ldots)$

4 For each formula given:

- **a** $y = x$
- **b** $y = x - 1$
- **c** $y = x - 2$
- **d** $y = x - 3$

  i copy and complete this table of values,

x	-2	-1	0	1	2
y					

  ii represent the relationship graphically. Draw all of the graphs on the same pair of axes and remember to label each line.

5 For each formula given:

a $y = 3x$

c $y = 7x$

b $y = 6x$

d $y = -7x$

   i copy and complete this table of values,

x	−2	−1	0	1	2
y					

   ii represent the relationship graphically. Draw all of the graphs on the same pair of axes and remember to label each line.

6 Express the relationship between the x and y values algebraically for each set of points.

a $(0,1), (1,2), (2,3)$

b $(0,2), (1,3), (2,4)$

c $(0,0), (1,2), (2,4)$

d $(0,0), (1,-2), (2,-4)$

e $(0,0), (1,-4), (2,-8)$

f $(0,0), (-4,1), (-8,2)$

7 For each set of points:

a $(-1,5), (0,5), (1,5)$

b $(-1,-5), (0,5), (1,5)$

c $(-1,-5), (0,0), (1,5)$

d $(-1,-1), (0,0), (1,1)$

e $(-1,1), (0,0), (1,1)$

   i determine whether you can draw a straight line through them,

   ii if it is possible to draw a straight line through them, write the equation of the line.

5.2 Method selection

In these questions you'll need to think carefully about which methods to apply.

For some questions you might need to use skills from earlier chapters.

1 Describe the relationship between x and y for the relationship shown on each graph.

a

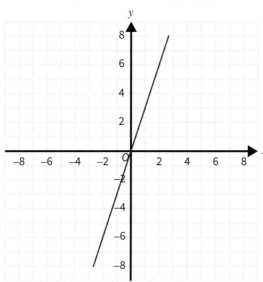

b

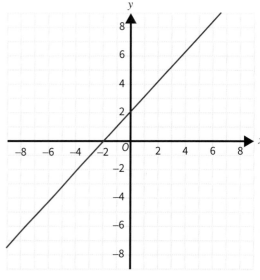

2 Find the correct equation in the box to describe each of the graphs.

$y = 3$	$y = x$
$y = x + 3$	$y = 3x$ $y = x - 3$
$x = 3$	$x = -3$
$y = -x$	$y = -3$

a
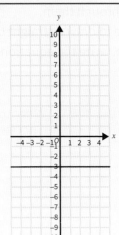

b
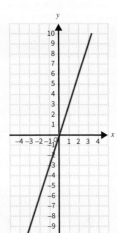

c
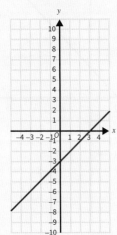

d
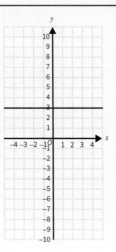

e
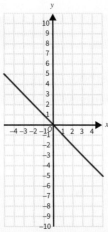

f
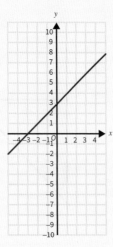

3 Draw a coordinate grid with x-axis from -12 to 12 and y-axis from -12 to 12. Represent each relationship graphically.

a y is 6 more than x

b y is 6 less than x

c y is x less than 6

d y is 6 times x

e x is 6 times y

4 Use each of the rules to complete the table of values. Show all your working and check your answers on a calculator.

a The y-coordinate is 13 less than the x-coordinate.

x	-25	6	8.3	25.4
y				

b The y-coordinate is 12 times the x-coordinate.

x	-17	3.5	13.7	184
y				

c $y = 25x$

x	-15	0.5	27	361
y				

d $y = 18 - x$

x	-21	-4.5	21	24.6
y				

e $y = -0.25x$

x	-29	-0.1	3.7	21.8
y				

5 For each table of values:

a

x	-2	0	8	20
y	-12	-10	-2	10

b

x	-5	0	8	10
y	-7.5	0	12	15

i describe the relationship between x and y,

ii represent the relationship graphically.

5.2 Purposeful practice

There may be more than one way to approach these questions.

Once you have answered a question one way, can you think of another way?

1 The graph of $y = -10x$ is drawn for x-values between -2 and 2
  a How many points are there on the line?
  b Write some points that lie on the line.
  c Write a point that does not lie on the line.

2 Find some points that lie in each of the sections of the Venn diagram.
  If you think a section is impossible to fill, explain why.

  a

  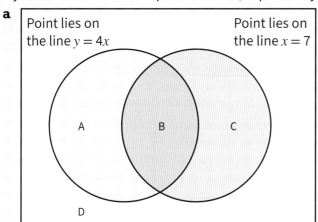

  b

  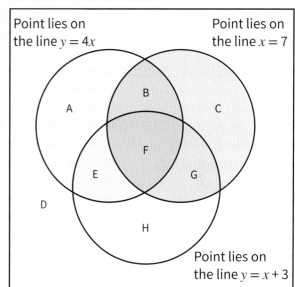

3 Here is a partially completed table of values.

x	-3	-1	0	2	5
y					25

  a Write some different rules that could be used to complete the table.
  b For each rule:
    i copy and complete the table,
    ii represent the rule graphically,
    iii describe the shape of the graph.

Watch out!

Some students have tried to answer the questions below but have unfortunately made some mistakes.

For each question do the following:

a   answer the question correctly

b   write down the mistake that each student has made

c   comment on why they might have made that mistake

d   write an explanation for each student to convince them (nicely!) that their answer cannot be correct.

1   Alanna and Fatima attempted to answer the question, "Draw a suitable coordinate grid and plot the point $(5, 7)$."

Here is Alanna's working:

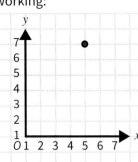

Here is Fatima's working:

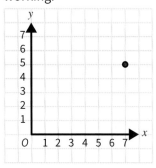

Here is Ben's working:

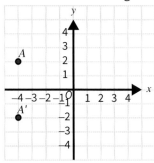

Here is Darpan's working:

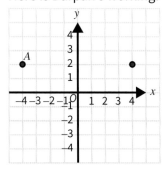

2   Ben and Darpan attempted to answer the question, "Reflect the point A in the y-axis and label it A'."

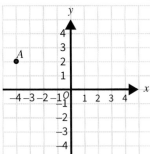

3   Jan and Zola tried to work out the answer to the question, "The points $(1, 5)$ and $(2, 10)$ lie on a line. Express the relationship between the x and y coordinates on the line algebraically."

Jan wrote:

$$y = x + 4$$

Zola wrote:

$$x = 5y$$

Check your understanding

Turn over to find the review questions

5.1 Plotting coordinates

You should now be able to...	Questions
describe and plot coordinates	1a, 1b, 2a, 3a
solve problems involving points on coordinate grids	1c, 1d, 2c, 3d
solve problems involving shapes on coordinate grids	1e − , 2b, 3b, 3c

5.2 Coordinates, formulae, and graphs

You should now be able to...	Questions
understand that in a horizontal and vertical line either x or y is constant	6
understand that a graph shows all the points (within a range) that satisfy a relationship	4d, e
plot points and draw a graph of an algebraic relationship	4a − c, 5

Chapter 5

1

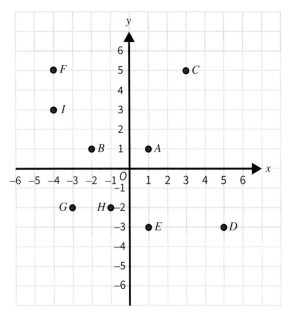

Look at the graph.

a Write the letters of the two coordinates that are shown in the first quadrant. [1 mark]

b Write the coordinates of point B. [1 mark]

c Write the coordinates of the midpoint between points D and E. [1 mark]

d Write the coordinates of the midpoint between points C and I. [2 marks]

AE and ED are two sides of a square.

e Write the coordinates of the fourth vertex of the square. [1 mark]

EH and HG are two sides of a parallelogram.

Josh says, "The fourth vertex of the parallelogram is at $(-2, -3)$."

f Is Josh correct? Explain your answer. [2 marks]

Philomena says, "The coordinates of the image of F after a reflection in the x-axis are $(4, 5)$."

g Is Philomena correct? Explain your answer. [2 marks]

2 A quadrilateral $PQRS$ has vertices at $P(3, 1)$, $Q(1, 3)$, $R(-1, 1)$ and $S(1, -5)$.

Use a grid with both the x and y axes drawn from –6 to 6

a Plot the points and draw the quadrilateral. [3 marks]

b Write the name of the quadrilateral. [1 mark]

The quadrilateral $P'Q'R'S'$ is a reflection of $PQRS$ in the y-axis.

c Write the coordinates of P', Q', R' and S'. [2 marks]

---

3 A rectangle $ABCD$ has vertices $A(-7, 5)$, $B(5, 5)$ and $C(5, -3)$.

Use a grid with both the x and y axes from –8 to 8.

a Plot the points A, B, and C. [2 marks]

b Now find the coordinates of point D. [1 mark]

The rectangle represents a swimming pool.

Each unit on the grid represents $1\,m$ in real life.

c Find:

  i the perimeter of the swimming pool, [2 marks]

  ii the area of the surface of the water in the swimming pool. [2 marks]

Life guards are stationed at the midpoints of each side of the pool.

d Write the coordinates of the location of the life guards. [2 marks]

4 y is three less than x

  a Write, using algebra, a relationship between x and y [1 mark]

  b Copy and complete this table of values.

x	−4	−2	0	2	4
y					

                                                 [2 marks]

  c Represent the relationship graphically. [2 marks]

  d Max says that the point $(3, 1)$ satisfies the relationship. Use your graph from part **c** to explain why Max is incorrect. [1 mark]

  e How many points lie on the line you have drawn in part **c**? [1 mark]

5 $y = 4x$

  a Write, in words, the relationship between x and y shown by the formula. [1 mark]

  b Represent this relationship graphically. [2 marks]

6 Use a coordinate grid to answer this question.

  a Draw each of these lines on a coordinate grid. Label each line with its equation.

    i $y = 7$ [1 mark]

    ii $x = -2$ [1 mark]

    iii $x = 0$ [1 mark]

Two students are discussing a method for drawing the line $x = 3$

Jasleen says, "You have to plot all of the points that lie on the line and join them up."

Sun-young says, "No, all you need to do is draw a horizontal line through 3 on the y-axis."

  b Explain why each student is incorrect and write a correct method. [2 marks]

Key words

Make sure you can write a definition for these key terms.

coordinate grid • x-axis • y-axis • quadrant • coordinate pair • origin

midpoint • reflection • vertex (plural: vertices) • graphically • algebraically

6 Perimeter and area

Here is an allotment with vegetable beds. Each bed is the same size. What information would you need to work out the length of wood needed for the edge of each bed? How would you work out how much space is available for planting?

What comes before?	This chapter	What comes after?
Primary school • Quadrilaterals and triangles **Book 1** • Place value • Properties of numbers • Arithmetic • Expressions and equations • Coordinates	• 6.1 Properties of triangles and quadrilaterals • 6.2 Perimeter • 6.3 Area	**Book 1** • Transformations **Book 2** • Perimeter, area, and volume • Polygons • Constructions **Book 3** • Pythagoras' Theorem • Trigonometry

Introduction

In this chapter you will explore the properties of different quadrilaterals and triangles, such as equal angles, equal side lengths, and parallel and perpendicular sides. This will help you to classify polygons and find missing angles or lengths.

You will also calculate the area and perimeter of quadrilaterals, triangles and composite shapes. Perimeter is the distance around the outside of a shape. For example, you would find the perimeter of a field to work out the length of a fence that would go all around it. Area is the space inside a boundary. For example, you would find the area of a room to work out how big the carpet inside it should be.

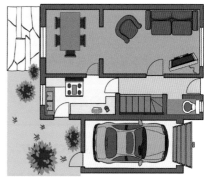

In this chapter you will learn how to...

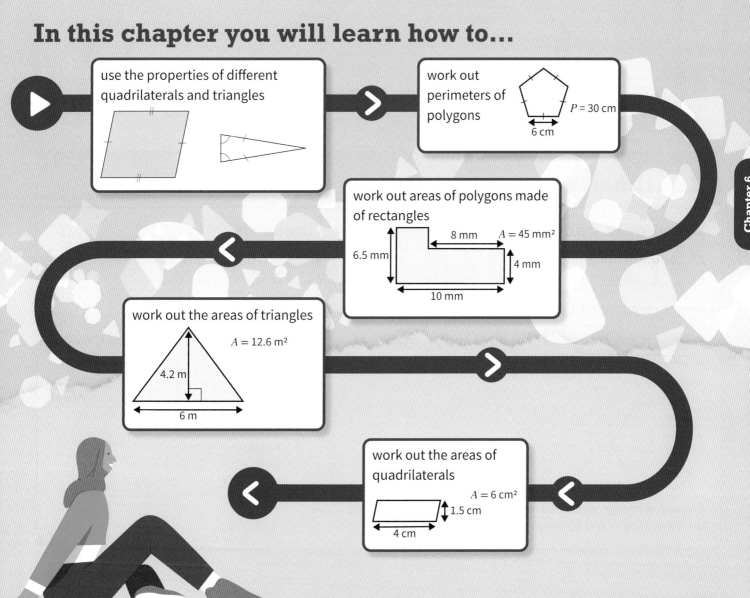

use the properties of different quadrilaterals and triangles

work out perimeters of polygons $P = 30$ cm, 6 cm

work out areas of polygons made of rectangles
8 mm $A = 45$ mm²
6.5 mm
4 mm
10 mm

work out the areas of triangles
$A = 12.6$ m²
4.2 m
6 m

work out the areas of quadrilaterals
$A = 6$ cm²
1.5 cm
4 cm

Reactivate your knowledge

If you can answer the questions on these pages then you should be ready for the chapter.

Some questions are there to help you to remember some maths from primary school and some are to help you remember maths from earlier in the book.

If you see this symbol 🔗 it tells you where that information was introduced in an earlier chapter. If you are struggling with those questions you could go back and read through it again.

6.1 Properties of triangles and quadrilaterals

You should know...

1. **that the sum of the angles in a triangle is 180°**

For example

$a + b + c = 180°$

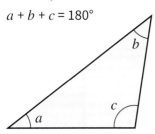

Check in

1. Find the missing angles in these triangles:

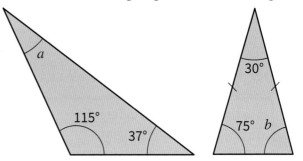

6.2 Perimeter

You should know...

2. **common units of length**

For example

mm means millimetres, which are a unit of length

3. **how many sides polygons have and properties of regular polygons**

For example

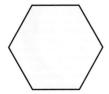

A hexagon has six sides. In a regular hexagon, all the sides are the same length and all the angles are the same size.

Check in

2. Which of these are units of length?

Litres, ml, cm, g, km, metres, tonnes, s, kg, hours

3. Write how many sides each of these regular polygons has:

   a octagon
   b pentagon
   c heptagon
   d nonagon

▶

4. how to draw polygons on coordinate grids

For example

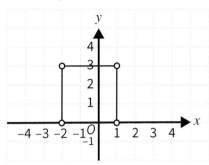

This square has vertices with coordinates $(-2,3)$, $(1,3)$, $(1,0)$, and $(-2,0)$

 Look back to Book 1 5.1.3

5. how to use an algebraic statement or formula to represent a relationship

For example

The expression $5 + x + y$ represents two different numbers, x and y, being added to 5

 Look back to Book 1 4.1.3

4. Draw each of these polygons on their own set of axes:

   a A triangle with vertices at $(4,5)$, $(1,2)$, and $(6,-2)$

   b A rectangle with vertices at $(-3,1)$, $(4,1)$, $(4,-4)$, and $(-3,-4)$

   c A parallelogram with vertices at $(-2,1)$, $(0,1)$, $(1,-3)$, and $(-1,-3)$

5. Write an expression to show each of these relationships:

   a a number, x, being added to 4

   b two lots of a number, y, being added to 10

   c three lots of one number, x, being added to a second number, y

6.3 Area

You should know...

6. how to find the area of a rectangle

For example

The area of a rectangle with sides 5 cm and 6 cm is $5 \times 6 = 30 \text{ cm}^2$

7. how to substitute variables into a formula

For example

Substituting $a = 16$ and $b = 3$ into the expression $\dfrac{a}{2} - b$ gives

$$\frac{16}{2} - 3 = 8 - 3 = 5$$

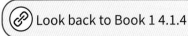 Look back to Book 1 4.1.4

Check in

6. Work out the area of a rectangle with side lengths:

   a 4 cm and 7 cm

   b 3 mm and 10.5 mm

   c 2.1 m and 17 m

7. By substituting, give the value of the expression $6x + \dfrac{y}{2}$ when

   a $x = 2$, $y = 8$

   b $x = 1.5$, $y = 10$

   c $x = 5$, $y = 7$

Chapter 6

Properties of quadrilaterals and triangles

6.1.1 Properties of quadrilaterals

Objective

You will:
- know and use the properties of different quadrilaterals

A **quadrilateral** is a **polygon** with four sides. Some quadrilaterals have sides of equal **length** or **parallel** sides and you can mark these with dashes or arrows.

Dashes show the sides that are equal in length.	Arrows show the sides that are parallel.	Arcs show the **angles** that are equal.
	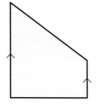	

You use double dashes, arrows, or arcs if a polygon has more than one set of equal lengths, parallel sides, or equal angles.

Square

All sides of equal length
Opposite sides parallel
4 right angles

Rectangle

Opposite sides of equal length
Opposite sides parallel
4 right angles

Parallelogram

Opposite sides of equal length
Opposite sides parallel
Opposite angles equal

Rhombus

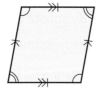

All sides of equal length
Opposite sides parallel
Opposite angles equal

Kite

2 pairs of sides of equal length
1 pair of equal angles

Trapezium (plural: trapezia)

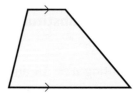

1 pair of parallel sides

If the angles in a polygon are all equal and its sides are all of equal length it is called a **regular** polygon. Otherwise, the polygon is **irregular**.

Worked example	Thinking	Your turn!
Label the missing side lengths and angles in this parallelogram. 7 cm / 80° / 6 cm / 100°	Which sides are of equal length? Which angles are equal?	Label the missing side lengths and the angle x in this kite. 3 cm / 100° / x / 8 cm
Missing lengths: 6 cm and 7 cm Missing angles: 100° and 80°	How do we show equal angles and equal side lengths?	

> In a parallelogram, the sides of equal length are opposite each other.

> In a parallelogram, opposite angles are equal.

> I can mark the equal angles and equal side lengths with arcs and dashes.

7 cm / 100° / 80° / 6 cm / 6 cm / 80° / 100° / 7 cm

▲ Example-problem pair 1

6.1.1 Fluency

In this exercise you can practise applying the mathematical methods that you have just learnt.

1 Are these statements true or false?
  a A square has four right angles.
  b A rectangle has exactly two right angles.
  c A rectangle has two pairs of equal sides.

2 $ABCD$ is a rectangle.

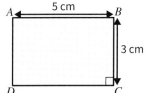

  A — 5 cm — B
  3 cm
  D — C

  a Write the length of side CD.
  b Write the length of side AD.

3 Are these statements true or false? If the statement is false, write a correct statement.
  a A parallelogram has two pairs of equal angles.
  b A rhombus has four sides of equal length.
  c None of the side lengths in a kite are equal.
  d A trapezium has one pair of parallel sides.

4 Ishita says that a parallelogram is a type of rhombus. Is Ishita correct? Explain your answer.

6.1.2 Properties of triangles

Investigate further

Draw some triangles. What do you notice about the largest angle and the longest side in each one?

Objective

You will:

- know and use the properties of different triangles

Triangles are polygons with three sides and three angles. There are different types of triangle, depending on the number of equal angles and sides of equal length.

Equilateral triangle

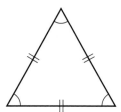

All sides of equal length
All angles equal, each 60°

Isosceles triangle

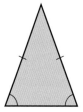

Two sides of equal length
Two equal angles

Scalene triangle

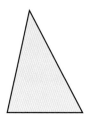

No sides of equal length
No equal angles

You can also name some triangles using their angles.

Right-angled triangle

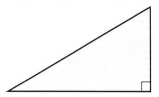

Obtuse-angled triangle

Worked example	Thinking	Your turn!
Write the size of the angle at A and the length of the side BC. What type of triangle is this? 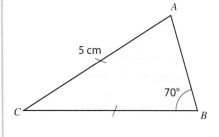	*What type of triangle is this and what other properties of the triangle can you state?*	All sides of this triangle have length 7 m. Write the size of each angle in the triangle. What type of triangle is this? 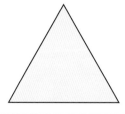

I can see that this is an isosceles triangle because two sides are equal in length. There must therefore be two equal angles.

Worked example	Thinking	Your turn!
The triangle is isosceles. The angle at A is $70°$ and BC is $5\,cm$ 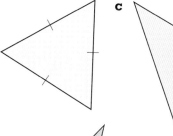	*Which angles are equal and which is different?* *Which sides have equal lengths?*	

> The angle where the two sides of equal length meet is different from the other two angles.

> Sides BC and AC are equal in length.

▲ Example-problem pair 1

6.1.2 Fluency

In this exercise you can practise applying the mathematical methods that you have just learnt.

1 Write the name of each of these triangles.

a

c

b

d

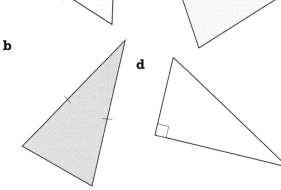

2 Are these statements true or false? If the statement is false, write a correct statement.
a An equilateral triangle has three $60°$ angles.
b All right-angled triangles are scalene.
c A scalene triangle has all three angles different sizes.
d A right-angled triangle has two other acute angles.

3 The diagram shows a square joined to an isosceles triangle.

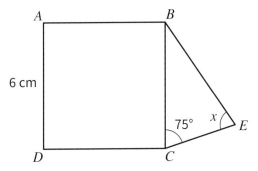

a Write down the length of side BE.
b Write down the size of angle x.

4 An isosceles triangle has an angle of $110°$.
Maria says that $110°$ can only be the different angle.
Is Maria correct? Explain your answer.

5 Are these statements true or false? If the statement is false, write a correct statement.
a An isosceles triangle can be right-angled.
b A scalene triangle can have a right angle.
c A right-angled triangle can also be equilateral.
d An isosceles triangle can be obtuse-angled.

6.1 Exercises

6.1 Intelligent practice

"Why is it intelligent?" You might notice a connection when you move on from one question to the next. You can use the Reflect, Expect, Check, Explain process to:

- *reflect* on what's different between each question and the one that came before
- decide how you *expect* this answer to be different
- complete the question and *check* your answer
- *explain* to yourself why your expectation was correct or incorrect.

Question 1a   **EXAMPLE**
Name the polygon.

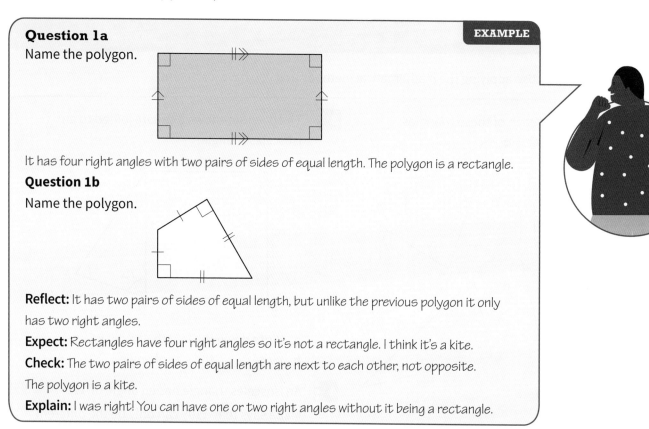

It has four right angles with two pairs of sides of equal length. The polygon is a rectangle.

Question 1b
Name the polygon.

Reflect: It has two pairs of sides of equal length, but unlike the previous polygon it only has two right angles.

Expect: Rectangles have four right angles so it's not a rectangle. I think it's a kite.

Check: The two pairs of sides of equal length are next to each other, not opposite. The polygon is a kite.

Explain: I was right! You can have one or two right angles without it being a rectangle.

1   Name each of these polygons.

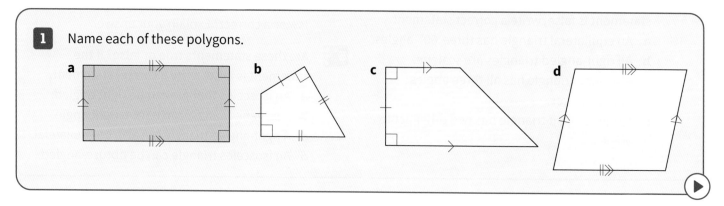

a   b   c   d

2 On a copy of each polygon, mark the correct notation.

a 4 sides of equal length

Opposite angles equal

2 pairs of parallel lines

b 2 sides of equal length

2 pairs of equal angles

1 pair of parallel lines

c 2 pairs of sides of equal length

2 pairs of equal angles

2 pairs of parallel lines

d 2 pairs of sides of equal length

4 right angles

2 pairs of parallel lines

3 Copy and complete the table by ticking which polygons always have each property.

		Kite	Parallelogram	Rectangle	Rhombus	Trapezium
a	Four right angles					
b	Four sides of equal length					
c	Two pairs of sides of equal length					
d	Two pairs of equal angles					
e	Two pairs of parallel sides					
f	One pair of parallel sides					
g	One pair of equal angles					

4 Draw a quadrilateral that could fit in each part of the table to make the statements true.

	Two pairs of sides of equal length	One pair of parallel sides
One pair of equal angles		
Two right angles		

5 Write which of these are

a quadrilaterals

b kites

c trapezia

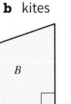
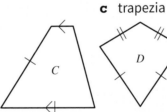
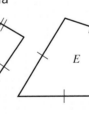
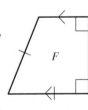

6 Write which of these triangles are isosceles and which are scalene.
If you don't have enough information to tell, write down why.

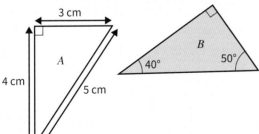
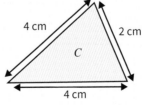
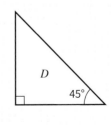

6.1 Method selection

In these questions you'll need to think carefully about which methods to apply.

For some questions you might need to use skills from earlier chapters.

1 Use a coordinate grid with axes labelled from −5 to 5 to answer each part of this question. Plot each group of coordinates. Join the points in order and name the polygon you make.
  a $(-3, 2), (0, -1), (3, 2), (0, 5)$
  b $(1, -2), (3, 0), (4, 0), (2, -2)$
  c $(-3, 1), (-1, -1), (-1, -3), (-5, 1)$
  d $(2, -5), (4, -4), (4, -3), (3, -3)$
  e $(-4, -2), (-2, -4), (-4, -5), (-5, -3)$

2 On a copy of each polygon, write an expression for each side length.

  a Square
  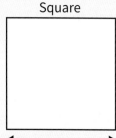
  a

  b Rectangle
  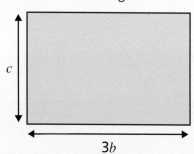
  c
  $3b$

  c Parallelogram
  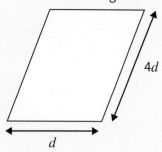
  $4d$
  d

3 Find the side lengths of the polygon shown in the diagram if
  a $d = 3$ **b** $d = 7$ **c** $d = 1.5$

  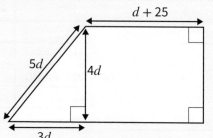
  $d + 25$
  $5d$
  $4d$
  $3d$

4 The diagram shows three triangles A, B, and C on a coordinate grid.
  a Name the type of each triangle.
  b Reflect triangles A, B, and C in the x-axis. Name the polygons made by combining each triangle with its reflection.

  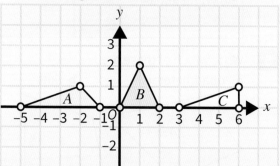

5 Use a coordinate grid with axes labelled from −5 to 5 to answer each part of this question. Plot each group of coordinates. Join the points in order and name the polygon you make.
  a $(1, 1), (0, -2), (-1, 1)$
  b $(1, 1), (0, -2), (-1, 0)$
  c $(1, 0), (0, -2), (-3, -1)$

6.1 Purposeful practice

There may be more than one way to approach these questions.
Once you have answered a question one way, can you think of another way?

1 In each diagram the polygon *ABCD* is a square.
What type of polygon is each of these? Explain each answer.

a *BFDE*   **b** *AFED*   **c** *BFDE*   **d** *EFGH*

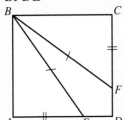 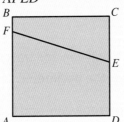 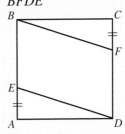 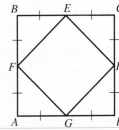

2 By joining two of the triangles *A*, *B*, and *C* shown in the diagram, find as many quadrilaterals as you can. You can use two copies of the same triangle or two different triangles. The lengths marked with a single dash are all equal and the lengths marked with two dashes are equal.

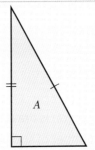 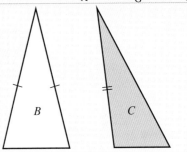

3 Here is a square *ABCD* that has been split into seven different pieces.

For each piece, name the type of polygon and work out its area in grid squares.

a *ABF*   **d** *JCH*   **g** *FGI*
b *AFD*   **e** *EDH*   **h** *DFIH*
c *BJIG*   **f** *EFIH*   **i** *BDHJ*

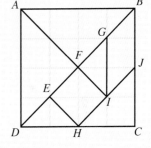

4 The diagram shows a square that has been divided into other polygons.
Write the name of the polygon in each part of the question.
The first one has been done for you.
ABF is a right-angled triangle.

a *ACEF*   **c** *BCEF*   **e** *DEF*
b *BCDF*   **d** *BCD*

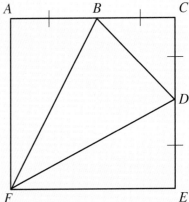

Perimeter

6.2.1 Introduction to perimeter

Objective

You will learn how to:

- work out perimeters using properties of polygons

Language

The word 'perimeter' comes from a Greek word, *perimetron*, where *peri-* means 'around' and *metron* means 'measure'.

If you start at one vertex of a polygon and travel around the sides until you return to the original vertex, you travel the **perimeter**.

To calculate the perimeter of a polygon, add together the lengths of its sides. The perimeter is a length, so the units are usually millimetres, centimetres, or metres.

Key point

The perimeter is the total length of all the sides of a polygon.

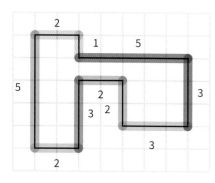

If a polygon is drawn on cm-square paper, you can find the perimeter by counting the number of squares that fit along each **edge**. Choose a vertex to start from. Count around the outer edge, noting the value of each length as you go, and stop when you get back to your starting vertex.

If the sides of this polygon were unfolded onto a straight line, the line would be $2 + 1 + 5 + 3 + 3 + 2 + 2 + 3 + 2 + 5 = 28$ cm long. So the perimeter is 28 cm.

For polygons not drawn on cm-square paper or drawn to scale, you may be given the side lengths instead.

Worked example	Thinking	Your turn!	
Find the perimeter of the polygon. 8 mm 6 mm 4 mm 5 mm 11 mm	*How do we calculate the perimeter of a polygon?*	Find the perimeter of the polygon. 7 cm 6 cm 8 cm 10 cm 5 cm	*I need to add all the side lengths.*
$6 + 8 + 4 + 5 + 11 = 34$ mm	*What units should we use?*		*Perimeter is a measure of length, and the side lengths are given in mm, so the units are mm.*

▲ Example-problem pair 1

If you want to work out the perimeter of a regular polygon, you can use the fact that all the sides are of equal length.

Worked example	Thinking	Your turn!
Find the perimeter of a square with a side of length 7 cm.	What do we know about the sides of this polygon? How do we find the perimeter?	Find the perimeter of an equilateral triangle with a side of length 9 m.
$4 \times 7 = 28$ cm	What units should we use?	

A square has four equal length sides.

I need the total length of all the sides.

The side length is given in cm so the units are cm.

▲ Example-problem pair 2

Investigate further 🔍

A pentagon is a five-sided polygon, a hexagon has six sides, a heptagon has seven sides, and an octagon is an 8-sided polygon. Investigate the names of polygons with more sides.

6.2.1 Fluency

In this exercise you can practise applying the mathematical methods that you have just learnt.

1 Each of these polygons has been drawn on cm-squared paper. Write the perimeter of each polygon.

a   b 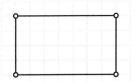 c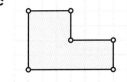

2 Find the perimeter of each of these polygons.

a 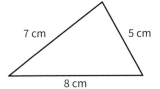 b 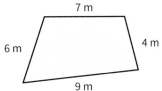 c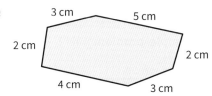

3 Find the perimeter of each of these regular polygons.

a 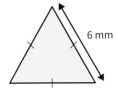 b 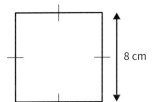 c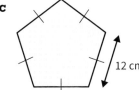

6.2.2 Finding the perimeter of polygons

Objective ☑

You will learn how to:
- work out perimeters using properties of polygons

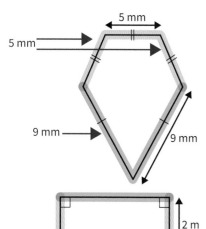

Sometimes you need to work out some of the side lengths of a polygon before you can work out the perimeter.

Some side lengths may be equal to ones you do know, and you can use properties of polygons to find unmarked side lengths. For example, in this polygon, the markings show that two of the unknown side lengths are 5 mm, and one of the unknown side lengths is 9 mm.

So the perimeter is $9 + 9 + 5 + 5 = 33$ mm

In a rectangle you know that the parallel sides are equal in length.

Perimeter $= 2 + 2 + 5 + 5 = 14$ m

Worked example	Thinking	Your turn!	
Find the perimeter of the parallelogram. 7 cm 2 cm	What do we know about side lengths in parallelograms? How do we work out the total perimeter?	Find the perimeter of the parallelogram. 9 mm 4 mm	I know that opposite sides are equal lengths, so the unmarked lengths are 2 cm and 7 cm.
			I add all four side lengths to find the perimeter.
Perimeter $= 7 + 7 + 2 + 2 = 18$ cm	What units should we use?		The sides of the polygon are measured in cm so the units are cm.

▲ Example-problem pair 1

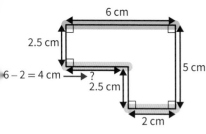

A **rectilinear shape** is made up of rectangles, and has straight sides joined at right angles. You can use your knowledge of rectangles to work out unknown side lengths.

In this shape the unknown side length and the 2 cm side add together to give the total **width** of 6 cm.

Perimeter $= 6 + 5 + 2 + 2.5 + 4 + 2.5 = 22$ cm

Check that the number of lengths you are adding together is the same as the number of sides of the polygon. Sometimes it is easy to miss one.

Worked example	Thinking	Your turn!
Find the perimeter of this rectilinear shape. 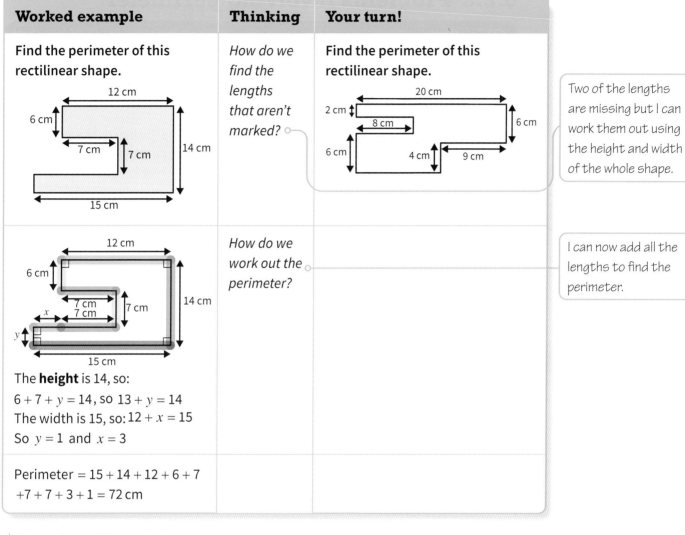	How do we find the lengths that aren't marked?	Find the perimeter of this rectilinear shape.

Two of the lengths are missing but I can work them out using the height and width of the whole shape.

	How do we work out the perimeter?	

The **height** is 14, so:

$6 + 7 + y = 14$, so $13 + y = 14$

The width is 15, so: $12 + x = 15$

So $y = 1$ and $x = 3$

I can now add all the lengths to find the perimeter.

Perimeter $= 15 + 14 + 12 + 6 + 7$
$+ 7 + 7 + 3 + 1 = 72$ cm

▲ Example-problem pair 2

6.2.2 Fluency

In this exercise you can practise applying the mathematical methods that you have just learnt.

1 Find the perimeter of each of these polygons.

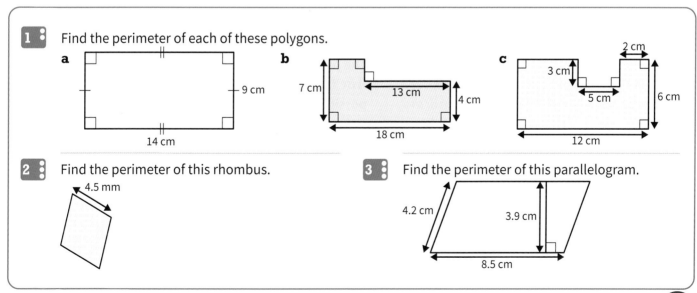

2 Find the perimeter of this rhombus.

4.5 mm

3 Find the perimeter of this parallelogram.

4.2 cm   3.9 cm

8.5 cm

6.2.3 Problems involving perimeter

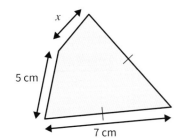

5 cm

x

7 cm

You may be given the perimeter of a polygon and asked to find the length of a side. For example, the perimeter of the polygon shown is 22 cm. Find the missing side length labelled x.

You know that two of the sides have length 7 cm. You can write a missing number calculation for the perimeter: $7 + 7 + 5 + \square = 22$

Add all the side lengths you know: $19 + \square = 22$

Using your knowledge of inverse operations, you can solve $19 + \square = 22$ with the related calculation $22 - 19 = \square$. So the missing side length is 3 cm.

Worked example	Thinking	Your turn!
Find the side length of a regular hexagon if the perimeter is 72 cm.	*What facts do we know about the polygon that could be useful in finding the perimeter?* *Can we write a missing number problem using this information?*	Find the side length of a regular octagon if the perimeter is 48 cm.
$6 \times \square = 72$ cm	*How can we find the missing number?*	
$72 \div 6 = 12$, so one side is 12 cm.		

A regular hexagon has six equal sides.

The number of sides multiplied by the side length is equal to the perimeter.

Dividing is the inverse of multiplying, so I will calculate $72 \div 6$

▲ Example-problem pair 1

Worked example	Thinking	Your turn!
The perimeter of the rectangle $ABCD$ is 18 units. Find the possible coordinates of B and C. 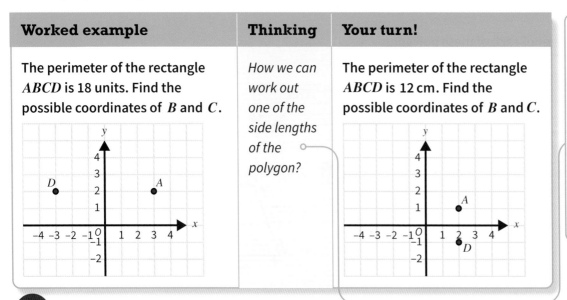	*How we can work out one of the side lengths of the polygon?*	The perimeter of the rectangle $ABCD$ is 12 cm. Find the possible coordinates of B and C.

The sides of the rectangle haven't been drawn but I can work out the distance between A and D, to find the length of side AD. There are 6 squares between −3 and 3 so the length of AD is 6 units.

Worked example	Thinking	Your turn!	
The length AD is 6 units. BC also has length 6 units. $6 + 6 + AB + CD = 18$ $12 + AB + CD = 18$ $AB + CD = 6$ AB and CD both have length 3 units.	*What do we know about the side lengths and perimeter of a rectangle?*		*The perimeter is the sum of all the side lengths. I know that opposite sides in a rectangle have equal lengths so the length of BC must also be 6, and AB and CD are the same length.*
B is 3 units above or below A, and C is 3 units above or below D. B is at $(3, 5)$ and C is at $(-3, 5)$. Or B is at $(3, -1)$ and C is at $(-3, -1)$.	*What do we know about the angles of a rectangle?*		*I know that all of the angles are right angles, and since AB is 3 units, B must be 3 units directly above or below A. Similarly C must be 3 units directly above or below D.*

🔺 Example-problem pair 2

6.2.3 Fluency

In this exercise you can practise applying the mathematical methods that you have just learnt.

1 The perimeter of an equilateral triangle is 36 cm. Find the side length of the triangle.

2 A rectangle has a perimeter of 18 m. Its length is 4 m. Find its width.

3 $ABCD$ is a rectangle. Points A and B are marked on the grid.

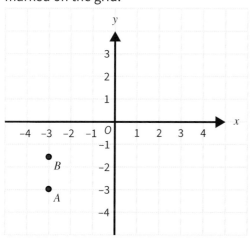

Given that the rectangle has a perimeter of 15 units, and point C has a positive x-coordinate, write the coordinates of points C and D.

4 The perimeter of this shape is 90 cm.

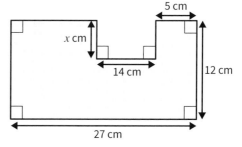

Find the value of x.

5 A hexagon has three sides of length x cm and three sides that are each 4 cm longer.

Write an expression for the perimeter in its simplest form.

6.2 Exercises

6.2 Intelligent practice

"Why is it intelligent?" You might notice a connection when you move on from one question to the next. You can use the Reflect, Expect, Check, Explain process to:

- *reflect* on what's different between each question and the one that came before
- decide how you *expect* this answer to be different
- complete the question and *check* your answer
- *explain* to yourself why your expectation was correct or incorrect.

EXAMPLE

Question 1a

Find the perimeter of this shape drawn on cm-square paper.

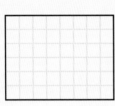

Starting at the top left, the perimeter is $8 + 6 + 8 + 6 = 28$ cm.

Question 1b

Find the perimeter of this shape drawn on cm-square paper.

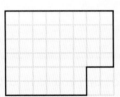

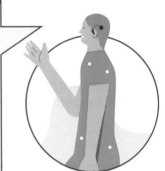

Reflect: The polygons are on the same size grid, but the one in the previous question had four sides and this polygon has six sides.

Expect: I think this polygon will have a longer perimeter.

Check: Starting at the top, perimeter $= 8 + 4 + 2 + 2 + 6 + 6 = 28$ cm

Explain: I was wrong! The horizontal sides have the same total length as in the previous question and so do the vertical sides. So the perimeter is the same.

---

1 Find the perimeter of these shapes drawn on cm-square paper.

a  b  c 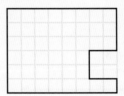 d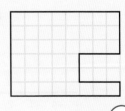

2 Find the perimeter of each of these regular polygons.

a 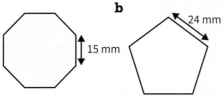 15 mm

b 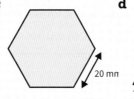 24 mm

c  20 mm

d 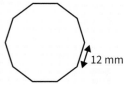 40 mm

e 12 mm

3 Find the perimeter of each of these rectilinear shapes. What do you notice about your answers?

a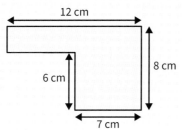
12 cm
8 cm
6 cm
7 cm

c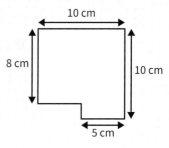
10 cm
8 cm
10 cm
5 cm

b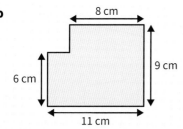
8 cm
9 cm
6 cm
11 cm

d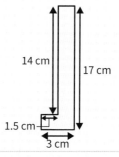
14 cm
17 cm
1.5 cm
3 cm

4 How many rectangles with integer side lengths and with a perimeter of 12 m are there? Write their lengths and widths.

5 Which expressions do **not** find the perimeter in km of the rectangle shown?

a $7 + 5 + 7 + 5$ b $2 \times (7 + 5)$ c $7 + 5 \times 2$ d $2 \times 7 + 2 \times 5$

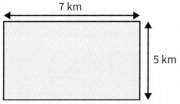
7 km
5 km

6 Write the unlabelled side lengths of these triangles so that the perimeter of each triangle is 33 cm. The four triangles are all different.

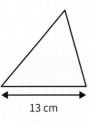
13 cm
Scalene
Triangle

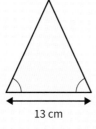
13 cm
Isosceles
Triangle

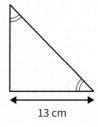
13 cm
Isosceles
Triangle

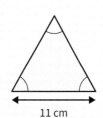
11 cm
Equilateral
Triangle

Chapter 6

6.2 Method selection

In these questions you'll need to think carefully about which methods to apply.

For some questions you might need to use skills from earlier chapters.

1 Find the perimeter of each of these triangles.

a

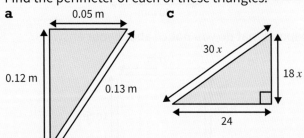

c

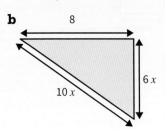

b

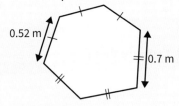

2 Find the perimeter of this hexagon.

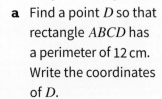

3 All the points are plotted on cm-square paper.

a Find a point D so that rectangle $ABCD$ has a perimeter of 12 cm. Write the coordinates of D.

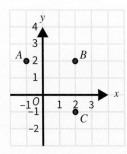

b Find a point C and a point D so that $ABCD$ is a rectangle with a perimeter of 10 cm and write their coordinates. Can you find another solution?

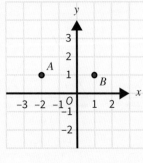

c AB is 5 cm in length. Find a point C and a point D so that $ABCD$ has a perimeter of 20 cm and write their coordinates. Can you find another solution?

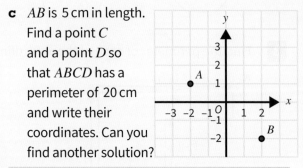

4 The perimeter of this polygon is 64 units. Find the missing length marked x.

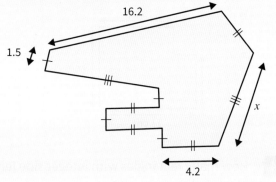

5 The larger shape is made up of three copies of the rectangle shown.

Write an expression for the perimeter of the larger shape in terms of x.

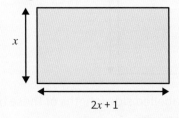

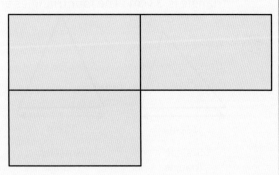

6.2 Purposeful practice

There may be more than one way to approach these questions.
Once you have answered a question one way, can you think of another way?

1 Find the perimeter of each of these shapes drawn on cm-square paper.

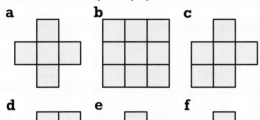

a **b** **c**

d **e** **f**

Which of the perimeters is the odd one out?

2 The perimeter of this equilateral triangle is 11 mm. Find the perimeter of the shape shown that is made up of seven copies of the triangle.

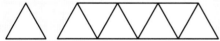

3 The perimeter of the smaller rectangle shown is 14 cm. Find the perimeter of the larger shape made up of four identical rectangles.

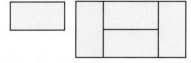

4 Find the perimeter of this rectilinear shape.

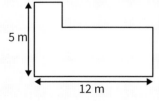

5 m

12 m

5 These three shapes are each made up of three identical rectangles. Which of the shapes has the smallest perimeter?

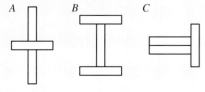

A   B   C

6 These three shapes are each made up of copies of the smaller rectangle. Which shape has a perimeter exactly double the smaller rectangle?

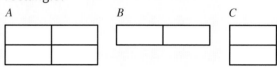

A   B   C

7 Order the shapes from smallest perimeter to largest perimeter.

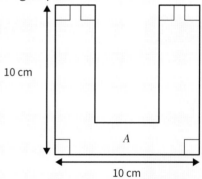

10 cm

10 cm

A

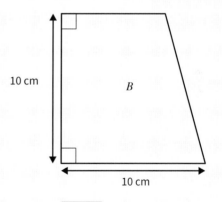

10 cm

10 cm

B

10 cm

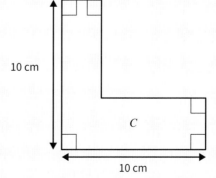

10 cm

10 cm

C

10 cm

6.3.1 Introduction to area

If you want to tile a floor, you need to find out how many tiles to buy to cover the floor. The measure of the floor space you need to cover is the **area**. You usually measure area in centimetre squares (cm^2) or metre squares (m^2).

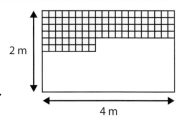

2 m

4 m

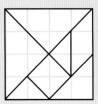
Key point 🗝

The area is the space inside a boundary. Area can be measured by counting the number of unit squares that fit into a polygon.

When a polygon is drawn on squared paper, you can find the area by counting the number of squares that fit exactly inside the polygon without gaps or overlaps.

The rectangle shown is drawn on cm-square paper and contains 35 squares, so the area is $35\,cm^2$

To find the area of the rectangle you don't have to count every square. You can see that this rectangle is a 7×5 array so that means it contains a total of $7 \times 5 = 35$ squares, an area of $35\,cm^2$

The triangle shown covers 2 whole squares and 4 half squares. The 4 half squares make 2 whole squares so the total area is $4\,cm^2$

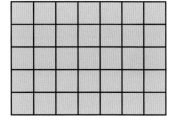

The polygon here contains 25 squares, so its area is $25\,cm^2$.

Instead of counting all the squares you could work this out as the total of a 2×2 array and a 7×3 array $(4 + 21 = 25)$. Or you could work out the area by noticing it is the same as the previous rectangle but with a 5×2 array removed $(35 - 10 = 25)$.

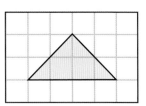

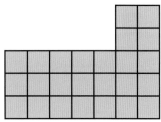

Worked example	Thinking	Your turn!
Find the area of the polygon drawn on cm-square paper.	What is an efficient way to find the area of this polygon?	Find the area of the polygon drawn on cm-square paper.

I see that this shape is a larger rectangle of 7×9 squares with a smaller square of 3×3 cut away.

$7 \times 9 = 63$ $3 \times 3 = 9$	How can we find how many squares there are?	

I subtract the area of the smaller square from the area of the larger rectangle.

$63 - 9 = 54 \text{ cm}^2$	What units do we use?	

The polygon is on cm-square paper, so I use cm^2.

▲ Example-problem pair 1

6.3.1 Fluency

In this exercise you can practise applying the mathematical methods that you have just learnt.

1 These polygons are on cm-square paper. Count squares and parts of squares to find their areas.

a    b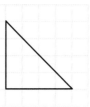

2 This polygon is on cm-square paper. Count squares and parts of squares to find its area.

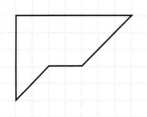

3 These polygons are on cm-square paper. Count squares and parts of squares to find their areas.

a 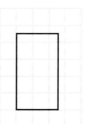   b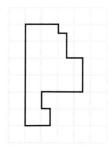

4 This polygon is on cm-square paper. Count squares and parts of squares to find its area.

a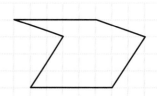

6.3.2 Area of polygons involving rectangles

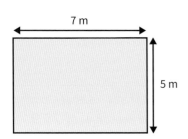

Objective ☑

You will learn how to:

- work out areas of composite shapes made of rectangles

If a polygon isn't drawn to scale, you can use other information to find the area. This rectangle has length 7 m and width 5 m marked, so its area is $7 \times 5 = 35\,m^2$.

Key point

You can find the area of any rectangle by multiplying the width and length.

A **composite shape** is made of two or more polygons put together. You can find the area of a composite shape by splitting it into polygons, finding the areas of the separate polygons, and then adding the areas together.

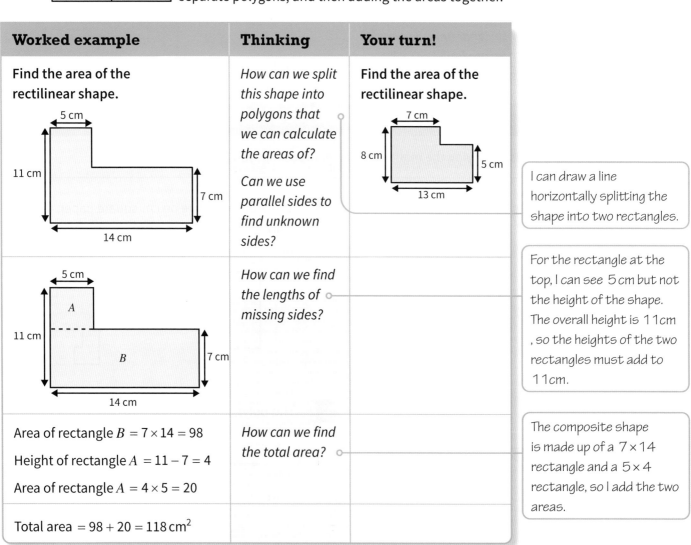

Worked example	Thinking	Your turn!
Find the area of the rectilinear shape.	How can we split this shape into polygons that we can calculate the areas of? Can we use parallel sides to find unknown sides?	Find the area of the rectilinear shape.
	How can we find the lengths of missing sides?	I can draw a line horizontally splitting the shape into two rectangles.
		For the rectangle at the top, I can see 5 cm but not the height of the shape. The overall height is 11cm, so the heights of the two rectangles must add to 11cm.
Area of rectangle $B = 7 \times 14 = 98$ Height of rectangle $A = 11 - 7 = 4$ Area of rectangle $A = 4 \times 5 = 20$	How can we find the total area?	The composite shape is made up of a 7×14 rectangle and a 5×4 rectangle, so I add the two areas.
Total area $= 98 + 20 = 118\,cm^2$		

▲ Example-problem pair 1

Composite shapes may be made of a polygon you know with another polygon cut out. You can work out the area of these by subtracting the area of the cut-out polygon from the larger polygon.

Make sure all the measurements you are working with are in the same units. Area units are squares of length units, so you might use mm^2, cm^2, m^2, or km^2.

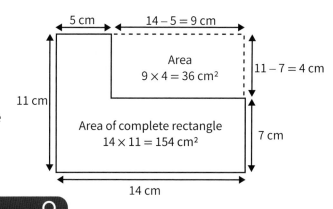

Area of composite shape

$154 - 36 = 116 cm^2$

Investigate further 🔍

Areas of land are often measured in different units. Research the units acre, are, and hectare. How do they relate to m^2 and km^2?

6.3.2 Fluency

In this exercise you can practise applying the mathematical methods that you have just learnt.

1 Work out the area of these rectangles.

a 6 cm, 2 cm

b 20 m, 8 m

c 30 cm, 7 cm

2 The diagram shows a polygon split into two rectangles.

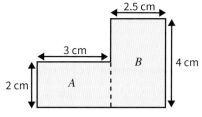

Work out the area of
a the polygon labelled A
b the polygon labelled B
c the whole polygon.

3 Calculate the area of these polygons.

a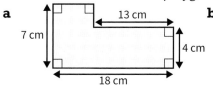

b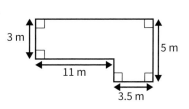

c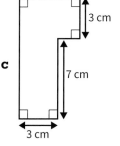

4 Calculate the area of these polygons.

a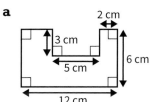

b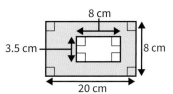

6.3.3 Area of triangles

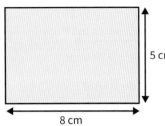

You can find the area of any rectangle by multiplying the length and width.

The rectangle has an area of $8 \times 5 = 40 \, \text{cm}^2$.

Each shaded triangle is exactly half the area of the rectangle, so each triangle has an area of $\frac{1}{2} \times 8 \times 5 = 20 \, \text{cm}^2$.

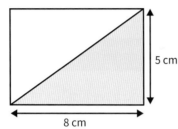 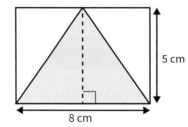 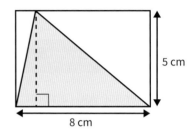

If you know the length of one side of the triangle (the **base length**) and the **perpendicular height** of the triangle measured from that base, then you can work out the area of the triangle.

Key point

The area of a triangle $= \frac{1}{2} \times$ base $\times$ perpendicular height

If you draw a rectangle around a triangle, where the base of the triangle is the same length as one side of the rectangle and the perpendicular height of the triangle is the same length as the other side of the rectangle, the area of the triangle is always half the area of the rectangle. Here are triangles with some of the lengths given. A rectangle has been drawn around each triangle to show how the formula works for each one.

 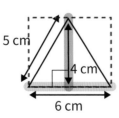 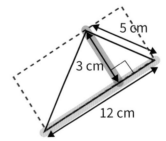 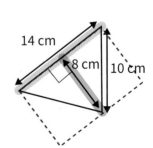

Worked example	Thinking	Your turn!	
Find the area of the triangle. 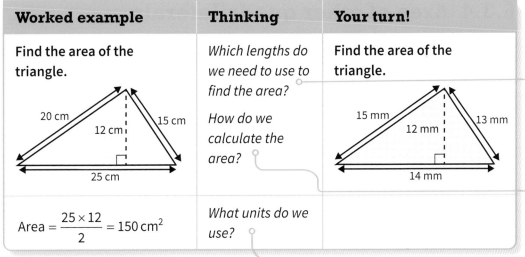 20 cm 15 cm 12 cm 25 cm	*Which lengths do we need to use to find the area?* *How do we calculate the area?*	Find the area of the triangle. 15 mm 13 mm 12 mm 14 mm	I need the base and the perpendicular height. 25 is the base and 12 is the perpendicular height as shown by the right angle.
Area $= \dfrac{25 \times 12}{2} = 150\,\text{cm}^2$	*What units do we use?*		I multiply the base and perpendicular height The units of the lengths are cm so I need to use cm^2.

▲ Example-problem pair 1

6.3.3 Fluency

In this exercise you can practise applying the mathematical methods that you have just learnt.

1 Work out the area of these triangles.

a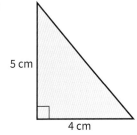
5 cm
4 cm

b
3 cm
6 cm

c
7 m
10 m

d
12 mm
5 mm

2 Work out the area of these triangles.

a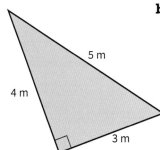
5 m
4 m
3 m

b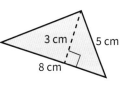
3 cm 5 cm
8 cm

c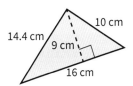
14.4 cm 10 cm
9 cm
16 cm

d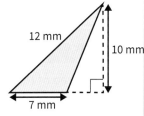
12 mm 10 mm
7 mm

3 Draw three different triangles which all have a base of 4 cm and a perpendicular height of 3 cm.
Explain why all three of the triangles you have drawn have an area of 6 cm².

6.3.4 Area of other quadrilaterals

Objective

You will learn how to:

- work out the area of different quadrilaterals

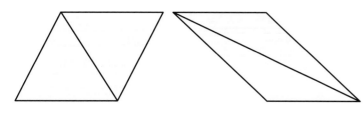

You can use the area of a triangle to help you find the area of quadrilaterals.

The area of a triangle is $\frac{1}{2} \times$ base $\times$ perpendicular height.

You can make a parallelogram from two copies of the same triangle.

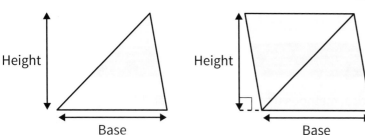

The area of a parallelogram is

$2 \times \frac{1}{2} \times$ base $\times$ perpendicular height, which you can simplify to base $\times$ perpendicular height.

Key point

The area of a parallelogram is given by base $\times$ perpendicular height.

A parallelogram has the same area as a rectangle with the same base and height.

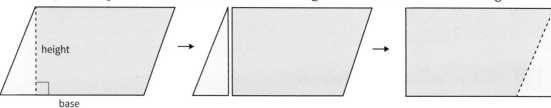

Worked example	Thinking	Your turn!	
Find the area of the parallelogram. 7 cm 3 cm 4 cm	Which lengths do we need to find the area? How do we calculate the area?	Find the area of the parallelogram. 8 mm 12 mm 11 mm	I need the base and perpendicular height. 7 cm and 3 cm are perpendicular lengths. 7 cm is the base and 3 cm is the height.
			I multiply the base and perpendicular height.
$7 \times 3 = 21$ Area $= 21\,\text{cm}^2$	What units do we use?		The units of the lengths are cm so I need to use cm^2.

▲ Example-problem pair 1

You can use the area of a parallelogram to help you work out the area of a trapezium. You know that a trapezium has one pair of parallel sides and a parallelogram has two pairs. If you put two identical trapezia together you can make one parallelogram:

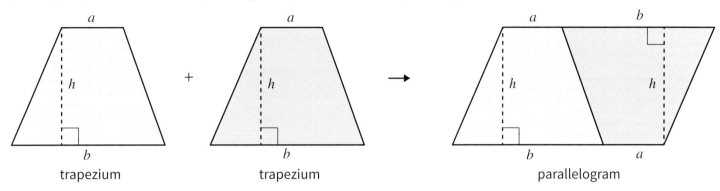

The parallelogram has base length of $a + b$ and height of h, so the area of the parallelogram is $(a + b) \times h$

The area of the trapezium is half of this.

Key point

The area of a trapezium is given by $\frac{1}{2}(a + b)h$, where a and b are the lengths of the parallel sides and h is the perpendicular distance between them.

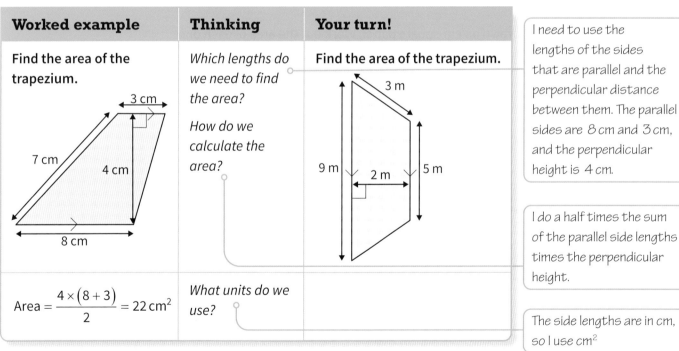

Worked example	Thinking	Your turn!
Find the area of the trapezium.	*Which lengths do we need to find the area?* *How do we calculate the area?*	Find the area of the trapezium.
Area $= \dfrac{4 \times (8 + 3)}{2} = 22\,\text{cm}^2$	*What units do we use?*	

I need to use the lengths of the sides that are parallel and the perpendicular distance between them. The parallel sides are 8 cm and 3 cm, and the perpendicular height is 4 cm.

I do a half times the sum of the parallel side lengths times the perpendicular height.

The side lengths are in cm, so I use cm²

▲ Example–problem pair 2

To find the area of other quadrilaterals, for example a kite, you can split the quadrilateral into two triangles.

Worked example	Thinking	Your turn!	
Find the area of the kite. 5 m, 4 m, 15 m, 4 m	Can we split the shape into two triangles? How do we calculate the area of one triangle?	Find the area of the kite. 11 cm, 3.5 cm, 12 cm, 3.5 cm	Yes, I can see two identical triangles with height 4 and base 15. I use half the base length times the height.
Area of one triangle = $\dfrac{15 \times 4}{2} = 30$	How do you use the triangle to find the area of the kite?		The kite is made up of two triangles, so I will multiply my area by 2.
Area of kite = $30 \times 2 = 60 \, \text{m}^2$	What are the units?		The side lengths are in m, so I use m^2.

▲ Example-problem pair 3

6.3.4 Fluency

In this exercise you can practise applying the mathematical methods that you have just learnt.

1 These polygons are drawn on cm-square paper. Work out the area of each one.

a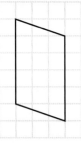

b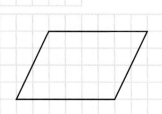

c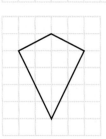

d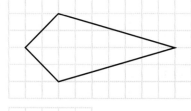

e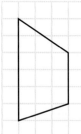

f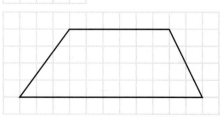

2 Work out the area of these polygons.

a

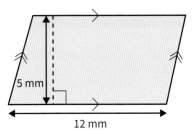

5 mm

12 mm

b

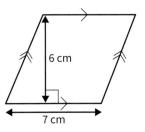

6 cm

7 cm

c

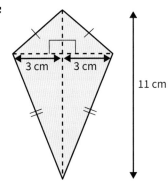

3 cm 3 cm

11 cm

d

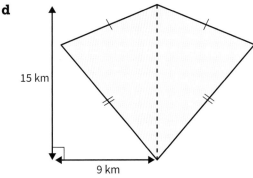

15 km

9 km

e

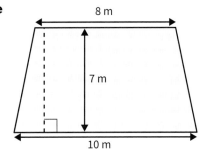

8 m

7 m

10 m

f

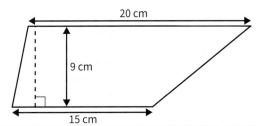

20 cm

9 cm

15 cm

3 Work out the area of these polygons.

a

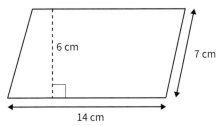

6 cm

7 cm

14 cm

b

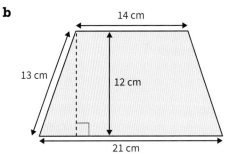

14 cm

13 cm

12 cm

21 cm

4 A trapezium can be split into two different triangles with the same height.

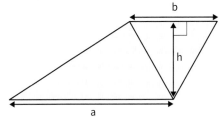

b

h

a

Write down, in terms of a, b, and h, the area of the two triangles.

From this, show that the area of the trapezium is given by the formula $\text{Area} = \dfrac{h(a + b)}{2}$

6.3.5 Problems involving area

Objective ☑

You will learn how to:

- solve problems involving areas of polygons

You work out the area of a composite shape by finding the area of each of the polygons it is made up of and adding these areas together.

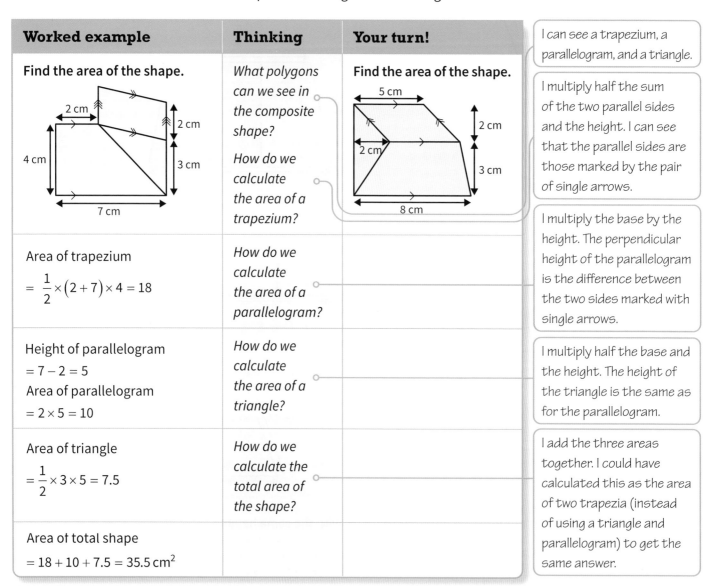

Worked example	Thinking	Your turn!	
Find the area of the shape.	*What polygons can we see in the composite shape?* *How do we calculate the area of a trapezium?*	**Find the area of the shape.**	I can see a trapezium, a parallelogram, and a triangle. I multiply half the sum of the two parallel sides and the height. I can see that the parallel sides are those marked by the pair of single arrows.
Area of trapezium $= \dfrac{1}{2} \times (2 + 7) \times 4 = 18$	*How do we calculate the area of a parallelogram?*		I multiply the base by the height. The perpendicular height of the parallelogram is the difference between the two sides marked with single arrows.
Height of parallelogram $= 7 - 2 = 5$ Area of parallelogram $= 2 \times 5 = 10$	*How do we calculate the area of a triangle?*		I multiply half the base and the height. The height of the triangle is the same as for the parallelogram.
Area of triangle $= \dfrac{1}{2} \times 3 \times 5 = 7.5$	*How do we calculate the total area of the shape?*		I add the three areas together. I could have calculated this as the area of two trapezia (instead of using a triangle and parallelogram) to get the same answer.
Area of total shape $= 18 + 10 + 7.5 = 35.5 \text{ cm}^2$			

▲ Example-problem pair 1

Given the area of a polygon and some of its lengths, you can work out an unknown length.

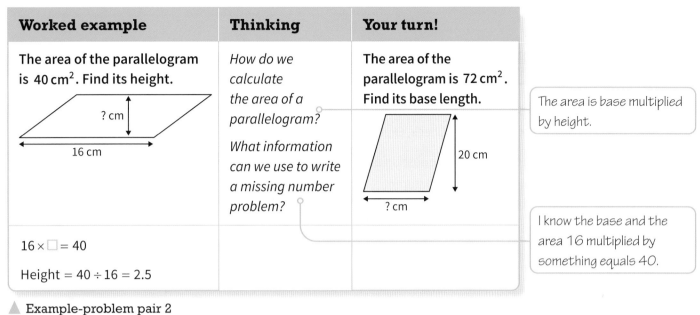

Worked example	Thinking	Your turn!
The area of the parallelogram is 40 cm². Find its height.	How do we calculate the area of a parallelogram? What information can we use to write a missing number problem?	The area of the parallelogram is 72 cm². Find its base length.

The area is base multiplied by height.

I know the base and the area 16 multiplied by something equals 40.

$16 \times \square = 40$

$\text{Height} = 40 \div 16 = 2.5$

▲ Example-problem pair 2

6.3.5 Fluency

In this exercise you can practise applying the mathematical methods that you have just learnt.

1 These polygons are drawn on cm-square paper. Work out the area of each one.

a 　　b 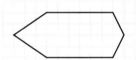　　c

2 a The area of a square is 25 cm². Work out the side length of the square.
 b A rectangle has area 45 cm². Its width is 5 cm. Work out its length.

3 Work out the area of these shapes.

a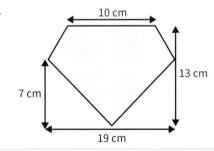

b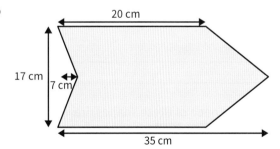

4 a A trapezium has area 21 m². The lengths of the parallel sides are 6 m and 8 m.
 Work out the perpendicular height of the trapezium.
 b A triangle has area 45 cm². The perpendicular height is 18 cm. Work out the base length of the triangle.

5 Decide if each of these statements are true or false. If the statement is false, write a correct statement.
 a The area of a square is the square of the side length.
 b The area of a rectangle is the sum of all four side lengths.
 c The area of a parallelogram is the product of the two different side lengths.

Chapter 6

6.3 Exercises

6.3 Intelligent practice

"Why is it intelligent?" You might notice a connection when you move on from one question to the next. You can use the Reflect, Expect, Check, Explain process to:

- *reflect* on what's different between each question and the one that came before
- decide how you *expect* this answer to be different
- complete the question and *check* your answer
- *explain* to yourself why your expectation was correct or incorrect.

Question 2a   **EXAMPLE**

Find the area of the polygon.

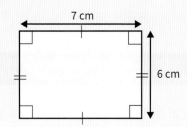

Area $= 7 \times 6 = 42\,cm^2$

Question 2b

Find the area of the polygon.

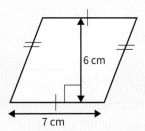

Reflect: This polygon has opposite sides parallel too but no right angles.

Expect: I think it will have the same area as the rectangle in a, $42\,cm^2$.

Check: Area of parallelogram $=$ base $\times$ height $= 6 \times 7 = 42\,cm^2$

Explain: I was right! The side lengths are different to in part a but the base and height are the same so the areas are the same.

---

1   Find the area of each of these shapes drawn on cm-square paper.

a   b   c

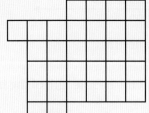 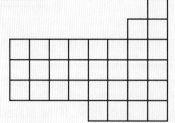 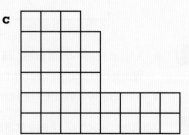

2 Find the area of each of these polygons.

a
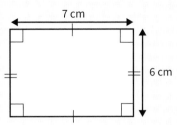

b
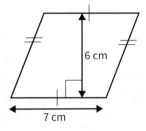

c
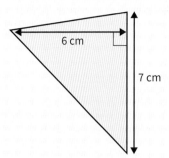

d
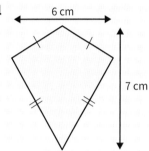

3 Find the area of each shaded shape.

a
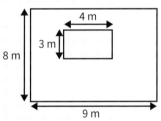

b
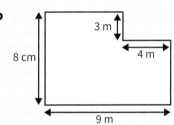

c
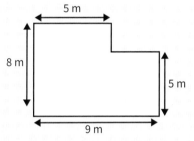

4 Find the missing length in each polygon so that the area is 24 mm².

a
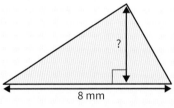

b
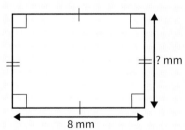

c
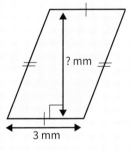

d
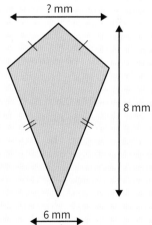

e

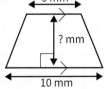

6.3 Method selection

In these questions you'll need to think carefully about which methods to apply.
For some questions you might need to use skills from earlier chapters.

1 Find as many rectangles as possible with integer lengths and area of $48\,cm^2$.
Write the length and width of each.

2 Find the side lengths of the squares with these areas.

a
9 cm²

b
16 cm²

c
21 cm²

d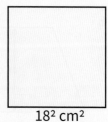
18² cm²

3 Copy the Venn diagram and write the letter for each polygon on the diagram.

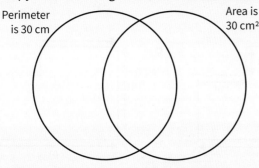

Perimeter is 30 cm   Area is 30 cm²

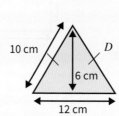

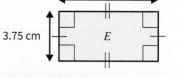

4 Length AB is drawn on a cm-square grid.
Write the possible coordinates of C if triangle
ABC has each of these areas.
Choose from the positions $C1$ to $C7$.
a $18\,cm^2$ **b** $9\,cm^2$ **c** $12\,cm^2$ **d** $15\,cm^2$

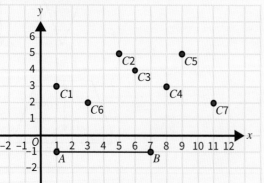

5 Find the area of the kite.

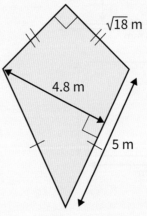

$\sqrt{18}$ m
4.8 m
5 m

6 Expressions a to d represent areas. Match each expression with the correct polygon.

a $17^2 + 8^2 + 5^2$ **c** $17^2 + 8^2 - 5^2$

b $17^2 - 8^2 + 5^2$ **d** $17^2 - 8^2 - 5^2$

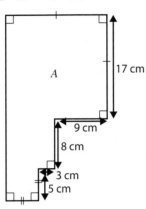

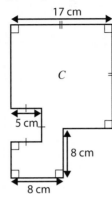

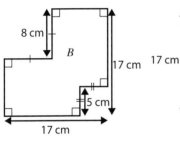

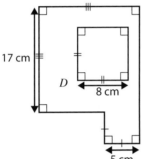

7 This rectangle is divided into four rectangles. This shape is made up of four rectangles.

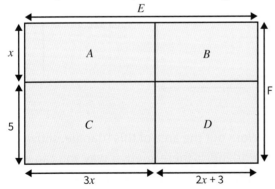

Write an expression in its simplest form for:

a the length of side E

b the length of side F

c the area of polygon D

d area of $A + B + C + D$

Write your answers as expressions in terms of x.

8 A rectangle has a length three times its width. The perimeter is 20 mm. What is the area of the rectangle?

9 Which of these shaded rectilinear shapes have the same areas?

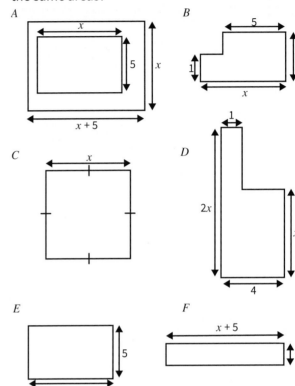

10 This rectangle is divided into four rectangles. Find the area of the rectangle marked x.

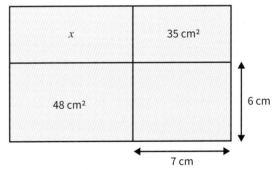

6.3 Purposeful practice

There may be more than one way to approach these questions.

Once you have answered a question one way, can you think of another way?

1 Find the length, y, marked on the triangle.

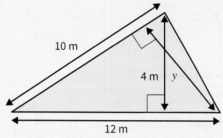

2 Find the length, z, marked on the parallelogram.

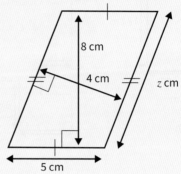

3 Both of these shapes are made up of rectangles.
Find the missing lengths x and y.

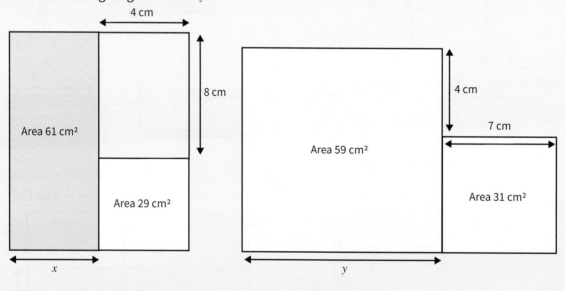

4 Find the side length, w, in this rectilinear shape. The green area $(A + B)$ is equal to the yellow area $(C + D)$.

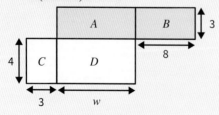

5 Work out the area of this triangle, showing your working. Is there another way you can work it out? Can you think of a third way?

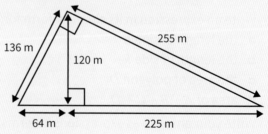

6 Compare the perimeter of the smaller polygon and the perimeter of the larger polygon in each of these pairs. What do you notice?

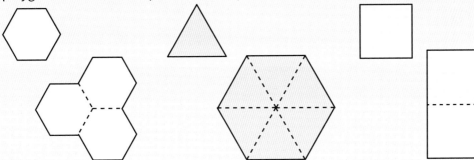

7 The shaded triangle is drawn so that the three vertices are on the edges of a rectangle. Find the area of the triangle.

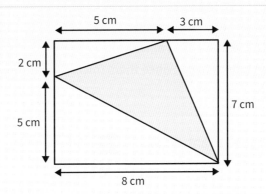

8 The area of this polygon is $190\,m^2$. The lengths x and y are integers. What are the possible values of x and y? Explain your answers.

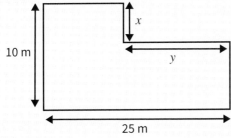

9 Andy says you cannot have a rectangle with length $12\,cm$ and an area of $6\,cm^2$.
He also says you cannot have a rectangle with length $12\,cm$ and a perimeter of $6\,cm$.
Are both, one or neither statements correct?

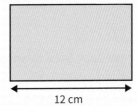

10 Find the total area of the shaded parts.

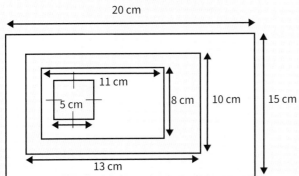

Watch out!

Some students have tried to answer the questions below but have unfortunately made some mistakes.
For each question do the following:

a answer the question correctly

b write down the mistake that each student has made

c comment on why they might have made that mistake

d write an explanation for each student to convince them (nicely!) that their answer cannot be correct.

1 Aisha and Bella have each tried to answer this question.
Name this polygon.

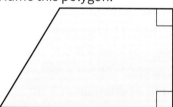

Aisha wrote: quadrilateral.
Bella wrote: kite

2 Danny and Cameron have each tried to answer this question.
Find the perimeter of the polygon shown.

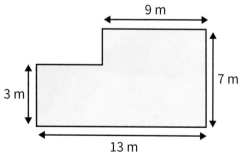

Danny wrote:
$13 + 3 + 7 + 9 = 32\,\text{m}$

Cameron wrote:
$13 + 7 + 9 + 3 + 9 + 3 = 44\,\text{m}$

3 Elliot and Fiona have each tried to answer the question:
Work out the length x on the rectangle. The perimeter of the rectangle is $35\,\text{cm}$.

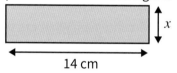

Elliot wrote: $35 - 14 = 21$
$\dfrac{21}{3} = 7\,\text{cm}$

Fiona wrote: $35 - 14 = 21$
$\dfrac{21}{2} = 10.5\,\text{cm}$

4 Nanako, Helen and Jan have each tried to answer the question:
Find the area of this polygon.

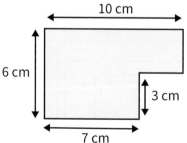

Nanako wrote: $10 \times 3 \times 7 \times 6 = 1260\,\text{cm}^2$
Helen wrote: $6 \times 10 - 7 \times 3 = 39\,\text{cm}^2$
Jan wrote: $6 \times 10 + 7 \times 3 = 81\,\text{cm}^2$

5 Joe and Kamil have each tried this question:
Work out the area of the triangle shown.

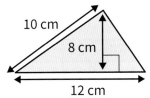

10 cm

8 cm

12 cm

Joe wrote: $10 \times 12 = 120$

$\dfrac{120}{2} = 60 \, cm^2$

Kamil wrote:

$10 \times 12 \times 8 = 960 \, cm^2$

Check your understanding

6.1 Properties of triangles and quadrilaterals

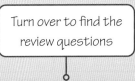
Turn over to find the review questions

You should now be able to...	Questions
know and use the properties of different quadrilaterals	1
know and use the properties of different triangles	2

6.2 Perimeter

You should now be able to...	Questions
work out perimeters using properties of polygons	3b, 4b, 5b, 6b, 7a, 8a
solve problems involving perimeters of polygons	9, 10

6.3 Area

You should now be able to...	Questions
work out areas of polygons on squared paper	3a
work out areas of composite polygons made of rectangles	8b
work out the area of triangles	5a
work out the area of different quadrilaterals	4a, 6a, 7b
solve problems involving areas of polygons	11

Chapter 6

Chapter 6 review questions

1 Copy this table.

	Square	Rectangle	Parallelogram	Kite	Trapezium
All four angles are equal in size					
Both pairs of opposite sides are equal in length					
Both pairs of opposite sides are parallel					

Put a tick into the box when the statement on the left is true. [3]

2 *ABC* is an isosceles triangle.

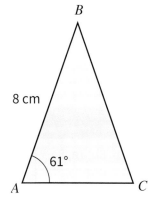

a Write down the length of side *BC*. [1]
b Write down the size of the angle at *C*. [1]

3 The diagram shows a shape drawn on cm-square paper.

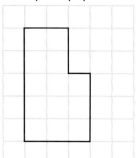

a Work out the area of the shape. [1]
b Work out the perimeter of the shape. [1]

4

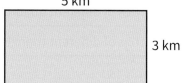

a Work out the area of the rectangle. [1]
b Work out the perimeter of the rectangle. [1]

5

a Work out the area of the triangle. [1]
b Work out the perimeter of the triangle. [1]

6

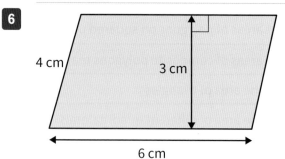

a Work out the area of the parallelogram. [1]
b Work out the perimeter of the parallelogram. [1]

7

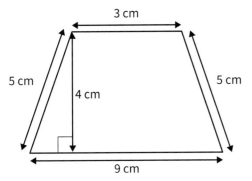

a Work out the perimeter of the trapezium. [1]

b Work out the area of the trapezium. [2]

8 For this rectilinear shape, work out the:
  a perimeter. [2]
  b area. [2]

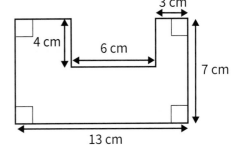

9 A regular nonagon has a perimeter of 135 m.
What is the length of one side of the nonagon? [2]

10 A rectangle has a perimeter of 184 mm.
The length is 3 times the width.
Find the length of the rectangle. [3]

11 Look at this diagram.

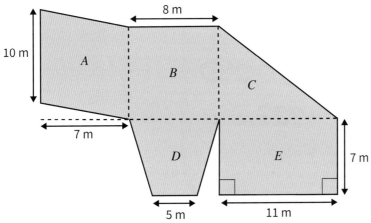

Polygon A is a parallelogram and polygon B is a rectangle.
Calculate the area of the whole shape. [5]

Key words

Make sure you can write a definition for these key terms.

*quadrilateral • polygon • length • parallel • angle • diagonal • square • rectangle • parallelogram
rhombus • kite • trapezium • regular • irregular • triangle • equilateral triangle • isosceles triangle
scalene triangle • right-angled triangle • obtuse-angled triangle • perimeter • edge • rectilinear shape
width • height • area • composite shape • base length • perpendicular height*

Chapter 6

7 Fractions

Lots of countries keep gold reserves in banks. The purity of gold is measured in carats. 24 carats means that 24 out of 24 parts are gold. These bars are 24 carats, which is pure gold. How pure is 18-carat gold as a fraction?

What comes before?	This chapter	What comes after?
Primary school • Fractions **Book 1** • Place value • Arithmetic	• 7.1 Working with fractions and decimals • 7.2 Comparing and ordering fractions • 7.3 Adding and subtracting fractions • 7.4 Multiplying and dividing fractions	**Book 1** • Fractions and ratio **Book 2** • Percentages and proportionality

Introduction

In this chapter you will develop your understanding of fractions, including working with negative fractions and mixed numbers. You will convert between fractions and decimals, order fractions, and find out when you need to find a common denominator.

To add or subtract fractions, you first need to make sure that all the fractions involved in the calculation have a common denominator. However, you can multiply or divide fractions without finding a common denominator. For example, $\dfrac{1}{2} \times \dfrac{1}{4} = \dfrac{1}{8}$

You can think of multiplying fractions as finding that fraction of an amount: $\dfrac{1}{2} \times \dfrac{1}{4}$ means 'find $\dfrac{1}{2}$ of $\dfrac{1}{4}$', so it is the same as $\dfrac{1}{4} \div 2$

In this chapter you will learn how to...

▶ write fractions for 1

$$\frac{6}{6} = 1$$

› convert between fractions and mixed numbers

$$-\frac{8}{3} = -2\frac{2}{3}$$

› convert between fractions and decimals

$$0.25 = \frac{25}{100}$$

compare and order fractions

$$\frac{7}{10} > \frac{5}{10} > -\frac{8}{10}$$

$$3\frac{1}{4} < \frac{7}{2} < \frac{18}{5}$$

‹ simplify fractions

$$\frac{8}{10} = \frac{4}{5}$$

add and subtract fractions

$$\frac{1}{3} + \frac{2}{9} = \frac{5}{9}$$

‹ multiply with fractions and mixed numbers

$$1\frac{1}{3} \times \frac{4}{5} = 1\frac{1}{15}$$

‹ divide with fractions

$$18 \div \frac{2}{5} = 45$$

Reactivate your knowledge

If you can answer the questions on these pages then you should be ready for the chapter.

Some questions are there to help you to remember some maths from primary school and some are to help you remember maths from earlier in the book.

If you see this symbol 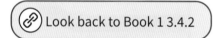 it tells you where that information was introduced in an earlier chapter. If you are struggling with those questions you could go back and read through it again.

7.1 Working with fractions and decimals

You should know...

1. how to add and subtract fractions with the same denominator

For example

$$\frac{4}{7} + \frac{2}{7} = \frac{4+2}{7} = \frac{6}{7}$$

You add the numerators and keep the denominators the same.

2. how to divide integers and decimals using short division

For example
$$5\overline{)12.^20}\quad = 2.4$$

🔗 Look back to Book 1 3.4.2

3. how to identify the place value of decimal digits

For example

0.438 712 is made up of 4 tenths $\left(\frac{4}{10}\right)$, 3 hundredths $\left(\frac{3}{100}\right)$, 8 thousandths $\left(\frac{8}{1000}\right)$, 7 ten-thousandths $\left(\frac{1}{10\,000}\right)$, 1 hundred-thousandth $\left(\frac{1}{100\,000}\right)$, and 2 millionths $\left(\frac{2}{1\,000\,000}\right)$.

🔗 Look back to Book 1 1.2.1

Check in

1. Work out:

a $\dfrac{1}{5} + \dfrac{3}{5}$

b $\dfrac{4}{11} + \dfrac{5}{11}$

c $\dfrac{11}{17} + \dfrac{2}{17}$

2. Using short division, work out:

a $21 \div 6$

b $7 \div 4$

c $17 \div 8$

3. Here is a number: $0.152\,968$. Write the value of each of these digits in words and as a fraction:

a 5

b 8

c 6

d 2

7.2 Comparing and ordering fractions and
7.3 Adding and subtracting fractions

You should know...

4. how to find the lowest common multiple (LCM) of two numbers

For example

The LCM of 12 and 14 is $2 \times 2 \times 3 \times 7 = 84$

 Look back to Book 1 2.3.6

5. how to compare and order decimal numbers

For example

9.2 is greater than 9.12, so we write $9.2 > 9.12$

These numbers have been written in ascending order (from least to greatest):

5.15, 5.191, 5.21, 5.221

 Look back to Book 1 1.3.3

6. how to compare and order positive and negative numbers

For example

These numbers have been written in ascending order (from least to greatest):

$-9, -3, -1, 0, 4, 5, 7$

 Look back to Book 1 3.1.1

Check in

4. Work out the LCM of these pairs of numbers:

   a 3 and 5

   b 10 and 15

   c 3 and 9

   d 24 and 72

5. Complete **a** and **b**.

   a Write the symbol < or > between each pair of numbers:

     i 0.7 ☐ 0.8

     ii 1.54 ☐ 1.45

     iii 13.305 ☐ 13.35

   b Order these numbers from least to greatest:

     4.76, 4.706, 4.67, 4.076

6. Order these numbers from least to greatest:

   0, −13, −19, 16, −15, 13, 10

7.4 Multiplying and dividing fractions

You should know...

7. how to use the distributive law of multiplication over addition

For example

$$4 \times \left(\frac{1}{2} + 5 \right) = \left(4 \times \frac{1}{2} \right) + \left(4 \times 5 \right) = 22$$

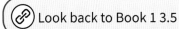 Look back to Book 1 3.5

Check in

7. Use the distributive law to copy and complete these calculations:

   a $5 \times \left(3 + \frac{1}{5} \right) = \left(\square \times 3 \right) + \left(\square \times \frac{1}{5} \right)$

   b $2 \times \left(6 + \frac{1}{3} \right) = \left(2 \times 6 \right) + \left(2 \times \frac{\square}{\square} \right)$

   c $7 \times \left(4 + 16 \right) = \left(7 \times \square \right) + \left(\square \times 16 \right)$

Chapter 7

Working with fractions and decimals

7.1.1 Wholes and parts

Objectives

You will:

- understand that 1 can be written in the form $\dfrac{n}{n}$

Fractions tell you about a part of a whole. The **denominator** tells you how many equal parts to split the whole into and the **numerator** tells you how many of these parts are being used.

For instance, $\dfrac{3}{5}$ means split the whole into five parts and use three of them, as shown in this bar model.

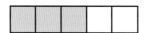

The number 1 can be written as a fraction too. All of these fractions represent the number 1. Notice how the numerator and denominator are the same. This is because in each fraction, 1 has been split into a number of parts, and all of the parts are being used.

$$\frac{3}{3}, \frac{8}{8}, \frac{100}{100}, \frac{12\,000}{12\,000}$$

Worked example	Thinking	Your turn!
Copy and fill in the blank so that the fraction equals 1 $$\dfrac{\Box}{7} = 1$$	*What do we know about the numerator and denominator if the fraction equals 1?*	Copy and fill in the blank so that the fraction equals 1 $$\dfrac{\Box}{9} = 1$$
$$\dfrac{7}{7} = 1$$		

The numerator and denominator must be the same.

▲ Example-problem pair 1

To equal 1, the numerator and denominator do not need to be integers, just equal, so

$\dfrac{0.5}{0.5}$ and $\dfrac{\frac{1}{2}}{\frac{1}{2}}$ are also equal to 1

Worked example	Thinking	Your turn!
Copy and fill in the blank so that the fraction equals 1 $\dfrac{2.6}{\square} = 1$	*What do we know about the numerator and denominator if the fraction equals 1?*	Copy and fill in the blank so that the fraction equals 1 $\dfrac{\square}{10.8} = 1$
$\dfrac{2.6}{2.6} = 1$		

The numerator and denominator must be the same.

▲ Example-problem pair 2

7.1.1 Fluency

In this exercise you can practise applying the mathematical methods that you have just learnt.

1 Write down the value of each fraction:

a $\dfrac{4}{4}$

b $\dfrac{12}{12}$

c $\dfrac{854}{854}$

2 Copy and complete each of these:

a $1 = \dfrac{7}{\square}$

b $1 = \dfrac{\square}{18}$

3 Copy and complete each of these:

a $8 \div 8 = \dfrac{\square}{8} = \square$

b $-11 \div -11 = \dfrac{-11}{\square} = \square$

4 What fraction of each of these shapes is shaded?

a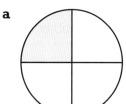

c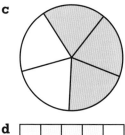

b

d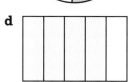

5 Write down the value of each fraction:

a $\dfrac{3.1}{3.1}$

b $\dfrac{\sqrt{5}}{\sqrt{5}}$

c $\dfrac{\frac{1}{3}}{\frac{1}{3}}$

Chapter 7

7.1.2 Improper fractions and mixed numbers

Objective

You will learn how to:

- convert between improper fractions and mixed numbers

If the numerator of a positive fraction is less than the denominator, then the fraction is less than 1 and is called a **proper fraction**.

$$\frac{2}{3} < 1$$

$$\frac{7}{12} < 1$$

If the numerator of a positive fraction is greater than the denominator, then the fraction is greater than 1 and is called an **improper fraction**.

$$\frac{12}{7} > 1$$

$$\frac{3}{2} > 1$$

The fraction $\frac{3}{2}$ looks like this on a bar model:

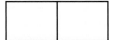 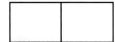

$\frac{3}{2}$ is the same as three halves. One whole shape only has two halves, so in order to add the other half you need split another whole in two and use one half.

This bar model shows you that $\frac{3}{2}$ is the same as $\frac{2}{2} + \frac{1}{2}$. Since $\frac{2}{2} = 1$, this means that $\frac{3}{2} = 1 + \frac{1}{2} = 1\frac{1}{2}$

When you write a number greater than 1 as an integer and a proper fraction, you call this a **mixed number**.

Here is the same number with three representations:

Bar model	Improper fraction	Mixed number
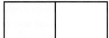	$\frac{3}{2}$	$1\frac{1}{2}$

Worked example	Thinking	Your turn!
Here is a fraction shown on a bar model.	How many parts is each whole split into?	Here is a fraction shown on a bar model.
Write the fraction as an improper fraction and as a mixed number.	How many parts are shaded?	Write the fraction as an improper fraction and as a mixed number.
Improper fraction: $\dfrac{5}{3}$		
Mixed number: $1\dfrac{2}{3}$		

Each whole is split into three equal parts.

There are five shaded, or one whole and two parts.

▲ Example-problem pair 1

As you know, the number line extends in two directions from zero. For every positive integer there is a negative integer the same size. This is true for fractions too: for every positive fraction, there is a negative fraction the same size. Negative fractions can be proper or improper, or written as mixed numbers, just like positive fractions.

7.1.2 Fluency

In this exercise you can practise applying the mathematical methods that you have just learnt.

1 Here are some fractions:

$\dfrac{1}{2}, \dfrac{8}{7}, \dfrac{2}{3}, \dfrac{9}{9}, \dfrac{11}{10}, \dfrac{5}{3}, \dfrac{12}{12}, \dfrac{19}{20}$

Sort these fractions into those

a less than one

b equal to one

c greater than one

2 Write each of these as a mixed number:

a $\dfrac{5}{4}$ **b** $\dfrac{9}{7}$ **c** $\dfrac{18}{5}$ **d** $\dfrac{31}{14}$

3 Write each of these as a mixed number:

a $\dfrac{42}{25}$ **b** $\dfrac{47}{19}$ **c** $\dfrac{97}{30}$ **d** $\dfrac{107}{42}$

4 Write each of these as an improper fraction:

a $1\dfrac{4}{5}$ **b** $2\dfrac{5}{6}$ **c** $3\dfrac{8}{9}$ **d** $5\dfrac{6}{11}$

5 Write each of these as a mixed number:

a $-\dfrac{12}{7}$ **b** $-\dfrac{19}{9}$

6 Write each of these as an improper fraction:

a $-1\dfrac{2}{3}$ **b** $-2\dfrac{1}{5}$

Chapter 7

7.1.3 Writing fractions as divisions and decimals

You have already seen that the fraction $\frac{2}{3}$ can be thought of as splitting the whole into three parts, then using two of them.

It can also be thought of as two wholes split into three parts. You can see these two representations as two different bar models:

One whole split into three parts, use two parts.

Two wholes split into three equal parts.

This means that you can think of $\frac{2}{3}$ as two wholes divided into three parts, or $2 \div 3$.

Any fraction can be thought of as the numerator divided by the denominator, and you use this idea to convert fractions into decimals, using short division.

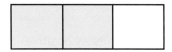

$$\frac{3}{5} = 3 \div 5$$

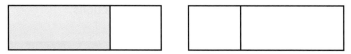

Calculator

To enter a fraction on a calculator, press ▣ or ▣.

Alternatively, type in the numerator, then ÷ , then the denominator, and then press =

To convert between a decimal and a fraction press the conversion key. It may look like S⇔D or FORMAT .

Worked example	Thinking	Your turn!
Convert $\dfrac{5}{8}$ to a decimal.	*What calculation does the fraction bar represent?* ○	Convert $\dfrac{9}{16}$ to a decimal.
$\dfrac{5}{8} = 5 \div 8 = 0.625$ $\begin{array}{r} 0.\ 6\ 2\ 5 \\ 8\overline{)5.^50^20^40} \end{array}$		

The fraction bar represents division.

▲ Example-problem pair 1

Calculators can only show a certain number of digits. For some fractions the decimal shown is not exactly the same number, just the digits that fit on the screen:

$\dfrac{1}{3} \neq 0.333333$

7.1.3 Fluency

In this exercise you can practise applying the mathematical methods that you have just learnt.

1 Irem says that $\dfrac{4}{5}$ represents the same number as $4 \div 5$

Is Irem correct? Explain your answer.

2 Barney says that $\dfrac{18}{144}$ is equal to 0.125

Use the converter key on your calculator to check Barney's answer.

3 Enter $\dfrac{14}{32}$ as a division on your calculator.

Write down the decimal equivalent of this fraction.

4 Convert each of these to a decimal:

  a $\dfrac{3}{4}$ **c** $\dfrac{7}{8}$ **e** $\dfrac{19}{5}$

  b $\dfrac{2}{5}$ **d** $\dfrac{21}{6}$ **f** $\dfrac{94}{8}$

5 Mishael says that 0.156 is equal to $\dfrac{39}{250}$

Use the converter key on your calculator to check Mishael's answer.

6 Malak enters $\dfrac{11}{36}$ into her calculator and uses the converter key to convert it to a decimal.

The calculator displays the number 0.3055555556

Malak says that the decimal equivalent of $\dfrac{11}{36}$ is longer than the number displayed on the calculator.

Is Malak correct? Explain your answer.

7 Convert each of these to a decimal:

  a $\dfrac{75}{8}$ **c** $\dfrac{65}{16}$

  b $\dfrac{142}{5}$ **d** $\dfrac{843}{12}$

8 Simon enters $\dfrac{17}{52}$ as a division into his calculator.

He says that the decimal equivalent of his number is exactly 0.3269230769 because that is what is shown on his calculator.

Is Simon correct? Explain your answer.

Chapter 7

7.1.4 Writing decimals as fractions

Objective

You will learn how to:
- write a decimal as a fraction
- convert between fractions and decimals on a calculator

Fractions and decimals are both ways of showing parts of a whole. You can convert decimals into fractions using your knowledge of place value from Chapter 1

Before converting a decimal into a fraction, you need to decide if it is a **terminating decimal** or a **recurring decimal**.

Decimals where the digits after the decimal point stop, or terminate, are called terminating decimals. 0.4, 0.28, 0.179, 0.123456 are examples of terminating decimals.

Calculator

Enter a decimal into your calculator and press $=$. The equivalent fraction is shown. Press 0 $\cdot$ 4 $=$. The calculator displays $\dfrac{2}{5}$.

When you write some numbers as a decimal the digits do not terminate but continue forever in a repeating pattern. These are called recurring decimals. You write a dot above the digits that repeat. For example:

$$\frac{4}{9} = 0.4444444... = 0.\dot{4}$$

$$\frac{28}{99} = 0.2828282828... = 0.\dot{2}\dot{8}$$

$$\frac{179}{999} = 0.179179179... = 0.\dot{1}7\dot{9}$$

You can write any terminating decimal as a fraction with a power of ten in the denominator.

For example, 0.1 is the same as $\dfrac{1}{10}$, since the 1 is in the tenths column. 0.43 has a 4 in the tenths column and a 3 in the hundredths column. It is forty-three hundredths, so it can be written as $\dfrac{43}{100}$

Worked example	Thinking	Your turn!
Write 2.713 as a mixed number and as an improper fraction	*What is the place value of the last decimal digit?*	Write 1.462 as a mixed number and as an improper fraction.
$0.713 = \dfrac{713}{1000}, 2 = \dfrac{2000}{1000}$ $2.713 = 2\dfrac{713}{1000} = \dfrac{2713}{1000}$		

The last digit is in the thousandths column so I can write 0.713 and 2 as fractions over 1000

▲ Example-problem pair 1

7.1.4 Fluency

In this exercise you can practise applying the mathematical methods that you have just learnt.

1 Complete each of these:

a $0.6 = \dfrac{6}{\square}$ **c** $0.54 = \dfrac{54}{\square}$

b $0.3 = \dfrac{\square}{10}$ **d** $0.78 = \dfrac{\square}{100}$

2 Write each of these as a single fraction:

a 0.7   **d** 0.6731   **g** 3.319

b 0.63   **e** 1.1   **h** 7.7139

c 0.127   **f** 2.17

3 Write each of these as both an improper fraction and a mixed number:

a 1.3

b 6.71

c 8.757

d 12.6517

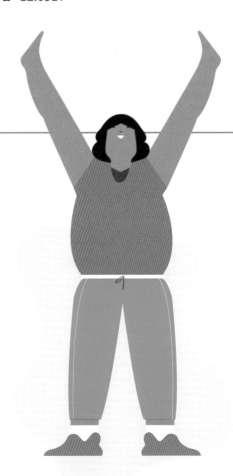

7.1.5 Simplifying fractions

Objective

You will learn how to:

*   write a fraction in its simplest form

You know that different fractions can represent the same number. $\frac{9}{9} = \frac{5678}{5678} = 1$ and $\frac{2}{4} = \frac{1}{2}$. These are examples of **equivalent fractions**. Often you will find it useful to work with fractions in their **simplest form**.

A fraction in its simplest form has an integer numerator and denominator that do not have any common factors (other than 1).

To simplify a fraction, you cancel common factors from the numerator and denominator. This means you divide both top and bottom by the same number. This doesn't change the value of the fraction.

You can simplify in stages, checking each answer for common factors. Or you can find the highest common factor (look back to Subsection 2.3.5) of the numerator and denominator and divide them both by this factor.

Worked example	Thinking	Your turn!	
Write the fraction $\frac{26}{104}$ in its simplest form.	*Can we spot any common factors?*	Write the fraction $\frac{8}{12}$ in its simplest form.	Both the numerator and denominator are even, so I know 2 is a common factor.
$\frac{26}{104} = \frac{26 \div 2}{104 \div 2} = \frac{13}{52}$	*Are there any more common factors?*		The numerator 13 is prime, so I just need to check if the denominator divides by it. $13 \times 4 = 52$
$= \frac{13 \div 13}{52 \div 13} = \frac{1}{4}$			

🔺 Example-problem pair 1

When fractions are in their simplest form both the numerator and denominator are integers. To simplify a fraction written with decimals, you start by multiplying the numerator and denominator by a number that will make them integers, using the same number for both. If a decimal has one decimal place, you can multiply it by 10 to make it an integer. If it has two decimal places, you can multiply it by 100.

Calculator

You can use your calculator to check if a fraction is in its simplest form. Type in $\dfrac{840}{1206}$ using the fraction key  or ▪, or the division key ÷ . Your calculator will display $\dfrac{140}{201}$

7.1.5 Fluency

In this exercise you can practise applying the mathematical methods that you have just learnt.

1 Simplify each of these fractions:

   a $\dfrac{2}{4}$ **c** $\dfrac{8}{24}$

   b $\dfrac{6}{9}$ **d** $\dfrac{48}{60}$

2 Complete **a** and **b**.

   a Find the highest common factor of each pair of numbers:

     i 34 and 51

     ii 108 and 144

     iii 216 and 600

   b Now simplify each of these fractions:

     i $\dfrac{34}{51}$

     ii $\dfrac{108}{144}$

     iii $\dfrac{216}{600}$

3 Write each of these as a fraction in its simplest form:

$$\dfrac{2}{3}, \dfrac{7}{14}, \dfrac{19}{20}, \dfrac{42}{48}, \dfrac{33}{60}, \dfrac{8}{21}, \dfrac{11}{44}, \dfrac{85}{100}$$

Which of these fractions are already in their simplest form?

4 Write each of these as a fraction in its simplest form:

   a $\dfrac{14.5}{20}$ **c** $\dfrac{7}{12.5}$

   b $\dfrac{6.4}{8}$ **d** $\dfrac{4}{6.4}$

Now check your answers. You may want to use your calculator. Did you get any wrong and can you work out why?

7.1 Exercises

7.1 Intelligent practice

"Why is it intelligent?" You might notice a connection when you move on from one question to the next. You can use the Reflect, Expect, Check, Explain process (page X) to:

- *reflect* on what's different between each question and the one that came before
- decide how you *expect* this answer to be different
- complete the question and *check* your answer
- *explain* to yourself why your expectation was correct or incorrect.

> **EXAMPLE**
>
> **Question 1a**
> State whether each fraction is equal to $1(=1)$, less than $1(<1)$ or greater than $1(>1)$.
>
> $\dfrac{1}{3}$
>
> The numerator is less than the denominator, so the fraction is less than 1.
>
> **Question 1b**
> State whether each fraction is equal to $1(=1)$, less than $1(<1)$ or greater than $1(>1)$.
>
> $\dfrac{2}{3}$
>
> **Reflect:** This is like question 1a but the numerator is larger.
> **Expect:** The numerator is still less than 3, so I think the fraction is less than 1.
> **Check:** Yes, $2 < 3$, so $\dfrac{2}{3} < 1$.
> **Explain:** I was right! The numerator did not pass 3 so the fraction was less than 1.

1 State whether each fraction is equal to $1(=1)$, less than $1(<1)$ or greater than $1(>1)$.

a $\dfrac{1}{3}$

b $\dfrac{2}{3}$

c $\dfrac{3}{3}$

d $\dfrac{4}{3}$

e $\dfrac{5}{3}$

f $\dfrac{2.5}{3}$

d $\dfrac{11}{2}$

e $\dfrac{22}{2}$

f $-\dfrac{22}{2}$

g $-\dfrac{21}{2}$

2 Convert each fraction from an improper fraction to a mixed number.

a $\dfrac{5}{2}$

b $\dfrac{6}{2}$

c $\dfrac{7}{2}$

3 Convert each fraction from a mixed number to an improper fraction.

a $1\dfrac{1}{5}$

b $1\dfrac{2}{5}$

c $1\dfrac{3}{5}$

d $2\dfrac{3}{5}$

e $20\dfrac{3}{5}$

f $-20\dfrac{3}{5}$

g $-2\dfrac{3}{5}$

4 Simplify each of these fractions.

a $\dfrac{2}{20}$ d $\dfrac{20}{20}$ g $\dfrac{25}{20}$

b $\dfrac{4}{20}$ e $\dfrac{200}{20}$ h $\dfrac{2.5}{20}$

c $\dfrac{10}{20}$ f $\dfrac{100}{20}$

5 Convert these fractions to decimals.

a $\dfrac{1}{2}$ d $\dfrac{5}{4}$

b $\dfrac{3}{2}$ e $\dfrac{5}{8}$

c $\dfrac{5}{2}$ f $\dfrac{5}{16}$

6 Write each of these decimals as a proper fraction or a mixed number in its simplest form.

a 0.3

b 0.6

c 0.9

d 0.09

e 0.009

f 0.999

g 1.999

h 9.999

i 9.333

j 3.333

k 3.3

l −3.3

7.1 Method selection

In these questions you'll need to think carefully about which methods to apply.

For some questions you might need to use skills from earlier chapters.

1 Copy and complete each statement using >, <, or =

a $\dfrac{8}{9}\Box 1$ c $\dfrac{16}{16}\Box 1$

b $\dfrac{9}{8}\Box 1$ d $\dfrac{24}{16}\Box 1$

2 You are given $304 = 2^4 \times 19, 512 = 2^9$

Write each of these fractions in their simplest form.

a $\dfrac{19}{304}$ c $\dfrac{304}{512}$

b $\dfrac{32}{304}$ d $\dfrac{608}{512}$

3 Write the number 1 as a fraction in three different ways.

4 Write the number $\dfrac{3}{2}$ as a fraction in three different ways.

5 Convert each number to a decimal.

a $\dfrac{4}{25}$

b $\dfrac{40}{25}$

c $4\dfrac{1}{25}$

d $\dfrac{41}{25}$

Chapter 7

6 Julia says, "The quickest way to convert a fraction to a decimal is to convert it so that its denominator is 10 or 100." Check Julia's method for the fractions given. Can you find equivalent fractions with a denominator of 10 or 100 for all of them? If not, what other method could you use to convert them to a decimal?

a $\dfrac{4}{5}$ **d** $\dfrac{1}{8}$

b $\dfrac{8}{5}$ **e** $\dfrac{7}{16}$

c $\dfrac{1}{4}$ **f** $\dfrac{2}{3}$

7.1 Purposeful practice

There may be more than one way to approach these questions.

Once you have answered a question one way, can you think of another way?

1 Here are two fractions with some of their digits hidden. Which fraction is greater? How do you know?

$$\dfrac{2\square\square4}{4\square\square\square} \qquad \dfrac{3\square\square\square}{2\square1\square}$$

2 Using all the digits from 1 to 4 once only, find all the fractions that are
   a less than 1 and can be simplified
   b greater than 1 and can be simplified
   c less than 1 and cannot be simplified
   d greater than 1 and cannot be simplified.

3 Leanne says that $\dfrac{2}{3}$ simplifies to $\dfrac{1}{1.5}$. Is Leanne correct? Explain your reasoning.

4 Here are five digits.

   5 1 2 4 6

   In each case, use each digit once to make
   a the greatest possible fraction
   b the least possible fraction
   c the fraction closest to or equal to 1

5 Copy and complete the Venn diagram with a fraction that fits each section.

Simplifies to $\frac{3}{4}$

Denominator is prime

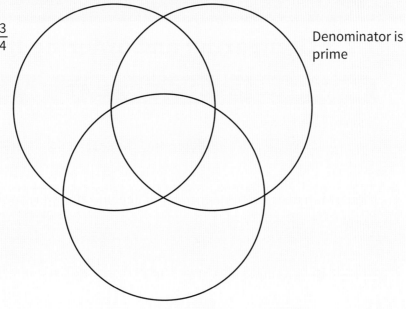

Less than 1

Are there any sections that cannot be filled? Explain your answer.

6 Match each fraction on the left with the equivalent division calculation on the right.

$\frac{8}{10}$ $1 \div 2$

$\frac{9}{12}$ $4 \div 5$

$\frac{8}{20}$ $3 \div 4$

$\frac{16}{32}$ $2 \div 5$

Comparing and ordering fractions

7.2.1 Comparing and ordering fractions

Objectives

You will learn how to:

- compare and order fractions using common denominators

If fractions have the same numerator or denominator, you can compare them fairly easily.

$$\frac{5}{33} > \frac{4}{33}$$ ◄──── fewer lots of $\frac{1}{33}$ and $\frac{3}{5} > \frac{3}{7}$ ◄──── dividing by a larger number than 5 so the result is smaller

For other fractions you can compare them by giving them the same denominator.

You use equivalent fractions to do this. Use the lowest common multiple of the two denominators as the **common denominator**.

For instance, to compare $\frac{5}{8}$ and $\frac{2}{3}$, you can convert them both into twenty-fourths:

$$\frac{5}{8} = \frac{5 \times 3}{8 \times 3} = \frac{15}{24}$$

$$\frac{2}{3} = \frac{2 \times 8}{3 \times 8} = \frac{16}{24}$$ ──── multiplying top and bottom by the same number does not change the value of the fraction

Since $\frac{15}{24} < \frac{16}{24}$, you can see that $\frac{5}{8} < \frac{2}{3}$

Worked example	Thinking	Your turn!	
Write these numbers in order from least to greatest. $\frac{5}{9}, \frac{8}{15}$ and $\frac{3}{5}$	*Are any clearly greater or less because they share a numerator or denominator?* *How do we make the fractions easier to compare?*	Write these numbers in order from least to greatest. $\frac{3}{4}, \frac{7}{10}$ and $\frac{5}{8}$	*No, I can't tell straight away if any are greater or less. They are all less than 1.* *I'll change the fractions so they have a common denominator. The LCM of 9, 15 and 5 is 45, so I will make the common denominator 45.*

Worked example	Thinking	Your turn!
$\dfrac{5}{9} = \dfrac{5 \times 5}{9 \times 5} = \dfrac{25}{45}$ $\dfrac{8}{15} = \dfrac{8 \times 3}{15 \times 3} = \dfrac{24}{45}$ $\dfrac{3}{5} = \dfrac{3 \times 9}{5 \times 9} = \dfrac{27}{45}$		
$\dfrac{24}{45} < \dfrac{25}{45} < \dfrac{27}{45}$ So $\dfrac{8}{15} < \dfrac{5}{9} < \dfrac{3}{5}$		

▲ Example-problem pair 1

7.2.1 Fluency

In this exercise you can practise applying the mathematical methods that you have just learnt.

1 Copy the pairs of fractions and write < or > between each pair to make the statements true.

   a $\dfrac{1}{6} \square \dfrac{1}{7}$ **b** $\dfrac{12}{17} \square \dfrac{13}{17}$

2 Copy each pair of fractions and write < or > between them to make the statement true. Write each pair of fractions using a common denominator to help you.

   a $\dfrac{7}{8} \square \dfrac{8}{9}$ **c** $\dfrac{7}{12} \square \dfrac{4}{7}$

   b $\dfrac{8}{11} \square \dfrac{4}{5}$ **d** $\dfrac{3}{4} \square \dfrac{37}{51}$

3 Copy the pairs of fractions and write < or > between each pair to make the statements true.

   a $\dfrac{9}{7} \square \dfrac{10}{7}$

   b $\dfrac{1}{2} \square \dfrac{1}{3}$

4 Write the fractions using a common denominator and use this to put the fractions in order, least first.

$$\dfrac{1}{2}, \dfrac{3}{4}, \dfrac{5}{8}, \dfrac{7}{10}, \dfrac{5}{6}, \dfrac{11}{20}$$

5 Write the fractions using a common denominator and use this to put the fractions in order, least first.

$$\dfrac{8}{5}, \dfrac{7}{4}, \dfrac{37}{20}, \dfrac{5}{3}, \dfrac{11}{6}, \dfrac{17}{10}$$

6 Copy the pairs of fractions and write < or > between each pair to make the statements true.

   a $-\dfrac{7}{6} \square -\dfrac{5}{6}$ **b** $-\dfrac{12}{13} \square -\dfrac{12}{17}$

7 Write the fractions using a common denominator and use this to put the fractions in order, least first.

$$\dfrac{6}{7}, \dfrac{8}{9}, -\dfrac{2}{3}, \dfrac{17}{21}, -\dfrac{5}{7}, -\dfrac{50}{63}$$

7.2.2 Comparing and ordering fractions by converting to decimals

Objective

You will learn how to:

- compare and order fractions by converting to decimals

Sometimes, it is helpful to convert your fractions into decimals. If you want to compare $\frac{1}{8}, \frac{3}{10}$ and $\frac{131}{1000}$, you could write them all as decimals.

$$\frac{1}{8} = 0.125 \qquad \frac{3}{10} = 0.3 \qquad \frac{131}{1000} = 0.131$$

Since $0.125 < 0.131 < 0.3$, you know that $\frac{1}{8} < \frac{131}{1000} < \frac{3}{10}$

To convert fractions to decimals you can use short division or your calculator. You may also use the decimal equivalents of some common fractions you have learned.

$$\frac{1}{2} = 0.5 \qquad \frac{1}{5} = 0.2$$

$$\frac{1}{4} = 0.25 \qquad \frac{3}{4} = 0.75$$

$$\frac{1}{8} = 0.125$$

You do not always need to convert the numbers you are comparing to the same format to order them. Check if some are negative and some are positive first, and then see which are less than or greater than 1.

Worked example	Thinking	Your turn!	
Write these numbers in order from least to greatest. $-\frac{1}{2}, \frac{1}{2}, \frac{5}{4}, \frac{3}{5}, \frac{52}{65}$	*Are any negative? Are any greater than 1?*	Write these numbers in order from least to greatest. $\frac{3}{4}, \frac{7}{10}, \frac{10}{7}, \frac{5}{8}, -\frac{4}{5}$	Yes $-\frac{1}{2}$ is the only negative number and $\frac{5}{4}$ is the only number greater than 1, so you only need to check the others.
$-\frac{1}{2} < 0$ and $\frac{5}{4} > 1$	*How do we make the fractions easier to compare?*		I could change the fractions so they have a common denominator but I'm going to use decimals – I know what a half is to start with.
$\frac{1}{2} = 0.5 \quad \frac{3}{5} = 0.6 \quad \frac{52}{65} = 0.8$			
$-\frac{1}{2} < \frac{1}{2} < \frac{3}{5} < \frac{52}{65} < \frac{5}{4}$			

▲ Example-problem pair 1

7.2.2 Fluency

In this exercise you can practise applying the mathematical methods that you have just learnt.

1 Convert the fractions to decimals and write each pair with the correct symbol, < or >, between them.

a $\dfrac{1}{2} \square \dfrac{3}{5}$

b $\dfrac{3}{10} \square \dfrac{1}{4}$

c $\dfrac{4}{5} \square \dfrac{3}{4}$

d $\dfrac{3}{4} \square \dfrac{9}{10}$

2 Write these numbers in ascending order.

$\dfrac{1}{4},\ 0.23,\ \dfrac{1}{5},\ 0.27,\ \dfrac{14}{50},\ \dfrac{29}{100}$

3 Write these numbers in ascending order.

$-0.1,\ \dfrac{7}{100},\ \dfrac{3}{20},\ -\dfrac{1}{5},\ 0.09,\ -\dfrac{3}{21}$

4 Convert each fraction to a decimal and use this to put the fractions in order, least first.

$\dfrac{7}{10},\ \dfrac{3}{4},\ \dfrac{4}{5},\ \dfrac{5}{8},\ \dfrac{11}{20},\ \dfrac{1}{2}$

5 Without using a calculator, write each pair with the correct symbol < or >.

a $\dfrac{1}{4} \square 0.23$

b $-\dfrac{4}{5} \square -0.81$

c $\dfrac{9}{5} \square \dfrac{17}{10}$

6 Write these numbers in ascending order.

$\dfrac{5}{6},\ 0.8,\ \dfrac{5}{7},\ -\dfrac{4}{5},\ -0.75,\ \dfrac{3}{4},\ -\dfrac{17}{20},\ \dfrac{77}{100}$

7 Convert each fraction to a decimal and use this to put the fractions in order, least first.

$\dfrac{3}{8},\ \dfrac{7}{20},\ \dfrac{5}{16},\ \dfrac{37}{100},\ \dfrac{361}{1000},\ \dfrac{2}{5},\ \dfrac{9}{25},\ \dfrac{173}{500}$

7.2.3 The infinite nature of the number line

Objective ☑️

You will learn how to:
- order positive and negative fractions and decimals:

Here is a number line from 0 to 10.

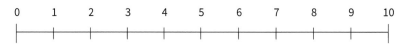

If you zoom in between 0 and 1 you can see more numbers.

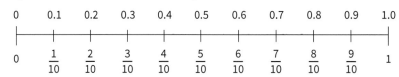

If you zoom in between 0.1 and 0.2 you can see more numbers.

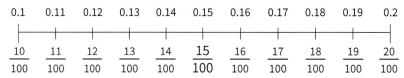

Any section of the number line has infinitely many numbers on it. You can always zoom in and see more. This means you can always find a number that sits between two others.

Worked example	Thinking	Your turn!
Find a fraction in its simplest form between $\dfrac{3}{4}$ and $\dfrac{7}{8}$.	*Which equivalent fractions will help us answer the question?*	Find a fraction in its simplest form between $\dfrac{1}{2}$ and $\dfrac{5}{9}$
$\dfrac{3 \times 2}{4 \times 2} = \dfrac{6}{8}$ $\dfrac{6 \times 2}{8 \times 2} = \dfrac{12}{16} \quad \dfrac{7 \times 2}{8 \times 2} = \dfrac{14}{16}$	*Should we use fractions or decimals to work out an answer?*	
$\dfrac{13}{16}$ is between $\dfrac{12}{16}$ and $\dfrac{14}{16}$ Or, $\dfrac{3}{4} = 0.75, \dfrac{7}{8} = 0.875$ Example, $0.8 = \dfrac{4}{5}$ $\dfrac{13}{16}$ and $\dfrac{4}{5}$ are between $\dfrac{3}{4}$ and $\dfrac{7}{8}$	*How many possible answers are there?*	

I can start by exchanging quarters for eighths and then eighths for sixteenths, and so on. My fraction should not have a decimal numerator or denominator.

I could convert both numbers to decimals and find a decimal between them, and then convert that to a fraction.

There's an infinite number!

▲ Example-problem pair 1

7.2.3 Fluency

In this exercise you can practise applying the mathematical methods that you have just learnt.

1 The number line shows whole numbers.

30　31　32　33　34　35

a Write a number greater than 32 and less than 33 and mark it on a copy of the number line.

b Write a number less than 35 and greater than 34 and mark it on a copy of the number line.

2 Answer the questions below.

a Write a number greater than 0.99 and less than 1

b Write a number greater than 0.9999 and less than 1

c How many numbers are there that are greater than 0.9999 and less than 1?

3 For each part, write a number that is between the two numbers.

a $\frac{1}{5}$ and 0.21

b 0.74 and $\frac{3}{4}$

c 1.35 and $1\frac{2}{5}$

d $3\frac{3}{10}$ and 3.34

4 Write a number between $\frac{1}{13}$ and $\frac{1}{12}$

5 Write a number between $\frac{3}{20}$ and $\frac{3}{19}$

6 Answer the questions below.

a How many fractions are there?

b How many decimals are there?

c How many positive fractions and decimals have a corresponding negative?

7.2 Exercises

7.2 Intelligent practice

"Why is it intelligent?" You might notice a connection when you move on from one question to the next. You can use the Reflect, Expect, Check, Explain process (page X) to:

- *reflect* on what's different between each question and the one that came before
- decide how you *expect* this answer to be different
- complete the question and *check* your answer
- *explain* to yourself why your expectation was correct or incorrect.

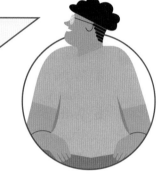

EXAMPLE

Question 1a

Copy and complete the statement with the correct symbol, < or >.

$\frac{1}{2} \square \frac{3}{5}$.

Since $\frac{1}{2} = \frac{5}{10} = 0.5$ and $\frac{3}{5} = \frac{6}{10} = 0.6$, $\frac{1}{2} < \frac{3}{5}$

Question 1b

Copy and complete the statement with the correct symbol, < or >.

$\frac{1}{2} \square \frac{2}{5}$

Reflect: This is like question 1a but the fraction on the right is smaller.

Expect: The fraction on the right is smaller so I think I will need to write > this time.

Check: $\frac{1}{2} = 0.5$ and $\frac{2}{5} = 0.4$, so $\frac{1}{2} > \frac{2}{5}$

Explain: I was right! The second fraction became smaller than $\frac{1}{2}$

---

1 Copy and complete each statement with the correct symbol, < or >.

a $\frac{1}{2} \square \frac{3}{5}$

b $\frac{1}{2} \square \frac{2}{5}$

c $\frac{1}{4} \square \frac{2}{5}$

d $\frac{1}{8} \square \frac{2}{5}$

e $\frac{9}{8} \square \frac{2}{5}$

2 Copy and complete each statement with the correct symbol, < or >.

a $\frac{3}{8} \square \frac{3}{16}$

b $\frac{3}{16} \square \frac{3}{32}$

c $\frac{3}{32} \square \frac{9}{32}$

d $\frac{9}{32} \square \frac{9}{40}$

e $\frac{32}{9} \square \frac{40}{9}$

3 Copy and complete each statement with the correct symbol, < or >.

a $-\frac{8}{11} \square -\frac{7}{10}$

b $-\frac{16}{11} \square -\frac{7}{10}$

c $-\frac{16}{11} \square -\frac{14}{10}$

d $-\frac{16}{12} \square -\frac{14}{9}$

e $-\frac{16}{24} \square -\frac{14}{18}$

4 Write a number between the two given.

  a 15 and 18

  b 15 and 16

  c 1.5 and 1.6

  d 0.15 and 0.16

  e 1.15 and 1.16

  f 11.5 and 11.6

  g 115 and 116

5 Find a fraction between the two given. Give your answer in its simplest form.

  a $\dfrac{1}{2}$ and $\dfrac{3}{4}$

  d $\dfrac{3}{4}$ and $\dfrac{7}{8}$

  b $\dfrac{1}{2}$ and $\dfrac{5}{8}$

  e $\dfrac{1}{2}$ and $\dfrac{9}{16}$

  c $\dfrac{5}{8}$ and $\dfrac{7}{8}$

7.2 Method selection

In these questions you'll need to think carefully about which methods to apply.

For some questions you might need to use skills from earlier chapters.

1 Draw arrows to show these fractions on a copy of the number line.

$$\dfrac{1}{2} \qquad \dfrac{3}{4} \qquad \dfrac{3}{8} \qquad \dfrac{7}{8}$$

2 Write these numbers in order, from greatest to least.

  a $\dfrac{3}{4}, \dfrac{7}{8}, \dfrac{1}{2}, \dfrac{9}{16}$

  d $-\dfrac{17}{200}, -\dfrac{1}{10}, -\dfrac{3}{50}, -\dfrac{7}{100}$

  b $\dfrac{2}{9}, \dfrac{4}{11}, \dfrac{8}{17}, \dfrac{2}{7}$

  e $\dfrac{1}{4}, 0.18, \dfrac{3}{10}, \dfrac{1}{5}$

  c $\dfrac{1}{5}, \dfrac{3}{10}, \dfrac{31}{100}, \dfrac{9}{25}$

  f $1.01, \dfrac{11}{10}, \dfrac{6}{5}, \dfrac{19}{20}$

3 There are 120 students in a year group.

5 students play the trumpet.

What fraction of the year group does not play the trumpet?

Give your answer in its simplest form.

4 In Sanjit's class there are 32 students. Sanjit says that $\dfrac{1}{5}$ of the class is left-handed. Explain how you know Sanjit must be wrong.

5 School A says that $\dfrac{3}{5}$ of their students attended maths club.

School B says that $\dfrac{2}{3}$ of their students attended maths club.

Which school had the bigger proportion of its students attend maths club?

6 Vish is asked to write a number between 0.34 and 0.4. He writes 0.5 and gives the reason, 'Because 5 is between 4 and 34.' Is Vish correct? Explain your reasoning.

7 A **unit fraction** is one whose numerator is 1. Find a unit fraction between each of these numbers.

a $\dfrac{1}{10}$ and $\dfrac{1}{8}$ **c** $\dfrac{1}{4}$ and $\dfrac{5}{12}$ **e** $\dfrac{1}{100}$ and $\dfrac{1}{80}$

b $\dfrac{1}{50}$ and $\dfrac{3}{50}$ **d** $\dfrac{1}{18}$ and $\dfrac{1}{9}$ **f** $\dfrac{1}{15}$ and $\dfrac{2}{15}$

7.2 Purposeful practice

There may be more than one way to approach these questions.
Once you have answered a question one way, can you think of another way?

1 Complete **a** and **b** below.

a Using all the digits from 1 to 8 once only, copy and complete this comparison statement.

$$\frac{\square}{\square} > \frac{\square}{\square} > \frac{\square}{\square} > \frac{\square}{\square}$$

b Now try part **a** again, giving a different answer but using the same digits.

2 Show that

a $\dfrac{5}{4}$ is between $\dfrac{6}{5}$ and $\dfrac{4}{3}$

b $\dfrac{13}{10}$ is between $\dfrac{6}{5}$ and $\dfrac{4}{3}$

3 Find five fractions that are between

$\dfrac{1}{3}$ and $\dfrac{2}{3}$ whose denominators are less than 25

4 Complete **a** and **b** below.

a Using the digits 1, 2, 3 and 4 once each, fill in the boxes to make the statement with a fraction and a decimal true.

$$\frac{\square}{\square} > \square.\square$$

b How many ways can you answer part **a**?

5 Here are Jane's test scores for last week.

Maths: 27 out of 30

English: 40 out of 50

Science: $7\frac{1}{2}$ out of 10

Write these subjects in order of Jane's success, from greatest to least.

6 a Copy and complete this Venn diagram with a fraction that fits each section.
If any of the section are impossible to fill, explain why

Greater than $\frac{1}{2}$

Denominator is prime

Less than 1

b How many fractions can go in the centre section?

7.3.1 Adding and subtracting fractions with a common denominator

Whenever you add or subtract, you collect numbers of the same counting unit. Ones, tens and hundreds are all integer counting units, so when you add $163 + 4$, you add the ones ($5 + 3$) to get 8 ones, you add the tens ($6 + 4$) to get 10 tens, but you exchange this for 1 hundred to get 208. Try setting this out as a column addition to see how this happens on paper.

The idea of collecting counting units is true for all addition and subtraction, including with fractions. You can add sevenths with sevenths:

2 sevenths + 3 sevenths = 5 sevenths

$$\frac{2}{7} \quad + \quad \frac{3}{7} \quad = \quad \frac{5}{7}$$

Here the counting unit is the unit fraction $\frac{1}{7}$ and you are adding 2 lots of $\frac{1}{7}$ to 3 lots of $\frac{1}{7}$ to get 5 lots of $\frac{1}{7}$. The bar model on the left illustrates this.

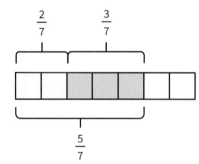

Worked example	Thinking	Your turn!
Work out $\frac{2}{5} + \frac{4}{5}$	*The denominators are the same. How does that help?*	Work out $\frac{5}{12} + \frac{1}{12}$
$\frac{2}{5} + \frac{4}{5} = \frac{2+4}{5} = \frac{6}{5}$		

Both fractions have the same counting unit, so I can just add the numerators.

▲ Example-problem pair 1

Since subtraction is the inverse of addition, using the same counting unit works in the same way. You must ensure your fractions have a common denominator before subtracting only the numerators.

7 twelfths − 5 twelfths = 2 twelfths

$$\frac{7}{12} \quad - \quad \frac{5}{12} \quad = \quad \frac{2}{12}$$

Notice that $\frac{2}{12}$ can be simplified to $\frac{1}{6}$. You should simplify your answers wherever possible.

Worked example	Thinking	Your turn!
Work out $\dfrac{12}{7} - \dfrac{5}{7}$	*The denominators are the same. How does that help?*	Work out $\dfrac{19}{8} - \dfrac{7}{8}$
$\dfrac{12}{7} - \dfrac{5}{7} = \dfrac{12-5}{7} = \dfrac{7}{7} = 1$		

Both fractions are in the same counting unit, so I can just subtract the numerators.

▲ Example-problem pair 2

7.3.1 Fluency

In this exercise you can practise applying the mathematical methods that you have just learnt.

1 This bar model represents the calculation

$$\frac{3}{5} + \frac{4}{5} = \frac{7}{5} = 1\frac{2}{5}$$

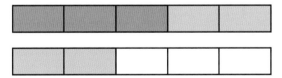

Draw bar models to represent each of these calculations. Work out the answer in each case.

a $\dfrac{2}{9} + \dfrac{5}{9}$ **c** $\dfrac{2}{6} + \dfrac{5}{6}$ **e** $\dfrac{4}{9} + \dfrac{7}{9} + \dfrac{5}{9}$

b $\dfrac{2}{3} + \dfrac{2}{3}$ **d** $\dfrac{6}{7} + \dfrac{5}{7}$

2 Sam says that, in order to add or subtract fractions, you need to have a common denominator as the counting unit.

Is Sam correct? Explain your answer.

3 Can these pairs of fractions can be added or subtracted without any additional working out? Explain your reasoning in each case.

a $\dfrac{3}{8}$ and $\dfrac{7}{8}$ **b** $\dfrac{4}{5}$ and $\dfrac{7}{10}$

c $\dfrac{14}{9}$ and $\dfrac{14}{27}$ **d** $\dfrac{1}{121}$ and $\dfrac{78}{121}$

4 Work out

a $\dfrac{3}{7} - \dfrac{2}{7}$ **c** $\dfrac{7}{13} - \dfrac{5}{13}$

b $\dfrac{3}{11} + \dfrac{4}{11}$ **d** $\dfrac{11}{15} + \dfrac{2}{15}$

5 Mat is calculating $\dfrac{5}{3} + 1$. His working and explanation is shown:

$\dfrac{5}{3} + 1 = \dfrac{5}{3} + \dfrac{5}{5}$ (write 1 as a fraction)

$= \dfrac{10}{8}$ (add the top numbers and the bottom numbers)

Explain the two mistakes that Mat has made and correct his working.

6 Work out

a $3\dfrac{2}{5} + 5\dfrac{2}{5}$ **c** $\dfrac{1}{7} - \dfrac{5}{7}$

b $4\dfrac{7}{11} - 3\dfrac{1}{11}$ **d** $\dfrac{8}{13} - \dfrac{12}{13}$

Chapter 7

7.3.2 Adding and subtracting fractions and mixed numbers

Objective

You will learn how to:

- add and subtract fractions and mixed numbers with different denominators

You can add fifths with fifths:

2 fifths + 9 fifths = 11 fifths

$$\frac{2}{5} + \frac{9}{5} = \frac{11}{5}$$

If you are adding fractions with different denominators, they have different counting units, so the addition is not so straightforward. This bar model shows $\frac{2}{5} + \frac{3}{10}$

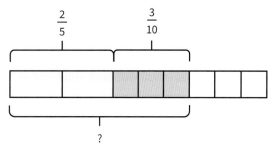

To work out the addition, you have to make an exchange for an equivalent fraction. In this case, you can exchange $\frac{2}{5}$ for $\frac{4}{10}$ $\left(\frac{2}{5} = \frac{2 \times 2}{5 \times 2} = \frac{4}{10} \right)$ as the bar model shows.

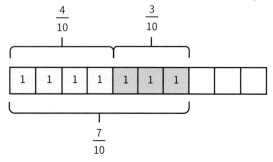

2 fifths + 3 tenths   (here the counting units are different)

$$\frac{2}{5} + \frac{3}{10} \qquad \text{(exchange } \frac{2}{5} \text{ for } \frac{4}{10} \text{ because } \frac{2}{5} \text{ is equivalent to } \frac{4}{10} \text{)}$$

$$\frac{4}{10} + \frac{3}{10} = \frac{7}{10}$$

The addition becomes 4 tenths + 3 tenths, which is 7 tenths. Notice how, once the denominators are the same, you only add the numerators.

Key point

To add fractions with different denominators, you find equivalent fractions that have the same denominator and then you add the numerators.

Worked example	Thinking	Your turn!
Work out $\dfrac{1}{16} + \dfrac{3}{4}$	*Are the denominators the same?*	Work out $\dfrac{2}{3} + \dfrac{5}{9}$
$\dfrac{3}{4} = \dfrac{3 \times 4}{4 \times 4} = \dfrac{12}{16}$		
$\dfrac{1}{16} + \dfrac{12}{16} = \dfrac{1+12}{16} = \dfrac{13}{16}$		

No, I need to make them the same. I can exchange quarters for sixteenths.

▲ Example-problem pair 1

Since subtraction is the inverse of addition, it works in the same way. You must ensure fractions have a common denominator before subtracting the numerators.

If you have mixed numbers you can make them improper fractions first.

Worked example	Thinking	Your turn!
Work out $1\dfrac{2}{7} - \dfrac{2}{3}$	*What can we do with the mixed number before we subtract?*	Work out $2\dfrac{1}{4} - \dfrac{3}{7}$
$1\dfrac{2}{7} = \dfrac{9}{7}$	*Are the denominators the same?*	
$\dfrac{9}{7} = \dfrac{9 \times 3}{7 \times 3} = \dfrac{27}{21}$ $\dfrac{2}{3} = \dfrac{2 \times 7}{3 \times 7} = \dfrac{14}{21}$		
$\dfrac{27}{21} - \dfrac{14}{21} = \dfrac{27-14}{21} = \dfrac{13}{21}$		

I can convert the mixed number to an improper fraction.

No, I can exchange both sevenths and thirds so that their denominators are 21.

▲ Example-problem pair 2

As with addition and subtraction of integers and decimals, you can use the associative and commutative properties of addition to add fractions in the order that is easiest for you. You can add and subtract the whole number parts of mixed numbers separately to make calculations easier.

7.3.2 Fluency

In this exercise you can practise applying the mathematical methods that you have just learnt.

1 Work out

a $\dfrac{3}{8} + \dfrac{1}{8}$

c $\dfrac{12}{13} - \dfrac{7}{13}$

b $\dfrac{6}{11} + \dfrac{4}{11}$

d $\dfrac{81}{100} - \dfrac{63}{100}$

2 Work out

a $1\dfrac{1}{3} + 2\dfrac{2}{3}$

c $6\dfrac{7}{9} - 4\dfrac{2}{9}$

b $2\dfrac{3}{8} + 3\dfrac{7}{8}$

d $11\dfrac{9}{20} - 7\dfrac{13}{20}$

3 Work out

a $\dfrac{1}{2} + \dfrac{1}{3}$

c $\dfrac{8}{11} - \dfrac{1}{4}$

e $-\dfrac{3}{5} + \dfrac{7}{12}$

b $\dfrac{7}{9} + \dfrac{4}{5}$

d $\dfrac{9}{10} - \dfrac{7}{8}$

4 Work out

a $3\dfrac{1}{4} + 2\dfrac{3}{8}$

c $3\dfrac{2}{3} + 8\dfrac{4}{9}$

e $8\dfrac{7}{12} - 4\dfrac{8}{9}$

b $5\dfrac{2}{5} + 6\dfrac{3}{4}$

d $7\dfrac{1}{2} - 4\dfrac{1}{3}$

f $-5\dfrac{1}{6} - 4\dfrac{7}{8}$

5 Berit is calculating $7\dfrac{3}{4} + 3\dfrac{5}{6} - 2\dfrac{1}{4}$. Her working is shown:

$$7\dfrac{3}{4} + 3\dfrac{5}{6} - 2\dfrac{1}{4} = 7\dfrac{3}{4} - 2\dfrac{1}{4} + 3\dfrac{5}{6} \quad \text{(line 1)}$$

$$= 5\dfrac{1}{2} + 3\dfrac{5}{6} \quad \text{(line 2)}$$

$$= 5\dfrac{6}{12} + 3\dfrac{10}{12} \quad \text{(line 3)}$$

$$= 8\dfrac{16}{12} \quad \text{(line 4)}$$

$$= 9\dfrac{1}{3} \quad \text{(line 5)}$$

a What law of arithmetic has Berit used in line 1 of her working?

b Explain how Berit could have simplified her working in line 3.

c Write out lines 3 to 5 of Berit's working using this simplification.

6 Riya is calculating $8\frac{3}{4} + 7\frac{5}{6} - 3\frac{1}{6}$. Her working is shown:

$$8\frac{3}{4} + 7\frac{5}{6} - 3\frac{1}{6} = 8\frac{3}{4} + 4\frac{4}{6} \qquad \text{(line 1)}$$

$$= 8\frac{3}{4} + 4\frac{2}{3} \qquad \text{(line 2)}$$

$$= 12 + \frac{9}{12} + \frac{8}{12} \qquad \text{(line 3)}$$

$$= 12 + \frac{17}{12} \qquad \text{(line 4)}$$

$$= 13\frac{5}{12} \qquad \text{(line 5)}$$

a What law of arithmetic has Riya used in line 1 of her working?

b What law of arithmetic has Riya used in line 3 of her working?

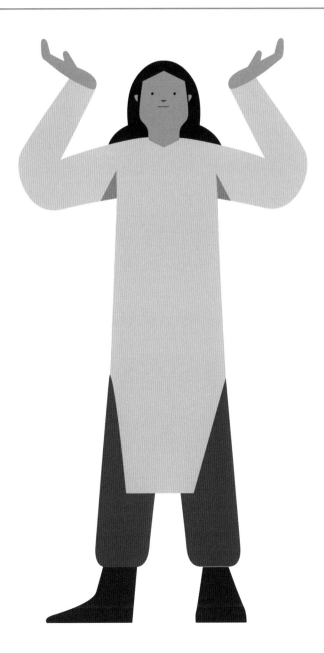

7.3 Exercises

7.3 Intelligent practice

"Why is it intelligent?" You might notice a connection when you move on from one question to the next. You can use the Reflect, Expect, Check, Explain process (page X) to:

- *reflect* on what's different between each question and the one that came before
- decide how you *expect* this answer to be different
- complete the question and *check* your answer
- *explain* to yourself why your expectation was correct or incorrect.

Question 1a   **EXAMPLE**

Work out $\dfrac{1}{15} + \dfrac{4}{15}$

The fractions have the same denominator, so $\dfrac{1}{15} + \dfrac{4}{15} = \dfrac{5}{15}$, which simplifies to $\dfrac{1}{3}$

Question 1b

Work out $\dfrac{6}{15} + \dfrac{4}{15}$

Reflect: The second fraction is the same and the first is $\dfrac{5}{15}$ more than in 1a.

Expect: Since the first fraction has increased by $\dfrac{5}{15}$, I think the answer will increase by $\dfrac{5}{15}$.

Check: $\dfrac{6}{15} + \dfrac{4}{15} = \dfrac{10}{15}$, which simplifies to $\dfrac{2}{3}$

Explain: I was right! The answer increased by the same amount as the numbers in the question.

---

1 Work out

a $\dfrac{1}{15} + \dfrac{4}{15}$ c $\dfrac{2}{5} + \dfrac{4}{15}$ e $\dfrac{2}{5} + \dfrac{6}{15}$

b $\dfrac{6}{15} + \dfrac{4}{15}$ d $\dfrac{2}{5} + \dfrac{5}{15}$

2 Work out

a $\dfrac{5}{12} + \dfrac{1}{4}$ c $\dfrac{3}{4} + \dfrac{5}{12}$

b $\dfrac{1}{4} + \dfrac{5}{12}$ d $2\dfrac{3}{4} + \dfrac{5}{12}$

3 Work out

a $\dfrac{3}{2} + \dfrac{5}{6}$ c $\dfrac{3}{8} + \dfrac{5}{6}$ e $\dfrac{3}{8} + \dfrac{1}{3} + \dfrac{1}{2}$

b $\dfrac{3}{4} + \dfrac{5}{6}$ d $1\dfrac{5}{6} + 1\dfrac{3}{8}$

4 Work out

a $\dfrac{1}{8} + \dfrac{2}{8}$ h $\dfrac{1}{5} - \dfrac{1}{8}$

b $\dfrac{2}{8} + \dfrac{1}{8}$ i $\dfrac{2}{5} - \dfrac{1}{8}$

c $\dfrac{2}{8} - \dfrac{1}{8}$ j $\dfrac{3}{5} - \dfrac{1}{8}$

d $\dfrac{1}{8} - \dfrac{2}{8}$ k $\dfrac{1}{8} - \dfrac{3}{5}$

e $\dfrac{1}{4} - \dfrac{2}{8}$ l $\dfrac{9}{8} - \dfrac{3}{5}$

f $\dfrac{1}{8} - \dfrac{1}{4}$ m $\dfrac{18}{8} - \dfrac{6}{5}$

g $\dfrac{1}{4} - \dfrac{1}{8}$ n $2\dfrac{3}{8} - \dfrac{6}{5}$

7.3 Method selection

In these questions you'll need to think carefully about which methods to apply.

For some questions you might need to use skills from earlier chapters.

1 Work out

    a $0.3 + 0.2$ **c** $4.3 - 1.2$ **e** $\dfrac{1}{5} + \dfrac{9}{30}$

    b $\dfrac{3}{10} + \dfrac{1}{5}$ **d** $4\dfrac{3}{10} - 1\dfrac{1}{5}$

2 Sharif eats $\dfrac{3}{8}$ of a pizza. Rebecca eats $\dfrac{1}{2}$ of the same pizza. What fraction of the pizza is left?

3 A metal bar is $\dfrac{5}{6}$ m long. It is cut into two sections, one of which is $\dfrac{1}{2}$ m long.

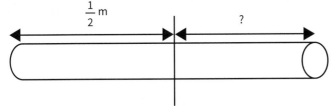

    a How long is the other section?

The metal bar weighs 18 kg and its mass is evenly distributed.

    b How much does each of the two parts weigh?

4 Find the perimeter of each shape.

    a

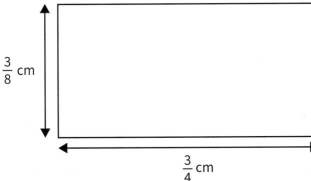

b

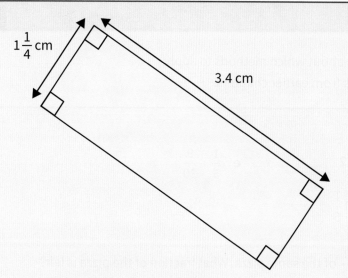

$1\frac{1}{4}$ cm

3.4 cm

c

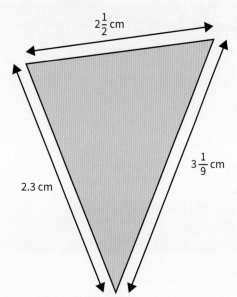

$2\frac{1}{2}$ cm

$3\frac{1}{9}$ cm

2.3 cm

5 Simplify these expressions

a $\dfrac{1}{2}x + \dfrac{1}{4}x$

b $20y - 5\dfrac{1}{3}y$

c $2p + 8q - \dfrac{3}{4}p + \dfrac{1}{5}q + \dfrac{1}{10}q$

6 The population of China is equal to the population of India plus $\dfrac{1}{100}$ of the world's population. If $\dfrac{9}{50}$ of the world's population lives in China, what fraction of the world's population lives in India?

7.3 Purposeful practice

There may be more than one way to approach these questions.

Once you have answered a question one way, can you think of another way?

1 Copy and complete the statements.

  a $\dfrac{\square}{6} + \dfrac{2}{3} = \dfrac{5}{6}$

  b $\dfrac{7}{9} - \dfrac{1}{\square} = \dfrac{11}{18}$

2 Copy and complete the statement.

  $\dfrac{5}{8} + \dfrac{1}{\square} = \dfrac{\square}{24}$

  The fraction on the right of the equals sign is in its simplest form. There are three possible answers – can you find them all?

3 From this list, find

  a the two fractions whose sum is closest to 1

  b the two fractions whose difference is closest to 0

  $\dfrac{1}{8}$ $\dfrac{3}{40}$ $\dfrac{3}{4}$ $\dfrac{1}{5}$ $\dfrac{11}{20}$ $\dfrac{2}{5}$

4 Find four different positive integers, a, b, c and d, to make an answer of $\dfrac{1}{4}$.

  Can you find more than one solution?

  $\dfrac{a}{b} - \dfrac{c}{d} = \dfrac{1}{4}$

5 Write five different fraction sums with answer $\dfrac{1}{2}$

6 A teacher wants to organise a trip for a group of students. $\dfrac{3}{8}$ of the students want to go to the fossil museum, $\dfrac{1}{6}$ of the students want to go to the technology museum and the rest want to go to the art gallery.

  a What fraction of the students want to go to the art gallery?

  b If the number of students is between 50 and 90, how many students are in the group?

7 Using the numbers 4, 5, 6 and 7 once each, copy and complete the expressions **a** and **b** to give

  a $\dfrac{\square}{\square} + \dfrac{\square}{\square}$

  b $\dfrac{\square}{\square} - \dfrac{\square}{\square}$

    i the greatest possible result

    ii the least possible result

Multiplying and dividing fractions

7.4.1 Multiplying fractions

Objectives

You will learn how to:

- multiply fractions

You have learnt that multiplication can be represented as an area model.
The multiplication 2×5 can be represented like this:

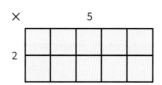

The area model shows the answer of 10.

This idea also works with fractions. $\frac{1}{2} \times \frac{1}{5}$ can be represented like this:

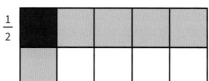

You shade or colour $\frac{1}{2}$ of the area horizontally and $\frac{1}{5}$ vertically. Where the shading

crosses over, you have the answer to the multiplication: $\frac{1}{10}$ of the area.

To multiply two fractions you multiply the numerators together and you multiply the denominators together.

Worked example	Thinking	Your turn!
Work out $\dfrac{5}{9} \times \dfrac{1}{3}$	*What process do we use to multiply two fractions?*	Work out $\dfrac{5}{8} \times \dfrac{2}{7}$
$\dfrac{5}{9} \times \dfrac{1}{3} = \dfrac{5 \times 1}{9 \times 3} = \dfrac{5}{27}$		

> I multiply the numerators and multiply the denominators.

▲ Example-problem pair 1

In mathematics, you can replace the word 'of' with multiplication, so if you want to find $\frac{3}{5}$ of 30, you work out $\frac{3}{5} \times 30$. You can convert 30 to an equivalent fraction, $\frac{30}{1}$, to multiply.

$$\frac{3}{5} \times \frac{30}{1} = \frac{3 \times 30}{5 \times 1} = \frac{90}{5} = 18$$

Worked example	Thinking	Your turn!
Work out $\frac{2}{3}$ of 50	What do we replace the word 'of' with? Will the answer be an integer?	Work out $\frac{2}{5}$ of 16
$\frac{2}{3} \times 50 = \frac{2}{3} \times \frac{50}{1} = \frac{100}{3} = 33\frac{1}{3}$		

I can replace 'of' with ×

The answer will not be an integer as 3 is not a factor of 50. I can write it as a mixed number or improper fraction.

▲ Example-problem pair 2

7.4.1 Fluency

In this exercise you can practise applying the mathematical methods that you have just learnt.

1 This area model represents the calculation

$$\frac{2}{3} \times \frac{4}{5} = \frac{8}{15}$$

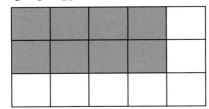

Draw area models to represent each of these calculations. Work out the answer in each case.

a $\frac{1}{2} \times \frac{3}{4}$ **c** $\frac{1}{6} \times \frac{4}{9}$

b $\frac{2}{3} \times \frac{5}{7}$ **d** $\frac{6}{7} \times \frac{4}{5}$

2 Alice says that if you want to find $\frac{2}{7}$ of 140, you divide 140 by $\frac{2}{7}$

Is Alice correct? Explain your answer.

3 Scott is working out $\frac{2}{3} \times \frac{2}{5}$. His working is shown:

$$\frac{2}{3} \times \frac{2}{5} = \frac{10}{15} \times \frac{6}{15} \text{ (Line 1)}$$

$$= \frac{60}{225} \quad \text{(Line 2)}$$

$$= \frac{4}{15} \quad \text{(Line 3)}$$

Explain the unnecessary step that Scott has included in line 1 of his working.

4 Answer **a** and **b** below.

a Dipika says that $\frac{3}{4} \times \frac{5}{6}$ is the same as $\frac{5}{6} \times \frac{3}{4}$
What law of arithmetic has Dipika used to justify her statement?

b Millie says that when working out $\frac{1}{2} \times \frac{3}{4} \times \frac{4}{5}$

you can work out $\frac{1}{2} \times \frac{3}{4}$ first, or you can

work out $\frac{3}{4} \times \frac{4}{5}$ first.

What law of arithmetic has Millie used to justify her statement?

Chapter 7

7.4.2 Multiplying proper and improper fractions

Objective

You will learn how to:

- multiply fractions

Sometimes, you can make a multiplication calculation simpler by cancelling common factors. Look at the calculation:

$$\frac{5}{9} \times \frac{2}{5}.$$

Notice how one fraction has a 5 in the numerator and the other has a 5 in the denominator. Because multiplication is commutative, you can write the calculation like this:

$$\frac{5}{9} \times \frac{2}{5} = \frac{5 \times 2}{9 \times 5} = \frac{2 \times 5 \div 5}{9 \times 5 \div 5} = \frac{2}{9}$$

It can be quicker to set it out like this:

$$\frac{{}^{1}\cancel{5}}{9} \times \frac{2}{\cancel{5}_{1}} = \frac{2}{9}$$

Note that you can only cancel a factor that is in a numerator and a denominator.

You cannot cancel factors that only appear in both numerators or both denominators.

Worked example	Thinking	Your turn!
Work out $\dfrac{8}{3} \times \dfrac{5}{16}$	Are there any common factors in any of the numerators and denominators?	Work out $\dfrac{5}{9} \times \dfrac{18}{7}$
$\dfrac{{}^{1}\cancel{8}}{3} \times \dfrac{5}{\cancel{16}_{2}} = \dfrac{5}{6}$		

▲ Example-problem pair 1

> I can see that 8 and 16 have a HCF of 8. I can simplify the calculation by dividing through top and bottom by 8 without changing the answer.

You can follow this method for proper and improper fractions. Always check your answer is in its simplest form.

You can use estimation to check whether your answer is the right size. If you multiply by a number between 0 and 1, your answer will be less than the original number. If you multiply by a number greater than 1, your answer will be greater than the original number.

7.4.2 Fluency

In this exercise you can practise applying the mathematical methods that you have just learnt.

1 Work out

a $\dfrac{1}{3} \times \dfrac{2}{5}$

b $\dfrac{3}{8} \times \dfrac{1}{5}$

c $\dfrac{3}{4} \times \dfrac{5}{7}$

d $\dfrac{6}{7} \times \dfrac{3}{5}$

2 Work out

a $\dfrac{1}{2} \times \dfrac{4}{5}$

b $\dfrac{2}{3} \times \dfrac{3}{4}$

c $\dfrac{8}{9} \times \dfrac{3}{4}$

d $\dfrac{6}{7} \times \dfrac{2}{3}$

e $\dfrac{8}{5} \times \dfrac{3}{4}$

f $\dfrac{9}{10} \times \dfrac{8}{3}$

g $\dfrac{4}{3} \times \dfrac{6}{5}$

h $\dfrac{9}{7} \times \dfrac{14}{3}$

3 Answer **a** and **b** below.

a Consider the calculation $\dfrac{6}{7} \times \dfrac{10}{11}$

Without doing the actual calculation, decide if the answer will be greater than, or less than, $\dfrac{6}{7}$

Explain how you know.

b Consider the calculation $\dfrac{8}{9} \times \dfrac{13}{12}$

Without doing the actual calculation, decide if the answer will be greater than, or less than, $\dfrac{8}{9}$

Explain how you know.

7.4.3 Multiplying mixed numbers

If you are multiplying mixed numbers, you can turn them into improper fractions first to make the calculation easier.

Worked example	Thinking	Your turn!
Work out $1\dfrac{3}{5} \times 3\dfrac{1}{2}$	*What should we do with mixed numbers before we multiply?*	Work out $1\dfrac{1}{3} \times 3\dfrac{1}{4}$
$1\dfrac{3}{5} = \dfrac{8}{5}$ and $3\dfrac{1}{2} = \dfrac{7}{2}$	*How can we make the multiplication simpler?*	
$\dfrac{\overset{4}{\cancel{8}}}{5} \times \dfrac{7}{\underset{1}{\cancel{2}}} = \dfrac{28}{5} = 5\dfrac{3}{5}$		

I can write mixed numbers as improper fractions.

I can cancel common factors in the numerators and denominators.

▲ Example-problem pair 1

When multiplying mixed numbers, you can also use an area model to help you.

Looking at $1\dfrac{3}{5} \times 2\dfrac{1}{2}$, you can set it out like this in a multiplication grid, by splitting $1\dfrac{3}{5}$

into $1 + \dfrac{3}{5}$ and $\dfrac{21}{2}$ into $2 + \dfrac{1}{2}$.

×	1	$\dfrac{3}{5}$
2	2	$\dfrac{6}{5}$
$\dfrac{1}{2}$	$\dfrac{1}{2}$	$\dfrac{3}{10}$

The sum of the products is $2 + \dfrac{1}{2} + \dfrac{6}{5} + \dfrac{3}{10}$

$= 2 + \dfrac{5}{10} + \dfrac{12}{10} + \dfrac{3}{10}$

$= 2 + \dfrac{20}{10}$

$= 4$

The grid shows how to use the distributive property of multiplication over addition to calculate the answer.

Worked example	Thinking	Your turn!
Work out $2\frac{1}{4} \times 1\frac{2}{3}$	To keep these as mixed numbers, what method could we use to multiply?	Work out $2\frac{5}{9} \times 1\frac{1}{2}$

×	2	$\frac{1}{4}$
1	2	$\frac{1}{4}$
$\frac{2}{3}$	$\frac{4}{3}$	$\frac{1}{6}$

$2 + \dfrac{4}{3} + \dfrac{1}{4} + \dfrac{1}{6}$

$= 3 + \dfrac{4}{12} + \dfrac{3}{12} + \dfrac{2}{12}$

$= 3\dfrac{9}{12} = 3\dfrac{3}{4}$

> I can use a multiplication grid and keep these as mixed numbers.

▲ Example-problem pair 2

7.4.3 Fluency

In this exercise you can practise applying the mathematical methods that you have just learnt.

1 Here is a calculation: $1\frac{1}{2} \times 2\frac{1}{4} = \frac{3}{2} \times \frac{9}{4} = \frac{27}{8}$

Use the same method to work out each of these.

a $1\frac{1}{3} \times 2\frac{1}{2}$ c $3\frac{1}{4} \times 2\frac{2}{5}$

b $2\frac{2}{3} \times 3\frac{1}{2}$ d $3\frac{1}{7} \times 1\frac{3}{8}$

2 Here is a calculation:

$1\frac{1}{3} \times 2\frac{1}{4} = \left(1 + \frac{1}{3}\right) \times \left(2 + \frac{1}{4}\right)$

$= 2 + \dfrac{1}{4} + \dfrac{2}{3} + \dfrac{1}{12}$

$= 2 + \dfrac{3}{12} + \dfrac{8}{12} + \dfrac{1}{12}$

$= 2 + \dfrac{12}{12}$

$= 3$

Use the same method to work out each of these.

a $2\frac{3}{4} \times 3\frac{1}{2}$ b $1\frac{4}{5} \times 2\frac{2}{3}$

3 Use a suitable method to work out each of these.

a $4\frac{1}{2} \times 3\frac{3}{4}$ c $4\frac{2}{3} \times 5\frac{1}{5}$

b $2\frac{4}{5} \times 3\frac{6}{7}$ d $3\frac{5}{8} \times 6\frac{1}{2}$

7.4.4 Using reciprocals to divide fractions

Objective

You will learn how to:
- rewrite a division as a multiplication by the reciprocal

You know from your work on place value in Chapter 1 that $\div 10$ is equivalent to $\times \dfrac{1}{10}$

In the same way, $12 \div 2 = 6$ is equivalent to $12 \times \dfrac{1}{2} = 6$. Dividing by 2 is the same as multiplying by $\dfrac{1}{2}$

Language

'Reciprocal' comes from the Latin *re* (back) and *pro* (forward) meaning 'back and forth'.

You call 2 and $\dfrac{1}{2}$ reciprocals. A **reciprocal** of a number is 1 divided by that number.

(Zero does not have a reciprocal but all other numbers do.)

Dividing by any number is the same as multiplying by its reciprocal.

You know that $\div 0.1$ or $\div \dfrac{1}{10}$ is equivalent to $\times 10$. In the same way, $\div \dfrac{1}{2}$ is equivalent

to $\times 2$ Dividing by $\dfrac{3}{4}$ is equivalent to multiplying by its reciprocal, $\dfrac{4}{3}$. To find the

reciprocal of a fraction you swap the numerator and the denominator.

Investigate further

Work out the reciprocal of each of 10, 1, 0.1, 0.01, 0.00001 and of $-10, -1, -0.1, -0.00001$. What do you notice?

Number	Reciprocal
2	$\dfrac{1}{2}$
3	$\dfrac{1}{3}$
$\dfrac{1}{5}$	5
$\dfrac{2}{5}$	$\dfrac{5}{2}$
$\dfrac{4}{3}$	$\dfrac{3}{4}$
$0.7 = \dfrac{7}{10}$	$\dfrac{10}{7}$
$1\dfrac{1}{2} = \dfrac{3}{2}$	$\dfrac{2}{3}$

Dividing by a number in the left column is the same as multiplying by its reciprocal in the right column, and vice versa.

Worked example	Thinking	Your turn!
Write the reciprocal of $\dfrac{3}{8}$	*How do we find the reciprocal of a fraction?*	Write the reciprocal of $\dfrac{2}{9}$
The reciprocal is $\dfrac{8}{3}$		

I swap the numerator and denominator.

▲ Example-problem pair 1

Calculator

You saw that $\dfrac{1}{10} = 10^{-1} = 0.1$ in Chapter 1. You can find the reciprocal of a number (or 1 divided by that number) by pressing the $\boxed{x^{-1}}$ key. On some calculators this might appear as $\boxed{\frac{1}{x}}$ or $\boxed{\blacksquare^{-1}}$.

7.4.4 Fluency

In this exercise you can practise applying the mathematical methods that you have just learnt.

1 Answer questions **a–d**.
  a Dividing by 10 is the same as multiplying by what fraction?
  b Dividing by 6 is the same as multiplying by what fraction?
  c Dividing by 20 is the same as multiplying by what fraction?
  d Dividing by 133 is the same as multiplying by what fraction?

2 Answer questions **a–d**.
  a Dividing by $\dfrac{1}{2}$ is the same as multiplying by what number?
  b Dividing by $\dfrac{1}{10}$ is the same as multiplying by what number?
  c Dividing by $\dfrac{1}{15}$ is the same as multiplying by what number?
  d Dividing by $\dfrac{1}{85}$ is the same as multiplying by what number?

3 Answer questions **a–d**.
  a Dividing by $\dfrac{2}{3}$ is the same as multiplying by what fraction?
  b Dividing by $\dfrac{4}{7}$ is the same as multiplying by what fraction?
  c Dividing by $\dfrac{8}{11}$ is the same as multiplying by what fraction?
  d Dividing by $\dfrac{87}{104}$ is the same as multiplying by what fraction?

Chapter 7

7.4.5 Divide a fraction by a whole number and a whole number by a fraction

Objective ☑

You will learn how to:

- divide a fraction by a whole number
- divide a whole number by a fraction

This bar model shows how $\dfrac{2}{7}$ divided by 3 is $\dfrac{2}{21}$

$\dfrac{1}{7}$ $\dfrac{1}{7}$

$\dfrac{1}{21}$ $\dfrac{1}{21}$

To work this out without a bar model, you can multiply by the reciprocal.

$$\frac{2}{7} \div 3 = \frac{2}{7} \times \frac{1}{3} = \frac{2}{21}$$

Worked example	Thinking	Your turn!
Work out $\dfrac{4}{5} \div 7$	*What calculation is the same as dividing by the whole number?*	Work out $\dfrac{9}{11} \div 4$
$\dfrac{4}{5} \div 7 = \dfrac{4}{5} \div \dfrac{7}{1} = \dfrac{4}{5} \times \dfrac{1}{7} = \dfrac{4}{35}$		

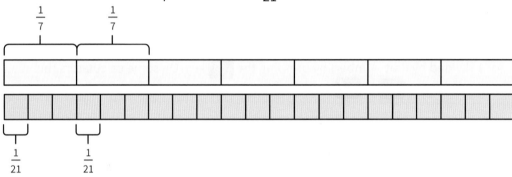

Dividing by 7 is the same as multiplying by its reciprocal, $\dfrac{1}{7}$

▲ Example-problem pair 1

Bar models can also show dividing a whole number by a fraction. This bar model shows $3 \div \dfrac{2}{5}$, thinking of it as 'how many times does $\dfrac{2}{5}$ fit into 3?'

1   1   1

$\dfrac{2}{5}$

Look at the bottom row, where each section is $\frac{2}{5}$. You can see that $7\frac{1}{2}$ of these fit into

3, so $3 \div \frac{2}{5} = 7\frac{1}{2}$ or $\frac{15}{2}$. To calculate this without a bar model, you can multiply by the

reciprocal of $\frac{2}{5}$

$$3 \div \frac{2}{5} = 3 \times \frac{5}{2} = \frac{15}{2} \text{ or } 7\frac{1}{2}$$

Worked example	Thinking	Your turn!
Work out $7 \div \frac{4}{5}$	*How can we rewrite the division?*	Work out $4 \div \frac{3}{2}$
$7 \div \frac{4}{5} = \frac{7}{1} \times \frac{5}{4} = \frac{35}{4} = 8\frac{3}{4}$		

Division is the same as multiplying by the reciprocal.

🔺 Example-problem pair 2

If you divide by a number between 0 and 1, your answer will be greater than the original number. If you divide by a number greater than 1, your answer will be less than the original number.

7.4.5 Fluency

In this exercise you can practise applying the mathematical methods that you have just learnt.

1 Draw bar models to represent each of these calculations. Work out the answer in each case.

a $\frac{1}{3} \div 2$ **c** $\frac{3}{5} \div 4$

b $\frac{2}{5} \div 3$ **d** $\frac{5}{6} \div 3$

2 Work out

a $4 \div \frac{1}{3}$ **c** $8 \div \frac{1}{7}$

b $6 \div \frac{1}{5}$ **d** $11 \div \frac{1}{9}$

3 Work out

a $3 \div \frac{2}{3}$ **c** $6 \div \frac{5}{7}$

b $4 \div \frac{3}{5}$ **d** $8 \div \frac{7}{9}$

4 Work out each of these, giving your answer as fraction in its simplest form.

a $\frac{4}{5} \div 7$ **c** $\frac{6}{7} \div 24$

b $\frac{5}{9} \div 12$ **d** $\frac{10}{11} \div 15$

5 Work out each of these, giving your answers in their simplest form.

a $5 \div \frac{5}{6}$ **c** $12 \div \frac{4}{5}$

b $10 \div \frac{2}{3}$ **d** $24 \div \frac{8}{9}$

6 Answer **a** and **b** below.

a Look at the calculation $4 \div \frac{10}{11}$ Without doing the actual calculation, decide if the answer will be less than or greater than 4. Explain how you know.

b Look at the calculation $3 \div \frac{13}{12}$ Without doing the actual calculation, decide if the answer will be less than or greater than 3. Explain how you know.

7.4.6 Divide a fraction by a fraction

Objective

You will learn how to:

- divide a fraction by a fraction

When you divide a fraction by a fraction, you can use a bar model to see the result. This bar model shows $\frac{8}{15} \div \frac{2}{5}$. The top bar shows $\frac{8}{15}$ while the middle bar shows that you can fit $1\frac{1}{3}$ lots of $\frac{2}{5}$ into the same amount.

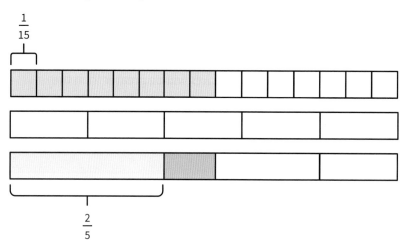

You can divide a fraction by a fraction in the same way that you divide an integer by a fraction, by multiplying by the reciprocal.

Worked example	Thinking	Your turn!
Work out $\frac{5}{11} \div \frac{9}{4}$	*How can we rewrite the division?*	Work out $\frac{7}{12} \div \frac{11}{5}$
$\frac{5}{11} \div \frac{9}{4} = \frac{5}{11} \times \frac{4}{9} = \frac{20}{99}$		

I multiply by the reciprocal.

▲ Example-problem pair 1

To find the answer to a division such as $\frac{9}{6} \div \frac{3}{2}$ efficiently, you can rewrite the division as a multiplication by the reciprocal, but then cancel common factors before multiplying.

Worked example	Thinking	Your turn!
Work out $\dfrac{9}{28} \div \dfrac{3}{7}$	*How can we rewrite the division?*	Work out $\dfrac{15}{8} \div \dfrac{5}{2}$
$\dfrac{9}{28} \div \dfrac{3}{7} = \dfrac{9}{28} \times \dfrac{7}{3}$	*Can we simplify the calculation before we multiply?*	
$\dfrac{9}{{}_4 28} \times \dfrac{{}^1 7}{3} = \dfrac{{}^3 9 \times 1}{4 \times 3_1}$ $= \dfrac{3}{4}$		

I multiply by the reciprocal.

Yes, I can cancel a common factor of 7 in the numerator and denominator.

🔺 Example-problem pair 2

Remember, you can use estimation to check whether your answer is the right size.

7.4.6 Fluency

In this exercise you can practise applying the mathematical methods that you have just learnt.

1 Work out

a $\dfrac{2}{3} \div \dfrac{1}{4}$ **b** $\dfrac{3}{4} \div \dfrac{1}{5}$ **c** $\dfrac{2}{5} \div \dfrac{1}{7}$ **d** $\dfrac{7}{8} \div \dfrac{1}{9}$

2 Work out

a $\dfrac{1}{2} \div \dfrac{3}{4}$ **b** $\dfrac{5}{6} \div \dfrac{7}{12}$ **c** $\dfrac{5}{8} \div \dfrac{3}{4}$ **d** $\dfrac{5}{12} \div \dfrac{7}{10}$

3 Work out

a $\dfrac{7}{18} \div \dfrac{14}{21}$ **b** $\dfrac{12}{25} \div \dfrac{18}{35}$ **c** $3\dfrac{3}{10} \div \dfrac{3}{5}$ **d** $8\dfrac{3}{11} \div \dfrac{7}{22}$

4 Answer **a** and **b** below.

  a Look at the calculation $\dfrac{8}{11} \div \dfrac{7}{8}$

    Without doing the actual calculation, decide if the answer will be less than or greater than $\dfrac{8}{11}$

    Explain how you know.

  b Look at the calculation $\dfrac{9}{10} \div \dfrac{15}{14}$

    Without doing the actual calculation, decide if the answer will be less than or greater than $\dfrac{9}{10}$

    Explain how you know.

7.4 Exercises

7.4 Intelligent practice

"Why is it intelligent?" You might notice a connection when you move on from one question to the next. You can use the Reflect, Expect, Check, Explain process (page X) to:

- *reflect* on what's different between each question and the one that came before
- decide how you *expect* this answer to be different
- complete the question and *check* your answer
- *explain* to yourself why your expectation was correct or incorrect.

> **EXAMPLE**
>
> **Question 1a**
>
> Work out these calculations. $10 \div 2$
>
> $10 \div 2 = 5$
>
> **Question 1b**
>
> Work out these calculations. $10 \times \frac{1}{2}$
>
> **Reflect:** The divide has changed to multiply and the 2 has changed to its reciprocal, $\frac{1}{2}$
>
> **Expect:** I think the answer will be the same, because dividing by a number is the same as multiplying by its reciprocal.
>
> **Check:** $10 \times \frac{1}{2} = \frac{10}{1} \times \frac{1}{2} = \frac{10}{2} = 5$
>
> **Explain:** I was right! The answer is the same.

1   Work out these calculations.

     a $10 \div 2$ **d** $5 \div 2$

     b $10 \times \dfrac{1}{2}$ **e** $25 \div 2$

     c $5 \times \dfrac{1}{2}$ **f** $25 \times \dfrac{1}{2}$

2   Find these products.

     a $\dfrac{1}{2} \times \dfrac{1}{8}$ **e** $\dfrac{1}{32} \times \dfrac{1}{4}$

     b $\dfrac{1}{8} \times \dfrac{1}{2}$ **f** $\dfrac{1}{4} \times \dfrac{1}{4}$

     c $\dfrac{1}{16} \times \dfrac{1}{2}$ **g** $\left(\dfrac{1}{4}\right)^2$

     d $\dfrac{1}{16} \times \dfrac{1}{4}$ **h** $\left(\dfrac{1}{4}\right)^3$

3   Work out these calculations.

     a $\dfrac{1}{10} \div 2$ **g** $2 \div \dfrac{1}{5}$

     b $\dfrac{1}{10} \div 4$ **h** $4 \div \dfrac{1}{5}$

     c $\dfrac{1}{10} \div 8$ **i** $\left(4 \div \dfrac{2}{5}\right) \div \dfrac{1}{4}$

     d $\dfrac{1}{5} \div 8$ **j** $\left(4 \div \dfrac{5}{2}\right) \div \dfrac{1}{4}$

     e $\dfrac{1}{5} \div 4$ **k** $\left(4 \div \dfrac{5}{2}\right) \div \dfrac{3}{4}$

     f $\dfrac{1}{5} \div 2$

4 Find the fractions of each amount.

a $\frac{1}{6}$ of 24

b $\frac{1}{6}$ of 12

c $\frac{1}{6}$ of 3

d $\frac{1}{6}$ of $\frac{1}{3}$

e $\frac{1}{6}$ of $\frac{1}{12}$

f $\frac{1}{6}$ of $\frac{1}{24}$

g $\frac{1}{24}$ of $\frac{1}{6}$

h $\frac{5}{24}$ of $\frac{1}{6}$

i $\frac{5}{24}$ of $\frac{1}{3}$

j $\frac{5}{4}$ of $\frac{1}{3}$ of 2

k $\frac{5}{4}$ of $\frac{2}{3}$ of 4

7.4 Method selection

In these questions you'll need to think carefully about which methods to apply.

For some questions you might need to use skills from earlier chapters.

1 Work out

a 0.3×0.2

b $\frac{3}{10} \times \frac{1}{5}$

c $4.8 \div 1.2$

d $4\frac{4}{5} \div 1\frac{1}{5}$

e $\frac{1}{5}$ of $\frac{9}{30}$

2 Michaela takes $\frac{3}{8}$ of a pizza. Sauda eats $\frac{1}{2}$ of Michaela's slice. What fraction of the original pizza did Sauda eat?

3 A cup uses up $\frac{2}{5}$ of a bottle of cola. How many cups can be filled from 4 bottles of cola?

4 Find the area of these shapes.

a

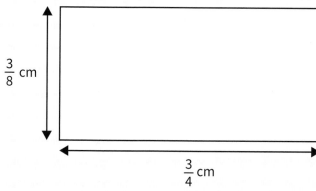

$\frac{3}{8}$ cm

$\frac{3}{4}$ cm

b

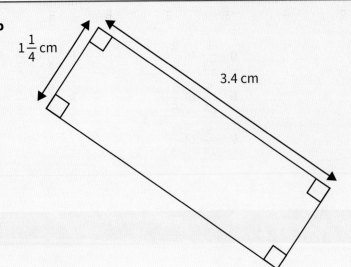

$1\frac{1}{4}$ cm

3.4 cm

c

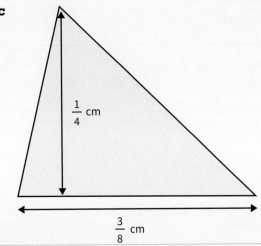

$\frac{1}{4}$ cm

$\frac{3}{8}$ cm

5 The population of China is approximately 1.4 billion. The population of Indonesia is approximately $\frac{1}{5}$ of this. What is the approximate population of Indonesia in millions?

6 Without working out the answer, explain which of these calculations has the greater answer, $\frac{3}{7} \times \frac{2}{5}$ or $\frac{3}{7} \div \frac{2}{5}$

7.4 Purposeful practice

There may be more than one way to approach these questions.

Once you have answered a question one way, can you think of another way?

1 Copy and complete these statements by finding integers that make each statement correct.

a $\dfrac{\square}{6} \times \dfrac{2}{3} = \dfrac{5}{9}$

b $\dfrac{7}{9} \div \dfrac{1}{\square} = \dfrac{\square}{3}$

2 From this list, find

a the two fractions that give the greatest product (multiplication)

b the two fractions that give the greatest quotient (division)

c the two fractions that give the product closest to 0

$$\dfrac{1}{8} \qquad \dfrac{3}{40} \qquad \dfrac{3}{4} \qquad \dfrac{1}{5} \qquad \dfrac{11}{20} \qquad \dfrac{2}{5}$$

3 Find four different positive integers, a, b, c and d, to make an answer of $\dfrac{1}{10}$. Can you find more than one solution?

$$\dfrac{a}{b} \div \dfrac{c}{d} = \dfrac{1}{10}$$

4 Write five different fraction multiplications with answer $\dfrac{1}{2}$

5 Write five different fraction divisions with answer $\dfrac{1}{2}$

6 Using any of the digits -5 to 5 at most once each, copy and complete the calculation to make

a the greatest possible quotient

b the least possible quotient

c the quotient closest to or equal to 0

$$\dfrac{\square}{\square} \div \dfrac{\square}{\square}$$

Watch out!

Some students have tried to answer the questions below but have unfortunately made some mistakes.

For each question do the following:

- **a** answer the question correctly
- **b** write down the mistake that each student has made
- **c** comment on why they might have made that mistake
- **d** write an explanation for each student to convince them (nicely!) that their answer cannot be correct.

1 Sarah and Paulo have tried to answer the question:

Write $\dfrac{4}{9}$ as a decimal.

Sarah wrote: $\dfrac{4}{9} = 4.9$

Paulo wrote $\dfrac{4}{9} = 0.49$

2 Liza has tried to answer the question:

Is $\dfrac{5}{5}$ equal to 1?

Liza wrote: No, because 5 is greater than 1

3 Ivan and Samina have tried to answer the question:

Fill in the blank to write an equivalent fraction:

$\dfrac{3}{8} = \dfrac{\square}{16}$

Ivan wrote: $\dfrac{3}{8} = \dfrac{2}{16}$

Samina wrote $\dfrac{3}{8} = \dfrac{11}{16}$

4 Pavlos and Nikki have tried to answer the question:

Is $\dfrac{1.5}{6}$ equivalent to $\dfrac{3}{12}$?

Pavlos wrote: They are not equivalent because you cannot have a decimal in a fraction.

Nikki wrote: No, because if you double it you get $\dfrac{3}{6}$.

5 Ewan and Olivia have tried to answer the question:

Work out $\dfrac{4}{7} \div \dfrac{1}{3}$

Ewan wrote: $\dfrac{7}{4} \times 3 = \dfrac{21}{4}$

Olivia wrote: $\dfrac{4}{7} \times \dfrac{1}{3} = \dfrac{4}{21}$

6 Ruben and Lily have tried to answer the question:

Work out $3 \times \dfrac{1}{5}$

Ruben wrote: $\dfrac{3}{15}$

Lily wrote: $\dfrac{1}{15}$

Check your understanding

Turn over to find the review questions

7.1 Decimals and fractions

You should now be able to...	Questions
Understand that 1 can be written in the form $\frac{n}{n}$	1
Convert between improper fractions and mixed numbers	2, 3
Write a fraction as a decimal	4
Write a decimal as a fraction	5, 6
Write a fraction in its simplest form	7
Convert between fractions and decimals using a calculator	8

7.2 Comparing and ordering fractions

You should now be able to...	Questions
Compare and order fractions by converting to decimals	9b
Compare and order fractions using common denominators	9a
Order positive and negative fractions and decimals	9c

7.3 Adding and subtracting fractions

You should now be able to...	Questions
Add and subtract fractions with common denominators	10a
Add and subtract fractions and mixed numbers with different denominators	10b, 11

7.4 Multiplying and dividing fractions

You should now be able to...	Questions
Multiply fractions	12
Multiply mixed numbers	13
Rewrite a division as a multiplication by the reciprocal	14, 15
Divide a fraction by a whole number	14a
Divide a whole number by a fraction	14b
Divide a fraction by a fraction	15

Chapter 7 review questions

1 Write the value of

   a $\dfrac{3}{3}$ [1]

   b $\dfrac{-793}{-793}$ [1]

2 Write each of these as a mixed number.

   a $\dfrac{19}{7}$ [1]

   b $-\dfrac{24}{5}$ [1]

3 Write each of these as an improper fraction.

   a $4\dfrac{1}{3}$ [1]

   b $-5\dfrac{5}{6}$ [1]

4 Convert each of these to a decimal.

   a $\dfrac{5}{8}$ [2]

   b $\dfrac{195}{12}$ [2]

5 Write 0.67 as a fraction.   [1]

6 Write 3.781 as a mixed number.   [1]

7 Write each of these fractions in their simplest form.

   a $\dfrac{48}{60}$ [1]

   b $\dfrac{7.5}{12}$ [2]

8 Use a calculator to convert $\dfrac{2808}{585}$ to a decimal   [1]

9 For each set of numbers, write them in order, starting with the least.

   a $\dfrac{7}{9}, \dfrac{11}{15}, \dfrac{4}{5}$ [2]

   b $\dfrac{576}{1600}, \dfrac{1314}{3600}, \dfrac{153}{500}$ [2]

   c $\dfrac{3}{11}, -0.6, \dfrac{29}{4}$ [2]

10 Work out

   a $\dfrac{11}{9} + \dfrac{13}{9}$ [1]

   b $\dfrac{8}{9} - \dfrac{4}{7}$ [2]

   Give your answer in simplest form.

11 Faryal has $3\dfrac{3}{4}$ litres of water in a jug.

   She pours in another $2\dfrac{2}{5}$ litres of water.

   How much water does Faryal now have in her jug?

   Give your answer as a mixed number.   [3]

12 Work out

   a $\dfrac{4}{5} \times 7$ [1]

   b $\dfrac{7}{9} \times \dfrac{3}{5}$ [2]

13 Pearl's patio measures $3\frac{4}{5}$ m by $2\frac{1}{2}$ m.

What is the area of Pearl's patio?

Give your answer as a mixed number in simplest form. [3]

14 Work out

a $\dfrac{8}{9} \div 4$ [1]

b $9 \div \dfrac{3}{4}$ [2]

15 Derek is making orange paint.

Each litre of orange paint requires $\dfrac{3}{14}$ of a litre of red paint.

He has $\dfrac{7}{8}$ of a litre of red paint.

How many litres of orange paint can Derek make?

Give your answer as a mixed number in simplest form. [3]

Key words

Make sure you can write a definition for these key terms.

fraction • denominator • numerator • proper fraction • improper fraction • mixed number
terminating decimal • recurring decimal • equivalent fractions • simplest form • common denominator
unit fraction • reciprocal

Chapter 7

Which ketchup is the best value?

£1.85

Tomato
KETCHUP
340 g

£2.30

Tomato
KETCHUP
510 g

£3.49

Tomato
KETCHUP
680 g

What comes before?	This chapter	What comes after?

What comes before?

Book 1
- Properties of numbers
- Expressions and equations
- Coordinates
- Perimeter and area
- Fractions

This chapter
- 8.1 Multiplicative relationships
- 8.2 Ratio tables and double number lines
- 8.3 Fractions in context
- 8.4 Applying ratios

What comes after?

Book 2
- Solving linear equations
- Percentages and proportionality

Book 3
- Non-linear sequences
- Expressions and formulae
- Standard form
- Linear and non-linear graphs

Introduction

In this chapter you will discover that there is a multiplicative relationship between any two numbers. For example, the multiplicative relationship between 4 and 8 is 2, because $4 \times 2 = 8$. You will represent multiplications as fractions, ratios, and diagrams and then practise finding fractions of amounts and sharing amounts into a ratio. Sharing something in the ratio 1:2 is the same as splitting the whole into two parts of $\frac{1}{3}$ and $\frac{2}{3}$.

People use multiplicative relationships all the time without even noticing it. For example, when a cook doubles a pancake recipe to feed twice as many people, they are using a multiplicative relationship.

300g flour
2 eggs
1/2 litre of milk
150g butter
pinch of salt
lemon or other topping

In this chapter you will learn how to...

show multiplicative relationships using ratios, fractions, and diagrams

5   :   3

find the multiplier between two numbers and find other pairs of numbers with the same multiplicative relationship

$4 = 0.8 \times 5$ $1.2 = 0.8 \times 1.5$

find a fraction of a given amount, and find the original amount given a fraction

11 is $\frac{1}{3}$ of 33

show multiplicative relationships using double number lines or ratio tables

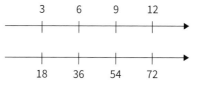

write one number as a fraction of another

$7 = \frac{7}{6}$ of 6

understand and use ratios

Jane and Davide share £45 in the ratio $7:2$. Jane gets £35 and Davide gets £10

use ratios to describe rates

The conversion rate of miles to kilometres is $1:1.6$

Reactivate your knowledge

If you can answer the questions on these pages then you should be ready for the chapter.

Some questions are there to help you to remember some maths from primary school and some are to help you remember maths from earlier in the book. If you see this symbol 🔗 it tells you where that information was introduced in an earlier chapter. If you are struggling with those questions you could go back and read through it again.

8.1 Multiplicative relationships

You should know...

1. how to complete a table of pairs of values that satisfy the same relationship

For example

All the values in the table satisfy the relationship

$y = 4x$

x	1	2	5	10	12
y	4	8	20	40	60

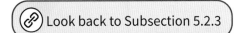 Look back to Subsection 5.2.3

Check in

1. Copy and complete each of these tables.

$y = 7x$

x	1	2	7	11	14
y	7	14			

$y = -2x$

x	1	2	6	9	15
y	-2	-4			

$y = 0.6x$

x	1	2	8	13	21
y	0.6	1.2			

8.2 Ratio tables, 8.3 Fractions in context, and 8.4 Applying ratios

You should know...

2. common units of length, mass, capacity, money, and area

For example

£ (pounds) and p (pence) are units of British money, and cm² is a unit of area

 Look back to Section 1.4

Check in

2. Look at these measures:

30 ml, 500 g, 2 litres, 50 mm², £1.45, 10 km, 42 kg, 2.6 m², 97 p, $\frac{1}{2}$ m

List the amounts that are measures of:

a money,   **d** mass,

b length,   **e** capacity.

c area,

3. how to simplify fractions

For example

$\dfrac{4}{10}$ simplified is $\dfrac{2}{5}$

$\dfrac{4}{10} = \dfrac{2}{5}$

$\div 2$

 Look back to Subsection 7.1.5

3. Simplify:

a $\dfrac{6}{10}$ **d** $\dfrac{18}{24}$

b $\dfrac{6}{9}$ **e** $\dfrac{12}{36}$

c $\dfrac{18}{12}$ **f** $\dfrac{26}{39}$

- - -

4. how to estimate the position of a decimal on a number line

For example

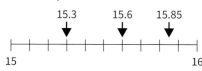

15.3   15.6   15.85

15   16

 Look back to Subsection 1.3.1

4. Copy and complete this number line and draw arrows to estimate the position of:

a 41.2

b 41. 55

c 41.79

41   42

- - -

5. how to plot and read points on a graph

For example

Point A has coordinates $(14, 7)$

Point B has coordinates $(17, 8.5)$

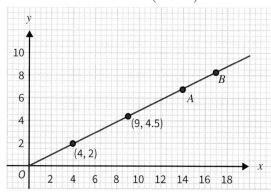

$(9, 4.5)$

$(4, 2)$

 Look back to Subsections 5.1.1 and 5.2.2

5. Copy this graph.

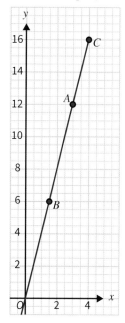

a Write the coordinates of points:

   i A **ii** B **iii** C

b On your copy, plot the points with coordinates:

   i $(2, 8)$ **ii** $(1, 4)$ **iii** $(3.5, 14)$

Multiplicative relationships

8.1.1 Writing multiplicative relationships as fractions and ratios

> ### Objective
>
> You will learn how to:
> - show a multiplicative relationship using a ratio, fraction, or diagram

Multiplicative relationships link any two numbers using multiplication or division. For example, the multiplicative relationship from 6 to 12 is ×2

You can describe multiplicative relationships with **fractions** and **ratios**. Here is a bar model.

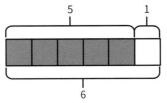

The shaded fraction is $\frac{5}{6}$ of the whole.

The unshaded fraction is $\frac{1}{6}$ of the whole.

The ratio of shaded to unshaded equal parts is

Number of shaded ⟶ 5 : 1 ⟵ Number of unshaded
parts   parts

You say this as "five to one."

Worked example	Thinking	Your turn!	
Write the ratio of shaded to unshaded parts in this bar model.	*How many shaded parts and how many unshaded parts are there?*	Write the ratio of shaded to unshaded parts in this bar model.	There are 6 shaded parts and 1 unshaded part.
6 : 1	*Which number should go first in the ratio?*		The question said 'shaded to unshaded' so the number of shaded parts should go first, which is 6.

▲ Example-problem pair 1

A ratio is a way to compare two (or more) quantities. The quantities can be unequal.

For example, pastry is made by mixing 1 part of butter to 2 parts of flour. The ratio of butter to flour is 1 to 2, which can be written as $1:2$. If Simon uses 50 g of butter, then 50 g is 1 part in the ratio. In this case, he would use 100 g of flour, or 2 parts in the ratio.

There are 3 equal parts in total, so the pastry is $\frac{1}{3}$ butter and $\frac{2}{3}$ flour.

You could show this as a bar model.

8.1.1 Fluency

In this exercise you can practise applying the mathematical methods that you have just learnt.

1 Look at this bar model:

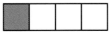

 a Write the ratio of shaded parts to unshaded parts.

 b What fraction of the bar model is shaded?

2 Look at this bar model:

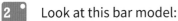

 a Write the ratio of shaded parts to unshaded parts.

 b What fraction of the bar model is shaded?

3 The ratio of shaded parts to unshaded parts in a bar model is $3:2$

 a Draw a bar model to illustrate this.

 b What fraction of the bar model is shaded?

4 Elise has some counters. $\frac{3}{8}$ of the counters are red and the rest are green.

 a Draw a bar model to illustrate this.

 b Write the ratio of red counters to green counters.

5 Arthur has 7 white chocolates and 8 milk chocolates.

 a Write the ratio of white chocolates to milk chocolates.

 b Write the number of white chocolates as a fraction of milk chocolates.

 c Write the number of milk chocolates as a fraction of all the chocolates.

Now check your answers. Did you get any wrong and can you work out why?

8.1.2 Multipliers

Between any two non-zero numbers there are two different kinds of relationship.

$3 \rightarrow 12$

The **additive relationship** is $+9$
The multiplicative relationship is $\times 4$

$45 \rightarrow 5$

The additive relationship is $+(-40)$
The multiplicative relationship is $\times \dfrac{1}{9}$

Key point

Additive relationships describe additions and subtractions.
Multiplicative relationships describe multiplications and divisions.
A **multiplier** is a way to describe the link between two numbers with multiplication by a single number. The multiplier from 4 to 12 is 3

Worked example	Thinking	Your turn!	
What is the relationship that links 8 to 24 using: **a** addition **b** multiplication?	*What calculation can we write to show each relationship?*	What is the relationship that links 4 to 16 using: **a** addition **b** multiplication?	What must I add to eight to get twenty-four? What must I multiply eight by to get twenty-four?
a $8 + \square = 24$ $8 + 16 = 24$	*How can we use inverse operations to find our answers?*		I know that $24 - 8 = 16$, so $8 + 16 = 24$. I know that $24 \div 8 = 3$ so $8 \times 3 = 24$
b $8 \times \square = 24$ $8 \times 3 = 24$			

▲ Example-problem pair 1

You can find a multiplicative relationship by combining multiplications and divisions into one operation.

Worked example	Thinking	Your turn!
What is the multiplier from 5 to 8?	Is the second number greater than the first?	What is the multiplier from 7 to 12?
$5 \times \square = 8$ 5 $\boxed{\times 8} \Rightarrow \boxed{\div 5} \Rightarrow 8$ 5 $\boxed{\times \frac{8}{5}} \Rightarrow 8$	What calculation can we write to show the relationship? How can we combine the operations here?	
The multiplier from 5 to 8 is $\dfrac{8}{5}$		

The second number is greater but it is not a multiple of the first number, so I need to multiply by a fraction greater than 1.

5 multiplied by what gives me 8?

Multiplying by the result and then dividing by the original number gives me two operations. I can combine these to make one multiplier.

▲ Example-problem pair 2

This process is the same, even when you work with negatives and decimals.

8.1.2 Fluency

In this exercise you can practise applying the mathematical methods that you have just learnt.

1 What is the relationship that links 6 to 9 using:
 a addition **b** multiplication?

2 What is the relationship that links 10 to 7 using:
 a addition **b** multiplication?

3 Find the multiplier from the first number to the second number in each pair of numbers.
 a 6 and 12 **d** 14 and 238
 b 10 and 100 **e** 16 and 384
 c 8 and 96

4 Find the multiplier from the first number to the second number in each pair.
 a 6.2 and 12.4 **d** −20 and −25
 b 8.4 and 21 **e** −50 and 75
 c 18 and −36

5 A multiplicative relationship has the form
 $y = ax$ where $y > x$
 Given that x is positive, what can you say about the value of a?

6 The multiplier from A to B is 2
 What is the multiplier from B to A?

7 The multiplier from A to B is 0.4
 What is the multiplier from B to A?

8 The multiplier from A to B is 4 and from B to C is 3. What is the multiplier from:
 a A to C **b** C to A?
 Now check your answers. You may want to use your calculator. Did you get any wrong and can you work out why?

Chapter 8

8.1.3 Equivalent multiplicative relationships

Objective

You will learn how to:

- find different pairs of numbers that satisfy the same multiplicative relationship

You know how to find the multiplicative relationship between two numbers. You can also use a multiplicative relationship to find other pairs of numbers with the same relationship.

Worked example	Thinking	Your turn!	
Write five pairs of numbers with a multiplicative relationship of × 7	*Let's draw a diagram to help us.*	Write five pairs of numbers with a multiplicative relationship of × 5	7 is the multiplier so that is in my diagram.
? →×7→ ?	*What number can we choose for our first box?*		I can choose any number for my first box and work out the other number by multiplying by seven.
10 →×7→ 70 3 →×7→ 21 0.1 →×7→ 0.7 12 →×7→ 84 −5 →×7→ −35	*Can we find a pair by choosing a number for the second box instead?*		I can choose any number for my second box and work out the first number by dividing by seven. I can then write my pairs.
10 → 70 3 → 21 0.1 → 0.7 12 → 84 −5 → −35			

▲ Example-problem pair 1

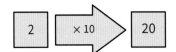

There are infinitely many pairs of numbers that satisfy a given multiplicative relationship. You can use one pair of numbers to help you find other pairs with the same multiplicative relationship.

For example, the numbers 2 and 20 have a multiplicative relationship of ×10

You can multiply both numbers by the same number (for example, 2) to find another pair with multiplicative relationship of ×10:

$2 \times 2 = 4$ and $20 \times 2 = 40$

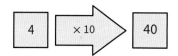

Or you could divide both numbers by the same number (for example, 2) to find another pair with the multiplicative relationship of ×10:

$2 \div 2 = 1$ and $20 \div 2 = 10$

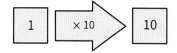

You can multiply or divide the pair of numbers by whatever you like, and as long as you multiply or divide both numbers by the same amount, the multiplicative relationship will remain the same.

8.1.3 Fluency

In this exercise you can practise applying the mathematical methods that you have just learnt.

1 Two numbers, A and B, satisfy a multiplicative relationship $A \rightarrow B$.

  a Write five pairs of numbers where the multiplier from A to B is:

    i 4   **iii** −5

    ii 15   **iv** −12

  b How many pairs of numbers are there for each of the multipliers in part **a**?

2 Two numbers, A and B, satisfy a multiplicative relationship $A \rightarrow B$.

Write five pairs of numbers where the multiplier from A to B is:

  a 2.5   **c** − 4.5

  b 3.1   **d** − 14.8

3 Two numbers, A and B, satisfy a multiplicative relationship $A \rightarrow B$.

In each of these cases, you are given A or B and the multiplier. Find the missing number.

  a $A = 7$, multiplier = 2.1

  b $A = 9$, multiplier = −5.8

  c $A = 13$, multiplier = 0.45

  d $B = 5.55$, multiplier = 3.7

  e $B = −34.02$, multiplier = −8.1

  f $B = 17.28$, multiplier = −0.24

4 A multiplicative relationship is $y = 2.5x$

  a On graph paper, draw a set of axes with x-axis from −5 to 5 and the y-axis from −13 to 13

  b Plot four pairs of numbers, (x, y), that satisfy the multiplicative relationship.

  c Draw a line illustrating the infinite set of points that satisfy the multiplicative relationship.

5 A multiplicative relationship is $y = -3.2x$

  a On graph paper, draw a set of axes with the x-axis from − 5 to 5 and the y-axis from − 16 to 16

  b Plot four pairs of numbers, (x, y), that satisfy the multiplicative relationship.

  c Draw a line illustrating the infinite set of points that satisfy the multiplicative relationship.

Now check your answers. You may want to use your calculator. Did you get any wrong and can you work out why?

Chapter 8

8.1 Exercises

8.1 Intelligent practice

"Why is it intelligent?" You might notice a connection when you move on from one question to the next. You can use the Reflect, Expect, Check, Explain process to:

- *reflect* on what's different between each question and the one that came before
- decide how you *expect* this answer to be different
- complete the question and *check* your answer
- *explain* to yourself why your expectation was correct or incorrect.

EXAMPLE

Question 2a

Write the ratio of shaded to unshaded sections.

The ratio is 2:5

Question 2b

Write the ratio of shaded to unshaded sections.

Reflect: This question looks the same as question 2a, but the shaded boxes are on the other side of the shape.

Expect: I expect that this means the order of the ratio will be different.

Check: shaded:unshaded is 2:5

Explain: I was incorrect! The ratio is shaded to unshaded parts instead of the order they appear in the diagram. The answer is still 2:5

1 For each diagram, write the ratio of shaded to unshaded sections.

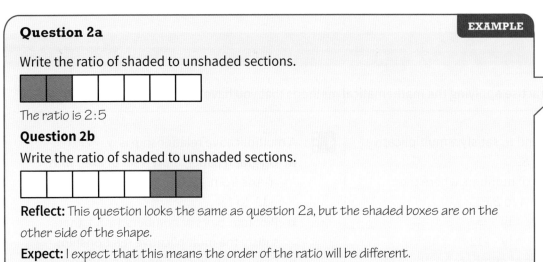

a

b   c

d

2 For each diagram, write the ratio of shaded to unshaded sections.

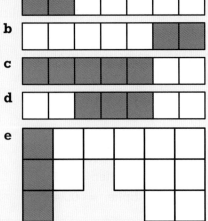

a

b

c

d

e

3 Each row of the grid describes a relationship. Copy the table and fill in the blanks. The first row has been done for you.

Diagram	Shaded:unshaded	Fraction of shapes unshaded
	2:1	$\frac{1}{3}$
		$\frac{3}{8}$
	3:2	
	2:3	
		$\frac{2}{3}$

4 Copy and complete the table of multipliers.

A	B	Multiplier from A to B	Multiplier from B to A
5	20		
10	20		
20	40		
10	40		
0.1	0.4		
0.4	0.4		
0.4	2		
2	0.4		
2	0.04		
200		0.0002	5000
20		0.0002	5000
	20	0.0002	5000
	5000	20	
	5000		20

5 Copy and complete the table of multipliers.

A	B	C	Multiplier from A to B	Multiplier from B to C	Multiplier from A to C
12	120	40			
6	60	40			
6	120	40			
6	40	120			
6	−40	−120			
6	−40	120			
6		120	−5		
−30		120	−5		
	−30			−2	10

8.1 Method selection

In these questions you'll need to think carefully about which methods to apply.
For some questions you might need to use skills from earlier chapters.

1 Each question part refers to the same shape.

  a $\frac{3}{8}$ of the shape is shaded. What fraction of the shape is unshaded?

  b The area of the shape is $32\,\text{cm}^2$. What is the area of the shaded part?

  c What is the ratio of shaded to unshaded parts?

  d How much more of the area needs to be shaded in order to give a shaded to unshaded ratio of $7:1$?

2 A rectangle has a perimeter of $26\,\text{cm}$.

  a How many possible different rectangles are there with integer side lengths? Draw these rectangles using centimetre squared paper.

  b Find the area of each rectangle.

  c For each of the rectangles drawn in part a, write the ratio length : width.

  d Shade each rectangle so the ratio of shaded to unshaded is $3:1$

  e For part d, how can you tell which rectangles can be shaded using only whole squares and which ones can't?

3 A muffin recipe uses $100\,\text{g}$ of flour for every $50\,\text{g}$ of butter.

  a If you use $250\,\text{g}$ of flour, how much butter should you use?

  b If you only had $30\,\text{g}$ of butter, how much flour would you use?

  c The original recipe makes 4 muffins, but you need six muffins. What multiplier could you use to adjust the recipe?

  d On square grid paper, draw a graph that shows the relationship between grams of flour (on the x-axis) and grams of butter (on the y-axis). Represent $4\,\text{g}$ by one square.

4 The cards show some pairs of numbers, A and B.

A	B
2	4

A	B
3.5	4.5

A	B
6	5

A	B
7.1	6.8

A	B
6.05	6.04

A	B
2.41	2.42

Without doing any calculations, write the pairs of numbers

  a a multiplier less than 1

  b a multiplier greater than 1

5 The multiplier from A to B is 0.5 and from B to C is 3

Josh says, "The multiplier from A to C is $0.5 + 3 = 3.5$"

Amrita says, "The multiplier from A to C is $0.5 \times 3 = 1.5$"

Which student is correct? Explain your answer.

8.1 Purposeful practice

There may be more than one way to approach these questions.
Once you have answered a question one way, can you think of another way?

1 Write a pair of numbers to go in each region of the Venn diagram.

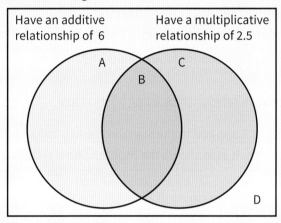

Have an additive relationship of 6 — Have a multiplicative relationship of 2.5

2 Write a pair of numbers to go in each region of the Venn diagram.

Have a multiplicative relationship of 3 — Have an additive relationship less than 1

3 The diagram shows some shaded and some unshaded squares.

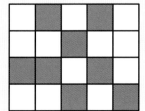

What relationships can you see between the shaded and unshaded squares? Can you express these relationships in different ways?

4 For a pair of numbers x and y, decide if each statement is always, sometimes or never true, and explain why.

a x and y have an equal multiplicative and additive relationship (the number you multiply to get from x to y is the same as the number you add).

b $x \rightarrow y$ is an equal additive relationship to $y \rightarrow x$

c If you add the additive relationship of $x \rightarrow y$ to the additive relationship of $y \rightarrow x$ the answer is 0

5 The numbers 2 and 3 have a multiplicative relationship.

Write down three pairs of numbers with the same relationship that are:

a both under 10

b both between 20 and 100

c both decimals

d both negative

e both greater than 1000

Do any of your pairs of numbers fit into more than one of these categories?

8.2 Representing multiplicative relationships

8.2.1 Proportional reasoning with ratio tables

> **Objective** ☑️
>
> You will learn how to:
> - use a ratio table to represent a multiplicative relationship

You can show equivalent multiplicative relationships using a ratio table.

This ratio table shows a multiplier of 7 applied to numbers in the first column to get to the numbers in the second column. It also shows the multiplicative relationship between the rows.

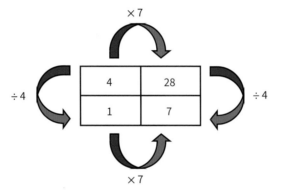

The ratio table shows that $4:28$ and $1:7$ have the same multiplicative relationship. They are equivalent ratios.

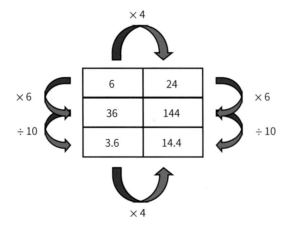

This ratio table shows that $6:24$, $36:144$, and $3.6:14.4$ are all equivalent ratios.

Worked example	Thinking	Your turn!
What is the missing number in this ratio table? <table><tr><td>5</td><td>13</td></tr><tr><td>15</td><td></td></tr></table>	*Which of the two multipliers will be most useful to us?*	What is the missing number in this ratio table? <table><tr><td>8</td><td>21</td></tr><tr><td>32</td><td></td></tr></table>
×3 ⟲ <table><tr><td>5</td><td>13</td></tr><tr><td>15</td><td></td></tr></table> ⟳ ×3	*What calculation should we use?*	
$13 \times 3 = 39$		

It's easier to use the multiplier between rows because it's an integer.

I'll work out 13×3 to find the missing value in my ratio table.

▲ Example-problem pair 1

8.2.1 Fluency

In this exercise you can practise applying the mathematical methods that you have just learnt.

1 Here is a ratio table:

<table><tr><td>2</td><td>4</td></tr><tr><td>5</td><td></td></tr></table>

  a What is the missing number in the table?
  b Complete this ratio statement: $2:4$ is equivalent to $5:\square$

2 Here is a ratio table:

<table><tr><td>3</td><td>9</td></tr><tr><td></td><td>21</td></tr></table>

  a What is the missing number in the table?
  b Complete this ratio statement:
    $3:9$ is equivalent to $\square:21$

3 Here is a ratio table:

<table><tr><td>4</td><td>10</td></tr><tr><td>20</td><td></td></tr></table>

  a What is the missing number in the table?
  b Write down two different pairs of equivalent ratios shown by the table.

4 Here is a ratio table:

<table><tr><td>3</td><td></td></tr><tr><td>9</td><td>45</td></tr></table>

  a What is the missing number in the table?
  b Write down two different pairs of equivalent ratios shown by the table.

5 Here is a ratio table:

<table><tr><td>4</td><td>1</td><td></td></tr><tr><td>1.6</td><td></td><td></td></tr></table>

4 cupcakes cost £1.60
Find the cost of 7 cupcakes.

6 Here is a ratio table:

<table><tr><td>5</td><td>1</td><td></td></tr><tr><td>3.75</td><td></td><td></td></tr></table>

5 brownies cost £3.75
Find the cost of 9 brownies.

Now check your answers. Did you get any wrong and can you work out why?

8.2.2 Simplifying ratios

Objective

You will learn how to:

- use a ratio table to simplify a ratio

Just like with fractions, you can simplify ratios. You have seen how to simplify fractions in Chapter 7. A ratio is in its simplest form when all the parts are integers and do not have any common factors other than 1

The diagram shows how you can simplify the ratio 0.3 : 7. You multiply both parts of the ratio by the same number. The ratio 3 : 70 is in its simplest form.

Worked example	Thinking	Your turn!	
Write the ratio 35 : 28 in its simplest form.	*How can I use a ratio table to help me*	**Write the ratio 55 : 50 in its simplest form.**	*I will put the numbers from the ratio in the top row and then divide them both by the same number.*
35 | 28	*How will we find the divisor?*		*I should use the highest common factor as the divisor, which is 7*
÷7 ⟳ 35 | 28 / 5 | 4 ÷7			
5 : 4			

▲ Example-problem pair 1

To simplify a fraction, you divide the numerator and denominator by the highest common factor.

To simplify a ratio, you divide all the parts by the highest common factor.

8.2.2 Fluency

In this exercise you can practise applying the mathematical methods that you have just learnt.

1 Look at this bar model:

Write, in simplest terms, the ratio of shaded parts to unshaded parts.

2 Look at this bar model:

Write, in simplest terms, the ratio of shaded parts to unshaded parts.

3 Look at this bar model:

Write, in simplest terms, the ratio of shaded parts to unshaded parts.

4 Look at this bar model:

Write, in simplest terms, the ratio of shaded parts to unshaded parts.

5 Simplify each of these ratios.
  a $6:4$
  b $10:15$
  c $80:100$
  d $1.2:2.4$
  e $5.5:7.5$

6 In a tank there are 18 blue fish and 24 yellow fish.
  a Write, in simplest terms, the ratio of blue fish to yellow fish.
  b Write, in simplest terms, the ratio of yellow fish to blue fish.

7 Simplify each of these ratios.
  a $2:4:6$
  b $10:15:20$
  c $40:50:60$
  d $120:100:60$

Now check your answers. You may want to use your calculator.
Did you get any wrong and can you work out why?

8.2.3 Proportional reasoning with double number lines

Objective

You will learn how to:

- use a double number line to represent a multiplicative relationship and connect it to other representations

Investigate Further 🔍

Where else have you seen double number lines? For example, what are the two measurements on a ruler? What are the two measurements on a set of weighing scales?

You can show multiplicative relationships on a **double number line** as well.

The 3 and 2 and 6 and 4 line up on this double number line to show equivalent relationships. So, 3 : 2 is equivalent to 6 : 4, and so on.

Like ratio tables, double number lines show multiple relationships between numbers.

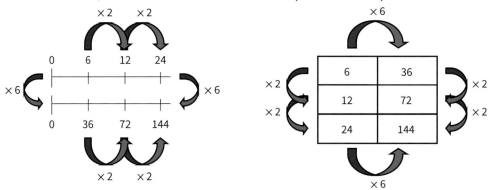

You can use more than one multiplier to solve more complex problems. The diagram below shows three ways you can answer the same question using a double number line.

4 pens cost £7. How much do 10 pens cost?

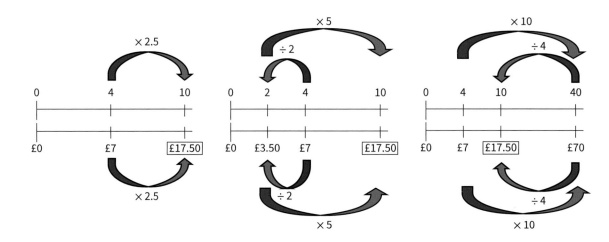

Each pen costs the same amount, so the multiplicative relationship between the number of pens and the total cost is always the same. The double number line shows that you can use the cost of a given number of pens to find the cost of any number of pens.

Worked example	Thinking	Your turn!
Six plants cost £27. Each plant costs the same amount. How much do 14 plants cost?	How can we use a simplified double number line here?	25 tickets cost £15. Each ticket costs the same amount. How much do 35 tickets cost?
6 14 ┼──────┼─────── ┼───┼────────── £27 [ ]	What would be a good intermediate step?	
×7 ÷3 2 6 14 ┼───┼──────┼ ┼───┼──────┼ £9 £27 [ ] ÷3 ×7	What calculations will give us what we need?	
$27 \div 3 = 9$ $9 \times 7 = £63$		

Side notes:
- I'll write the number of plants on the top number line and the cost below.
- If I add the cost of two plants to my number line, I can scale that up to 14 more easily.
- I'll divide the number of plants and the cost by 3 to find the cost of 2 plants, and then multiply by 7 to get my answer.

▲ Example-problem pair 1

8.2.3 Fluency

In this exercise you can focus on practising applying the mathematical methods that you have just learnt.

1 Three greeting cards cost £1.50
   a Work out the price of one greeting card.
   b Work out the cost of 20 cards.

2 Five pencils cost £1.25. Bill wants to buy seven pencils.
   a Show this on a double number line.
   b How much will Bill have to pay?

3 12 books cost £54. Phil wants to buy five books.
   a Show this on a double number line.
   b How much will Phil have to pay?

4 String costs £1.20 for 50 metres.
   a Use a double number line to work out how much you would expect to pay for 30 metres.
   b Write down any assumptions you have made.

Now check your answers. Did you get any wrong and can you work out why?

8.2.4 Plotting graphs for ratios

Objective

You will learn how to:

- use a double number line to represent a multiplicative relationship and connect it to other representations

You can draw a graph to show every pair of values that satisfy a given multiplicative relationship.

For example, if you look at a multiplicative relationship in the ratio $2:3$, you can plot this on a graph where the x-coordinate is the first part of the ratio and the y-coordinate is the second part of the ratio.

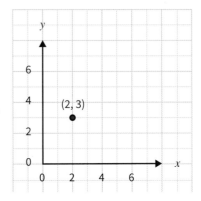

You can plot other values that are in the ratio $2:3$ on the same set of axes. You can then join all of these points with a straight line. Every single point on this line, including all the points on the line between the points that are plotted, shows a pair of values that are in the same ratio $2:3$

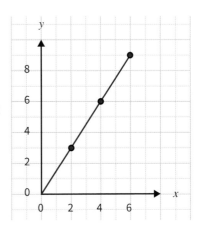

Relationships like this are called linear relationships because a multiplicative relationship where the ratio between all of the points is the same makes a straight line. You will learn more about representing linear relationships with algebra in the next two books.

Worked example	Thinking	Your turn!
Plot a graph that shows the multiplicative relationship shown on this double number line.	What would be a sensible scale to use for our axes?	Plot a graph that shows the multiplicative relationship shown on this double number line

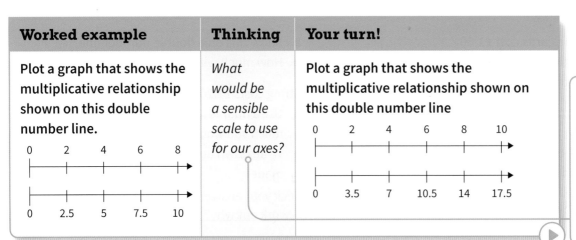

My x-axis (top number line) needs to go from 0 to at least 8. My y-axis (bottom number line) needs to go from 0 to at least 10

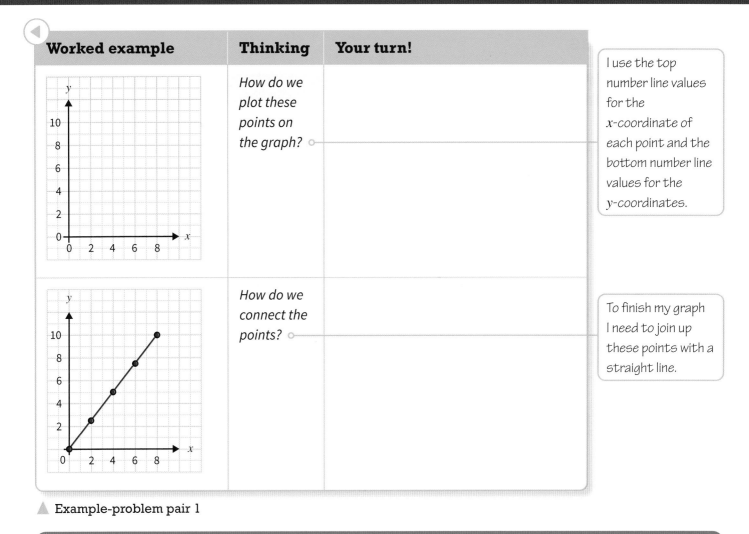

Worked example	Thinking	Your turn!

Worked example

How do we plot these points on the graph?

I use the top number line values for the x-coordinate of each point and the bottom number line values for the y-coordinates.

How do we connect the points?

To finish my graph I need to join up these points with a straight line.

▲ Example-problem pair 1

8.2.4 Fluency

In this exercise you can practise applying the mathematical methods that you have just learnt.

1 Here is a double number line:

1   2   3   i   5

3   6   9   ii   iii

a Copy the double number line and fill in the three missing numbers.

b Using an x-axis from 0 to 5 and a y-axis from 0 to 15, plot the points shown by the double number line.

2 Here is a double number line:

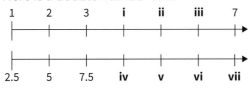

1   2   3   i   ii   iii   7

2.5   5   7.5   iv   v   vi   vii

a Copy the double number line and fill in the seven missing numbers.

b Using an x-axis from 0 to 7 and a y-axis from 0 to 18, draw a graph of the points shown by the double number line.

3 This table shows a multiplicative relationship between two numbers, x and y

x	1	2	3	4	5	6
y	0.8	1.6				

a Copy and complete the table.

b Show this relationship on a double number line.

c Draw a graph to illustrate this relationship.

Now check your answers. Did you get any wrong and can you work out why?

8.2 Exercises

8.2 Intelligent practice

"Why is it intelligent?" You might notice a connection when you move on from one question to the next. You can use the Reflect, Expect, Check, Explain process to:

- *reflect* on what's different between each question and the one that came before
- decide how you *expect* this answer to be different
- complete the question and *check* your answer
- *explain* to yourself why your expectation was correct or incorrect.

Question 4a **EXAMPLE**

Copy and complete the ratio table.

4	40
24	

The missing value is 240.

Question 4b

Copy and complete the ratio table.

4	3
24	

Reflect: This is like question 4a, but there's a 3 instead of a 40

Expect: I'd expect my answer to be less than 24

Check: Using the multiplier downwards, $4 \times 6 = 24$, so $3 \times 6 = 18$

Explain: I was right! My answer is less than 24 this time.

---

1 Write the ratio shown by each double number line. Give your answer in its simplest form.

a
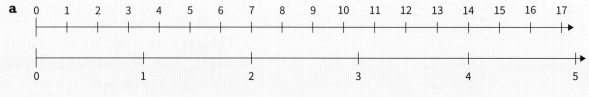

b
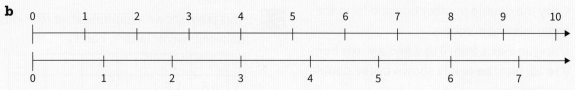

c
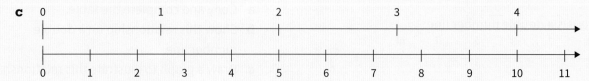

2 Use each graph to complete the double number lines.

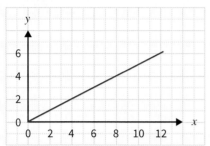

a

| x | 5 | 6 | 7 | 8 | 9 | 10 |

y: ☐ ☐ ☐ ☐ ☐ ☐

b

y: ☐ ☐ ☐ ☐ ☐ ☐

| x | 5 | 6 | 7 | 8 | 9 | 10 |

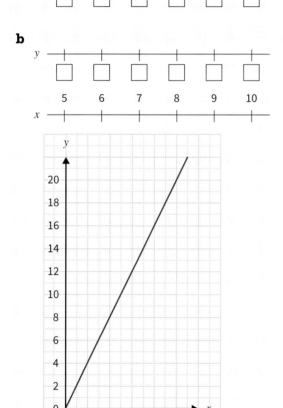

3 A paint shop sells 21 litres of paint for £35. You can buy any amount you need.

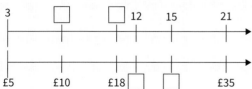

3 ☐ ☐ 12 15 21

£5 £10 £18 ☐ ☐ £35

a How many litres can you buy for £10?
b How much does 12 litres of paint cost?
c How much does 15 litres of paint cost?
d How much paint can you get for £18?

4 Copy and complete each ratio table.

a

4	40
24	

d

4	
8	3

b

4	3
24	

e

4	3
	1
	8

c

4	3
8	

5 Use the ratio tables to answer these questions.

a Four pens cost £1.20. How much do five pens cost?

4	1.2
5	

b Four pens now cost 80p. How many can I buy for £1.20?

4	0.8
	1.2

6 Use any representation you have seen in this section to answer these questions.

a Three drinks cost £4.20. How much do nine drinks cost?
b Six cakes cost £4.20. How much do three cakes cost?
c Nine books cost £67.50. How much do ten books cost?
d Three bus tickets costs £12.60. How much do ten tickets cost?
e Six plants cost £22.50. How much do ten plants cost?
f Nine metres of wire costs £31.50. How much does eleven metres cost?

Chapter 8

8.2 Method selection

In these questions you'll need to think carefully about which methods to apply.

For some questions you might need to use skills from earlier chapters.

1 Write each of these in its simplest form, where possible.

a $7:28$

b $7a:28a$

c $7a:28b$

d $\dfrac{7}{100}:\dfrac{28}{10}$

e $\dfrac{7}{35}:\dfrac{28}{25}$

f $29a+6b-5a:-7b+6a-2b$

2 In each set of equivalent ratios, find the missing value.

a $3:4=\square:12$

b $3:4=12:\square$

c $6:\square:12=9:36:\square$

d $-8:\square:5=\square:6:10$

e $4(y+2):\square(y-1)=2y+4:3(y-1)$

3 Seven drinks cost £22.40

a How much is one drink?

b How much change is there from £30 if you buy one drink?

4 Decide if the relationship is additive or multiplicative.

a Two pens cost 50 p and three pens cost 75 p.

b After two weeks Janice has saved £6 and after six weeks she has saved £10.

c Three boxes contain 12 plates and eight boxes contain 32 plates.

5 Write the ratio of shaded to unshaded parts in each diagram.

a

b

c

d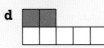

6 Answer questions **a** to **c**.

a The shape is made up of four squares, each with an area of $25\,\text{cm}^2$. What's the perimeter of the shape?

25 cm²

b Copy and complete the ratio table and write the ratios it shows.

25	4
125	

c Find the area and perimeter of the whole rectangle shown.

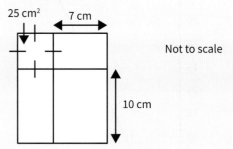

25 cm² 7 cm

Not to scale

10 cm

7 Each question changes a little bit.

Work out each answer by reading the questions carefully.

a There are 15 marbles in a bag. Nine of them are blue, the rest are red. What is the ratio of blue to red marbles?

b There are 15 marbles in a bag. 10 of them are blue, the rest are red. What is the ratio of blue to red marbles?

c There are 15 blue marbles and 10 red marbles in a bag. What fraction of marbles are blue?

8.2 Purposeful practice

There may be more than one way to approach these questions.

Once you have answered a question one way, can you think of another way?

1 Write a ratio that could go in each region on the Venn diagram.

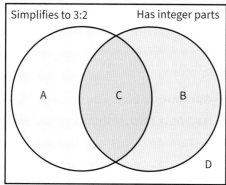

2 Write a ratio that could go in each region on the Venn diagram.

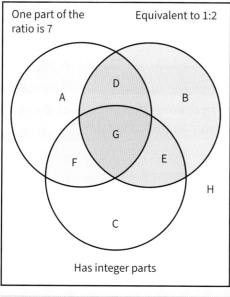

3 Point A and point B are shown on a coordinate grid. The line through A and B goes through the origin, but the scales on the x and y axes have not been given.

In each case, you are given the coordinates of A or B and need to work out the coordinates of the other point.

The axes' scales are different for each question part.

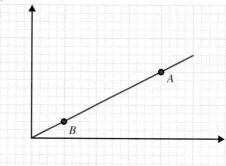

a A is at $(8, 4)$ B is at _____
b A is at _____ B is at $(8, 4)$
c A is at _____ B is at $(4, 8)$
d A is at $(4, 8)$ B is at _____
e A is at $(2, 4)$ B is at _____
f A is at $(p, 2p)$ B is at _____
g A is at _____ B is at $(p, 2p)$
h A is at _____ B is at $(p, 3p)$
i A is at $(3p, p)$ B is at _____

4 Write a reason for each of the four diagrams being the odd one out.

A

B

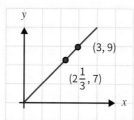

C

D

Fractions in context

8.3.1 Find a fraction of a given amount

Objective

You will learn how to:

- find a fraction of a given amount

You can use fractional multipliers to find fractions of amounts.

You often say 'lots of' when you first learn your times tables. The word 'of' in 'a fraction of …', relates to multiplication in the same way, only now, instead of finding an integer 'lot of', you're finding a fractional 'lot of'.

To enter a fraction on a calculator, press

 or ▪▢.

Alternatively, type in the numerator, then ÷ , then the denominator and then press = .

To convert to a decimal press S⇔D

or FORMAT .

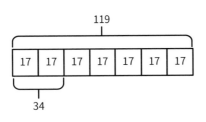

To find $\frac{2}{7}$ of 119, you can draw a bar model to represent dividing 119 by 7 and multiplying the answer by 2

Or you can calculate this in one step as $\frac{2}{7} \times 119 = 34$ using your calculator.

Key point

You calculate the fraction of an amount by dividing that amount by the denominator of the fraction and multiplying by the numerator.

Worked example	Thinking	Your turn!	
Find $\frac{3}{5}$ of 360	*What does the bar model look like for this situation?*	Find $\frac{5}{6}$ of 360	My bar model needs five sections, and the whole is worth 360. Each section is worth $360 \div 5 = 72$
360 72 | 72 | 72 | 72 | 72			
$72 \times 3 = 216$	*How can we check this?*		I can use my calculator to work out $\frac{3}{5} \times 360 = 216$

▲ Example-problem pair 1

You can also find a fraction of a fraction. To find $\frac{1}{2}$ of $\frac{3}{4}$ you can calculate $\frac{1}{2} \times \frac{3}{4} = \frac{3}{8}$

In Chapter 7 you learnt how to multiply fractions by multiplying the numerators together and multiplying the denominators together.

8.3.1 Fluency

In this exercise you can practise applying the mathematical methods that you have just learnt.

1 Use a bar model to find:

a $\frac{1}{4}$ of 8

b $\frac{1}{5}$ of 55

c $\frac{1}{3}$ of 30

d $\frac{1}{6}$ of 72

2 Use a calculator to find:

a $\frac{1}{8}$ of 60

b $\frac{1}{12}$ of 288

c $\frac{1}{20}$ of 83

d $\frac{1}{150}$ of 345

3 Find:

a $\frac{3}{4}$ of 40

b $\frac{2}{3}$ of 24

c $\frac{3}{5}$ of 75

d $\frac{5}{8}$ of 64

4 Answer questions **a** and **b**.

a $\frac{1}{7}$ of 343 is 49. What is $\frac{2}{7}$ of 343?

b $\frac{1}{9}$ of 252 is 28. What is $\frac{4}{9}$ of 252?

5 Find:

a $\frac{2}{3}$ of 3.9

b $\frac{3}{4}$ of 4.8

c $\frac{4}{5}$ of 8.2

d $\frac{3}{7}$ of 4.2

6 Giving your answer as a fraction in its simplest terms, find:

a $\frac{2}{5}$ of $\frac{10}{11}$

b $\frac{5}{6}$ of $\frac{12}{25}$

c $\frac{5}{8}$ of $\frac{40}{51}$

d $\frac{11}{12}$ of $\frac{60}{101}$

Now check your answers. You may want to use your calculator. Did you get any wrong and can you work out why?

Chapter 8

8.3.2 Finding the whole

Objective

You will learn how to:

- find the original amount, given a fraction of an amount and the fraction

To find an original amount from a given fraction of an amount, you can use a bar model in a slightly different way.

Before, you looked at how to find $\frac{1}{7}$ of 119. If instead you want to find a number where $\frac{1}{7}$ of it is 119, you can use a bar model like this:

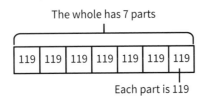

The whole has 7 parts

Each part is 119

The whole is 119×7. This gives an answer of 833

The fraction you are working with may have a numerator that's not 1. You can still use a bar model to help you.

For example, $\frac{3}{4}$ of a number is 432. What is the number?

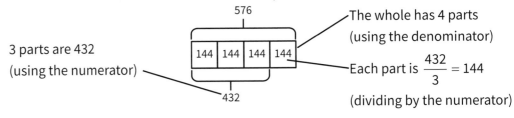

3 parts are 432
(using the numerator)

576

The whole has 4 parts
(using the denominator)

Each part is $\frac{432}{3} = 144$
(dividing by the numerator)

432

The whole is $144 \times 4 = 576$ (multiplying by the denominator)

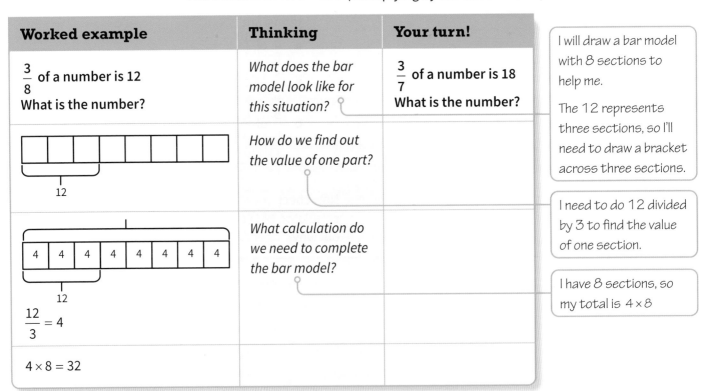

Worked example	Thinking	Your turn!	
$\frac{3}{8}$ of a number is 12 What is the number?	*What does the bar model look like for this situation?*	$\frac{3}{7}$ of a number is 18 What is the number?	I will draw a bar model with 8 sections to help me. The 12 represents three sections, so I'll need to draw a bracket across three sections.
[bar model with 8 sections, 12]	*How do we find out the value of one part?*		
[bar model: 4 4 4 4 4 4 4 4, 12] $\frac{12}{3} = 4$	*What calculation do we need to complete the bar model?*		I need to do 12 divided by 3 to find the value of one section. I have 8 sections, so my total is 4×8
$4 \times 8 = 32$			

▲ Example-problem pair 1

In each case, you divide by the numerator of the fraction you already have and then multiply by the denominator. This is still the case even if the amounts involved are decimals or fractions themselves.

For example, when $\frac{2}{3}$ of a number is $\frac{3}{4}$, you can divide $\frac{3}{4}$ by 2 (the numerator) to give $\frac{3}{8}$ and then multiply by 3 (the denominator). The original number is $\frac{9}{8}$.

8.3.2 Fluency

In this exercise you can practise applying the mathematical methods that you have just learnt.

1 Answer questions **a** to **f**.

a $\frac{1}{4}$ of a number is 3. What is the number?

b $\frac{1}{3}$ of a number is 5. What is the number?

c $\frac{1}{5}$ of a number is 6. What is the number?

d $\frac{1}{8}$ of a number is 7. What is the number?

e $\frac{1}{7}$ of a number is 20. What is the number?

f $\frac{1}{11}$ of a number is 12. What is the number?

2 Answer questions **a** to **f**.

a $\frac{3}{4}$ of a number is 12. What was the number?

b $\frac{2}{3}$ of a number is 20. What was the number?

c $\frac{2}{5}$ of a number is 8. What was the number?

d $\frac{5}{6}$ of a number is 25. What was the number?

e $\frac{3}{7}$ of a number is 36. What was the number?

f $\frac{9}{11}$ of a number is 108. What was the number?

3 Answer questions **a** to **f**.

a $\frac{3}{4}$ of a number is 4.8. What was the number?

b $\frac{4}{5}$ of a number is 3.6. What was the number?

c $\frac{3}{8}$ of a number is 3.3. What was the number?

d $\frac{3}{4}$ of a number is $\frac{3}{7}$. What was the number?

e $\frac{5}{8}$ of a number is $\frac{10}{17}$. What was the number?

f $\frac{6}{7}$ of a number is $\frac{18}{35}$. What was the number?

Now check your answers. You may want to use your calculator. Did you get any wrong and can you work out why?

8.3.3 Write one number as a fraction of another

Objective

You will learn how to:

- write one number as a fraction of another

The table shows the results of a survey of students in a class about their pets.

Has a dog	Doesn't have a dog	Total
14	16	30

The fraction of students that have a dog is $\frac{14}{30}$, as 14 students have a dog and there are 30 students overall. This simplifies to $\frac{7}{15}$

The number of students that have a dog as a fraction of those that don't is $\frac{14}{16}$, as 14 students have a dog, and 16 students don't have a dog. This simplifies to $\frac{7}{8}$

The number of students that don't have a dog as a fraction of those that do is $\frac{16}{14}$, as 16 students don't have a dog and 14 students do. This simplifies to $\frac{8}{7}$

"Write the number of A as a fraction of B" (for whatever A and B are in the question) means write the fraction $\frac{\text{number of } A}{\text{number of } B}$ of B and simplify.

Worked example	Thinking	Your turn!	
Write the number of people that don't play cricket as a fraction of the people that do.	What's the numerator and the denominator?	Write the number of people that don't play tennis as a fraction of the people that do.	The question says 'people that don't play cricket as a fraction of the people that do', so my numerator is the number for 'doesn't play cricket' and my denominator is the number for 'plays cricket'.
<table><tr><th>Plays cricket</th><th>Doesn't play cricket</th><th>Total</th></tr><tr><td>20</td><td>30</td><td>50</td></tr></table>	What parts of the table do we need for the numerator and denominator?	<table><tr><th>Plays tennis</th><th>Doesn't play tennis</th><th>Total</th></tr><tr><td>40</td><td>20</td><td>60</td></tr></table>	
$\dfrac{\text{Doesn't play cricket}}{\text{Plays cricket}} = \dfrac{30}{20}$	Have we simplified our fraction?		I now need to substitute in the values for the worded headers for each part of my fraction.
The fraction of people that don't play cricket is $\dfrac{30}{20} = \dfrac{3}{2}$			No. 20 and 30 have a common factor of 10

▲ Example-problem pair 1

The important skill when answering questions like these is in reading and finding the information, rather than in calculating. Sometimes you might need to find the numerator or denominator from a situation described using words, tables, or Venn diagrams.

You might need to use fractions or decimals as numerators and denominators.

Remember that fractions represent division, so $\frac{1}{3}$ as a fraction of $\frac{3}{5}$ means $\frac{1}{3} \div \frac{3}{5}$, which is the same as $\frac{1}{3} \times \frac{5}{3} = \frac{5}{9}$

8.3.3 Fluency

In this exercise you can practise applying the mathematical methods that you have just learnt.

1 Answer questions **a** to **c**.

  a Write the number of shaded parts as a fraction of the number of unshaded parts.
  b Write the number of shaded parts as a fraction of the whole shape.
  c Write the number of unshaded parts as a fraction of the whole shape.

2 Answer questions **a** to **c**.

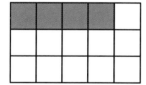

  a Write the number of shaded parts as a fraction of the number of unshaded parts.
  b Write the number of shaded parts as a fraction of the whole shape.
  c Write the number of unshaded parts as a fraction of the whole shape.

3 There are 5 boys and 6 girls in a maths club.
  a Write the number of boys as a fraction of the number of girls.
  b Write the number of girls as a fraction of the number of boys.
  c Write the number of boys as a fraction of the whole group.
  d Write the number of girls as a fraction of the whole group.

4 There are 8 pink shapes and 11 orange shapes in a bag.
  a Write the number of pink shapes as a fraction of the number of orange shapes.
  b Write the number of orange shapes as a fraction of the number of pink shapes.
  c Write the number of pink shapes as a fraction of the total number of shapes.
  d Write the number of orange shapes as a fraction of the total number of shapes.

5 Ethel buys a loaf of bread for £1.20 and a pack of butter for £1.55
  a Write the price of the loaf of bread as a fraction of the price of the pack of butter.
  b Write the price of the pack of butter as a fraction of the price of the loaf of bread.
  c Write the price of the loaf of bread as a fraction of the total that Ethel spent.
  d Write the price of the pack of butter as a fraction of the total that Ethel spent.

6 Write:
  a $\frac{1}{2}$ as a fraction of $\frac{3}{4}$
  b $\frac{1}{5}$ as a fraction of $\frac{1}{2}$
  c $\frac{3}{8}$ as a fraction of $\frac{9}{10}$
  d $\frac{8}{9}$ as a fraction of $\frac{2}{3}$

Now check your answers. Did you get any wrong and can you work out why?

8.3 Exercises

8.3 Intelligent practice

"Why is it intelligent?" You might notice a connection when you move on from one question to the next. You can use the Reflect, Expect, Check, Explain process to:

- *reflect* on what's different between each question and the one that came before
- decide how you *expect* this answer to be different
- complete the question and *check* your answer
- *explain* to yourself why your expectation was correct or incorrect.

EXAMPLE

Question 1a

Find $\dfrac{1}{5}$ of 210

$\dfrac{210}{5} = 42$

Question 1b

Find $\dfrac{1}{6}$ of 210

Reflect: This is like question 1a, but the denominator is bigger.

Expect: I'd expect my answer to be bigger because my denominator is bigger.

Check: $\dfrac{210}{6} = 35$

Explain: I was incorrect! Because I'm dividing by a bigger number my answer will be smaller!

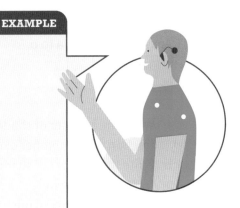

---

1 Give your answers as mixed numbers where appropriate.

a Find $\dfrac{1}{5}$ of 210

b Find $\dfrac{1}{6}$ of 210

c Find $\dfrac{1}{3}$ of 210

d Find $\dfrac{1}{30}$ of 210

e Find $\dfrac{1}{7}$ of 210

f Find $\dfrac{1}{7}$ of 105

g Find $\dfrac{2}{7}$ of 105

h Find $\dfrac{4}{7}$ of 105

i Find $\dfrac{4}{5}$ of 105

j Find $\dfrac{2}{5}$ of 210

k Find $\dfrac{5}{6}$ of 420

l Find $\dfrac{5}{6}$ of 42

m Find $\dfrac{5}{6}$ of 21

n Find $\dfrac{5}{6}$ of 20

o Find $\dfrac{6}{5}$ of 20

2 For each question, find the original number.

a $\dfrac{1}{5}$ of a number is 30

b $\dfrac{1}{6}$ of a number is 30

c $\dfrac{1}{3}$ of a number is 30

d $\dfrac{2}{3}$ of a number is 30

e $\dfrac{5}{6}$ of a number is 30

f $\dfrac{5}{6}$ of a number is 60

g $\dfrac{5}{12}$ of a number is 60

h $\dfrac{5}{13}$ of a number is 60

i $\dfrac{5}{14}$ of a number is 60

j $\frac{5}{7}$ of a number is 60

k $\frac{5}{7}$ of a number is 55

l $\frac{5}{7}$ of a number is 56

m $\frac{7}{5}$ of a number is 56

3 Answer questions **a** to **g**.

a Find $\frac{3}{5}$ of 25

b Work out $\frac{3}{5} \times 25$

c Work out $\frac{3}{5} \div 25$

d Work out the missing number: $\frac{3}{5} = \frac{\square}{25}$

e Work out the missing number: $\frac{3}{5} = \frac{\square}{225}$

f Copy and complete $\frac{3}{5} = \frac{225}{\square}$

g If $\frac{3}{5}$ of a group arrived by bus, what fraction didn't arrive by bus?

h What is the reciprocal of $\frac{3}{5}$?

i Work out 0.3×25

4 The Venn diagram shows the results of a survey that asked students in a class if they like gaming or baking.

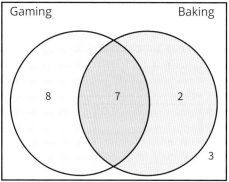

Simplify your answers where possible.

a How many students that liked gaming took part in the survey?

b What fraction of students in the survey liked gaming?

c What fraction of those that like baking also liked gaming?

d What fraction of those that like gaming also liked baking?

e What is the number of students that like baking as a fraction of those that don't?

8.3 Method selection

In these questions you'll need to think carefully about which methods to apply.

For some questions you might need to use skills from earlier chapters.

1 This shape is a rectangle. Give each answer in its simplest form.

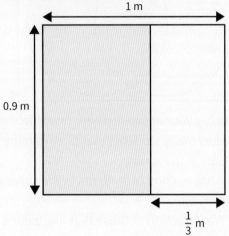

1 m

0.9 m

$\frac{1}{3}$ m

a What is the perimeter of the unshaded rectangle as an improper fraction?

b What is the perimeter of the shaded rectangle as an improper fraction?

c What is the ratio of the unshaded to the shaded area?

d What is the area of the unshaded region as a fraction of the area of the shaded region?

e What is the perimeter of the unshaded region as a fraction of the perimeter of the shaded region?

f What is your answer to part e as a decimal? What do you notice about your answers to parts d and e?

2 This shape is a rectangle.

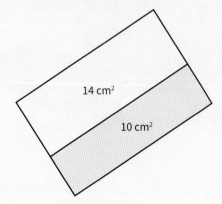

14 cm²

10 cm²

a What fraction of the rectangle is shaded?

b What is the shaded part as a fraction of the unshaded part?

c If the longest edge of the rectangle is 6 cm, what is the perimeter of the rectangle?

3 The diagram shows the results of a survey Manpreet took to find out how students in her class travelled to school. Simplify your answers where possible.

Car	ЖІ
Bus	ЖІ ІІІ
Bike	ІІ
Walk	ЖІ ЖІ

a How many students did Manpreet ask?

b What fraction of people walk to school?

c What is the number of students that travel by car as a fraction of those that walk?

d What is the number of students that travel by car as a fraction of those that travel by bike?

e What is the number of students that walk as a fraction of students that cycle?

4 Answer parts **a** to **c**.

a Find $\frac{1}{3}$ of 21

b $\frac{1}{3}$ of a number is 21. What is the number?

c What fraction of 21 is 3?

5 Barnaby, Carole, and Dakshika share some money.

a Barnaby gets $\frac{2}{5}$ of the money and has £14.50 Calculate the amount of money the three people share.

b Carole gets $\frac{8}{25}$ of the money. Calculate the amount of money that Carole gets.

c Work out Dakshika's share as a fraction of the total.

8.3 Purposeful practice

There may be more than one way to approach these questions.
Once you have answered a question one way, can you think of another way?

1 Write a fraction-of-an-amount question that can go in each region of the Venn diagram. An example has been given.

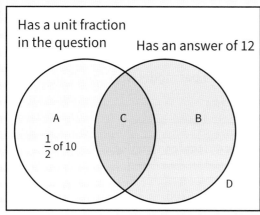

Has a unit fraction in the question

Has an answer of 12

A

$\frac{1}{2}$ of 10

C

B

D

2 Write a fraction-of-an-amount question that can go in each region of the Venn diagram. An example has been given.

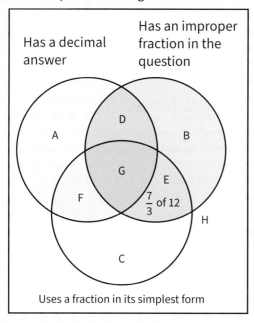

Has a decimal answer

Has an improper fraction in the question

A

D

B

G

E

F

$\frac{7}{3}$ of 12

H

C

Uses a fraction in its simplest form

3 Work out the missing number.

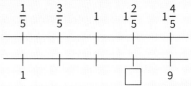

$\frac{1}{5}$ $\frac{3}{5}$ 1 $1\frac{2}{5}$ $1\frac{4}{5}$

1 □ 9

4 Siôn thinks of a number.

When he works out $\frac{4}{5}$ of the number, he gets $\frac{9}{10}$

a Siôn says, "If I had worked out $\frac{9}{10}$ of my number I would have got $\frac{4}{5}$"

Is Siôn correct? Explain your answer.

b Work out what Siôn gets if he works out $\frac{7}{8}$ of his number.

c Work out what fraction of his number Siôn has worked out if he gets $\frac{11}{20}$

5 When A is multiplied by B, the answer is 3

Write down, where possible, a pair of numbers that satisfy each of these conditions.

a A and B are integers.

b A is an integer and B is a fraction.

c A and B are both fractions.

d A is a decimal and B is an integer.

e A is a decimal and B is a fraction.

f A and B are both negative integers.

g A and B are both negative fractions.

h A is a negative number and B is a positive number.

Applying ratios

8.4.1 Dividing quantities in ratio

Objective ☑

You will learn how to:
- share an amount into a ratio

Investigate further 🔍

Road signs show the steepness of a road using a percentage. What would this look like if a ratio was used instead?

10 %

You can use a bar model to help you split a quantity into a given ratio.

To split £364 in the ratio $3:4$, you can draw a bar model with 7 parts in total.

You can think of this as finding $\frac{3}{7}$ and $\frac{4}{7}$ of the whole.

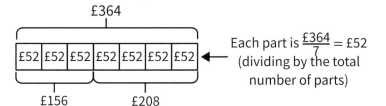

£364

| £52 | £52 | £52 | £52 | £52 | £52 | £52 |

£156   £208

Each part is $\frac{£364}{7} = £52$ (dividing by the total number of parts)

£364 split in the ratio $3:4$ is £156:£208

To split £400 into the ratio $1.2:0.8$, first write the ratio in its simplest form.

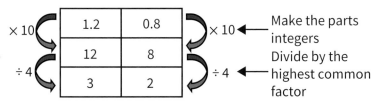

× 10	1.2	0.8	× 10
÷ 4	12	8	÷ 4
	3	2	

Make the parts integers

Divide by the highest common factor

Use a ratio table to help you.

Then use a bar model to help you find $\frac{3}{5}$ and $\frac{2}{5}$ of £400

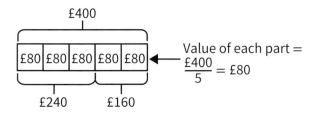

£400

| £80 | £80 | £80 | £80 | £80 |

£240   £160

Value of each part = $\frac{£400}{5} = £80$

£400 split in the ratio $1.2 : 0.8$ is £240 : £160

Worked example	Thinking	Your turn!
Jered and Keely share £350 in the ratio $2:3$. How much do they each get?	*Is the ratio in its simplest form?*	Abdoul and Beth share £350 in the ratio $4:3$. How much do they each get?
£350 [bar model with 5 parts]	*What is the total number of parts we have?*	

Yes. 1 is the only common factor of 2 and 3

I need to draw a bar model with five parts and a whole of £350

▲ Example-problem pair 1

Worked example	Thinking	Your turn!
£350 £70 £70 £70 £70 £70	What calculation do we need to do to complete the bar model?	
£350 £70 £70 £70 £70 £70 £140 £210 Jered has £140 Keely has £210	What is the order of the two parts?	

I need to find the value of one part of the bar model by doing £350 divided by 5

I can now add up the value of two parts and three parts and label my bar model.

▲ Example-problem pair 1

A bar model can also be used if you have a ratio with more than two sections. For example, say you needed to share £600 in the ratio $1:2:3$, you can draw a bar model with $1 + 2 + 3 = 6$ equal parts.

You can think of this as finding $\frac{1}{6}$, $\frac{2}{6}$, and $\frac{3}{6}$ of the whole, where each equal part is $\frac{£600}{6} = £100$

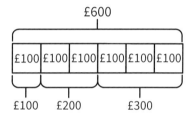

8.4.1 Fluency

In this exercise you can practise applying the mathematical methods that you have just learnt.

1 When Zaina shares £5 between herself and Sascha in the ratio $2:3$, Zaina gets £2 and Sascha gets £3

What would they get if Zaina shared:
- **a** £10
- **b** £20
- **c** £50
- **d** £0.50?

2 Share:
- **a** £40 in the ratio $3:5$
- **b** 70 kg in the ratio $7:3$
- **c** 80 ml in the ratio $1:4$
- **d** £900 in the ratio $5:13$

3 Share:
- **a** 70 litres in the ratio $3:11$
- **b** £550 in the ratio $7:4$

- **c** 960 grams in the ratio $5:7$
- **d** 561 cm in the ratio $8:3$

4 Share:
- **a** 7.8 kg in the ratio $1:2$
- **b** $\frac{3}{4}$ in the ratio $5:1$
- **c** 75 kg in the ratio $3.1:1.9$

5 Share:
- **a** 8.5 tonnes in the ratio $5:11:1$
- **b** $\frac{10}{11}$ in the ratio $2:3:5$
- **c** 5.6 litres in the ratio $1.3:2.6:3.1$

Now check your answers. You may want to use your calculator. Did you get any wrong and can you work out why?

Chapter 8

8.4.2 Using ratio to find missing parts

You will learn how to:

*   find one part of a whole, given another part and the ratio

You can also use a bar model for more complex problems with ratios, in a similar way as you did for fractions.

For instance, Anna and Bavel share some money in the ratio $1:3$

Anna gets £60. How much does Bavel get?

There are $1 + 3 = 4$ parts altogether so you need to draw 4 parts on the diagram.

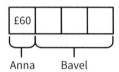

Each part is worth £60.

If you add up the three parts that make up Bavel's amount, you get £180

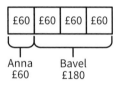

If Anna and Bavel share some money in the ratio $1:3$ and Bavel gets £60, we can work out how much Anna gets.

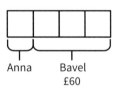

Three parts are worth £60. You divide by 3 to get the amount in one part. This gives Anna's amount of £20.

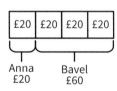

Worked example	Thinking	Your turn!	
Jered and Keely share money in the ratio $2:3$ Jered gets £30. How much does Keely get?	*How many parts are there altogether?* *What type of bar model will help us solve this?*	Abdoul and Beth share some money in the ratio $4:3$. Abdoul gets £30. How much does Beth get?	*I need to draw a bar model with five boxes.* *My bar model will have a bracket around two parts for Jered and three parts for Keely.*
Jered ⎵ Keely ⎵	*Where does the amount go on our bar model?*		*The question tells me Jered has £30, so I need to write this under Jered's bracket.*

Worked example	Thinking	Your turn!
 Jered £30 Keely	*What calculation do we need to complete the bar model?*	
£15 £15 £15 £15 £15 Jered £30 Keely £45	*What information do we need from our bar model to answer the question?*	
Keely gets £45.		

To find the amount for one part, I need to divide the £30 by 2 to get £15. Now I can fill in the rest of the bar model.

The question says Keely has three parts, so I work out the value of three parts.

▲ Example-problem pair 1

8.4.2 Fluency

In this exercise you can practise applying the mathematical methods that you have just learnt.

1 Martin and Chloe share money in the ratio $3:4$
   a List equivalent fractions to find out how much Chloe has if Martin has £15
   b List equivalent fractions to find out how much Martin has if Chloe has £32

2 Answer questions **a** to **c**.
   a Millie shares some sweets between herself and her friend in the ratio $5:9$
   Her friend gets 27 sweets.
   How many sweets does Millie get?
   b Manvi divides up some money between herself and her brother in the ratio $5:7$
   Manvi gets £30
   How much money does her brother get?
   c Cecil shares some lettuce between himself and Martha in the ratio $8:3$
   Martha gets 42 g of lettuce.
   How much lettuce does Cecil get?

3 Answer questions **a** to **c**.
   a Adam divides some money between himself, Paul, and Dino in the ratio $4:3:5$
   Adam gets £1.20
   How much money do Paul and Dino each get?
   b Clyde shares some lemonade between himself, Damia, and Saynab in the ratio $6:5:2$
   Damia gets 320 ml.
   How much lemonade do Clyde and Saynab each get?
   c Karen shares some paint between herself, Sophie, and Charlie in the ratio $7:3:4$
   Charlie gets 1.8 litres of paint.
   How much paint do Karen and Sophie each get?

Now check your answers. You may want to use your calculator. Did you get any wrong and can you work out why?

Chapter 8

8.4.3 Using ratios to find the whole

Objective

You will learn how to:

- find the whole, given one part of a whole and the ratio

You can use one of the numbers in the ratio and the ratio itself to find the whole amount.

For example, Mike and Devi share some money in the ratio 1 : 3. If Devi has £90, how much money do Mike and Devi have altogether?

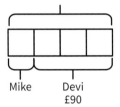

Mike   Devi
£90

You're told that Devi has 3 equal parts which is equivalent to £90, so 1 equal part must be equivalent to £90 divided by 3,

90 ÷ 3 = £30

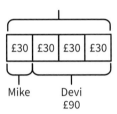

Mike   Devi
£90

There are 4 equal parts in total, so the whole amount must be £30 × 4 = £120

You can check this by adding the two amounts. Mike has 1 equal part, which is equivalent to £30. Devi has 3 equal parts, which is equivalent to £90, so altogether they have £30 + £90 = £120

Worked example	Thinking	Your turn!
The ratio of blue fish to yellow fish in a tank is 2 : 3 There are 8 blue fish. How many fish are there in the tank altogether?	*How many parts will our bar model have?*	The ratio of black sheep to white sheep in a field is 4 : 5 There are 12 black sheep. How many sheep are in the field altogether?
 blue yellow	*What calculation can we use to find 1 equal part?*	

I will draw a bar model with 2 parts for the blue fish and 3 parts for the yellow fish, so there will be 5 parts altogether.

There are 8 blue fish, which is 2 equal parts. That means an equal part is $\frac{8}{2} = 4$ fish

Worked example	Thinking	Your turn!
  blue 8 yellow	*What calculation do we need to find the whole amount?*	
There are $5 \times 4 = 20$ fish altogether.	*How can we check the answer?*	

There are 5 equal parts in total, so I need to do 5×4

I can find the number of yellow fish and add that to the number of blue fish.

▲ Example-problem pair 1

8.4.3 Fluency

In this exercise you can practise applying the mathematical methods that you have just learnt.

1 Answer questions **a** to **c**.

a Kimaya divides a sum of money between her and her brother in the ratio $3:2$
Kimaya gets £18
How much money did Kimaya divide up?

b Riya shares some porridge between her and her sister in the ratio $5:4$
Riya gets 200 g of porridge.
How much porridge was there to begin with?

c Scott shares some dog biscuits between Lilo and Barney in the ratio $7:5$
Lilo gets 28 biscuits.
How many biscuits did Scott start with?

2 Answer questions **a** to **c**.

a Oliver divides some money between himself and Felicity in the ratio $5:12$
Felicity gets £6
How much money did Oliver divide up?

b Stefan shares some juice between himself and Joanna in the ratio $4:3$
Stefan gets 840 ml.
How many litres of juice did Stefan start with?

c Mickey shares some beetroot between himself and Polly in the ratio $2:3$
Mickey gets 3.2 kg of beetroot.
How much beetroot did Mickey start with?

3 Answer questions **a** to **c**.

a Jenna divides some money up between herself and two friends in the ratio $4:3:2$
Jenna gets £24
How much money did Jenna divide up?

b Pauline shares some sherbet between herself and two friends in the ratio $8:5:3$
Pauline gets 960 g.
How many kilograms of sherbet did Pauline start with?

c Ari divides some money between himself and his sister in the ratio $1.6:3.2$
Ari gets £32.
How much money did Ari divide up?

Now check your answers. You may want to use your calculator. Did you get any wrong and can you work out why?

8.4.4 Using ratios when given the difference

Objective ☑

You will learn how to:

- find one part of a whole, given another part and the ratio

In some ratio problems you are told the value of the difference between the numbers in the ratio.

For these problems a comparative bar model, or a stacked bar model, can help. These models have a bar for each part of the ratio.

For example, Anna and Bavel share some money in the ratio 1:3. Bavel gets £60 more than Anna. How much do they each get?

Draw the two parts of the ratio stacked instead of side-by-side. You can see that Bavel has two more parts than Anna.

These two parts are worth £60. So each part is worth £60 ÷ 2 = £30

The completed bar model looks like this. You can see that Anna has £30 and Bavel has £90

£60

Anna

Bavel

£60

Anna	£30		
Bavel	£30	£30	£30

Worked example	Thinking	Your turn!	
Lakshmi and Martin share money in the ratio 2:5 Martin gets £30 more than Lakshmi. How much did they share?	What model could help us here? ○ Where does the amount go on our ○ bar model?	Carol and Dina share money in the ratio 3:5 Dina gets £30 more than Carol. How much did they share?	The question says Martin gets more than Lakshmi, so I can use a stacked bar model for the question. I'll use the numbers in the ratio as the numbers of parts.
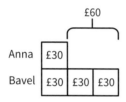 £30 Lakshmi Martin	What calculation do we need to do to complete the bar model?		Martin has £30 more than Lakshmi, so the three extra parts for Martin are worth £30

I need to divide £30 by 3 to get the value of one part.

Worked example	Thinking	Your turn!
£30 Lakshmi | £10 | £10 | Martin | £10 | £10 | £10 | £10 | £10 |	*What information do we need from our bar model to answer the question?*	
$7 \times 10 = £70$ Lakshmi and Martin shared £70		

> The question is asking me for the total amount shared, so I need to find the total of all the parts in my bar model.

▲ Example-problem pair 1

As before, you can also apply these strategies to ratios with more than two parts. For example, a bag is filled with red, yellow, and blue counters in the ratio $2:3:1$. There are 4 more yellow counters than red counters.

You can see from the bar model that each part is worth 4 counters. You can use this to work out the number of counters in each colour and the total number of counters.

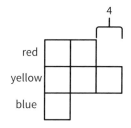

8.4.4 Fluency

In this exercise you can practise applying the mathematical methods that you have just learnt.

1 Paul and Ali share rice in the ratio $2:5$. Ali gets 15 kg more rice than Paul.
 a Draw a stacked bar model to illustrate this situation.
 b Use your bar model to work out how much rice each of them gets.

2 Ayano and Sanjay share money in the ratio $3:7$. Sanjay gets £40 more than Ayano.
 a Draw a stacked bar model to illustrate this situation.
 b Use your bar model to work out how much money each of them gets.

3 Frankie and Wayne share chocolate in the ratio $3:5$. Wayne gets 60 g more than Frankie.

 Work out how much chocolate each of them gets.

4 Milena and Sunny share sweets in the ratio $7:10$. Sunny gets 33 more sweets than Milena. Work out how many sweets each of them gets.

5 James and Jamal share cookies in the ratio $8:3$. James gets 10 more cookies than Jamal. Work out how many cookies they shared.

6 Elena, Gertrude, and Hanna share some money in the ratio $2:5:7$. Hanna gets £15 more than Elena.

 Work out how much money each of them gets.

Now check your answers. You may want to use your calculator. Did you get any wrong and can you work out why?

8.4.5 Using ratios to describe rates

Rates are a common example of multiplicative relationships.

Like ratios, rates describe the relationship between two quantities, but in rates the quantities are measurements.

A rate can be indicated by a ratio or the word **'per'** or 'for every'. For example, the **conversion rate** between Polish Złoty (zł) and British pounds is 1:0.19, so 1 zł is worth £0.19 or 19p.

A constant rate means that there is the same multiplicative relationship between all pairs of values, and the rate does not change over time. No matter how much money you exchange, you will always receive 19p for every 1 zł. You can plot a constant rate as a straight line on a graph in the same way as you did for ratios.

When you plot a rate on a graph, the graph will always go through the origin. This is because of the multiplicative relationship. If one of the values is zero, then no matter what multiplier you use, the other value must also be zero.

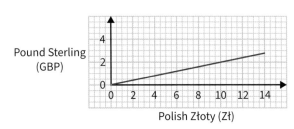

Pound Sterling (GBP) / Polish Złoty (Zł)

Worked example	Thinking	Your turn!
Carpet is priced at a constant rate of £27 per square metre. Plot a graph to show this.	*How do I know this is a multiplicative relationship?* *How can I work out the coordinates I need to plot?*	Wood flooring is priced at a constant rate of £36 per square metre. Plot a graph to show this.

Square metres	1	2	3	4	5
£	27	54	81	108	135

How do I plot these points on the graph?

The question says 'constant rate' and 'per'.

I can use the rate £27 per 1 square metre to set up a ratio table.

I use the area value for the x-coordinate of each point and the pounds for the y-coordinate. I join the points with a straight line.

Worked example	Thinking	Your turn!
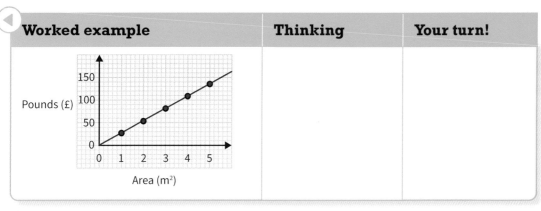		

▲ Example-problem pair 1

8.4.5 Fluency

In this exercise you can practise applying the mathematical methods that you have just learnt.

1 The ratio table shows the rate of exchange from pounds (£) to euros (€).

£	1	2	5
€	1.2	2.4	6

Use the ratio table to work out:
a how many euros you would get for £4
b how many pounds you would get for €12
c how many pounds you would get for €15.60

2 The double number line shows the conversion between gallons and litres:

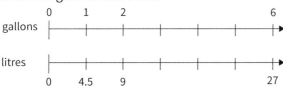

Use the double number line to work out:
a how many litres are in 4 gallons
b how many gallons are in 54 ℓ
c how many litres are in 8 gallons
d how many gallons are in 40.5 ℓ.

3 The rate of exchange from UK pounds (£) to US dollars ($) is £1 = $1.25
a Copy and complete this ratio table showing this exchange rate.

£	1	2	
$	1.25		8.75

b Draw a graph to show the exchange rate.

c Draw a double number line to show the exchange rate.

4 The conversion from ounces (oz) to grams (g) is 1 oz = 28 g.
a Copy and complete this ratio table showing this conversion.

oz	1	2	
g			140

b Use the ratio table to work out:
i the number of grams in 3 oz
ii the number of ounces in 280 g
iii the number of grams in 8 oz
iv the number of ounces in 364 g.

5 Water flows into a bucket at a constant rate of 1.5 ℓ per minute.
a Draw a graph to show this rate for the first 10 minutes.
b Use your graph to find:
i how much water is in the bucket after 6 minutes
ii how much water is in the bucket after 8 minutes
iii how long it takes to get 7.5 litres of water in the bucket.

Now check your answers. You may want to use your calculator. Did you get any wrong and can you work out why?

Chapter 8

8.4 Exercises

8.4 Intelligent practice

"Why is it intelligent?" You might notice a connection when you move on from one question to the next. You can use the Reflect, Expect, Check, Explain process to:

* *reflect* on what's different between each question and the one that came before
* decide how you *expect* this answer to be different
* complete the question and *check* your answer
* *explain* to yourself why your expectation was correct or incorrect.

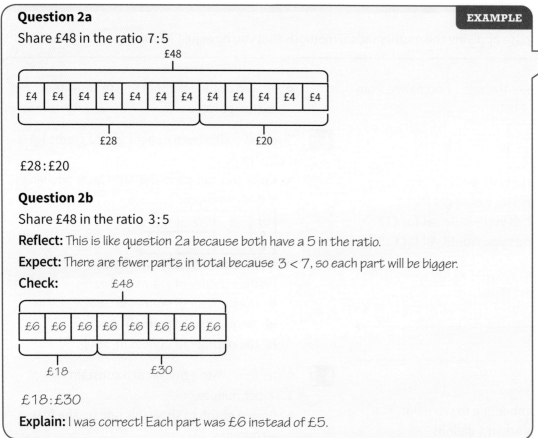

Question 2a   EXAMPLE

Share £48 in the ratio 7:5

£28:£20

Question 2b

Share £48 in the ratio 3:5

Reflect: This is like question 2a because both have a 5 in the ratio.

Expect: There are fewer parts in total because 3 < 7, so each part will be bigger.

Check:

£18:£30

Explain: I was correct! Each part was £6 instead of £5.

---

1   Answer questions **a** and **b**.

    a   John shares £10 in the ratio 2:3 with his friend Hasan. John gets £4 and Hasan gets £6. How much would they get each if John shares £100 in the ratio 2:3?

    b   Aisha shares £10 in the ratio 1:4 with her friend Ben. Aisha gets £2 and Ben gets £8. How much would they get each if Aisha shared £100 in the ratio 1:4?

2   Complete questions **a** to **k**.

    a   Share £48 in the ratio 7:5

    b   Share £48 in the ratio 3:5

    c   Share £48 in the ratio 1:5

    d   Share £48 in the ratio 1:3

    e   Share £24 in the ratio 1:3

    f   Share £24 in the ratio 3:1

    g   Share £2.40 in the ratio 1:3

    h   Share £2.40 in the ratio 1:4

i Share £2.40 in the ratio $1:4:3$

j Share £2.40 in the ratio $0.5:3.5$

k Share £2.40 in the ratio $0.5:3.5:2$

3 Reema and Sam share some money in the ratio $5:3$

a Use equivalent ratios to find out how much Sam has when Reema has £30

b Use equivalent ratios to find out how much Reema has when Sam has £30

c If Reema has £180, how much did they share?

d If they share £180, how much does Reema have?

e If Sam has £180, how much does Reema have?

f If Reema has £180 more than Sam, how much did they share?

g After splitting the money, Reema decides to split their money evenly so they have the same amount. She gives Sam £180. How much do they each have now?

8.4 Method selection

In these questions you'll need to think carefully about which methods to apply.

For some questions you might need to use skills from earlier chapters.

1 There are 270 students in the year group. Answer these questions about the year group.

a If $\frac{2}{3}$ of students don't have a pet, how many do?

b The ratio of walking to getting the bus is $2:3$. How many more students get the bus?

c Students study either French or Spanish. There are twice as many students studying French as Spanish. How many are studying Spanish?

d If $\frac{1}{5}$ of the school is in the year group, how many students are there altogether?

2 Alice and Jacinda share some money in the ratio $4:5$

a If they share £360, how much do they each get?

b What fraction of the money does Jacinda get?

c If Jacinda gets £360 more than Alice, how much did they both have to begin with?

d If Jacinda spends £360 and has £160 left, how much did Alice and Jacinda have altogether to begin with?

e If Alice gets £360, how much does Jacinda get?

f If Jacinda gets £360, how much did Alice and Jacinda have altogether to begin with?

g If Alice gives half her money to her brother and has £360 left, how much did Jacinda get?

3 Answer questions **a** and **b**.

a Work out the missing number: $\frac{3}{4} = \frac{\square}{84}$

b Copy and complete $3:4 = \square:84$

4 The graph shows the amount of time, t minutes, that it takes to add an amount of water, y litres, to a large barrel. The barrel has a capacity of 420 litres.

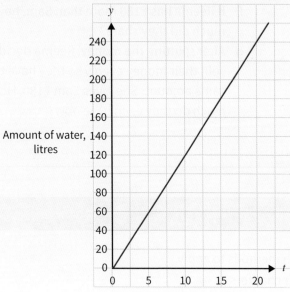

Time, minutes

a Copy and complete this ratio table connecting t and y.

t	2	5	10		
y		60		180	240

b Use the ratio table or the graph to work out:
   i the amount of water in the barrel after 8 minutes
   ii the amount of water in the barrel after 11 minutes
   iii the amount of time it takes to add 108 litres of water to the barrel
   iv the amount of time it takes to add 156 litres of water to the barrel.

c Calculate the amount of time it would take to fill the whole barrel at the same rate.

5 Use a suitable method to work out each of these problems.

a Min and Kyle divide some money in the ratio 5:7
Kyle gets £3.78. How much does Min get?

b Laura and Malak divide some sweets in the ratio 3.5:2.5
Malak gets 20 sweets. How many sweets does Laura get?

c Billy, Conor, and Dhanya share some counters in the ratio 5:7:8
Conor gets 42 counters. How many counters does Dhanya get?

d Faizal, Gemma, and Morwenna share some flour in the ratio 1.2:1.6:1.7
Faizal gets 360 g. How much flour does Morwenna get?

e Halima and Dan share some peanuts in the ratio 3:5. Dan gets 12 more peanuts than Halima. How many peanuts do they have altogether?

6 The rate at which Fluffy the cat eats his food is constant. Fluffy eats 30 g of food in 10 seconds.

a Find:
   i how long it takes Fluffy to eat 15 g of food
   ii how much food Fluffy eats in 4 seconds
   iii how long it takes Fluffy to eat 75 g of food.

b Complete this rate: Fluffy eats at a rate of _____ g per second.

8.4 Purposeful practice

There may be more than one way to approach these questions.
Once you have answered a question one way, can you think of another way?

1 Complete questions **a** and **b**.
  a Which of these questions will give integer answers?
    i Share £24 in the ratio $1:1$
    ii Share £24 in the ratio $1:2$
    iii Share £24 in the ratio $1:3$
    iv Share £24 in the ratio $1:4$
    v Share £24 in the ratio $1:5$
  b Find all the simplified ratios in the form $a:b$ that will give integer answers to 'Share £24 in the ratio $a:b$'.

2 Find all the simplified ratios in the form $a:b:c$ that will give positive integer answers to 'Share £6 in the ratio $a:b:c$'.

3 The graph shows the rate at which a bath fills with water.

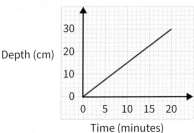

Use the graph, or other methods, to answer these questions.
  a What is the depth of the water after 10 minutes?
  b What is the depth of the water after 16 minutes?
  c How long does it take to fill the bath to a depth of 21 cm?
  d How long does it take to fill the bath to a depth of 27 cm?
  e Amar says, "It will take 40 minutes to fill the bath to a depth of 60 cm."
    Give two reasons why Amar's statement might be incorrect.

4 A business divides some money between teams in the ratio of the number of people in each team $6:8:9$
  a Given that each team gets an integer amount of money, find:
    i the smallest amount that the business can divide up
    ii the smallest amount greater than £100 that the business can divide up
    iii the smallest amount greater than £1000 that the business can divide up.
  b If the business divides £1966.50 between the teams, how much does the smallest team get?
  c If the largest team gets £1386, how much money did the business divide up?
  d If the middle team get £164 more than the smallest team, how much does the smallest team get?

5 The exchange rate from pounds (£) to US dollars ($) is £1 = $1.20
  a Draw a graph to illustrate this exchange rate. Use an y-axis from 0 to 100
  b Using the graph, or other methods, find:
    i the number of dollars that can be exchanged for £60
    ii the number of dollars that can be exchanged for £82.50
    iii the number of pounds that can be exchanged for $48
    iv the number of pounds that can be exchanged for $56.40
  c The exchange rate changes to £1 = $1.15
    A tourist travelling to the US changes £845 into dollars at this new exchange rate.
    How much less did they get than if they had exchanged their money at the old rate?

Chapter 8

Watch out! exercise

Some students have tried to answer the questions below but have unfortunately made some mistakes.

For each question do the following:

a answer the question correctly

b write down the mistake that each student has made

c comment on why they might have made that mistake

d write an explanation for each student to convince them (nicely!) that their answer cannot be correct.

---

1 Ethan and Frankie have both tried to complete this ratio table:

2	4
8	

a Ethan wrote:

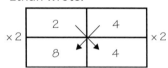

b Frankie wrote:

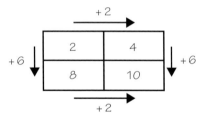

2 Keith and Lamees both try and share £330 in the ratio $2:4:5$

a Keith wrote: $£330 \div 2 = £165$ so the shares are £330, £660, and £825

b Lamees wrote: $£330 \div 11 = £30$ so each share is £30

3 Maya, Nusrat, and Oliver are working out the multiplier from A to B if the multiplier from A to C is 4 and the multiplier from B to C is 3

a Maya wrote:

The multiplier from A to B is $4 - 3 = 1$

b Nusrat wrote:

The multiplier from A to B is $3 \div 4 = 0.75$

c Oliver wrote:

The multiplier from A to B is $4 \times 3 = 12$

---

4 Paul, Quentin, and Eun-Jeong use this graph to convert £50 to dollars.

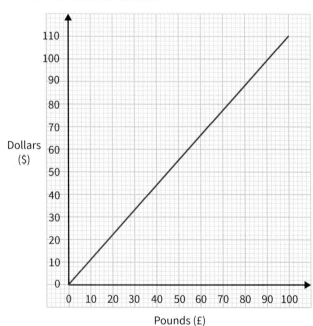

a Paul wrote: £50 is about $45

b Quentin wrote: $£50 = \$5500$

c Eun-Jeong wrote: $1.2 \times 50 = \$60$

Check your understanding

Turn over to find the review questions

8.1 Multiplicative relationships

You should now be able to...	Questions
understand that two numbers can be connected by addition/subtraction or multiplication/division	18a
show a multiplicative relationship using a ratio, fraction, or diagram	1, 2, 3, 4a, 17c
find the multiplier between two numbers	5, 6, 7
find different pairs of numbers that satisfy the same multiplicative relationship	18b

8.2 Representing multiplicative relationships

You should now be able to...	Questions
use a ratio table to represent a multiplicative relationship	18b
use a ratio table to simplify a ratio	18b, 18d
use a double number line to represent a multiplicative relationship and connect it to other representations	18c

8.3 Fractions in context

You should now be able to...	Questions
find a fraction of a given amount	8, 9
find the original amount given a fraction of an amount and the fraction	10, 11
write one number as a fraction of another	1b, 2b, 3b, 4b, 12

8.4 Applying ratios

You should now be able to...	Questions
share an amount into a ratio	13, 14, 17a, 17b
find the whole, given one part of a whole and the ratio	16
find one part of a whole, given another part and the ratio	15
use ratios to describe rates	18e

Chapter 8 review questions

1 Look at this bar model:

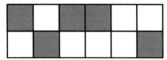

  a Write the ratio of shaded to unshaded. [1]
  b What fraction of the bar is shaded? [1]

2 Look at this grid:

  a Write the ratio of shaded to unshaded. [1]
  b What fraction of the bar is shaded? [1]

3 Delight has a bag containing 18 counters. 11 of the counters are green and the rest of the counters are purple.
  a What is the ratio of green counters to purple counters? [1]
  b What fraction of the counters are purple? [1]

4 There are 28 iced cakes and 24 plain cakes in a box.
  a Write, in simplest terms, the ratio of iced cakes to plain cakes. [1]
  b Write the number of iced cakes as a fraction of the number of plain cakes. [1]

5 Five bananas cost 65 pence.
  a How much do 20 bananas cost? [1]
  b How much do 12 bananas cost? [1]

6 18 pineapples cost £6.30
  a How much do 6 pineapples cost? [1]
  b How much do 5 pineapples cost? [1]

7 Ishani bought 7 litres of petrol and it cost £11.55
How much petrol could Ishani buy if instead she spent £25 on petrol? [2]

8 Work out:
  a $\frac{1}{6}$ of 54 [1]
  b $\frac{3}{5}$ of 95 [1]

9 Rayen's fruit shop has 85 grapefruit.
She sells $\frac{2}{17}$ of the total number of grapefruit.
How many grapefruit does Rayen sell? [2]

10 $\frac{1}{12}$ of a number is 9
What is the number? [1]

11 Ismail and Dorothy have some pies. Ismail has 18 pies. This is $\frac{3}{7}$ of the total.
How many pies does Dorothy have? [2]

12 Karl carries out a survey of the favourite food of his classmates.
His results are shown in the table.

Food	Number of students
Pizza	7
Pasta	5
Curry	8
Fish and chips	6

  a How many students are in Karl's class? [1]
  b What fraction of the students like pasta? [1]
  c What is the number of students who like fish and chips as a fraction of those who like curry? [1]
  d What is the number of students who like curry as a fraction of those who like fish and chips? [1]
  e What is the number of students who like curry as a fraction of those who like pizza? [1]

13 Philomena and Amrit share £190 in the ratio 7:3
How much does each of them get? [2]

14 Will and Megan share a £1.2 million lottery win in the ratio 0.6 : 1
How much does each of them get? [2]

15 Beatrice and Yuan share some money in the ratio 6 : 5
Beatrice has £48
How much does Yuan have? [2]

16 Felicity and Joshva share some sweets in the ratio 8 : 3
Felicity gets 35 more sweets than Joshva.
How many sweets do they share in total? [2]

17 Belinda, Carrie, and Elspeth share 420 beads in the ratio 7 : 4 : 3
  a How many beads does Belinda get? [1]
  b How many beads do Carrie and Elspeth each get? [2]
  Belinda finds that 100 of her beads are yellow and the rest are red.
  c Write the number of yellow beads to the number of red beads as a simplified ratio. [2]

18 $A = 3$ and $B = 11.25$
  a Write down two possible relationships that connect A and B. [1]
  b The table shows some other values of A and B.

A	3	6	1	
B	11.25	22.5		15

  Copy and complete the table. [1]
  c Show the relationship between A and B on a double number line. [1]
  d Write the ratio $A : B$ in the form $1 : n$. [1]
  e Your answer to part **d** represents the exchange rate from Pounds (£) to Tunisian Dinar.
  Calculate the number of Tunisian Dinar that can be bought with £50. [1]

Key words

Make sure you can write a definition for these key terms.

multiplicative relationship • fraction • ratio • additive relationship
multiplier • double number line • rate • per • conversion rate

These pictures show paper sizes. A typical sheet of printer paper is A4. What is the relationship between A5 and A4 paper? What is the relationship between A5 and A3 paper?

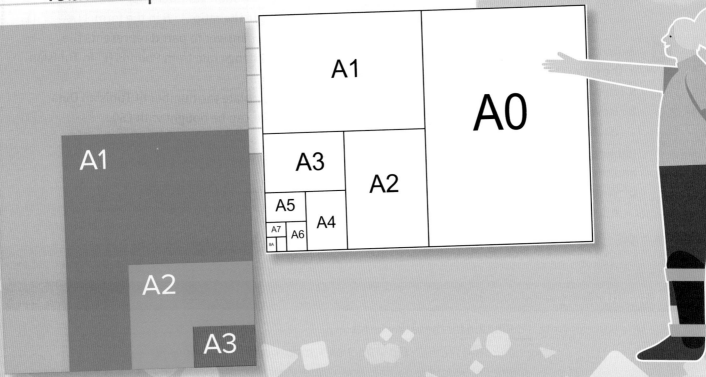

What comes before?	This chapter	What comes after?
Primary school • Angles • Shapes **Book 1** • Coordinates • Fractions and ratios	• 9.1 Translations • 9.2 Rotations • 9.3 Reflections • 9.4 Scale diagrams • 9.5 Enlargements	**Book 2** • Polygons **Book 3** • Similarity and congruence **GCSE** • Geometry

Introduction

In this chapter you will explore different types of transformations, including translations, rotations, and reflections. You will learn how to recognise, carry out, and describe these transformations. The original shape or picture is called the object and the transformed shape or picture is the image. Enlargement is another type of transformation explored in this chapter. In an enlargement all the lengths of an object are multiplied by the same number (called the scale factor) to create the image.

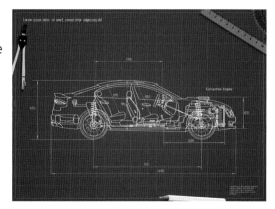

You will also learn how distances in real life can be shown on scale diagrams. For example, engineers draw a plan when they design a new car. This is a scale diagram of the lengths of its dimensions. A scale of 1 cm to 30 cm means every 1 cm on the diagram represents 30 cm in real life.

In this chapter you will learn how to...

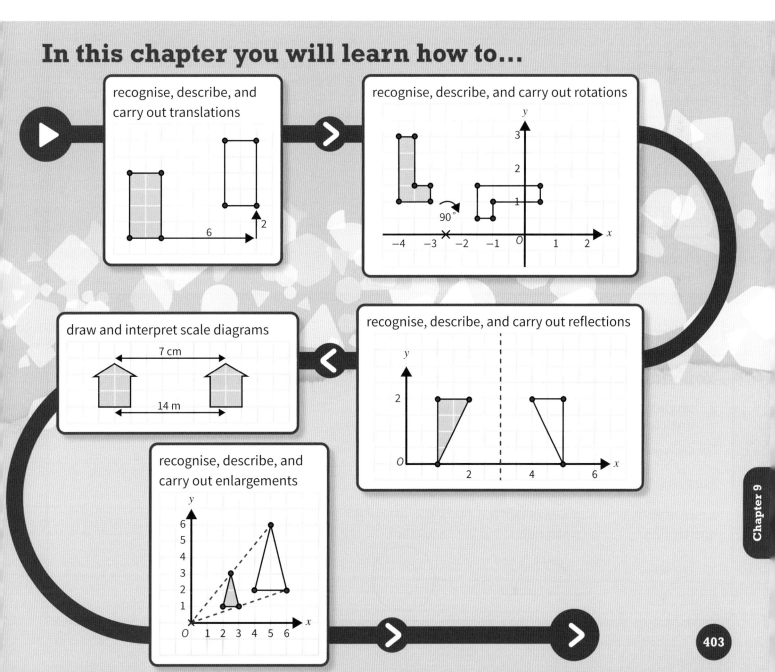

recognise, describe, and carry out translations

recognise, describe, and carry out rotations

draw and interpret scale diagrams

7 cm

14 m

recognise, describe, and carry out reflections

recognise, describe, and carry out enlargements

Reactivate your knowledge

If you can answer the questions on these pages then you should be ready for the chapter.

Some questions are there to help you to remember some maths from primary school and some are to help you remember maths from earlier in the book. If you see this symbol 🔗 it tells you where that information was introduced in an earlier chapter. If you are struggling with those questions you could go back and read through it again.

9.1 Translations

You should know...

1. how to draw shapes on coordinate grids

For example

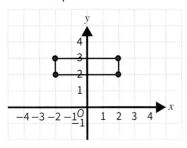

This rectangle has vertices with coordinates $(-2, 3)$, $(2, 3)$, $(2, 2)$, and $(-2, 2)$.

 Look back to Subsection 5.1.3

 Look back to Section 6.1

Check in

1. Draw each of these shapes on their own set of axes:

   a a triangle with vertices at $(1, 2)$, $(3, 5)$ and $(3, 2)$,

   b a parallelogram with vertices at $(-2, 1)$, $(-5, 3)$, $(-3, 5)$, $(0, 3)$,

   c a square with vertices at $(-1, -1)$, $(1, -1)$, $(1, -3)$, $(-1, -3)$.

9.2 Rotations

You should know...

2. angles can measure turns in a clockwise or anticlockwise direction

For example

clockwise   anticlockwise

A turn of 90° is a quarter-turn.

A turn of 180° is a half-turn.

A turn of 360° is a full turn.

Check in

2. How many 90° turns are in:

   a a quarter-turn,

   b a half-turn,

   c a full turn?

9.3 Reflections

You should know...

3. how to reflect points in axes

For example

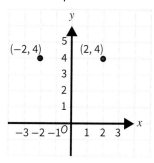

The point $(2, 4)$ is the image of a reflection of the point $(-2, 4)$ in the y-axis.

 Look back to Subsection 5.1.2

---

4. how to find the midpoint of points on a coordinate grid using their coordinates

For example

The midpoint of $(14, -2)$ and $(6, 8)$ is $(10, 3)$ since:

- the midpoint of the x-coordinates is $(14 + 6) \div 2 = 10$
- the midpoint of the y-coordinates is $(-2 + 8) \div 2 = 3$

 Look back to Subsection 5.1.2

Check in

3. Work out the coordinates of the images of:

a the point $(-6, 1)$ reflected in the y-axis,

b the point $(3, -5)$ reflected in the y-axis,

c the point $(-6, 1)$ reflected in the x-axis,

d the point $(3, -5)$ reflected in the x-axis.

4. Give the coordinates of the midpoint of:

a $(5, 7)$ and $(-3, 3)$,

b $(12, 8)$ and $(0, 16)$,

c $(-4, 13)$ and $(11, 19)$,

d $(-1, -5)$ and $(-21, 7)$.

9.4 Scale diagrams

You should know...

Check in

5. how to use ratio tables to work out quantities that are multiplicatively related

For example

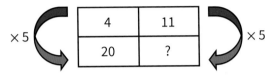

4	11
20	?

The missing number in this ratio table is 55, because
$11 \times 5 = 55$

🔗 Look back to Subsection 8.1.2

5. Work out the missing number in these ratio tables

a

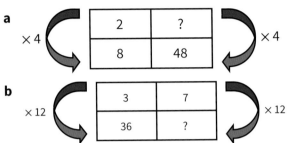

2	?
8	48

b

3	7
36	?

6. how to convert between units of length

For example

$1\,m = 100\,cm$

$25\,mm = 2.5\,cm$

$3.4\,m = 3400\,mm$

$5000\,m = 5\,km$

🔗 Look back to Subsection 1.4.1

6. Work out:

a 4000 mm in m,

b 6.7 m in cm,

c 3 km in m,

d 1.8 cm in mm.

7. how to work out one part, given the other part and the ratio

For example

Tom and Maryam share some grapes in the ratio 5:7
If Tom has 25 grapes, how many does Maryam have?

$25 \div 5 = 5$ for each part.

$5 \times 7 = 35$, so Maryam has 35 grapes.

🔗 Look back to Subsection 8.4.3

7. Sunita and Cillian share some raisins. Sunita has 24 raisins. Work out how many Cillian has if the ratio is:

a 4:7

b 6:11

c 12:5

9.5 Enlargements

You should know...

8. how to calculate the multiplier for any two numbers

For example

The multiplier that links 6 to 11 is $\dfrac{11}{6}$

because $6 \times \dfrac{11}{6} = 11$

 Look back to Subsection 8.1.1

Check in

8. Calculate the multiplier that links

   a 3 to 17

   b 2.5 to 10

   c 18 to 5

   d 14.6 to 8.2

Translations

Language 📖

The word 'translate' can mean to transfer words from one language to another. In maths it means to move (or transfer) a shape from one position to another without changing its shape, size, or orientation.

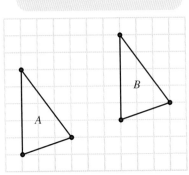

9.1.1 Introduction to translation

Objective ☑

You will:

- recognise a translation and know which features of an object are affected by translation

Look at triangles A and B on the grid. Triangles A and B are **congruent** which means they are the same shape and size. The **orientation** of the two triangles is also the same. They are the same 'way around'.

The **position** of the triangles on the grid is different. Triangle A has been moved six boxes to the right and two boxes up to the position of triangle B. When doing **transformations**, the original shape (triangle A in this case) is called the **object** and the transformed shape (triangle B in this case) is called the **image**.

Key point 🔑

Moving an object without changing its shape, size, or orientation is called **translation**.

Worked example	Thinking	Your turn!
Explain which shape represents a translation of shape A.	*What is meant by a translation?*	**Explain which shape represents a translation of shape A.**
Shape C is a translation of Shape A. It has been moved but its size and orientation have stayed the same.		A translation will be the same size and orientation.

▲ Example-problem pair 1

9.1.1 Fluency

In this exercise you can practise applying the mathematical methods that you have just learnt.

1 Look at these diagrams.

In each diagram write which of the shapes are translations of shape A.

a

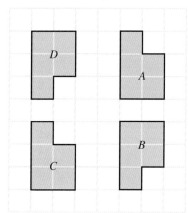

b

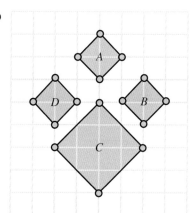

2 Look at these shapes.

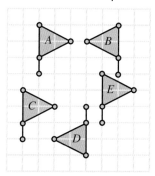

a Write the letters of two shapes that are translations of shape A.

b Marlon says that shape B is a translation of shape D since they are the same size.

Is Marlon correct? Explain your answer.

3 Look at these shapes.

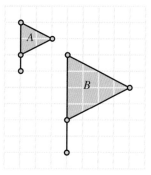

Cara says that shape B is a translation of shape A since it is the same orientation and has moved down and to the right.

Is she correct? Explain your answer.

4 Shape B is a translation of shape A.

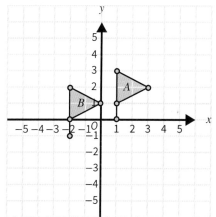

Write the coordinates of the image of each of these points under this translation.

a $(-2, -1)$ **c** $(-1, 0)$

b $(0, 1)$ **d** $(0, 0)$

Now check your answers. Did you get any wrong and can you work out why?

9.1.2 Describing translations

Objective

You will learn how to:

- describe a translation

In the diagram, object A has been translated seven units right and five units down to give its image A'.

To work out how the shape has been translated, you can choose any of the vertices and see where it has moved to. Whichever vertex you choose, you should get the same answer because all vertices are moved in the same way.

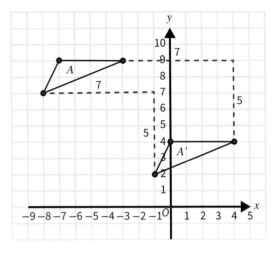

So you can describe the transformation of A to A' as a translation of:

- seven units in the positive x-direction,
- five units in the negative y-direction.

Key point

Translation is described by giving:

- the units moved in the positive or negative x-direction,
- the units moved in the positive or negative y-direction.

Worked example	Thinking	Your turn!
$A'B'C'D'$ is the image of $ABCD$ following a transformation. Describe the transformation.	*Have the size and shape changed?*	$A'B'C'D'$ is the image of $ABCD$ following a transformation. Describe the transformation.

No. I can see the position has changed and I also need to check if the orientation has changed.

Worked example	Thinking	Your turn!
This is a translation of eight units in the negative x-direction and six units in the negative y-direction.	*How do we work out the change in position?*	

I need to choose a vertex and see how I would need to move it horizontally and vertically.

▲ Example-problem pair 1

Translations can also be described using a **column vector**. A vector tells you how much you move and in what direction. The top number describes movement in the x-direction and the bottom number describes movement in the y-direction.

For example, the vector $\begin{pmatrix} 7 \\ -5 \end{pmatrix}$ describes a translation of seven units in the positive x-direction and five units in the negative y-direction.

9.1.2 Fluency

In this exercise you can practise applying the mathematical methods that you have just learnt.

1 Shape B is a translation of shape A four units right and one unit up.

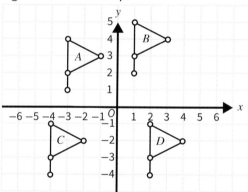

Describe these translations:

a A to C,   **c** B to A,

b A to D,   **d** D to C.

2 Look at the shapes in question 1.

Shape D is a translation of shape A five units in the positive x-direction and five units in the negative y-direction.

Describe these translations in the same way:

a A to B,   **c** B to C,

b A to C,   **d** B to D.

3 Look at these shapes.

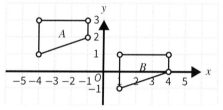

Shape B is a translation of shape A five units in the positive x-direction and two units in the negative y-direction.

Describe the translation of shape B to shape A in the same way. What do you notice?

4 Look at the shapes in question 1.

Shape D is a translation of shape A by vector $\begin{pmatrix} 5 \\ -5 \end{pmatrix}$

Use vectors to describe these translations:

a A to C,   **c** B to A,

b C to D,   **d** D to B.

Now check your answers. Did you get any wrong and can you work out why?

Chapter 9

9.1.3 Translating objects

If you want to draw the image of a shape that has been transformed, you can start by finding the coordinates of each of the vertices. Then you can draw the transformed shape by connecting the coordinates.

For example, here triangle ABC has been translated seven units in the negative x-direction and four units in the positive y-direction to give the image $A'B'C'$. Notice how every vertex has been translated in the same way.

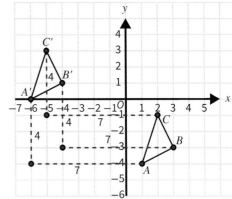

Worked example	Thinking	Your turn!
Translate shape $ABCD$ nine units in the positive x-direction and one unit in the positive y-direction. Label the image $A'B'C'D'$.	*What is the first step?*	Translate shape $ABCD$ eight units in the positive x-direction and one unit in the positive y-direction. Label the image $A'B'C'D'$.
	How do we complete the diagram?	

I need to choose a vertex to translate first then repeat for the other vertices.

I need to label the vertices correctly.

9.1.3 Fluency

In this exercise you can practise applying the mathematical methods that you have just learnt.

1 Use a copy of this grid to answer this question.

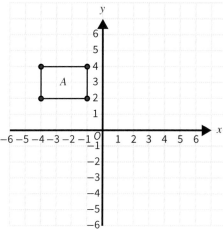

a Translate shape A four units right and one unit up. Label the image B.

b Translate shape A five units right and two units down. Label the image C.

c Translate shape A one unit left and three units down. Label the image D.

2 Use a copy of this grid to answer this question.

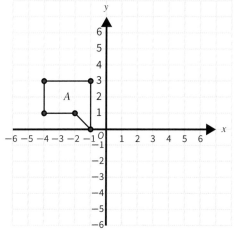

a Translate shape A three units in the positive x-direction and two units in the positive y-direction. Label the image B.

b Translate shape A two units in the negative x-direction and three units in the positive y-direction. Label the image C.

c Translate shape A six units in the positive x-direction and five units in the negative y-direction. Label the image D.

3 Use a copy of this grid to answer this question.

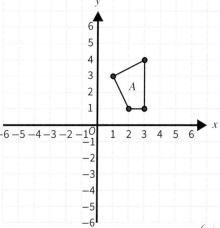

a Translate shape A using vector $\begin{pmatrix} 1 \\ -4 \end{pmatrix}$ Label the image B.

b Translate shape B using vector $\begin{pmatrix} -5 \\ 1 \end{pmatrix}$ Label the image C.

c Translate shape C using vector $\begin{pmatrix} 2 \\ 4 \end{pmatrix}$ Label the image D.

d Write the vector that you would use to translate shape A onto shape D directly.

Now check your answers. Did you get any wrong and can you work out why?

9.1 Exercises

9.1 Intelligent practice

"Why is it intelligent?" You might notice a connection when you move on from one question to the next. You can use the Reflect, Expect, Check, Explain process to:

- *reflect* on what's different between each question and the one that came before
- decide how you *expect* this answer to be different
- complete the question and *check* your answer
- *explain* to yourself why your expectation was correct or incorrect.

> **EXAMPLE**
>
> **Question 1a**
> Write a sentence to describe the transformation from A to B.
> *Translation of five units in the positive x-direction.*
> **Question 1b**
> Write a sentence to describe the transformation from A to C.
> **Reflect:** *Shape A has been translated five to the right as in question 1a, but it has also been translated down.*
> **Expect:** *I think that the x-direction part of the answer will be the same as for question 1a but there will also be a part in the y-direction.*
> **Check:** *The translation is five units in the positive x-direction and four units in the negative y-direction.*
> **Explain:** *I was right! The translation still involves five units in the positive x-direction, but also involves a translation in the y-direction.*

1 Use a copy of this grid to answer this question.

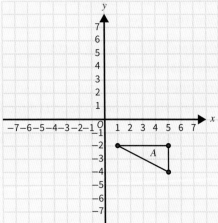

a Translate shape A six units left and label the image B.

b Translate shape A six units left and four units up and label the image C.

c Translate shape A one unit right and four units up and label the image D.

2 Look at triangles A–D.

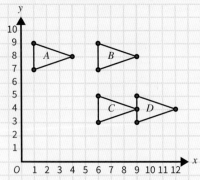

Write a sentence to describe the transformation from:

a A to B, **c** A to D,

b A to C, **d** D to A.

3 Describe the transformations from question 2 using vectors.

4 Look at triangles *P–S*.

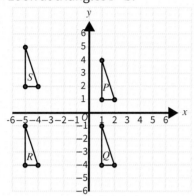

Write a sentence to describe the transformation from:

a *P* to *Q*,   **c** *P* to *S*,

b *P* to *R*,   **d** *S* to *P*.

5 Describe the transformations from question 4 using vectors.

6 Use a copy of this grid to answer this question.

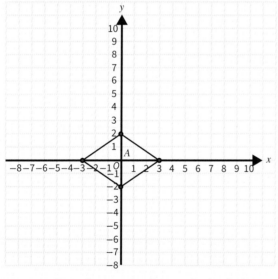

a Translate shape *A* by four units in the positive *y*-direction and label the image *B*.

b Translate shape *A* by four units in the negative *y*-direction and label the image *C*.

c Translate shape *A* by six units in the positive *x*-direction and four units in the negative *y*-direction and label the image *D*.

d Translate shape *A* by six units in the positive *x*-direction and eight units in the positive *y*-direction and label the image *E*.

7 Use a copy of this grid to answer this question.

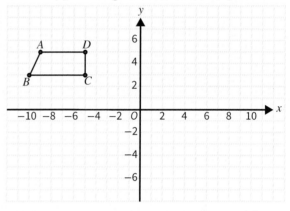

a Translate shape *ABCD* by the vector $\begin{pmatrix} 6 \\ 0 \end{pmatrix}$ and label the image *A'B'C'D'*.

b Translate shape *ABCD* by the vector $\begin{pmatrix} 6 \\ -9 \end{pmatrix}$ and label the image *A''B''C''D''*.

c Translate shape *ABCD* by the vector $\begin{pmatrix} 14 \\ -9 \end{pmatrix}$ and label the image *A'''B'''C'''D'''*.

8 State the coordinates of the point $(-3, 8)$ following a translation by vector:

a $\begin{pmatrix} 7 \\ 0 \end{pmatrix}$ **b** $\begin{pmatrix} 7 \\ -2 \end{pmatrix}$ **c** $\begin{pmatrix} 8 \\ -2 \end{pmatrix}$ **d** $\begin{pmatrix} 8 \\ -1 \end{pmatrix}$

9 Describe the translation that transforms the point $(-11, 2)$ to the point:

a $(-11, 3)$,   **c** $(0, 4)$,

b $(-11, 4)$,   **d** $(11, 4)$.

9.1 Method selection

In these questions you'll need to think carefully about which methods to apply.

For some questions you might need to use skills from earlier chapters.

1 The point A has coordinates $(3, -1)$.

The point B is the reflection of point A in the x-axis.

The point C is the reflection of point A in the y-axis.

a Draw triangle ABC.

b Translate triangle ABC five units in the negative x-direction and four units in the positive y-direction and label the image $A'B'C'$.

2 A, B, and C are three vertices of a rectangle. The fourth vertex of the rectangle is D.

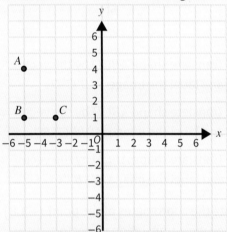

a What are the coordinates of D?

The rectangle is translated right eight units and down ten units. The image of D under this translation is D'.

b What are the coordinates of D'?

c What is the midpoint of D and D'?

3 The area of triangle PQR is $25\,\text{cm}^2$.

The triangle is translated right two units and up five units to give triangle $P'Q'R'$.

What is the area of triangle $P'Q'R'$?

4 A quadrilateral has vertices at $(1, -3)$, $(9, -3)$, $(5, 2)$, and $(2, 2)$.

a Write the name of the quadrilateral.

The quadrilateral is drawn on a grid where one unit = $1\,\text{cm}$.

b Calculate the area of the quadrilateral.

c Draw the image of the quadrilateral after it has been translated four units in the negative x-direction and five units in the positive y-direction.

5 Parallelogram A has vertices at $(-6, -2)$, $(-3, -2)$, and $(-2, 3)$.

a What are the coordinates of the fourth vertex?

The parallelogram is drawn on a grid where one unit = $1\,\text{cm}$.

b Calculate the area of parallelogram A.

Parallelogram B is shown in the diagram.

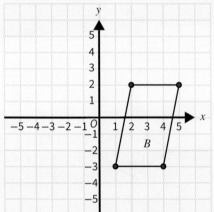

c Describe the transformation that transforms parallelogram A to parallelogram B.

6 The point $A(10, -5)$ is translated by the vector $\begin{pmatrix} 3 \\ 9 \end{pmatrix}$ then by the vector $\begin{pmatrix} 2 \\ -4 \end{pmatrix}$ to the point A'.

a What are the coordinates of A'?

b Describe the single transformation that will transform point A to A'.

7 The graph shows the line that satisfies the rule $x = 3$

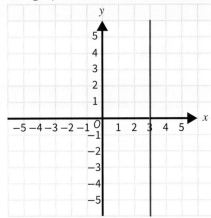

Every point on the line is translated by the vector $\begin{pmatrix} 1 \\ 2 \end{pmatrix}$

Write the rule that all the points will now satisfy.

9.1 Purposeful practice

There may be more than one way to approach these questions. Once you have answered a question one way, can you think of another way?

1 Use a copy of triangle A to answer this question.

    a Draw two different translations of triangle A and label them B and C.
    b Explain how you know that triangles B and C are translations of triangle A.
    c Draw two triangles that are not translations of shape A and label them D and E.
    d Explain why D and E are not translations of shape A.

2 Look at this diagram.

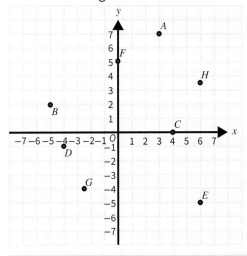

    a Pick some pairs of points from the diagram and describe the translation that transforms one to another.
    b For each of your translations in part a, describe the translation that would transform the image back to the object. What do you notice?

3 **a** Draw a quadrilateral on a coordinate grid and label it A.
    b Translate quadrilateral A by the vector $\begin{pmatrix} -5 \\ 2 \end{pmatrix}$ and label it B.
    c Translate quadrilateral B by the vector $\begin{pmatrix} 7 \\ -6 \end{pmatrix}$ and label it C.

    d Translate quadrilateral C by the vector $\begin{pmatrix} -2 \\ 4 \end{pmatrix}$ and label it D.
    e What do you notice? Can you explain why this has happened?

Rotations

9.2.1 Introduction to rotation

Objective

You will learn how to:

- recognise a rotation and know which features of an object are affected by rotation

Look at quadrilaterals A and A' on the grid.

Quadrilaterals A and A' are congruent, but the orientation of A and A' is different, so you know that this is not a translation. This type of transformation is a **rotation**: shape A is turned through an angle to give A'.

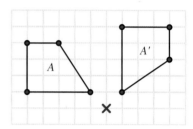

Language 📖

The word 'rotate' comes from the Latin word *rota*, which means 'wheel'. A wheel rotates in a circle.

A shape is rotated around a fixed point, called the **centre of rotation**. The centre of rotation does not change under the rotation, but the shape will rotate around it. In the diagram, the centre of rotation is shown by a cross.

Key point 🔑

Turning an object is called a rotation.
The centre of rotation is a fixed point that an object rotates around.

Worked example	Thinking	Your turn!
The diagram shows three different transformations of shape A. Two of the transformations are rotations with centre of rotation $(7, 7)$.		The diagram shows three different transformations of shape A. Two of the transformations are rotations with centre of rotation $(7, 6)$.

Worked example	Thinking	Your turn!
Which of the triangles B, C, and D is not a rotation of triangle A?	*What is meant by a rotation?*	Which of the triangles B, C, and D is not a rotation of triangle A?
Triangles B and D are rotations of triangle A, but triangle C is not (it is a reflection).		

> I need to check whether the shape has changed orientation and if it has been 'turned' to its new position.

▲ Example-problem pair 1

9.2.1 Fluency

In this exercise you can practise applying the mathematical methods that you have just learnt.

1 Which of shapes B, C, and D represent a rotation of shape A?

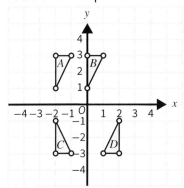

2 Look at these shapes.

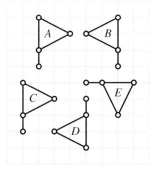

a Write the letters of two shapes that are rotations of shape A.

b Write the letters of two shapes that are rotations of shape C.

c Marian says that shape D is a rotation of shape E.
Is Marian correct? Explain your answer.

3 A shape is rotated.
Are these statements always true, always false, or sometimes true and sometimes false?
Explain your answers.

a The image of the shape under the rotation is the same size.

b The image of the shape under the rotation is in the same orientation.

c The image of the shape under the rotation is in the same position.

4 Shape B is a rotation of shape A.
The centre of rotation is $(1, 0)$.
Write the coordinates of the image of each of these points under the same rotation:

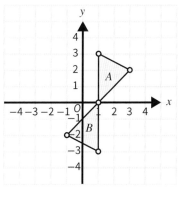

a $(2, 0)$,
b $(3, 1)$,
c $(1, 0)$,
d $(-1, -3)$.

e Eddie says that the centre of rotation $(1, 0)$ does not change under the rotation because it is one of the vertices of the shape.
Ellie says that the centre of rotation does not change even if it is *not* one of the vertices of the shape.
Who is correct? Explain your answer.

Now check your answers. Did you get any wrong and can you work out why?

9.2.2 Rotate an object

Objective

You will learn how to:

- rotate an object

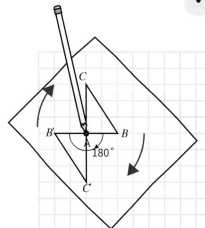

You can use tracing paper to help you rotate a shape. Trace the shape, then place your pencil at the centre of rotation and turn the paper through the angle required. Copy the image of the shape from the tracing paper onto the diagram.

For example, to rotate triangle ABC by 180° clockwise about the point A you trace the shape, put your pencil at the point A, then rotate the tracing paper 180° clockwise. The image of B is B' and the image of C is C', but the point A stays the same since it is the centre of the rotation.

When you are drawing the image, remember to use a ruler and check that the image is congruent to the object.

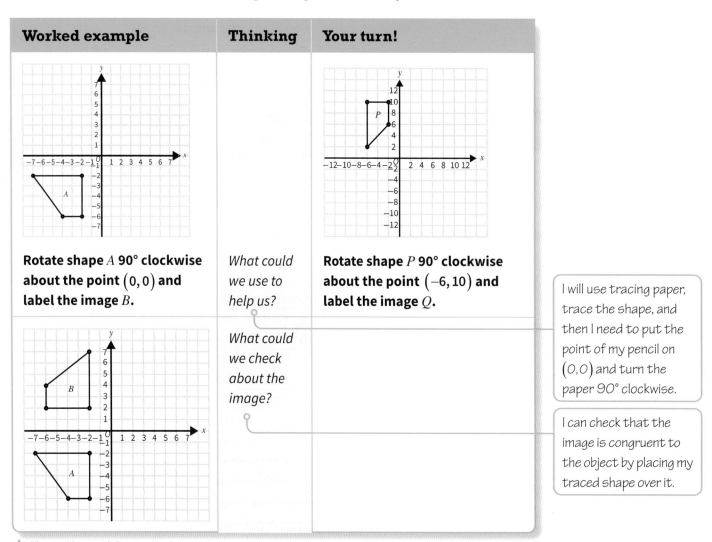

Worked example	Thinking	Your turn!

Rotate shape A 90° clockwise about the point $(0, 0)$ and label the image B.

What could we use to help us?

What could we check about the image?

Rotate shape P 90° clockwise about the point $(-6, 10)$ and label the image Q.

> I will use tracing paper, trace the shape, and then I need to put the point of my pencil on $(0,0)$ and turn the paper 90° clockwise.

> I can check that the image is congruent to the object by placing my traced shape over it.

▲ Example-problem pair 1

9.2.2 Fluency

In this exercise you can practise applying the mathematical methods that you have just learnt.

1 Use a copy of this grid to answer this question.

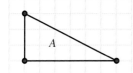

a Draw shape A after it has been rotated 180° and label it B.

b Draw shape A after it has been rotated 90° clockwise and label it C.

c Draw shape A after it has been rotated 270° clockwise and label it D.

2 Use a copy of this grid to answer this question.

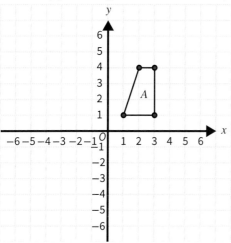

a Rotate shape A 180° about $(1,1)$. Label the image B.

b Rotate shape A 90° clockwise about $(2,3)$. Label the image C.

c Rotate shape A 270° clockwise about $(-1,0)$. Label the image D.

d Rotate shape A 90° anticlockwise about $(1,-3)$. Label the image E.

3 Copy the diagram and answer this question.

a Rotate shape A 90° clockwise about point P. Label the image B.

b Rotate shape A 180° about point Q. Label the image C.

c Rotate shape A 270° clockwise about point R. Label the image D.

4 Use a copy of this grid to answer this question.

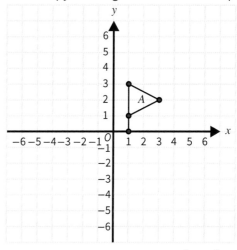

a Rotate shape A 180° about $(1,-1)$. Label the image B.

b Rotate shape B 90° clockwise about $(0,-1)$. Label the image C.

c Rotate shape C 180° about $(0,-2)$. Label the image D.

d Describe fully a single rotation that could have been used to rotate shape A to shape D directly.

5 Copy the diagram and answer this question.

a Rotate shape A 45° clockwise about centre P. Label the image B.

b Rotate shape A 135° anticlockwise about centre P. Label the image C.

c Rotate shape A 225° anticlockwise about centre P. Label the image D.

Now check your answers. Did you get any wrong and can you work out why?

9.2.3 Describing rotations

Investigate Further

What happens when you rotate a shape by 360°? How about 450°? Can you write a rule to explain how to draw or describe a rotation of more than 360°?

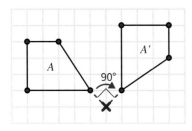

Objective

You will learn how to:

- describe a rotation

To describe a rotation fully you need to specify:

- the angle of rotation,
- the direction of rotation (clockwise or anticlockwise),
- the centre of rotation.

You can use tracing paper to help you find the centre of rotation. Trace the shape, then try putting your pencil at different points and rotating until you find the point that gives the correct position of the image.

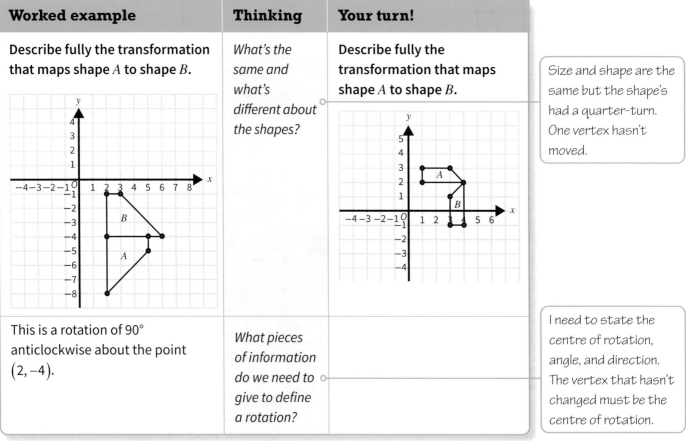

Worked example	Thinking	Your turn!	
Describe fully the transformation that maps shape A to shape B.	*What's the same and what's different about the shapes?*	**Describe fully the transformation that maps shape A to shape B.**	Size and shape are the same but the shape's had a quarter-turn. One vertex hasn't moved.
This is a rotation of 90° anticlockwise about the point $(2, -4)$.	*What pieces of information do we need to give to define a rotation?*		I need to state the centre of rotation, angle, and direction. The vertex that hasn't changed must be the centre of rotation.

▲ Example-problem pair 1

9.2.3 Fluency

In this exercise you can practise applying the mathematical methods that you have just learnt.

1 Look at these shapes.

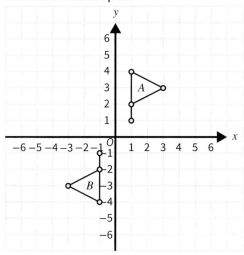

a Describe the rotation of shape A to shape B.
b Describe the rotation of shape B to shape A.
c Karl says that shape A is the image of itself under a 360° rotation about the origin.
Is Karl correct? Explain your answer.
d Ashley says that shape B is the image of shape A under a 540° rotation about the origin.
Is Ashley correct? Explain your answer.

2 Describe each of these rotations.

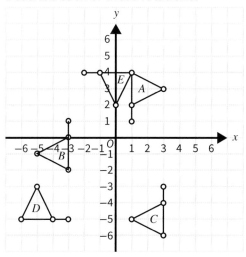

a A to B **c** A to D
b A to C **d** A to E

3 Describe each of these rotations.

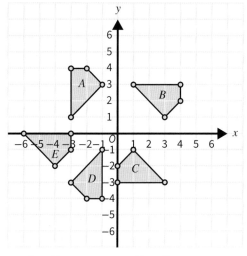

a A to B **c** C to D
b B to C **d** D to E

4 Here are some rotations. All rotations have the same centre.

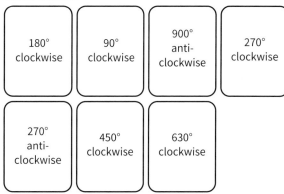

Use a table to sort the rotations into groups of equivalent rotations.

Now check your answers. Did you get any wrong and can you work out why?

9.2 Exercises

9.2 Intelligent practice

"Why is it intelligent?" You might notice a connection when you move on from one question to the next. You can use the Reflect, Expect, Check, Explain process to:

- *reflect* on what's different between each question and the one that came before
- decide how you *expect* this answer to be different
- complete the question and *check* your answer
- *explain* to yourself why your expectation was correct or incorrect.

Question 1a   EXAMPLE

Is shape *B* a rotation of shape *A*?

Yes, shape *A* has been turned a quarter-turn to give shape *B*.

Question 1b

Is shape *C* a rotation of shape *A*?

Reflect: Shape *B* has been turned another quarter-turn to give shape *C*.

Expect: I think that shape *C* is a rotation of shape *A* since it is a rotation of shape *B*.

Check: Shape *A* has been turned half a turn to give shape *C*.

Explain: I was right! Two quarter-turns give a half-turn so shape *C* is a rotation of half a turn of shape *A*.

---

1 Look at these shapes.

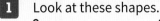

a Is shape *B* a rotation of shape *A*?

b Is shape *C* a rotation of shape *A*?

c Is shape *D* a rotation of shape *C*?

d Is shape *E* a rotation of shape *D*?

e Is shape *E* a rotation of shape *A*?

a Is shape *B* a rotation of shape *A*?

b Is shape *C* a rotation of shape *A*?

c Is shape *C* a rotation of shape *B*?

d Is shape *D* a rotation of shape *B*?

e Is shape *D* a rotation of shape *C*?

f Is shape *E* a rotation of shape *D*?

g Is shape *F* a rotation of shape *E*?

2 Look at these shapes.

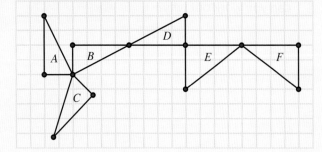

3 Draw the triangle after it has been rotated:

a 90° clockwise and label the image *B*,

b 90° anticlockwise and label the image *C*,

c 270° clockwise and label the image *D*,

d 180° anticlockwise and label the image *E*,

e 180° clockwise and label the image *F*.

4 On a single copy of the grid:

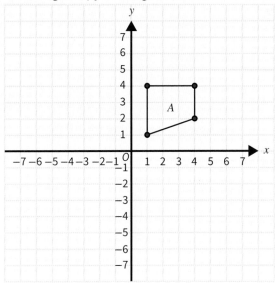

a rotate shape A 180° about the point $(0,0)$ and label the image B,

b rotate shape A 180° about the point $(4,2)$ and label the image C,

c rotate shape A 180° about the point $(4,0)$ and label the image D,

d rotate shape D 180° about the point $(4,0)$ and label the image E.

5 On a single copy of the grid:

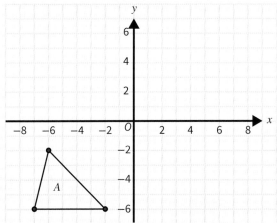

a rotate shape A 90° clockwise about the point $(0,0)$ and label the image B,

b rotate shape A 90° anticlockwise about the point $(0,0)$ and label the image C,

c rotate shape A 90° anticlockwise about the point $(-6,0)$ and label the image D,

d rotate shape D 90° clockwise about the point $(-6,0)$ and label the image E.

6 Look at these shapes.

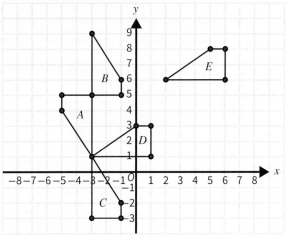

Describe fully the transformation from:

a shape A to shape B.

b shape A to shape C.

c shape A to shape D.

d shape A to shape E.

e shape E to shape A.

f shape E to shape C.

g shape C to shape E.

7 Use a separate copy of this diagram to answer each question part.

a Rotate triangle ABC 180° about the cross and label the image $A'B'C'$.

b Rotate triangle ABC 90° anticlockwise about the cross and label the image $A'B'C'$.

c Rotate triangle ABC 90° clockwise about the cross and label the image $A'B'C'$.

d Rotate triangle ABC 135° clockwise about the cross and label the image $A'B'C'$.

e Rotate triangle ABC 200° clockwise about the cross and label the image $A'B'C'$.

f Rotate ABC 200° clockwise about the point B and label the image $A'B'C'$.

9.2 Method selection

In these questions you'll need to think carefully about which methods to apply.

For some questions you might need to use skills from earlier chapters.

1 Look at these shapes.

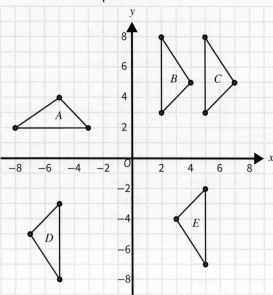

Describe fully the transformation that maps:

a A to B,   **d** C to B,   **g** D to E,

b B to A,   **e** C to D,   **h** E to D.

c B to C,   **f** D to C,

2 Copy the diagram and answer this question.

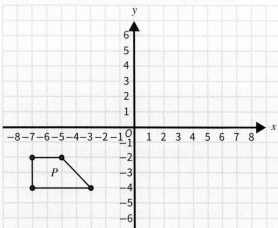

a Rotate shape P 180° about the point $(0,0)$ and label the image Q.

b Rotate shape P 90° clockwise about the point $(-2,0)$ and label the image R.

c Translate shape P nine units in the positive x-direction and one unit in the negative y-direction and label the image S.

3 Copy the diagram and answer this question.

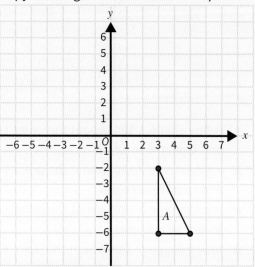

a Copy triangle A.

  i Translate triangle A seven units in the negative x-direction and one unit in the positive y-direction. Label the image A'.

  ii Rotate A' 90° clockwise about the point $(0,0)$ and label the image A''.

b Describe fully the single transformation that maps A to A''.

4 A parallelogram has vertices at $A(-5,-5)$, $B(0,-5)$, $C(2,-2)$, and D.

a Draw the parallelogram and write the coordinates of the point D.

b If each box on the grid is a 1 cm square, what is the area of the shape?

The parallelogram is rotated 90° clockwise about the point $(2,-2)$.

c Which vertex of the parallelogram does not move in the rotation?

d What is the image of point A under this rotation?

e What is the area of the rotated parallelogram?

9.2 Purposeful practice

There may be more than one way to approach these questions. Once you have answered a question one way, can you think of another way?

1 Use a copy of triangle A to answer this question.

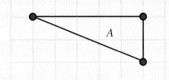

a Draw two different rotations of triangle A and label them B and C.

b Explain how you know that triangles B and C are rotations of triangle A.

c Draw two triangles that are not rotations of triangle A and label them D and E.

d Explain why D and E are not rotations of triangle A.

2 Use a copy of this diagram for this question.

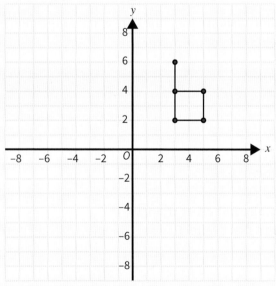

a For each part, write the centre of rotation you choose.

  i Choose a centre of rotation and rotate shape A 90° clockwise. Label the image B.

  ii Choose another centre of rotation and rotate shape B 90° clockwise. Label the image C.

  iii Choose another centre of rotation and rotate shape C 90° clockwise. Label the image D.

  iv Choose another centre of rotation and rotate shape D 90° clockwise. Label the image E.

b Describe fully the transformation that maps A to E.

3 Look at these triangles.

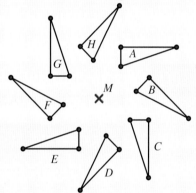

a Which triangle is described in each case?

  i Image of triangle A following rotation of 90° clockwise about the point M.

  ii Image of triangle A following rotation of 135° anticlockwise about the point M.

  iii Image of triangle A following rotation of 540° anticlockwise about the point M.

  iv Image of triangle A following rotation of 405° clockwise about the point M.

b Choose some pairs of triangles and describe fully the rotation that connects them.

c Describe each of your rotations in part b in a different way.

9.3.1 Introduction to reflection

Objective

You will learn how to:

- recognise a reflection and know which features of an object are affected by reflection

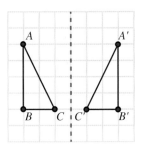

Look at the triangles ABC and $A'B'C'$ in the diagram.

The two triangles are congruent. However, you know that $A'B'C'$ is not a translation of ABC since its orientation has changed. Also, you know that $A'B'C'$ is not a rotation of ABC since triangle ABC is labelled anticlockwise but $A'B'C'$ is labelled clockwise – the 'sense' of the object has changed.

Instead, this is a third type of transformation called a **reflection**.

Triangle ABC has been reflected in the dashed line. This dashed line is the **mirror line**.

Language 📖

The word 'reflection' comes from the Latin word *reflex*, which means 'bent back'.

Each point on the image is the same distance from the mirror line as the matching point on the object, but on the other side of the mirror line.

Key point

A reflection is a type of transformation that 'flips' an object over a mirror line.

Worked example	Thinking	Your turn!
Explain whether triangles B, C, and D are reflections of triangle A.	*Are they all the same size and shape and can we flip them onto A?*	Explain whether triangles B, C, and D are reflections of triangle A.

Each of the triangles B, C, and D are the same size and shape as A but B has been translated, not reflected.

Worked example	Thinking	Your turn!
Triangles A, B, C, and D are all congruent. Triangles C and D are both reflections of triangle A. Triangle B is not a reflection of triangle A (it is a translation).		

▲ Example-problem pair 1

A reflection acts on all points in the coordinate grid. The only points that do not change position are those on the mirror line itself.

9.3.1 Fluency

In this exercise you can practise applying the mathematical methods that you have just learnt.

1 Which of shapes B, C, and D represent a reflection of shape A?

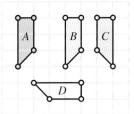

2 Look at these shapes.

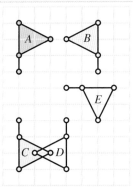

a Write the letters of two shapes that are reflections of shape A.

b Write the letters of two shapes that are reflections of shape C.

c Bharat says that both the orientation and the size changes when a shape is reflected. Is Bharat correct? Explain your answer.

3 A shape is reflected in a mirror line. Decide if each of these statements is true or false.

a If the shape is reflected in a vertical mirror line, the orientation stays the same.

b If the shape is reflected in a diagonal mirror line, the orientation changes.

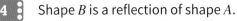

4 Shape B is a reflection of shape A.

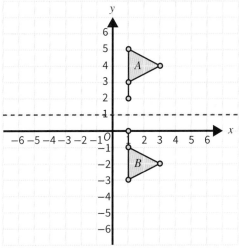

Write the coordinates of the image of each of these points under the same reflection.

a $(2,0)$ **c** $(-1,0)$

b $(3,-1)$ **d** $(-2,-3)$

e Emile says that the points with coordinates $(3,1)$ and $(5,1)$ will not move under the reflection shown. Is Emile correct? Explain your answer.

Now check your answers. Did you get any wrong and can you work out why?

9.3.2 Describing reflections

Objective

You will learn how to:

- draw a mirror line for a reflection

Every point on the image is the same distance from the mirror line as every point on the object. You can use this fact to work out where the mirror line is. You may be able to do this by counting squares or the diagonals of squares.

For example, in the diagram, you can see that the distance between:

- vertex A and its image A' is 10 squares,
- vertex B and its image B' is 8 squares,
- vertex C and its image C' is 4 squares.

The mirror line will then pass through the midpoints of the lines joining each vertex and its image, as shown.

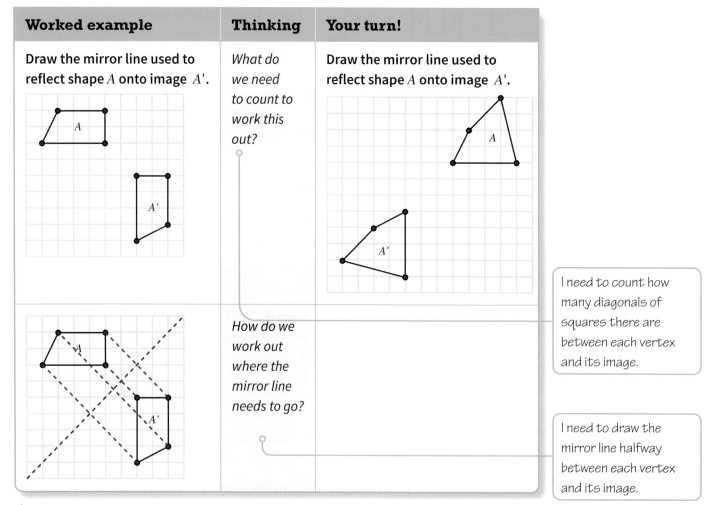

Worked example	Thinking	Your turn!
Draw the mirror line used to reflect shape A onto image A'.	*What do we need to count to work this out?*	Draw the mirror line used to reflect shape A onto image A'.
	How do we work out where the mirror line needs to go?	

I need to count how many diagonals of squares there are between each vertex and its image.

I need to draw the mirror line halfway between each vertex and its image.

▲ Example-problem pair 1

When the mirror line is not horizontal or vertical you can count diagonally across the squares instead, as shown in the Example-problem pair, or you could measure the distance between each vertex and its image.

In Chapter 5 you learnt how to write the equation of a vertical or horizonal line. When you are shown a reflection on a set of axes you can describe the mirror line by giving the equation of the line. For example, in the diagram, the triangle ABC has been reflected in the line $y = 2$ (the y-coordinate of every point on the line is 2).

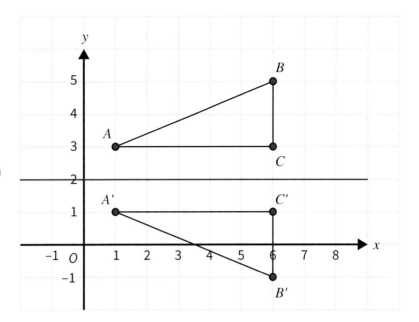

9.3.2 Fluency

In this exercise you can practise applying the mathematical methods that you have just learnt.

1 Use a copy of this diagram to answer this question.

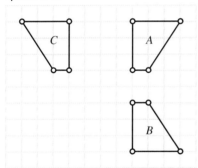

Draw the mirror line that was used to reflect:
a shape A onto shape B,
b shape A onto shape C.

2 Use a copy of this diagram to answer this question.

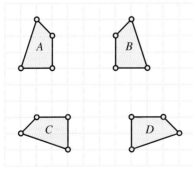

Draw the mirror line that was used to reflect:
a shape A onto shape B,
b shape B onto shape C,
c shape C onto shape D.

3 Use a copy of this grid to answer this question.

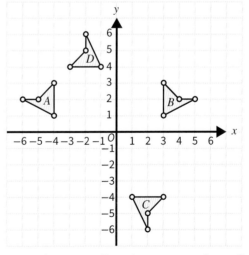

Draw the mirror line that was used to reflect:
a shape A onto shape B,
b shape A onto shape C,
c shape A onto shape D.

Chapter 9

9.3.3 Reflecting objects

Objective

You will learn how to:

- reflect an object in a given line

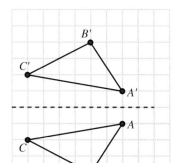

To reflect a shape in a horizontal or vertical mirror line:

- count the squares from a vertex to the mirror line,
- draw the image of this vertex the same distance on the other side of the mirror line,
- repeat for the other vertices,
- join the vertices to draw the image.

If the mirror line is diagonal, then you will need to count the diagonals of the squares instead, as in this next example.

Worked example	Think-ing	Your turn!

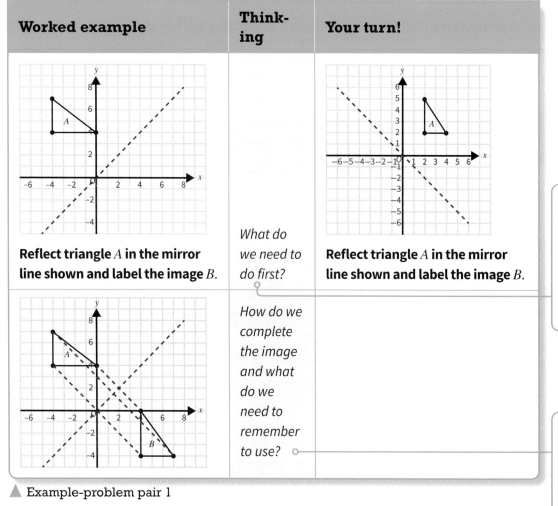

Worked example: Reflect triangle A in the mirror line shown and label the image B.

Thinking: What do we need to do first?

Your turn! Reflect triangle A in the mirror line shown and label the image B.

First I draw a line from each vertex to the mirror line, meeting it at right angles, and then extend it on the other side of the mirror line.

Thinking: How do we complete the image and what do we need to remember to use?

I count the diagonals of the squares to mark the images of the vertices and then use a ruler to draw the shape.

▲ Example-problem pair 1

9.3.3 Fluency

In this exercise you can practise applying the mathematical methods that you have just learnt.

1 Use a copy of this grid to answer this question.

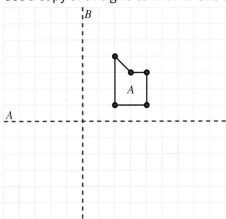

a Reflect shape A in line A.
Label the image B.
b Reflect shape A in line B.
Label the image C.

2 Use a copy of this grid to answer this question.

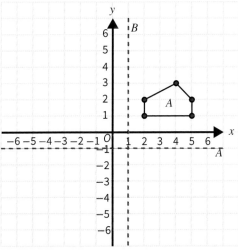

a Reflect shape A in line A
Label the image B.
b Reflect shape A in line B
Label the image C.

3 Use a copy of this grid to answer this question.

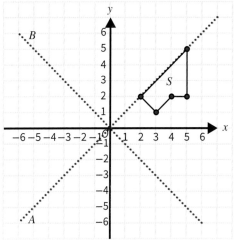

a Reflect shape S in line A
Label the image T.
b Reflect shape S in line B
Label the image U.

4 Use a copy of this grid to answer this question.

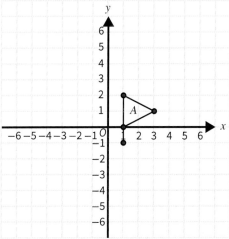

a Reflect shape A in the line $y = -2$
Label the image B.
b Reflect shape B in the line $x = -1$
Label the image C.
c Reflect shape C in the line $y = x$
Label the image D.
d Reflect shape D in the line $y = -x$
Label the image E.

Now check your answers. Did you get any wrong and can you work out why?

9.3 Exercises

9.3 Intelligent practice

"Why is it intelligent?" You might notice a connection when you move on from one question to the next. You can use the Reflect, Expect, Check, Explain process to:

- *reflect* on what's different between each question and the one that came before
- decide how you *expect* this answer to be different
- complete the question and *check* your answer
- *explain* to yourself why your expectation was correct or incorrect.

> **Question 1a**   EXAMPLE
>
> Is shape B a reflection of shape A?
>
> Yes.
>
> **Question 1b**
>
> Is shape B a reflection of shape A?
>
> **Reflect:** *This is similar to question 1a, except triangle A is one unit taller.*
>
> **Expect:** *Triangle B is also one unit taller so I think it is still a reflection.*
>
> **Check:** *I was right! It is a reflection.*
>
> **Explain:** *It is a reflection since every vertex of triangle B is the same distance from the mirror line as for triangle A.*

1   Is shape B a reflection of shape A in the mirror line shown in each case?

a

c

e

b

d

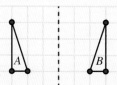

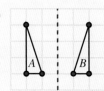

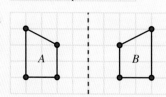

2   On a copy of each diagram, draw the mirror line for each reflection.

a

b

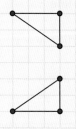

c

e

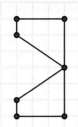

d

3 On a copy of each diagram, draw the mirror line for each reflection.

a **b**

c **d**

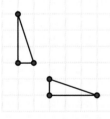
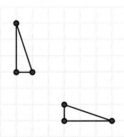

e

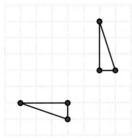

4 Give the equation of the mirror line for each reflection.

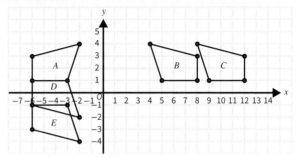

a A to B **c** A to D **e** E to A
b A to C **d** A to E

5 Copy the diagram.

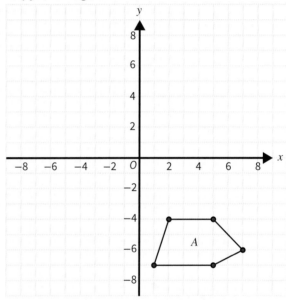

Then draw the reflection of shape A in the mirror line with equation:

a $x = 1$ and label the image B,
b $x = -1$ and label the image C,
c $y = 1$ and label the image D,
d $y = -1$ and label the image E.

9.3 Method selection

In these questions you'll need to think carefully about which methods to apply.

For some questions you might need to use skills from earlier chapters.

1 Describe fully the transformation that maps the first shape onto the second shape in each of these pairs.

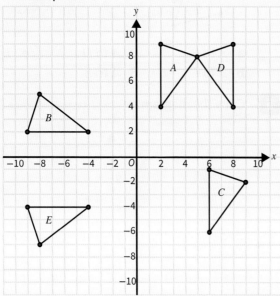

a A to B
b B to A
c A to C
d C to A

e A to D
f D to A
g B to E
h E to B

i E to D
j D to E

2 Use a copy of this diagram to answer this question.

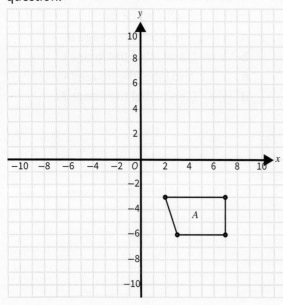

a Rotate shape A 180° about the point $(0,0)$ and label the image B.

b Reflect shape A in the x-axis and label the image C.

c Translate shape A eight units in the negative x-direction and two units in the positive y-direction and label the image D.

3 Use a copy of this diagram to answer this question.

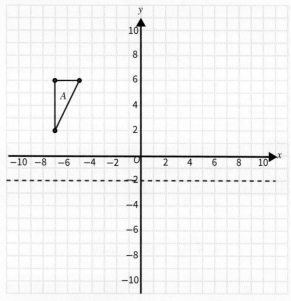

a Reflect triangle A in the line shown and label the image B.

b Reflect triangle B in the y-axis and label the image C.

c Translate triangle C two units in the positive x-direction and label the image D.

d Reflect triangle D in the line shown and label the image E.

e Describe fully the single transformation that maps A to E.

4 Use a copy of this diagram to answer this question.

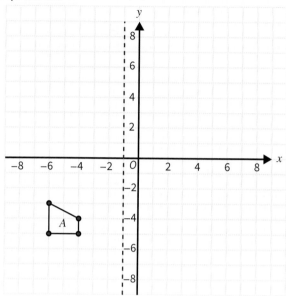

a Rotate A 180° about the point $(0,0)$ and label the image A'.

b Reflect A' in the line shown and label the image A''.

c Translate A'' two units in the positive x-direction and two units in the positive y-direction and label the image A'''.

d Describe fully the single transformation that maps A to A'''.

5 Look at this graph.

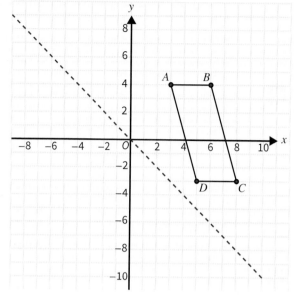

a Write the name of quadrilateral $ABCD$.

b Assuming that each box on the grid is a $1\,cm$ square, what is the area of shape $ABCD$?

c Reflect shape $ABCD$ in the mirror line shown and label the image $A'B'C'D'$.

d Write the area of shape $A'B'C'D'$.

6 A rectangle has vertices at $A(-12,-7)$, $B(-11,-4)$, $C(-5,-6)$, and D.

a Draw the rectangle and write the coordinates of the point D.

The rectangle is reflected in the line $x = -5$

b Which vertex of the rectangle does not change in the reflection?

c What is the image of point A under this reflection?

9.3 Purposeful practice

There may be more than one way to approach these questions. Once you have answered a question one way, can you think of another way?

1 Use a copy of this diagram to answer this question.

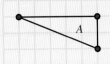

    a Reflect triangle A in two different mirror lines and label the images B and C.
    b Explain how you know that triangles B and C are reflections of triangle A.
    c Draw two triangles that are not reflections of triangle A and label them D and E.
    d Explain why triangles D and E are not reflections of triangle A.

2 Use copies of this diagram to answer this question.

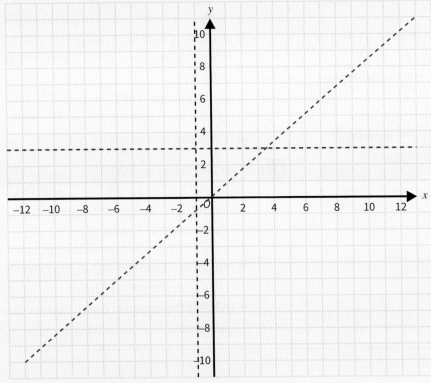

    a Draw a triangle on a copy of the diagram.
    b Reflect your triangle in each of the mirror lines shown.
    c Make another copy of the diagram and draw a quadrilateral.
        Reflect it on each of the mirror lines shown.

3 Use a copy of this diagram to answer this question.

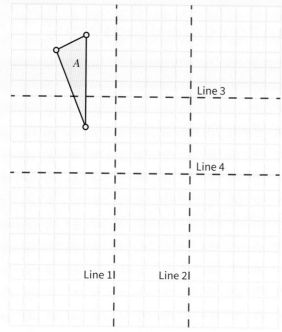

a On a copy of the diagram shown:
   i reflect triangle A in line 1 and label its image B,
   ii reflect triangle B in line 2 and label its image C.
b Describe the single transformation that maps A to C.
c What happens if the reflections are carried out in the opposite order (line 2 first then line 1)?
d Investigate what happens if the positions of the lines are changed.

4 Use a copy of the diagram given in question 3 to answer this question.
a Reflect triangle A in line 3 and label its image D.
b Reflect triangle D in line 4 and label its image E.
c Describe the single transformation that maps A to E.
d What happens if the reflections are carried out in the opposite order (line 4 first then line 3)?
e Investigate what happens if positions of the lines are changed.

5 Use a copy of this diagram to answer this question.

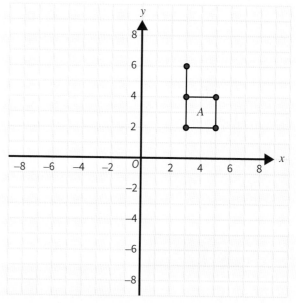

a For each part, either draw or write the equation of the mirror line you are using.
   i Reflect shape A in a horizontal mirror line and label the image B.
   ii Reflect shape B in a vertical mirror line and label the image C.
   iii Reflect shape C in another horizonal mirror line and label the image D.
   iv Reflect shape D in another vertical mirror line and label the image E.
b Describe fully the transformation that maps A to E.

9.4.1 Introduction to scale diagrams

Scale diagrams are used to represent objects, shapes, or places. For example, you might want to draw a diagram of a house **to scale**. This means that the lengths in the diagram are in the same proportion as in the actual house.

If a room in real life is 5 metres long and 3 metres wide then you might draw it in a scale diagram as 5 cm long and 3 cm wide. This would be using a scale of 1 cm to represent 1 m.

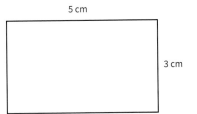

You can use different scales to make scale drawings. For example, you could use a scale of 3 cm to represent 1 m instead. Then the rectangle would be 15 cm long and 9 cm wide.

Two scale drawings of the same object will be **similar**, which means that they are the same shape, with the same angles, but a different size. For two shapes to be similar, the ratio of their side lengths must be the same. For example, in the scale drawing shown, the ratio of the length to the width is 5 : 3

Worked example	Thinking	Your turn!
A kitchen is the shape of a rectangle whose length is three times its width.		A playground is the shape of a rectangle whose length is five times its width.
On a scale drawing of the kitchen its width is 6 cm. What is the length of the kitchen on the scale drawing?	*What do we know about scale drawings?*	On a scale drawing of the playground its width is 4 cm. What is the length of the playground on the scale drawing?
Length of kitchen in scale drawing $= 3 \times 6$ $= 18\,cm$		

The ratio of the lengths must be the same in the scale drawing as in real life.

▲ Example-problem pair 1

9.4.1 Fluency

In this exercise you can practise applying the mathematical methods that you have just learnt.

1 The diagram shows three scale drawings. Two of the scale drawings represent the same room on a diagram.

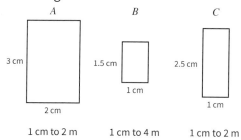

A   B   C

3 cm   1.5 cm   2.5 cm

1 cm

2 cm   1 cm

1 cm to 2 m   1 cm to 4 m   1 cm to 2 m

Write the letter of the scale drawing that *does not* represent the same room.

2 In a bedroom, the door is twice as far from the bed as the wardrobe is from the bed.

On a scale diagram of the bedroom, the door is 8 cm from the bed.

How far is the wardrobe from the bed on the scale diagram?

3 In a town, the leisure centre is three times as far from the library as the railway station is from the library.

On a scale diagram of the town, the railway station is 13 cm from the library.

What is the distance between the leisure centre and the library on the scale diagram?

4 In a kitchen, the fridge is a certain distance from the sink, and the cooker is one-quarter of that distance from the sink.

On a scale diagram of the kitchen, the fridge is 8.4 cm from the sink.

How far is the cooker from the sink on the scale diagram?

5 The length of a plant cell is three times its width.

On a scale diagram the cell's length is 15 cm.

How wide is the cell on the scale diagram?

Now check your answers. Did you get any wrong and can you work out why?

Chapter 9

9.4.2 Interpreting scale diagrams

Objective

You will learn how to:

- interpret a scale diagram

A common type of scale diagram is a map. The scale for a map can be written using a ratio. You learnt about these in Chapter 8. For example, if 1 cm on the map represents 1 km in real life, then the scale can be written as:

- 1 cm : 1 km or
- 1 : 100 000 (since there are 100 000 cm in a kilometre).

Key point

The scale for a map can be written as the ratio $a : b$ where a is the length on the map and b is the distance in real life.

You can use the scale of the map to work out the distance in real life.

For example, this map uses a scale of 2 cm to represent 1 km.

This may also be written as 2 cm : 1 km or 2 : 100 000 (which can be simplified to 1 : 50 000).

On this map 2 cm represents 1 km in real life, therefore:

- 4 cm on the map will represent 2 km in real life so the block of flats is 2 km from the supermarket,
- 6 cm on the map will represent 3 km in real life so the school is 3 km from the supermarket,
- 3 cm on the map will represent 1.5 km in real life so the school is 1.5 km from the block of flats.

You may need to measure the lengths on the map or scale diagram yourself using a ruler.

Worked example	Thinking	Your turn!
The scale of a map is 1 cm : 3 km. The length of a road on the map is 5 cm. Find the length of the road in real life.	*What can we use to help us?*	The scale of a map is 1 cm : 5 km. The length of a road on the map is 2 cm. Find the length of the road in real life.

I can use a ratio table to help me.

Worked example	Thinking	Your turn!

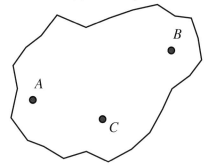

$\times 5$

1 cm	3 km
5 cm	15 km

$\times 5$

What do we know about the lengths?

Length of road = $3 \times 5 = 15\,$km

> I need to write the length on the map and in real life at the top, the other length at the bottom, and then think about what I need to multiply by to complete the table.

▲ Example-problem pair 1

9.4.2 Fluency

In this exercise you can practise applying the mathematical methods that you have just learnt.

1 On the map, 1 cm represents 5 km.

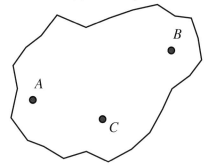

a How far is town A from town B, in km?
b How far is town A from town C, in km?
c How far is town B from town C, in km?

2 The diagram represents a picnic blanket drawn using a scale of 1 : 40

What are the length and width of the blanket, in cm?

3 The diagram represents a boat sail, drawn using a scale of 1 : 400

What are the lengths of the sides of the sail, in metres?

4 The diagram represents a hall in a public building, drawn using a scale of 1 : 2000

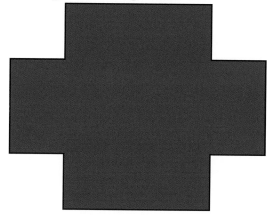

What is the perimeter of the hall, in metres?

5 The map is drawn using a scale of 1 : 250 000

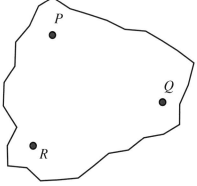

a How far is town P from town Q, in km?
b How far is town R from town P, in km?
c How far is town R from town Q, in km?

Now check your answers. Did you get any wrong and can you work out why?

9.4.3 Drawing scale diagrams

Objective

You will learn how to:

- draw a scale diagram

You need to be able to use a ruler accurately to draw scale diagrams.

The first step is to use the scale to work out the lengths involved, and then carefully draw these on your diagram. You can use ratio tables to work out the lengths. You saw ratio tables in Chapter 8.

Worked example	Thinking	Your turn!
A garden is a rectangle of width 4 m and length 6 m. Make a scale drawing of the garden using 3 cm to represent 1 m.	*How can we use a ratio table to help us?*	A patio is a rectangle of width 3 m and length 5 m. Make a scale drawing of the patio using 2 cm to represent 1 m.

To find the width:

3 cm	1 m
12 cm	4 m

×4 ... ×4

Width in scale drawing = 4 × 3 = 12 cm

To find the length:

3 cm	1 m
18 cm	6 m

×6 ... ×6

Length in scale drawing = 6 × 3 = 18 cm

18 cm

12 cm

What do we need to remember to use when drawing the scale diagram?

> I need to write the length on the scale drawing and in real life at the top of a ratio table and then work out what I need to multiply by.

> I need to use a ruler to draw this accurately.

▲ Example-problem pair 1

When using a scale on a map, you need to know the directions of the compass points.

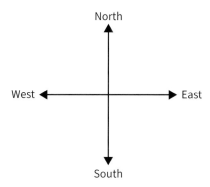

9.4.3 Fluency

In this exercise you can practise applying the mathematical methods that you have just learnt.

1 Alphaville is 25 km West of Betatown.

Draw a scale map with scale 1 cm to 5 km to represent this.

2 A phone mast is 38 m tall.

Draw a scale diagram of the phone mast using a scale of 1 cm to 4 m.

3 A rectangular pond is 120 cm long and 80 cm wide.

Draw a scale diagram of the pond using a scale of 1:20

4 A rectangular table mat is 40 cm long and 25 cm wide.

Draw a scale diagram of the mat using a scale of 1:5

5 A flag is in the shape of a right-angled triangle.

The two sides that meet at the right angle are 150 cm and 90 cm in length.

a Draw a scale diagram of the flag using a scale of 1:15

b Use your drawing to find the length of the third side of the flag.

6 A circular archery target has a diameter of 120 cm.

There is a second circle with diameter 70 cm in the middle of the target.

Draw a scale diagram of the target using a scale of 1:20

7 Gammaland is 30 km South of Deltapolis.

Draw a scale map with scale 1:500 000 to represent this.

8 Kappaville is 15 km due north of Pitown and 20 km due west of Zetapolis.

a Draw a scale map with scale 1:250 000 to represent this.

b Use your drawing to find the distance from Pitown to Zetapolis.

Now check your answers. Did you get any wrong and can you work out why?

9.4 Exercises

9.4 Intelligent practice

"Why is it intelligent?" You might notice a connection when you move on from one question to the next. You can use the Reflect, Expect, Check, Explain process to:

- *reflect* on what's different between each question and the one that came before
- decide how you *expect* this answer to be different
- complete the question and *check* your answer
- *explain* to yourself why your expectation was correct or incorrect.

Question 1a   **EXAMPLE**

Part of the roof of a building is in the shape of a right-angled triangle whose base is four times its height. Can the diagram shown be used as a scale drawing of the roof?

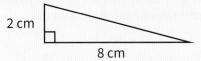
2 cm
8 cm

Yes, since the base is four times the height.

Question 1b
Can this diagram be used a scale drawing of the roof?

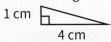
1 cm
4 cm

Reflect: Comparing this to question 1a, the base and height have both been divided by two.

Expect: I think this means that it can be used as a scale drawing of the roof.

Check: The base, 4 cm, is four times the height, 1 cm.

Explain: I was right! This can be used as a scale drawing of the roof since the base is four times the height.

---

1 Part of the roof of a building is in the shape of a right-angled triangle whose base is four times its height. For each of the drawings shown, write whether it could be used as a scale drawing of the roof.

a
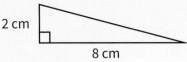
2 cm
8 cm

c
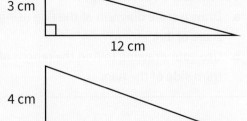
3 cm
12 cm

b
1 cm
4 cm

d
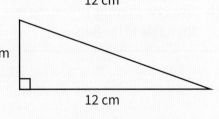
4 cm
12 cm

e

4 cm
16 cm

f

0.4 cm
1.6 cm

g

1.4 cm
2.6 cm

2 A map uses a scale of 1 cm to represent 5 km.

Find the length of a road in real life if its length on the map is:

  a 1 cm,   **c** 4 cm,   **e** 30 cm,

  b 2 cm,   **d** 5 cm,   **f** 0.3 cm.

3 A scale model of a train uses a scale of 1 : 8

Find the width of a part of the train if its width on the scale model is:

  a 1 cm,   **c** 6 cm,   **e** 120 cm,

  b 3 cm,   **d** 12 cm,   **f** 1.2 cm.

4 A map uses a scale of 2 : 300 000

Find the distance, in kilometres, between two towns in real life if the distance on the map is:

  a 2 cm,   **c** 5 cm,   **e** 25 cm,

  b 10 cm,   **d** 50 cm,   **f** 2.5 cm.

5 The floor of an office is the shape of a rectangle with a length of 12 m and a width of 9 m.

Make a scale drawing of the floor of the office using:

  a 1 cm to 1 m,   **c** 2 cm to 3 m,

  b 2 cm to 1 m,   **d** 3 cm to 2 m.

6 Draw a dot in the centre of your page and label it 'Town A'.

Use a scale of 1 cm : 5 km to show the relative positions of the other towns using the information given.

  a Town B is 10 km east of Town A.

  b Town C is 20 km east of Town A.

  c Town D is 20 km south of Town A.

  d Town E is 40 km south of Town A.

  e Town F is 40 km north of Town A.

  f Town G is 8 km north of Town A.

  g Town H is 16 km west of Town A.

7 A flowerbed is the shape of a square with side length 60 cm.

Make a scale drawing of the flowerbed using the scale:

  a 1 : 30   **b** 1 : 15   **c** 2 : 15   **d** 4 : 15

8 A map uses the scale 1 : 250 000

Find the distance on the map between two places if the distance in real life is:

  a 5 km,   **c** 100 km,   **e** 0.5 km,

  b 10 km,   **d** 1 km,   **f** 4.5 km.

9.4 Method selection

In these questions you'll need to think carefully about which methods to apply.
For some questions you might need to use skills from earlier chapters.

1 Here is a scale diagram of a rectangular area of lawn.

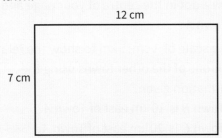

12 cm

7 cm

Work out the dimensions of the lawn in real life if the scale that has been used is

a   1 cm to represent 1 m,
b   2 cm to represent 1 m,
c   1 cm to represent 2 m,
d   1:200
e   1:50

2 This diagram shows the length and width of a rectangular area of lawn.

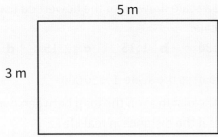

5 m

3 m

Make a scale drawing of the lawn using the scale

a   1 cm to represent 1 m,
b   1 cm to represent 2 m,
c   1:200
d   1:50

3 A scale drawing of a square courtyard uses the scale 1:20

a   Work out the side length of the courtyard if the side length in the scale drawing is 30 cm.
b   Work out the area of the courtyard:
   i   in the scale drawing,
   ii in real life.

4 This is a scale drawing of the roof of a car. The scale used is 1:45

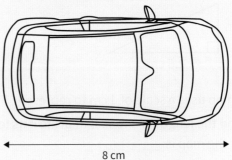

8 cm

a   Work out the actual length of the car.
b   A new scale diagram is drawn using the scale 1:40
   Work out the length of the car in the new scale diagram.
c   A scale model is made of the car. The length of the model is 5 cm.
   Work out the scale that was used to make the model.

5 The table shows information about the distance between towns on different maps.

Copy and complete the table.

Scale of the map	Distance on the map	Distance in real life
1 cm : 3 km	12 cm	
1 cm : 5 km		18 km
2 cm : 3 km	17 cm	
	5 cm	40 km
1 : 200 000	24 cm	
1 : 2 000 000		18 km
	6.5 cm	39 km

6 A scale drawing of a bee uses a scale of 30:1

a   Work out the real-life length of the bee if its length in the scale drawing is 24 cm.
b   Work out the length of the bee in the scale drawing if its actual length is 1.3 cm.

9.4 Purposeful practice

There may be more than one way to approach these questions. Once you have
answered a question one way, can you think of another way?

1 Here is a scale drawing of a window.

6 cm

4 cm

Draw three different possible scale drawings of
the same window.

2 Make a scale drawing of your classroom using
three different scales. Write the scale that you
use in each case.

3 The dimensions of the front cover of a book are
shown in the diagram.

15 cm

20 cm

  a Make a scale drawing of the cover of the
book using the scale 1:5
  b Find the area of your scale drawing.
  c Find the area of the cover of the actual
book.
  d Work out in its simplest form the ratio of the
area of the scale drawing to the actual area.
  e Repeat parts a–d using different scales. In
each case write the scale you use. See if you
can spot a pattern.

9.5.1 Introduction to enlargement

> ### Objective
>
> You will learn how to:
> - recognise an enlargement and know which features of an object are affected by enlargement

So far you have seen three types of transformation: translation, rotation, and reflection. For all of these transformations, the image is congruent to the object. Another type of transformation you need to know about is **enlargement**. In an enlargement, the image is similar to the object.

> ### Key point
>
> The image of an object following an enlargement is similar to the object.

16 cm

4 cm

2 cm | A |

8 cm | B |

B is an enlargement of A as they are similar shapes. An enlargement is described using a **scale factor**.

> ### Key point
>
> The scale factor of an enlargement is the number that all the lengths are multiplied by in the transformation.

In the diagram the scale factor is 4 because the width and the length of A are both multiplied by four to give the width and length of B.

Worked example	Thinking	Your turn!
	What must be true about the two rectangles if B is an enlargement of A?	
Explain whether rectangle B is an enlargement of rectangle A.		**Explain whether rectangle B is an enlargement of rectangle A.**

> If B is an enlargement of A then the two rectangles must be similar.

Worked example | Thinking | Your turn!

For rectangle A, the ratio of the width to the length is $2:4$

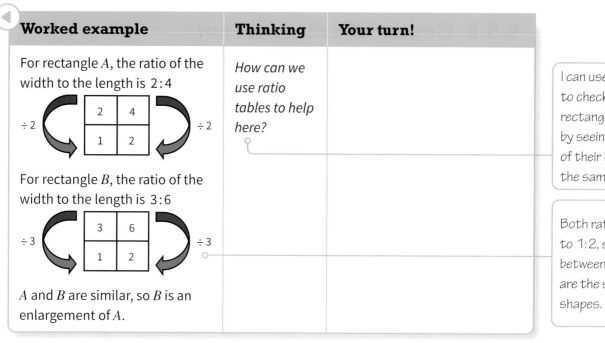

How can we use ratio tables to help here?

I can use a ratio table to check if the two rectangles are similar by seeing if the ratios of their lengths are the same.

For rectangle B, the ratio of the width to the length is $3:6$

A and B are similar, so B is an enlargement of A.

Both ratios simplify to $1:2$, so the ratios between the lengths are the same in both shapes.

▲ Example-problem pair 1

9.5.1 Fluency

In this exercise you can practise applying the mathematical methods that you have just learnt.

1 Look at the shapes below.

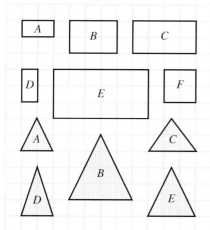

a Which two rectangles are enlargements of rectangle A?

b Which two triangles are enlargements of triangle A?

b Malak enlarged triangle C and drew triangle D. What scale factor has Malak used?

c Malak enlarged triangle E and drew triangle F. What scale factor has Malak used?

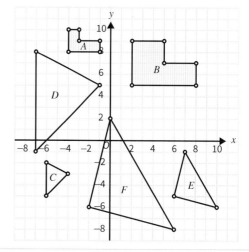

2 Look at the shapes on the grid.

a Malak says that shape B is an enlargement of shape A since the height and width doubled. Is he correct? Explain your answer.

3 Square P has sides of $12\,cm$. What scale factor does Doug use to draw:

a Square B with sides of $18\,cm$

b Square C with sides of $4\,cm$

9.5.2 Centre of enlargement

Objective

You will learn how to:

- recognise an enlargement and know which features of an object are affected by enlargement

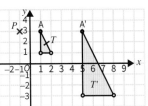

As well as the scale factor, the **centre of enlargement** is needed when describing an enlargement. Look at the diagram of rectangles A and B. Notice that the distance of each point from the centre of enlargement on the object, A, has been multiplied by three to give its position in the image, B. The orientation of the shape stays the same following an enlargement by a positive scale factor.

To work out the position of an image after an enlargement, find the distance from the centre of enlargement to a point on the object then multiply that by the scale factor, this gives you the distance to the corresponding point on the image. An enlargement acts on all points in the coordinate grid. The only point that does not change position is the centre of enlargement.

Key point

To decide if a transformation is an enlargement about a given centre of enlargement, check that:

- the side lengths are correct (they have been multiplied by the scale factor),
- the orientation of the shape is correct,
- the position of one vertex of the shape is correct.

Worked example	Thinking	Your turn!	
Explain whether the diagram shows an enlargement of scale factor 3 about the centre of enlargement P. Both are right-angled triangles. Base of image $= 1 \times 3 = 3$ Height of image $= 2 \times 3 = 6$ So the triangles are similar. The smaller triangle has been enlarged by a scale factor of 3.	*What do we need to check to decide whether this shows an enlargement?* *How can we check if the size of the image is correct?*	Explain whether the diagram shows an enlargement of scale factor 2 about the centre of enlargement Q. 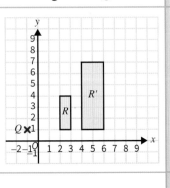	*I need to check if both the size and the position of the image are correct.* *To check the size I need to check if the base and height of the object have been multiplied by the scale factor.*

Worked example	Thinking	Your turn!	
The orientation of the image and object is the same.	*What is the second thing we need to check?*		I need to check that the image is the same 'way around' as the object.
Consider the corresponding points A and A' as shown. Distance from P to $A = 2$ Distance from P to $A' = 6$ So the image is in the correct position since the distance has also been multiplied by the scale factor of 3.	*How can we check if the position of the image is correct?*		I need to choose any vertex on the object and its corresponding vertex on the image and check that the distance from the centre of enlargement has been multiplied by the scale factor.

▲ Example-problem pair 1

9.5.2 Fluency

In this exercise you can practise applying the mathematical methods that you have just learnt.

1 Look at this diagram.

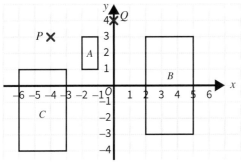

a Mel says that rectangles B and C are enlargements of rectangle A, with B using centre P and C using centre Q.
Is she correct? Explain your answer.

b Cai says that the centre of enlargement doesn't change under an enlargement.
Is he correct? Explain.

2 Look at these flags.

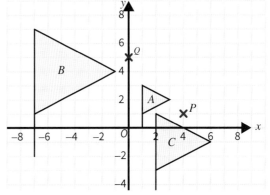

a Ania says that flags B and C are both enlargements of flag A. Is she correct?

b Samit says that the centre of enlargement is point $P(4, 1)$ for flag B and point $Q(0, 5)$, for flag C. Is he correct? Explain your answer.

3 Shape B is an enlargement of shape A with centre P.

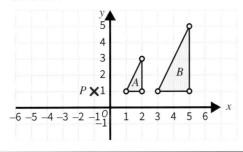

Write the coordinates of the image of each of these points under the same enlargement:

a $(0, 1)$,   **c** $(-1, 0)$,   **e** $(-1, 1)$.

b $(2, 0)$,   **d** $(-2, 3)$,

9.5.3 Drawing enlargements

Objective

You will learn how to:

- enlarge an object

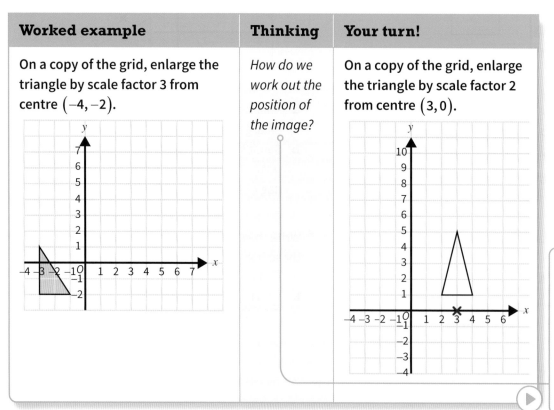

When you enlarge a shape, you use a given scale factor and centre of enlargement.

First draw a line through the centre of enlargement and one of the vertices of the shape.

You then need to measure the distance from the centre of enlargement to the vertex and multiply it by the scale factor. The image of the vertex will be this new distance from the centre along the line.

For example, to enlarge by a scale factor of 2, if the distance from the centre of enlargement to the vertex A is 5 cm, then the distance from the centre of enlargement to the image, A', of this vertex will be 10 cm.

Repeat this process for the other vertices and then join them to form the image.

The orientation of the shape will stay the same when you enlarge by a positive scale factor. So if the enlargement is to be done on a grid, you can use this method for just one of the vertices and then complete the rest of the image using that point and the scale factor.

Worked example	Thinking	Your turn!
On a copy of the grid, enlarge the triangle by scale factor 3 from centre $(-4, -2)$.	*How do we work out the position of the image?*	On a copy of the grid, enlarge the triangle by scale factor 2 from centre $(3, 0)$.

I can start by drawing a line from the centre and through one of the vertices. Then I multiply the distance along the line by three to get the position of the image of this vertex.

Worked example	Thinking	Your turn!
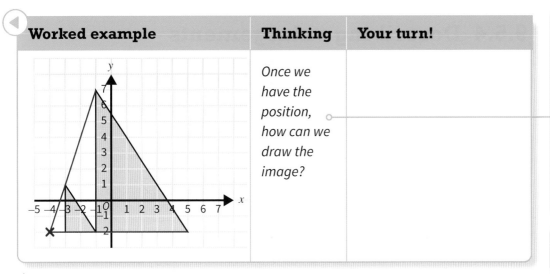	*Once we have the position, how can we draw the image?*	

I can repeat the process for the other two vertices, or I can draw the image in the same orientation as the object, starting from this vertex and remembering to multiply all the side lengths by the scale factor.

Investigate Further 🔍

Try enlarging an object by a negative scale factor.

▲ **Example-problem pair 1**

Scale factors can also be fractions or decimals — the method is the same. A positive scale factor less than 1 will give an image that is smaller than the object.

9.5.3 Fluency

In this exercise you can practise applying the mathematical methods that you have just learnt.

1 Copy shapes A and P onto a grid.

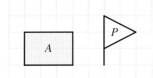

a Enlarge shape A by:
  i scale factor 2. Label the image B.
  ii scale factor 3. Label the image C.
b Enlarge shape P by:
  i scale factor 2. Label the image Q.
  ii scale factor 3. Label the image R.

2 ⠿ Use a copy of this grid to answer this question.

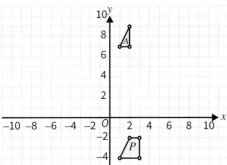

a Enlarge shape A by:
  i scale factor 2, centre of enlargement

$(-1, 8)$. Label image B.
  ii scale factor 3, centre of enlargement $(4, 10)$. Label image C.
b Enlarge shape P by:
  i scale factor 3, centre of enlargement $(0, -4)$. Label image Q.
  ii scale factor 4, centre of enlargement $(4, -2)$. Label image R.

3 ⠿ Use a copy of this grid to answer this question.

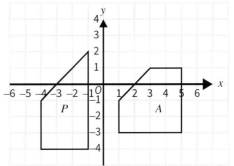

a Enlarge shape A by scale factor $\frac{1}{2}$, centre of enlargement $(5, 3)$. Label the image B.
b Enlarge shape P by scale factor $\frac{1}{3}$, centre of enlargement $(-10, -1)$. Label the image Q.

9.5.4 Describing enlargements

Objective

You will learn how to:

- describe an enlargement

When describing an enlargement you must state:

- the scale factor,
- the position of the centre of enlargement.

You find the scale factor by dividing a side length of the image by the corresponding side length of the object:

$$\text{Scale factor} = \frac{\text{side length of image}}{\text{side length of object}}$$

You find the centre of enlargement by drawing lines through corresponding vertices on the object and the image. The place where these lines intersect is the centre of the enlargement.

For example, here the object is a square with side length 2 cm and the image is a square with side length 10 cm.

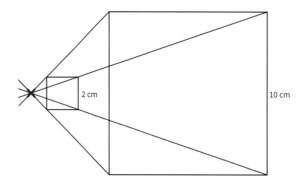

$$\text{Scale factor} = \frac{\text{side length of image}}{\text{side length of object}} = \frac{10}{2} = 5$$

Worked example	Thinking	Your turn!
Describe the enlargement from shape A to shape B. 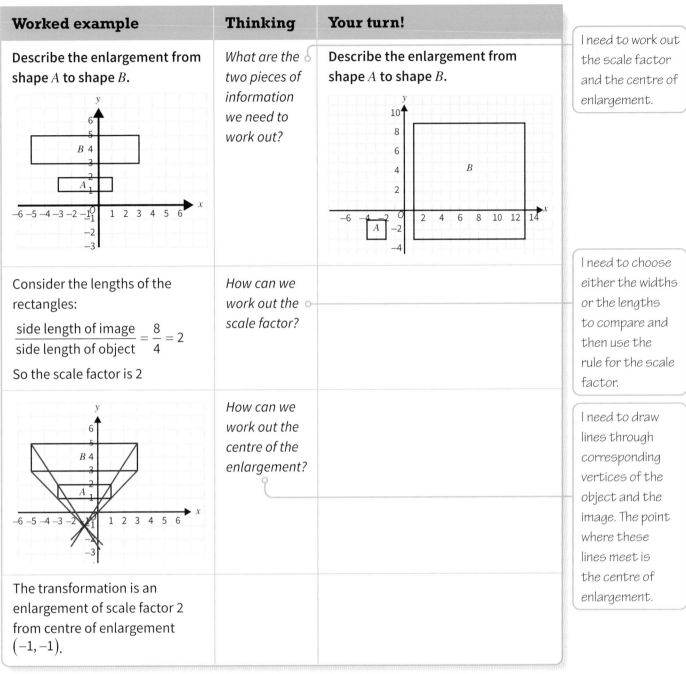	*What are the two pieces of information we need to work out?*	**Describe the enlargement from shape A to shape B.**
Consider the lengths of the rectangles: $$\frac{\text{side length of image}}{\text{side length of object}} = \frac{8}{4} = 2$$ So the scale factor is 2	*How can we work out the scale factor?*	
	How can we work out the centre of the enlargement?	
The transformation is an enlargement of scale factor 2 from centre of enlargement $(-1, -1)$.		

I need to work out the scale factor and the centre of enlargement.

I need to choose either the widths or the lengths to compare and then use the rule for the scale factor.

I need to draw lines through corresponding vertices of the object and the image. The point where these lines meet is the centre of enlargement.

▲ Example-problem pair 1

Remember, the scale factor can be a fraction or decimal. A positive scale factor less than 1 will give an image which is smaller than the object.

9.5.4 Fluency

In this exercise you can practise applying the mathematical methods that you have just learnt.

1 Rectangles *B–D* are enlargements of rectangle *A*.

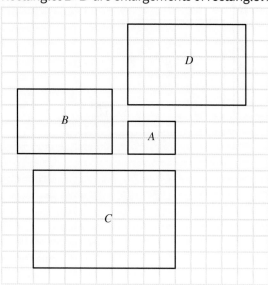

Write the scale factor of enlargement from:
a *A* to *B*,
b *A* to *C*,
c *A* to *D*.

2 Rectangles *B* and *C* are enlargements of rectangle *A*.

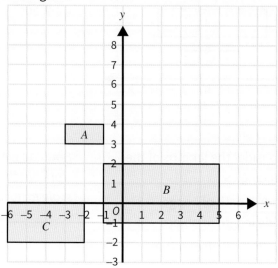

a *B* is an enlargement of *A*.
Write the scale factor and centre of enlargement.

b *C* is an enlargement of *A*.
Write the scale factor and centre of enlargement.

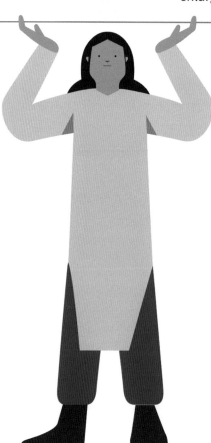

3 Flags *B–D* are enlargements of flag *A*.

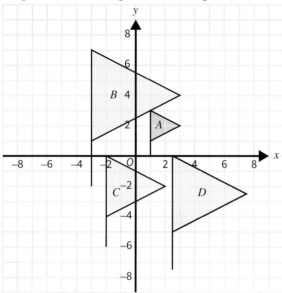

a *B* is an enlargement of *A*.
Write the scale factor and centre of enlargement.

b *C* is an enlargement of *A*.
Write the scale factor and centre of enlargement.

c *D* is an enlargement of *A*.
Write the scale factor and centre of enlargement.

4 Triangles *B* and *C* are enlargements of triangle *A*.

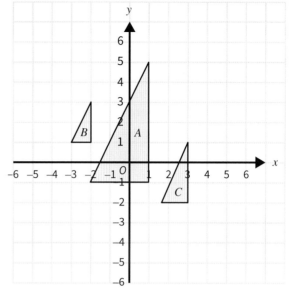

a *B* is an enlargement of *A*.
Write the scale factor and centre of enlargement.

b *C* is an enlargement of *A*.
Write the scale factor and centre of enlargement.

Now check your answers. Did you get any wrong and can you work out why?

9.5 Exercises

9.5 Intelligent practice

"Why is it intelligent?" You might notice a connection when you move on from one question to the next. You can use the Reflect, Expect, Check, Explain process to:

- *reflect* on what's different between each question and the one that came before
- decide how you *expect* this answer to be different
- complete the question and *check* your answer
- *explain* to yourself why your expectation was correct or incorrect.

EXAMPLE

Question 2a

Enlarge triangle A by scale factor 2 from centre $(0, 0)$.

The points of the enlarged triangle will be twice as far away from the centre as for triangle A.

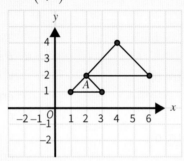

Question 2b

Enlarge triangle A by scale factor 2 from centre $(1, 0)$.

Reflect: *The scale factor is the same as in question 2a, but the centre of enlargement is different.*

Expect: *I think that the triangle will be the same size as in question 2a but in a different position.*

Check:

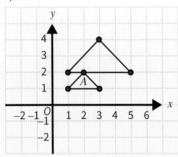

Explain: *I was right! The triangle has a base of 4 and a height of 2 as in question 2a but its position has changed.*

1 Use a new copy of this grid to answer each part of the question.

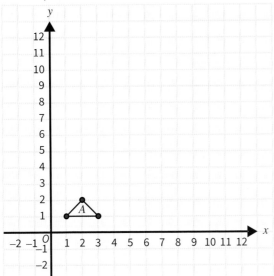

Enlarge triangle A:

a by scale factor 2 from centre $(0,0)$,

b by scale factor 2 from centre $(1,0)$,

c by scale factor 2 from centre $(1,1)$,

d by scale factor 3 from centre $(1,1)$,

e by scale factor 3 from centre $(-1,1)$,

f by scale factor 3 from centre $(-1,0)$.

2 Use a new copy of this grid to answer each part of the question.

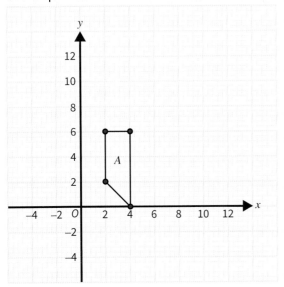

Enlarge shape A

a by scale factor 2 from centre $(0,0)$,

b by scale factor 2 from centre $(-2,0)$,

c by scale factor 2 from centre $(-2,2)$,

d by scale factor $\frac{1}{2}$ from centre $(-2,2)$,

e by scale factor $1\frac{1}{2}$ from centre $(-2,2)$.

3 In each part of the question decide whether the transformation from triangle A to triangle B is an enlargement and write the scale factor if it is.

a

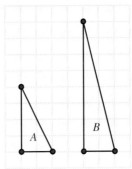

b

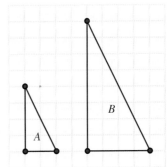

c

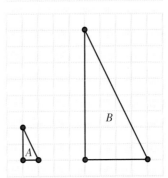

d

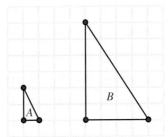

e

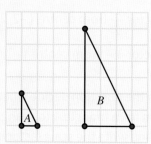

f

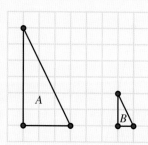

b

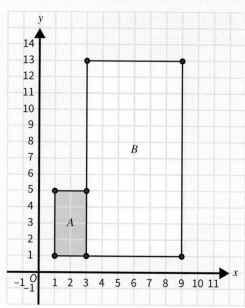

4 Describe fully the transformation from rectangle *A* to rectangle *B* in each case.

a

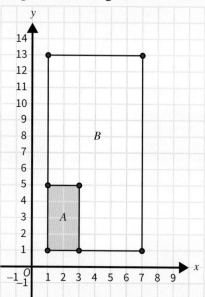

c

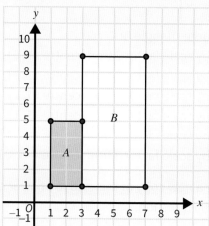

d

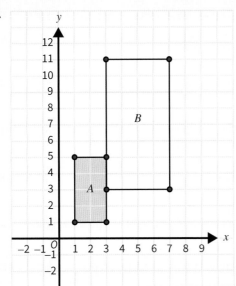

e

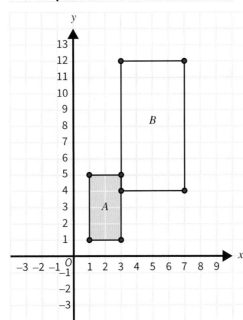

f

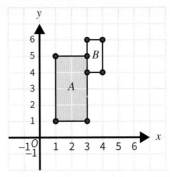

g

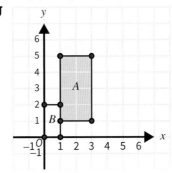

9.5 Method selection

In these questions you'll need to think carefully about which methods to apply.

For some questions you might need to use skills from earlier chapters.

1 Triangles A–D are all transformations of each other.

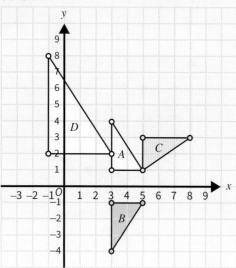

Describe fully the transformation that maps triangle:

a A to B, **c** A to C, **e** A to D,

b B to A, **d** C to A, **f** D to A.

2 Use a copy of this grid to answer this question.

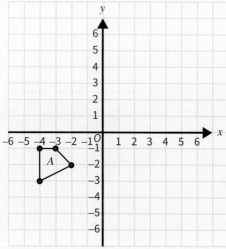

a Rotate shape A 180° about the point $(0, 0)$ and label the image B.

b Reflect shape A in the x-axis and label the image C.

c Enlarge shape A by scale factor 3 centre $(-6, -4)$ and label the image D.

3 Use square grid paper or graph paper to answer this question.

a Draw coordinate axes with x from −11 to 11 and y from −4 to 4.

A square has three vertices at $(1, -1)$, $(3, -2)$, and $(4, 0)$

b Draw the square on your diagram and label it A.

c Write the coordinates of the fourth vertex of the square.

d Enlarge the square by scale factor 2 centre $(-2, -1)$ and label the image B.

e Reflect square B in the y-axis and label the image C.

4 A triangle has vertices at A, B, and C.

The coordinates of vertex A are $(6, 9)$.

Find the coordinates of the image of A following enlargement of:

a scale factor 3 from centre $(0, 0)$,

b scale factor 3 from centre $(3, 0)$,

c scale factor 3 from centre $(3, 3)$,

d scale factor $\dfrac{1}{3}$ from centre $(3, 3)$,

e scale factor $\dfrac{1}{3}$ from centre $(6, 9)$.

9.5 Purposeful practice

There may be more than one way to approach these questions. Once you have answered a question one way, can you think of another way?

1 Look at this triangle.

a Draw three different enlargements of triangle A and label them B, C, and D.

b Explain how you know that triangles B, C, and D are enlargements of the same triangle.

c Draw two triangles that are not enlargements of triangle A and label them E and F.

d Explain why E and F are not enlargements of triangle A.

2 Use a copy of this grid to answer this question.

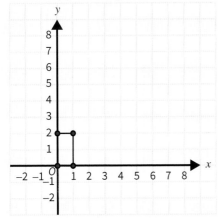

a Draw an enlargement of this shape by scale factor 2 and centre $(0, 0)$. Label the image A.

b Draw an enlargement of this shape by scale factor 2 and centre $(-2, -1)$. Label the image B.

c Describe fully the transformation that maps A to B.

d On a new copy of the grid, repeat parts a–c for different centres of enlargement. Can you spot a pattern?

3 Repeat question 2 on a larger grid using a scale factor of 3. Try to predict what patterns you might see and then draw the enlargements to see if you were correct. Now try different scale factors.

Watch out! exercise

Some students have tried to answer the questions below but have unfortunately made some mistakes.

For each question do the following:

a answer the question correctly

b write down the mistake that each student has made

c comment on why they might have made that mistake

d write an explanation for each student to convince them (nicely!) that their answer cannot be correct.

---

1 Taisiya and Paul attempted to answer the question, "Reflect triangle A in the line $y = 0$ and label the image B."

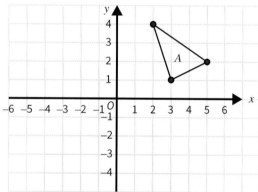

Here are Taisiya and Paul's working:

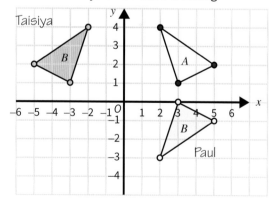

2 Lily and Sian attempted to answer the question, "Enlarge triangle ABC by scale factor 3 about the centre of enlargement shown and label the vertices of the image $A'B'C'$."

Here is Lily's working:

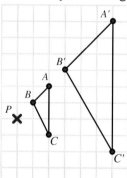

Here is Sian's working:

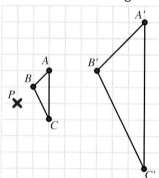

Check your understanding

Turn over to find the review questions

9.1 Translations

You should now be able to...	Questions
recognise a translation and know which features of an object are affected by translation	1b
describe a translation	1b
translate an object	2b

9.2 Rotations

You should now be able to...	Questions
recognise a rotation and know which features of an object are affected by rotation	1c, 1d, 7b
rotate an object	2c, 6b
describe a rotation	1c, 1d

9.3 Reflections

You should now be able to...	Questions
recognise a reflection and know which features of an object are affected by reflection	1a, 7a
draw a mirror line for a reflection	6c
reflect an object in a given line	2a, 6a

9.4 Scale diagrams

You should now be able to...	Questions
know how distances on a scale diagram represent distances in real life	4
interpret a scale diagram	4
draw a scale diagram	3

9.5 Enlargements

You should now be able to...	Questions
recognise an enlargement and know which features of an object are affected by enlargement	7c
enlarge an object	5
describe an enlargement	8

1

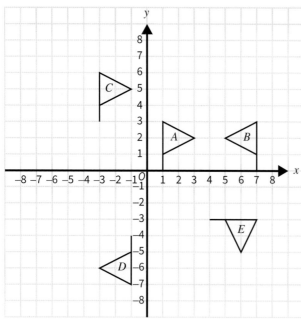

Flags B–E are all transformations of flag A.

Write the single transformation that maps:

a A onto B, [2 marks]

b A onto C, [2 marks]

c A onto D, [2 marks]

d A onto E. [2 marks]

2 A rectangular football pitch is $70\,\text{m}$ wide and $120\,\text{m}$ long.

Draw a scale diagram of the football pitch using a scale of $1:2000$ [2 marks]

3 A map is drawn using a scale of $1:50\,000$

On the map, the distance from the cinema to the market place is $4\,\text{cm}$.

a How far, in km, is the cinema from the market place in real life? [2 marks]

The town hall is $6\,\text{km}$ from the railway station.

b How far, in cm, is the town hall from the railway station on the map? [2 marks]

4 Use a copy of this grid to answer this question.

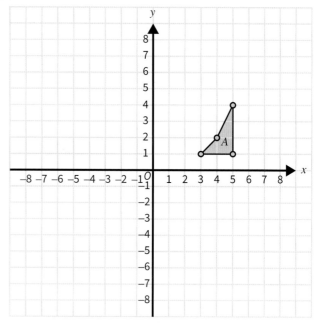

a Reflect shape A in the line $y = x$
Label the image B. [2 marks]

b Translate shape A using vector $\begin{pmatrix} -5 \\ -4 \end{pmatrix}$
Label the image C. [2 marks]

c Rotate shape A by $90°$ anticlockwise about centre $(1, -2)$.
Label the image D. [2 marks]

5 Decide if each of these statements is true or false.

If the statement is false, write a correct statement.

a In a reflection, points on the mirror line do not change. [1 mark]

b In a rotation, there are no invariant points. [1 mark]

c In an enlargement by scale factor 2, every point on the image is three times as far from the centre of enlargement as the corresponding point on the object. [1 mark]

6 Use a copy of this grid to answer this question.

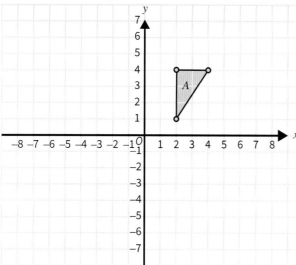

a Enlarge triangle A by scale factor 2, using centre $(0, 0)$. Label the image B. [2 marks]
b Enlarge triangle A by scale factor 3, using centre $(6, 5)$. Label the image C. [2 marks]
c Enlarge triangle A by scale factor 0.5, using centre $(4, -4)$. Label the image D. [2 marks]

7 Use a copy of this grid to answer this question.

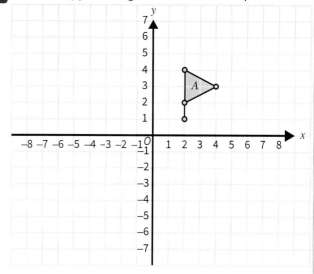

a Reflect shape A in the line $y = -1$ Label the image B. [2 marks]
b Rotate shape B 180° using centre $(-1, -1)$. Label the image C. [2 marks]
c Describe the single transformation that maps shape A onto shape C. [2 marks]

8 Look at this graph.

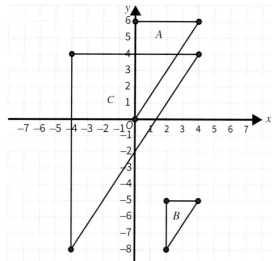

a C is an enlargement of A.
Write down the scale factor and centre of enlargement. [2 marks]
b C is an enlargement of B.
Write down the scale factor and centre of enlargement. [2 marks]
c Describe the transformation that maps C onto B. [1 mark]

Key words

Make sure you can write a definition for these key terms.

congruent • orientation • position • transformation • object • image • translation • column vector
rotation • centre of rotation • reflection • mirror line • scale diagram • to scale • similar
enlargement • scale factor • centre of enlargement

Glossary

absolute value   A number's distance from zero, e.g. 3 and −3 both have an absolute value of 3

additive inverse   What you need to add to a number to make zero, e.g. the additive inverse of 3 is −3

additive relationship   A relationship describing additions and/or subtractions.

algebraically   Using a formula, equation or expression to describe something.

angle   The amount one line has been turned in relation to the other when 2 lines meet at a point.

area   The space inside a boundary.

ascending   Going up in order of size from smallest to largest.

associative law   The associative law says that you can group calculations involving only addition or only multiplication in any way you like.
The grouping can be shown using brackets,
e.g. $60 + 3 + 10 + 5 = (60 + 10) + (3 + 5)$

base   In index notation, the base is the number upon which the exponent is to operate, e.g. in 5^3, 5 is the base.

base length   The length of a side which is perpendicular to the height of the polygon. (The base is often, but not always, at the 'bottom' of the polygon.)

centre of enlargement   When the object and image of an enlargement have their corresponding points joined by straight lines, then all those lines will cross at a common point called the centre of enlargement.

centre of rotation   A fixed point that an object rotates around.

coefficient   The number the variable or variables are multiplied by.

collect like terms   Simplifying an expression by adding the like terms.

common denominator   A common denominator of two or more fractions is a number into which all of their denominators will divide.

commutative law   The commutative law means that if you have a string of additions or multiplications, you can do them in any order and the result will always be the same, e.g. $3 \times 4 = 4 \times 3$

composite number   An integer greater than 1 that is not prime.

composite shape   A shape made of two or more shapes put together.

congruent   The same in shape and size.

constant   A term that does not involve a variable.

conversion rate (*or* exchange rate)   A statement of how a value in one system may be given as an equivalent value in the other system.

coordinate grid   A space with a grid in the background and axes, where position is defined using coordinates.

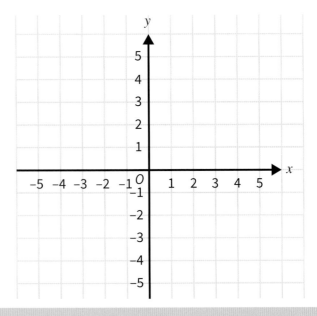

coordinate pair   A coordinate pair is written (x, y) where x is the position from the origin in the x-direction and y is the position from the origin in the y-direction.

cubed   To cube a number is to multiply three copies of the number together (multiply it by itself and then by itself again), e.g. 2 cubed is $2^3 = 2 \times 2 \times 2 = 8$

cube number   The result of multiplying three copies of a number (a number multiplied by itself and then by itself again).

cube root $\sqrt[3]{}$ The inverse of cubing, e.g. $\sqrt[3]{8} = 2$

decagon   A polygon with 10 sides.

denominator   The bottom number in a fraction, which shows the number of equal parts that the whole is split into.

descending   Going down in order of size from largest to smallest.

diagonal   A straight line within a polygon joining two vertices that are not joined by a side.

digit   Digits or numerals are the single symbols 0, 1, 2, 3, 4, 5, 6, 7, 8, and 9. They are numbers but can also be put together to make larger numbers.

distributive law   The distributive law describes how two operators may be used together when linked in a particular way, e.g. 26×5 can be calculated as $5 \times (20 + 6) = (5 \times 20) + (5 \times 6)$

dividend   The amount in a division operation which is to be shared out, e.g. in $20 \div 5$, 20 is the dividend.

divisor   The amount in a division operation among which the dividend must be shared, e.g. in $20 \div 5$, 5 is the divisor.

double number line   Two number lines with different but related scales that show the relationship between pairs of numbers in a similar way to a ratio table.

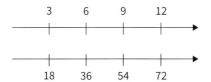

edge   One of the lines defining the outline of a shape.

enlargement   A transformation in which the distances between every pair of points in the object are multiplied by the same amount to produce the image.

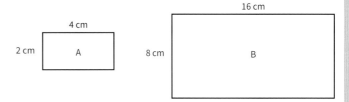

equation   A statement which shows two algebraic expressions that are equal, e.g. $2x + 3 = 7$

equilateral triangle   A triangle with 3 sides of equal length and 3 angles each equal to $60°$

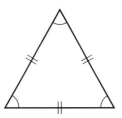

equivalent fractions   Fractions that are equal in value to each other.

even   A whole number which, when divided by 2, has no remainder.

expand brackets   Write an expression so that it does not have any brackets by multiplying the term next to the brackets by each of the terms inside the brackets, e.g. expanding the brackets of $3(x + 2)$ gives $3x + 6$

exponent (*or* index)   The name we give to the number 2 in the expression 5^2. We say the exponent (or index) of 5 is 2

expression   A combination of symbols that can include numbers, variables and mathematical operations (such as +, −, × or ÷). It does NOT include an equals sign (=) or inequalities ($\neq$, $<$, $\leq$, $>$, $\geq$).

factor   A factor of a number divides that number exactly (without a remainder).

factor pair   Two numbers that give a particular product when multiplied together.

factorise   To find the factors of a number or algebraic expression or to express it in factors. Factorising an expression means writing it using brackets, taking a common factor in front of the brackets, e.g. writing $3x + 6$ as $3(x + 2)$

formula   A statement, usually written as an equation, giving the exact relationship between certain quantities, so that, when one or more values are known, the value of one particular quantity can be found.

fraction   A measure of how something is to be divided up or shared out. Fractions involve the whole being divided into equal parts with a certain number of those parts being used.

fully factorise   An expression is fully factorised into a single set of brackets if the highest common factor of the terms inside the brackets is 1, e.g. $15p - 5p$ is fully factorised as $5p(3 - p)$

function machine   A function machine tells you how to use an input number to calculate an output number.

input → ×3 → −1 → output

generalise   To generalise in mathematics is to make statements, often using algebra, about the rules that will always work.

graphically   Drawing a line or curve where every point on it satisfies a relationship is called representing the relationship graphically.

height   The distance or measurement from the bottom to the top of something.

heptagon   A polygon with 7 sides.

hexagon   A polygon with 6 sides.

highest common factor (HCF)   The greatest integer that is a factor of two or more given integers. In algebra, the HCF is the greatest term that is a factor of two or more given terms.

identity   An equation that is true for all values of the variable or variables.

image   The transformed shape following a transformation. If A is the object then the image is referred to as A'.

improper fraction   A positive fraction where the numerator is greater than the denominator.

index form (*or* index notation)   A way of indicating how a number (or symbol) must be operated on by using another number written as an exponent to the first, e.g. 5^3

inequality   A comparison of two expressions or values that are not equal. The symbols <, ≤, >, ≥, and ≠ may be used.

inverse   The inverse of an operation reverses the effect of that operation, e.g. multiplication is the inverse of division, and subtraction is the inverse of addition.

integer   Any positive or negative whole number, or zero.

irregular   An irregular shape is one where the angles are NOT all the same size and/or the sides are NOT all the same length.

isosceles triangle   A triangle with 2 sides of equal length and 2 angles of equal size.

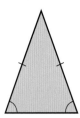

kite   A quadrilateral with 2 pairs of adjacent sides of equal length and 1 pair of equal angles.

leading zero   An extra zero at the start of a number which does not affect its value, e.g. all three zeros in 00 021 395

length   How long something is.

like terms   Like terms involve exactly the same variable, or variables, so they can be simplified by adding (collecting) them together.

lowest common multiple (LCM)   The smallest integer that is a multiple of two or more given integers.

metric system   A measuring system based on powers of 10

midpoint   The point exactly halfway between two points.

minuend   The number to be subtracted from, e.g. in $7 - 2$, 7 is the minuend.

mirror line   The fixed line used in making a reflection.

mixed number   A number greater than 1 written as an integer and a proper fraction.

multiple   A multiple of a given number is the product of that number and an integer.

multiplicative relationship   A relationship describing multiplications and/or divisions.

multiplier   A way to describe the link between two numbers with multiplication by a single number, e.g. the multiplier from 3 to 12 is 4, and the multiplier from 12 to 3 is $\dfrac{1}{4}$

negative number   A number less than 0

nonagon   A polygon with 9 sides.

numerator   The top number in a fraction, which shows the number of equal parts that are being used.

object   The original shape when doing a transformation.

obtuse-angled triangle   A triangle where one angle is greater than $90°$

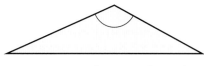

octagon   A polygon with 8 sides.

odd   A whole number which, when divided by 2, has a remainder of 1.

orientation   Facing in a certain direction in relation to something else.

origin   The point with coordinates $(0, 0)$

parallel   Two lines are parallel if they are always the same distance apart and would never meet if extended.

parallelogram   A quadrilateral with 2 pairs of parallel sides of equal length and opposite angles that are equal.

partitioning   Writing as an equivalent calculation involving addition (or subtraction), e.g. 26 could be partitioned as $12 + 14$

pentagon   A polygon with 5 sides.

per   For each, e.g. a price of $60\,p$ per kilogram means that each kilogram costs $60\,p$.

perimeter   The complete distance around the outer sides of a 2D shape.

perpendicular height   The height measured at right-angles from the base.

polygon   Any closed 2D shape with only straight sides.

position   Where an object can be found; its place or location.

positive number   A number greater than 0

power   The result of multiplying a given number of copies of a number (multiplying a number by itself a given number of times).

power of 10   The result of multiplying (or dividing) a given number of copies of 10

prefix   A letter or group of letters joined to the front of a word to change or add to its meaning.

prime factor   The prime factors of a number are all those factors of the number which are themselves prime numbers.

prime factorisation (*or* prime factor decomposition)   The process of writing a number as the product of its prime factors.

prime number   An integer greater than 1 that has exactly two factors: 1 and itself.

product   The result given by a multiplication operation.

proper fraction   A positive fraction where the numerator is less than the denominator.

quadrant   One of the 4 areas that a coordinate grid can be split into using the x-and y-axes. The quadrants are labelled first to fourth anti-clockwise, starting with the top right quadrant.

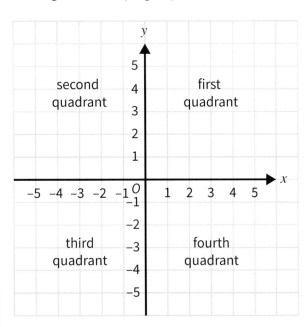

quadrilateral   A polygon with 4 sides.

quotient   The result given by a division operation.

rate   A measure of how quickly an amount changes relative to another.

ratio   A way to describe the multiplicative relationship between two or more quantities, e.g. the ratio 3 : 1 describes a relationship where the first quantity is 3 times the size of the second.

reciprocal   A reciprocal of a number is 1 divided by that number, e.g. 2 is the reciprocal of $\frac{1}{2}$ and $\frac{1}{2}$ is the reciprocal of 2

rectangle   A quadrilateral with 2 pairs of opposite sides of equal length and 4 right angles.

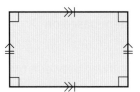

rectilinear shape   A shape made up of rectangles, with straight sides joined at right angles.

recurring decimal   Decimals where the digits do not terminate but continue forever in a repeating pattern, shown by a dot above the digits that repeat, e.g. 0.232323… is written as $0.\dot{2}\dot{3}$

reflection   A transformation that 'flips' an object over a fixed straight line, such that a point in the object and its corresponding point in the image are both the same perpendicular distance from, and on opposite sides of, the mirror line.

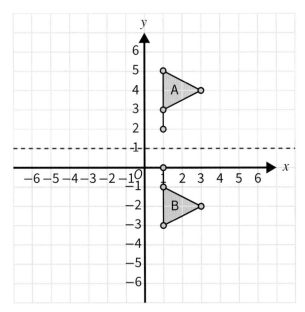

regular   A regular shape is one where all the sides are equal in length and all the angles are equal in size.

rhombus   A quadrilateral with all sides of equal length where the opposite angles are equal.

right-angled triangle   A triangle where one angle is equal to 90°

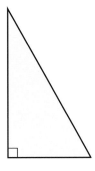

rotation   A transformation that turns an object around a fixed point.

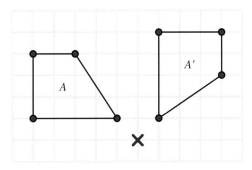

scale diagram   A diagram with measurements in proportion to those of the original.

scale factor   The number that all the lengths are multiplied by in an enlargement.

scalene triangle   A triangle where all the sides are different lengths and all the angles are different sizes.

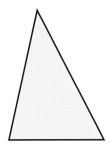

similar   Two shapes are similar if their respective angles are equal, and the ratios of the lengths of their respective sides are equal.

simplest form   A fraction in its simplest form has an integer numerator and denominator that do not have any common factors (other than 1).

simplify   Writing an expression with fewer parts.

solution   A solution to an equation is a value for a variable that satisfies the equation (makes it true).

square   A quadrilateral with all sides of equal length and 4 right angles.

squared   To square a number is to multiply it by itself (multiply two copies of the number), e.g. $5^2 = 5 \times 5 = 25$

square number   The result of multiplying a number by itself (multiplying two copies of a number).

square root $\sqrt{}$ The inverse of squaring, e.g. $\sqrt{25} = 5$

substitute   Replace a variable or unknown with a numerical value.

subtrahend   The number being subtracted, e.g. in $7 - 2$, 2 is the subtrahend.

sum   The result of an addition calculation.

term   A term is a number, a variable, or two or more numbers or variables multiplied together, e.g. $4y$, 2 and $3x^2$ are terms in the expression $4y + 2 + 3x^2$

terminating decimal   Decimals where the digits after the decimal point stop, or terminate, e.g. 0.2

to scale   With measurements in proportion to those of the original object.

trailing zero   An extra zero at the end of a decimal number, which does not change the value of the number.

transformation   A change carried out under specific rules, especially the operations that may be used on an object to affect its position, shape, or size.

translation   Moving an object without changing its shape, size, or orientation.

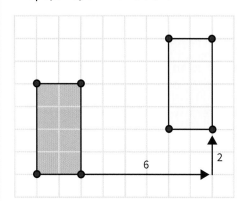

trapezium (plural: trapezia)   A quadrilateral with 1 pair of parallel sides.

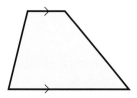

triangle   A polygon with 3 sides.

unit fraction   A fraction with a numerator of 1 and a denominator that is an integer.

variable   A letter that can represent different numbers, e.g. x is a variable in the expression $4x + 2$

vector (*or* column vector)   A (column) vector can be used to describe a translation, with the top number describing the movement in the x-direction and the bottom number describing the movement in the y-direction, e.g. $\begin{pmatrix} 3 \\ -4 \end{pmatrix}$ describes a movement of $+3$ in the x-direction (to the right) and -4 in the y-direction (downwards).

vertex (plural: vertices)   A corner on a shape, where the sides or edges meet.

width   The distance or measurement of something from side to side.

***x*-axis**   The horizontal number line on a coordinate grid.

***y*-axis**   The vertical number line on a coordinate grid.

zero pair   A number and its additive inverse.

Answers

Complete answers to Watch out! exercises and the Chapter review questions are supplied on Kerboodle.

1 Place value

Reactivate your knowledge

1.1 Place value in integers

1 a 4370 **b** 56 300 **c** 2000

1.2 Place value in decimals

2 a $\dfrac{3}{1000}$ **b** $\dfrac{14}{100}$ or $\dfrac{7}{50}$ **c** seven tenths

3 a 480 **b** 7200 **c** 35 000 **d** 36 000

4 a 14 **b** 6 **c** 0.09 **d** 0.51

1.3 Ordering and comparing numbers

5

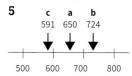

	c	a	b
	591	650	724

500 600 700 800

1.4 Measures

6 a Mass **b** Volume **c** Length

1.1 Place value in integers

1.1.1 Understanding place value of integers

Your turn! 1 80 000 or eighty thousand

1.1.1 Fluency

1 a 70 **b** 40 000 **c** 8 000 000

2 a twenty-three thousand and seventy-six
b one million, four hundred and thirty-two thousand, six hundred and seven

3 a 17 820 **b** 4 816 601 | **4 a** 40 000 **b** 100 000 000

5 a 50 000 000 **b** 10 000 000 000

6 a seven hundred and twenty thousand and forty-one
b nine million, forty-two thousand and seven
c three million and sixty

7 a 85 007 **b** 907 063 **c** 8 064 304

8 a 0134 **b** 000 040 056 **c** None **d** 008 901 320

9 a one hundred and twenty-three million, seven hundred and six thousand, and forty-one
b 470 654 301

1.1.2 Representing place value of integers using powers of 10

Your turn! 1 1000

Your turn! 2
a $7 \times 100000 + 8 \times 10000 + 9 \times 1000 + 5 \times 10 + 3 \times 1$
b $7 \times 10^5 + 8 \times 10^4 + 9 \times 10^3 + 5 \times 10^1 + 3 \times 10^0$

1.1.2 Fluency

1 a 2 **b** 3 **c** 1 | **2** 7

3 a 5 **b** 6

4 a $5 \times 1000 + 2 \times 100 = 5 \times 10^3 + 2 \times 10^2$
b $7 \times 10000 + 8 \times 1000 + 2 \times 100 = 7 \times 10^4 + 8 \times 10^3 + 2 \times 10^2$
c $9 \times 10000 + 1 \times 1000 + 3 \times 10 = 9 \times 10^4 + 1 \times 10^3 + 3 \times 10^1$
d $1 \times 100000 + 4 \times 10000 + 5 \times 1000 + 6 \times 100 + 7$
$= 1 \times 10^5 + 4 \times 10^4 + 5 \times 10^3 + 6 \times 10^2 + 7 \times 10^0$

5 Six hundred and two million, two hundred and fourteen thousand, and seventy-six

1.1 Exercises

1.1 Intelligent practice

1 a Three hundred/300 **d** Three thousand/3000
b Three hundred/300 **e** Thirty thousand/30 000
c Three hundred/300 **f** Three hundred thousand/300 000

2 a 5 **b** 2 **c** 2 **d** 2

3 a 5 **b** 5 **c** 5 **d** 0

4 a 735 **b** 7035 **c** 7035 **d** 70 350

5 a 93 851 **b** 98 315 **c** 90 051 **d** 90 051 **e** 90 015

6 a The zeros are not needed. We consider place value starting in the ones column. In the number 00 567, the digits 5/6/7 will have the same value if we remove the zeros.
b Both zeros are needed. In the number 56 700 the digits 5/6/7 will change value if we remove the zeros.

1.1 Method selection

1 Table headings: <u>Millions</u>, <u>Hundred thousands</u>, <u>Ten thousands</u>, Thousands, Hundreds, Tens, Ones;
First row: <u>1 000 000</u>, <u>100 000</u>, 10 000, <u>1000</u>, 100, 10, 1;
Second row: 10^6, <u>10^5</u>, <u>10^4</u>, <u>10^3</u>, 10^2, 10^1, <u>10^0</u>

2 a 10 **b** 100 **c** 1000 **d** 3600 **e** 36 000 000

3 a = **b** ≠ **c** = **d** =

4 Answers include:
$2 \times 1000 + 3 \times 100 + 0 \times 10 + 4 \times 1$; $2 \times 1000 + 3 \times 100 + 4 \times 1$
$2 \times 10^3 + 3 \times 10^2 + 0 \times 10^1 + 4 \times 1$; $2 \times 10^3 + 3 \times 10^2 + 4 \times 10^0$

5 There are many answers, one is: 700, 1700, 2700, 3700, 4700

6 Columns are in groups of three, with each group of three going 'one …/ten …/hundred …' where the … is ones/thousands/millions, etc.

7 0045, 0405, 0450, 4005, 4050, 4500

8 Paul is not correct. The reason is that 80 000 is in the ten thousands and 7000 is in the thousands.

9 Because 3×10^4 is in the ten thousands and 4×10^3 is in the thousands

1.1 Purposeful practice

1 The first number has five digits, the second only has four digits, so the first is greater.

2 a There are many answers. One is:

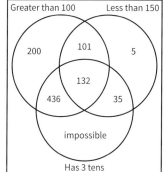

The section labelled 'Has 3 tens' and the section outside the circles are impossible because there is no number that is both less than or equal to 100 and greater than or equal to 150

b Any number from 130 to 139 can go in the centre section.

477

1.1 Purposeful practice contin.

3 a 65 410   **b** 01 456   **c** 65 401   **d** 10 456   **e** 60 145

4 a i Any solution with 4 and 3 in the tens places and 1 and 2 in the ones places, e.g. $41 + 32$

    ii Any solution with 1 and 2 in the tens places and 3 and 4 in the ones places, e.g. $13 + 24$

    iii $43 - 12$

    iv $34 - 21$

  b Greatest sum: $432 + 1$ or $431 + 2$; least sum remains the same; greatest difference: $432 - 1$; least difference remains the same

5 a 123 456 789   **c** 498 765 321   **e** 698 754 321

  b 987 654 321   **d** 412 356 789

6 a 2987   **b** 198 765   **c** 12 345

1.2 Place value in decimals

1.2.1 Understanding place value in decimals

Your turn!   Three hundred thousandths

1.2.1 Fluency

1 a 0.5   **b** 0.002

2 a Twelve hundredths   **b** Forty-five thousandths

3 a 0.7   **b** 0.17 | **4 a** 0.0009   **b** 0.000 08

5 a 0.000 007   **b** 0.000 000 006

6 a Two thousand, four hundred and fifty-six ten thousandths

  b Three hundred and sixty-four ten thousandths

  c Nine hundred and forty-one thousand, two hundred and forty-five millionths

  d Eight hundred and seventy-five thousand and sixteen millionths

7 a 0.507 (accept 500.007)   **c** 0.1417

  b 0.0085   **d** 0.871 657

8 a 0.4<u>0</u>   **c** 0.145 000 0<u>30</u>   **e** none

  b 0.024 <u>500</u>   **d** 0.005 000 000 <u>100</u>

9 19.000 065

1.2.2 Representing place value in decimals using powers of 10

Your turn! 1   100 000

Your turn! 2

a $7.89053 = 7 \times 1 + 8 \times 0.1 + 9 \times 0.01 + 0 \times 0.001 + 5 \times 0.0001$
$+ 3 \times 0.000 01$

b $7.89053 = 7 \times 10^{0} + 8 \times 10^{-1} + 9 \times 10^{-2} + 0 \times 10^{-3} + 5 \times 10^{-4}$
$+ 3 \times 10^{-5}$

1.2.2 Fluency

1 a -2 **b** -1 **c** -3

2 2 | **3 a** -3 **b** -6

4 a $5 \times 0.1 + 6 \times 0.01 = 5 \times 10^{-1} + 6 \times 10^{-2}$

  b $8 \times 0.1 + 7 \times 0.01 + 1 \times 0.001 = 8 \times 10^{-1} + 7 \times 10^{-2} + 1 \times 10^{-3}$

  c $7 \times 0.1 + 2 \times 0.001 + 1 \times 0.0001 = 7 \times 10^{-1} + 2 \times 10^{-3} + 1 \times 10^{-4}$

  d $3 \times 0.01 + 6 \times 0.0001 = 3 \times 10^{-2} + 6 \times 10^{-4}$

5 Three and seven hundredths, five thousandths, two ten thousandths, one hundred thousandth and three ten millionths

1.2.3 Multiplying and dividing by positive powers of 10

Your turn! 1   230 | **Your turn! 2**   0.004 58

1.2.3 Fluency

1 a 340   **b** 5700   **c** 9.1   **d** 69.751

2 a 23 000   **c** 6 310 000 000   **e** 0.694 125

  b 3 600 000   **d** 0.0452   **f** 0.947 254 63

3 a 6120   **c** 820 000   **e** 6.79

  b 341 000   **d** 127 300 000   **f** 1.2354

4 a 6 100 000   **b** 4 510 200 000   **c** 0.067 512 4   **d** 641 312

5 a 540 000   **b** 16 200 000 000   **c** 870   **d** 91 500

1.2.4 Multiplying and dividing by negative powers of 10

Your turn! 1   0.0105 | **Your turn! 2**   540

1.2.4 Fluency

1 a 5.2   **b** 0.73   **c** 850   **d** 61

2 a 0.046   **c** 0.0927   **e** 8 430 000

  b 0.059   **d** 64 500   **f** 69 870

3 a 0.081   **b** 0.007 61   **c** 4500   **d** 347 900

4 a 5.31   **b** 73 200 000 000   **c** 821.46

5 a 672   **b** 19 200   **c** 0.000 075 4

1.2 Exercises

1.2 Intelligent practice

1 a 3   **c** 0.03 or $\dfrac{3}{100}$ **e** 30

  b 0.3 or $\dfrac{3}{10}$ **d** 0.3 or $\dfrac{3}{10}$ **f** 0.003 or $\dfrac{3}{1000}$

2 a 5   **b** 5   **c** 4   **d** 0

3 a 5   **b** 0   **c** 0   **d** 4

4 a 0.735   **b** 0.7035   **c** 0.7035   **d** 7.0305

5 a 0.938 51   **c** 0.900 51   **e** 0.900 15

  b 0.983 15   **d** 0.900 51

6 a The zeros are not needed. If you remove the zeros the 5, 6, and 7 stay in the same place so their value does not change.

  b Both zeros are needed. If you remove the zeros, the other digits move place.

1.2 Method selection

1 Table headings: Ones, Tenths, Hundredths, <u>Thousandths</u>, <u>Ten thousandths</u>, <u>Hundred thousandths</u>, Millionths;

First row: 1, 0.1, 0.01, <u>0.001</u>, <u>0.000 1</u>, 0.000 01, <u>0.000 001</u>;

Second row: 1, $\dfrac{1}{10}$, $\dfrac{1}{100}$, $\dfrac{1}{1000}$, $\dfrac{1}{10\,000}$, $\dfrac{1}{100\,000}$, $\dfrac{1}{1\,000\,000}$

Third row: $\underline{10^{0}}$, 10^{-1}, $\underline{10^{-2}}$, $\underline{10^{-3}}$, 10^{-4}, $\underline{10^{-5}}$, $\underline{10^{-6}}$

2 a 10   **c** 0.1   **e** 1000   **g** 360 000

  b 0.1   **d** 0.01   **f** 0.001   **h** 0.000 036

3 a $=$ **b** $\neq$ **c** $=$ **d** $=$

4 There are several ways to expand 23.045:

$2 \times 10 + 3 \times 1 + 0 \times 0.1 + 4 \times 0.01 + 5 \times 0.001$

(or the same with the third term not written)

$2 \times 10 + 3 \times 1 + 0 \times \dfrac{1}{10} + 4 \times \dfrac{1}{100} + 5 \times \dfrac{1}{1000}$

(or the same with the third term not written)

$2 \times 10^{1} + 3 \times 10^{0} + 0 \times 10^{-1} + 4 \times 10^{-2} + 5 \times 10^{-3}$

(or the same with the third term not written)

5 There are many answers. Here is one: 0.87, 0.77, 0.67, 0.57, 0.47

6 a $\times 1000$ **d** $\times 0.01$ **g** $\times 10$

  b $\times 100\,000$ **e** $\times 0.0001$ **h** $\times 1$

  c $\times 1\,000\,000$ **f** $\times 0.000\,01$

7 a $\div 1000$ **d** $\div 0.01$ **g** $\div 1$

  b $\div 1\,000\,000$ **e** $\div 0.0001$ **h** $\div 10\,000$

  c $\div 1\,000\,000$ **f** $\div 0.000\,001$

8 Jayla is correct that $0.00007 < 0.0008$, but her reason is wrong. It is because 0.0008 is 8 ten thousandths but 0.000 07 is 7 hundred thousandths, and hundred thousandths are less than ten thousandths.

9 4×10^{-3} is 4 thousandths, 3×10^{-4} is 3 ten thousandths. Thousandths are greater than ten thousandths.

1.2 Purposeful practice

1 a There are many answers. Here is one.

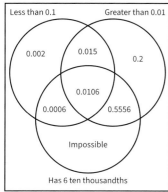

The bottom region cannot be filled. It has to be less than 0.01 but greater than 0.1, which is impossible.

b Any number of the form $0.0xy6$, where x and y are digits from 1 to 9, will fit in the centre section

2 a 0.1789 **b** 0.9871 **c** 80.179
d 9.8701 (9.8710 would contain a trailing, therefore unnecessary, 0)
e 7.0189

3 The first number has 6 tenths, the second 7 tenths, so the second is greater

4 a Any answer with 8 and 7 in the one places, e.g. $8.5 + 7.6$
b Any answer with 5 and 6 in the ones place, e.g. $5.7 + 6.8$
c $8.7 - 5.6$ **d** $7.5 - 6.8$

5 a 0.501 **b** 0.019 876 543 2 **c** 0.102

6 There are many answers. One answer is:
$0 \times 10^0 + 5 \times 10^{-1} + 8 \times 10^{-2} + 6 \times 10^{-3}$ (0.586)
$0 \times 10^0 + 5 \times 10^{-1} + 7 \times 10^{-2} + 6 \times 10^{-3}$ (0.576)
$0 \times 10^0 + 5 \times 10^{-1} + 6 \times 10^{-2} + 6 \times 10^{-3}$ (0.566)
$0 \times 10^0 + 5 \times 10^{-1} + 5 \times 10^{-2} + 6 \times 10^{-3}$ (0.556)

7 a i $5 \times 10^1 + 9 \times 10^0 + 2 \times 10^{-2}$
ii $5 \times 10^2 + 9 \times 10^1 + 2 \times 10^{-1}$
iii $5 \times 10^4 + 9 \times 10^3 + 2 \times 10^1$
iv $5 \times 10^{-1} + 9 \times 10^{-2} + 2 \times 10^{-4}$
v $5 \times 10^{-2} + 9 \times 10^{-3} + 2 \times 10^{-5}$
The digits stay the same but the powers of 10 change. The index goes up by the number of zeros in the multiplier for 10, 100, and 10 000, and down in the same way for 0.1 and 0.01
b i $5 \times 10^{-1} + 9 \times 10^{-2} + 2 \times 10^{-4}$
ii $5 \times 10^{-2} + 9 \times 10^{-3} + 2 \times 10^{-5}$
iii $5 \times 10^1 + 9 \times 10^0 + 2 \times 10^{-2}$
iv $5 \times 10^2 + 9 \times 10^1 + 2 \times 10^{-1}$
v $5 \times 10^4 + 9 \times 10^3 + 2 \times 10^1$
The digits stay the same but the powers of 10 change. The index goes down by the number of zeros in the divisor for 10 and 100 and up in the same way for 0.1, 0.01, and 0.0001

1.3 Ordering and comparing numbers

1.3.1 Placing integers and decimals on number lines

Your turn! 1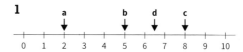

1.3.1 Fluency

1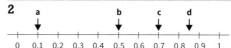

2

3 a 3 **b** 9 **c** 4.5
4 a 20 **b** 60 **c** 70
5 a 0.3 **b** 0.6 **c** 0.95

6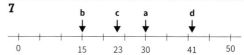

7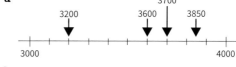

1.3.2 Comparing the size of integers and decimals

Your turn! 1 $23\,502 > 23\,052$ | **Your turn! 2** $15.045 < 15.45$

1.3.2 Fluency

1 a > **b** > **c** <
2 a < **b** > **c** > **d** = **e** > **f** =
3 a < **b** < **c** > **d** <

1.3.3 Ordering integers and decimals

Your turn! 1 2008, 2800, 8020, 8200

Your turn! 2 1.064, 1.406, 1.46, 1.604

1.3.3 Fluency

1 a 42, 402, 420, 1402, 4002 **b** 61, 106, 601, 610, 1060, 1600
2 a 0.0506, 0.056, 0.506, 0.56, 5.6
b 0.1032, 1.0302, 1.032, 1.302, 1.32
c 703.142, 7031.42, 7301.42, 37 012.4, 70 314.2, 730 142
d 6420.273, 46 202.73, 64 202.73, 624 072.3, 642 027.3, 6 420 273
3 a 1.9×10^{-6}, 2×10^5, two million, 19 541 321
b Eighteen million, 1.82×10^7, 181 364 510, 18×10^8
c $921\,0000 \times 10^{-9}$, 9 200 000, ninety-two million, 9.21×10^6

1.3 Exercises

1.3 Intelligent practice

1 a

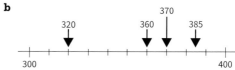

b

1.3 Intelligent practice contin.

1 c

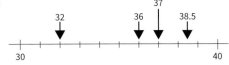

d

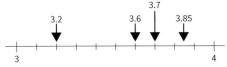

The arrows look like they are in the same position in each answer. This is because each number is the same proportion along the line in each part.

2 a 14, 22, 27   **d** 150, 350   **g** 1.51, 1.53, 1.565
  b 140, 220, 270   **e** 2, 3.5, 5.25
  c 170, 250, 300   **f** 0.5, 1.5, 3, 4.75, 5.5

3 a

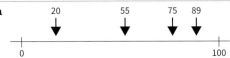

b

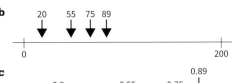

c

4 a 123, 132, 213, 231, 312, 321
  b 1.23, 1.32, 2.13, 2.31, 3.12, 3.21
  c 0.001 23, 0.0231, 0.0321, 0.213, 0.312, 1.32

5 a >   **b** >   **c** <   **d** >   **e** =

1.3 Method selection

1 a <   **b** >   **c** <   **d** >

2 a >   **b** =   **c** <

3 0.321, $1 \times 1 + 3 \times 0.1 + 2 \times 0.01$, two point one three, 12.3, twenty-three and one-tenth, $3 \times 10^2 + 1 \times 10^1 + 2 \times 10^{-2}$

4 12×10^{10}, 1.2×10^9, twelve million, 1 200 000, one hundred and twenty thousand

5

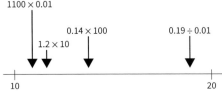

6

1.3 Purposeful practice

1 a 40   **b** 196   **c** 9   **d** 3.3   **e** 14.5

2 a 15   **b** 7   **c** 19   **d** 4.5   **e** 11.2   **f** 2.35

2 g You find the difference from the middle to the endpoint and then go the same difference the other way.

3 Bath, Barnsley, Barnet, Barry, Barking

4 a 23.8   **c** 23.8   **e** 23 800
  b 2.38   **d** 2380   **f** 238

5 23.569, 23.596, 23.659, 23.695

1.4 Measures

1.4.1 The metric system

Your turn! 1   45 000 nm , 4000 mm, 450 cm, 40 m, 0.45 km

1.4.1 Fluency

1 a grams (accept any sensible unit of mass)
  b metres (accept any sensible unit of length)
  c litres (accept any sensible unit of capacity)

2 a 0.35 cm, 30 cm, 35 cm, 350 cm
  b 8.5 g, 80 g, 85 g, 850 g

3 a >   **b** <

4 a 4.5   **b** 0.067   **c** 860

5 a 71 000   **b** 3.7   **c** 52 000 000

6 a 7.2 cm, 720 mm, 7 m, 0.72 km
  b 8.5 g, 0.08 kg, 85 g, 0.85 kg
  c 120 ml, 1020 ml, 1.2 *l*, 12 *l*

7 a 3100   **b** 0.085   **c** 120   **d** 95 000 000

8 a ×10   **b** ×100 000   **c** ÷1 000 000

1.4.2 Money and time

Your turn! 1   15 300 p   **Your turn! 2**   8 minutes

Your turn! 3   8640 minutes

1.4.2 Fluency

1 a £   **b** Hours, minutes, seconds

2 a 3.70   **b** 910   **c** 14.71   **d** 1793

3 a 240   **b** 6   **c** 480   **d** 12   **e** 23 400

4 a £2.53, 2530 pence, £253, 253 000 pence
  b 837 pence, £83.72, £837, 83 720 pence

5 a 135 minutes, 2 hours and 17 minutes, 8280 seconds, 2.4 hours
  b 29 124 seconds, 8.1 hours, eight hours and nine minutes, 490 minutes

1.4 Exercises

1.4 Intelligent practice

1 a <   **b** <   **c** <   **d** >

2 a 0.5 kg   **d** 50 000 m   **g** 0.5 *l*
  b 0.005 kg   **e** 50 000 000 mm
  c 5000 m   **f** 5 *l*

3 a 250 mm   **d** 25 000 000 000 µg
  b 250 000 µm   **e** 0.025 Gg
  c 25 000 000 mg   **f** 0.025 tonnes

4 a £156   **b** 1560 p   **c** 156 p

5 a 240 seconds   **c** 96 h
  b 14 400 seconds   **d** $\frac{1}{6}$ or 0.167 days

1.4 Method selection

1 a 62 *l* , 62 dl, 62 cl, 62 ml
  b 7 kg, 700 g, 70 000 mg, 700 000 µg
  c 2 500 000 cm, 2.5 km, 250 m, 2500 mm
  d £24.10, 2145 p, £2.41, 214.5 p

2 a 0.75 *l*, 75 dl, 7500 cl, 0.75 kl
b 1.5 Mg, 15 tonnes, 150 000 kg, 1.5 Gg

3 a = **b** < **c** = **d** >

4 a = **b** < **c** = **d** =

5 No, it weighs 130 g and 1.2 kg is 1200 g

6 85 min, 1½ h, 1 h 45 min, 125 min, 2.2 h

1.4 Purposeful practice

1 1.88 m or 188 cm **2** 14 g heavier

3 10.5 km **4** 1.5 bottles

5 a The five might include any of 1.8 kg, 0.0018 Mg, 0.0018 tonnes, 0.000 001 8 Gg, 1 800 000 mg, 1 800 000 000 μg
b The five might include any of 20 000 m, 20 000 000 mm, 2 000 000 cm , 20 000 000 000 μm, 20 000 000 000 000 nm, 0.02 Mm, 0.000 02 Gm
c 2.5 *l*, 0.0025 kl, 0.000 002 5 Ml, 0.000 000 002 Gl, 2500 ml, 2 500 000 μl, 25 dl

6 1.875 kg **7** 25 laps

Chapter 1 summary

Watch out! (full answers on Kerboodle)

1 a They are the same number. **2 a** 0.6010 = 0.601

3 a 0.304 < 0.34 **4 a** 1.4 **5 a** 4.57

6 a 0.045 km **7 a** 0.01 or $\frac{1}{100}$

8 a 4800 **9 a** 30 minutes **10 a** 540 minutes

2 Properties of numbers

Reactivate your knowledge

2.1 Multiples

1 a 36 **b** 77 **c** 40

2 a 6×4 or 4×6 **b** 1×7 or 7×1 **c** 8×2 or 2×8

2.2 Powers and roots

3 a 1, 4, 9, 16, 25, 36, 49, 64, 81, 100, 121, 144
b 5 arrays of square numbers

4 a 7.3 **b** 3.4 **c** 5.7 **d** 5.0

2.3 Factors and prime factorisation

5 a 9 **b** 9 **c** 5 **d** 12

2.1 Multiples

2.1.1 Understanding multiples

Your turn! 1 8, 16, 24, 32, 40

Your turn! 2 No

2.1.1 Fluency

1 3, 6, 9, 12, 15

2 11, 22, 33, 44, 55, 66, 77, 88, 99, 110

3 a False **b** True **c** True **d** False

4 14, 28, 42, 56 **5** 23, 46, 69, 92, 115, 138

6 34, 68, 102, 136, 170 **7** 85, 170, 255, 340

8 a It is not a multiple: it is 20 more than 210 and 20 is not a multiple of 7
b It is a multiple: it is 70 more than 210 and 70 is 10×7

9 a $96 = 42 + 54 = 7 \times 6 + 9 \times 6$, so 96 will also be a multiple of 6
b $138 = 42 + 42 + 54 = 7 \times 6 + 7 \times 6 + 9 \times 6$, so 138 will also be a multiple of 6

2.1.2 Divisibility rules

Your turn! 1 No

2.1.2 Fluency

1 a True **c** True **e** True
b False **d** True **f** False

2 a and c (both even numbers)

3 a, b and d (e.g. digits sum multiple of 3)

4 All of them (e.g. digits sum multiple of 9)

5 Yes; digits sum to a multiple of 3

6 Yes; digits sum to a multiple of 9

7 Yes; even and digits sum to a multiple of 3

8 No; last two digits not divisible by 4

2.1 Exercises

2.1 Intelligent practice

1 a 72 **c** 48 **e** 48 **g** 48
b 72 **d** 48 **f** 48 **h** 48

2 a True; e.g. digit sum divisible by 9
b True; e.g. digit sum divisible by 9
c False; e.g. digit sum not divisible by 9
d True; e.g. digit sum divisible by 9
e True; e.g. digit sum divisible by 3
f True; e.g. divisible by 3 and even
g False; e.g. divisible by 3 but not even

3

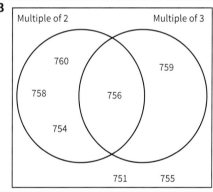

4 a 728 **b** 741 **c** 2

2.1 Method selection

1 28 is a multiple of 2, 4; 42 is a multiple of 2, 3, 6; 70 is a multiple of 2, 5

2 12 **3** No

4 90 **5** 30 boxes and 48 packs

6 a Yes, 154 or 514 **c** Not possible
b Not possible **d** Yes, 145 or 415

7 6 or 0 **8** 15th

9 No; 170 is a multiple of 17, but 67 is not

10 234 **11** Wednesday

12 21st multiple of 22 **13** 1, 2, 3, 4, 6, 8, 12

2.1 Purposeful practice

1 1, 2, 7, 14; largest number is 14

2 4 codes: 420, 441, 462, 483

2.1 Purposeful practice contin.

3 a 500; yes   **b** 299; no   **c** 425; yes

4 123, 234, 345, 456, 567, 678, 789 are all multiples of 3

5 2, 5, 8 | **6** 884 | **7** It's not

8 11 or 23 or 35 | **9** 352

2.2 Powers and roots

2.2.1 Square and cube numbers

Your turn! 1   81 | **Your turn! 2**   27

2.2.1 Fluency

1 $5 \times 5 \times 5$ | **2 a** 2   **b** 2   **c** 3   **d** 3

3 a 1   **b** 64   **c** 125

4 a 36   **b** 675   **c** 128   **d** 200   **e** 144   **f** 576

5 a 31   **b** 39   **c** 98   **d** 224   **e** 50   **f** 42

2.2.2 Understanding square roots

Your turn! 1   9

2.2.2 Fluency

1 a 7   **b** 11

2 a 19   **b** 28   **c** 91

3 a 6.5   **b** 8.9

4 a 12   **b** 13   **c** 15

5 a 17.8   **b** 21.7   **c** 30.4

6 4, 16, 25, 49, 121; they are square numbers

7 a 20   **b** 21   **c** 12   **d** 17

2.2.3 Understanding cube roots

Your turn! 1   3 | **Your turn!2**   8

2.2.3 Fluency

1 a 9   **b** 8   **c** 12

2 a 3.4   **b** 6.4

3 a 4   **b** 10   **c** 7   **d** 11

4 a 5.3   **b** 7.5   **c** 9.2   **d** 9.7

5 8, 27, 216, 1000

6 18; $\sqrt[3]{27} = 3$, $\sqrt[3]{216} = 6$, $3 \times 6 = 18$

7 a 6   **b** 5

2.2.4 Higher powers of numbers

Your turn! 1 9^6

2.2.4 Fluency

1 2, 4, 8, 16 | **2** $6 \times 6 \times 6 \times 6$

3 a 4   **b** 5   **c** 7

4 a 3, 9, 27, 81   **b** 4, 16, 64, 256   **c** 5, 25, 125, 625

5 a 5^2 **b** 2^3 **c** 4^4 or 2^8 **d** 5^4

6 a 200   **b** 144   **c** 4500

7 a 512   **b** 1800   **c** 675 000

8 a 4, 128, 256   **b** 9, 81, 243   **c** 25, 125, 625, 3125

2.2 Exercises

2.2 Intelligent practice

1 a $5 \times 5 \times 5$ **d** 7×7

   b $3 \times 3 \times 3 \times 3 \times 3$ **e** $2 \times 2 \times 2 \times 2 \times 2 \times 2 \times 2$

   c Part b is larger   **f** Part e is larger

2 a 3^6 **b** 9^4 **c** 6^3 **d** 4^9 **e** c, a, b, d

3 a 10 000   **b** 625   **c** 64   **d** 64   **e** 81

4 a 11   **b** 11   **c** 121

5 a 36   **b** 42.25   **c** 49   **d** Jaylah is incorrect

6 a 10   **b** 11   **c** 12

7 a 2^3 **b** 2^7 **c** 9^7 **d** 9^7 **e** 9^9

2.2 Method selection

1 a 25   **b** 27   **c** 64

2 a 5^2 **b** 15^2

3 a $100 = 10^2$ **b** $1089 = 33^2$ **c** $2744 = 14^3$ **d** $1296 = 6^4$

4 a $20 = \sqrt{400}$ **b** $30 = \sqrt{900}$ **c** $2000 = \sqrt{4\,000\,000}$

5 a 81 and 4 or 49 and 36   **c** 25 and 9 or 225 and 1

   b 125 and 64

6 a 4 and 5   **b** 8 and 9   **c** 12 and 13

7 a 343   **b** 15   **c** 1.331   **d** 1.6   **e** 40.841 01   **f** 30

8 a 5   **b** 5   **c** 6   **d** 4

2.2 Purposeful practice

1 a 12   **b** 27   **c** 48

2 The digits 2, 3, 7, and 8 cannot be the last digit in a square number.

3 a Not a square number; the ones digit is 3

   b Not a square number; the ones digit is 2

   c Could be a square number; it is 27^2

   d Not a square number; the ones digit is 7

4 a, b; $4^4 = 2^8 = 256$ | **5** 42

6 a Yes   **b** No   **c** Yes

2.3 Factors and prime factorisation

2.3.1 Understanding factors of numbers

Your turn! 1   1, 2, 4, 5, 10, 20 | **Your turn! 2**   No

2.3.1 Fluency

1 a 1, 5   **b** 1, 2, 3, 4, 6, 12

   c 1, 2, 3, 4, 5, 6, 8, 10, 12, 15, 20, 24, 30, 40, 60, 120

2 a True   **b** False   **c** True   **d** False

3 a 1, 2, 4, 5, 8, 10, 20, 25, 40, 50, 100, 200

   b 1, 3, 5, 9, 15, 25, 45, 75, 225

   c 1, 2, 4, 5, 10, 17, 20, 34, 68, 85, 170, 340

   d 1, 2, 4, 5, 8, 10, 20, 25, 40, 50, 100, 125, 200, 250, 500, 1000

4 3, 5, 36, 40 | **5** 8, 15

6 a Even   **c** Odd   **e** Odd

   b Odd   **d** Even   **f** Odd

2.3.2 Prime numbers

Your turn! 1   No, e.g. it's divisible by 3

Your turn! 2   10, 12, and 144 are composite; 11 is prime

2.3.2 Fluency

1 two; 1; itself

2 2, 3, 5, 7, 11, 13 | **3** 13, 17, 19

4 29, 67, 89 | **5** $93 = 3 \times 31$

6 73 does not divide by 2, 3, 5, or 7

7 101 | **8** 1041 divides by 3

9 887 does not divide by 2, 3, 5, 7, 11, 13, 17, 19, 23, or 29

2.3.3 Prime factorisation

Your turn! 1 $60 = 2^2 \times 3 \times 5$

2.3.3 Fluency

1 **a** $2^2 \times 3$ **b** $2 \times 3^2 \times 5$ **c** $2^2 \times 5^2$ **d** $2^4 \times 3^2$

2 **a** $2^3 \times 3 \times 5$ **c** $2^6 \times 5$ **e** $2 \times 5^2 \times 13$
 b $2^3 \times 5^2$ **d** $5^2 \times 19$ **f** $2^3 \times 5^3$

3 **a** $7^2 \times 11$ **b** $7 \times 11 \times 13$ **c** $7^2 \times 17$ **d** $7^3 \times 11 \times 13$

2.3.4 Using prime factorisation to identify properties of numbers

Your turn! 1 $392 = 2 \times 2 \times 2 \times 7 \times 7$

Your turn! 2 $675 = 3^3 \times 5^2$

2.3.4 Fluency

1 **a** No **b** Yes **c** No **d** Yes

2 **a** Yes **b** No **c** Yes **d** Yes **e** No **f** Yes

3 **a** Both **b** Neither **c** Cube **d** Square **e** Square

2.3.5 Highest common factor using prime factorisation

Your turn! 1 21

2.3.5 Fluency

1 **a** 2 **b** 20

2 **a** 8 **b** 4 **c** 12 **d** 24

3 **a** 5 **b** 15 **c** 15 **d** 5

4 **a** 2 **b** 18 **c** 12 **d** 12

5 **a** 4 **b** 20 **c** 11 **d** 145

2.3.6 Lowest common multiple using prime factorisation

Your turn! 1 210

2.3.6 Fluency

1 **a** 35 **b** 24 **c** 45 **d** 54

2 **a** 765 **b** 450 **c** 225 **d** 1530

3 **a** 2170 **b** 540 **c** 1560 **d** 6480

4 **a** 4350 **b** 6300 **c** 12 705 **d** 120

2.3 Exercises

2.3 Intelligent practice

1 **a** 1, 2, 4, 7, 14, 28 **c** 1, 7, 11, 77
 b 1, 2, 3, 6, 7, 14, 21, 42 **d** 1, 7

2 **a** 2 **b** 2 **c** 2 **d** 2
 e They all have two factors and are prime numbers

3 **a** 3 **b** 7 **c** 5
 d They all have an odd number of factors and are square numbers

4 **a** 2×7 **d** $2 \times 5 \times 7$ **g** $2 \times 2 \times 5 \times 5 \times 5$
 b $2 \times 2 \times 7$ **e** 5×7 **h** $2 \times 5 \times 5$
 c $2 \times 2 \times 2 \times 5 \times 7$ **f** $2 \times 2 \times 5 \times 5 \times 5 \times 7$ **i** $2 \times 2 \times 5 \times 5 \times 5 \times 5$

5 **a** 189, 198, 918 **b** 198, 918 **c** 198, 918 **d** 189, 918

6 **a** 5 **c** $2 \times 5 = 10$ **e** $2 \times 5 = 10$ **g** 1
 b 5 **d** $2 \times 5 = 10$ **f** $2 \times 3 = 6$

7 **a** 42 **b** 30 **c** 30 **d** 30 **e** 90 **f** 180

2.3 Method selection

1 **a** $42 = 2 \times 3 \times 7$ **b** 2, 3, 7 **c** 1, 6, 14, 21, 42

2 83, 89

3 **a** 1, 2, 3, 4, 6, 8, 12, 16, 24, 48 **c** 1, 2, 4, 8, 16; Tallest = 16
 b 1, 2, 4, 8, 16, 32

4 40

5 **a** True **b** False **c** True **d** False

6 $585 = 3^2 \times 5 \times 13$; $455 = 5 \times 7 \times 13$

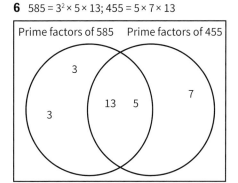

Prime factors of 585	Prime factors of 455
3	7
3	13 5

7 $187 = 11 \times 17$; $935 = 5 \times 11 \times 17$
 LCM = 935, since it is a multiple of 187

8 **a** $450 = 2 \times 3^2 \times 5^2$ (not all of the exponents are even)
 b multiply by 2 **c** 30

9 **a** 98×6 **b** 28×21 **c** 14×42

10 1890

11 $1728 = 2^6 \times 3^3$, so it is a cube number

2.3 Purposeful practice

1 28

2 **a** 1 **b** 2 **c** 4 **d** 6 **e** 16

3 2, 3, 4, 5, 6, 8, 10, 11, 12, 13

4 **a** $1764 = 2 \times 2 \times 3 \times 3 \times 7 \times 7$, so it is a square number
 b $2221 = 2221$, so it is prime
 c $2310 = 2 \times 3 \times 5 \times 7 \times 11$, so it is a multiple of 11
 d $2744 = 2 \times 2 \times 2 \times 7 \times 7 \times 7$, so it is a cube number

5 **a** True **b** False **c** False **d** True

6 Five (33, 34, 35, 38, 39)

7 51 (factors are 1, 3, 17, 51), 91 (factors are 1, 7, 13, 91), or any prime multiple, p, of 19 (factors are 1, 19, p, $19 \times p$)

8 **a** 9:15 a.m. **b** 8

9 6 (this counts e.g. 5×63 and 63×5 as the same array)

10 899; multiply the two numbers **11** 638

12 1; all numbers are divisible by 1 and themselves

13 There are infinite multiples of any two or more numbers

14 Square numbers have all even exponents of their prime factors. If you multiply two square numbers the result will also have all even exponents. E.g.
 $4 = 2^2$ $25 = 5^2$ $100 = 2^2 \times 5^2$

Chapter 2 summary

Watch out! (full answers on Kerboodle)

1 **a** 9^5 **2** **a** 216

3 **a** $2 \times 2 \times 3 \times 3 \times 5$ **4** **a** 6

5 **a** 60 **6** **a** 8

7 **a** 1, 2, 4, 7, 14, 28

3 Arithmetic

Reactivate your knowledge

3.1 Addition and subtraction with negative integers

1

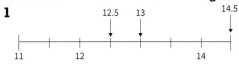

2 a 114 > 113   **b** 71.5 < 71.9   **c** 92.2 > 86.7

3.2 Multiplication and division with negative integers,
3.3 Addition and subtraction with decimals, and
3.4 Multiplication and division with decimals

3 a 6×4, $24 \div 4$ **b** 1×7, $7 \div 7$ **c** 8×2, $16 \div 2$

4 a 3, 6, 9, 12, 15, 18, 21, 24, 27, 30
   b 7, 14, 21, 28, 35, 42, 49, 56, 63, 70
   c 12, 24, 36, 48, 60, 72, 84, 96, 108, 120

5 a E.g. $563 = 500 + 60 + 3$ **c** E.g. $20\,937 = 20\,900 + 30 + 7$
   b E.g. $6293 = 6200 + 93$

6 a 243   **b** 230.75   **c** 62.3

7 a 480   **b** 35 000   **c** 30   **d** 80

8 a 1640   **b** 873 000   **c** 2.405   **d** 6.3822

9 a 4.8503   **b** 82   **c** 19 300   **d** 658 000

3.5 Efficient calculations

10 a 289   **b** 91.125   **c** 10.4976   **d** 59 049

11 a 18   **b** 4.4 (to 1 d.p.) **c** 8   **d** 3.5 (to 1 d.p.)

3.1 Addition and subtraction with negative integers

3.1.1 Negative integers

Your turn! 1 $-4 < -2$

Your turn! 2 $-58, -55, -52, -50, 0, 53, 57$

3.1.1 Fluency

1

2 a −7   **b** −1   **c** 5

3 a −2   **b** 4   **4** $-4, -3, 0, 1, 6$

5 a >   **b** <   **c** >   **d** =   **e** >

6

7 $15, 11, 6, 2, -6, -12$ **8** $-3, -2, -1, 0, 1$

9 $-5, -4, -3, -2, -1, 0$

3.1.2 Addition with negative integers

Your turn! 1 5

3.1.2 Fluency

1 a 18   **c** 4   **e** −3   **g** 12   **i** −10
   b −1   **d** −3   **f** 3   **h** −9   **j** −17

2 a −9   **b** −13   **c** −9   **d** −19   **e** 18   **f** −3

3 a <   **b** <

3.1.3 Introduction to subtraction with negative integers

Your turn! 1 5

3.1.3 Fluency

1 a 5   **b** −2   **c** 4   **d** −5   **e** −1   **f** 2

2 a −12   **b** 8   **c** −9   **d** 11

3 a <   **b** >   **c** >   **d** <

3.1.4 More addition and subtraction with negative integers

Your turn! 1 9

3.1.4 Fluency

1 a 8 **b** −5 **c** 4 **d** −4 **e** −23 **f** 16 **g** 66 **h** −73

2 a + **b** − **c** −

3 a 20 **b** 25 **c** −31 **d** 85 **e** −37 **f** 129

4 a < **b** > **c** > **d** <

3.1 Exercises

3.1 Intelligent practice

1 a 2   **c** −16   **e** −20   **g** 20   **i** 4   **k** 2
   b −2   **d** −160   **f** −20   **h** 2   **j** 2

2 a True   **c** True   **e** False   **g** True
   b False   **d** False   **f** True   **h** True

3 See table below

	Original	Rewritten	Model	Answer
a	$-3 - -5$	$-3 + (+5)$	(−1)(−1)(−1) + (+1)(+1)(+1)(+1)(+1)	2
b	$-5 + -3$	$-5 + (-3)$	(−1)(−1)(−1)(−1)(−1) + (−1)(−1)(−1)	−8
c	$-3 + 5$	$-3 + 5$	(−1)(−1)(−1) + (+1)(+1)(+1)(+1)(+1)	2
d	$6 + -5 + 3$	$6 + (-5) + 3$	(+1)(+1)(+1)(+1)(+1)(+1) + (−1)(−1)(−1)(−1)(−1) + (1)(1)(1)	4
e	$6 - 5 - 3$	$6 + (-5) + (-3)$	(+1)(+1)(+1)(+1)(+1)(+1) + (−1)(−1)(−1)(−1)(−1) + (−1)(−1)(−1)	−2
f	$5 - 6 - 3$	$5 + (-6) + (-3)$	(+1)(+1)(+1)(+1)(+1) + (−1)(−1)(−1)(−1)(−1)(−1) + (−1)(−1)(−1)	−4

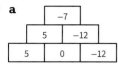

3.1 Method selection

1 −2 °C

2 820, 297, 438, 42, 356

3 a

```
        -7
    5       -12
  5     0     -12
```

c

```
        15
    7       8
  8    -1     9
```

b

```
        -8
   -5       -3
 -13     8    -11
```

d

```
        -8
  -16       8
 -11    -5    13
```

4 a −3   **c** 5   **e** −4   **g** −6
   b −17   **d** −7   **f** 20

5 a triangle: − 3, star: 5   **b** rhombus: − 4, cloud: − 9

6 a 358   **b** 1215   **c** 48

3.1 Purposeful practice

1 E.g. −2 − 2 − 5 − (−5) = −4   −2 − 2 + 5 + (−5) = −4

−2 + 2 − 5 − (−5) = 0   −2 + 2 + 5 − (−5) = 10

−2 + 2 + 5 + (−5) = 0   2 − (−2) + 5 − (−5) = 14

−2 − 2 − 5 + (−5) = −14   2 − (−2) + 5 + (−5) = 4

2 a 1, − 7, 9   **b** −15, 17

3 a E.g. −2 − 1 ; 0 − 3 ; 3 − 6
   b E.g. 1 + −2 + (−2) ; 6 − 8 + (−1)

4 a No   **b** 6 answers: 1, − 1, 11, − 11, 27, − 27

5 a i Place 2 in the centre space   **ii** 3
   b, c, d Student answers

6 a i −2   **ii** −2   **iii** 2   **iv** 2   **v** Student answers
   b All zero
   c i −4   **ii** −4   **iii** 4   **iv** 4   **v** Student answers
   d Student answers

7 a ⊖ + ⊖ = ⊖   **j** ⊕ + ⊖ = 0

b ⊕ + ⊖ = ⊕   **k** ⊖ − ⊖ = ⊖

c ⊖ + ⊕ = ⊕   **l** ⊕ − ⊕ = ⊕

d ⊕ + ⊖ = ⊖   **m** ⊖ + ⊖ = ⊖

e ⊖ + ⊕ = ⊖   **n** ⊕ − ⊕ = ⊖

f ⊕ − ⊕ = ⊕   **o** ⊖ + ⊕ = ⊕

g ⊖ − ⊕ = ⊖   **p** ⊕ − ⊖ = ⊕

h ⊕ − ⊕ = ⊖   **q** ⊖ + ⊕ = ⊖

i ⊖ − ⊖ = ⊕

3.2 Multiplication and division with negative integers

3.2.1 Multiplying integers

Your turn! 1 −6, − 12, − 18, − 24

3.2.1 Fluency

1 a 20   **b** −21   **c** −30   **d** −32   **e** −27

2 a 240   **b** −120   **c** −350   **d** −3200   **e** −2700

3 −7, − 14, − 21, − 28, − 35   **4** −12, − 24, − 36, − 48, − 60, − 72

5 a 156   **b** −120   **c** −140
   d Student explanations, e.g. multiplying two positive or two negative numbers gives a positive answer. If the signs are different, the answer is negative.

6 a >   **b** >   **c** <   **d** <

3.2.2 Multiplying two or more negative numbers

Your turn! 1 57

3.2.2 Fluency

1 a 21   **b** 24   **c** 72   **d** 88

2 a 60   **c** 72   **e** 175   **g** 186
   b 120   **d** 105   **f** 152   **h** 287

3 a 36   **b** 64   **c** −27   **d** 10 000   **e** 625   **f** −32
Student explanations for each part, e.g. raising a negative number to an even power gives a positive answer whereas if the power is odd, the answer is negative. Positive numbers raised to any power are always positive.

3.2.3 Dividing integers

Your turn! 1 −4 | **Your turn! 2** −34

3.2.3 Fluency

1 a 5   **b** −8   **c** −5   **d** 9

2 a 8   **b** −25   **c** −20   **d** 21
Student explanations, e.g. dividing two positive or two negative numbers gives a positive answer. If the signs are different, the answer is negative.

3 a −5   **b** −20   **c** −17   **d** −14   **e** 13   **f** 12

3.2 Exercises

3.2 Intelligent practice

1 a 72   **c** −72   **e** −720   **g** −7200   **i** −7200
   b −72   **d** 72   **f** −720   **h** 7200   **j** 7200

2 a 9   **d** 9   **g** −180   **j** −60
   b −9   **e** −90   **h** 18   **k** 90
   c −9   **f** 9   **i** −60   **l** −30

3 a

×	10	−5
10	100	−50
8	−80	40

c

×	22	−17
−5	−110	85
7	154	−119

b

×	12	−7
−10	−120	70
12	144	−84

4 a 9   **c** −27   **e** 810 000
   b 9   **d** 81   **f** −24 300 000

3.2 Method selection

1 a 270 000 000 , two hundred and seventy million
b 32 200 000 , thirty-two million, two hundred thousand
c 3 624 000 , three million, six hundred and twenty-four thousand
d 125 , one hundred and twenty-five
e 1500 , one thousand five hundred
f 10 288, ten thousand, two hundred and eighty eight

2 a $-3, -6, -9, -12, -15$ **d** $-4, -8, -12, -16, -20$
b $-9, -18, -27, -36, -45$ **e** $-40, -80, -120, -160, -200$
c $-12, -24, -36, -48, -60$ **f** $-80, -160, -240, -320, -400$

3 225 feet below

4 a Sum $= 10$, Product $= 16$ **i** 6, 2
b 9, Sum $= 7$ **j** -4, Sum $= 2$
c 6, 3   **k** Sum $= -11$, Product $= 30$
d Sum $= 10$, Product $= 24$ **l** 3, Sum $= 7$
e Sum $= 8$, Product $= 16$ **m** 1, 12
f $-9, 2$ **n** Sum $= -1$, Product $= -30$
g $-6, -3$ **o** Sum $= -7$, Product $= -30$
h 8, Product $= 32$

5 a

$\times$	-7	-3
-7	49	21
-3	21	9

d

$\times$	9	-7
4	36	-28
-5	-45	35

b

$\times$	-7	-3
-7	49	21
3	-21	-9

e

$\times$	-6	-8
-6	36	48
8	-48	-64

c

$\times$	5	-4
5	25	-20
4	20	-16

f

$\times$	-9	7
-4	36	-28
-5	45	-35

3.2 Purposeful practice

1 a $-5 \times 8 + (-9) = -49$ **d** $-9 \times (-5) - 8 = 37$
b $-5 \times (-9) + (-7) = 38$ **e** $-9 \times 6 - (-5) = -49$
c $-9 \times 6 + 8 = -46$ **f** $-7 \times 8 - (-5) = -51$

2 Student answers for example:
A $-7 + 2$ **B** -1×5 **C** $7 \times (-3)$ **D** $-6 - 4$

3 Student answers, for example:
A $3 \times (-2) + 4$ **D** $\dfrac{5 \times (-1) + 4 - 3}{2}$ **G** $\dfrac{-8}{4}$
B $5 \times 2 - 16 + 4$ **E** $\dfrac{3 \times (-4)}{2} + 4$ **H** $-3 + 1$
C $4 - 6$ **F** $\dfrac{3 \times 4 - 8}{-2}$

4 For example:
a $-3 \times 8 - (-7)$ **b** $8 \times (-7) - 4 - (-3)$ **c** $(-7) \times (-3) + 4$

3.3 Addition and subtraction with decimals

3.3.1 Adding and subtracting positive decimals

Your turn! 1 34.23

3.3.1 Fluency

1 a 48.8   **b** 182.6   **c** 92.3   **d** 181.8

2 a 178.1   **c** 24.4   **e** 20.1414
b 373.474   **d** 85.74   **f** 11.8689

3 1000   **4** 350

3.3.2 Negative decimals

Your turn! 1 $<$

3.3.2 Fluency

1 Any five decimals greater than 43.1

2 a -0.5 **b** 0.1   **c** 0.4

3 a -4.5 **b** 1.5   **c** 3.5

4 $-4.8, -2.8, -2.2, 2, 3, 3.6, 4$

5 a $>$ **b** $<$ **c** $=$ **d** $>$

6

7 a Any five integers greater than -7
b Any five decimals less than -3.5

8 Any three decimals between -5 and -3 (not inclusive)

9 a Infinitely   **c** Corresponding
b Infinitely   **d** Infinitely

3.3.3 Adding and subtracting positive and negative decimals

Your turn! 1 27.32   **Your turn! 2** -44.78

3.3.3 Fluency

1 a -3.4 **b** 7.89   **c** -2.67 **d** -0.39

2 a -6.37 **b** -27.18 **c** -5.86 **d** 1.94

3 a $<$ **b** $<$ **c** $>$ **d** $<$ **e** $>$ **f** $<$

3.3 Exercises

3.3 Intelligent practice

1 a i -0.5 **iii** -0.05 **v** 0.55
   ii -0.2 **iv** 0.2   **vi** 0.85
 b i -0.08 **iii** -0.025 **v** 0.045
   ii -0.05 **iv** 0.02   **vi** 0.08
 c i -1.5 **iii** -0.65 **v** -0.15
   ii -1.1 **iv** -0.5 **vi** 0.3

2 a $<$ **c** $<$ **e** $<$ **g** $<$ **i** $>$
 b $>$ **d** $>$ **f** $>$ **h** $<$

3 a 7.7   **c** 18.1   **e** 8.9   **g** 0.89
 b 8.1   **d** 18.14   **f** 0.89

4 a 7.5   **c** 2.1   **e** 44.2   **g** 4.42
 b 7.5   **d** 1.9   **f** 4.42   **h** 4.42

5 a 0   **e** -6.7 **i** 0.93   **m** -70.01
 b -0.3 **f** -0.67 **j** 0.93   **n** -70.01
 c 0.3   **g** -0.93 **k** 9.3
 d -6.7 **h** 0.67   **l** 9.3

3.3 Method selection

1 a

	1.6	
0.4	1.2	
1.2	−0.8	2

c

	−35.16	
−18.23	−16.93	
−7.2	−11.03	−5.9

b

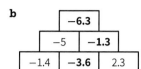

	−6.3	
−5	−1.3	
−1.4	−3.6	2.3

d

	−27.93	
−12.48	−15.45	
5.02	−17.5	2.05

2 a −2.8   **c** −2.7   **e** −3.6   **g** 10.97
b −7   **d** −0.7   **f** 24.3

3 a −2.5   **d** −55   **g** −4.5   **j** −63.8
b 17.5   **e** 2.27   **h** −6.9
c 2.5   **f** 8.8   **i** 30.06

4 a 5.3   **b** 15.18   **c** 17.13

3.3 Purposeful practice

1 a E.g. 6.3 + 5 + 4.21 = 15.51 ; 1.5 + 2 + 3.46 = 6.96
b 1.5 + 2 + 3.46

2 a E.g. 6.5 − 1 − 2.34 = 3.16 ; 1.2 − 6 − 5.43 = −10.23
b 3.5 − 1 − 2.46 = 0.04

3 For example:
a A 3.5 + 2.3   **b A** 1.4 − 3.57
   B 1.52 + (−6.22)   **B** 4.54 − 9.24
   C −6 + 1.3   **C** 2.9 − 7.6

3.4 Multiplication and division with decimals

3.4.1 Multiplying positive decimals

Your turn! 1   0.000 08   **Your turn! 2**   19.836

3.4.1 Fluency

1 a 12 000   **b** 320 000   **c** 2 700 000

2 a 9.43   **b** 33.28   **c** 49.29

3 a 0.021   **c** 0.000 16   **e** 0.000 003 5
b 0.003   **d** 0.000 024

4 a 4.68   **c** 38.908   **e** 18.2182
b 14.484   **d** 42.09

5 b and **f** are different.

3.4.2 Dividing positive decimals

Your turn! 1   9.8   **Your turn! 2**   18.75

3.4.2 Fluency

1 a 4   **b** 40   **c** 0.06

2 a 7.8   **b** 1.16   **c** 12.36

3 a 40   **b** 500   **c** 80   **d** 30 000

4 a 2370   **b** 1650   **c** 11 600   **d** 49 000

5 a 16 000   **b** 1 000 000   **c** 280 000

6 b and **f** are different.

3.4.3 Multiplying and dividing negative decimals

Your turn! 1   3.107   **Your turn! 2**   −68

3.4.3 Fluency

1 a 4.48   **b** −21.58   **c** −56.7

2 a −1.7   **b** −1.24   **c** 14.53

3 a −0.02   **c** −0.000 042
b 0.0024   **d** −0.000 003 6

4 a −60   **b** 300   **c** −80   **d** 0.6

5 a −5.46   **b** 8.532   **c** −57.28   **d** 17.1226

6 a 1140   **b** −1320   **c** −9600   **d** 55 000

7 d and **f**   **8 c** and **e**

3.4 Exercises

3.4 Intelligent practice

1 a 5.16   **c** 14.28   **e** 0.2856
b 7.14   **d** 2.856   **f** 0.2856

2 a 0.72   **c** 0.234   **e** 0.243   **g** 2.432 43
b 0.144   **d** 0.234   **f** 0.0243   **h** 0.243 243

3 a 2.16   **c** 2.16   **e** 0.216   **g** 0.017 28
b 0.002 16   **d** 0.0216   **f** 0.004 32

4 a −2.4   **c** −4.8   **e** −3.6   **g** 720   **i** −144
b 2.4   **d** 14.4   **f** −0.072   **h** −720

5 a 2.52   **d** 0.042   **g** 180   **j** 21   **m** 60
b 1.4   **e** 4200   **h** 1.8   **k** −21
c 0.014   **f** 140   **i** 0.9   **l** −21

6 a 0.45   **b** 0.3   **c** 0.3   **d** −3   **e** −0.9

3.4 Method selection

1 a 0.015; fifteen thousandths
b 0.368; three hundred and sixty-eight thousandths
c 0.0312; three hundred and twelve ten-thousandths
d 1375; one thousand three hundred and seventy-five
e 24 000; twenty-four thousand

2 a Sum = 7.4, Product = 8.4   **e** Sum = 5.8, Product = 8.4
b Sum = 6.7, Product = 4.2   **f** Sum = 7.1, Product = 8.4
c 6, Sum = 6.4   **g** 4, Sum = −1
d 2, Product = 0.8   **h** −4, Sum = −19

3 a

×	0.3	0.7
2.6	0.78	1.82
3.9	1.17	2.73

c

×	3.27	0.555
−0.2	−0.654	−0.111
−3.8	−12.426	−2.109

b

×	0.08	0.12
5.73	0.4584	0.6876
1.8	0.144	0.216

4 30   **5** No, the parcels weight 72 kg

6 58 pieces (493 cm so 7 cm left)

7 a 30 000 pencils   **d** 6 tickets   **g** 12 boxes
b £1470   **e** 30 books   **h** 7.35 cm
c £2.45   **f** £88.20

3.4 Purposeful practice

1 a 12, 12.25, 30, 30.25, 42.25, 110.25

b Multiply the whole number before and after and add a quarter $(n+0.5)(n-0.5) = n^2 - 0.25$ so $n^2 = (n+0.5)(n-0.5) + 0.25$

2 Student answers, for example:

A 2×4 **B** 0.5×16 **C** 1.4×6.5 **D** $56 \div 8$

3 Student answers, for example:

A 2×6 **D** $15.5 + (-3.5)$ **G** $-10 \div (-2)$

B 0.5×12 **E** $-15 + 27$ **H** 1.3×7

C $20.59 + 0.1$ **F** $1.5 \times (-3)$

4 a i 2.5×3.4 **ii** 3.2×4.5 **iii** 3.5×4.2

   b i $3.5 \div 2.4$ **ii** $2.3 \div 4.5$ **iii** $3.5 \div 4.2$

5 a E.g. 25 m of gold, blue and silver or 175 m of green

   b One fabric: 175 m of green

3.5 Efficient calculations

3.5.1 The commutative and associative laws

Your turn! 1 1120

3.5.1 Fluency

1 a Student explanations, e.g. you can change the order of the numbers in addition and multiplication calculations.

   b i 27   **ii** 57   **iii** 180   **iv** 2900

2 a Student explanations, e.g. you can add or multiply numbers in any order.

   b i 190   **ii** 1300   **iii** 28   **iv** 131

3 **a**, **b**, **e** and **g** are all true; for the false ones, review student explanations.

4 a Student explanations, e.g. subtracting a negative is the same as adding, then the commutative law is used to change the order of the operations so that the calculation is easier to do.

   b i 2   **ii** 4.49   **iii** 10.78   **iv** 4.77

5 a Student explanations, e.g. the associative law has been used to calculate -2×-5 before multiplying by 2.1

   b i 36   **ii** 81   **iii** 832   **iv** -923

3.5.2 Factorising numbers to multiply and divide

Your turn! 1 660   **Your turn! 2** 43

3.5.2 Fluency

1 a Student explanations, e.g. 45 and 12 are decomposed into 9×5 and 2×6, then $5 \times 2 = 10$ and the calculation becomes $54 \times 10 = 540$

   b i 910   **iii** 840   **v** 30 500

     ii 990   **iv** 3600   **vi** 64 800

2 a Student explanations, e.g. dividing by 6 has been split into dividing by 3 and then by 2 to make the calculation easier.

   b i 55   **iii** 35   **v** 240

     ii 87   **iv** 250   **vi** 540

3 a -70 **c** 7.7   **e** 54

   b 40   **d** -6.3 **f** -8.4

3.5.3 The distributive law

Your turn! 1 133

3.5.3 Fluency

1 a Student explanations, e.g. you can split a 2-digit number into the tens and the units and multiply each part separately.

   b i 54   **ii** 144   **iii** 110   **iv** 252

2 a Student explanations, e.g. the distributive law has been used on the first number and then the second number to make the calculation easier.

   b i 224   **ii** 276   **iii** 399   **iv** 552   **v** 1428

3 a Student explanations, e.g. the 153 has been split into two parts so each part can be divided separately, before adding the answers.

   b i 17   **ii** 23   **iii** 24   **iv** 34   **v** 39

4 a Student explanations, e.g. 99 has been changed to $100 - 1$ and then the distributive law has been used to make the calculation easier.

   b i 178.2   **ii** 441   **iii** 1248.75   **iv** 2495

3.5.4 Priority of operations

Your turn! 1 5   **Your turn! 2** 4.53

3.5.4 Fluency

1 a 35   **b** 48   **c** 3

2 a 9.84   **b** 9.96   **c** 100

3 a 42   **b** 31   **c** 24   **d** 26   **e** -8

4 a 24.16   **c** 53.9   **e** 540.24

   b -48.34 **d** 1014.058

5 a 9   **b** 37   **c** 4   **d** 56

6 Using estimations: $4 \times (2+3) \div (10-6) = 4 \times 5 \div 4 = 5$

7 Using estimations:

$(4+2)^2 - (8+2) \div (12 - 5 \times 2) = 36 - 10 \div 2 = 31$

3.5 Exercises

3.5 Intelligent practice

1 a 24   **c** 4   **e** 2.4   **g** 184

   b 240   **d** 24   **f** 18.4

2 a 120   **d** 26   **g** 76   **j** 120

   b 120   **e** 34   **h** 68   **k** 260

   c 120   **f** 46   **i** 80   **l** 2.6

3 a 9   **c** 31   **e** 36   **g** 10   **i** 10

   b 25   **d** 31   **f** 14   **h** 10

4 a 3.4   **c** 5.44   **e** 4.32

   b 3.4   **d** 4.24   **f** 4.26

5 a 39   **b** 60   **c** 51   **d** 84

6 a 3   **b** 300   **c** 3   **d** 12

7 a 58   **c** 108   **e** 130

   b 88   **d** 304   **f** 420

8 a 84   **c** 27   **e** 6.1   **g** 2.1   **i** 0.9

   b 45   **d** 10   **f** 1.1   **h** 2.1

9 a 4   **e** 3   **i** 4   **m** 28   **q** -60

   b 3.25   **f** 3   **j** -12 **n** 1.5   **r** 180

   c 39   **g** -3 **k** -1 **o** 0   **s** -1080

   d 14.4   **h** -24 **l** 18   **p** 18

3.5 Method selection

1 a 5   **b** 8   **c** 2   **d** 8

2 a $\times$ **c** $+$ **e** $\div$ **g** $+ \times$

   b $\div$ **d** $-$ **f** $\times -$

3 a $3 \times (2+7) - 1 = 26$ **d** $(2+3) \times (4+7) = 55$

   b $6 \times (2+3) \times 5 = 150$ **e** $2 + (3 \times 5 - 7) \times 4 = 34$

   c $7 + 5 \times (2-3) = 2$

4
a B		**c** G		**e** D		**g** C	
b A		**d** H		**f** E		**h** F	

5 Three bottles of water

6 a i 10 000 **iii** 300 000   **d i** 200 **iv** 360
     ii 100 000   **ii** 8000 **v** 20 m
  b 20   **iii** 400
  c i 1000 **ii** 2

7 £43.10

8 No. The boxes total 1317.5 kg, which exceeds the lift's limit.

3.5 Purposeful practice

1 a $-4 \times 6 + 5 = -19$ **f** $5 \times 6 - -4 = 34$
   b $-5 \times -6 + 4 = 34$ **g** $4 \times -5 - 6 = -26$
   c $-6 \times 7 + 3 = -39$ **h** $3 \times 7 - -6 = 27$
   d $-3 \times -7 + 6 = 27$ **i** $-3 \times 6 - -7 = -11$
   e $2 \times -5 + -8 = -18$ **j** $2 \times -5 - -8 = -2$

2 For example:
   A $(2 + 2 + 1) \times 3$ **E** $(-1 + 3) \times (2 + 6) - 1$
   B $(2 + 1)^2 + 5 + 1$ **F** $-7 + 5^2 + 2 - 5$
   C $5^2 - 6 \times 2 + 2$ **G** $-3 + 8 + 9 + 1$
   D $(-1 + 4)^2 \times 2 - 3$ **H** $2 \times 6 + 4 - 1$

3 There are 54 possible calculations.

4 a Associative   **d** Distributive
   b Commutative   **e** Distributive
   c Commutative   **f** Distributive and commutative

5 It is possible to make all integers 1-20

Chapter 3 summary

Watch out!

1 a $(-10) + (-8) = -18$			**2 a** 10	
3 a 30	**4 a** 0		**5 a** 10	
6 a 1	**7 a** 17		**8 a** 3.2	

4 Expressions and equations

Reactivate your knowledge

4.1 Introduction to algebra

1 a 108	**b** 56	**c** 33	
2 a $\dfrac{5}{11}$	**b** $\dfrac{30}{13}$	**c** $4 \div 25$	**d** $19 \div 6$
3 a 16	**b** 1	**c** 144	
4 a 2	**c** -6	**e** -2	
b -8.05	**d** -8.1	**f** -9.86	
5 a -15	**b** 12	**c** -2	**d** 5
6 a 3	**b** 5	**c** 58	**d** 28

4.2 Formulae and equations and 4.3 Simplifying equations

7 a 8	**b** 4	**c** 7	**d** 5

4.4 Using the distributive law

8 a 2	**b** 15	**c** 12	**9 a** 85	**b** 342	**c** 36

4.1 Introduction to algebra

4.1.1 Algebraic thinking

Your turn! 1   **a** 12 years old   **c** $x + 8$ years old
                  b 17 years old

4.1.1 Fluency

1 a 6	**b** 7	**c** 13	**d** $n + 3$
2 a 6	**b** 7	**c** 17	**d** $n - 3$
3 a 5	**b** 15	**c** 21	**d** $n \times 2 + 1$
4 a 3	**b** 6	**c** 12.5	**d** $\dfrac{n}{2}$ or $n \div 2$

5 a £15   **b** $£\left(\dfrac{x}{20} + 5\right)$ or $£(x \div 20 + 5)$

   c $£\left(\dfrac{x-1}{20} + 5\right)$ or $£(x - 1) \div 20 + 5$

   d $£\left(\dfrac{3 \times x}{20} + 5\right)$ or $£(3 \times x) \div 20 + 5$

4.1.2 Algebraic notation

Your turn! 1 a $3q$ pens   **b** nq pens

4.1.2 Fluency

1 **a**, **c** and **f** are expressions

2 a 2	**b** 3	**c** 1	**d** 2
3 a $5x$	**b** $7y$	**c** $-4a$	**d** $\dfrac{b}{3}$
4 a $5x$	**b** nx	**c** $2nx$	
5 a 2	**b** 3	**c** 2	**d** 3

6 a $\dfrac{6}{w}$	**b** 6^2 or 36	**c** y^2	**d** x^3	**e** $2yz$
7 a $3x^3$	**b** $8x^2$	**c** $2my$	**d** $\dfrac{12x^2 y}{c}$	

4.1.3 Generalising relationships

Your turn! 1   **a** 20 minutes   **c** $\dfrac{x}{3} + 10$ minute
                 b 30 minutes

4.1.3 Fluency

1 a $x + 5$ **b** $y - 7$ **c** $8x$ **d** $\dfrac{z}{3}$

2 $5n$

3 a $2x$ **b** x^2 **c** $\dfrac{x}{y}$ **d** $3x + 2y$ **e** $2\dfrac{x}{y}$ **f** x^2

4 a $a + b$ **b** $b - a$ **c** ab **d** $2a$

5 a £2   **b** $£(3y - 10)$ **6 a** $£(4x + 12)$ **b** $£(4x + 6y)$

7 $n + n + 1 + n + 2 = 3n + 3$ **8** $3n$

4.1.4 Substitution

Your turn! 1   37   **Your turn! 2** -67

4.1.4 Fluency

1 a 7	**b** 13	**c** 37	**d** -5
2 a 7	**b** 22	**c** 157	**d** -33
3 a 6	**b** 9	**c** 17	**d** -1
4 a 3	**b** 15	**c** 80	**d** 8
5 a 15	**b** -39	**c** 30	**d** 15
6 a 50	**b** 29	**c** -60	**d** 33

4.1 Exercises

4.1 Intelligent practice

1
a $3a$
b $3a$
c $\dfrac{a}{3}$
d $\dfrac{3}{a}$

2
a a
b a
c a
d $\dfrac{1}{a}$

3
a $2a$
c a^2
e $6a^2$
g $\dfrac{a^2}{6}$
i $6a^3$

b $2a$
d $6a^2$
f $6a^2$
h $\dfrac{6}{a^2}$

4
a $8c$
c cd
e $8cd$
g $\dfrac{cd}{8}$
i $8cd^2$

b c
d cd
f $8cd$
h $8c^2d$

5
a 4
b 8
c 12
d 15
e 9
f 0
g 0
h −1.5

6
a 4
b −4
c 0
d 8
e 24
f 0
g −24
h −8

4.1 Method selection

1 9 less than a number $= x - 9$, 9 more than a number $= x + 9$, a number subtracted from 9 $= 9 - x$, 9 lots of a number $= 9x$, a number divided by 9 $= \dfrac{x}{9}$, 9 divided by a number $= \dfrac{9}{x}$, a number added to itself $= 2x$, a number multiplied by itself $= x^2$, the sum of two different numbers $= x + y$, the product of two different numbers $= xy$, the difference between two different numbers $= x - y$ (or $y - x$)

2 12, 6, 3, 9, −6, 6, 27, $\dfrac{1}{3}$, 36, −9, 15

3 1st column: $2 \times a$ (or $a \times 2$), $a \div 2$, $6 - 2 \times a$, $3 \times a \times a \div 2$
2nd column: $6a$, $a + 6$, $6 - a$, $\dfrac{6}{a}$, $6a + 2$, a^2, $6a^2$
3rd column: 60, 20, 16, −4, 0.6, 5, 62, −14, 100, 600, 150
4th column: −18, −6, 3, 9, −2, −1.5, −16, 12, 9, 54, 13.5

4
a 70
b 238
c −122
d 4
e 259.6

5
a 38
b 2515
c −387
d 333
e 54.27

6
a $\dfrac{a^2}{b} + 3ab$
c $\dfrac{ab^2}{3} - 3a^2b + \dfrac{b}{3a}$

b $3ab + a^3 - 6b$
d $\dfrac{2a}{b^2} + 15ab^3$

4.1 Purposeful practice

1 Expressions using x, y and 8
Find pairs written differently but meaning the same, for example:
$x + y$ and $y + x$, $8xy$ and $8yx$ and so on.

2
a Examples of expressions with value 50 when $x = 5$, such as $10x$, $x + 45$
b Examples of expressions with value 50 when $x = -5$, such as $-10x$, $x + 55$
c Expression that has value 50 for both 5 and −5 is $2x^2$

3
a When $x = 3$

$3x = 9$	$3 - x = 0$	$\dfrac{3}{x} = 1$
$x + 3 = 6$	$3 + x = 6$	$x + x + x = 9$
$\dfrac{x}{3} = 1$	$(3x)^2 = 81$	$3x^2 = 27$

$x - 3 = 0$

b Expressions evaluated with a different value of x; those with the same value stated

3
c
i $x + 3$ and $3 + x$, $x + x + x$ and $3x$
ii Examples of pairs that sometimes have the same value are:
$x - 3$ and $3 - x$ have same value when $x = 3$
$\dfrac{x}{3}$ and $\dfrac{3}{x}$ have same value when $x = 3$
iii Pairs that can never be equal are:
$x - 3$ and $x + 3$
Also, the following pairs, but it is unlikely students will be able to verify:
$x - 3$ and $3x^2$ $x - 3$ and $(3x)^2$ $3 - x$ and $\dfrac{3}{x}$

4
a Student's answers
b Student's answers
D and E: Not possible to fill since if a number is a multiple of 4 then it cannot be prime.

4.2 Formulae and equations

4.2.1 Function machines

Your turn! 1   38   **Your turn! 2**   24

4.2.1 Fluency

1
a 9
b 26
c 3
d −8

2
a 11
b 39
c 3
d −11

3
a 25
b 95
c 5
d −30

4
a 16
b 20
c 8
d −10

4.2.2 Formulae and substitution

Your turn! 1   8   **Your turn! 2**   −96

4.2.2 Fluency

1 c and e   **2 a** $y = 9$ **b** $y = 24$ **c** $y = 3$

3 a $y = 19$ **b** $y = 39$ **c** $y = 59$ **d** $y = -41$ **e** $y = 4$

4
a 13
b 9.5
c 26
d 15.75

5
a 9
b 51
c 33
d 13.5

6
a 21
b −20
c −9.6
d 7.65

4.2.3 Creating formulae using function machines

Your turn! 1 $y = 6x + 5$ **Your turn! 2** $y = 6(x + 5)$

4.2.3 Fluency

1
a $28\,\text{cm}^2$
b $96\,\text{cm}^2$
2 a $26\,\text{cm}$
b $50\,\text{cm}$

3
a $y = x - 8$
b $y = 8x$
c $y = x + 8$

4
a i $x \rightarrow \boxed{+8} \rightarrow y$
ii $y = x + 8$

c i $x \rightarrow \boxed{-2} \rightarrow y$
ii $x - 2$

b i $x \rightarrow \boxed{\times 4} \rightarrow y$
ii $y = 4x$

d i $x \rightarrow \boxed{\div 3} \rightarrow y$
ii $y = \dfrac{x}{3}$

5
a $y = 3(x + 8)$
c $y = \dfrac{3x + 8}{2}$

b $y = 3x + 8$
d $y = 2(3x - 8)$

6
a i $x \rightarrow \boxed{-4} \rightarrow \boxed{\times 7} \rightarrow y$
ii $y = 7(x - 4)$

b i $x \rightarrow \boxed{+6} \rightarrow \boxed{\div 2} \rightarrow y$
ii $y = \dfrac{x + 6}{2}$

4.2.4 Equations and inequalities

Your turn! 1 $4x - 3 = 9$ **Your turn! 2**   No

4.2.4 Fluency

1   a, d and f   **2**   **a**   Yes   **b**   No

3   **a** $x + 3 = 10$ **b** $6x = 10$

4   **a** $3(x - 2) = 10$ **b** $\dfrac{3(x-2)}{5} = 10$ **c** $x^2 - 2 = 10$

5   **a**   Equation   **b**   Expression   **c**   Equation   **d**   Equation

6   **a**   No   **c**   No   **e**   Yes
     b   Yes   **d**   No   **f**   No

7   **a**   No   **b**   No

4.2 Exercises

4.2 Intelligent practice

1   **a** $y = 35$ **d** $y = 100$ **g** $y = 16.5$
     b $y = 70$ **e** $y = 96$ **h** $y = 18$
     c $y = 73$ **f** $y = 33$ **i** $y = 18$

2   **a**   12   **b**   24   **c**   25   **d**   −25

3   **a**   15   **b**   35   **c**   38   **d**   56

4   **a**   **i**   29   **ii**   29   **c**   **i**   25   **ii**   361
     b   **i**   137   **ii**   137

5   **a**   Yes   **c**   No   **e**   Yes
     b   Yes   **d**   Yes   **f**   No

4.2 Method selection

1   **a** $3x + 5$, $x^2 + 3x$, $9 - x$, $xy + y^2$
     b $7x - 14 = 2$, $x + 5 = 2x$ (may also have $y = 2x$)
     c $A = \dfrac{1}{2}bh$, $y = 2x$
     d $3x > 18$, $x \neq 6$

2   **a**   52   **b**   42

3   **a** $2(x + 7) = 20$ or $2x + 14 = 20$ or $x + 7 = 10$
     b $4x = 20$

4   **a** $2(x + y)$ or $2x + 2y$ **b** $2(2x + y)$ or $4x + 2y$

5   **a** $A = xy$ **b** $A = 2xy$ **c** $A = 2x^2$

6 $n = 1, P = 7$, Yes $n = 6, P = 37$, Yes
   $n = 2, P = 13$, Yes $n = 7, P = 43$, Yes
   $n = 3, P = 19$, Yes $n = 8, P = 49$, No
   $n = 4, P = 25$, No $n = 9, P = 55$, No
   $n = 5, P = 31$, Yes $n = 10, P = 61$, Yes

7   **a**   9   **b**   **i**   14   **ii**   7

8   **a**   **i** $C = 50t + 90$ **ii**   £240
     b   **i** $C = 50t + P$ **ii**   £$(150 + P)$
     c   **i** $C = Ht + P$ **ii**   £$(3H + P)$

9   **a** $y = 18, z = 36$ **e** $y = 8450$, $z = 16\,900$
     b $y = 0, z = 0$ **f** $y = 5.12$,
     c $y = 72, z = 144$ $z = 10.24$
     d $y = 72, z = 144$

10   **a**   **i**   3 or −3   **ii**   7 or −7
     b   When $x = 2$, $\sqrt{2 \times 2 - 5} = \sqrt{-1}$ but you cannot find the square root of a negative number

11   **a**   Yes   **c**   No   **e**   Yes   **g**   Yes   **i**   Yes
      b   No   **d**   Yes   **f**   No   **h**   No

4.2 Purposeful practice

1   **a**   Examples of function machines
     b   Formulae written from their function machines
     c   Student's answers. Note that multiplying and dividing can be done in either order, as can adding and subtracting functions
       a) $x \rightarrow + 4 \rightarrow x\,6 \rightarrow y$ b) $y = 6(x + 4)$

2   **a**   Examples of equations or inequalities that are satisfied by $x = 8$ or $x < 8$ are, for example, $2x = 16$, $x - 4 = 4$, $x + 2 < 15$
     b   Alter equations and inequalities so that $x = 5$ satisfies them, for example, $2x = 10$, $x - 4 = 1$, $x + 2 < 15$

3   E.g. $P = 3r + s + t$, $A = 2r^2$, $A = st$, $s = r$, $t = 2r$

4   **a**   Student's answers
     b   Student's answers
       E: Not possible since if $a > 5$ then b would have to be negative in order for $a + b \geq 5$,
       but then ab would be a negative value so not equal to 20

4.3 Simplifying expressions

4.3.1 Identifying like terms

Your turn! 1 a   −3   **b**   5   **c**   −8

4.3.1 Fluency

1   **a**   Four   **b**   4

2   **a**   140   **b** $14x$ **3**   **a**   10   **b**   −2

4 $4a$, $3a$, $-5a$, $2a$, $4a$, $-4a$, $12a$
     a^2, $4a^2$, $-3a^2$
     6, -7, 10
     $5b$
     $-b^2$

5   **a** $-7x$, $+8x$, $+4x$ **b** $-3x^2$ **c**   −5

6   **a** $-3q$ **b** $-3p^2$ **c**   There are no terms like $8p$

7 $\dfrac{1}{4}$

8 $4ab$, $3ab$, $-2ab$, $6ab$, $-ab$, $-2ab$
     a^2b, $-3a^2b$
     $2ab^2$, $7b^2a$, $4ab^2$
     $12a^2b^2$

9   **a**   **i** $-4xy$, $-7xy$ **ii** $2x^2y$
     b   The power of y should be the same in both terms.

4.3.2 Simplifying expressions

Your turn! 1 $-3x - 2y$ **Your turn! 2** $2x^2 + 2x - 1$

4.3.2 Fluency

1   **a** $13x$ **c** $8p - 2q$ **e** $3x - 3y + 6z$
     b $4a + 3b$ **d** $-14a + 4b$

2   **a** $12x^2$ **e** $-3p^2 + 5p$
     b $6x^2$ **f** $6x + 3y + x^2 + 3y^2$
     c $15x + 8x^2$ **g** $-c^2 - 7c + 3d - 11d^2 + e$
     d $11a - 3a^2$ **h** $5x^2 + 4 - 4y^2 + 7x + 3y$

3   **a** $8ab + 10ab^2$ **d** $9xy + 5x^2y + 2x^3y$
     b $14x + 14xy$ **e** $12xy - 5x^2y + 4xz - 2xy^2 - 3yz$
     c $6p^2q + 13pq^2 - 11p^2$

4.3 Exercises

4.3 Intelligent practice

1 a 13   **b** $8 + x$ **c** $2x$ **d** $5x$ **e** $7x$

2 a 30   **b** 60   **c** $5x$ **d** $10x$

3 a $4d$ **f** 0   **k** $3d + 8e$ **p** $-5d + 5e$
   b $3d + e$ **g** $-2e$ **l** $3d + 6e$ **q** $d + 5e$
   c $2d + 2e$ **h** $2d$ **m** $3d + 5e$ **r** $d - 9e$
   d $2d + 2e$ **i** $3d$ **n** $5d + 5e$ **s** $1 - 9e$
   e $2d$ **j** $3d + 2e$ **o** $-d + 5e$ **t** $1 - 9e$

4 a $2x^2$ **f** $-5x^2 + 5x$ **k** $8x^2 - 5x - 5$
   b $6x^2$ **g** $-5x^2 + x$ **l** $8x^2 - 3x - 7$
   c $5x^2 + x$ **h** x **m** $8x^2 - 3x - 7$
   d $5x^2 + 3x$ **i** $3x^2 + x$
   e $5x^2 + 5x$ **j** $3x^2 - 5x$

5 a $8x + y$ **k** $-7y^2 + 6xy$
   b $8x + y^2$ **l** $-7y^2$
   c $3x + y^2 + 5xy$ **m** $-7y^2 - 3xy + 3xy^2$
   d $3x + y^2 + 5xy + 2x^2$ **n** $-5x^2 - 2y^2 - 3xy + 3xy^2$
   e $6x + y^2 + 5xy$ **o** $-5x^2 - 2y^2 - 3xy + 3x^2y$
   f $3x + y^2 + 8xy$ **p** $-5x^2 - 2y^2$
   g $3x + y^2 - 2xy$ **q** $-5x^2 - 2xy^2$
   h $3x + 2y^2 - 2xy$ **r** $-5x^2 - 2xy^2 + 6x^2y$
   i $3x - 3y^2 + 3xy$ **s** $-7xy^2 + 6x^2y$
   j $3x - 7y^2 + 3xy$

4.3 Method selection

1 a i 3   **ii** x, y **iii** 3   **iv** 1   **b** 17

2 a i 3   **ii** x, y **iii** –5   **iv** 3   **v** 4   **b** 28

3 a 24   **b** $12x$ **c** 24

4 a 252   **b** $5x^2 + x$ **c** 252

5 a $2x + 4$ **c** $2x + 8$ **e** $6x + 3y$
   b $2x + y$ **d** $2x + 3y$

6 a $2x + 8y$ **b** $3x + 5y$ **c** $6y - 5$

7 a $3x + 3y, 2x + y, x + 2y$
   b $8x, 5x - y, 3x + y$
   c $17x + 3y, 10x + 4y, x - 6y$
   d $2x + 4y - 2, x + 3y, -3x - 3y + 7$
   e $3x^2 + 8x, 2x^2 + 5x, x^2 + 3x$
   f $16x^2 - 3x + 1, 7x^2 + 5x - 3, 7x^2 + 3$
   g $-3y^2 + 3x + 2y, x^2 - 4y^2 + 4x, -x^2 + y^2 - x + 2y$
   h $x^2 + 7x^2y + xy^2 + xy, x^2 + 4x^2y - 2xy, xy^2 + 5xy$

8 a $2x$ **d** xy **g** $y - x$ **j** xy^2
   b $2x$ **e** xy **h** $6xy$
   c x^2 **f** $x + y$ **i** x^2y

9 a $3a$ **f** $a + 3a^2$ **k** $ab^2 + 3a^2 - a^2b$
   b $4a + b$ **g** $a + 2a^2$ **l** $ab^2 + 3ab - a^2b$
   c $-2a + b$ **h** $ab + 2a^2$ **m** $ab^2 + 2a^2b$
   d $3a^2 + b$ **i** $ab + 3a^2 - a^2b$
   e $a + 3ab$ **j** $3a^2$

10 a 60   **c** 13   **e** 15   **g** 129
   b 42   **d** 23   **f** 156   **h** −270

11 a $x\boxed{+}3x = 4x$
   b $2x\boxed{-}x + 3y = x + 3y$
   c $5x\boxed{+}6x\boxed{+}y\boxed{-}3y = 11x - 2y$
   d $\boxed{-}7x\boxed{-}6y\boxed{+}5y\boxed{-}4x = -11x - y$

11 e $x\boxed{\times}x = x^2$
   f $x\boxed{\times}y\boxed{\times}3 = 3xy$
   g $5x^2y\boxed{+}3yx\boxed{-}8x^2y = 3xy - 3x^2y$
   h $5xy^2\boxed{+}8yx\boxed{-}4x^2y\boxed{-}9xy - yx^2 = -xy\boxed{-}5x^2y + 5xy^2$

4.3 Purposeful practice

1 a $2x + 6y$
   b Expressions for length and width to give perimeter of $8x + 10y$ for example $4x$ and $5y$

2 a Expressions that simplify to x
   b Expressions that simplify to $x + 1$
   c Expressions that simplify to $x^2 - x + 1$

3 Correct pyramids

4 a $3x + 5x + 3 - 8x = 4$ is never true,
     $2x + 7 - 8x + 7x = 3x + 2x - 1$ is sometimes true,
     $6x - 9 - 4x + 13 = 2x + 5$ is never true,
     $x^2 + 7x - 5x + 3x^2 - 2x = 36$ is sometimes true,
     $-xy + 3x - 2y + 7xy - 3x = 6xy - 2y$ is always true.
   b Those that are always true are called identities

4.4 Using the distributive law

4.4.1 Expanding brackets

Your turn! 1 $4cd - 3d$ **Your turn! 2** $4c^2 - 3c$

4.4.1 Fluency

1 a $2x + 14$ **b** $10 + 2y$ **c** $2x + 2y$

2 a $3x + 6$ **c** $9x - 18$ **e** $6p - 48$
   b $4y + 28$ **d** $7a - 28$ **f** $15 - 5x$

3 a $x^2 + 4x$ **d** $3x^2 + 24x$ **g** $30p - 6p^2$
   b $2x^2 + 5x$ **e** $6a^2 + 8a$ **h** $42q - 35q^2$
   c $2x^2 - 8x$ **f** $12a^2 - 9a$

4 a $8x + 8y$ **d** $-8x^3 + 4x^2y + 12x^2$
   b $6x^2 - 4xy + 8x$ **e** $7.5a^2 - 9ab$
   c $6x^3 - 10x^2y$ **f** $0.6x^2y - 0.8xy^2 + 0.4xy$

4.4.2 Expanding and simplifying

Your turn! 1 $2x^2 + 7x + 3$

4.4.2 Fluency

1 a $3x + 5$ **b** $7x - 19$

2 a $5x + 4$ **b** $10x + 10$ **c** $x + 16$ **d** $18x + 3$

3 a $3x + 26$ **d** $13ab - 27b - 2a$
   b $55 - 5x$ **e** $10a - 8b + 11ab$
   c $4a + 26b + 6ab$ **f** $2a^2 + 6ab - 2b^2$

4 a He has written 3 in front of the second bracket rather than 2; correct expression: $2(3x - y) + 2(4x + 3y)$
   b $14x + 4y$

5 a $2p^3q - 3p^3 - 4p^2q$ **c** $-8xy^2 + 17x^2y$
   b $2x^3y^2 - 5x^3y$ **d** $30x^4y^2 - 14x^2y^3$

4.4.3 Identifying algebraic factors

Your turn! 1   **a** $2 \times 11 \times x \times y$ **b** $(-1) \times 2 \times 2 \times 2 \times 3 \times x \times x \times x$

Your turn! 2   **a** 4   **b** $11x$

4.4.3 Fluency

1 a 2×3 **b** 2×5 **c** 5×7 **d** $2 \times 3 \times 7$

2 a $x \times y$ **e** $3 \times 7 \times x \times x$
 b $x \times x$ **f** $2 \times 3 \times 5 \times x \times x$
 c $2 \times 3 \times 3 \times x$ **g** $2 \times 2 \times 2 \times 3 \times x \times x$
 d $3 \times 7 \times x$

3 a $2 \times 2 \times 2 \times 3 \times x \times x \times x \times y$ **d** $2 \times 2 \times 2 \times 3 \times x \times x \times x \times y \times y$
 b $2 \times 2 \times 2 \times 3 \times x \times y$ **e** $2 \times 2 \times 2 \times 3 \times x \times x \times x \times y \times y \times z$
 c $2 \times 2 \times 2 \times 3 \times x \times y \times y$

4 a 3 **b** y **c** 5

5 a $7x$ **c** $3x$ **e** $5b$ **g** $8z$
 b $9y$ **d** $6a$ **f** $5p$

6 a $3z$ **b** $8a$ **c** $5xy$

4.4.4 Factorising expressions

Your turn! 1 $3a(5a - 6)$

4.4.4 Fluency

1 a $4(a + 4)$ **c** $3(y - 2)$ **e** $3(3x - 11)$
 b $6(x + 3)$ **d** $4(2a - 3)$ **f** $6(3p + 10)$

2 a $x(x + 2)$ **d** $3x(3x + 4)$ **g** $4b(3b - 4)$
 b $3a(a + 3)$ **e** $4(4p^2 + 5)$ **h** $3y(3y - 7)$
 c $2a(a - 3)$ **f** $2x(9x + 7)$

3 a $3a(b + 2)$ **d** $4xy(2y + 3x)$
 b $5p(q - 1)$ **e** $3xy(2 + x - 3y)$
 c $3xy(2x + 1)$

4.4 Exercises

4.4 Intelligent practice

1 a $6 + 14$ **e** $3x - 21$ **i** $10x - 45$
 b $10 + 14$ **f** $5x - 35$ **j** $10x^2 - 45x$
 c $15 + 21$ **g** $5x - 5$ **k** $10x^2 - 45xy$
 d $3x + 21$ **h** $10x - 5$ **l** $-10x^2 + 45xy$

2 a $24 + 3x$ **e** $28 - 4y$ **i** $32y + 20y^2$
 b $21 + 3x$ **f** $28 - 20y$ **j** $32y - 20y^2$
 c $21 + 3y$ **g** $28 + 20y$ **k** $32x - 20xy$
 d $28 + 4y$ **h** $28y + 20y^2$ **l** $32x^2 - 20xy$

3 a $20 + 6$ **g** $-20a^2 + 30a$
 b $20 + 30$ **h** $-20a^2 + 30ab$
 c $10a + 30$ **i** $-20a^2 + 30ab - 10ac$
 d $10a - 30$ **j** $-20a^2 + 30ab - 10a^2c$
 e $10a^2 - 30a$ **k** $20a^2 - 30ab + 10a^2c$
 f $-10a^2 + 30a$ **l** $20a^2 - 30abc + 10a^2c$

4 a $5x + 22$ **g** $-15x - 17$
 b $5x + 23$ **h** $-15x^2 - 20x + 3$
 c $5x - 17$ **i** $-15x^2 + 20x + 3$
 d $10x - 17$ **j** $-15x^2 + 20xy + 3$
 e $-10x + 23$ **k** $-15x^2 + 20xy - 3$
 f $-10x - 17$ **l** $-15x^2y + 20xy^2 - 3$

5 a $5x + 21$ **g** $-21x^2 + 25x - 6$
 b $5x - 9$ **h** $-11x^2 + 9x$
 c $5x - 21$ **i** $-11x^2 - 6xy + 15x$
 d $-x + 9$ **j** $-11x^2 + 9xy$
 e $7x + 9$ **k** $10x^2y - 6xy^2 - 21x^2 + 15xy$
 f $-11x + 9$ **l** $10x^2y - 6xy^2 - 7x + 5y$

6 a 6 **c** 6 **e** $6x$ **g** $6x$ **i** $3y$
 b 6 **d** 6 **f** 6 **h** $6xy$

7 a $3(5 + 2)$ **h** Does not factorise
 b $3(a + 2)$ **i** $a(3a - 4)$
 c $3(a + 2)$ **j** $3a(a - 8)$
 d $3(a + 2)$ **k** $3a(3a - 8)$
 e $3(a + 4)$ **l** $-3a(3a + 8)$
 f $3(a - 4)$ **m** $-3a(3ab + 8)$
 g Does not factorise **n** $-3ab(3a + 8)$

8 a $5(2x + 1)$ **h** $5(2x^2 - 3y)$
 b $5(1 + 2x)$ **i** $5(2x^2 - 3y^2)$
 c $5(1 - 2x)$ **j** $5x(2x - 3y^2)$
 d $5(3 - 2x)$ **k** $5xy(2x - 3y)$
 e $5(3 - 2x^2)$ **l** $x(10xy - 15y^2 + 1)$
 f $5x(3 - 2x)$ **m** $xy(10x - 15y + 1)$
 g $5x(2x - 3)$ **n** $xy(10x - 15y + xy)$

4.4 Method selection

1 a $1, 2, 3, 4, 6, 9, 12, 18, 36$ **c** 9
 b $2 \times 2 \times 3 \times 3$ **d** $9(4x + 5)$

2 a $2(2x + 7)$ **b** 22 **c** $8x + 28$

3 a $x(3x - 5)$ **b** 28 **c** $12x^2 - 20x$

4 a $3(x + 5) = \boxed{3}x + \boxed{15}$ **h** $\boxed{9}(5x - \boxed{1}) = 45x - 9$
 b $9(x + \boxed{4}) = \boxed{9}x + 36$ **i** $x(3x + \boxed{7}) = \boxed{3x^2} + 7x$
 c $7(\boxed{x} - 4) = 7x \boxed{-} 28$ **j** $\boxed{5x}(5x + \boxed{6}) = 25x^2 + 30x$
 d $2(3x - 4) = \boxed{6}x - \boxed{8}$ **k** $\boxed{13x}(\boxed{3}x + \boxed{1}) = 39x^2 + 13x$
 e $8(\boxed{3}x + 7) = 24x + \boxed{56}$ **l** $3y(3x + \boxed{11}) = \boxed{9xy} + 33y$
 f $\boxed{4}(x - 5) = 4x \boxed{-} \boxed{20}$ **m** $3xy(2y + 5y) = 6\boxed{x^2y} + 15\boxed{xy^2}$
 g $\boxed{3}(\boxed{6}x + 5) = 18x + 15$ **n** $\boxed{4xy}(2y - 4) = 8xy^2 - \boxed{16xy}$

5 a $(2x + 6)\,\text{cm}^2$ **f** $7\,\text{cm}$
 b $(2x + 18)\,\text{cm}$ **g** $(7 - 4x)\,\text{cm}$
 c $(x + 4)\,\text{cm}$ **h** $(3x^2 + 2x)\,\text{cm}^2$
 d $(14x + 35)\,\text{cm}^2$ **i** $(1 + 3y)\,\text{cm}$
 e $(26 - 6x)\,\text{cm}$ **j** $15x\,\text{cm}$

6 a Yes **c** No **e** Yes **g** No
 b No **d** No **f** Yes

7 a $6(x + 4)$ **d** $3(x^2 - 1)$ **g** $12xy(2x - y)$
 b $6(x + 3)$ **e** $2(6x - 2)$
 c $8(5 - x)$ **f** $x(6y + 3x)$

8 a True for all values of x **c** True for all values of x
 b Not true for all values of x **d** Not true for all values of x

9 a $0.3x + 2.1$ **d** $0.32x + 2.4$
 b $3x - 7.5$ **e** $-0.3x - 9.5$
 c $14.4 - 72x$ **f** $7.05x + 5.97y$

10 $8x + 20$ **11** $14x + 2$

12a $48x - 30$ **b** $44x - 32$ **13** $18x + 31y$

14 $2(2x + 3) + 2(4x - 1) = 4x + 6 + 8x - 2$
  $= 12x + 4 = 4(3x + 1)$

15 $3x + 7 + 2(3x + 7) + 8x - 1 + 8x - 1 - 9$
  $= 19x - 4 + 6x + 14 = 25x + 10 = 5(5x + 2)$

4.4 Purposeful practice

1 Examples of expressions using the terms provided, for example:
$4x(x+7) = 4x^2 + 28x, 2(y-3) + 4x = 2y - 6 + 4x$

2 Expressions that multiply to give $24x + 36$

3 Expressions that multiply to give $63x^2 - 42x$

4 a Student's answers, expressions could be given in factorised or expanded form
  b Student's answers, expressions could be given in factorised or expanded form

Chapter 4 summary

Watch out!

1 a $3a^2$ **2 a** $y = 7(x+4)$ or $y = 7x + 28$

3 a $6x + 5y$ **4 a** The expression cannot be simplified

5 a $m^2 - m$ **6 a** $6x(3x-2)$

5 Coordinates

Full answers with graphs are available on Kerboodle

Reactivate your knowledge

5.1 Plotting coordinates

1 a D, G **b** A, J **c** B, E, I

2 a $(1,4)$ **b** $(3,0)$ **c** $(5,1)$

5.2 Coordinates, formulae and graphs

3 a e.g. 2, 1; 10, 5; 1, 0.5
  b e.g. $x = 1$, $y = 17$; $x = 16$, $y = 2$; $x = 9$, $y = 9$
  c e.g. $x = 1$, $y = 5$; $x = 10$, $y = 50$; $x = 7$, $y = 35$

5.1 Plotting coordinates

5.1.1 Coordinates in all four quadrants

Your turn! 1 Points correctly plotted

5.1.1 Fluency

1 A $(2,3)$ C $(-4,2)$ E $(-2,-4)$
   B $(3,4)$ D $(4,-2)$

2 Points correctly plotted

3 Points correctly plotted on axes from −6 to 6

5.1.2 Points and midpoints on coordinate grids

Your turn! 1 The midpoint is $(0,-4)$

5.1.2 Fluency

1 a i $(1,4)$ **ii** $(3,3)$ **b** E

2 a i $(-2,-3)$ **ii** $(2,3)$
  b i $(1.5,3)$ **ii** $(1,0)$ **iii** $(4.5,0)$

3 a i $(5,3)$ **ii** $(-5,-3)$
  b i $(-0.5,1)$ **ii** $(1,-1.5)$ **iii** $(3.5,-0.5)$

4 a $(2,10)$ **b** $(10,-10)$ **c** $(-6,16)$ **d** $(-14,-18)$

5.1.3 Shapes on coordinate grids

Your turn! 1 S has coordinates $(-3,-1)$

5.1.3 Fluency

1 a Points correctly plotted   **b** Rectangle

2 a Points correctly plotted   **b** D $(-4,-3)$

3 a Points correctly plotted   **b** Parallelogram

4 D $(4,-6)$ | **5 a** S $(-4.5,-3)$ **b** D $(0,2)$

6 A' $(2,1)$ B' $(4,2)$ C' $(4,5)$ D' $(2,4)$

5.1 Exercises

5.1 Intelligent practice

1 A $(2,1)$ C $(-3,2)$ E $(-3,-2.5)$
   B $(2,2)$ D $(-3,0)$ F $(0,-2.5)$

2 Points correctly plotted

3 a $(4,3)$ **f** $(8,10)$ **k** $(-10,-15)$
  b $(3,4)$ **g** $(-8,10)$ **l** $(-0.1,-0.15)$
  c $(6,8)$ **h** $(-8,-10)$ **m** $(0.9,-0.15)$
  d $(6,8)$ **i** $(-80,-100)$
  e $(7,9)$ **j** $(-40,-60)$

4 a Square   **d** Square   **g** Parallelogram
  b Square   **e** Rectangle   **h** Parallelogram
  c Rectangle   **f** Rectangle

5 a $(2,5)$ **c** $(3,0)$ **e** $(-3,0)$
  b $(3,5)$ **d** $(-3,0)$ **f** $(-1.5,0)$

6 a $(4,0)$ **c** $(6,-2)$ **e** $(12,0)$ **g** $(-3,0)$
  b $(4,-2)$ **d** $(6,0)$ **f** $(-12,0)$

7 a $(2,4)$ **c** $(4,4)$ **e** $(1,-4)$
  b $(4,4)$ **d** $(4,-4)$

5.1 Method selection

1 a A $(-4,0)$ or F $(2,0)$ **h** Square
  b H $(0,-5)$ **i** Isosceles
  c E $(5,1)$ or B $(2,6)$ **j** right-angled/scalene
  d D $(-1,-3)$ **k** A or F
  e $(2,3)$ **l** $(1,3)$
  f $(2,2)$ **m** $(5,3)$
  g $(2.5,-4)$

2 a Rectangle   **b** 30 cm   **c** 50 cm^2

3 $(7,20.5)$

4 First row: $(3,9)$, $(7,1)$, $(5,5)$;
  Second row: $(-2,8)$, $(-8,-6)$, $(-5,1)$;
  Third row: $(5,-4)$, $(2,12)$, $(3.5,4)$;
  Fourth row: $(13,-1)$, $(11,15)$, $(12,7)$;
  Fifth row: $(-19,-11)$, $(19,24)$, $(0,6.5)$;
  Sixth row: $(-13,21)$, $(5,-27)$, $(-4,-3)$

5 a S $(-8,-1)$
  b $P'(6,1)$, $Q'(6,5)$, R, $(-8,5)$, S, $(-8,1)$

6 a Points correctly plotted and joined in order
  b Square   **c** 4.8 cm   **d** 1.44 cm^2

7 a D $(0,-2)$
  b E $(-2,7)$, F $(-7,4)$, G $(-4,-1)$, H $(1,2)$
  c Square

8 R $(18,5)$ S $(23,12)$

5.1 Purposeful practice

1 a Any point in the first quadrant, e.g. $(2,5)$, $(6,0.1)$
  b Any point in the second quadrant, e.g. $(-2,5)$, $(-6,0.1)$
  c Any point in the third quadrant, e.g. $(-2,-5)$, $(-6,0.1)$
  d Any point in the fourth quadrant, e.g. $(2,-5)$, $(6,-0.1)$
  e Any point on the x-axis, e.g. $(2,0)$, $(-6,0)$
  f Any point on the y-axis, e.g. $(0,5)$, $(0,-0.1)$
  g $(0,0)$

2 a $(3,7)$ and $(-3,7)$ OR $(3,-5)$ and $(-3,-5)$ OR $(0,4)$ and $(0,-2)$

  b Infinite number of solutions, with vertices of the form
$(0,0)$, $(a,0)$, (a,a), $(0,a)$, or $(0,0)$, $(2a,0)$, (a,a), $(a,-a)$;
(a can be positive or negative)

  c Infinite number of solutions, with vertices of the form
$(2,1)$, $(a+2,1)$, $(a+2,a+1)$, $(2,a+1)$, or $(2,1)$, $(2a+2,1)$,
$(a+2,a+1)$, $(a+2,-a+1)$;
(a can be positive or negative)

3 Four points that form a rectangle with area of $30\,\text{cm}^2$

4 Four points that form a rectangle with perimeter of $20\,\text{cm}$

5 Two points with a midpoint of $(3,5)$

5.2 Coordinates, formulae, and graphs

5.2.1 Horizontal and vertical lines

Your turn! 1 $x=-3$

5.2.1 Fluency

1 a, b Points correctly plotted and joined with a straight line

  c The x-coordinate can take any value.
The y-coordinate is always equal to 3
OR $y=3$

2 a, b Points correctly plotted and joined with a straight line

  c The x-coordinate is always equal to 2 and
the y-coordinate can take any value.
OR $x=2$

3 a Vertical line passing through $(5,0)$

  b Vertical line passing through $(-2,0)$

  c Horizontal line passing through $(0,4)$

  d Horizontal line passing through $(0,-6)$

4 a $x=1$ **b** $x=-7$ **c** $y=-3$ **d** $y=4.5$

5 a Horizontal line passing through $(0,2.5)$

  b Vertical line passing through $(-3.2,0)$

  c Vertical line passing through $(5.8,0)$

  d Horizontal line passing through $(0,-1.3)$

5.2.2 Graphs of relationships

Your turn! 1   The point $(-2,-0.5)$ does not lie on the line because the y-coordinate is not 4 times the x-coordinate.

5.2.2 Fluency

1 a The y-coordinate is 5 times the x-coordinate

  b Points correctly plotted and joined with a straight line

  c Yes

2 a i, ii, v, and vii

  b The y-coordinate is always 4 less than the
x-coordinate

  c $0.5-4=-3.5$ so the point does lie on the line

3 a The y-coordinate is -1 times the x-coordinate

  b Points correctly plotted and joined with a straight line

  c Yes since $2178\times-1=-2178$

4 a The y-coordinate is the x-coordinate squared

  b It is not possible to draw a straight line through the points, you
would need to draw a curve

5.2.3 Representing relationships algebraically and graphically

Your turn! 1   The graph is a straight line.

5.2.3 Fluency

1 a i $(1,3)$ **iv** $(0,2)$ **vii** $(-3,-1)$

    ii $(2,4)$ **v** $(-1,1)$

    iii $(3,5)$ **vi** $(-2,0)$

  b, c Points correctly plotted and joined with straight line

2 a i $(1,3)$ **iii** $(0,0)$ **v** $(-2,-6)$

    ii $(2,6)$ **iv** $(-1,-3)$

  b, c Points correctly plotted and joined with a straight line

3 a y values: $-6, -5, -4, -3, -2, -1, 0$

  b Points correctly plotted and joined with a straight line

4 a y values: $-6, -4, -2, 0, 2, 4, 6$

  b Points correctly plotted and joined with a straight line

5 a Straight line passing through $(-2,-2)$, $(0,0)$, and $(2,2)$

  b Straight line passing through $(-2,-1)$, $(0,0)$, and $(2,1)$

6 a Points correctly plotted and joined with a straight line

  b $y=4x$

7 $y=-3x$

8 a y values: $-7, -2, 1, 2, 1, -2, -7$

  b Points correctly plotted and joined with a curved line

  c A curve

5.2 Exercises

5.2 Intelligent practice

1 a yes   **b** no   **c** yes   **d** yes   **e** yes

2 a yes   **b** yes   **c** no   **d** yes   **e** no

3 a $(20,10)$ **b** $(10,5)$ **c** $(-10,-5)$ **d** $(-1,-0.5)$ **e** $(0,0)$

4 a i y values: $-2,-1,0,1,2$

  b i y values: $-3,-2,-1,0,1$

  c i y values: $-4,-3,-2,-1,0$

  d i y values: $-5,-4,-3,-2,-1$

  a–d ii Points correctly plotted and joined with straight lines.
Lines are parallel and 1 square apart.

5 a i y values: $-6,-3,0,3,6$

  b i y values: $-12,-6,0,6,12$

  c i y values: $-14,-7,0,7,14$

  d i y values: $14,7,0,-7,-14$

  a–d ii Points correctly plotted and joined with straight lines

6 a $y=x+1$ **c** $y=2x$ **e** $y=-4x$

  b $y=x+2$ **d** $y=-2x$ **f** $y=-\dfrac{1}{4}x$

7 a Yes; $y=5$ **d** Yes; $y=x$

  b No   **e** No (equation is $y=x^2$)

  c Yes; $y=5x$

5.2 Method selection

1 a y is three times x (or $y = 3x$)
  b y is two more than x (or $y = x + 2$)

2 a $y = -3$ **c** $y = x - 3$ **e** $y = -x$
  b $y = 3x$ **d** $x = 3$ **f** $y = x + 3$

3 a Straight line passing through $(-12, -6)$, $(0, 6)$, and $(6, 12)$
  b Straight line passing through $(-6, -12)$, $(0, -6)$, and $(12, 6)$
  c Straight line passing through $(-6, 12)$, $(0, 6)$, and $(12, -6)$
  d Straight line passing through $(-2, -12)$, $(0, 0)$, and $(2, 12)$
  e Straight line passing through $(-12, -2)$, $(0, 0)$, and $(12, 2)$

4 a y values: $-38, -7, -4.7, 12.4$
  b y values: $-204, 42, 164.4, 2208$
  c y values: $-375, 12.5, 675, 9025$
  d y values: $39, 22.5, -3, -6.6$
  e y values: $7.25, 0.025, -0.925, -5.45$

5 a i y is 10 less than x; $y = x - 10$
    ii Points correctly plotted and joined with a straight line
  b i y is 1.5 times x; $y = 1.5x$
    ii Points correctly plotted and joined with a straight line

5.2 Purposeful practice

1 a An infinite number
  b Any examples of points with x-values between -2 and 2 that lie on $y = -10x$, including use of decimals and fractions
  c Any point that doesn't lie on the line $y = -10x$

2 a Section A: Points that lie on $y = 4x$ but not $x = 7$
    Section B: $(7, 28)$
    Section C: Points that lie on $x = 7$ but not $y = 4x$
    Section D: Points that do not lie on $x = 7$ or $y = 4x$
  b Section A: Points that lie on $y = 4x$ but not $x = 7$ or $y = x + 3$
    Section B: $(7, 28)$
    Section C: Points that lie on $x = 7$ but not $y = 4x$ or $y = x + 3$
    Section D: Points that do not lie on $x = 7$, $y = 4x$ or $y = x + 3$
    Section E: $(1, 4)$
    Section F: Not possible, if $x = 7$ then for $y = 4x$ you must have $y = 28$ but for $y = x + 3$ you must have $x = 10$
    Section G: $(7, 10)$
    Section H: Points that lie on $y = x + 3$ but not $y = 4x$ or $x = 7$

3 Likely examples (described in words or algebra):
  $y = 5x$ (graph is a straight line)
  $y = x + 20$ (graph is a straight line)
  $y = 25$ (graph is a straight line)
  $y = 30 - x$ (graph is a straight line)
  $y = x^2$ (graph is a curve)

Chapter 5 summary

Watch out! (full answers on Kerboodle)

1 a
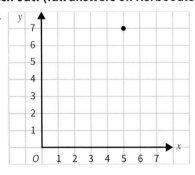

2 a
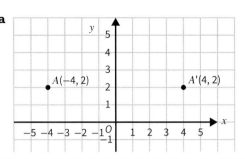

3 a $y = 5x$

6 Perimeter and area

Reactivate your knowledge

6.1 Properties of quadrilaterals and triangles

1 a $28°$ **b** $75°$

6.2 Perimeter

2 cm, km, metres

3 a 8   **b** 5   **c** 7   **d** 9

4 a
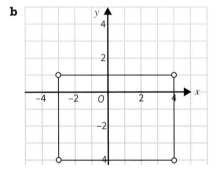

b

c
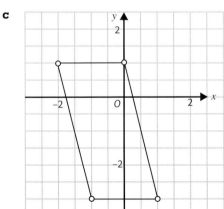

5 **a** $x+4$ **b** $2y+10$ **c** $3x+y$

6.3 Area

6 **a** $28\,\text{cm}^2$ **b** $31.5\,\text{mm}^2$ **c** $35.7\,\text{m}^2$

7 **a** 16 **b** 14 **c** 33.5

6.1 Properties of quadrilaterals and triangles

6.1.1 Properties of quadrilaterals

Your turn! 1 $3\,\text{cm}$, $8\,\text{cm}$, $100°$

6.1.1 Fluency

1 **a** True **b** False **c** True

2 **a** $5\,\text{cm}$ **b** $3\,\text{cm}$

3 **a** True **c** False; two pairs of adjacent sides are equal
b True **d** True

4 Ishita is not correct. A rhombus always has all four side lengths equal, whereas a parallelogram does not always.

6.1.2 Properties of triangles

Your turn! 1 $60°$, equilateral

6.1.2 Fluency

1 **a** Equilateral **b** Isosceles **c** Scalene **d** Right-angled

2 **a** True
b False; an isosceles triangle can have a right angle
c True
d True

3 **a** $6\,\text{cm}$ **b** $75°$

4 Maria is correct. $110°$ cannot be one of the equal angles otherwise the triangle would have another $110°$ angle and a triangle can only have one obtuse angle.

5 **a** True
b True
c False; equilateral triangles have three equal angles of $60°$
d True

6.1 Exercises

6.1 Intelligent practice

1 **a** Rectangle **c** Trapezium
b Kite **d** Parallelogram

2 **a**   **c**

b   **d**

3 **a** Rectangle
b Rhombus
c Kite, parallelogram, rectangle
d Parallelogram, rhombus
e Parallelogram, rectangle, rhombus
f Trapezium
g Kite

4 For example:

	Two pairs of sides of equal length	One pair of parallel sides
One pair of equal angles		
Two right angles		

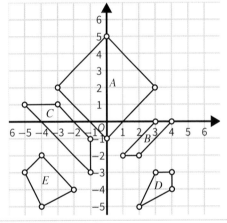

5 **a** $B, C, D, E,$ and F **b** D and E
c C and F

6 Isosceles: C and D, Scalene: A and B, Not enough information: E

6.1 Method selection

1 **a** Square **d** Kite
b Parallelogram **e** Quadrilatera
c Trapezium

2 **a** all four sides labeled a
b horizontal sides labeled $3b$, vertical sides labeled c
c horizontal sides labeled d, diagonal sides labeled $4d$

3 **a** 28, 15, 12, 9 **c** 26.5, 7.5, 6, 4.5
b 32, 35, 28, 21

4 **a** A: scalene obtuse-angled triangle,
B: isosceles triangle, C: scalene right-angled triangle
b A: kite, B: rhombus, C: isosceles triangle

5 **a** Isosceles triangle **c** Scalene triangle
b Isosceles triangle

6.1 Purposeful practice

1 **a** Kite **c** Parallelogram
b Trapezium **d** Square

2 Student answer

6.1 Purposeful practice contin.

3 **a** Right-angled isosceles triangle, 4 squares
   b Right-angled isosceles triangle, 4 squares
   c Parallelogram, 2 squares
   d Right-angled isosceles triangle, 2 squares
   e Right-angled isosceles triangle, 1 square
   f Square, 2 squares
   g Right-angled isosceles triangle, 1 square
   h Trapezium, 3 squares
   i Trapezium, 6 squares

4 **a** Square   **d** Right-angled isosceles triangle
   b Kite   **e** Right-angled scalene triangle
   c Trapezium

6.2 Perimeter

6.2.1 Introduction to perimeter

Your turn! 1   36 cm   **Your turn! 2**   27 m

6.2.1 Fluency

1 **a** 16 cm   **b** 22 cm   **c** 20 cm
2 **a** 20 cm   **b** 26 m   **c** 19 cm
3 **a** 18 mm   **b** 32 cm   **c** 60 cm

6.2.2 Finding the perimeter of polygons

Your turn! 1   26 mm   **Your turn! 2**   76 cm

6.2.2 Fluency

1 **a** 46 cm   **b** 50 cm   **c** 42 cm
2 18 mm
3 25.4 cm

6.2.3 Problems involving perimeter

Your turn! 1   6 cm

Your turn! 2

$B\left(-2,1\right), C\left(-2,-1\right)$ **or** $B\left(6,1\right), C\left(6,-1\right)$

6.2.3 Fluency

1 12 cm   **2** 5 m
3 $C\left(3,-1.5\right)$ and $D\left(3,-3\right)$ **4** 6 cm
5 $6\left(x+2\right)$ or $6x+12$

6.2 Exercises

6.2 Intelligent practice

1 **a** 28 cm   **b** 28 cm   **c** 32 cm   **d** 34 cm
2 **a** 120 mm   **b** 120 mm   **c** 120 mm   **d** 120 mm
   e 120 mm
3 **a** 40 cm   **b** 40 cm   **c** 40 cm   **d** 40 cm
4 Three rectangles: $1 \times 5, 2 \times 4, 3 \times 3$
5 **c**, because it is 17 cm not 24 cm like the others.
6 13 cm, any two other values that add up to 20 cm
   13 cm, 10 cm, 10 cm
   13 cm, 13 cm, 7 cm
   11 cm, 11 cm, 11 cm

6.2 Method selection

1 **a** 0.3 m   **c** $48x + 24 = 24\left(2x+1\right)$
   b $16x + 8 = 8\left(2x+1\right)$
2 3.66 m

3 **a** $\left(-1,-1\right)$
   b $\left(1,-1\right)$ and $\left(-2,-1\right)$ or $\left(1,3\right)$ and $\left(-2,3\right)$
   c One possible solution is $\left(3,1\right)$ and $\left(7,-2\right)$
4 12.5 units   **5** $12x + 4$

6.2 Purposeful practice

1 **a** 12 cm   **b** 12 cm   **c** 12 cm
   d 12 cm   **e** 12 cm   **f** 14 cm
2 33 mm   **3** 28 cm
4 34 m   **5** C
6 A **7** B, C, A

6.3 Area

6.3.1 Introduction to area

Your turn!   57 cm^2

6.3.1 Fluency

1 **a** 12 cm^2 **b** 8 cm^2 **2** 18.5 cm^2
3 **a** 11.25 cm^2 **b** 14.25 cm^2 **4** 20 cm^2

6.3.2 Area of polygons involving rectangles

Your turn! 1   86 cm^2

6.3.2 Fluency

1 **a** 12 cm^2 **b** 160 m^2 **c** 210 cm^2
2 **a** 6 cm^2 **b** 10 cm^2 **c** 16 cm^2
3 **a** 87 cm^2 **b** 50.5 m^2 **c** 34.5 cm^2
4 **a** 57 cm^2 **b** 132 cm^2

6.3.3 Area of triangles

Your turn! 1   84 mm^2

6.3.3 Fluency

1 **a** 10 cm^2 **b** 9 cm^2 **c** 35 m^2 **d** 30 mm^2
2 **a** 6 m^2 **b** 12 cm^2 **c** 72 cm^2 **d** 35 mm^2
3 All triangles with this base and perpendicular height have the
   same area $\left(6\,\text{cm}^2\right)$ since the area is equal to half of the base
   multiplied by the height.

6.3.4 Area of other quadrilaterals

Your turn! 1   88 mm^2 **Your turn! 2**   14 m^2
Your turn! 3   42 cm^2

6.3.4 Fluency

1 **a** 15 cm^2 **b** 24 cm^2 **c** 10 cm^2 **d** 18 cm^2
   e 13.5 cm^2 **f** 34 cm^2
2 **a** 60 mm^2 **b** 42 cm^2 **c** 33 cm^2 **d** 135 km^2
   e 63 m^2 **f** 157.5 cm^2
3 **a** 84 cm^2 **b** 210 cm^2
4 $\dfrac{1}{2}ah + \dfrac{1}{2}bh = \dfrac{h\left(a+b\right)}{2}$

6.3.5 Problems involving area

Your turn! 1   34.5 cm^2 **Your turn! 2**   3.6 cm

6.3.5 Fluency

1 **a** 12 cm^2 **b** 32 cm^2 **c** 18 cm^2
2 **a** 5 cm   **b** 9 cm
3 **a** 153.5 cm^2 **b** 408 cm^2
4 **a** 3 m   **b** 5 cm

5 a True
 b False; the area of a rectangle is the product of the two different side lengths.
 c False; the area of a parallelogram is the product of the base length and the perpendicular height.

6.3 Exercises

6.3 Intelligent practice

1 a $31\,cm^2$ **b** $31\,cm^2$ **c** $31\,cm^2$

2 a $42\,cm^2$ **b** $42\,cm^2$ **c** $21\,cm^2$ **d** $21\,cm^2$

3 a $60\,m^2$ **b** $60\,m^2$ **c** $60\,m^2$

4 a $6\,mm$ **b** $3\,mm$ **c** $8\,mm$ **d** $6\,mm$ **e** $3\,mm$

6.3 Method selection

1 1×48, 2×24, 3×16, 4×12, 6×8

2 a $3\,cm$ **c** $\sqrt{21}\,cm$ or $4.58\,cm$ (2 d.p.)
 b $4\,cm$ **d** $18\,cm$

3

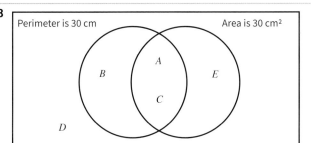

Perimeter is 30 cm   Area is 30 cm²
B A E C D

4 a $C2(5,5)$ or $C5(9,5)$ **c** $C1(1,3)$ or $C4(8,3)$
 b $C6(3,2)$ or $C7(11,2)$ **d** $C3(6,4)$

5 $21\,m^2$

6 a A **b** D **c** C **d** B

7 a $5x + 3$ **c** $10x + 15$
 b $x + 5$ **d** $(5x + 3)(x + 5) = 5x^2 + 28x + 15$

8 $18.75\,mm^2$

9 A and C, D and E, B and F

10 $40\,cm^2$

6.3 Purposeful practice

1 $4.8\,m$ | **2** $10\,cm$

3 $x = 4\,cm$, $y = 7\,cm$ | **4** 12

5 Area $= 17\,340\,m^2$

6 The perimeter of the larger polygon is double that of the smaller polygon

7 $20.5\,cm^2$

8 $x = 3$, $y = 20$ $x = 5$, $y = 12$
 $x = 4$, $y = 15$ $x = 6$, $y = 10$

 The product of x and y must be $60\,m^2$

9 False; $12\,cm$ by $0.5\,cm$ creates an area of $6\,cm^2$
 True; $12\,cm + 12\,cm$ is already over $6\,cm$

10 $233\,cm^2$

Chapter 6 summary

Watch out! (full answers on Kerboodle)

1 a Trapezium | **2 a** $40\,m$

3 a $3.5\,cm$ | **4 a** $51\,cm^2$

5 a $48\,cm^2$

7 Fractions

Reactivate your knowledge

7.1 Working with fractions and decimals

1 a $\dfrac{4}{5}$ **b** $\dfrac{9}{11}$ **c** $\dfrac{13}{17}$

2 a 3.5 **b** 1.75 **c** 2.125

3 a Five hundredths; $\dfrac{5}{100}$

 b Eight millionths; $\dfrac{8}{1\,000\,000}$

 c Six hundred-thousandths; $\dfrac{6}{100\,000}$

 d Two thousandths; $\dfrac{2}{1000}$

7.2 Comparing and ordering fractions and 7.3 Adding and subtracting fractions

4 a 15 **b** 30 **c** 9 **d** 72

5 a i $<$ **ii** $>$ **iii** $<$ **b** 4.076, 4.67, 4.706, 4.76

6 $-19, -15, -13, 0, 10, 13, 16$

7.4 Multiplying and dividing fractions

7 a $5 \times \left(3 + \dfrac{1}{5}\right) = (5 \times 3) + \left(5 \times \dfrac{1}{5}\right)$

 b $2 \times \left(6 + \dfrac{1}{3}\right) = (2 \times 6) + \left(2 \times \dfrac{1}{3}\right)$

 c $7 \times (4 + 16) = (7 \times 4) + (7 \times 16)$

7.1 Working with fractions and decimals

7.1.1 Wholes and parts

Your turn! 1 9 | **Your turn! 2** 10.8

7.1.1 Fluency

1 a 1 **b** 1 **c** 1

2 a 7 **b** 18 | **3 a** 8 and 1 **b** -11 and 1

4 a $\dfrac{1}{4}$ **b** $\dfrac{5}{8}$ **c** $\dfrac{3}{5}$ **d** $\dfrac{4}{5}$

5 a 1 **b** 1 **c** 1

7.1.2 Improper fractions and mixed numbers

Your turn! 1 $\dfrac{11}{4}, 2\dfrac{3}{4}$

7.1.2 Fluency

1 a $\dfrac{1}{2}, \dfrac{2}{3}, \dfrac{19}{20}$ **b** $\dfrac{9}{9}, \dfrac{12}{12}$ **c** $\dfrac{8}{7}, \dfrac{11}{10}, \dfrac{5}{3}$

2 a $1\dfrac{1}{4}$ **b** $1\dfrac{2}{7}$ **c** $3\dfrac{3}{5}$ **d** $2\dfrac{3}{14}$

3 a $1\dfrac{17}{25}$ **b** $2\dfrac{9}{19}$ **c** $3\dfrac{7}{30}$ **d** $2\dfrac{23}{42}$

4 a $\dfrac{9}{5}$ **b** $\dfrac{17}{6}$ **c** $\dfrac{35}{9}$ **d** $\dfrac{61}{11}$

5 a $-1\dfrac{5}{7}$ **b** $-2\dfrac{1}{9}$ | **6 a** $-\dfrac{5}{3}$ **b** $-\dfrac{11}{5}$

7.1.3 Writing fractions as divisions and decimals

Your turn! 1 0.5625

7.1.3 Fluency

1 Yes: a fraction represents division

2 Barney is correct | **3** 0.4375

4 a 0.75 **c** 0.875 **e** 3.8
b 0.4 **d** 3.5 **f** 11.75

5 Mishael is correct | **6** Yes, the 5 recurs

7 a 9.375 **b** 28.4 **c** 4.0625 **d** 70.25

8 No, there might be more digits than can be displayed on his calculator.

7.1.4 Writing decimals as fractions

Your turn! 1 $\dfrac{1462}{1000}$, $1\dfrac{462}{1000}$

7.1.4 Fluency

1 a 10 **b** 3 **c** 100 **d** 78

2 a $\dfrac{7}{10}$ **c** $\dfrac{127}{1000}$ **e** $\dfrac{11}{10}$ **g** $\dfrac{3319}{1000}$

b $\dfrac{63}{100}$ **d** $\dfrac{6731}{10\,000}$ **f** $\dfrac{217}{100}$ **h** $\dfrac{77\,139}{10\,000}$

3 a $\dfrac{13}{10}$; $1\dfrac{3}{10}$ **c** $\dfrac{8757}{1000}$; $8\dfrac{757}{1000}$

b $\dfrac{671}{100}$; $6\dfrac{71}{100}$ **d** $\dfrac{126\,517}{10\,000}$; $12\dfrac{6517}{10\,000}$

7.1.5 Simplifying fractions

Your turn! 1 $\dfrac{2}{3}$

7.1.5 Fluency

1 a $\dfrac{1}{2}$ **b** $\dfrac{2}{3}$ **c** $\dfrac{1}{3}$ **d** $\dfrac{4}{5}$

2 a i 17 **ii** 36 **iii** 24
b i $\dfrac{2}{3}$ **ii** $\dfrac{3}{4}$ **iii** $\dfrac{9}{25}$

3 $\dfrac{7}{14}=\dfrac{1}{2}$, $\dfrac{42}{48}=\dfrac{7}{8}$, $\dfrac{33}{60}=\dfrac{11}{20}$, $\dfrac{11}{44}=\dfrac{1}{4}$, $\dfrac{85}{100}=\dfrac{17}{20}$

$\dfrac{2}{3}$, $\dfrac{19}{20}$, $\dfrac{8}{21}$ are already in their simplest form.

4 a $\dfrac{29}{40}$ **b** $\dfrac{4}{5}$ **c** $\dfrac{14}{25}$ **d** $\dfrac{5}{8}$

7.1 Exercises

7.1 Intelligent practice

1 a <1 **c** $=1$ **e** >1
b <1 **d** >1 **f** <1

2 a $2\dfrac{1}{2}$ **c** $3\dfrac{1}{2}$ **e** 11 **g** $-10\dfrac{1}{2}$
b 3 **d** $5\dfrac{1}{2}$ **f** -11

3 a $\dfrac{6}{5}$ **c** $\dfrac{8}{5}$ **e** $\dfrac{103}{5}$ **g** $-\dfrac{13}{5}$
b $\dfrac{7}{5}$ **d** $\dfrac{13}{5}$ **f** $-\dfrac{103}{5}$

4 a $\dfrac{1}{10}$ **c** $\dfrac{1}{2}$ **e** 10 **g** $\dfrac{5}{4}$
b $\dfrac{1}{5}$ **d** 1 **f** 5 **h** $\dfrac{1}{8}$

5 a 0.5 **c** 2.5 **e** 0.625
b 1.5 **d** 1.25 **f** 0.3125

6 a $\dfrac{3}{10}$ **d** $\dfrac{9}{100}$ **g** $1\dfrac{999}{1000}$ **j** $3\dfrac{333}{1000}$
b $\dfrac{3}{5}$ **e** $\dfrac{9}{1000}$ **h** $9\dfrac{999}{1000}$ **k** $3\dfrac{3}{10}$
c $\dfrac{9}{10}$ **f** $\dfrac{999}{1000}$ **i** $9\dfrac{333}{1000}$ **l** $-3\dfrac{3}{10}$

7.1 Method selection

1 a $<$ **b** $>$ **c** $=$ **d** $>$

2 a $\dfrac{1}{16}$ **b** $\dfrac{2}{19}$ **c** $\dfrac{19}{32}$ **d** $\dfrac{19}{16}$

3 Any fraction with equal numerator and denominator

4 Any fraction with a numerator 1.5 times the denominator

5 a 0.16 **b** 1.6 **c** 4.04 **d** 1.64

6 a $\dfrac{8}{10}=0.8$ **c** $\dfrac{25}{100}=0.25$ **e** $\dfrac{4375}{10\,000}=0.4375$

b $\dfrac{16}{10}=1.6$ **d** $\dfrac{125}{1000}=0.125$ **f** $0.\dot{6}$

7.1 Purposeful practice

1 The second is greater than 1 and the first is less than 1, so the second fraction is greater.

2 a $\dfrac{12}{34}, \dfrac{14}{32}$ **b** $\dfrac{34}{12}, \dfrac{32}{14}$

c $\dfrac{12}{43}, \dfrac{13}{24}, \dfrac{13}{42}, \dfrac{14}{23}, \dfrac{21}{34}, \dfrac{21}{43}, \dfrac{23}{41}, \dfrac{24}{31}, \dfrac{31}{42}, \dfrac{32}{41}$

d $\dfrac{23}{14}, \dfrac{24}{13}, \dfrac{31}{24}, \dfrac{34}{21}, \dfrac{41}{23}, \dfrac{41}{32}, \dfrac{42}{13}, \dfrac{42}{31}, \dfrac{43}{12}, \dfrac{43}{21}$

3 Leanne is incorrect because a simplified fraction must have an integer numerator and denominator

4 a $\dfrac{6542}{1}$ **b** $\dfrac{1}{6542}$ **c** $\dfrac{65}{124}$

5 E.g.

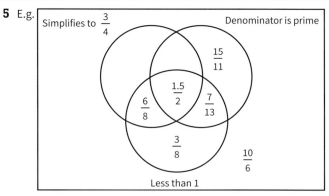

All fractions that simplify to $\dfrac{3}{4}$ are also less than 1. So 'simplifies to $\dfrac{3}{4}$' and the overlap between 'simplifies to $\dfrac{3}{4}$' and 'denominator is prime' are empty.

6 $\dfrac{8}{10}=4\div5$; $\dfrac{9}{12}=3\div4$; $\dfrac{8}{20}=2\div5$; $\dfrac{16}{32}=1\div2$

7.2 Comparing and ordering fractions

7.2.1 Comparing and ordering fractions

Your turn! 1 $\frac{5}{8}, \frac{7}{10}, \frac{3}{4}$

7.2.1 Fluency

1 a > **b** <

2 a < **b** < **c** > **d** >

3 a < **b** > $\quad$ **4** $\frac{1}{2}, \frac{11}{20}, \frac{5}{8}, \frac{7}{10}, \frac{3}{4}, \frac{5}{6}$

5 $\frac{8}{5}, \frac{5}{3}, \frac{17}{10}, \frac{7}{4}, \frac{11}{6}, \frac{37}{20}$

6 a < **b** < $\quad$ **7** $-\frac{50}{63}, -\frac{5}{7}, \frac{2}{3}, \frac{17}{21}, \frac{6}{7}, \frac{8}{9}$

7.2.2 Comparing and ordering fractions by converting to decimals

Your turn! 1 $-\frac{4}{5}, \frac{5}{8}, \frac{7}{10}, \frac{3}{4}, \frac{10}{7}$

7.2.2 Fluency

1 a < **b** > **c** > **d** <

2 $\frac{1}{5}, 0.23, \frac{1}{4}, 0.27, \frac{14}{50}, \frac{29}{100}$ $\quad$ **3** $-\frac{1}{5}, -\frac{3}{21}, -0.1, \frac{7}{100}, 0.09, \frac{3}{20}$

4 $\frac{1}{2}, \frac{11}{20}, \frac{5}{8}, \frac{7}{10}, \frac{3}{4}, \frac{4}{5}$ $\quad$ **5 a** > **b** > **c** >

6 $-\frac{17}{20}, -\frac{4}{5}, -0.75, \frac{5}{7}, \frac{3}{4}, \frac{77}{100}, 0.8, \frac{5}{6}$

7 $\frac{5}{16}, \frac{173}{500}, \frac{7}{20}, \frac{9}{25}, \frac{361}{1000}, \frac{37}{100}, \frac{3}{8}, \frac{2}{5}$

7.2.3 The infinite nature of the number line

Your turn! 1 E.g. $\frac{19}{36}$

7.2.3 Fluency

1 a E.g. 32.5 **b** E.g. $34\frac{1}{2}$

2 a E.g. 0.991 **b** E.g. 0.99995 **c** An infinite amount

3 a E.g. 0.205 **b** E.g. 0.745 **c** E.g. 1.36 **d** E.g. 3.31

4 E.g. $\frac{25}{312}$ $\quad$ **5** E.g. $\frac{29}{190}$

6 a An infinite amount **c** All of them
$\quad$ **b** An infinite amount

7.2 Exercises

7.2 Intelligent practice

1 a < **b** > **c** < **d** < **e** >

2 a > **b** > **c** < **d** > **e** <

3 a < **b** < **c** < **d** > **e** >

4 There are many possible answers for this question, e.g.

a 16 **c** 1.51 **e** 1.152 **g** 115.4
b 15.5 **d** 0.151 **f** 11.53

5 There are many possible answers for this question, e.g.

a $\frac{5}{8}$ **b** $\frac{9}{16}$ **c** $\frac{3}{4}$ **d** $\frac{13}{16}$ **e** $\frac{17}{32}$

7.2 Method selection

1

2 a $\frac{7}{8}, \frac{3}{4}, \frac{9}{16}, \frac{1}{2}$ $\quad$ **d** $-\frac{3}{50}, -\frac{7}{100}, -\frac{17}{200}, -\frac{1}{10}$

b $\frac{8}{17}, \frac{4}{11}, \frac{2}{7}, \frac{2}{9}$ $\quad$ **e** $\frac{3}{10}, \frac{1}{4}, \frac{1}{5}, 0.18$

c $\frac{9}{25}, \frac{31}{100}, \frac{3}{10}, \frac{1}{5}$ $\quad$ **f** $\frac{6}{5}, \frac{11}{10}, 1.01, \frac{19}{20}$

3 $\frac{115}{120} = \frac{23}{24}$

4 $\frac{1}{5}$ cannot be written as $\frac{\text{integer}}{32}$ as 5 is not a factor of 32

5 School B

6 Vish is not correct. He has confused tenths and hundredths with tens and ones.

7 a $\frac{1}{9}$ **c** $\frac{1}{3}$ **e** $\frac{1}{90}$

b $\frac{1}{25}$ **d** $\frac{1}{12}$ **f** $\frac{1}{10}$

7.2 Purposeful practice

1 a, b E.g. $\frac{4}{5} > \frac{3}{6} > \frac{2}{7} > \frac{1}{8}$ or $\frac{4}{6} > \frac{3}{5} > \frac{2}{8} > \frac{1}{7}$

2 a $\frac{6}{5} = \frac{72}{60}$ and $\frac{4}{3} = \frac{80}{60}$ so, since $\frac{5}{4} = \frac{75}{60}, \frac{6}{5} < \frac{5}{4} < \frac{4}{3}$

b $\frac{6}{5} = \frac{36}{30}$ and $\frac{4}{3} = \frac{40}{30}$ so, since $\frac{13}{10} = \frac{39}{30}, \frac{6}{5} < \frac{13}{10} < \frac{4}{3}$

3 E.g. $\frac{9}{24}, \frac{10}{24}, \frac{11}{24}, \frac{12}{24}, \frac{13}{24}$

4 a E.g. $\frac{4}{1} > 2.3, \frac{4}{1} > 3.2, \frac{4}{2} > 1.3, \frac{4}{3} > 1.2, \frac{3}{1} > 2.4, \frac{3}{2} > 1.4$

b 6

5 Maths: $\frac{27}{30} = \frac{90}{100}$; English: $\frac{40}{50} = \frac{80}{100}$; Science: $\frac{7\frac{1}{2}}{10} = \frac{75}{100}$

6 a One possible answer is:

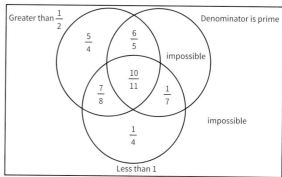

b Infinitely many.

7.3 Adding and subtracting fractions

7.3.1 Adding and subtracting fractions with a common denominator

Your turn! 1 $\frac{6}{12} = \frac{1}{2}$ $\quad$ **Your turn! 2** $\frac{12}{8} = \frac{3}{2}$

7.3.1 Fluency

1 a $\frac{7}{9}$ **c** $\frac{7}{6} = 1\frac{1}{6}$ **e** $\frac{16}{9} = 1\frac{7}{9}$

b $\frac{4}{3} = 1\frac{1}{3}$ **d** $\frac{11}{7} = 1\frac{4}{7}$

2 Yes: you need to use a common denominator so that you are adding fractions of the same 'type'

3 **a** Yes; they share a common denominator
 b No; they do not share a common denominator
 c No; they do not share a common denominator (even though they have a common numerator)
 d Yes; they share a common denominator

4 **a** $\dfrac{1}{7}$ **b** $\dfrac{7}{11}$ **c** $\dfrac{2}{13}$ **d** $\dfrac{13}{15}$

5 He has written 1 as $\dfrac{5}{5}$ instead of $\dfrac{3}{3}$ and then added the numerators and denominators.
 Correct working: $\dfrac{5}{3}+\dfrac{3}{3}=\dfrac{8}{3}=2\dfrac{2}{3}$

6 **a** $8\dfrac{4}{5}$ **b** $1\dfrac{6}{11}$ **c** $-\dfrac{4}{7}$ **d** $-\dfrac{4}{13}$

7.3.2 Adding and subtracting fractions and mixed numbers

Your turn! 1 $\dfrac{11}{9}=1\dfrac{2}{9}$ **Your turn! 2** $\dfrac{51}{28}=1\dfrac{23}{28}$

7.3.2 Fluency
1 **a** $\dfrac{4}{8}=\dfrac{1}{2}$ **b** $\dfrac{10}{11}$ **c** $\dfrac{5}{13}$ **d** $\dfrac{18}{100}=\dfrac{9}{50}$

2 **a** 4 **b** $6\dfrac{1}{4}$ **c** $2\dfrac{5}{9}$ **d** $3\dfrac{4}{5}$

3 **a** $\dfrac{5}{6}$ **b** $1\dfrac{26}{45}$ **c** $\dfrac{21}{44}$ **d** $\dfrac{1}{40}$ **e** $-\dfrac{1}{60}$

4 **a** $5\dfrac{5}{8}$ **c** $12\dfrac{1}{9}$ **e** $3\dfrac{25}{36}$
 b $12\dfrac{3}{20}$ **d** $3\dfrac{1}{6}$ **f** $-10\dfrac{1}{24}$

5 **a** The commutative law
 b She could have used a simpler common denominator since 2 and 6 share a common factor
 c $5\dfrac{3}{6}+3\dfrac{5}{6}=8\dfrac{8}{6}=9\dfrac{1}{3}$

6 **a** The associative law **b** The commutative law

7.3 Exercises

7.3 Intelligent practice
1 **a** $\dfrac{5}{15}\left(=\dfrac{1}{3}\right)$ **b** $\dfrac{10}{15}\left(=\dfrac{2}{3}\right)$ **c** $\dfrac{10}{15}\left(=\dfrac{2}{3}\right)$ **d** $\dfrac{11}{15}$ **e** $\dfrac{12}{15}\left(=\dfrac{4}{5}\right)$

2 **a** $\dfrac{8}{12}\left(=\dfrac{2}{3}\right)$ **b** $\dfrac{8}{12}\left(=\dfrac{2}{3}\right)$ **c** $\dfrac{14}{12}\left(=\dfrac{7}{6}\right)$ **d** $\dfrac{38}{12}\left(=\dfrac{19}{6}\right)$

3 **a** $\dfrac{14}{6}\left(=\dfrac{7}{3}\right)$ **b** $\dfrac{19}{12}$ **c** $\dfrac{29}{24}\left(=1\dfrac{5}{24}\right)$ **d** $\dfrac{77}{24}\left(=3\dfrac{5}{24}\right)$ **e** $\dfrac{29}{24}$

4 **a** $\dfrac{3}{8}$ **e** 0 **i** $\dfrac{11}{40}$ **m** $\dfrac{42}{40}\left(=\dfrac{21}{20}\right)$
 b $\dfrac{3}{8}$ **f** $-\dfrac{1}{8}$ **j** $\dfrac{19}{40}$ **n** $\dfrac{47}{40}$
 c $\dfrac{1}{8}$ **g** $\dfrac{1}{8}$ **k** $-\dfrac{19}{40}$
 d $-\dfrac{1}{8}$ **h** $\dfrac{3}{40}$ **l** $\dfrac{21}{40}$

7.3 Method selection
1 **a** 0.5 **b** $\dfrac{1}{2}$ **c** 3.1 **d** $3\dfrac{1}{10}$ **e** $\dfrac{1}{2}$

2 $\dfrac{1}{8}$ **3** **a** $\dfrac{1}{3}$ m **b** 10.8 kg and 7.2 kg

4 **a** $2\dfrac{1}{4}$ cm **b** $9\dfrac{3}{10}$ cm **c** $7\dfrac{41}{45}$ cm

5 **a** $\dfrac{3}{4}x$ **b** $\dfrac{44}{3}y$ **c** $\dfrac{5}{4}p+\dfrac{83}{10}q$ **6** $\dfrac{17}{100}$

7.3 Purposeful practice
1 **a** 1 **b** 6

2 $\dfrac{5}{8}+\dfrac{1}{12}=\dfrac{17}{24}$; $\dfrac{5}{8}+\dfrac{1}{3}=\dfrac{23}{24}$; $\dfrac{5}{8}+\dfrac{1}{6}=\dfrac{19}{24}$

3 **a** $\dfrac{3}{4}+\dfrac{1}{5}=\dfrac{11}{20}+\dfrac{2}{5}=\dfrac{19}{20}$ **b** $\dfrac{1}{8}-\dfrac{3}{40}=\dfrac{1}{20}$ **4** E.g. $\dfrac{2}{3}-\dfrac{5}{12}$

5 Any five pairs of fractions with a sum of $\dfrac{1}{2}$

6 **a** $\dfrac{11}{24}$ **b** 72

7 **a** **i** $\dfrac{7}{4}+\dfrac{6}{5}$ **ii** $\dfrac{4}{6}+\dfrac{5}{7}$ **b** **i** $\dfrac{7}{4}-\dfrac{5}{6}$ **ii** $\dfrac{5}{6}-\dfrac{7}{4}$

7.4 Multiplying and dividing fractions
7.4.1 Multiplying fractions

Your turn! 1 $\dfrac{10}{56}=\dfrac{5}{28}$ **Your turn! 2** $\dfrac{32}{5}=6\dfrac{2}{5}$

7.4.1 Fluency
1 **a** $\dfrac{3}{8}$ **b** $\dfrac{10}{21}$ **c** $\dfrac{2}{27}$ **d** $\dfrac{24}{35}$

2 No: to find a fraction *of* an amount, you multiply by the fraction.

3 He has converted each fraction to an equivalent fraction with a common denominator.

4 **a** The commutative law **b** The associative law

7.4.2 Multiplying proper and improper fractions

Your turn! 1 $1\dfrac{3}{7}$

7.4.2 Fluency
1 **a** $\dfrac{2}{15}$ **b** $\dfrac{3}{40}$ **c** $\dfrac{15}{28}$ **d** $\dfrac{18}{35}$

2 **a** $\dfrac{2}{5}$ **c** $\dfrac{2}{3}$ **e** $\dfrac{6}{5}$ **g** $\dfrac{8}{5}$
 b $\dfrac{1}{2}$ **d** $\dfrac{4}{7}$ **f** $\dfrac{12}{5}$ **h** 6

3 **a** Less than: you are multiplying by a fraction less than 1
 b Greater than: you are multiplying by a fraction greater than 1

7.4.3 Multiplying mixed numbers

Your turn! 1 $4\dfrac{1}{3}$ **Your turn! 2** $3\dfrac{5}{6}$

7.4.3 Fluency
1 **a** $\dfrac{10}{3}$ **b** $\dfrac{28}{3}$ **c** $\dfrac{39}{5}$ **d** $\dfrac{121}{28}$

2 **a** $9\dfrac{5}{8}$ **b** $4\dfrac{4}{5}$

3 **a** $16\dfrac{7}{8}$ **b** $10\dfrac{4}{5}$ **c** $24\dfrac{4}{15}$ **d** $23\dfrac{9}{16}$

7.4.4 Using reciprocals to divide fractions

Your turn! 1 $\dfrac{9}{2}$

7.4.4 Fluency

1 a $\dfrac{1}{10}$ **b** $\dfrac{1}{6}$ **c** $\dfrac{1}{20}$ **d** $\dfrac{1}{133}$

2 a 2 **b** 10 **c** 15 **d** 85

3 a $\dfrac{3}{2}$ **b** $\dfrac{7}{4}$ **c** $\dfrac{11}{8}$ **d** $\dfrac{104}{87}$

7.4.5 Divide a fraction by a whole number and a whole number by a fraction

Your turn! 1 $\dfrac{9}{44}$ **Your turn! 2** $\dfrac{8}{3} = 2\dfrac{2}{3}$

7.4.5 Fluency

1 a $\dfrac{1}{6}$ **b** $\dfrac{2}{15}$ **c** $\dfrac{3}{20}$ **d** $\dfrac{5}{18}$

2 a 12 **b** 30 **c** 56 **d** 99

3 a $\dfrac{9}{2}$ **b** $\dfrac{20}{3}$ **c** $\dfrac{42}{5}$ **d** $\dfrac{72}{7}$

4 a $\dfrac{4}{35}$ **b** $\dfrac{5}{108}$ **c** $\dfrac{1}{28}$ **d** $\dfrac{2}{33}$

5 a 6 **b** 15 **c** 15 **d** 27

6 a Greater than: dividing by a fraction less than 1 is the same as multiplying by a fraction greater than 1.
b Less than: dividing by a fraction greater than 1 is the same as multiplying by a fraction less than 1.

7.4.6 Divide a fraction by a fraction

Your turn! 1 $\dfrac{35}{132}$ **Your turn! 2** $\dfrac{3}{4}$

7.4.6 Fluency

1 a $\dfrac{8}{3}$ **b** $\dfrac{15}{4}$ **c** $\dfrac{14}{5}$ **d** $\dfrac{63}{8}$

2 a $\dfrac{2}{3}$ **b** $\dfrac{10}{7}$ **c** $\dfrac{5}{6}$ **d** $\dfrac{25}{42}$

3 a $\dfrac{7}{12}$ **b** $\dfrac{14}{15}$ **c** $\dfrac{11}{2}$ **d** 26

4 a Greater than: dividing by a fraction less than 1 is the same as multiplying by a fraction greater than 1.
b Less than: dividing by a fraction greater than 1 is the same as multiplying by a fraction less than 1.

7.4 Exercises

7.4 Intelligent practice

1 a 5 **c** $\dfrac{5}{2}$ **e** $\dfrac{25}{2}$
b 5 **d** $\dfrac{5}{2}$ **f** $\dfrac{25}{2}$

2 a $\dfrac{1}{16}$ **c** $\dfrac{1}{32}$ **e** $\dfrac{1}{128}$ **g** $\dfrac{1}{16}$
b $\dfrac{1}{16}$ **d** $\dfrac{1}{64}$ **f** $\dfrac{1}{16}$ **h** $\dfrac{1}{64}$

3 a $\dfrac{1}{20}$ **d** $\dfrac{1}{40}$ **g** 10 **j** $\dfrac{32}{5}$
b $\dfrac{1}{40}$ **e** $\dfrac{1}{20}$ **h** 20 **k** $\dfrac{32}{15}$
c $\dfrac{1}{80}$ **f** $\dfrac{1}{10}$ **i** 40

4 a 4 **d** $\dfrac{1}{18}$ **g** $\dfrac{1}{144}$ **j** $\dfrac{5}{6}$
b 2 **e** $\dfrac{1}{72}$ **h** $\dfrac{5}{144}$ **k** $\dfrac{10}{3}$
c $\dfrac{1}{2}$ **f** $\dfrac{1}{144}$ **i** $\dfrac{5}{72}$

7.4 Method selection

1 a 0.06 **b** $\dfrac{3}{50}$ **c** 4 **d** 4 **e** $\dfrac{3}{50}$

2 $\dfrac{3}{16}$ **3** 10

4 a $\dfrac{9}{32}$ cm² **b** $\dfrac{17}{4}$ cm² **c** $\dfrac{3}{64}$ cm²

5 280 000 000 or 280 million

6 The division will give a bigger answer, as dividing by a number between 0 and 1 increases a value, while multiplying by a number between 0 and 1 decreases it.

7.4 Purposeful practice

1 a $\dfrac{5}{6} \times \dfrac{2}{3} = \dfrac{5}{9}$
b Any integer solution where the number in the first box is $\dfrac{3}{7}$ of the number in the second box

2 a $\dfrac{3}{4} \times \dfrac{11}{20} = \dfrac{33}{80}$ **b** $\dfrac{3}{4} \div \dfrac{3}{40} = 10$ **c** $\dfrac{1}{8} \times \dfrac{3}{40} = \dfrac{3}{320}$

3 E.g. $\dfrac{1}{4} \div \dfrac{5}{2} = \dfrac{1}{10}$

4 Any calculation with answer $\dfrac{1}{2}$ when simplified

5 Any calculation with answer $\dfrac{1}{2}$ when simplified

6 a $\dfrac{5}{1} \div \dfrac{2}{4}$ or $\dfrac{5}{2} \div \dfrac{1}{4}$
b $\dfrac{-5}{1} \div \dfrac{2}{4}$ or $\dfrac{-5}{2} \div \dfrac{1}{4}$ (the negative sign can go anywhere)
c The first numerator must be 0; the other boxes can be filled with any number

Chapter 7 summary

Watch out! (full answers on Kerboodle)

1 a $0.\dot{4}$ **2 a** Yes, $\dfrac{5}{5} = 1$ **3 a** $\dfrac{3}{8} = \dfrac{6}{16}$

4 a $\dfrac{1.5 \times 2}{6 \times 2} = \dfrac{3}{12}$, so they are equivalent.

5 a $\dfrac{4}{7} \div \dfrac{1}{3} = \dfrac{4}{7} \times \dfrac{3}{1} = \dfrac{12}{7}$ **6 a** $3 \times \dfrac{1}{5} = \dfrac{3}{5}$

8 Ratio and proportion

Reactivate your knowledge

8.1 Multiplicative relationships

1 a $y = 49, 77, 98$ **b** $y = -12, -18, -30$ **c** $y = 4.8, 7.8, 12.6$

8.2 Ratio tables and double number lines, 8.3 Fractions in context, and 8.4 Applying ratios

2 a £1.45, 97 p **c** 50 mm², 2.6 m² **e** 30 ml, 2 litres
b 10 km, $\dfrac{1}{2}$ m **d** 500 g, 42 kg

3 a $\dfrac{3}{5}$ **b** $\dfrac{2}{3}$ **c** $\dfrac{3}{2}$ **d** $\dfrac{3}{4}$ **e** $\dfrac{1}{3}$ **f** $\dfrac{2}{3}$

4

5 a $A\ (3,12)$ $B\ (1.5,6)$ $C\ (4,16)$
  b Points $(2,8)$, $(1,4)$, and $(3.5,14)$ correctly plotted.

8.1 Multiplicative relationships

8.1.1 Writing multiplicative relationships as fractions and ratios

Your turn! 1   2:3

8.1.1 Fluency

1 a 1:3   **b** $\dfrac{1}{4}$ | **2 a** 2:5   **b** $\dfrac{2}{7}$

3 a

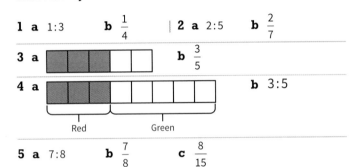

  b $\dfrac{3}{5}$

4 a   **b** 3:5

Red   Green

5 a 7:8   **b** $\dfrac{7}{8}$ **c** $\dfrac{8}{15}$

8.1.2 Multipliers

Your turn! 1   **a** $+12$ **b** $\times 4$ | **Your turn! 2** $\dfrac{12}{7}$

8.1.2 Fluency

1 a $+3$ **b** $\times\dfrac{3}{2}$ (or $\times 1.5$) | **2 a** $+(-3)$ **b** $\times\dfrac{7}{10}$ (or $\times 0.7$)

3 a 2   **b** 10   **c** 12   **d** 17   **e** 24

4 a 2   **b** 2.5   **c** -2 **d** 1.25   **e** -1.5

5 a is greater than 1 | **6** 0.5

7 2.5 | **8 a** 12   **b** $\dfrac{1}{12}$

8.1.3 Equivalent multiplicative relationships

Your turn! 1   There are infinitely many answers, where one number is five times the other.

8.1.3 Fluency

1 a Student answers, for example,
  i 2, 8   **ii** 3, 45   **iii** 2, −10   **iv** −4, 48
  b An infinite amount

2 Student answers, for example,
  i 2, 5   **ii** 3, 9.3   **iii** 4, −18   **iv** −5, 74

3 a 14.7   **c** 5.85   **e** 4.2
  b −52.2   **d** 1.5   **f** −72

4 Graph of $y = 2.5x$ correctly plotted, straight line passing through points $(-4,-10)$, $(0,0)$, and $(4,10)$. Any four points plotted on the line.

5 Graph of $y = -3.2x$ correctly plotted, straight line passing through points $(-5,16)$, $(0,0)$, and $(5,-16)$. Any four points plotted on the line.

8.1 Exercises

8.1 Intelligent practice

1 a 3:5   **b** 3:5   **c** 3:5   **d** 3:5

2 a 2:5   **b** 2:5   **c** 5:2   **d** 3:4   **e** 3:11

3 Missing information by column:
  Diagram: Diagram with 3 shaded and 2 unshaded shapes, Diagram with 2 shaded and 3 unshaded shapes, Diagram with 1 shaded and 2 unshaded shapes
  Shaded : unshaded: 5:3, 11:1, 5:7, 1:2
  Fraction of unshaded shapes: $\dfrac{3}{8}, \dfrac{1}{12}, \dfrac{7}{12}, \dfrac{2}{3}$

4 Missing information by column:
  A: 100 000, 250, 100 000
  B: 0.04, 0.004
  Multiplier from A to B: 4, 2, 2, 4, 4, 1, 5, 0.2, 0.02, 0.05
  Multiplier from B to A: 0.25, 0.5, 0.5, 0.25, 0.25, 1, 0.2, 5, 50, 0.05

5 Missing information by column:
  A: 6
  B: -30, 150
  C: 60
  Multiplier from A to B: 10, 10, 20, $\dfrac{20}{3}$, $\dfrac{-20}{3}$, $\dfrac{-20}{3}$, -5
  Multiplier from B to C: $\dfrac{1}{3}, \dfrac{2}{3}, \dfrac{1}{3}, 3, 3, -3, -4, \dfrac{4}{5}$
  Multiplier from A to C: $\dfrac{10}{3}, \dfrac{20}{3}, \dfrac{20}{3}, 20, -20, 20, 20, -4$

8.1 Method selection

1 a $\dfrac{5}{8}$ **b** 12 cm^2 **c** 3:5   **d** 16 cm^2

2 a Rectangles of dimensions 1×12, 2×11, 3×10, 4×9, 5×8, 6×7
  b 12 cm^2, 22 cm^2, 30 cm^2, 36 cm^2, 40 cm^2, 42 cm^2
  c 12:1, 11:2, 10:3, 9:4, 8:5, 7:6
  d

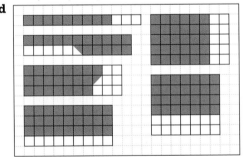

  e If the area is a multiple of four, you can shade in whole squares.

3 a 125 g   **b** 60 g   **c** $\dfrac{3}{2}$
  d

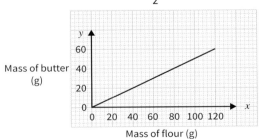

Mass of butter (g)

Mass of flour (g)

4 Less than 1:6 and 5, 7.1 and 6.8, 6.05 and 6.04
  Greater than 1:2 and 4, 3.5 and 4.5, 2.41 and 2.42

5 Amrita is correct: to find the multiplier from A to C, you multiply the two multipliers together.

8.1 Purposeful practice

1 E.g. A 2 and 8; B 4 and 10; C 5 and 12.5; D 3 and 7

2 E.g. A 1.5 and 4.5; B $\dfrac{1}{3}$ and 1; C 4 and 4.5; D 0.5 and 4

3 E.g. Ratio of shaded to unshaded $= 8:12 = 4:6 = 2:3$
Ratio of unshaded to shaded $= 12:8 = 6:4 = 3:2$
Fraction of squares shaded $= \dfrac{8}{20} = \dfrac{4}{10} = \dfrac{2}{5}$
Fraction of shaded to unshaded $= \dfrac{8}{12} = \dfrac{4}{6} = \dfrac{2}{3}$
The multiplier from shaded to unshaded is $\times 1.5$

4 **a** Sometimes true: 2 to 4 is $+2$ and $\times 2$
  b Sometimes true: only when $p = q$
  c Always true because they are inverses of each other

5 **a** E.g. 4 and 6, 5 and 7.5, 6 and 9
  b E.g. 30 and 45, 50 and 75, 60 and 90
  c E.g. 2.2 and 3.3, 4.4 and 6.6, 10.2 and 15.3
  d E.g. -2 and -3, -4 and -6, -10 and -15
  e E.g. 2000 and 3000, 4000 and 6000, 1 000 000 and 1 500 000
Some numbers may fit into different categories.

8.2 Representing multiplicative relationships

8.2.1 Proportional reasoning with ratio tables

Your turn! 1 84

8.2.1 Fluency

1 **a** 10   **b** 10   **2 a** 7   **b** 7

3 **a** 50   **b** $4:10 = 20:50$ and $4:20 = 10:50$

4 **a** 15   **b** $3:15 = 9:45$ and $3:9 = 15:45$

5 1 costs £0.40; 7 cost £2.80   **6** 1 costs £0.75; 9 cost £6.75

8.2.2 Simplifying ratios

Your turn! 1 $11:10$

8.2.2 Fluency

1 $2:3$ **2** $1:3$ **3** $1:3$ **4** $3:2$

5 **a** $3:2$ **b** $2:3$ **c** $4:5$ **d** $1:2$ **e** $11:15$

6 **a** $3:4$ **b** $4:3$

7 **a** $1:2:3$ **b** $2:3:4$ **c** $4:5:6$ **d** $6:5:3$

8.2.3 Proportional reasoning with double number lines

Your turn! 1 £21

8.2.3 Fluency

1 **a** £0.50   **b** £10

2 **a** Double number line with 7 intervals; 5 and 7 correctly marked on top number line; £1.25 marked on bottom number line, aligned below 5
  b £1.75

3 **a** Double number line with 12 intervals; 5 and 12 correctly marked on top number line; £54 on bottom number line, aligned below 12
  b £22.50

4 **a** £0.72
  b That the length and cost of string are in a multiplicative relationship

8.2.4 Plotting graphs for ratios

Your turn! 1 Graph of $y = \left(\dfrac{7}{4}\right)x$ correctly plotted, straight line passing through $(0,0)$, $(4,7)$, and $(8,14)$

8.2.4 Fluency

1 **a i** 4   **ii** 12   **iii** 15
  b Graph of $y = 3x$ correctly plotted, straight line passing through $(0,0)$, $(1,3)$, $(2,6)$, $(3,9)$, $(4,12)$, and $(5,15)$

2 **a i** 4 **ii** 5 **iii** 6 **iv** 10 **v** 12.5 **vi** 15 **vii** 17.5
  b Graph of $y = \left(\dfrac{5}{2}\right)x$ correctly plotted, straight line passing through $(0,0)$, $(1,2.5)$, $(2,5)$, $(3,7.5)$, $(4,10)$, $(5,12.5)$, $(6,15)$, and $(7,17.5)$

3 **a** $y = 2.4, 3.2, 4.0, 4.8$
  b Double number line with 6 intervals; 1, 2, 3, 4, 5, and 6 correctly marked on top number line; 0.8, 1.6, 2.4, 3.2, 4.0, and 4.8 marked on the bottom number line, aligned to the numbers on top number line
  c Graph of $y = \left(\dfrac{4}{5}\right)x$ correctly plotted, straight line passing through $(0,0)$ and $(5,4)$

8.2 Exercises

8.2 Intelligent practice

1 **a** $7:2$ **b** $4:3$ **c** $2:5$

2 **a** 2.5, 3, 3.5, 4, 4.5, 5   **b** 10, 12, 14, 16, 18, 20

3 **a** 6 litres **b** £20 **c** £25 **d** 10.8 litres

4 **a** 240 **b** 18 **c** 6 **d** 1.5 **e** $\dfrac{4}{3}$ and $\dfrac{32}{3}$

5 **a** £1.50 **b** 6

6 **a** £12.60 **c** £75 **e** £37.50
  b £2.10 **d** £42 **f** £38.50

8.2 Method selection

1 **a** $1:4$ **c** $a:4b$ **e** $5:28$
  b $1:4$ **d** $1:40$ **f** $8a+2b:2a-3b$

2 **a** 9 **b** 16 **c** 24, 18 **d** 3, -16 **e** 6

3 **a** £3.20 **b** £26.80

4 **a** multiplicative **b** additive **c** multiplicative

5 **a** $2:3$ **b** $3:5$ **c** $3:2$ **d** $2:5$

6 **a** 40 cm
  b 20; $25:4 = 125:20$ and $25:125 = 4:20$
  c Area $= 180\,\text{cm}^2$, perimeter $= 54\,\text{cm}$

7 **a** $3:2$ **b** $2:1$ **c** $\dfrac{3}{5}$

8.2 Purposeful practice

1 Student answers, e.g. A $7.5:5$; B $1:3$; C $6:4$; D $0.3:0.1$

2 Student answers, e.g. A $7.5:7$; B $0.5:1$; C $6:4$; D $3.5:7$; E $2:4$; E $2:4$; F $7:3$; G $7:14$; H $0.2:0.1$

3 **a** $(2,1)$ **d** $(1,2)$ **g** $(4p,8p)$
  b $(32,16)$ **e** $(0.5,1)$ **h** $(4p,12p)$
  c $(16,32)$ **f** $(0.25p,0.5p)$ **i** $(0.75p,0.25p)$

4 Student answers

8.3 Fractions in context

8.3.1 Find a fraction of a given amount

Your turn! 1 300

8.3.1 Fluency

1 a 2   **b** 11   **c** 10   **d** 12

2 a 7.5   **b** 24   **c** 4.15   **d** 2.3

3 a 30   **b** 16   **c** 45   **d** 40

4 a 98   **b** 112

5 a 2.6   **b** 3.6   **c** 6.56   **d** 1.8

6 a $\frac{4}{11}$ **b** $\frac{2}{5}$ **c** $\frac{25}{51}$ **d** $\frac{55}{101}$

8.3.2 Finding the whole

Your turn! 1 42

8.3.2 Fluency

1 a 12   **b** 15   **c** 30   **d** 56   **e** 140   **f** 132

2 a 16   **b** 30   **c** 20   **d** 30   **e** 84   **f** 132

3 a 6.4   **b** 4.5   **c** 8.8   **d** $\frac{4}{7}$ **e** $\frac{16}{17}$ **f** $\frac{3}{5}$

8.3.3 Write one number as a fraction of another

Your turn! 1 $\frac{1}{2}$

8.3.3 Fluency

1 a $\frac{3}{5}$ **b** $\frac{3}{8}$ **c** $\frac{5}{8}$

2 a $\frac{4}{11}$ **b** $\frac{4}{15}$ **c** $\frac{11}{15}$

3 a $\frac{5}{6}$ **b** $\frac{6}{5}$ **c** $\frac{5}{11}$ **d** $\frac{6}{11}$

4 a $\frac{8}{11}$ **b** $\frac{11}{8}$ **c** $\frac{8}{19}$ **d** $\frac{11}{19}$

5 a $\frac{24}{31}$ **b** $\frac{31}{24}$ **c** $\frac{24}{55}$ **d** $\frac{31}{55}$

6 a $\frac{2}{3}$ **b** $\frac{2}{5}$ **c** $\frac{5}{12}$ **d** $\frac{4}{3}$

8.3 Exercises

8.3 Intelligent practice

1 a 42   **d** 7   **g** 30   **j** 84   **m** 17.5

   b 35   **e** 30   **h** 60   **k** 350   **n** $16\frac{2}{3}$

   c 70   **f** 15   **i** 84   **l** 35   **o** 24

2 a 150   **d** 45   **g** 144   **j** 84   **m** 40

   b 180   **e** 36   **h** 156   **k** 77

   c 90   **f** 72   **i** 168   **l** 78.4

3 a 15   **c** $\frac{3}{125}$ **e** 135   **g** $\frac{2}{5}$ **i** 7.5

   b 15   **d** 15   **f** 375   **h** $\frac{5}{3}$

4 a 15   **b** $\frac{3}{4}$ **c** $\frac{7}{9}$ **d** $\frac{7}{15}$ **e** $\frac{9}{11}$

8.3 Method selection

1 a $\frac{37}{15}$ **b** $\frac{47}{15}$ **c** 1:2   **d** $\frac{1}{2}$ **e** $\frac{37}{47}$

   f 0.79, they are not the same.

2 a $\frac{5}{12}$ **b** $\frac{5}{7}$ **c** 20 cm

3 a 25   **b** $\frac{2}{5}$ **c** $\frac{1}{2}$ **d** $\frac{5}{2}$ **e** 5

4 a 7   **b** 63   **c** $\frac{1}{7}$

5 a £36.25   **b** £11.60   **c** $\frac{7}{25}$

8.3 Purposeful practice

1 A E.g. What is $\frac{1}{5}$ of 25?   **C** E.g. What is $\frac{1}{3}$ of 36?

   B E.g. What is $\frac{2}{3}$ of 18?   **D** E.g. What is $\frac{7}{8}$ of 40?

2 A E.g. What is $\frac{2}{4}$ of 15?   **E** E.g. What is $\frac{3}{2}$ of 4?

   B E.g. What is $\frac{9}{6}$ of 12?   **F** E.g. What is $\frac{5}{6}$ of 14?

   C E.g. What is $\frac{1}{4}$ of 20?   **G** E.g. What is $\frac{5}{4}$ of 13?

   D E.g. What is $\frac{20}{15}$ of 8?   **H** E.g. What is $\frac{6}{8}$ of 16?

3 7

4 a No he is not correct. He has multiplied his number by $\frac{4}{5}$, not divided it.

   b $\frac{63}{64}$ **c** $\frac{22}{45}$

5 a 1 and 3   **e** E.g. 4.5 and $\frac{2}{3}$

   b E.g. 6 and $\frac{1}{2}$ **f** −1 and −3

   c E.g. $\frac{8}{2}$ and $\frac{3}{4}$ **g** E.g. $-\frac{1}{2}$ and $-\frac{18}{3}$

   d E.g. 0.1 and 30   **h** Not possible

8.4 Applying ratios

8.4.1 Dividing quantities in ratio

Your turn! 1 Abdoul gets £200 and Beth gets £150

8.4.1 Fluency

1 a £4 and £6   **c** £20 and £30

   b £8 and £12   **d** £0.20 and £0.30

2 a £15 and £25   **c** 16 ml and 64 ml

   b 49 kg and 21 kg   **d** £250 and £650

3 a 15 l and 55 l   **c** 400 g and 560 g

   b £350 and £200   **d** 408 cm and 153 cm

4 a 2.6 and 5.2   **b** $\frac{5}{8}$ and $\frac{1}{8}$ **c** 46.5 and 28.5

5 a 2.5, 5.5, and 0.5   **c** 1.04, 2.08 and 2.48

   b $\frac{2}{11}, \frac{3}{11}$ and $\frac{5}{11}$

8.4.2 Using ratio to find missing parts

Your turn! 1 £22.50

8.4.2 Fluency

1 a $\frac{15}{20}$ so £20   **b** $\frac{24}{32}$ so £24

2 a 15   **b** £42   **c** 112 g

3 a £0.90 and £1.50   **c** 3.15 ℓ and 1.35 ℓ

   b 384 ml and 128 ml

8.4.3 Using ratios to find the whole

Your turn! 1 27

8.4.3 Fluency

1 a £30 **b** 360 g **c** 48

2 a £8.50 **b** 1.47 ℓ **c** 8 kg

3 a £54 **b** 1.92 kg **c** £96

8.4.4 Using ratios when given the difference

Your turn! 1 £120

8.4.4 Fluency

1 a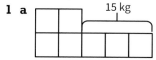

b Ali gets 25 kg and Paul gets 10 kg

2 a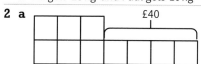

b Sanjay gets £70 and Ayano gets £30

3 Frankie gets 90 g and Wayne gets 150 g

4 Milena gets 77 sweets and Sunny gets 110 sweets

5 22 cookies

6 Elena gets £6, Gertrude gets £15, and Hanna gets £21

8.4.5 Using ratios to describe rates

Your turn! 1 Graph of $y = 36x$ correctly plotted, y-axis labeled 'Pounds (£)' and x-axis labeled 'Area (m²)'

8.4.5 Fluency

1 a 4.80 **b** 10 **c** 13

2 a 18 **b** 12 **c** 36 **d** 9

3 a £ = 7, $ = 2.5
 b Graph of $y = \left(\dfrac{5}{4}\right)x$ correctly plotted, straight line passing through $(0, 0)$ and $(4, 5)$, y-axis labeled 'Dollars ($)' and x-axis labeled 'Pounds (£)'

c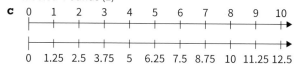

4 a oz = 5, g = 28, 56
 b i 84 **ii** 10 **iii** 224 **iv** 13

5 a Graph of $y = \left(\dfrac{3}{2}\right)x$ correctly plotted, straight line passing through $(0, 0)$, $(2, 3)$, and $(10, 15)$, y-axis labeled 'Litres' and x-axis labeled 'Time (minutes)'
 b i 9 ℓ **ii** 12 ℓ **c** 5 min

8.4 Exercises

8.4 Intelligent practice

1 a John gets £40, Hasan gets £60
 b Aisha gets £20, Ben gets £80

2 a £28 and £20 **d** £12 and £36
 b £18 and £30 **e** £6 and £18
 c £8 and £40 **f** £18 and £6

2 g £0.60 and £1.80 **j** £0.30 and £2.10
 h £0.48 and £1.92 **k** £0.20, £1.40, and £0.80
 i £0.30, £1.20, and £0.90

3 a £18 **c** £288 **e** £300 **g** £720
 b £50 **d** £112.50 **f** £720

8.4 Method selection

1 a 90 **b** 54 **c** 90 **d** 1350

2 a Alice gets £160 and Jacinda gets £200 **d** £936
 e £450
 b $\dfrac{5}{9}$ **f** £648
 c £3240 **g** £900

3 a 63 **b** 63

4 a $t = 15, 20$; $y = 24, 120$
 b i 96 ℓ **ii** 132 ℓ **iii** 9 min **iv** 13 min
 c 35 min

5 a £2.70 **b** 28 **c** 48 **d** 510 g **e** 48

6 a i 5 seconds **ii** 12 grams **iii** 25 seconds **b** 3

8.4 Purposeful practice

1 a i, ii, iii and v
 b 1:1 1:2, 2:1 1:3, 3:1 1:5, 5:1
 1:7, 3:5, 5:3, 7:1
 1:11, 5:7, 7:5, 11:1
 1:23, 5:19, 7:17, 11:13, 13:11, 17:7, 19:5, 23:1

2 1:2:3, 1:3:2, 2:1:3, 2:3:1, 3:1:2, 3:2:1, 1:1:4, 1:4:1, 4:1:1, 1:1:1

3 a 15 cm **b** 24 cm **c** 14 min **d** 18 min
 e The rate of filling may change; the bath might be less than 60 cm deep

4 a i £23 **ii** £115 **iii** £1012
 b £513 **c** £3542 **d** £492

5 a Graph of $y = \left(\dfrac{6}{5}\right)x$ correctly plotted, straight line passing through $(0, 0)$, $(50, 60)$, and $(100, 120)$, y-axis labeled 'Dollars ($)' and x-axis labeled 'Pounds (£)'
 b i $72 **ii** $99 **iii** £40 **iv** £47 **c** $42.25

Chapter 8 summary

Watch out! (full answers on Kerboodle)

1 a 16 **2 a** The shares are £60, £120, and £150

3 a If A to C is 4 and B to C is 3, then A to B is $4 \div 3 = \dfrac{4}{3}$

4 a £50 = $55

9 Transformations

Full answers with graphs are available on Kerboodle

Reactivate your knowledge

9.1 Translations

1 a Points correctly plotted and joined to make a triangle
 b Points correctly plotted and joined to make a parallelogram
 c Points correctly plotted and joined to make a square

9.2 Rotations

2 a 1   **b** 2   **c** 4

9.3 Reflections

3 a $(6,1)$ **b** $(-3,-5)$ **c** $(-6,-1)$ **d** $(3,5)$

4 a $(1,5)$ **b** $(6,12)$ **c** $(3.5,16)$ **d** $(-11,1)$

9.4 Scale diagrams

5 a 12   **b** 84

6 a 4 m   **b** 670 cm   **c** 3000 m   **d** 18 mm

7 a 42   **b** 44   **c** 10

9.5 Enlargements

8 a $\dfrac{17}{3}$ **b** 4   **c** $\dfrac{5}{18}$ **d** $\dfrac{41}{73}$

9.1 Translations

9.1.1 Introduction to translation

Your turn! 1 B; shape, size, and orientation have stayed the same but the position has changed.

9.1.1 Fluency

1 a C **b** B and D

2 a C and E **b** No: they must also be in the same orientation

3 She is incorrect. To be a translation, the shape must not only be in the same orientation, but must also be the same size. Here, shape B is not the same size as shape A.

4 a $(-5,-2)$ **b** $(-3,0)$ **c** $(-4,-1)$ **d** $(-3,-1)$

9.1.2 Describing translations

Your turn! 1   Translation of 9 units in the $-$ x-direction and 4 units in the $+$ y-direction.

9.1.2 Fluency

1 a 1 unit left and 5 units down   **c** 4 units left and 1 unit down
   b 5 units right and 5 units down   **d** 6 units left

2 a 4 units in the $+$ x-direction and 1 unit in the $+$ y-direction
   b 1 unit in the $-$ x-direction and 5 units in the $-$ y-direction
   c 5 units in the $-$ x-direction and 6 units in the $-$ y-direction
   d 1 unit in the $+$ x-direction and 6 units in the $-$ y-direction

3 5 units in the $-$ x-direction and 2 units in the $+$ y-direction; it is the same but with $+$ and $-$ swapped around

4 a $\begin{pmatrix} -1 \\ -5 \end{pmatrix}$ **b** $\begin{pmatrix} 6 \\ 0 \end{pmatrix}$ **c** $\begin{pmatrix} -4 \\ -1 \end{pmatrix}$ **d** $\begin{pmatrix} -1 \\ 6 \end{pmatrix}$

9.1.3 Translating objects

Your turn!   Image drawn with vertices $A'(4,-4)$, $B'(4,0)$, $C'(6,0)$, $D'(6,-3)$

9.1.3 Fluency

1 a Image B vertices $(0,3),(0,5),(3,5),(3,3)$
   b Image C vertices $(1,0),(1,2),(4,2),(4,0)$
   c Image D vertices $(-5,-1),(-5,1),(-2,1),(-2,-1)$

2 a Image B vertices $(-1,3),(-1,5),(2,5),(2,2),(1,3)$
   b Image C vertices $(-6,4),(-6,6),(-3,6),(-3,3),(-4,4)$
   c Image D vertices $(2,-4),(2,-2),(5,-2),(5,-5),(4,-4)$

3 a Image B vertices $(3,-3),(2,-1),(4,0),(4,-3)$
   b Image C vertices $(-2,-2),(-3,0),(-1,1),(-1,-2)$
   c Image D vertices $(0,2),(-1,4),(1,5),(1,2)$

d $\begin{pmatrix} -2 \\ 1 \end{pmatrix}$

9.1 Exercises

9.1 Intelligent practice

1 a Image B with vertices at $(-5,-2),(-1,-2),(-1,-4)$
   b Image C with vertices at $(-5,2),(-1,2),(-1,0)$
   c Image D with vertices at $(2,2),(6,2),(6,0)$

2 a Translation of 5 units in positive x-direction (right)
   b Translation of 5 units in positive x-direction (right) and 4 units in negative y-direction (down)
   c Translation of 8 units in positive x-direction (right) and 4 units in negative y-direction (down)
   d Translation of 8 units in negative x-direction (left) and 4 units in positive y-direction (up)

3 a $\begin{pmatrix} 5 \\ 0 \end{pmatrix}$ **b** $\begin{pmatrix} 5 \\ -4 \end{pmatrix}$ **c** $\begin{pmatrix} 8 \\ -4 \end{pmatrix}$ **d** $\begin{pmatrix} -8 \\ 4 \end{pmatrix}$

4 a Translation of 5 units in negative y-direction (down)
   b Translation of 6 units in negative x-direction (left) and 5 units in negative y-direction (down)
   c Translation of 6 units in negative x-direction (left) and 1 unit in positive y-direction (up)
   d Translation of 6 units in positive x-direction (right) and 1 unit in negative y-direction (down)

5 a $\begin{pmatrix} 0 \\ -5 \end{pmatrix}$ **b** $\begin{pmatrix} -6 \\ -5 \end{pmatrix}$ **c** $\begin{pmatrix} -6 \\ 1 \end{pmatrix}$ **d** $\begin{pmatrix} 6 \\ -1 \end{pmatrix}$

6 a Image B with vertices at $(-3,4),(0,6),(3,4),(0,2)$
   b Image C with vertices at $(3,-4),(0,-2),(-3,-4),(0,-6)$
   c Image D with vertices at $(3,-4),(6,-2),(9,-4),(6,-6)$
   d Image E with vertices at $(3,8),(6,10),(9,8),(6,6)$

7 a Image vertices at $A'(-3,5),B'(-4,3),C'(1,3),D'(1,5)$
   b Image vertices at $A''(-3,-4),B''(-4,-6),C''(1,-6),D''(1,-4)$
   c Image vertices at $A'''(5,-4),B'''(4,-6),C'''(9,-6),D'''(9,-4)$

8 a $(4,8)$ **b** $(4,6)$ **c** $(5,6)$ **d** $(5,7)$

9 a $\begin{pmatrix} 0 \\ 1 \end{pmatrix}$ or Translation of 1 unit in positive y-direction (up)

   b $\begin{pmatrix} 0 \\ 2 \end{pmatrix}$ or Translation of 2 units in positive y-direction (up)

   c $\begin{pmatrix} 11 \\ 2 \end{pmatrix}$ or Translation of 11 units in positive x-direction (right) and 2 units in positive y-direction (up)

   d $\begin{pmatrix} 22 \\ 2 \end{pmatrix}$ or Translation of 22 units in positive x-direction (right) and 2 units in positive y-direction (up)

9.1 Method selection

1 a Triangle drawn with vertices $A\ (3,-1)$, $B\ (3,1)$, $C\ (-3,-1)$
   b Triangle drawn with vertices $A'\ (-2,3)$, $B'\ (-2,5)$, $C'\ (-8,3)$

2 a $(-3,4)$ **b** $(5,-6)$ **c** $(1,-1)$ **3** 25 cm²

4 a Trapezium   **b** 27.5 cm²
   c Image drawn correctly with vertices at $(-3,2),(-2,7),(1,7),(5,2)$

5 a $(-5,3)$ **b** 15 cm²

   c $\begin{pmatrix} 7 \\ -1 \end{pmatrix}$ Translation 7 units in positive x-direction and 1 unit in negative y-direction

6 a $(15,0)$ **b** Translation by vector $\begin{pmatrix} 5 \\ 5 \end{pmatrix}$ **7** $x = 4$

9.1 Purposeful practice

1 a Triangles A, B, and C should be translations of each other

b They are the same shape, size and orientation but have been moved to a new position

c Triangles D and E should not be translations of triangle A

d e.g. their size or orientation might be different; need reasons that are correct for student's triangles

2 a Descriptions using words or vector, e.g. A to B is a translation 8 units in negative x-direction and 5 units in negative y-direction/translation by vector $\begin{pmatrix} -8 \\ -5 \end{pmatrix}$

b The reverse translations have the same magnitude with the signs reversed

3 a Any quadrilateral labelled A.

b A translated by vector $\begin{pmatrix} -5 \\ 2 \end{pmatrix}$ and labelled B

c B translated by vector $\begin{pmatrix} 7 \\ -6 \end{pmatrix}$ and labelled C

d C translated by vector $\begin{pmatrix} -2 \\ 4 \end{pmatrix}$ and labelled D (same as A)

e Quadrilateral D is in the same position as A. For the x-coordinates you subtract 5 then add 7 then subtract 2, $-5 + 7 - 2 = 0$, so you end up at the same x-coordinate as you started. For the y-coordinates you add 2 then subtract 6 then add 4, $2 - 6 + 4 = 0$, so you end up at the same y-coordinate as you started.

9.2 Rotations

9.2.1 Introduction to rotation

Your turn! 1 D is not a rotation of A.

9.2.1 Fluency

1 D

2 a D and E **b** D and E

c Yes: the orientation and position have changed but the size is the same

3 a Always true: size does not change under a rotation

b Sometimes true and sometimes false: orientation will change, except in the case of rotation through 360°

c Sometimes true and sometimes false: position will change, except in the case of rotation through 360°

4 a $(0,0)$ **b** $(-1,-1)$ **c** $(1,0)$ **d** $(3,3)$

e Only Ellie is completely correct. The centre of rotation does not change under any rotation, whether it is a vertex of the shape or not.

9.2.2 Rotate an object

Your turn! 1 Image Q drawn correctly with vertices at $(-14, 10)$, $(-6, 10)$, $(-6, 6)$, $(-10, 6)$

9.2.2 Fluency

1 a 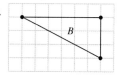   **b** 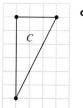   **c**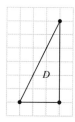

2 a Image B vertices at $(-1, 1)$, $(1, 1)$, $(0, -2)$, $(-1, -2)$

b Image C vertices at $(0, 2)$, $(0, 4)$, $(3, 3)$, $(3, 2)$

c Image D vertices at $(-2, 4)$, $(-2, 2)$, $(-5, 3)$, $(-5, 4)$

d Image E vertices at $(-3, -1)$, $(-3, -3)$, $(-6, -2)$, $(-6, -1)$

3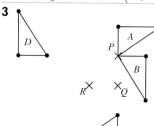

4 a Image B drawn with points at $(1, -2)$, $(1, -3)$, $(1, -5)$, $(-1, -4)$

b Image C drawn with points at $(-1, -2)$, $(-2, -2)$, $(-4, -2)$, $(-3, 0)$

c Image D drawn with points at $(1, -2)$, $(2, -2)$, $(4, -2)$, $(3, -4)$

d A rotation 90° clockwise (or 270° anticlockwise) about $(0, -1)$

5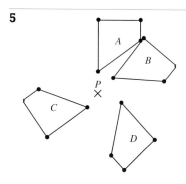

9.2.3 Describing rotations

Your turn! 1 Rotation about $(4, 2)$ of 90° anticlockwise.

9.2.3 Fluency

1 a 180° rotation about the origin

b 180° rotation about the origin

c Yes: rotating an object 360° means it finishes where it starts

d Yes: rotating through 540° means rotating through a full turn and then another 180°

2 a 180° rotation about $(-1, 1)$ **b** 180° rotation about $(2, -1)$

c 90° anticlockwise rotation about $(2, -4)$

d 90° rotation clockwise about $(1, 4)$

3 a 90° clockwise rotation about $(0, 0)$

b 180° rotation about $(2, 0)$

c 90° anticlockwise rotation about $(0, -4)$

d 90° anticlockwise rotation about $(-4, -3)$

4 180° clockwise and 900° anticlockwise;
90° clockwise, 270° anticlockwise and 450° clockwise;
270° clockwise and 630° clockwise

9.2 Exercises

9.2 Intelligent practice

1 a Yes   **b** Yes   **c** Yes   **d** No   **e** No

2 a Yes   **b** Yes   **c** Yes   **d** Yes   **e** Yes   **f** No   **g** No

3 a   **b**   **c**   **d**   **e**

9.2 Intelligent practice Contin.

4 a Image B vertices at $(-1,-1),(-1,-4),(-4,-4),(-4,-2)$
b Image C vertices at $(7,3),(7,0),(4,0),(4,2)$
c Image D vertices at $(7,-1),(7,-4),(4,-4),(4,-2)$
d Image E vertices at $(1,1),(1,4),(4,4),(4,2)$

5 a Image B vertices at $(-6,2),(-6,7),(-2,6)$
b Image C vertices at $(6,-2),(6,-7),(2,-6)$
c Image D vertices at $(-4,0),(0,4),(0,-1)$
d Image E vertices at $(-2,-6),(-7,-6),(-6,-2)$

6 a Rotation of 180° about $(-3,5)$
b Rotation of 180° about $(-3,1)$
c Rotation of 90° clockwise (or 270° anticlockwise) about $(-3,1)$
d Rotation of 90° clockwise (or 270° anticlockwise) about $(2,1)$
e Rotation of 90° anticlockwise (or 270° clockwise) about $(2,1)$
f Rotation of 90° clockwise (or 270° anticlockwise) about $(-3,6)$
g Rotation of 90° anticlockwise (or 270° clockwise) about $(-3,6)$

7 a ✗ **b** ✗ **c**

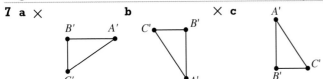

d **e** ✗ **f**

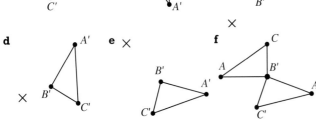

9.2 Method selection

1 a Rotation of 90° clockwise (or 270° anticlockwise) about $(0,0)$
b Rotation of 90° anticlockwise (or 270° clockwise) about $(0,0)$
c Translation 3 units in the $+x$-direction/by vector $\begin{pmatrix}3\\0\end{pmatrix}$
d Translation 3 units in the $-x$-direction/by vector $\begin{pmatrix}-3\\0\end{pmatrix}$
e, f Rotation of 180° about $(0,0)$
g Translation 10 units in the positive x-direction and 1 unit in the positive y-direction/by the vector $\begin{pmatrix}10\\1\end{pmatrix}$
h Translation 10 units in the negative x-direction and 1 unit in the negative y-direction/by the vector $\begin{pmatrix}-10\\-1\end{pmatrix}$

2 a Image Q with vertices at $(3,4),(7,4),(7,2),(5,2)$
b Image R with vertices at $(-6,1),(-6,5),(-4,5),(-4,3)$
c Image S with vertices at $(6,-5),(2,-5),(2,-3),(4,-3)$

3 a i Image A' with vertices at $(-4,-1),(-2,-5),(-4,-5)$
ii Image A'' with vertices at $(-1,4),(-5,2),(-5,4)$
b Rotation of 90° clockwise (or 270° anticlockwise) about $(4,3)$

4 a Points A, B, C plotted correctly, point D plotted as (-3,-2)
b 15 cm² **c** C **d** $(-1,5)$ **e** 15 cm²

9.2 Purposeful practice

1 a Triangles A, B and C should be rotations of each other
b They are the same shape and size but orientation is different
c Triangles D and E should not be rotations of triangle A
d E.g. sizes might be different, or they may have been reflected not rotated; need reasons that are correct for the triangles drawn

2 a Shapes A, B, C, D, and E shown on a grid. Each shape should be a 90° clockwise rotation of the previous shape, around a centre of rotation that is stated.
b A translation, described fully using either words or vectors

3 a i C **ii** F **iii** E **iv** B
b Examples of rotations, each should be fully defined. E.g. F to H is rotation of 90° clockwise about the point M.
c Alternative ways of expressing answers to **b**, e.g. F to H could also be a rotation of 270° anticlockwise about point M or a rotation of 450° clockwise about point M.

9.3 Reflections

9.3.1 Introduction to reflection

Your turn! 1 B and C are reflections, D is not.

9.3.1 Fluency

1 C

2 a B and C **b** A and D
c No: he is correct that the orientation changes, but the size will remain the same

3 a False **b** True

4 a $(2,2)$ **b** $(3,3)$ **c** $(-1,2)$ **d** $(-2,5)$
e Yes: both points lie on the mirror line and the mirror line is invariant under a reflection.

9.3.2 Describing reflections

Your turn! 1

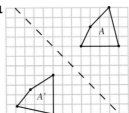

9.3.2 Fluency

1

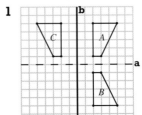

2

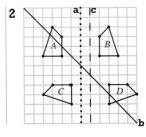

3 a Vertical straight line passing through $(0,-0.5)$
b Diagonal straight line $y = x$ passing through $(-6,-6),(0,0),(6,6)$
c Diagonal straight line $y = -x$ passing through $(-6,6),(0,0),(6,-6)$

9.3.3 Reflecting objects

Your turn! 1 Image B vertices at $(-2,-2),(-2,-4),(-5,-2)$

9.3.3 Fluency

1

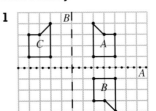

2 a Image B vertices $(2,-3),(5,-3),(5,-4),(4,-5),(2,-4)$
b Image C vertices $(-3,1),(-3,2),(-2,3),(0,2),(0,1)$

3 a Image T vertices $(2,2),(1,3),(2,4),(2,5),(5,5)$
   b Image U vertices $(-2,-2),(-1,-3),(-2,-4),(-2,-5),(-5,-5)$

4 a Image B with points $(1,-3),(1,-4),(1,-6),(3,-5)$
   b Image C with points $(-3,-3),(-3,-4),(-3,-6),(-5,-5)$
   c Image D with points $(-3,-3),(-4,-3),(-6,-3),(-5,-5)$
   d Image E with points $(3,3),(3,4),(3,6),(5,5)$

9.3 Exercises

9.3 Intelligent practice

1 a Yes   **b** Yes   **c** Yes   **d** Yes   **e** No

2 a   b   c   d   e

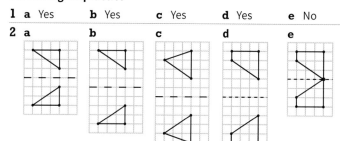

3 a   b

 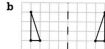

c   d   e

 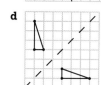

4 a $x=1$ **b** $x=3$ **c** $y=1$ **d** $y=0$ **e** $y=0$

5 a Image B vertices $(1,-7),(-3,-7),(-5,-6),(-3,-4),(0,-4)$
   b Image C vertices $(-3,-7),(-7,-7),(-9,-6),(-7,-4),(-4,-4)$
   c Image D vertices $(1,9),(5,9),(7,8),(5,6),(2,6)$
   d Image E vertices $(1,5),(5,5),(7,4),(5,2),(2,2)$

9.3 Method selection

1 a Rotation 90° anticlockwise (or 270° clockwise) about $(0,0)$
   b Rotation 90° clockwise (or 270° anticlockwise) about $(0,0)$
   c Translation 4 units in the positive x-direction and 10 units in the negative y-direction/ by vector $\begin{pmatrix}4\\-10\end{pmatrix}$
   d Translation 4 units in the negative x-direction and 10 units in the positive y-direction/ by vector $\begin{pmatrix}-4\\10\end{pmatrix}$
   e, f Reflection in the line $x=5$ (or show line on diagram)
   g, h Reflection in the line $y=-1$ (or show line on diagram)
   i Rotation 90° clockwise (or 270° anticlockwise) about $(6,-6)$
   j Rotation 90° anticlockwise (or 270° clockwise) about $(6,-6)$

2 a Image B with vertices at $(-2,3),(-7,3),(-7,6),(-3,6)$
   b Image C with vertices at $(2,3),(3,6),(7,6),(7,3)$
   c Image D with vertices at $(-1,-1),(-1,-4),(-5,-4),(-6,-1)$

3 a Image B drawn with vertices at $(-7,-6),(-5,-10),(-7,-10)$
   b Image C drawn with vertices at $(7,-6),(7,-10),(5,-10)$
   c Image D drawn with vertices at $(9,-6),(9,-10),(7,-10)$
   d Image E drawn with vertices at $(9,2),(7,6),(9,6)$
   e Reflection in the line $x=1$ (or draw line on diagram)

4 a Image A' drawn with vertices at $(4,4),(4,5),(6,5),(6,3)$
   b Image A'' drawn with vertices at $(-8,3),(-8,5),(-6,5),(-6,4)$
   c Image A''' drawn with vertices at $(-6,5),(-6,7),(-4,7),(-4,6)$
   d Reflection in the line $y=1$

5 a Parallelogram   **b** $21\,\text{cm}^2$
   c Image with vertices $A'(-4,-3),B'(-4,-6),C'(3,-5),D'(3,-8)$
   d $21\,\text{cm}^2$

6 a $(-6,-9)$ **b** C **c** $(2,-7)$

9.3 Purposeful practice

1 a Triangles B and C should be reflections of triangle A with mirror lines shown
   b Each point on the image is on the opposite side but the same distance from the mirror line as the object
   c Triangles D and E should not be reflections of triangle A
   d E.g. their size might be different, or they may have been rotated not reflected; need reasons that are correct for the triangles drawn

2 a, b Triangle drawn and reflected in each of the mirror lines
   c Quadrilateral drawn and reflected in each of the mirror lines

3 a

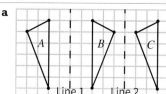

Line 1   Line 2

   b Translation 10 units right
   c Produces a translation 10 units left
   d Investigate lines in different positions

4 a,b

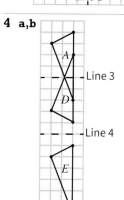

   c Translation of 10 units down
   d Produces a translation of 10 units up

5 a Shapes A,B,C,D,E shown on a grid. Each shape should be a reflection of the previous in a mirror line that is drawn or given as an equation.
   b Should be a translation, described fully using either words or vectors

9.4 Scale diagrams

9.4.1 Introduction to scale diagrams

Your turn! 1 20 cm

9.4.1 Fluency

1 C **2** 4 cm   **3** 39 cm   **4** 2.1 cm   **5** 5 cm

9.4.2 Interpreting scale diagrams

Your turn! 1 10 km

9.4.2 Fluency

1 a 20 km   **b** 10 km   **c** 13 km (Accept ±1 km)

2 120 cm by 80 cm (Accept ±8 cm)

3 8 m, 10 m, and 14 m (Accept ±0.8 m)

4 500 m (Accept between 452 m and 548 m)

5 a 8.75 km   **b** 7.5 km   **c** 9.5 km (Accept ±0.5 km)

9.4.3 Drawing scale diagrams

Your turn! 1 Student diagram: rectangle should be 10 cm by 6 cm

9.4.3 Fluency

1 Student diagram: distance is 5 cm

2   Student diagram: distance is 9.5 cm

3   Student drawing: rectangle should be 6 cm by 4 cm

4   Student drawing: rectangle should be 8 cm by 5 cm

5   **a**   Student drawing: right-angle triangle   **b**   1.75 m
     with shorter sides 10 cm and 6 cm

6   Student drawing: concentric circles of diameters 6 cm & 3.5 cm

7   Student diagram: distance is 6 cm

8   **a**   Student drawing: vertical distance 6 cm   **b**   25 km
     and horizontal distance (right) 8 cm

9.4 Exercises

9.4 Intelligent practice

1   **a**   Yes   **b**   Yes   **c**   Yes   **d**   No   **e**   Yes   **f**   Yes   **g**   No

2   **a**   5 km   **b**   10 km   **c**   20 km   **d**   25 km   **e**   150 km   **f**   1.5 km

3   **a**   8 cm   **b**   24 cm   **c**   48 cm   **d**   96 cm   **e**   960 cm   **f**   9.6 cm

4   **a**   3 km   **b**   15 km   **c**   7.5 km   **d**   75 km   **e**   37.5 km **f**   3.75 km

5   Student drawings of rectangles with dimensions:
     a 12×9 cm   **b** 24×18 cm   **c** 8×6 cm   **d** 18×13.5 cm

6   Student diagram drawn to scale using these distances from the dot representing Town A:
     a   Town B 2 cm right   **e**   Town F 8 cm above
     b   Town C 4 cm right   **f**   Town G 1.6 cm above
     c   Town D 4 cm below   **g**   Town H 3.2 cm left
     d   Town E 8 cm below

7   Student drawings of squares with side:
     a   2 cm   **b**   4 cm   **c**   8 cm   **d**   16 cm

8   **a**   2 cm **b**   4 cm   **c**   40 cm   **d**   0.4 cm   **e**   0.2 cm   **f**   1.8 cm

9.4 Method selection

1   **a**   7 m and 12 m   **c**   14 m and 24 m   **e**   3.5 m and 6 m
     b   3.5 m and 6 m   **d**   14 m and 24 m

2   Student drawings of rectangles with dimensions:
     a 3×5 cm   **b** 2.5×1.5 cm   **c** 2.5×1.5 cm   **d** 10×6 cm

3   **a**   600 cm / 6 m   **b**   **i**   900 cm²   **ii**   360 000 cm² / 36 m²

4   **a**   360 cm / 3.6 m   **b**   9 cm   **c**   1 cm to represent 72 cm / 1:72

5   Entries for each row shown with missing values underlined:
     1 cm:3 km, 12 cm, <u>36 km</u>;
     1 cm:5 km, <u>3.6 cm</u>, 18 km;
     2 cm:3 km, 17 cm, <u>25.5 km</u>;
     <u>1 cm:8 km or 1:800 000</u>, 5 cm, 40 km;
     1:200 000, 24 cm, <u>48 km</u>;
     1:2 000 000, <u>0.9 cm</u>, 18 km;
     <u>1 cm:6 km or 1:600 000</u>, 6.5 cm, 39 km

6   **a**   0.8 cm / 8 mm   **b**   39 cm

9.4 Purposeful practice

1   Examples of rectangles where the length is 1.5 times the width

2   Scale drawings of the classroom using different scales

3   **a**   Student scale drawing of rectangle with dimensions 3 cm by 4 cm
     b   12 cm²   **c**   300 cm²   **d**   1:25
     e   Examples of different scale drawings, ratio of areas should be
         1:25 in all cases

9.5 Enlargements

9.5.1 Introduction to enlargement

Your turn! 1 A and B are similar rectangles so yes, B is an enlargement of A.

9.5.1 Fluency

1   **a** C and E **b** B and E

2   **a**   No: the top length of the image should be two squares, not
     three as in the diagram
     b   Scale factor 3   **c**   Scale factor 2

3   **a**   Scale factor $1\frac{1}{2}$ or $\frac{3}{2}$ **b**   Scale factor $\frac{1}{3}$

9.5.2 Centre of enlargement

Your turn! 1 The shape has doubled in size but the distance from the centre has not, so, no, it is not an enlargement.

9.5.2 Fluency

1   **a**   No: B is an enlargement from centre P, but C does not have
     the correct dimensions to be an enlargement from Q
     b   Yes: the centre of enlargement is the only invariant point
     under an enlargement

2   **a**   Yes she is correct. Flag B uses SF 3 and flag C uses SF 2
     b   He is correct that the centre of enlargement for C is $(0,5)$ but
     he is not correct that the centre for B is $(4,1)$ it is $(5,1)$

3   **a** $(1,1)$ **b** $(5,-1)$ **c** $(-1,-1)$ **d** $(-3,5)$ **e** $(-1,1)$

9.5.3 Drawing enlargements

Your turn! 1 Image correctly drawn with vertices at $(1,2)$, $(3,10)$, $(5,2)$

9.5.3 Fluency

1   **a**   **i**   Correctly drawn image B with sides 6 x 4 squares
         ii   Correctly drawn image C with sides 9 x 6 squares
     b   **i**   Correctly drawn image Q - height 6 squares, width 4 squares
         ii   Correctly drawn image R - height 9 squares, width 6 squares

2   **a**   **i**   Image B with vertices at $(3,6)$, $(5,10)$, $(5,6)$
         ii   Image C with vertices at $(-5,1)$, $(-2,7)$, $(-2,1)$
     b   **i**   Image Q with vertices at $(3,-4)$, $(6,2)$, $(9,2)$, $(9,-4)$
         ii   Image R with vertices at $(-8,-10)$, $(-4,-2)$, $(0,-2)$, $(0,-10)$

3   **a**   Image B with vertices at $(3,0)$, $(3,1)$, $(4,2)$, $(5,2)$, $(5,0)$
     b   Image Q with vertices at $(-7,0)$, $(-7,2)$, $(-8,2)$, $(-8,1)$

9.5.4 Describing enlargements

Your turn! 1 Enlargement of SF 6, from centre of enlargement $(-5,-3)$

9.5.4 Fluency

1   **a**   2   **b**   3   **c**   2.5

2   **a**   SF 3, centre $(-4,5)$ **b**   SF 2, centre $(0,8)$

3   **a**   SF 3, centre $(3,1)$ **b**   SF 2, centre $(4,6)$ **c**   SF 2.5, centre $(0,5)$

4   **a**   SF $\frac{1}{3}$, centre $(-3.5,2)$ **b**   SF $\frac{1}{2}$, centre $(5,-3)$

9.5 Exercises

9.5 Intelligent practice

1   **a**   Image drawn with vertices at $(2,2)$, $(4,4)$, $(6,2)$
     b   Image drawn with vertices at $(1,2)$, $(3,4)$, $(5,2)$
     c   Image drawn with vertices at $(1,1)$, $(3,3)$, $(5,1)$
     d   Image drawn with vertices at $(1,1)$, $(4,4)$, $(7,1)$
     e   Image drawn with vertices at $(5,1)$, $(8,4)$, $(11,1)$
     f   Image drawn with vertices at $(5,3)$, $(8,6)$, $(11,3)$.

2 a Image drawn with vertices at $(4,4),(4,12),(8,12),(8,0)$
b Image drawn with vertices at $(6,4),(6,12),(10,12),(10,0)$
c Image drawn with vertices at $(6,2),(6,10),(10,10),(10,-2)$
d Image drawn with vertices at $(0,2),(0,4),(1,4),(1,1)$
e Image drawn with vertices at $(4,2),(4,8),(7,8),(7,-1)$

3 a No **c** Yes, SF 4 **e** Yes, SF 3
b Yes, SF 2 **d** No **f** Yes, SF $\dfrac{1}{3}$

4 a SF 3 centre $(1,1)$ **e** SF 2 centre $(-1,-2)$
b SF 3 centre $(0,1)$ **f** SF $\dfrac{1}{2}$ centre $(5,7)$
c SF 2 centre $(-1,1)$
d SF 2 centre $(-1,-1)$ **g** SF $\dfrac{1}{2}$ centre $(-1,-1)$

9.5 Method selection

1 a Reflection in the x-axis/the line $y=0$
b Reflection in the x-axis/the line $y=0$
c Rotation of 90° clockwise/270° anticlockwise about $(5,1)$
d Rotation of 90° anticlockwise/270° clockwise about $(5,1)$
e Enlargement of scale factor 2 from centre $(7,0)$
f Enlargement of scale factor $\dfrac{1}{2}$ from centre $(7,0)$

2 a Image B drawn with vertices at $(3,1),(2,2),(4,3),(4,1)$
b Image C drawn with vertices at $(-4,1),(-4,3),(-2,2),(-3,1)$
c Image D drawn with vertices at $(0,-1),(0,5),(3,5),(6,2)$

3 a Coordinate axes correctly drawn
b Points correctly plotted and square A drawn **c** $(2,1)$
d Image B with vertices at $(4,-1),(6,3),(10,1),(8,-3)$
e Image C with vertices at $(-10,1),(-6,3),(-4,-1),(-8,-3)$

4 a $(18,27)$ **b** $(12,27)$ **c** $(12,21)$ **d** $(4,5)$ **e** $(6,9)$

9.5 Purposeful practice

1 a Three different enlargements of triangle A
b Show that they are similar shapes; that the ratio of the sides is the same $(\text{base}:\text{height}=2:3)$
c Two triangles that are not enlargements of triangle A
d Show that triangles in part c are not similar to A

2 a Image A drawn correctly with vertices at $(0,0),(0,4),(2,4),(2,0)$
b Image B drawn correctly with vertices at $(2,1),(2,5),(4,5),(4,1)$
c Translation 2 units in the positive x-direction and 1 unit in the positive y-direction/by vector $\begin{pmatrix}2\\1\end{pmatrix}$
d Enlargements of scale factor 2 but from different centres of enlargement, then a description of the translation

3 a Image A drawn correctly with vertices at $(0,0),(0,6),(3,6),(3,0)$
b Image B drawn correctly with vertices at $(4,2),(4,8),(7,8),(7,2)$
c Translation 4 units in the positive x-direction and 2 units in the positive y-direction/by vector $\begin{pmatrix}4\\2\end{pmatrix}$
d Enlargements of scale factor 3 but from different centres of enlargement, then a description of the translation. Repeat for different scale factors.

Chapter 9 summary

Watch out! (full answers on Kerboodle)

1 a Image B drawn correctly with vertices at $(3,-1),(5,-2),(2,-4)$

2 a

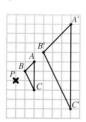

Index